Scuba America

Volume One
The Human History of Sport Diving

Scuba America

Volume One
The Human History of Sport Diving

To Bob - who has been so helpful. Thanks.
Really, Oceans of Thanks,
Keep having fun
in all you do.
Zale Parry
1-24-01

by
Zale Parry
and

Albert Tillman

#38

To Bob fellow historian
keeping our memories intact
Albert Tillman

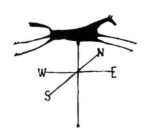

Whalestooth Publishing
Olga, WA

Copyright 2001 by Zale Parry and Albert Tillman
All Rights Reserved
Whalestooth Publishing, Olga, Wa 98279
www.whalestooth.com
in cooperation with
Scuba America Historical Center
www.divinghistory.com

Library of Congress Cataloging-in-Publication Data
Parry, Zale
Tillman, Albert

Scuba America I/by Zale Parry and Albert Tillman

ISBN#1-928638-03-1
first edition

Production management by Thomas Tillman
Cover: Original Oil Painting by Jo Bailey Vartanian

DEDICATION

To all of you who have been generous and patient with the production of this book. To name the helpful people would require another volume. We learned that there were wonderful people all through the history of diving, some renown and many more behind the scenes. They all helped us have confidence in writing this book and enforced humility, too.

Many of you could have been employed in the time of Phillip of Macedonia who had a guy with a pig bladder on a stick come into his chamber at odd times and hit him on the head to remind him that he was not immortal, superior or perfect. Thanks to all of you who helped us write this and kept us respectful of our responsibility.

TABLE OF CONTENTS

THE INTRODUCTION

BY DICK ANDERSON

One could write a book, a thick book, about the positive impact that Al Tillman and Zale Parry had on scuba diving in the United States and worldwide.

Zale and Al were two of the first divers I met after I went to work for U.S.Divers Corporation in the summer of 1951.

Zale was so beautiful (she still is) she always got more stares than glances.

And, Zale was one of the primary factors in making scuba diving more than "a man's sport." Women could dive and dive well, and Zale proved it!

Then Hollywood grabbed her. She became an actress and stunt lady. In 1954, she made an international women's record depth-dive to 209 feet, an experiment to test the Hope-Page non-return valve mouthpiece which became a standard feature in double-hose regulators. Zale is a diver of the first water!!!

Al Tillman seemed to have two major goals: One was the promotion of scuba diving - and the other was <u>safety</u> in scuba diving.

Dick Anderson at the Sparling School of Diving in 1953.

As the founder of the Los Angeles County Underwater Instructors' Program, Al set a precedent in our country and worldwide that has no doubt saved thousands of lives.

Al's concept and promotion of the International Underwater Film Festival offered divers, and potential divers, a view and insight to all aspects of the sport. In fact, Al Tillman talked me into making my first 16mm dive film.

Al Tillman and Zale Parry are two of the most dedicated people I have ever met. They've been putting this series of books together for a couple of decades! They give an accurate insight to the birth and growth of scuba diving in America. Generations to come will profit from this knowledge. Without their efforts much of the early history would have faded into oblivion.

Three Cheers *for Al and Zale!!!*

PREFACE

This is not a book about all the efforts to go underwater over the past centuries. There were many impressive and courageous events in humans' attempt to be fish. This is a human history of a grand, new sport that arose in American leisure during the last half of the 20th Century. It was a propitious time. Americans were evolving in many new ways along social, economic, and cultural lines. They were a generation that had lived through a devastating depression and an enormous war, which toughened them and propelled them into creating a new order of things, a stability and prosperity to be a foundation for having fun and joy in life.

There were jobs again in many fields, pay checks, money available beyond survival needs that they called discretionary.

They could choose to go to the movies, buy toys, a new car, a home, take a vacation and buy products and services for the pleasure they brought. The year 1950 was chosen to be the starting point of what we will call the Golden Years of Skin and Scuba Diving...and year 2000 marks the 50th Anniversary as we arbitrarily have designated it.

There was a lot of sport diving before 1950, basically that of the breath-holding free divers or skin divers. Some adventurous water athletes had found ways to go underwater back in the 1930's when bringing home food from the sea motivated them greatly.

The 1950 date was the start of a new American society, one in which the young men intended to make up for a half decade of life lost to the war, and a new economic group was created, the middle class, which was where most Americans would fit from then on.

S.C.U.B.A. (Self-Contained Underwater Breathing Apparatus) which attracted the masses was an exotic machine that would allow everyone to go where only highly skilled skin divers had gone (and even deeper), was something everyone wanted to try and many did. Scuba was not a sudden new invention of 1950 but came along in various forms before then. The main scuba invention that carried the day and swept into the American consciousness was the Aqua Lung developed by Jacques Yves-Cousteau and Emile Gagnan.

But even before the Aqua Lung, there were scuba constructions that should be noted here as a pre-history so that it is realized that most of the time ideas are running concurrent and being executed in many parts of the world.

In America's Midwest, where there are no oceans, a group of men came together to initiate devices and knowledge about diving with self-contained breathing apparatus. *Scuba America* was fortunate in getting first hand reports from key figures of that group. The greatest source of lucid accounts of that time in the late 1930's came from listening to and reading correspondence from Edgar End, M.D. of the Medical College of Wisconsin. Additional back up information came from group members Jack Browne, Max Gene Nohl, Ivan Hans Vestrem, Colonel John D. Craig and James Lockwood.

Dr. End wrote us (authors Zale Parry and Al Tillman) as follows but in excerpted form:

"Dear Al and Zale,

I have always been a little irked that Cousteau gets credit for inventing scuba while we had ours in 1937 and used it on Craig's expedition to the West Indies in 1938. We never patented the scuba and never made a penny off of it. However, when Jack Browne started DESCO, (Diving Equipment Supply Company) we continued to make scuba for U.S. Navy frogmen, UDT Mine Disposal... We also put Jack Browne to a record 550 feet in a wet pot in 1945.

Signed

Doc End"

Going on with this recall by Dr. End and his group, they credit Dr. Christian J. Lambertsen of the University of

Pennsylvania's School of Medicine with coining the acronym, S.C.U.B.A., in 1954. They solved the problems of physiology and engineering by fearlessly trying everything themselves. While everyone prophesied an early death for them, none of them ever lost his life in a diving accident.

Dr. End believed modern diving was born when Max Gene Nohl returned to Milwaukee from MIT (Massachusetts Institute of Technology) in 1936 with a functioning self-contained diving suit. By 1937 it became a compact scuba. There were no dive shops to walk into and buy something like...a corrugated hose - so it all had to be made from scratch. Nohl broke depth records with it and it served John Craig well, filming movies on the Silver Shoals treasure reefs in the Caribbean.

In almost every corner of America, young men were inventing and building underwater breathing devices using garden hoses, metal buckets, tire pumps, and surplus high altitude respiratory gear. E. R. Cross commercially put out a scuba called the Sport Diver in the late 1940's, basically similar to a plan for making one in a 1947 issue of *Popular Science Magazine*.

America could well have been the birth place of scuba, the Aqua Lung that ignited the interest of the general American public. It took the American newly developing life style to give the French product a rampant marketplace. From 1950 on, diving captured the imagination of everyone looking for something new, something exciting that had never been done before.

We (authors) were immersed in many of the events covered in *Scuba America*, created some of them, witnessed the rest, and were friends and colleagues of most of the founders of sport diving.

In the early 1970's one of the best divers and outstanding underwater photographers in diving, Ron Church, died of a damaged brain at too early an age. We had our epiphany - that all of us pioneers of sport diving could be gone at any moment and with us would go the wonderful impressions and stories that future generations ought to hear. The origins of this exciting activity, the events and people who created sport diving, would never be known.

In an almost thirty-year-quest to gather information through printed materials, magazines, books, letters and personal interviews, *Scuba America* finally emerged as a four-volume set of comprehensive books in the new 21st Century. Here are 50 years of the 100 events and 100 people who made it all happen. It is mainly a human interest approach, in narrative form that we hope is entertaining and factual. Everything is in the eye of the beholder and we agonized over varied impressions of the same happening. We certainly disagreed on a number of things but we tried to cover both sides, or all sides and views. It was a long frustrating labor of love, love for diving, and the wonderful years of opportunity to be part of the birth and growth of this new experience into the unknown.

We often stifled screams and yells of irritation in our solitudes of research and writing, but at the process not each other. We both experienced great and sad moments in our personal lives but we learned to encourage and support each other over all these years. We consoled each other when someone who had generously helped us asked with impatience, "Where's the book?"

Here's the book! We hope that it will refresh your memory, recharge your enthusiasm for diving and reveal things you always wondered about or confirm what you already thought.

Great events may have been missed in our compiling a list of 100 which in itself was a horrendous task. And we certainly have overlooked some great divers in selecting our 100 founders.

If you'd like, go ahead and write in people and events you feel should be in this book. In fact we actually have not identified number one hundred in events or people, so go on, you write in your choice when you get to that point.

Authors

Zale Parry and Albert A. Tillman

1

Invention of the Aqua Lung

Defining Event: Cousteau Stands on his Head

It took an ambitious diver and a valve engineer to finally come up with the "perfect" recreational diving system. They were Frenchmen, Jacques-Yves Cousteau and Emile Gagnan.

Cousteau had been the leader of a trio of pioneer skin divers-together from 1936 on. He was the more polished spokesman of the talented trio and the other two, Frederic Dumas and Phillipe Tailliez, let him assume the public image role. They all had the dream of breath-holding divers to be able to stay down and observe life there for an extended period of time.

It meant improving what breathing systems had been invented to this point to enable the swimming diver. Cousteau took his ideas and those of LePrieur and others to a

Jacques-Yves Cousteau makes the first Aqua Lung dive. Marne River, France, 1943.
The Cousteau Society

Emile Gagnan, an engineer with a commercial gas company, Air Liquide. Conscripted to do underwater work in Toulon Harbor where the French fleet had been scuttled to avoid capture, Cousteau's team had the opportunity to try diving systems. The outshoot of it was the realization that apparatus existed to provide diving free from surface air if there was some way to control the compressed air so it would flow to the diver only as needed.

PRECURSORS TO THE AQUA LUNG

There were many precursors to the Aqua Lung. But the history leading up to a self-contained breathing apparatus is filled with other discoveries that paved the way.

There are myths and fantasy stories galore. The ancient Sumerians of 5000 BC had a king who tied rocks to his feet and breathing surface air through a tube of seaweed , searched for a plant to provide eternal life. Aristotle told of Alexander the Great using underwater breathing apparatus in the form of diving bells. Leonardo Da Vinci had lots of drawings of undersea breathing devices.

A major guideline for inventors of the past century and a half was Jules Verne's *20,000 Leagues Under The Sea* which imagined much of the diving equipment used by modern diving. Cousteau said, ..."Like many poets, Verne led the way for science to follow." Augustus Siebe in England, about this same time, actually created a lot of this dreamed-up equipment.

Probably, the most influencing development leading to the Aqua Lung, the self-contained underwater breathing apparatus (S.C.U.B.A.) as it is referred to generically, was in 1865. A French Naval Lieutenant Auguste Denayrouse and a mining engineer Benoit Rouquayrol did produce a scuba unit but because air couldn't yet be compressed to adequate pressures, giant tanks were required. They gave it up and went back to air supplied from a surface hose.

The dreaded decompression sickness, the bends, showed up as divers went deeper and stayed longer, and it got great attention as workers in pressurized shafts worked underwater to put in bridge pilings.

Another Frenchman, Paul Bert, showed up in 1878 to explain how the body couldn't exhaust waste product fast enough and nitrogen bubbles would form in the blood stream to block circulation. A Scottish medical doctor, John Haldane, developed the first decompression tables for the Royal Navy which guided divers in interval ascents to allow time for excess nitrogen to be naturally eliminated.

In 1878, Henry Fleuss came up with a self-contained regenerating breathing apparatus that used a caustic soda to purify exhaled carbon dioxide. This was a closed circuit system. By 1911, Sir Robert Davis of England streamlined the Fleuss unit into a light cylinder with increased oxygen pressure. But the closed circuit idea was extremely dangerous at depths below 30 feet where divers breathed nine times more oxygen than in air at normal pressure. Along came Frenchman, Yves LePrieur, who developed the first high-pressure cylinder using ordinary air and his regulating device patterned after the Rouquayrol-Denayrouse design. This device allowed exhalation to escape into water under the edge of the diver's mask, eliminating the recirculation of breathed air.

Cousteau and Emile Gagnan actually were diving with the LePrieur device in 1937. But the system seemed too complicated and would break down often.

Much credit must go to the many who experimented and invented before Cousteau and Gagnan.

TESTING THE IDEA

By summer of 1943, after six months of additional experimentation, the demand device worked effectively. By October 1943, it was put to an ultimate test by Frederic Dumas diving to 200 feet in open water off Marseilles for fifteen minutes.

It might have been snatched up by the military, French or Germans, except for the telltale bubbles of exhalation in an open circuit type scuba. Rebreathers were closed circuit and detection resistant. The "AQUA LUNG", as Cousteau's group decided to call it, was destined to be, it would seem, a grand new toy for civilian divers to use sight seeing and exploring. The Cousteau team used it for such purposes until the patented device went into the market place in 1946.

Jacques-Yves Cousteau, Georges, Philippe Tailliez, Jean Pinard, Frederic Dumas and Guy Morandiere in 1946.   Marine Nationale Comismer

It was not a booming sales success at first in the European region probably because most people were a little afraid of the idea. But the Cousteau group kept pushing its potential with Dumas diving to 306.9 feet in August 1947. In September 1947, a French Navy officer reached a 397 feet depth record but surfaced unconscious and died a short time later. A limit seemed to be evident.

It would take the American market and American competitors with slightly different versions of the Aqua Lung to pressure the Company Air Liquide (on whose Board of Directors Cousteau's father-in-law sat) to increase production of this reliable and low cost breathing unit to meet the demands of sport diving in America.

IN PURSUIT OF COUSTEAU'S LIFETIME DREAM

Cousteau with this frustration of all the free diving pioneers in the 1930's tried his hand at inventing a breathing device. Even as an eleven year old. Taking a blueprint of a two-hundred ton floating crane, he proceeded to build an electric powered model with his Meccano Toy Building Set.

In 1938, while on Navy duty aboard a French Cruiser, Cousteau designed an oxygen rebreathing lung-built it out of a brass box and motorcycle innertube following the principle then being used to escape submarines (Momsen Lung). Misled by experts telling him oxygen was safe down to 45 feet, he over-did with his first closed circuit scuba and was fished out unconscious after a violent oxygen convulsion. A redesign and second attempt had the same result. Cousteau moved his thinking from the danger of oxygen to considering the helmet diving using compressed air to 200-feet, then being used by commercial and salvage divers. But he did not like the lack of freedom of suit, boots, helmet and lines.

World War II exploded and by November 1942, the Germans moved into Southern France. The French sunk their Navy fleet in the Mediterranean to keep it from the enemy. Lieutenant Cousteau was discharged. Cousteau then took on the development of a self-contained-air-lung full time. He had no idea that the great passport to innerspace, the Aqua Lung, would be born out of an automobile gadget.

Simone Cousteau becomes the first woman to use the Aqua Lung. *Cousteau Society*

Cousteau would be financed by Air Liquide, A French company, and there he would team up with Emile Gagnan. Gagnan, a retiring and shy man, was an engineering genius in the field of air pressure apparatus. He had designed a regulator to use cooking gas in autos instead of gasoline.

Here is a photo of the original Cousteau-Gagnon regulator . *Cousteau Society*

It was many weeks before the two men realized what they were seeking to control air in a breathing apparatus was sitting out in the parking lot.

The redesign of the car gas regulator was not a simple crossover to underwater use. One chamber of the Aqua Lung would fill with water to aid the flow of air into a dry chamber to supply the diver. Air flow stops when the pressures become equal in wet and dry chambers and the diver's lungs. There was not instant success. Cousteau took the prototype into the dirty Marne River outside Paris in January 1943 with Gagnan watching from shore. Gagnan was elated to see bursts of bubbles and then alarmed to see the bubbles cease entirely. Sensing failure and Cousteau's demise, Gagnan threw off his coat and began untying his shoes. Cousteau appeared to explain, "I was standing on my head and it gets hard to breathe upside down and runs wide open standing up. It was okay when I was swimming horizontally. How can we go up and down?," he queried.

Dejected they drove back to Paris but they suddenly understood what had happened and began shouting at each other.

"The exhaust valve is six-inches higher than the air take on the back. It's the difference in the water pressure. The air flow is suppressed."

And so as in all inventions, a simple adjustment, placing the exhaust near the center of the regulator diaphragm turned the ultimate corner for this marvelous tool-toy.

Cousteau took the adjusted regulator back in the water and did flips and rolls and headstands with a steady supply of air. His head popped the surface and he cried to Gagnan, "That's it!" They then patented the adjusted device as the Aqua Lung.

The invention of the Aqua Lung sits atop a mountain of efforts over the centuries, to allow man to be like a fish. Ideally, every diver should have

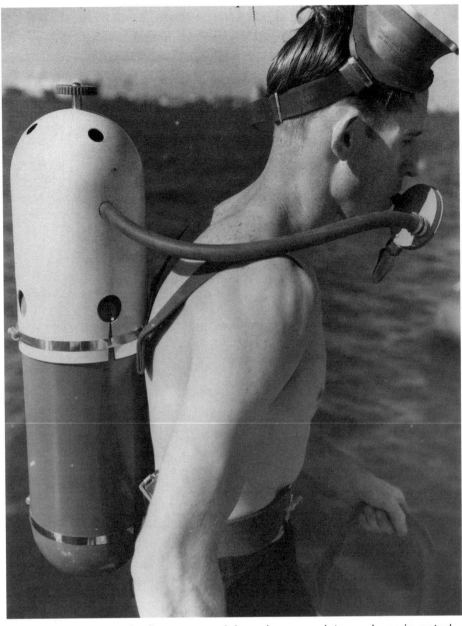

The Sport Diver was the first commercial one hose regulator and was invented by E.R. Cross.
E.R. Cross Collection

surgically implanted gills but that has remained an unattainable God-like miracle over the years. Looking back we see wonderful but limited devices carved and painted into ancient walls. Predominant is the diving bell, an open topped giant container turned upside down and lowered into the water. The air captured within it is compressed to the water pressure surrounding it. It is a humorous but onerous thought that without the Aqua Lung, scuba divers would have to rent a trailer to get their personal two-ton diving bells to their diving venues.

Dr. Christian J. Lambertsen coined the acronym, S.C.U.B.A., for Self-Contained Underwater Breathing Apparatus, in 1954. The acronym has become such a standard part of the English language that *Websters* and all other dictionaries now define it as a word in itself and it is no longer considered as an acronym in popular society.

Aqua Lung lost its brand name exclusive-market-control, and manufacturing companies arose to challenge it with alternative scuba equipment.

The National Research Council's 1959 booklet, *A History Of Self-Contained Diving And Underwater Swimming*, defines S.C.U.B.A. as self-contained apparatus therefore with no surface attachments to aid in breathing. In addition, a breath holding free diver with a lung full of air is using no apparatus and is therefore eliminated from the

Here is a shot of the Sport Diver after a spearfishing dive and lobster catch. Note the surplus cartridge belt that many early divers used for a weight belt.

Homer Lockwood

definition. Submersibles, chambers and armored suits don't fit either, but the bell does, because it adapts the diver to the depth rather than protecting him from it.

The diving bell had a long run as the only scuba method for military use, shipwreck salvaging and obtaining food for some 2000-years. Alexander the Great used one and Aristotle in 300 B.C. talked about a "kettle"-a bell-used by Greek sponge divers. The bell in many forms operated on a simple physics principle: An inverted open ended vessel is submerged in water, the water can enter the vessel by compressing the air trapped inside it.

By the year 1600, improvements to the diving bell involved barrels of air attached outside the bell with air hoses leading inside.

The English astronomer, Sir Edmund Halley of Halley Comet fame, made a simple innovation for renewing the supply of air in the bell, raising and lowering two 36 gallon barrels with hoses coming out of the bottom and extending into the bell. The barrels were alternatingly refilled at the surface providing a constant supply of fresh air.

With that development, the bell moved out of the self-contained underwater breathing apparatus interpretation. A pump replaced the barrels for getting a constant flow of air to the diver. The bell shrunk to a diving "hard hat" helmet. An era of helmet-hose-diving more or less began by the year 1800.

More precursors, continuing attempts to create the scuba that was almost perfectly safe and truly self-con-

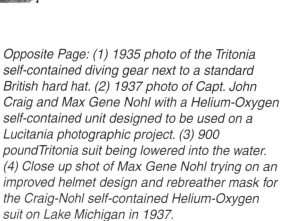

Opposite Page: (1) 1935 photo of the Tritonia self-contained diving gear next to a standard British hard hat. (2) 1937 photo of Capt. John Craig and Max Gene Nohl with a Helium-Oxygen self-contained unit designed to be used on a Lucitania photographic project. (3) 900 poundTritonia suit being lowered into the water. (4) Close up shot of Max Gene Nohl trying on an improved helmet design and rebreather mask for the Craig-Nohl self-contained Helium-Oxygen suit on Lake Michigan in 1937.

Above: (1) Drawing of an early diving setup. (2) Ed Lamphier working with an experimental diver on an early S.C.U.B.A. suit. (3-4) Popular Science Magazine provided the instructions for many early divers who made their own S.C.U.B.A. or surface-supplied systems.

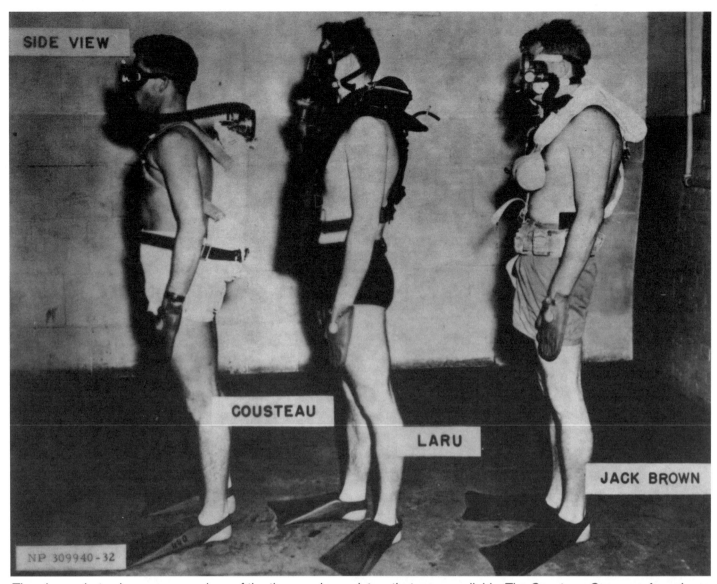

SIDE VIEW

COUSTEAU

LARU

JACK BROWN

NP 309940-32

The above photo shows a comparison of the three early regulators that were available. The Cousteau-Gaagnon Aqua Lung came out on top and revolutionized recreational diving. Note: The Cousteau regulator is being worn backwards in this photo.   U.S. Government

tained with no dependence on surface supply of air, were numerous in many places throughout the world during the nineteenth century and the important ones have already been noted. But there is even more that went before the Aqua Lung.

Some scuba inventions were bizarre looking but had elements of brilliance. A German Friedreich van Drieberg devised a box with bellows supplied with air by tubes to surface, then to a mouthpiece, and a piston connected to a diver's head-crown activated the bellows, with the reverse action of the bellows sucking up the exhausted air. He called it the Triton but it still had to seek surface air. Therefore, the vital principle of compressed air being used underwater, as recognized by Halley with diving bells in the year 1716, was introduced. It was another step on the way to the Aqua Lung.

In America in 1935, a Brooklyn, New York, machinist, Charles Condert, had the plans drawn up for a compressed air suit that took compressed air from a reservoir with no surface air supplied and leaked it into a rubberized suit by operating a valve-cock, with respired air escaping through a small aperture in the head covering. It was used many times by Condert at shallow twenty-foot depths but he drowned when the air tube broke underwater.

This may have been the truly first successful compressed air scuba. Condert's application was printed up in a journal and gave guidance and encouragement to other scuba inventors around the world.

As always controversy was rampant throughout diving. The English were adamant about their primary role in developing S.C.U.B.A. led by Sir Robert Davis, who claimed a light diving apparatus he designed in the year 1911 for his own firm of Siebe Gorman & Co. was the first.

After Condert, two Frenchmen in the year 1865, Rouquoyrol, a mining engineer, and Denayrouse, a Navy Lieutenant, came up with a "self-contained diving suit," but alas, it still had to have air pumped from the surface. But it did have an air reservoir which gave the diver some backup when topside pumps failed. Old French Navy diving manuals stated that it could be used to a depth of 66 feet. By the year 1880, several countries looked upon it favorably. Jules Verne's *20,000 Leagues Under the Sea*, written in 1869,

Jacques Cousteau and Emile Gagnon.

U.S. Divers

carried references to it as the basis for Nemo's own design which stored air in a reservoir for ten hours.

Verne's concept would have required ten cylinders to accommodate the pressure containment suggested. Verne seemed to be unaware of the problems of decompression, which in 1870 became clarified in Paul Bert of France's writings on barometric pressure.

PHOTOGRAPHY THE BIG INCENTIVE

Brothers, Louis and A. Bouton, Louis a zoology professor, both of France, were motivated by a great interest in underwater photography and seeking lateral mobility for it. They tried free diving and then available scuba. There is not much information available about Bouton-scuba except they used the traditional helmet and suit plus a steel cylinder of air compressed to 2,850 pounds per square inch (psi).

The military needs, especially with submarine escape, spurred England through its renowned manufacturer of diving equipment, Siebe, Gorman & Co. and Germany's Draegerwerk to develop oxygen rebreathers. By year 2000 electronically monitored rebreathers threatened to revolutionize the sport of diving.

Francois Villarem and Emile Gagnon uncertain about the one hose follow up to Aqua Lung.

Both England and Germany competed to devise the perfect scuba. Westfalea of Germany in the year 1912 was using a mixed gas scuba suit containing 30% oxygen and 70% nitrogen usable to 200 feet. Siebe Gorman came right back preceding World War I with their Fleuss-Davis scuba which let divers mix air and oxygen from two cylinders, useful to a 66 foot depth.

World War I was a latent period for scuba development; submarines seemed to be doing what was necessary. However, a filming of *20,000 Leagues Under The Sea* by J. E. Williamson in 1915 in the United States did employ an oxylite scuba for "Underwater Walkers". The oxylite used to purify the self-contained air supply got used up fast and on one occasion during filming, fouled gas seemed to make drunken maniacs out of the actors and they attacked each other.

Helmet-hose diving continued well after World War I to be the preferred approach to underwater submergence. It was improved technically by efforts in the United States, France and Italy. But scuba lurked nearby and in France the effort was concentrated on open circuit for civilian use and in Italy on close circuit for military. The United States military in the 1930's concentrated on rebreathers as well, but the United

Scuba Instructor and movie star Buster Crabbe with Rene Bussoz and Hal Messinger in 1949 try out the first Aqua Lungs in the US.   *Rene Bussoz*

States with the world supply of helium did develop a self-contained suit using the helium for respiration.

Importantly, the pioneer work of Dr. J. S. Haldane in devising a procedure for decompression and further studies by Americans, Dr. Edgar End, Dr. Albert R. Behnke, Elihu Thompson, William Shaw, and others, provided new visions on how scuba should function. Helium provided comparison results with nitrogen. Mixed gas-use was always on inventors' mind and a prime effort was when Dr. End and John D. Craig oversaw Gene Nohl's record setting dive on December 1, 1937 using helium oxygen mixture-scuba to 420 feet in Lake Michigan.

It is important to again recall Le Prieur's great contribution to the Aqua Lung invention. In 1926 Le Prieur, a Captain in the French Navy, got a French patent for a scuba apparatus. It involved a steel cylinder 1950 pounds per square inch (psi) with a hose to a mouthpiece, using goggles and no suit or helmet. Inventions inspire accessory inventions, and the De Corlier swim fins became available by the 1930's to aid in the use of the Le Prieur. The first model only allowed a short period of bottom time because the unit involved a wasteful steady flow of air to the diver. To control it would require a balanced demand regulator.

Goggle diving, skin diving, breathhold diving grew in popularity in the 1930's and all of the early pioneers such as Cousteau, Dumas, Talliez (French), Hass (Austrian), Gilpatric (American), and a large contingency of United States divers in Southern California and Florida began the parade to mass interest in sport diving. All of them were thinking about staying down longer and the need for a safe scuba device.

We reached 1942 and the dawn of the open circuit scuba era with Cousteau's Aqua Lung.

AMERICA WAITING

In the late 1940's in America, everywhere, young men were tracking to war surplus stores that had mushroomed up. They bought high altitude oxygen regulators, hose and small 38 cubic foot tanks and fire extinguishers. The clever ones adjusted them to work underwater. Alas, there was aluminum inside the unit that the salt water corroded quickly. A leading invention was by pioneer, icon, Ellis Royal Cross. It was the first marketed single hose scuba. But busy with his Sparling School of Diving in 1948, he could not find the time to go into commercial production and distribution. Much in demand for lectures on diving, he gave a talk on diving at the Redondo Beach Rod & Gun Club. In the audience, a wide-eyed, alert, 42 year old man, Homer Lockwood, stayed after to volunteer to put these conversion units together. And, so the Sport Diver scuba from military surplus parts became available but it had a short life immediately preceding the Aqua Lung arrival in the U.S.A. Only 39 units were ever sold, some through a *Popular Mechanics Magazine* mail order advertisement, at the cost of $50.00 which included a war surplus 38 cubic foot CO_2 tank purged and full of air. But with the discovery of the corrosive vulnerability, it saw a quick demise.

SPORT DIVING'S PRIMARY ROLE IN EQUIPMENT DEVELOPMENT

Everything we've gotten in sport diving has trickled down from the military, the science field and the commercial diving industry. The equipment, the technology, the medical understandings, the training...and underwater photography.

Not quite.

Taking pictures underwater was the best way of sharing the great things seen before anyone else and everyone else seemed to want to see in pictures what it was that excited divers down there.

For early divers it was like showing off pictures of something they owned...whatever was in that picture at the moment was theirs. If someone else eventually got a picture of the same thing, well, they had the "first edition", and it was uniquely as they saw it, perhaps in its original state of creation. If Adam and Eve had a camera, we'd have a better idea of what Eden was like.

This drive to share the experience with others, who had never been there and perhaps never would, made sport diving the prime mover for developing the equipment over and beyond the scientific and military efforts.

Jacques Cousteau still found joy in his Aqua Lung a half century after its invention. Cousteau Society

Philip Halsman, a photographer, had been diving with Yves Le Prieur scuba gear which was invented in 1926. Halsman had used it since 1931 and at that time it was the most popular scuba device. It had a full face mask. Halsman taught Dimitri Rebikoff, a non-swimmer, how to use it in 1948. Rebikoff would recall, "I would sink feet first, walk on the bottom, run out of air and ascend by the anchor line."

In 1949, Henri Broussard, President of the Submarine Alpine Club in Cannes, France, got Rebikoff to move to Cannes for purposes of solving lighting problems for underwater photography. Broussard pushed Dimitri into switching from Le Prieur's unit to Cousteau's Aqua Lung.

Rebikoff responsible for so many underwater inventions would say that he could very well have improved Le Prieur's S.C.U.B.A. and come up with the equivalent of the Aqua Lung. Divers in garages and workshops across America and Europe were trying to invent the "AQUA LUNG" that Cousteau and Gagnan were first to produce.

Underwater photography was certainly the major driving force that brought scuba and the Aqua Lung into existence. It was true with Cousteau in those early years when he was trying to make films by holding his breath and being frustrated. The taking of game, sight-seeing, exploring wrecks and caves and numerous other interests fall just under photography as catalysts.

Jacques Cousteau would say, "With the Aqua Lung, my childhood dreams triggered by Jules Verne imagination, that of flying and breathing underwater, would be achieved, not only for myself but the whole world."

And with the Aqua Lung's 1950 arrival on American shores, the half century history of scuba diving in America would begin.

2
BOOKS THAT TURNED US ON

DEFINING EVENT: THE SILENT WORLD

"At night I had often had visions of flying by extending my arms as wings. Now I flew without wings. Since that first Aqua Lung flight, I have never had a dream of flying." So said Jacques-Yves Cousteau in his classic book *The Silent World,* Harper and Row, 1953. The sub-title is "a story of undersea discovery and adventure, by the first men to swim at record depths with the freedom of fish."

The book was an honest, human attempt to describe the first sensations and adventures of the man who came to represent scuba diving in the public's eye. For divers in those pioneer days, the early 1950's of its publication, the book was encouraging and motivating to move from breath holding to using this new device for flying under-water and to try and duplicate Cousteau and his crew's adventures.

In *Exploring the Deep Frontier,* pioneer diver, Al Giddings, frequently refers and quotes from *The Silent World* which "he read and eagerly reread" to be able to write dramatically about early diving moments and feelings about using scuba. *The Silent World* captured the essence of diving for all time and nothing in writing has come along over the years to surpass it.

Cousteau had been skin diving almost a decade be-fore scuba took over his devotion to this new sport. Ameri-can divers, skin divers, were going under with crude free diving equipment in 1936 when Cousteau began. There were even crude scuba homemade units being tried in

The Silent World inspired a generation of early pioneer divers.

America. Some used compressed air. The dangerous rebreather family was also available as scuba, commer-cially made, but with highly limited capability.

Silent World was a grand reassuring testimonial to the Aqua Lung which could well have been the generic word for tank diving but since it was a patented trade mark it opened the door to the acronym, scuba, a typical military approach of naming their tools with a long phrase, thus Self-Contained Underwater Breathing Apparatus-S.C.U.B.A. coined by Dr. Christian J. Lambertsen at the University of Pennsylvania in 1954.

Cousteau was encouraged to write *Silent World* by an American journalist, James Dugan, who became ac-quainted with him during World War II. Although the book credits authorship to Captain J. Y. Cousteau with Frédéric Dumas, there is a short excerpt in the front that notes that James Dugan aided in *Silent World* preparation. Many people familiar with Cousteau and with James Dugan's style suspect that it was Dugan who shaped Cousteau's stories and feelings into literature.

Twenty Thousand Leagues Under the Sea became a hit movie and has been remade several times. *Stackpole*

The book is truly a classic of exploration and has held up as the scuba book beyond all others. Cousteau addresses many of his mistakes and dramatically expresses what millions of scuba divers in the years to follow publication would feel and would find the words to describe it in Jacques Cousteau's book.

He explains that being of this new species of Menfish, one feels "our flesh feeling what the fish scales know". His first view underwater with goggles sparked this reaction, "One Sunday morning in 1936.......standing up to breathe I saw a trolley car, people, electric light poles... I put my eyes under again and civilization vanished with one last bow... I was in a jungle never seen by those who floated on the opaque roof."

Divers were introduced to "rapture of the deep" by *Silent World*. Cousteau's experiences with this "drunkenness" and his research into Albert Behnke's early nitrogen narcosis work for the United States Navy led him to write about its effect: "If a passing fish seems to require air, the crazed diver may tear out his air pipe or mouth grip as a supreme gift." ...an off repeated description in the early days of scuba. *Silent World* covered the gamut of sunken ships, cave diving, submersibles, befriending sea creatures, shark encounters, and in many ways could be used as a beginning manual for diving 50 years later—a highly entertaining manual.

The book jacket is a colorful but mundane photo of a diver poling through bushes of coral. It is distinctive. On the jacket inside lapel, it says, "Jules Verne's imagination is matched by the reality of the 5,000 dives Cousteau and Dumas have made into the last unknown."

The publisher Harper and Row reprinted *Silent World* many times and many thousand of copies have flooded the world in the past 50 years.

Al Tillman recalls: "I read the October 1952 *National Geographic* article which was the forerunner to *The Silent World* ...but it was the book, a literary time capsule that simply illuminated the whole scuba experience. It echoed my own feelings and gave permission to let the athletic lure of skin diving go and embrace scuba diving which opened the floodgates of much greater adventure potential. Hey, Cousteau's gang did dumb things just like me. It is the first thing I'd hand to any new comer to diving to read."

The pioneer divers in interview all praised *The Silent World* as one of if not *the* greatest motivating force in their transition from free diving to scuba diving. John Cronin, CEO of the U.S. Divers Company in its zenith and co-founder of PADI, credited *The Silent World* with creating the industry of sport diving in the beginning.

Stanton Waterman, Diving's foremost silver tongued lecturer-cinematographer who has been diving since the beginning of the 50 year history recalls, "I read *Silent World*, closed my cranberry farm because I felt I could do what Cousteau was doing and I wanted to do what Cousteau was doing, so I packed up and went to the Bahamas to operate a charter boat dive business."

JULES VERNE LIGHTED THE WAY

The "Jules Verne imagination" initiated all modern science fiction. His prophetic writings were fulfilled by many actual inventions in the Twentieth Century. His classic 1869 *Twenty Thousand Leagues Under the Sea* ignited a great interest in the underwater world and led young inventors to try and actually create the described devices. Cousteau was captivated by the book and certainly some of the inspiration for the Aqua Lung must have germinated from reading it. It has been reprinted in many forms, even a pop-up version, and continues to thrill the reader as an exciting story even in the modern age of mega technological developments.

Twenty Thousand Leagues Under the Sea described diving that would come into existence over a century later. Jules Verne had Captain Nemo dive where no one had ever gone before. He walked through Atlantis! "I was treading underfoot the mountains of this continent, touching my hand to those ruins a thousand generations old, ... I was walking on the very spot where the contemporaries of the first man had walked."

No other books have come along to match up to the influence that these two, Cousteau and Verne, have had on sport diving. Some divers would lobby for Hans Hass's *Diving to Adventure,* 1951, as being as important to sport diving but it was primarily about skin diving. His other books were oriented to the use of the rebreather SCUBA. For the young pioneers of the 1940's and early 1950's, Hass came closer to their experiences than Cousteau did.

Finally, *Twenty Thousand Leagues Under the Sea* has been put into film form several times and the motion pictures have empowered the book. It is true, as well, that *Silent World*, the movie, gave tremendous support to *Silent World*, the book.

OTHER INSPIRING BOOKS

Here is an annotated list of other adventure books that fall into a lesser category but all had an effect of drawing people into diving and going underwater. How-To-Manuals, books on marine life and anthologies are not covered here because although informative, they do not represent the literary-lure sirens that ignited the fires within adventurers to be.

• *Beneath the Sea* - William L. (Bill) High

Best Publishing Company, Flagstaff, Arizona, 1998

One of sport diving's pioneers tells his memoirs as a marine biologist and leader of various sport diving's big events.

"I rode the back of a wild killer whale; descended more than one thousand feet beneath the sea; lived for weeks on the ocean floor; was "attacked" by brown bears, sharks, giant octopuses and sea lions. I watched the Japanese bomb Pearl Harbor and dove among the war dead of Truk Lagoon. I was shipwrecked on a desolate Alaska shore. I had conversations with the distinguished Ambassador Clare Booth Luce, chatted with John Wayne, shared company with the father of saturation diving, Dr. George Bond, met Lyndon Johnson under most unusual circumstances and had a couple of run-ins with Jacques Cousteau.

• *Blue Water Hunting and Freediving* - Terry Maas

Blue Water Free Divers, 1955

This is a book that covers the real heroes and athletes of sport diving - the underwater hunters and free divers. It reveals both the difference and the linkage between free diving and scuba diving.

"...the streamlined diver levels off easily at 25 feet. He experiences an exhilaration known only to trained free divers. His mental ease and special physiological adaptations make him feel as if he has no need to breathe - now or ever. It is narcotic. Peaceful. Part of him feels as if he could remain suspended beneath the waves forever.

...The enveloping water is supportive and filled with beauty. The diver is free. Free of bulky and noisy scuba gear. Free to roam with wild animals. Free to fly gracefully in any direction.

• *Cousteau* - Richard Munson

William Morrow and Company, 1989

This book shows balanced, unauthorized revelations about the world's most famous adventurer. It reveals the flaws and the greatness of Cousteau who was credited with authoring over 80 books.

• *Dive to Adventure* - Jack McKenney

Panorama Publications Ltd., 1983

McKenney was a great diver, cinematographer, and writer. He died young but left a treasury of underwater films. He was pulled into diving when he saw the movie, *The Frogmen*, at 13 and then shortly after discovered the books of Hans Hass. Jack always wanted to be Hans Hass but instead he became his equal. This book is ideal for attracting young people into diving.

McKenney had made more dives on the Andrea Doria than anyone (49) and most of this book is about the trials and tribulations. Here's a bit from one of his close call experiences:

"...pulling hand over hand, far exceeding the normal rate of ascent, exhaling whenever I could. Don't let me passout-not now! sixty feet, 50 feet, where was I..."

It takes the reader on the scene of what was the hardest diving in history.

• *Exploring the Deep Frontier* - Dr. Sylvia Earle and

Al Giddings, National Geographic Society, 1980

Two pioneer divers gave a personal touch to their view of diving history in general.

Al Giddings observed, that most of the early divers were spearfishermen - Hans Hass, Cousteau *and* Al Giddings. He remembers as the most exciting days of his life as diving down 60 feet in cold, murky water. "I'd know I'd reached the bottom when I could see the eyes of dozens of enormous lingcod resting on the sand, looking up at me as if I'd just dropped in from another universe."

• *I Thought I Saw Atlantis* - Al Tillman

Whalestooth Publishing, 1998

This memoir book of a pioneer scuba diver tells the humbling experiences encountered on the way to founding a number of sport diving's leading organizations from NAUI to UNEXSO.

Here's one experience:

"The kelp parted and the sun glinted through. A sparkling green flashed up at me. The green ran 30 feet and more. It seemed like the bottom was solid jade. This was the source of jade, long finger reefs of it. This was a virtual sea of jade."

• *Lady with a Spear* - Dr. Eugenie Clark

Harper & Brothers Publishers New York. 1951

A woman pioneer, who would eventually go with scuba into virgin venues of the sea and make the definitive statement about sharks. It was a book to excite people about free diving but in particularly to attract to diving the female gender.

"Genie", as her friends call her, expressed:

"Goggling in the beautiful clear water around Bimini had one disadvantage. Diving among the delicate lavender and canary-yellow sea fans, I would look up through the magnifying face mask and see a barracuda watching me.

.... I was diving with a little knife with which to cut some of the sea fans loose. I wanted to dry them and bring them back to my family for souvenirs - unlike most marine animals they keep their colors well. As I was heading for the surface with two lovely fans, I met a barracuda. He didn't make a move but just looked at me calmly - with no sign of the fear that other fishes have. I felt as if a policeman had caught me stealing flowers from a park and I let the sea fans drop back to the bottom."

• *Manta* - Dr. Hans Hass
Rand McNally, 1952
This book is translated from German and stands beside Hass' *Diving to Adventure* as pre-*Silent World* tomes of excitement to the early young divers. Hans Hass was a closed circuit scuba diver by the time he wrote this account of diving on Mantas (at that time rarely seen "monsters".)
Hass tells of his first encounter:
"The sight that I now confronted appeared incredible. ...the huge beast had come even nearer. ...I could see one eye and above it two projecting devil's horns...."

• *Men and Sharks* - Dr. Hans Hass
Doubleday & Company, Inc. Garden City, New York, 1954
Hass doesn't dispel the historical fear of sharks in this book but his are the first diver's experience with sharks. If nothing else, he found yelling at them drives them off.

• *Men Beneath the Sea* - Dr. Hans Hass
St. Martin's Press, 1973
It's hard to pick out another impact book from the large publication that Hans Hass has had over the years right on through year 2000. For many divers, Hans Hass was the inspiring solitary diver versus the Cousteau Calypso team. He covers in this book his own and his famous diving friends' adventures. In it we see his changeover similar to Cousteau's concern with the loss of the ocean environment.

• *Sea Fever* - Sir Robert Marx
Doubleday and Company, 1972
Robert Marx has been diving's most prolific author after Cousteau and his storytelling of some of diving's legendary figures holds you in its grip.
Marx on a Teddy Tucker find:
"The Seventh day on the wreck was the most exciting day of Tucker's life. He discovered the most valuable single item of treasure ever recovered from an old shipwreck (valued at $2,000,000 in the 1950's) . ....he stuck his head in (the hole) and saw a magnificent emerald-studded gold cross."

• *Sunken Treasure* - Robert E. Burgess
Dodd Mead, 1988
There's no doubt the idea of sunken treasure has been the most exotic motivator for going diving. Only a few divers ever fulfilled the dream and struck it rich. This book covers six who did.
Here is one of the moments described:
"...Twenty-six-year-old Susan Nelson was on the bottom searching the craters dug by the mighty blowers - ". ...suddenly I kicked and there was a gold bar. I kicked again and there was another gold bar and suddenly there

I was holding four gold bars in my hands, and I was a little in awe. I was hyperventilating underwater. I said, 'Oh, my Lord.' "

• *The Blue reef* - Walter Starck

Alfred A. Knopf, 1979

This noted marine biologist describes what scuba diving and the magic of a coral reef are all about from a field expedition to Eniwetok Atoll.

Suspended in the muted light of a night dive, by himself, he recalls:

"It was an eerie sensation to float suspended in almost complete blackness. My only company was the half-seen shadows of fish moving in front of my face.

....I pondered those of the creatures around me. They have lived with the same problems for the past 50 million years or more and have learned to cope with their surroundings and neighbors. ....as I swam slowly up through clouds of silvery bubbles, I seemed to be suspended in time...."

• *The Compleat Goggler* - Guy Gilpatric

Skin Diver Magazine Reprint, 1960

Gilpatric was an American journalist diving on the French Riviera in the 1930's. No one else was diving at the time but Cousteau's interest was triggered by seeing Gilpatric using goggles and spearing fish. His book is probably the first complete book describing the diving experience. Hans Hass got his first introduction to skin diving from Guy Gilpatric. Gilpatric was a grand story teller and he cautioned these young men, (eventually to become legends in diving) - "Never dive too close to steep rocks, because that's where enormous specimens...hide in crevices and caves...(the octopus) will embrace anything that passes too close, and pull it into the hole with incredible force."

It was suspected Gilpatric was not trying to recruit more divers to invade his private territory. But he did.

• *The Last of the Blue Water Hunters* - Carlos Eyles

Watersport Publishing Co., 1985

This is a moving narrative of one passionate free diver on a solitary "last dive" and the foundation of what scuba diving was built on. The author reflects:

"My thoughts are not on new territories to explore but on old ones that have disappeared, the rich untouched ocean that the fathers (the pioneer divers) experienced fifty years ago. If I could find a seam in time that is where I would go. Not to hunt, but to see and feel the teeming life that existed here on the island and along the coastline.

The bottom is thick with lobsters, many as long as your leg. ...abalone big as dinner plates hang on every available rock..."

• *The Living Sea* - Jacques-Yves Cousteau with

James Dugan

Harper and Row, 1963

James Dugan as Cousteau's voice, putting Cousteau's journal notes into a book form, created literature that was indeed the Pied Piper that led the general public into diving.

Diving on the S.S. Thistlegorm, a World War II shipwreck, those two super-hero divers, Frédéric Dumas and Albert Falco, report they saw "The Thing." It was a prodigious dark-green wall of flesh, a single slab-sided animal that barred their progress aft. Dumas and Falco were stupefied. It was beyond the remotest connection with any fish they had ever seen. Dumas said, "There were army tanks on the deck. When the Thing passed near them, it seemed as big as a truck." They called it the Truckfish but later found out it was a giant wrasse.

• *The Ocean World of Jacques-Yves Cousteau* - (A series in 15 volumes) Jacques-Yves Cousteau

The Danbury Press, 1973

The series demonstrates the leap from the *Silent World* of adventure into the unknown to Cousteau's changed attitude toward the oceans he conquered.

In his introduction, he sounds the warning that man's spoilation can kill the ocean. If the ocean dies then so will all life on this planet which is unique in that it is the only celestial body where we know life is possible. The ocean is where life originated.

This series was preceded by one translated from French - *The Underwater Discoveries of Jacques-Yves Cousteau* in 1970, and contains one particular volume that covers sharks which is required reading for divers.

James Dugan, David Stith and George Youmans and colleagues.   Joe Dorsey

• *World Beneath the Sea* - James Dugan

National Geographic Society, 1967

The author was Cousteau's literary voice according to many accounts and a brilliant writer. This, his last book, before he died at sea in 1967, is mostly his final take on the sea's mysteries that captivated him. In this book he goes behind the scenes. He recalls George Bond pointing out that Dugan's admired hero, Edmond Halley, (Halley's Comet fame) tested a wooden diving bell to 80 feet for 90 minutes without knowledge of decompression sickness. "A few minutes more," Bond said, "and Halley might have died." The book is filled with in-depth views of diving's most impactful happenings.

Scuba America may have missed a few books along the way but certainly, feels strongly about this selection. The shame is that more of the early divers didn't keep journals and write their personal accounts.

The books cited were expressions of heart and soul and captured some of the early wonder at seeing things no one had ever seen before. These writers were the divers who metaphorically walked through the fog and into a mountain and on the other side found a brilliant, awesome and glorious Shangrila but one that seemed to have no boundaries. Indeed they could fly and discover something akin to Eden and they *knew it*. As well as they wrote, they all shook their heads and said it was too large an experience for words, it had to be felt in person. But their words were better than they thought and seduced thousands upon thousands of people over the years into wanting to have the same experiences. Hopefully, many more books are to be written not only to lead people into diving but to help veteran divers with the words to express the magical feeling of going underwater.

3

SKIN DIVER MAGAZINE

DEFINING EVENT: FIRST ISSUE - DECEMBER 1951

The Skin Diver

A MAGAZINE FOR

SKIN DIVERS AND SPEARFISHERMEN

Featuring---

NOVEMBER
SPEARFISHING AT
LA PAZ
By Ronald Drummond

CALIFORNIA
SHEEPSHEAD
By Conrad Limbaugh

MIDWINTER
SKIN DIVING DERBY

THE PEARL DIVERS
OF HIKUERU
By Don Clark

CLUB NEWS FROM —
The Seals of Santa Barbara
Muirmen
Santa Anita Neptunes
Bottom Scratchers
Los Angeles Neptunes
Sea-Downers
Dolphins
Southern Calif. Skin Divers

DECEMBER

Photo By Larry Kronquist, Laguna Beach

First Issue

Before *The Skin Diver* magazine, communication between divers was about as good as Indian smoke signals on a rainy day. Divers wanted their diving spots to themselves and resented any other diver who intruded. They barely grunted if they got close to each other.

Now this may be somewhat exaggerated because there were a few clubs where divers came together to share ideas and inventions and as Jim Christiansen always said, "Lied to each other about fish." It was 1950, the beginning of diving's recorded history period. A paucity of any books on diving also ripened the atmosphere for uniting divers and allowing them to talk to each other on a national scale.

One day two big guys in their early twenties bounced the idea of a diving magazine off each other. The bulk of divers at the time were dedicated free diving spearfishermen and Jim Auxier and Chuck Blakeslee belonged to the Dolphin Club

Jim Aucier and Chuck Blakeslee hold half of a 462 pound clam shell from the Marshall Islands that was on display in the Skin Diver Magazine offices.   *Skin Diver Magazine*

of Compton/South Gate, California, which was a typical band of "walrus-type divers". (Chuck Blakeslee, in looking around him and at the original Bottom Scratcher Club, decided there were a lot of "walrus-type guys" into diving, including Jim Auxier and himself.)

Jim Auxier was a linotype operator and thoroughly trained printer for Chambers Printing in South Gate, California. He set all the HOT type for *The Skin Diver* for the first two years of the magazine before it had outgrown the capabilities of Chambers to handle the numbers of such a large printing. (The magazine eventually was printed at Pacific Press, the largest west coast printer.) Chuck Blakeslee was a lab technician and assistant to a Ph.D. in Bacteriology for Texaco for several years. He had also developed a speargun, The Barracuda, which gave him access to many of the west coast potential manufacturers/distributors who were later to advertise in the magazine. Thank God for their day jobs which helped pay the bills as the two pursued their passion for skin diving and turned it into a successful special interest magazine.

Jim and Chuck were both thoughtful, cautious personalities. Decisions to go ahead, try something new, expand would never come easy. Slow and sure they were, but when determined, their decisions were of rock solid sensible substance. Six- hundred and forty-one dollars sounds like tip money for the week nowadays for someone like...Oh...Robert Petersen or Bill Gates. But in 1951 when Jim and Chuck managed to scrape it together out of grocery money, they settled down in Jim's garage and Chuck's bedroom to publish 2000 copies of a magazine they would call "*Skin Diver*". They put their passion for this exciting new sport in its early free diving form into ink and paper.

They had put the call out to diving clubs by hand-addressed letters asking for club news and adventure stories. No literary masterpieces tumbled in, but the response was encouraging. Somebody would have to edit it all down to a meaningful best, and Jim Auxier took on the role and the logistical job of getting it printed. The subscriptions would have to pay some of the way eventually, but to get *Skin Diver* before the diving public eye, the magazine would have to be sold to dive shops. The real money to support any magazine has to come from advertising, and Chuck Blakeslee, as co-owner and co-publisher with Jim, took on the stressful job of getting advertisers. The major unveiling probably was at the National Sporting Goods Association Show in 1955.

Chuck Blakeslee and Jacques Cousteau at the Skin Diver Magazine offices.

In 1951, from the first issue, *The Skin Diver* was on the news-stands, first through the Drown News Agency in Long Beach, California, and the Sunset Agency in Los Angeles. Some of the large stores that also distributed the magazine were Aqua Lung Incorporated of Miami, Florida, Abercrombie and Fitch, and Richards in New York. Chuck distributed the magazines to individual dive and sporting goods shops in the Los Angeles basin such as Mel Fisher's, Sparling School of Diving, Woody's in Compton, California, Long Beach Sporting Goods, and Tex's Sporting Goods in Santa Monica. Returned and unsold issues were recycled and used for promotional material.

The first issue, published in December 1951, was a peephole-look at all of diving around the country. The cover was champion spearfisherman, Doc Nelson Mathison, with a gigantic White Sea Bass slung over his wet shoulder. The cover was in a duo-tone, green and black, while the rest of the magazine was in black and white. The back cover ad, also in two colors, from Voit Rubber Company, renowned for its rubber basketballs and footballs and well-recognized, helped sell their masks and fins.

A total of sixteen pages made up the Number 1 issue. It was a skinny one but substantially full of exciting stories about activities and information for the world to read. News included the first annual Midwinter Skin Diving Derby held on December 15, 1951. "Underwater fishermen *and* women from Monterey to San Diego, California, explored the kelp beds and underwater reefs for big fish, abalone, and lobster in an effort to win one of the prizes offered...prizes consisted of Aqua Lungs, rubber suits, spears, guns, masks, flippers and a variety of other equipment amounting to almost a thousand dollars." The article said that competition was keen since the world's best underwater divers tried their luck. The derby was held as a voice and means to build a "war chest" of money in support of the Southern Council of Conservation Clubs and the Ocean Fish Protective League.

Later issues declared "...all manuscripts and photography submitted to *The Skin Diver* for publication are accepted free of any obligation to *The Skin Diver* and its staff and no remuneration will be made for any such material contributed."

There were about 100 clubs in America by 1953, and most of them were submitting copy to the magazine. By then, the magazine had swollen to 48 pages and published 57,000 copies a month. (By year 2000, *Skin Diver Magazine* would reach 154 pages and have a paid circulation of 211,960 copies with 1.1 million in total readership.) The original subscription rate was $3.00 a year at 25 cents per copy; $5.00 for two years at 21 cents per copy; $10 for five years at 17 cents per copy; $4.00 a year for Foreign (other than U.S. Possessions) and Lifetime subscription was $50. By year 2000 the subscription for one year was $49.85. When an advertisement insert in the magazine was used, it was discounted for a final cost of $9.97 per year. Canadian orders added $13.00 per year, and foreign orders added $15.00 per year for surface mail postage. All payment was to be in United States funds. The modern magazine was state-of-the-art graphics, full color throughout, and a typical cover was like the May 2000 one - a blonde, female scuba diver palming a nudibranch in color-coordinated equipment, photographed by the editor, and probably computer enhanced, surrounded by a menu of articles within. Interestingly, despite the wonderful underwater photography being done and rapid progress in graphics, the pioneer divers admire most the 1950's and 1960's covers with paintings by John Steele, who went on to become a celebrated

Jim Auxier

wildlife artist.

Auxier and Blakeslee worked hard at publishing *Skin Diver Magazine*, and throughout their thirteen-year ownership, it was the national, then international "chat room", as it might be called, in year 2000 jargon. What it told was at a human level of what you might hear from voices around a beach campfire after a dive.

The magazine after the first issue started to attract some writings by individuals who would become famous divers. Andreas Rechnitzer was one, and after he had submitted "*Early History of Skin Diving*" for the first issue, he wrote in his best academic style about marine biology students diving, "but much supplemental observational assistance can come from the amateur...to be sure most of the interest displayed by skin divers is on a gastronomical level...securing palatable protein." Along that line of diving to eat, many readers submitted recipes and some, as Allen Petrie, wrote a column for a time.

By the end of the first year, news and articles were coming in from divers on the East and West Coasts of the United States such as Rod White of the Seals of Santa Barbara, California, and Richard Crosby of Long Island, New York, who wrote several good articles. Other writers sent material from Haiti (Gustav Dalla Valle), Ceylon (Rodney Jonklass), Tasmania (Len Staples), Maupiti in the Society Islands- Tahiti (Don Clark), the Red Sea (Dr. Eugenie Clark), Japan, while a member of UDT in the Korean conflict (John Riffe), as well as articles from Fiji and Mexico. How did the magazine get around the world so quickly? By 1963 when *The Skin Diver* was sold to Petersen Publications the magazine was read in 90 countries!

The cover of the February 1952 issue was a photo by Jerry Greenberg, often considered by the pioneer divers as *the* best underwater photographer, (and the only one who got *SDM* to pay for material saying, "I'm a professional.") The cover pictured Florida diver, Alex Drimba, smiling and sitting on top of a pile of huge groupers, a picture that later diver/environmentalists would call an unnecessary slaughter. On the cover it said, "A Magazine for Skin Divers and Spearfishermen." There would be many pictures of speared fish, even using the new scuba, and an occasional shot such as a bare-skinned, cookie cutter-masked Lamar Boren coming out of the water with his hands full of lobster.

Chuck Blakeslee

The early *SDM* masthead read "Jim Auxier, Editor; Chuck Blakeslee, Associate Editor; published at PO Box 128, Lynwood, California. In June 1952 Chuck assumed the title Associate Editor and Advertising Manager and finally his title was changed to Advertising Manager. The first editorial laid out the goals and purposes of the new publication: "...you as a skin diver will find this magazine interesting from cover to cover because it was compiled, written and published with you as its reader... The name...was picked because it includes everyone interested and participating in underwater fishing and hunting. Our policies are few and can be readily adjusted according to the trend or season. We make no claims on our journalistic talents; therefore, *The Skin Diver* has many writers - all experts - not necessarily experts at writing but experts on the subject written about..." The magazine's primary purpose was that of a monthly publication creating a further interest in skin diving and spearfishing and in providing an advertising medium for manufacturers and retail merchants of equipment used by the underwater fishing and hunting enthusiast.

Two club reports in February 1952 were "parallel universes" of California and Florida diving. Al Tillman's report on the Santa Anita Neptunes talked about varying weather and water of the winter season and asked the magazine to promote competitive skin diving leagues, technique descriptions by the best divers, and friendlier atmospheres at local diving areas - "Don't grunt, say, 'Hello'." Across America the Miami Neptunes (no connection to the aforementioned) had President, Ed Sutherland, telling *SDM* readers that the best depth for spearfishing was

30-35 feet.

The first advertising selling at eight cents per word featured Fisher Sporting Goods (Mel Fisher) in Torrance, California, (a chicken farm) claiming, "If it's underwater equipment - I've got it." Mel announced in the ad that he manufactured CO_2 gas guns and exploding heads and made underwater movies on order. Sea Net, a pioneer in manufacturing mask and fins, located at 1428 Maple Avenue in Los Angeles, had a two-thirds page pushing their National Frogman Club; join for a dollar. Mart Toggweiler, probably the first charter dive boat Captain/owner, advertised his 42 foot diesel cruiser, "Maray", going to Catalina Island for skin diving with a note of "Privacy for mixed groups." René Sports was pushing Italian Frogman Suits at $29.95, Aqua Lungs, and Arbalete Spearguns.

The 1952 Los Angeles Neptunes report by Woody Dimel moaned about commercial divers taking 60 dozen abalone a day and the need for all clubs to get together in a council and fight legislation, or "We will find ourselves pushed out of the water and all our skin diving gear useful only to decorate our den walls...Florida is facing that problem right now (1952)." The Sea Downers (California Club) told of Pat O'Malley joining the august rank within the Club of King Sea Downers with an 11 pound lobster (or bug), the requirements being to get 3 abalone (abs) on one dive, spear a 15 pound fish and get a 9 pound bug.

Lots of spearfishing. That's what it seemed in the early 1950's. That's what diving was all about, and the magazine had to go in that direction. As the high priests of that early era, Wally Potts and Jack Pradonovich, had this to say, "There were gangs of fish everywhere, dozens of abalone in every crack, 2 or 3 lobster in every hole; it seemed an abundance that would never run out." No one envisioned in the future having to search all day for a fish or one abalone. The Coronado Wetbacks talked about going down to Guaymas, Mexico, where club President, Pete Glynn, and others shot big fish and had them swim off, "to die, perhaps, but die in freedom"...and that "The rod and reel boys were eating fish with holes in their sides."

Did *Skin Diver Magazine* encourage this wantonness or was it just the messenger? One has to visualize that the ocean, just invaded, was a figurative candy store to hungry kids, the sea of buffalo on the plains of frontier America. Hindsight of modern divers might see this as greed, but *then* it was the heart of the hunter genetically thrusting forth.

The Magazine turned a corner in 1955 when it made a greater transition to scuba diving coverage, despite the fact that scuba equipment had been advertised from the first issue and had been in use by many divers. The title "*Skin Diver*" stayed the same and would through year 2000. The high cost of scuba equipment may have delayed its usage by large numbers of divers. More sophisticated manufacturers with expanded advertising helped make the transition. As with the individuals and clubs, *SDM* moved to a 50/50 between skin diving and scuba diving.

Themed editions of the magazine were tried in 1956 with an underwater photography issue. There was also one on regulators because divers, for the most part, assumed this "machine" they were using was some magic little box, and Auxier and Blakeslee felt divers were smarter than that. Certainly the photography issue catalyzed this new activity in the new sport. It was a positive move as spearfishermen set records for large fish and eventually burned out on giant unnecessary takes. Even the Bottom Scratchers got fed up with just killing fish, especially with the tonnage approach of competitive meets, and they had an epiphany when a new fish they had been gunning down was identified by member, Dr. Carl Hubbs of Scripps Institution of Oceanography, as an extremely rare species that had drifted from the South into La Jolla waters. The Scratchers began to make camera cases instead of guns, and members like Lamar Boren and Ron Church became the best underwater photographers in diving.

The Magazine didn't just recognize underwater photography as a parallel activity to spearfishing, it was going to make it happen. It sponsored the first prototype of a Film Festival in 1955 with Los Angeles County's Bill Starr setting it up at his "day job site", Gompers Junior High School in Los Angeles, and featuring the underwater movies of Dimitri Rebikoff. Auxier and Blakeslee also got Los Angeles County's Al Tillman to do a film show with Gustav Dalla Valle and Jim Christiansen on stage to raise money to send the National Spearfishing Team to

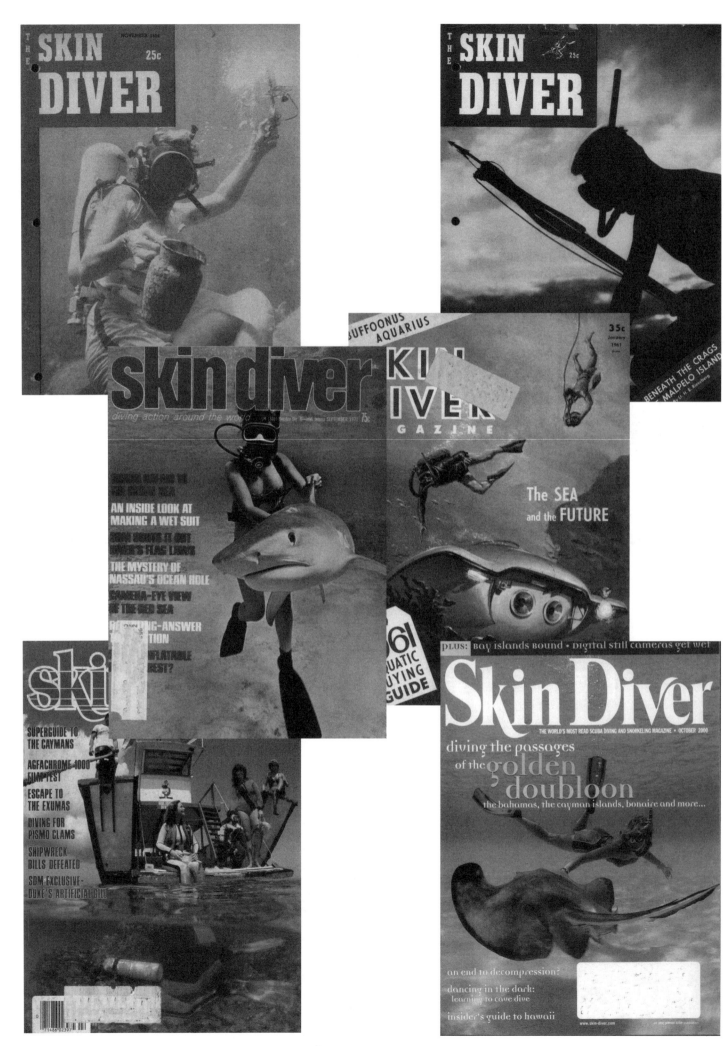

SOME OF THE BEST COVERS FROM THE PAST 50 YEARS.

Europe. In 1957 *SDM* jumped in to sponsor and publicize the first underwater photographic competitions in conjunction with the Los Angeles County Underwater Unit and the newly formed Underwater Photographic Society Los Angeles Chapter.

The conscience of the Magazine, actually Jim's and Chuck's consciences, didn't always act instantly but eventually courageously. They supported the Los Angeles County training programs in every way. Jim and Chuck became Los Angeles County certified instructors from the start. Al Tillman recalls that the Magazine printed many of the programs of Los Angeles County Underwater Unit. The story of making the first training film, *Introduction to Skin Diving,* the Junior Frogman Program, the International Underwater Film Festival started in 1957, and much on diving safety, such as an article on what color works best underwater to be noticed from a safety standpoint (white!), all were endorsed by *Skin Diver Magazine.*

Even though retailers and manufacturers were leery of the growing power of instructors, *SDM* let Neal Hess, a graduate of the Los Angeles County Instructor Certification, start a column in 1959 called *Dive Patrol*, an idea he had thought up while he was back at Harvard Business School. *Dive Patrol* was to parallel the Ski Patrol of that industry, but consultation with the ski industry moguls yielded, "You don't have casualties, you have fatalities; the patrol idea won't work." Of course, they were right and instead, the idea of a National Association of Underwater Instructors was purloined from a similar idea promulgated by Los Angeles County in 1958, aimed at a week-long instructors course at Catalina Island (cancelled because Los Angeles County Administrators didn't feel official activities could cross boundaries of the County). The name Dive Patrol became *Instructors Corner.* Hess listed himself as certified by Los Angeles County and Training Director for the Boston YMCA.

Hess was providing recognition as an instructor to anyone who mailed a request and their written course outline to him. Sort of a mail order certification, but it did provide a worthwhile mailing list for promoting the first NAUI Course in Houston in the summer of 1960 to coincide with the first convention of the newly formed Underwater Society of America. Neal Hess was an astute businessman, and he went after the manufacturers for financial support and set up a tentative arrangement to have NAUI serve as the Society's training arm. Some of the Councils were howling because they already had put good training programs in place with club's "safety officers".

The Illinois Club Council, the Southwest Council Instruction Program (SCIP) and the YMCA Program in New England questioned the NAUI idea. In turn, they were irritated at *SDM*'s support of it.

Hess got Al Tillman together with John Jones, Jr. who had a well-formed instruction program under the Fort Lauderdale Chapter of the Red Cross in Florida. They proceeded to adapt the Los Angeles County Instruction Program to a national perspective. Hess went to work and under *SDM* aegis lined up big name speakers like Dr. Andreas Rechnitzer, Hal Lattimore, Dr. George Bond, Dr. Albert Behnke, and Harry Vetter. Hess, Tillman and Jones were part of the teaching staff. It was a booming success but not possible without the patronage of *Skin Diver Magazine.*

Nobody made it easy for Auxier and Blakeslee, there was always opposition to whatever fork in the road they took. Underwater Society of America felt *SDM* should just roll over and be their mouthpiece for the Society's emergence. They wanted more coverage or "they'd put out their own magazine". A host of strong club and council leaders were at the USOA helm and were used to getting their way but when together they squabbled for power. Good men all, like Carl Hauber of the Illinois Council and First President, Ben Davis of Canada, David Stith, James Dugan, and Fred Calhoun. Auxier and Blakeslee worried it through in their usual stoic manner. (Al Tillman recalls how his own hyper full-steam-ahead approach when he worked for SDM seemed to be ignored by Jim Auxier, who sat like a great Buddha in his throne-office. An idea told eagerly to Jim would get no response, but three days later Auxier would tell Tillman to "Go ahead with the idea..." and Tillman already had forgotten the idea. What they did was give the Society a special pullout supplement in the magazine. The Society never showed much gratitude for the boost and like everybody else might not have survived the first years without *Skin Diver Magazine.* A note from Chuck's wife, Jeri, explained that *Skin Diver Magazine* never received outside money from anyone to do anything for clubs. It was a *SDM* courtesy.

NAUI had incorporated nonprofit with Tillman as President, Jones as Vice President and Hess as Executive Secretary. Hess in his great business sense saw NAUI as a money cow, a major commercial enterprise in the years ahead, while Tillman and Jones were steeped in public service. With NAUI leadership split down the middle, Auxier stepped in and decided that public service was the path to take. Hess resigned and Tillman took over complete management of NAUI in 1961. *Skin Diver Magazine* created a position on the magazine called Director of Public Affairs, and in that office Tillman would guide NAUI, the Film Festival, the Museum and other projects that were great promotions for *SDM* but loss leaders.

Skin Diver Magazine introduced women into the "all male sport" of diving. The 1955 photography issue had a woman on the cover with an underwater camera. Inside the pages more and more women were showing up in the pictures, sometimes as divers' sidekicks or worse as "sex objects" to draw the leers of the hormone-driven young male divers. The *SDM* bathing beauty pages were called Miss Driftwood, leading to a popular feature called a Miss Beach Temptress Contest which became Miss International Beach Temptress up through 1964. Numerous pictures of young women in revealing bathing suits posed by diving equipment.

Sex really reared its ugly head when in 1960 the cover featured a well-endowed woman from Fiji in a grass skirt and halter. Eyebrows went up in many places, and bundles of magazines were returned. "What's going on?" worriedly wondered the editors. Looking closely, it appeared the halter had slipped down and the top half of a nipple was showing, or was it just a print shadow? Whatever it was, the "Puritans marched" on the Magazine. Auxier and Blakeslee, straight-arrow family men, hastened to correct the impression. John Gaffney, who was *SDM*'s advertising salesman at the time (later to publish a rival magazine, *Dive Magazine* and head-up National Association of Skin Diving Stores) chortled and urged Jim and Chuck to put in a nude diver centerfold and sell millions of magazines. At another point in time, libraries rejected the magazine because the title, "Skin Diver", seemed risqué or something.

Auxier and Blakeslee were very fair to women all during their ownership. They respected women, and anything that showed women in a lesser role in society wasn't their doing. It was just going along with the way of things in that time period. In 1956 they added the first full-time employee to their meager editorial staff. It was a fresh and personable woman diver, Connie Johnson, who had just arrived in California from the Midwest. Her outlook as a woman and new diver shaped and humanized the publication and she really edited stories into correct literature, eventually to become Managing Editor.

For pictures of spearfishing championships and other special events, Auxier and Blakeslee could always depend on their friend, another legendary figure in diving's development, Homer Lockwood. Spearfisher-champ, writer, and an outstanding topside and underwater photographer, Homer, took the photographs with his Graflex camera and an old Model C Leica camera using a homemade, lucite-underwater-housing designed to completely adjust the shutter speed, aperture and focus underwater. Two years later, his Rolleimarin pictures were seen in the magazine. In the year 2000, a grand old man at 91, Homer Lockwood, came to *Scuba America*'s aid with his prize collection of all the early copies of *Skin Diver Magazine*. Auxier and Blakeslee counted on another friend who pitched-in with stories and photography. He was inventor-engineer, Rory Page, of the Hope-Page Non-Return Valve fame.

Gene Parker, "Mr. Diver-Down-Flag", came on staff as an Associate Editor in New York. Ross Olney, another Associate Editor, questioned copy - "Tillman, in your manual you say, 'Where 150 feet waves...' What's your source?" The magazine was conscientious about factual material.

Dead fish pictures rapidly disappeared in the latter part of the 1950's, replaced by actual photos of what live creatures could be seen underwater.

Color didn't come easily to the magazine. One color photo separation could cost $1,000. Remember, they printed 2000 whole copies of the first magazine for $637. Printers weren't yet competent at doing color, and

A recent photograph of Jim Auxier and Chuck Blakeslee.

Scuba America Archives

many's the time Jim Auxier with an eye loupe squinted over his printer's eye to find the dots out of register in the proofs, and they went back several times before Jim was satisfied. But color *had* to be perfect. If you looked around at other magazines, in particular *National Geographic*, black and white retired grudgingly, and different color processes evolved fuzzily to the brilliant detail of year 2000 publications. *Skin Diver Magazine* got color separations from *National Geographic*'s 1927 issue of the first underwater color photographs ever to reprint in a promotional feature for the International Underwater Film Festival.

The first disaster in a very limited color attempt had to do with an ad for shark repellent. John Gaffney pushed to put blood-red ink in the ad symbolizing a shark attack, and the advertising manufacturers "went bananas," as they were saying then. They threatened to pull all their ads in the magazine if it was going to scare the public. Color probably arrived in full glory with the 1963 issue of *SDM* when the powers that were at that time decided to publish the winners of the underwater photographic competitions that were then run by the International Underwater Film Festival out of new magazine headquarters in Hollywood.

Auxier and Blakeslee weren't afraid to become a sponsor of technological changes in diving. They put the magazine behind the famous Hannes Keller Dive to 1000 feet off Santa Catalina Island in 1962. A highly controversial dive. (Why do it so publicly? *That* was the purpose, to create an awareness that things about diving would, and could, change.) Criticism ran high because of two deaths. The dive still established that with the computer, decompression could be shortened and done on a curve rather than steps...and well, a lot of the divers from that era still don't completely understand it. The *SDM* report on the dive by Al Tillman and the film made about it compared it to Lindbergh's ill-structured flight across the Atlantic to open up the field of aviation.

The handwriting was always on the wall for Auxier and Blakeslee. There would be other diving magazines eventually, but SDM controlled the thinking in diving for over a decade. They had served divers, had integrity and sold a vast amount of brand names of equipment. Robert Petersen with his *Hot Rod* and hunting conglomerate of magazines, with its cross-over advertising, tried to get a magazine called *Water World* into competition but despite effective writers like Bill Barada, the magazine never seemed to represent the real divers, and it never captured their imaginations during the 1950's. Petersen would be in wait for years before he moved on diving again. There were newsletters all over the place put out by councils of diving clubs and a magazine in Florida called *Waterbug* made a short half-hearted effort. *Skin Diver Magazine* was just the big respected fish that ate the rest of them. In later years (1964) the most formidable challenge came from John Gaffney and his *Dive* Magazine. Gaffney, a former *SDM* employee, had unified dive shops into a powerful pressure group and sales force. But once again *SDM* had thoroughly entrenched itself against rebel forces.

In 1964, *Skin Diver Magazine* experienced the monster change in its first 13 years of existence. Auxier and Blakeslee sold out to Robert Petersen and his magazine empire. The two first owners figuratively using "spit, duct tape and baling wire" to hold together the publishing of a single-interest, contained-market magazine just got tired. They were always pressured by the councils and clubs to take stands, such as the long debate over the "Divers Flag," which was about ways the stripes should run. Whose hand signals should be national standards? What would be the stand on the use of scuba in spearfishing? Add to that, the grumbling advertisers who always found fault with *Skin Diver Magazine's* positions and directions...and were very slow paying for ads, making collections of due bills a challenging task for Chuck Blakeslee. The two originators were just plain beat, and Petersen kept dangling a luring offer over the years.

A deal was made and the two creators, Jim at 35 and Chuck at 38, retired from publishing, Jim to go on to operate an amusement arcade and commercial real estate in Big Bear, California, and Chuck to own and manage his avocado ranch and commercial real estate in Carpinteria, California. The specifics of the deal are not known, but rumor has it that each of them walked away with $100,000. They would also receive the accounts receivable which were considerable, the real estate, and some mailing equipment. Jim stayed on with Petersen for three years to oversee the transition. NAUI and the Underwater Film Festival traveled with *SDM* to be located in Petersen's Hollywood Headquarters.

The next two years saw the magazine relentlessly change. The graphics, the color were top drawer, as Petersen's ace graphics artist, Art Smith, became a vital force in the new look. Connie Johnson stayed on with Jim Auxier and even after Petersen moved to his Sunset Tower to really maintain some continuity to the Magazine. Connie was a crafts person and could put the magazine mechanically together in the dark.

The NAUI page which set up much of the thinking in diving instruction was still a prime feature and the International Film Festival received full coverage with some financial support. Both programs were furnished an office with a secretary, and Al Tillman was retained as Director of Public Affairs. Eventually, in 1965 Petersen's accounting gnomes saw no financial profit coming from NAUI or Festival involvement and convinced Petersen to let the two projects go. (Both were nonprofit corporations that Petersen couldn't control.) Additionally, Tillman interpreted from an interview with Bill Barada a decade later, that Barada, as the new Marketing Director, had warned Petersen that they'd lose advertising support from the newly developing *other* training agencies and from manufacturers who were still unsure of NAUI's rising power. Auxier, as a lameduck publisher/editor, couldn't stop the move.

Looking back over the Auxier-Blakeslee reign, there are a stable of writers who ultimately became legends in diving. Certainly Bev Morgan, who many say is invested with the spirit of American diving's first hero. Connie Limbaugh, epitomized the diver the *Skin Diver Magazine* readers wanted to be - a writer, scientist, photographer, inventor, excellent diver and everything that fictitious Mike Nelson purported to be. Bev, as an adventurer, wrote the first *series* of articles about his diving, sailing cruise half way around the world that was slam-bang motivating. You could earmark it as *Skin Diver Magazine's* first revelations of diving travel, which would become the major thrust of the magazine's later years.

Skin Diver Magazine was not without humor, as in the first years when a Carl Kohler wrote funny replies to letters to the editors and drew up distinctive cartoons about diving worthy of *MAD Magazine*. But the crown prince of humor was a young diver of extraordinary diving ability, and much like Bev, was an inventor of diving equipment and had the spirit of E. R. Cross in his soul. Dick (or Bev) could be our answer, our pure American solution, to The Frenchman, Jacques-Yves Cousteau. But everybody wants to only say, "*that* Dick Anderson, he's funny". Go to dinner with him and he puts a napkin on his head to get the waitress' attention, recalls Al Tillman. *Skin Diver Magazine* gave Dick his first public voice and his humorous looks at other divers, diving history, himself, the equipment, René Bussoz or Gustav Dalla Valle. He had us all snickering and laughing out loud. This irreverence fit the emerging counterculture times. Americans who were laughing at Lucy Arnaz, Jackie Gleason and Milton

Berle, at least America's divers, found a place for him and took him to heart. His films captured his humor, too, and snapped audiences' eyes open after watching ten minutes of other films of Garibaldi's or manganese nodules on the bottom of the sea. Who else would be on a gold diving trip and on film break open an egg in a frying pan to find a gold nugget in it? The humor seemed never to stop. He would not suffer any editing of his material for *Skin Diver Magazine*, sending along a large butcher knife with an article submission - "Okay, now go ahead and do your damn editing." Harry Reisberg and Robert Marx, two prolific writers, got the wreck and treasure juices going with their articles.

When Auxier finally departed in 1966, the magazine was pretty well ingested into the Petersen system, one where an ad, whatever it was about, went into a dozen special-interest magazines, the more popular magazines carrying the weaker ones. *Skin Diver Magazine* was a *strong* one, covering a sport that wouldn't fade to a small bunch of aficionados but would grow technologically with more and more saleable merchandise. Petersen had bought himself a plum of a magazine, well established in a mushrooming field. He did buy it at a plateauing time with Cousteau's films and *Sea Hunt*-magic practically gone. But the jet age and travel were just around the corner, and a good investment it was.

In talking with Jim Auxier and Chuck Blakeslee 25 years after the magazine began, their lament was missing the early days. There was something clean and pure about diving then, and excitingly new.

Al Tillman recalls meeting Chuck Blakeslee slogging up the cliff trail at Palos Verdes sunken barge area (Hey, that's my spot, Chuck.) with a sack of abalone and fish and a kid under his arm, with pretty diving wife, Jeri, pulling up another kid and an innertube. "So early?" asked Al. Chuck said, "Got to go get the magazine *out*." It was like that with both Auxier and Blakeslee, good people and great divers, putting out a magazine that seemed stained with salt water and fish scales from their last dives. Their Magazine, the original Magazine, was the super glue that held the fraternity of divers together and defined it in those founding days.

4

THE DIVE SHOP

DEFINING EVENT: DIVE N' SURF

Sparling School of Deep Sea Diving in 1947. The Sparling School and its owner, E. R. Cross, are legends in the diving industry.

E.R. Cross

Nothing held sport diving together better than the linchpin-dive shop. Put the gigantic impact of Cousteau Specials, *Sea Hunt*, magazines like *Skin Diver* aside, we're talking about something very personal in a multitude of communities.

The local neighborhood dive shop did not have an easy birth. It often started in the corner of an automotive transmission garage, a motorcycle shop, a department store, or the close-by hardware store... even the backroom of a barber shop. Sometimes it operated out of the trunk of a car of a diver turned entrepreneur.

It was not easy to get commercial equipment in the early 1950's. The manufacturers of regulators were just tooling-up after an under estimation of the potential market. Although there were a number of them producing the low end skin diving gear of mask and fins, the idea of sport diving was looked upon as a novelty recreation. The pioneer divers were a hardy lot, mostly athletes, and represented an extremely small percentage of the general population in America. The 1950's were a do-it-yourself era. Homemade equipment provided a challenge and sense of achievement. There was great pride in doing this new and exotic activity with something the individual constructed on his garage workbench.

When we talked to DACOR owner, Don Davison, in 1976, he was probably most pleased with a sort of scuba he put together with an anesthesiologist's regulator, surgical tubing and old acetylene tanks - in 1935! More pleased than about all of the other scuba equipment his company would produce many years later. A great majority of the first generation of divers fondly recall the attempts to breathe underwater with buckets, garden hoses, tire pumps and old surplus military equipment.

It always was the second phase of constructing a device for oneself to move to making more of the same for others - and selling them. E. R. Cross had put together a scuba called Sport Diver a few years before Cousteau's Aqua Lung arrived on American shores, and although it was a flawed device, a hard-breather, Cross with Homer Lockwood's help put together and sold several hundred. When we look farther back, there's the amazing and not well known creations of Jack Browne. Way ahead of his time, Browne had a lung (featured in the October 1945 Popular Mechanics Magazine). His lung, a closed circuit unit, was several years ahead of Cousteau's Aqua Lung and being tested for military use by the Navy's Experimental Diving Unit.

Jack Browne wasn't even the legal age of 21 when he formed the Diving Equipment and Supply

Bob Lorenz's Water Gill was possibly the first dive shop in California.

Company (DESCO) in Milwaukee, Wisconsin. As Browne told us in the 1970's, "Look in a current catalog of a big diving company..." and there's not much difference from what he had. He sold DESCO in 1946, at the time the largest equipment manufacturing plant in the world.

DESCO became a big mail order supplier for sport diving and featured what could be considered a walk-in dive shop, too. By the 1950's, Divemaster bought out DESCO and a young ex-UDT officer, Dick Bonin, learned the dive- shop-business, running one for Divemaster in Chicago, Illinois.

There was a growing number of adventurous persons, mostly men, who wanted to buy ready-made equipment and try diving. Suddenly, there was a consumer outlet of enough size to start up small manufacturing efforts. Rene Bussoz, who got the first shipment of Aqua Lungs (six) to this country, started a company called U.S. Divers; Richard Klein, a barbell producer, set up a diving division in his Healthways Company; the Davisons' created the DACOR Company to especially service the middle of America. Voit, a sporting goods company of some stature, came in with a strong rubber-goods diving line and shortly thereafter, with scuba.

Someone now had to connect up the manufacturers and the diving consumers. Mail Order direct from the product companies was a starting effort but the hazards inherent in diving and using the equipment really indicated that more direct contact was required. Clubs were experiencing their inception and growth-boom at this time and were doing a kind of pick-up job of instructing new members as they joined, and they were buying a unit or two that got passed around. But the club, operating like a cooperative, could also put together a group order and buy direct from the manufacturer.

But clubs were fickle affairs at best, meeting off and on, dissolving with the loss or retirement of a sparkplugleader who kept it all going. Divers needed a country store with a cracker barrel and potbellied stove to sit around and tell stories as it had been in the frontier days of America.

Suddenly, individual divers in all parts of America, decided to open a small storefront place to sell equipment - the birth of the dive shop. While sporting good stores carried a corner with this new novelty activity, the specialized dive store could probably put a sign in the window "Diving spoken here." New enthusiasts found more than a sales clerk ready to sell them something - they found a real diver full of stories and passion for diving. The dive store was a fun place to hang out.

No one, not many anyway, quit their career jobs to just be a shopkeeper. In most cases a wife or girlfriend 'managed' the store after the diving-male opened the shop, ran off to his subsistence job, and returned later in the day. Many had to dig in the cookie jar for small savings, took small business administration loans, got money from relatives or simply bluffed their way with a lot of creditors.

Ski N. Dive in Westwood was the second store in the family. It used to be a drug store on the road to Mandalay where Don and George bought bubble gum as kids. They grew up two blocks away. D. O. Brauer

As everyone, especially manufacturers, recalls there were few businessmen among the early shop owners. Most of them had no experience with profit and loss, balance sheets, depreciation schedules, insurance, business taxes and all the rest of the functional anatomy of efficient operation as a commercial enterprise. "I don't want to do no arithmetic," said one. On a good day, the water flat, the sun out, a real diver would put up the "closed" sign, toss his gear in a pack and roar off to a favorite diving spot - ignoring the fact that his diving customers would be motivated, too, and wanting to buy, rent equipment and get an airfill. It was just simply that they were divers first and then, businessmen. By 2000, those roles became almost 180^0 reversed.

Getting products to sell was not an easy process. Investing in rental gear was even harder. Manufacturers needed those shops to distribute what they produced — the incidental selling of diving gear in department stores and sporting good stores did not generate the volume for manufacturers to fully expand and tool-up. Chuck Buchanan, who helped John Gaffney construct the National Association of Diving Stores (NASDS), told us, as many on the shop-side did, that the industry, basically the manufacturers, failed to put up much money to publicize diving and counted on serendipitous, occasional attention from the media and television. Al Tillman recalls when John Gaffney would launch a tirade against the manufacturers, not just for their failure to promote diving, but the cavalier way they treated the small shops. "By the time the stores got the product, there was a small margin of profit, and if the merchandise sat on the shelf very long, rent and electric bills didn't get paid. But the manufacturers got their money and left the poor-guy out in the field selling for them to twist in the wind," bellowed Gaffney.

It is a dangerous thing to stereotype the shop owner of those pioneering days, for there were a variety of start-up-situations, unusual financing and certainly a diverse set of personalities. Taking a look geographically, the history of the dive shop can be seen best by describing some of these specific shops.

We may be too personal here, but our research indicates the shoreline of California, especially Southern California, was the most fertile grounds for the incubation of the early dive shops. Certainly there was the weather, the great kelp beds, ample game and the outdoor nature of the young veterans and their families after the 1940's era of World War II. Industries spawned off the war created many jobs, created migration to California and the first concepts of a discretionary income - money to spend on recreation.

Of course, Rene's Sporting Goods in Westwood near the University of California, Los Angeles, California, (UCLA) was more dive shop than sporting goods after it featured the first Aqua Lungs in America back in 1949.

Valley Scuba Haus. Typical dive shop in the 1950's.
Scuba America Archives

But most pioneer divers from the greater Los Angeles area remember the Water Gill Shop on Lincoln Boulevard near Santa Monica as the first diving only shop in town. A small dark hole in the wall space in a building with no parking, it was owned by a hardhat diver named Bob Lorenz, who had the dark curly-haired look of a waterfront tough guy. The store had a meager inventory of masks, fins and snorkels available on the dimly lit shelves, and the oily, dank smell of an Ingersoll Rand Compressor thumping away in a back crowded cubby hole. Bob or his wife were there to take care of your needs when they found the time - for it seemed that the Lorenzes were always in the process of getting Bob ready to go out on a commercial dive for someone. If you were to swing down to the industrial area of Wilmington near the Los Angeles harbor, you would have located the Sparling School of Diving, a hardhat diving operation that the legendary Ellis Royal Cross, Master U.S. Navy Diver, had taken over with a Small Business Administration loan.

Cross was focused on the training of hardhat (or helmet divers as many call them today) for the many underwater jobs developing around post-war waterfront construction. Noted divers like Dick Anderson and Nick Icorn went through the program. Cross also had a small skin and scuba diving equipment outlet that was not in a good walk-in traffic location. In fact, most divers got lost trying to find it. Cross was an encyclopedia of diving information and divers respected anything he said. Al Tillman remembers raiding the family petty cash sugar bowl and going to Cross to get something better than long johns to keep him warm. "Cross was very serious, all business, intimidating to a degree, handsome and fit, and when he told you something about diving, it was as if he was speaking for Poseidon and King Neptune. I didn't have the money to get a full dry suit; that's all there was at that time. So Cross convinced me that a shorty top would do the trick. After all, you only need to keep your heart warm, which circulates and warms the blood. Sounded good to me, but I still cautiously wondered out loud, why no sleeves? Cross assured me sleeves would just get in the way, and he tapped his heart like he was putting coins in a vending machine and reminded me ..."The heart, that's what you want to keep warm." Hey, he could have told me to stick a hot poker up you know where and I'd have taken it as gospel. Well, as you might guess, water creeped up the indentation of the small of my back when I took the shorty top diving. I never lost my admiration for Cross, as the guru of diving, but I realized from that first experience that he was also a shrewd shopkeeper."

While the foregoing glimmerings of the stereotype dive shop of 1950's were reflecting a slow regeneration of a place-time-at-leisure America, the next decade would see a country living an old American dream - a new car, a house in suburbia, two kids, a dog and family values - and a desire to try all the new toys available. We might have thought of building a bomb shelter in the backyard next to the ubiquitous barbecue, because the Korean War happened in the early 1950's and a cold war with Communist Russia was permeating the world atmosphere. Families got one of those new 35mm cameras and took pictures, while skiing was booming along side of golf, tennis and camping. Diving and surfing were the new kids on the block in individual sports. They both needed the ocean but usually each attracted a different kind of person.

Water people, the beach addicts, tried it. No finer example of this is better represented than by four young Los

Angeles County lifeguards - Bev Morgan, Ramsey Parks, Bob and Bill Meistrell. They were outstanding surfers, swimmers and divers with a ferocious passion. Before Bev Morgan had to leave the County Service in 1955, after setting up the first public classes with Al Tillman, genius-Bev and Hap Jacobs, a surfboard builder, had already been in the dive-shop/surfing business, Dive N' Surf. The two partners sanded balsa blocks into boards and pumped air at a small-structure-setting on the famous rock siding in Redondo Beach, California. The waves crashed that rocky fringe before a Marina went in, right on over the road and flooded the grocery store across the street where

Bev Morgan and the Meistrell Brothers in front of Dive 'N Surf.

Meistrell Collection

Roger Hess, the butcher, soon to be a Los Angeles County instructor and charter boat captain, cut meat for customers like Al Tillman and Bill Starr. A precarious location in a precarious business, but Bev had great vision. When the surf was up, it was unlikely you'd find the store open, as the proprietors were out, off shore waiting for a perfect break. The surf boards kept it all going. The rent was cheap.

It was 1953 when Bill Meistrell, who was fresh out of the military, and surfing champion, Dale Velzy, wanted to open a dive shop in Topanga Canyon. "We went out there to look for a place to rent. We were ready to give them the money," Bill said. Then a telephone call that night changed their minds to join Bev in business in Redondo Beach. There was a friendship already with Bev. "As a matter of fact, Bev married my girlfriend when I went into the service," Bill said laughing. "Then when I came out of the military service, Bev asked if I wanted to go into the business with him." That phone call changed the pursuit for the Topanga Canyon dive shop. Instead, the partners of the Dive N' Surf shop changed. Bev Morgan and only Bill Meistrell "set the deal together and I (Bill) got my picture and diamond ring back from my ex-girlfriend. My brother, Bob, wouldn't go into business with me until a few weeks later.

"We borrowed the $1,800 from our mother. The first day we were in the

Original Diving Locker in 1959 with assorted halibut spearfisherman. Chuck Nicklin is in the center.

The Diving Locker

Joe Dorsey's Divers Den. *Dorsey Collection*

dive shop-business we sold a 15-cent *Skin Diver Magazine*. Total sales for the day. When we went home, Mom asked, 'What were the gross receipts for the day?' We said 15 cents. 'That isn't very good. Where are all the money-numbers here?'

"It wasn't until 1955 when the Meistrells received the first government wet suit-order in the world from the U.S. Navy Coronado Island Base. Three-hundred wet suits, paid with a check of $11,000, proved scuba diving was profitable. "We were so proud of that check that we had to show it to her before we even cashed it," tells Bill. That tickled Mother Meistrell and the twins were now convinced that a dive shop was worth operating.

Redevelopment upgraded the property values. The store called Dive N' Surf moved to a new building farther inland in Redondo Beach. Bev and Hap went separate ways, and the Meistrel twins' partnership financed the new building.

Bob and Bill Meistrel brought into Dive N' Surf a responsible attitude crowned by integrity. No one ever felt that they got less than a square deal from them. Bev was restless to see the world, and Al Tillman remembers Bev swearing he'd never be pinned down by a 9-to-5 alarm clock-job, which his own mother seemed to suffer through raising him in downtown Los Angeles. Bev opened a branch, Dive N' Surf, in a great location, La Jolla, California, but the lure of Wind N' Sea waves kept him out of the store too much. Soon he sold out to the Meistrels and took off with lifeguard friends to sail and dive exotic places.

The twins made custom wet suits that set a standard never exceeded and their Redondo shop became a classic role model for all shops. They built an in-shop pool, provided Los Angeles County Certified instruction, sold boats and motors and the top line of diving equipment. It was a full-service diving shop with air, equipment sales, rentals, instruction and repairs. But

Inside view of the Diver's Den. *Joe Dorsey Collection*

beyond that was a reputation for a superior wet suit, and although they did mail order on it, the crème de la crème was to go to the shop and have Bob or Bill take your measurements.

Most important as a customer, Zale Parry remembers, that upon entering Dive N' Surf, the shopper was always greeted, and at the same time entertained with the latest episode or diving adventure in the lives of the owners. Treated like a queen or king. But it was the fussy, meticulous, motion picture industry that counted on the Meistrells for wet suit-wardrobe for any actor needing cold water protection. It was not necessarily a scuba diving actor, although Dive N' Surf did suit-up the cast for the Sea Hunt series and a list of other productions. Cowboys and Indians had a wet suit that fit perfectly under their costume if the script called for water-entry-falls in lakes and rivers. Gary Cooper and Lloyd Bridges were a few of that nobility the Meistrells pleased.

GO UNDERWATER AND REALLY LIVE!

AQUA-LUNG CLASSES

"I will make a diver out of you." Having taught over 4,400 novices to be confident lung divers, we guarantee that in one compact lesson, you too can start to "Really Live"!!

MEL'S AQUA SHOP
RIVIERA VILLAGE
1911 So. Catalina Ave.
REDONDO BEACH, CALIFORNIA
FRontier 5-6714

Many shops had their own training program along with sales. Mel Fisher's one lesson training consisted of little more than "stick it in your mouth and breathe."   *Skin Diver Magazine.*

Just across town in the shadow of Palos Verdes huge marine terraces that had risen from the sea, was Mel's Aqua Shop in the early 1950's. But before the shop opened in Hollywood Riviera (next to Palos Verdes), Mel Fisher was selling diving equipment, pumping air, distributing chicken feed and selling eggs from a large shack on his parents' farm in Torrance, California. Al Tillman, reminiscing with Bill Starr in the 1970's, got a lot of laughs out of stopping off at Mel's to get air on the way to a dive. Sometimes Mel was there and Dolores, his wife, too, his Ma, and his toddler son in a playpen in the middle of the limited space. Mel's, at one point in time, was the major volume retailer in America, but the displayed-inventory didn't seem all that much. But Mel Fisher was a grand salesman and merchandiser. He didn't try to sell you a mask or a regulator but instead would be cackling over a nugget or vial of platinum ("Everybody's looking for gold, and this is far and away more valuable.") with that sly slit-eyed grin of his. So you got excited about gold diving and treasure wrecks and Mel sold you a dredge plus all the diving gear you could carry out. Al Tillman recalls his wife, Ruth, using saved household money to buy a complete outfit - regulator, Bel Aqua suit, converted fire extinguisher tank - as a package Christmas present for him for about $99. As they say, Mel sold a whole lot of sizzle while waving a treasure map under your nose.

Mel used the Hermosa Beach Hotel indoor pool for his classes which in the beginning, before he and Dolores became certified Los Angeles County instructors, were accomplished in a session or two. Pioneer divers remembered how Mel had his own television show and showed movies he and Doc Nelson E. Mathison had shot. Al Tillman recalls turning his rough footage of diving for the half-ton Jade nugget (now in the Los Angeles County Museum of Natural History) over to Mel to edit and put on his TV show. Mel showed big fish and treasure to excite and recruit a lot of new divers.

Bill Hogan got started with a shop about this same time, as did Bev and Mel, and eventually had a shop with the first built-in-pool right at the pier in Long Beach, California. He was full-service plus running dive charter boat trips off the end of the pier. Hogan was good at display and was one of first to put a fully-equipped mannequin in the front window.

Out in San Fernando Valley, Herb and Shirley Hughes set up Cal Aquatics in the 1950's, with Shirley defining the role of the female wife shop-manager. "Herb was in my college diving club, the Devilfish, which I advised," Al Tillman relates, "and he bought my Aqua Lung setup getting into the shop business. In those days, you needed rentals and would pick up gear from divers who were upgrading."

Shirley Hughes devoted more than a quarter of a century of her life in the Cal Aquatics shop. With the decorator-touch of a Martha Stuart-comfort, color and carpeting, Shirley graced the place. The Hughes' made a great team. Their accounts included the motion picture/television industry, too, as did Dive N' Surf, with plenty of gear and their special wet suits.

They were just a bunch of divers, those early shop owners, with few having any business sense, something they had to pick up to survive. Tom Hemphill, one of NAUI's year 2000 top leaders, told us that he felt you could probably make a diver out of a businessman rather than the other way around. Many of the early shops went

bankrupt before the owner metamorphosed from a gungho-diver into a knowledgeable businessman. Working long hours, many of those just going diving "because we needed to test the equipment (Ha Ha)," didn't create the profit needed and in many cases, as Bill Hogan and Chuck Buchanan told us, it splits up a marriage. Diving, the shop, the instruction, the trips and the rest becomes the "other woman."

Down Coast from the Los Angeles region, shops, like Lyle Hoskin's in Newport Beach, got great volume by being in a boat- haven of wealthy people, John Wayne and his yacht-crew and guests as an example. Further South is the incubator divingland of San Diego with Mexico in its back-

Ma and Joe Dorsey looking over a powerhead.   *Joe Dorsey*

yard, the Coronado Islands, the first club, The Bottom Scratchers, Scripps Institution of Oceanography and a plethora of famous diving pioneers.

Some of those pioneers like Conrad Limbaugh and Dr. Wheeler North put together a consortium of colleagues and opened the original Diving Locker (In time, there would be branch Diving Lockers.) They found a handsome water athlete, Chuck Nicklin, to come in as a partner/manager, who also turned out to be good businessman and award winning underwater photographer. Nicklin inevitably bought out his partners, and through the decades, the main shop survived and flourished under children and grandchildren who came into the business. The original shop was near the Crystal Pier. Across town in the 1950's, two divers, Bill Hardy and Bill Johnson, operated a prime pioneer shop, called San Diego Divers Supply. Bill Johnson ran the popular Bottom Scratcher Charter Boat to take their students out. Later, he acquired the Sand Dollar Charter Boat. Many other small shops popped up in the early years but most were composites, combining co-businesses, such as a tennis school adding on a dive store.

Back in the Los Angeles region, the first Ski N' Dive shop was opened by two brothers who had been in the air conditioning business, Don and George Brauer. Skiing was hot in the 1950's, and their plan was to let skiing carry the early years and diving to follow the ski industry-lead of taking the pedantic seriousness out of diving and make it social and fun as skiing had done. They were somewhat irreverent in so doing. Hard-core leaders in the industry often frowned and felt they went too far at times. But boy! did they promote - taking boat- loads of divers to Catalina, having as many as 500 fun-loving types on the beach for beer and barbecues. And they filmed all of it to show on their promotional television show, *Territory Underwater*. It changed many of the shops' philosophy. You didn't have to scare people into buying your instruction or equipment. Their shop club in the hundreds of members, the Squid Diddlers, was one big frolic.

It all worked for them and at a formative meeting of NASDS, the Brauers boasted a shop could gross a million dollars a year. Chuck Nicklin shook his head then stated most shops pulled in a $50,000 gross, some $100,000 and a rare few in a good year $300,000. The Brauers did the million dollar gross over several years.

An interesting note is that the Brauers both got certified as instructors by Los Angeles County and sent their employees to enroll and do the same. Their classes met the Los Angeles County standards, but the Brauers were not happy with a government agency controlling any part of how they operated and influenced other shops along this line. However, when Mel Fisher was selling more equipment than most all of the other shops put together, the Brauers, figuratively, led the mob with torches to get the County to condemn Mel's "quicky classes." Mel could have grinned and ignored it all, but he and Dolores came to Los Angeles County, were conscientious candidates, graduated head of the class, and Mel changed his teaching ways. He deserved to find the Atocha eventually.

Up North in California where the weather was always iffy, early in the 1950's, Ed Brawley, noted for the Professional Diving Instructor College (1970's and on), had a small store smack in the heart of downtown San Francisco. Ed never exuded much charm, but he knew his diving and his customers weathered his manner to absorb his smarts.

Close-by in an industrial section of San Francisco, by the 1960's, Al Giddings and his partner, LeRoy French, opened a branch of The Bamboo Reef. While Al managed that one, LeRoy setup another Bamboo Reef shop in the affluent region of Marin County. One catered to a blue-collar crowd, the other to a duded-up professional group. Both LeRoy and Al were top-notch divers and gold medal underwater photographers. Al Tillman remembers visiting both shops in the early 1960's and being impressed with the two roommates from college days who could "do it all in diving." Tillman says, "Al Giddings was a big husky guy who was a kind of Wright Brothers-Edison, working in a wire caged-work area in the back of the store, creating equipment-innovations, especially, camera cases. (Ultimately, he would dive with a digital movie camera, the size of a Volkswagen he had created, to film IMAX movies.) While there, Tillman helped him move about a dozen or so antique display cases that he'd just captured at an auction when the famous store, Gumps, cut back. Al's shop looked like a workshop, while LeRoy's had the fancy-air of a boutique. Their shops finally sold to other people; the San Francisco one went to Sal Zamiti, a graduate of Jim Cahill's New England Divers. We can't mention them all but there was Duffy's in Monterey and Stan's in San Jose; two top-shop operations that serviced the strong Central California Council of Diving Clubs.

Probably, the main things that differed the stores and made some successful, had to do with the owners' personalities, plus the full inventories tastefully displayed in large, well-lighted spaces. But all of them were run by real divers. That's the language that was spoken, and early divers wanted to hang out near these gurus.

FLORIDA

Florida was a warm, laid-back place with virgin tropical diving reefs in the 1940's and 1950's. Paul Arnold is a name that comes up often when pioneers talk about diving's beginnings in this region - he was the distributor for Aqua Lung (more or less the equivalent of Rene Bussoz) on the East Coast.

Charles Diercksmeier, recalled in 1975, how he and Paul Arnold ran a retail store called the Aqua Lung Center in downtown Miami, Florida. There was a weird assortment of eccentrics coming in the door everyday in the mid-1950's interested in this weird contraption for breathing underwater.

According to Dirck's vivid memory none exceeded the gypsy brothers and their wives who drove up in a dank, smelly car with no doors. They just threw air tanks and speared fish in on the seats and went to sell them to local restaurants.

They got air regularly but one brother began complaining that he was getting a short-fill or something. It turns out that as he breathed air in it was escaping through a perforated ear drum he'd picked up in earlier diving. Those were the "days of great ignorance" as Paul Arnold used to call them.

Lew Maxwell arrived on the scene, bought Arnold out and proceeded to open five dive shops in the Keys and Southern Florida. Maxwell was a keen diver and shrewd businessman. He knew with five stores he could volume-buy from manufacturers. The stores were called The Florida Frogman.

In one store, Lew Maxwell hired a young diver on a deal that the diver and he would split profits. Lew controlled sales, he thought, by being the provider of equipment as a distributer. Noticing a good number of divers going in and out, he could see the sales slips didn't match-up with inventory. Checking it out, he found out the young manager was buying from Ma Klein and selling on the side. Lew ran across the disappointing young diver a while later when he was the bellhop who had to carry Lew's luggage up to a room at a Miami hotel. The 'Original Florida Frogman' was Lew Maxwell, as he called himself.

But nothing stays the same, and soon competition arose in the 1950's. Jordan Klein, who began running a charter boat in 1948, decided to open a shop in 1953 called Marineland in a prime location on Biscayne Boulevard in Central Miami. Pioneer divers remember the store as well-designed, with the sharp management of Jordan's Mother, "Ma Klein," as everybody fondly called her. Tillman recalls stopping in, searching for Jordan to build a plexiglass case for his 16mm Kodak camera and finding a diminutive lady who seemed a bit harsh and all business. But it was a most successful operation, even to the point of Jordan selling the name to Marineland of Florida and changing his business name to Underwater Sports, Inc. Doing great volume, the Kleins picked up the Aqua Lung distributorship. That was a power that kept competitive shops from opening too close.

Mike Kevorkian opened a shop called Tarpon in Hialeah by the race track (horse race bettors often had money and a desire to take risks, and diving seemed like a risk attraction to them.) Mike had a speargun called the Tarpon. The inventor became his partner. But to open the store, he had to buy Aqua Lungs through Ma Klein. One day he walked into Underwater Sports, Inc. shop and Mrs. Klein pushed a dozen Cressi Masks and Fins on him. She said, "Sell them or bring them back." Mike decided on a small storefront with palm tree waving in front, where he'd sell and he did. Kevorkian had a warm, flamboyant personality. Customers trusted him - a trait found in most of the shop owners who survived the first years. Little shops erupted all over Florida in the late 1950's and bait shops and sporting good stores displayed small inventories as well.

NEW ENGLAND

Up coast in the New England area, Jim Cahill, a personable UDT officer, got discharged and began selling equipment - and teaching. One of his first students at the Huntington YMCA was Frank Scalli, who helped guide all of the training agencies at various times later, and would become U.S. Divers' sales manager. Cahill set up New England Divers, put the brand on equipment, and got exclusive distributorship deals with U.S. Divers, Healthways, DACOR and just about every manufacturer.

The big volume shops actually got manufacturers to put their shop names as the brand of some products - Hardy and Johnson in San Diego as an example. Small shops were being set up. Dry suits and wet suits were making the region into a year-round-diving venue. Frank Scalli had a shop in conjunction with a sporting goods shop in Nantucket, Massachusetts, on the side from his "day job" and had the built-in consumption of the Boston

Sea Rovers, for whom he was the training officer. But New England Divers ruled, and shops who could not go direct to the manufacturers because of small orders, benefited from New England Divers warehousing. They could get orders overnight, too, or pick parts and equipment up at the warehouse, which was also a retail shop in Beverly, Massachusetts. Lots and lots of these shops were testing the waters in the late 1950's and most of them didn't make it through a year.

In the heart of New York City, Cougar Sports owned by the Schuck Brothers, got into diving as an adjunct to fishing equipment store which got its start

Repair station at Ski 'N Dive around 1960.   D. O. Brauer

because of John Schuck discovering and getting the exclusive on a magical fish lure. Marvelously, the diving business was starting to boom with its fresh excitement and soon pushed the old recreation of fishing aside.

Joe Dorsey's Divers Den in Baltimore, Maryland, was reliably and continuously a role-model dive shop. Dorsey himself was a tough diver but dearly loved by his customers. He moved with the times but he was of the old school with a diver's mentality. He did exciting things like find giant six-inch fossil sharks' teeth. He was a top graduate of the NAUI First Instructor Course in Houston, Texas. He retired after 34 years of being a dive store owner/operator and the industry recognized him with its highest honor - the Reaching Out Award in the Diving Equipment Marketing Association's (DEMA) Hall of Fame.

MIDWEST - SOUTH - to - NORTHWEST

Chicago and Milwaukee were beds of great diving activity due to their locations on Lake Michigan. Vern Pedersen was one of first to set up shop, a diving specialty shop, and bought out Jack Browne's DESCO. Diving pioneers like Fred Roberts (who would write the definitive book on regulators) and Ralph Ericksen (who founded PADI with John Cronin) tried their hands at the retail business. There was Gene Betz in Minneapolis and Phil Bayouth in Oklahoma City, Dave Woodward's WOCO Diving School in Spokane, and The Underwater Sports Shops of Gary Keffler and Dale Dean rocked Seattle.

The dive shops pumped air furiously on weekends, taught classes during the week and had one huge rental mess to clean up on Mondays. Trying to get their personal diving in often found shop owners a bit gruff or putting up a closed sign on the door. Most were great divers and heroes to their customers. They missed some sales here and there but they never lost their followings.

Sometimes in these first shops of the pioneer years. things were rather messy and pieces of equipment to sell got buried back in cases or even closets. Really attractive equipment display probably owes much to the pegboard revolution and the attempts to train shop owners in display at DEMA Conventions and other dealer association seminars. NASDS did a good job along this line. So did Harry Rice when he was at U.S. Divers as Sales Manager.

The evolution of standards and training agencies dictated greatly to where diving was going to manufacturers and shops. Shops could see how the instructors influenced new divers. The industry didn't really trust these independent instructors and as a former DEMA Chief, Chuck Buchanan, told us in 1970's, "The shops especially resented Los Angeles County in the 1950's, and then NAUI in the 1960's as taking control of divers away from the shops." NASDS and SSI were shop oriented training agencies. PADI had moved in that direction, too, (although SSI and NASDS called themselves schools quickly to shift the power.) The YMCA struggled with a national system and was pretty much made up of some strong and some weak local Y-Programs which had some bad incidents of YMCA's buying direct from manufacturers and jobbers. This squeezed out the retail dive shop.

Tillman remembers how UNEXSO's dive shop depended on being the exclusive outlet for equipment to support an expensive operation but was hurt by the Freeport, Bahamas, YMCA importing equipment, then selling it to members at discounted prices. The 1960's saw the specialty store taking over from the adjunct status in sporting goods and department stores. Some large retailers like Sears got Aqua Lungs with its JCHiggins Brand attached, sold them cheaper than Aqua Lungs, but it didn't work even at lower prices. People wanted an Aqua Lung if they were going to "risk their lives in this dangerous sport."

As clubs diminished as a focal instrument for keeping divers in the water, *Sea Hunt* disappeared, Cousteau's films on TV became cartoonish and repetitive, the Vietnam War subsided but had taken away many young male potential customers, and the economy floundered. Dive shops suffered. By 1969, manufacturers and shops needed to find new boosters.

The dive shops had to step in and generate new interest and new spending, stop competing with each other, and take on the skiing and golf competition. The dive shop needed to use instruction as a major profit-center. Instruction became a leading product, and training agencies were pushed to create more diving beyond the classroom (The agencies were saying that the dropout rate was around 70% in the first year after basic training).

And so a number of things happened. Dive Shops expanded the Charter Boat business, both independents and ones owned directly by the shops. The training agencies during the 1970's were now ballooning certification into confined water and classroom teaching. The open water-diver classification would only be available when multi-open water dives under supervision were achieved by the students. Four open water dives became a standard put up by the National Scuba Training Committee of ANSI (American National Standards Institute). It brought the diver back into the shop for rentals, purchases and the charter trips to make the open water dives profitable, sometimes included in the course tuition, but often this was added on. A course tuition had risen to an average $300. Air and all kinds of additional safety devices were sold because students were now going into the real ocean.

Advanced specialty diving courses had been brewing for a long time. Los Angeles County and NAUI both had distinctive encampments and seminars on underwater photography, deep diving, search and recovery, marine biology programmed-in to keep the recreational diver aware of what to do with the new-found skill (or the diver would drop out). Los Angeles County had a large Advanced Diving Program created by Morgan 'Clint' Degn. Going into the 1960's and into the 1970's, it covered all the specialties in one broad spectrum course. The largest class had over one hundred enrollees. Many then went on to the Instructor and Divemaster Courses.

A third important move by dive shops was to stage local diving events from photo contests to pumpkin-carving to water clean-up projects to underwater board games of checkers or chess. Dive shops couldn't sit back and let the clubs do it by the 1970's, for the clubs had begun to fade away to some degree. The motto, as Fred Calhoun often told us is, "to stop talking about diving and get the diver in the water with all his gear - often."

By the 1970's destination resorts and travel were new products to sell to diving customers. Skin Diver Magazine became loaded with resort and travel advertising. Travel agencies were packaging exotic diving location trips, and consequently during the 1970's, the shops became travel agencies on the side. Some local diving suffered as divers saved up money and time for the jet trip to dive. But the newly affluent divers coming into the sport bought top-of-the-line equipment, all of it. Thereby, it made up for loss of local diving sales. Anyway, the suffering environment from impact and pollution was not the wonderful underwater world it used to be. It certainly didn't measure

Bob Rutherford and students at the original Aquatic Center Dive Shop in 1957.   Bob Rutherford

up to the graphic splendor shown on television.

A multitude of manufacturers were hustling five times the products available in previous decades; it kept shop owners whirling, trying to stock everything available. The customer wanted the new jet fin they saw on TV or a special prescription mask. Shops, poorly financed in their beginnings, suddenly, could afford all examples of inventory. The early shops resorted to putting empty boxes on shelves to create the illusion that they were complete and ready to sell anything. Some say Ma Klein master-minded that marketing deception. Manufacturers wanted to take orders in September just after "the season" rather than in January at the National Sporting Goods Association or DEMA Convention Trade Shows (a factor that hurt DEMA's Convention during a long period.), The manufacturers, where they were selling direct to retailers in many cases, or a cooperative of shops (Gaffney used to chortle that he'd designed that strategy) wanted to estimate their production and move it out to dealers. The dealers had to warehouse inventory but if they bought it early, there were discounts. Those who couldn't pay up-front took advantage of "dating" - whereby a shop could get equipment on credit and if they paid up by May, they got as much as a 40% discount; by July it went to 20% and wait until September, full price was required.

Even with this, manufacturers ended up with surpluses and would in desperation "dump off" gear in large quantities to large discount stores where the prices beat local dive shops. In turn, retail shops skating on thin financial ice, would discount severely, have big sales, unload surplus inventory to stay in business, creating a domino effect, by taking away customers from a cross-town shop holding its prices.

By the 1980's, dive shops had aligned themselves with one or another training agency, all of which had decided that diving was going to be funneled through the dive shops. Dive shops then signed up to be a PADI Official Dive Center. If full-service, it was designated a five-star shop. NASDS and SSI were based on the exclusive dive shop classification. Even NAUI, who believed in the dignity with pride of the independent instructor, had to finally "fall in line" to a degree. The dive shops in some cases were required to use a specific agency's instructors, certified by them, plus buy all student materials from the agency. In turn PADI or SSI or any of the rest of the agencies did mass marketing and arranged insurance programs based on numbers of enrollees. The weekend instructor had to go with these policies to avoid the growing octopus of liability.

The 1980's saw some dive shops merge into larger mall type operations - the big sporting goods stores. A major case of this is the Sports Chalet in Southern California (which had 23 stores by year 2000.) It carried lines of all the major individual adventure sports, of which diving evolved as a super section. Sports Chalet goes back to an original store in La Crescenta, California, nestled in this hilly town away from the ocean. Deeply entrenched in snow-ski equipment for years, Sports Chalet's Norbert Olberz, CEO, waded into scuba sales in 1959.

Diving really caught up with the economy and recreation interest of a new breed of affluent people by the 1980's. It had its own on-premises pools, and the instructor/dive masters were trained as much to be sales-staff as anything. R.E.I. in the Northwest is another example of the larger mall adventure-stores. The new breed of diver was connected to the label dive "store" rather than dive-shop.

The stores of the 1980's had to be attractively decorated and clean, have everything fully available on sight and browsing was encouraged after a charming, "Can I help you?" is asked of everyone. In the old days, there was often a grumpy proprietor trying to figure out his accounts and wanting to get outdoors to go diving. The new divers are, in large part of the high-tech generation. A shop has to be ready to talk about the latest advances. These divers wanted to try out new, computer-driven devices. They often saw gear as the lure rather than the underwater world itself.

Another factor in the 1980's, the shop owner was often more businessman than diver. He needed to be into the computer world. He needed to know how to sell design and color, the equipment decorations over functions - as the equipment looked different but was often quite similar in effect and quality.

By the 1990's shops were thoroughly entrenched in diving computers, the glitzy look, space-age materials, travel and the newly arrived ultimate experience, the live-aboard. The economy was smoking. The public was buying everything put in front of them. Fixed-income people, the older population from the pioneer years of diving, were bemoaning the high prices, the disappearance of their good-old diving areas, the threat of a fishless ocean, and the hyper, high-tech, pace of their lives. Dive shops had to fall in line and pushed the specialty courses, such as Ice Diving and Cave Diving, which people took as a course whether they ever did that kind of diving or not. The new generation of divers felt guilty if they didn't have the latest diving gadget or look - or talk the new language of diving, about dive profiles and down-loading.

The grand risk of going underwater with dangerous monsters all about, the thrill of living the fantasy of *20,000 Leagues Under The Sea*, the fear of the bends and the whole awesome process of scuba and skin diving had been diminished by elaborate equipment that took the diver diving rather than the diver taking simple basic gear he really needed. Instead of shark-fear, divers were demanding to see sharks and to hand-feed them. Statues and trail markers were being put underwater for sanctuaries created where things can not be taken. Virgin unexplored places may only exist in Borneo or some very remote ocean region, if at all. Jacque Cousteau is one, so is Dimitri Rebikoff, E. R. Cross, Gustav Dalla Valle, Mel Fisher - most of the colorful characters that put zest and testosterone into diving in the early days.

The new diving is what shops have had to accept and make work in some way or another. It is a monster challenge and the industry will depend on people spending huge sums of money for exotic experiences. The little, old hole-in-the-wall dive shop can't re-emerge to be that place to swap fish stories and compare homemade diving gimmicks. Yet as 2000 arrived, there was a retro movement, as free divers, young and old, and spearfishermen shunted scuba aside to dive "like they used to." Right along side of that, paradoxically, is the new rebreather and mixed gases and submersibles that dive shops have to rebuild facilities to handle, including going "back to school" to understand.

Ventura Marina Divers Supply on Anchors Way decorated to attract attention.   *Scuba America Archives*

Whatever happens in the future, nothing else but the dive shop has been as much at the center of where diving was at any point in time over the fifty year history.

NOTES

IMPORTANT EVENTS THAT SHUT DOWN SOME DIVE SHOPS

1. 1980 Mt. St. Helen's eruption [on May 18th, just before diving season] tumbled local economy and Tom Hemphill in Vancouver operated, as usual, but business dropped off and he had to move on.

2. Pollution hits from population density, sewage, shut down a lot of island paradises, killed off marine life and shops suffered. Santa Monica Bay, California, is contaminated.

3. Shark attacks like the Pamperin event in La Jolla, California, that gets wide publicity drives people/divers out of water and shops don't have customers.

4. *Jaws*, along same line, even though it was a fiction scared people about the ocean.

5. A big industry or military base supporting a local economy closes down, there are no paychecks to spend.

6. The stock market fluctuations drive the economy, arrest public spending when it's a Bear Market.

7. Cave drowning particularly in Florida, shuts down access to that kind of diving and local shops that depend on it. They have to shift programs or go under.

8. Worst job is making collections. Dive shop customers have a record of not paying-up when they have bad dive experiences.

9. Manufacturers forcing a minimum order policy. Advertising a product that manufacturers don't have ready.

SHOPS SUCCEED FOR VARIOUS REASONS

The following are excerpts from shop owner-interviews over the years.

1. Dive N' Surf had a good wet suit but came up with a great name "Body Glove" that got picked up by the fashion industry. A dive shop that comes up with an appealing new idea can upgrade its business greatly.

2. Shops with great relationships with clubs have a captured-customer block.

3. The serendipitous feature news story about diving that gets in the paper on slow-news days or the planted-story about a great find by a customer or achievement by dive shop staff, an award, etcetera.

4. Being able to have the latest equipment on display in shop, being able to afford it, especially if "news of it is in the media."

Computers/gauges become big money-item to replace regulators. There are twelve brands of "retractors" selling for an average of $25 each that attach something to you.

5. Nothing beats good air sold cheap to get traffic and impulse buying through a shop.

6. When a shop knows where its profit centers are, the ones based on the labor-intense factor, they often realize the quick purchases of buckles and snaps, small bits of hardware for repairs over the long haul take no labor-time and represents $3 to $15 small sales that have great volume - whereas, to sell a regulator takes staff time to set it up on a tank, and is a significant cost because the customer is "shopping" and a low percentage of sales are incurred by the effort. Buyers of the large items want "to think about it." Sell small!

7. The in-house pool became a necessity for successful stores. For example, the Sports Chalet's store in the Fallbrook Mall, Canoga Park, California, has the pool with the entry off the dive equipment sales-area with a street window on a heavily trafficked mall-pathway. A major initial cost, it saves time and is a great attraction to lure people into store.

8. Nothing beats top-of-the-line, personable, knowledgeable personnel impassioned about diving, with inventory congruent with shops personnel. The staff should all be as motivated and act like shop owners.

9. Great trips controlled by the shop, staffed with most skilled and caring dive masters, deluxe treatment given to diving customers, stable safe boats, good food and water made a shop look good.

The 1959 Skin Diver Magazine ran a feature on the "New Look in Dive Shops." The new Underwater Sports Shop in Long Beach, CA was the feature store with 3,000 square feet of space dedicated to diving equipment, a large showroom, workshop, compressor room and specially designed 20 x 45 foot pool for handling up to 24 students per week.

5

U. S. Divers Company

Defining Event: The Cronin Era and the Cousteau Image

The U.S. Divers Company was the General Motors of diving. It had the power to direct the course of sport diving over all the decades. Sometimes admired and sometimes hated, it stayed king of the hill despite a number of mistakes and being challenged by new manufacturers along the way.

It all started with two skinny Frenchmen. One of them, René Bussoz was owner of an upgrade sporting goods store at 1045 Broxton Avenue in the stylish Westwood area of Los Angeles next to UCLA. Tennis and hunting gear were major parts of its inventory. It was a clean, orderly store with glass display cases and a relatively small inventory on the surrounding shelves of the approximately 1,000 square feet of floor space.

René made a good living from it, had a boat and a nice Bel Aire home with a swimming pool. Movie stars, sports figures, students and university professors were his customers. But he didn't get really rich until later.

The most popular story recalled by divers of the 1940's and 1950's was that while vacationing in Paris in 1948 and admiring his reflection in a sporting goods window, suddenly a strange tubed-machine entered his vision. So what kind of sport is this, he thought?

Inquiring inside, he was introduced to the Aqua Lung, a way for swimmers to breathe underwater. Interesting product, he mused, an attention getter, but most likely an impractical novelty.

Perhaps he could put it in his store window in Westwood and draw people into the store out of curiosity. This was the kind of thing that might capture Burt Lancaster's imagination, and instead of just looking in the window, come on into the store. So he arranged to have a few, six goes the report, shipped to Los Angeles.

René Bussoz told us that he saw them as a loss-leader. He'd just sell them off for whatever cost in order to have them for awhile. They would stimulate some foot traffic. He had no idea that there was a solid market of skin divers out across America, but particularly in Southern California. Many of the skin divers were veterans of World War II (1940-1945). Many were garage-workshop tinkerers who tried to construct a way to breathe underwater with bucket helmets, garden hoses, bicycle pumps, and surplus high altitude oxygen systems. Some had heard of Cousteau (the other skinny Frenchman) and his Aqua Lung.

René just didn't know they were there, those do-it-yourself free divers making spears and floats and other items. René had fins, mask, and arbalete-spearguns, but he was interested in and catered to an upper economic class.

The six units came in and René Bussoz invited some friends out on his and Bob Vincent's boat to try them.

One of those friends was actually a customer, his gardener, and diving enthusiast who had tried diving during World War II in the South Pacific. Glenn McCall had come into René's store to buy binoculars and René brought out a thing called the Aqua Lung. Glenn asked, "What is that?" He was one of those friends, and another was Tarzan himself, Olympic Swimming Champion, Johnny Weissmuller. Another friend was Champion Swimmer, "Flash Gordon" Buster Crabbe, (who later graduated from NAUI's 1962 instructors course in the Gloucester, Massachusetts).

GLENN MCCALL TO THE RESCUE

The Aqua Lungs, all six of them, were assembled already when René received them from France, but on the tryout dive, they didn't work properly. So René had McCall put his experience with homemade units to work trying to get them working properly. In his garage, McCall found the major problem in the second stage of the regulator. "I had to bend the metal," McCall told us; "There were no convenient screws to adjust." René had been disgusted with "the damn things" and had been ready to write the machines off.

But McCall, the engineer, was intrigued and saw a definite possibility in these Aqua Lungs and felt he knew how to fix what was wrong. He did, and René put them back in the window.

FIRST OWNERS

Meanwhile, Dr. Willis E. Pequegnat, editor of the Journal of Entomology and Zoology at the time, replied to René's desire to advertise the Aqua Lung. "But not without a personal test in a pool," said Pequegnat who brought one to Pomona College. "I tried it and bought it," he said. "I used the device for obtaining specimens for use in teaching marine ecology and experimental embryology at the Kerckhoff Marine Laboratory Corona del Mar, California. Then I got support from the Office of Naval Research to conduct a study of submarine reefs off Laguna Beach and Corona del Mar." Users were the advertisers.

Divers studying marine biology at UCLA under Dr. Boyd Walker saw the window display of the Aqua Lung and talked the department chairman into buying a couple of the first units to use in the field research. Connie Limbaugh was one of the students and Ken

Glenn McCall with 21 1/2 Lb. lobster with two legal sized abalones attached. Santa Cruz Island, 1952. Glenn McCall Collection

Norris another. Word of mouth did the rest. Back in Woods Hole, another oceanography student, David M. Owen, was introducing the Aqua Lung into the field studies of that institution's program. Dave Owen put out a book that lighted the way for all the manuals yet to come. Its title was *The Manual For Free Divers.*

René had sold the first shipment of six and still didn't think he had more than a novelty on his hands. The story goes that he notified Aqua Lung manufacturer, Air Liquide (a French company Cousteau got involved with through his father-in-law), that he wouldn't be ordering more because the "U.S. market was saturated."

Then an avalanche of interest flowed through René's store in the next year or so. That vast market of spearfishing free divers was knocking on his door. That first shipment of six was claimed to have been purchased by dozens of divers wanting to establish their pioneer credentials in the new sport. The units all had a metal plate on the regulator that gave its number. That first shipment, as far as we can determine went, probably to UCLA (2), *Jordan Klein, Paul Arnold, Dr. Willis E. Pequegnat. And the other owners are still being sought.*

Cousteau's eldest son, Jean-Michel, recalled in interview that a representative from Air Liquide first brought the units to René, a bit in reverse of the story that René had discovered the Aqua Lung in Paris in 1947.

Bill Barada claimed to have traded René a prototype dry suit for one of those early units. "It came with a 38 cubic foot tank, which meant about 15 minutes of air. So I just took it along on my free dives and used it when I got hung-up in an especially difficult extraction of a lobster from its hole. I just never saw it as a replacement for free diving."

René got the message quickly, for he was a crafty and shrewd businessman according to all the pioneer divers who did business with him. He retained Glenn McCall for the next ten years to assemble and repair the regulators which "Were made and ordered from Europe - all in parts." No one seems to know how to pin down the exact year, although Glenn believes it was 1947 when René brought in the parts for about 1200 regulators in those early years of the late 1940's and early 1950's.

One of those early units was bought by Eddie Shain of Duarte, California, who was a member of the spin-off branch of the Los Angeles Neptunes Dive Club, called the Santa Anita Neptunes. Eddy generously took it along on club trips and let all the members use it. (There was no instruction or guiding manuals of note at this time.) It was Al Tillman's first chance to use one and like most free divers, he was both leery and skeptical about such a device, even while using it. "Some of us were seeing it as sissy-diving, but then it took me awhile to accept the snorkel," recalls Tillman.

We have to credit René with quickly realizing that he had a runaway product *exclusively* in his clutches. It would dwarf the sales of all the other sporting goods in time. He picked up distributors from friends such as "playboy," Paul Arnold, who took it into the Florida region and opened the Aqua Lung Center with Charles Diercksmeier. Jordan and his Mother, Anne Klein, were soon distributing out of their Miami store. Lew Maxwell eventually took over Arnold's distributorship. René went to the National Sporting Goods Show in Chicago, recruited more distributors, and sold units directly.

SHOWCASED NSGA CONVENTION - 1955

In the first years that scuba diving was represented at the National Sporting Goods Association Convention held at the Morrison Hotel in Chicago, Illinois, the exhibits for companies were presented in the actual hotel rooms. Beds were removed, some tables replaced for larger, longer ones and the dressers used as counters for the merchandise demonstrations or display. Sporting goods, all kinds from here to breakfast, were there for dealers to order or buy on the spot. Tennis, archery, bodybuilding weights with motion apparatuses, and especially, salt and freshwater fishing equipment were big shows. Represented along with golf, billiards, bowling and other ballgames, indoor and outdoor sports were the shoes and costumes that went with all of the other paraphernalia. But this was the year that scuba and skin diving gear started to radiate brightly. The convention was not open to the public. It was 1955.

Zale Parry who was at the show recalls, "It was February, a wind-blowing cold-kind of season. From the U.S. Divers Company hotel room-exhibit, René Bussoz sold a set of pressed-steel double tanks to a King Kong-diver dealer for cash. As the diver happily carried the doubles down the stairs of the hotel, he swore they weighed about 45 pounds each. Heavy. The next day, the diver dressed in a Barada Bel Aqua Dry Suit, the double-tank setup, mask and fins, went to Lake Michigan with a group of dry-topside buddy observers to try them out. Off the end of the pier, he went alone to the bottom of the Lake in about a 35-40 foot depth. The guy couldn't get back! Couldn't go down either. Buddies were worried until they realized he was so heavy; he walked to shore. It was the first double-set of tanks ever sold. René never gave the diver his money back."

Michigan with its collection of Great Lakes would join Florida as a key distribution point for Renés Aqua Lung sales. There was John Irving in the New England area and Vern Pederson in Chicago.

DICK ANDERSON - THE KID-HIS VERSION

If we need to laugh at this point at the serious business of getting the premier diving company started, then we need to turn to Dick Anderson. His stories aren't always absolutely accurate, but they are fun to listen to and he certainly was on hand at many of sport diving's major events.

Dick Anderson showed up at René's with a want ad for a "laborer". He was only 18 and had been doing labor on the docks in Alaska (That's what you get for reading Jack London).

It was 1950, and Anderson was one of those enthusiastic, going-free divers without any money. As Anderson tells it, "Only a week or so earlier I had dropped into René Sports to look longingly at the Aqua Lung. Sterling Hayden (movie star of the era) was looking at the same unit, but he could afford it." René saw in Anderson the future generation of buyers he must cultivate, and of course as an 18 year old, he could be hired at the California minimum wage of $1.25 an hour. As Harry Rice, who René hired to be his sales manager at a National Sporting Goods Show, would say, "René was shrewd but he was...well...stingy, and it was hard to convince him you had to spend money to make money."

Dick Anderson may have seemed cheap labor at first, but he was a learner and he listened to the stories of René's enterprises as he worked. Some of these stories came from Glenn McCall who had been elevated from René's gardener to become "the factory" putting Aqua Lungs together from parts with the same tools he had worked on for lawn mowers. According to Dick, the story he got was René had been in the U.S. Office of War Information during World War II making French propaganda for broadcasts in Europe. He went back to Paris to open three sportswear shops. On a recreation vacation to America, he discovered and fell in love with Westwood. In 1947 he opened René Sports. As Anderson tells it, René had gone on a buying trip to Paris (He handled mask and fins and other accessories from European companies.) and had setup a rendezvous to meet a young lady in front of a sporting goods store when he saw a window-displayed Aqua Lung with a card saying "be like a fish...call Jacques Cousteau," with a phone number. Forget the girl, René got a hold of Jacques and told him he wanted to sell Aqua Lungs, which until then had been sold only in Europe by Air Liquide, a welding company in France.

Cousteau had just been in America trying to get someone to handle the Aqua Lung there so he thought "René was nuts." Anderson said that René, with financial aid of a partner, Maurice Oliver, obtained 20 units wholesale from Cousteau. (This contrasts with the six in other accounts.) In the United States, a big problem arose. Where do you fill the French tanks which didn't have a U. S. ICC-rating? So they snuck over to UCLA and got them surreptitiously filled. Eventually, René had U.S. made tanks.

Glenn McCall went about teaching Dick Anderson everything about the Aqua Lung. McCall says that René had Aqua Lungs in 1947, the year after McCall had come out of the service. "I was one of those thousands of veterans who were around in the late 1940's, anxious to live some years the war had taken away and full of adventure. We were René's market." Glenn says he had unit #12 which cost him $140, tank, valve, and regulator, but he didn't use it as much when he was out free diving with the likes of Herb Sampson, Doc Mathison and Hal Messinger.

"Anderson," recalls McCall, "came in with some idea that there was some big awesome mystery in this little machine, but he clicked in fast." Anderson remembers, "The role of each part, chamber and air channel was instantly quite obvious...it all suddenly fell in place, and a few days later I was repairing regulators and giving repair instructions to the U.S. Navy Underwater Demolition Team. I began giving Aqua Lung diving instruction to preferred customers in the pool of Renés posh Bel Aire home."

Glenn McCall as it has been related here, had built homemade units during World War II (and eventually put a unit on the market called *Water Gill* in 1948) while in the service. He was the perfect representative to introduce the Aqua Lung to the Coronado Island Underwater Demolition Team Unit under L. E. "Mac" McLarty, who said that the UDT was trying to get away from the use of rebreathers.

This period around 1948-1949 appears to have been a major year for scuba, as Cousteau's first black and white movies were shown around to clubs in the United States by Cousteau himself. (Cousteau was also over to check on how René was doing with the first shipment of Aqua Lungs.) There was also an article by James Dugan about Cousteau and the Aqua Lung entitled, *The First of the Menfish* which appeared in the December 1948 issue of *Science Illustrated.* Commander Francis Douglas Fane of the Submersible Operations Platoon, U.S. Navy, followed up reading that article with directly ordering ten units for testing from Air Liquide. Woods Hole Institution and Scripps Institution of Oceanography obtained some, too.

BIRTH OF U.S. DIVERS

René had his partner pull out saying, "These things are too much trouble to sell...it costs a dollar to make a dollar." René went ahead and formed the U.S. Divers Company. Then he put up a sign over the *back* door at René Sports. It was a strong name, had industrial strength, and gave the aura of government quality control.

Then a bonanza hit. No one is *exactly sure* how it came about. René received a huge order for Aqua Lungs from the U.S. Navy. It was big money compared to the trickle going out to individual divers. The big hang-up at first was simply no place to fill the French tanks, and some divers shipped the tanks via parcel post back to the new U.S. Divers Company to be filled. René had to put a Rix Compressor in his upstairs toilet at the Sports store.

Anderson pointed out that the French manufactured Aqua Lung was rather crude. There were flaws in the cast metal that let air seep out. Now René had decided to avoid importing the valves and hardware, especially with the three months delay in getting parts, so he arranged with a Chicago valve and fitting manufacturer, the Bastian-Blessing Company, to produce them. B and B advised him the regulator parts could be made by them, too, they had been making complicated regulators for other purposes for years. They made René realize that this was no magic machine of secret French genius. Make them U.S. and forget about import duties.

René, with this information and the big Navy order in the hundreds of thousands of dollars,

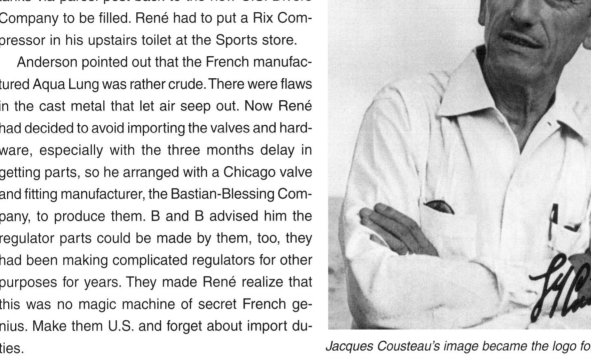

Jacques Cousteau's image became the logo for U.S. Divers.

rushed to France to meet with Cousteau at Air Liquide and get the exclusive rights to manufacture and sell the Aqua Lung in the United States. For it, the not as shrewd Cousteau, who was more interested in the movie business at the time, along with Gagnon, his co-inventor, would get a modest royalty. At this point, a distributor in Burlington, Vermont, which was handling the Eastern region, was discontinued. Now René had a powerful exclusive on a product that had no competition. With this power he was confident in forming the U.S. Divers Company.

The sports store in Westwood was just too small for the blooming business. U.S. Divers opened a large plant and offices not too far away at 11201 West Pico Boulevard, Los Angeles, California. Harry Rice, the Sales Manager in the early days of U.S. Divers, reiterated to us that René was a charming guy and an okay boss to work for because he respected Harry's years of selling footballs and basketballs...but René didn't like to spend money. René didn't think he needed salesmen out on the road taking orders, which had always been the crux of a successful manufacturer. René used *Skin Diver Magazine* to reach the divers with full-page ads and a small one in *National Geographic Magazine.* René felt there was a small niche-market with civilian divers, a big market with the Navy but the general public was not ready to go into a scary place like the ocean and try to breathe there.

SELLING OFF U.S. DIVERS

Even as he became a multimillionaire, René still battled against his past. One was his failure to really understand the diving market. An interesting note is that René's father invented the slot machine, and René had been importing slot parts for Las Vegas. The second thing that caught up to him was his somewhat questionable ploy of bringing parts into the country, rather than a fully assembled product, thus avoiding high tariffs.

Al Tillman remembers going to court with Mel Fisher and Bev Morgan to testify about what constituted a completed product, such as a mask or Aqua Lung, and if merely assembling in the U.S. Divers "factory" justified the avoidance of duty. René breezed by that snag, but the stress of it contributed to his deciding to sell off U.S. Divers in 1957.

U.S. Divers was in a wonderful position in the early 1950's. It had the exclusive on a product that as yet had no competition and it controlled its manufacture. Diving clubs were just emerging and mushrooming up everywhere. They fully encouraged a device by which divers everywhere could talk to each other - *Skin Diver Magazine. SDM* was created by two great free divers who were smart enough to realize the new "bubble machine" was just too alluring not to take over every diver's imagination, if not his pocketbook as yet. Diving had to change. Daredevils who walked into the sea to the awe of spectators on the beach had to yield to the mass public's involvement.

U.S. Diver's first catalogs in 1953 and 1954 said in the opening page - "Until the invention of the Aqua Lung, only highly trained specialists could explore the underwater world. This was an expensive adventure, full of risks. Now, thanks to this self-contained diving unit, any experienced and healthy swimmer can dive among the wonders of the deep, below 100 feet and up to one hour, unhampered by hoses or lines." It should be noted that in this 1954 catalog there is no mention of Cousteau.

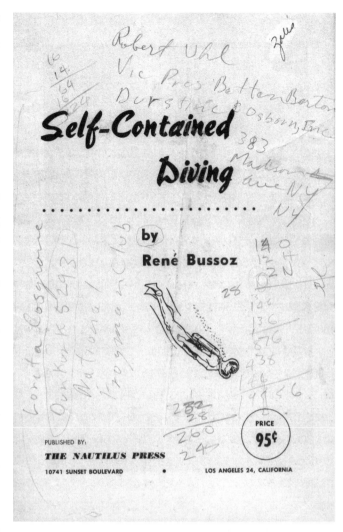

René Bussoz wrote one of the first manuals on how to use the Aqua Lung.

The heroes of diving were still the champion free diving spearfishermen like the Pender Brothers of Florida and Jim Christiansen of California, but only in the ranks of divers, not the public. Little did anyone realize that Dick Anderson, René's $1.25 an hour kid-worker and Aqua Lung repairman, was destined to become one of the scuba diving legends. Another young diver, a teacher from Canada but French in origin, with a sexy seductive continental accent showed up on René's doorstep. René, as Anderson tells it, had him teach Sam Lecocq, the new guy, everything he knew about the Aqua Lung.

Anderson had adventure in his bones, gold and treasure in his heart, and he parted ways with René Sports and U.S. Divers. He went with Mel Fisher to Florida to seek treasure wrecks. Sam Lecocq would learn everything about scuba and also move on later in 1954 to join Dick Klein at Healthways, noted for its weights and fitness equipment.

The military lock that René had during the 1950's was extended by supplying the movies with Aqua Lung equipment. The movie, *The Frogmen*, with Dana Andrews, came out in the excitement of the Korean War and the public had its heroes in these extraordinary athletes in uniform, underwater with Aqua Lungs.

By the mid 1950's, it was estimated there were nearly one million divers in the USA, skin and scuba diving. Some $250,000 worth of Aqua Lungs had been sold by 1953 with 80% of sales in California. In October of 1952, *National Geographic* published an article entitled *Fishmen Explore A New World Undersea* and suddenly Cousteau's name was on everybody's lips. The public admired the UDT Frogmen, but Cousteau's fishmen were closer to who they were now, and *they* still were the male veterans of World War II and the Korean War. *National Geographic* backed Cousteau in grand fashion with articles over the next few years, and television producer, David Wolper, put the Captain and his crew on TV with a series of underwater specials. James Dugan helped Cousteau write and publish the classic, *The Silent World*, which in turn was made into a lush color film that stirred many in America to give scuba diving a try. All of this, on top of a springing-up of clubs, the 1951 publication of *Skin Diver Magazine*, and formal instruction being organized, gave U.S. Divers an open road to success. U.S. Divers also picked up great exposure by going into a demonstration tank at the Los Angeles Sportmen Show in 1957. That year René netted $30,000.

U.S. DIVERS CHALLENGED

However, the hold U.S. Divers had on scuba diving in America became threatened by manufacturers of different scuba regulators entering the market.

Healthways, the company that picked up Dick Anderson and Sam Lecocq at different times, had two inventive and mechanical geniuses on board. Healthways, headquartered in Los Angeles, managed to bypass the limited patent on the Aqua Lung, which only covered the exhaust hose and flapper type exhaust valve located at the diaphragm. The Aqua Lung was challenged by Healthways' DIVAIR Regulator, which was actually manufactured by the L.G. Arpin Company of New Jersey.

There was a shaking of the U.S. Divers Company complacency as the DIVAIR picked up sales in 1954, which encouraged others to try to enter the area. The Garrett AiResearch Corporation in Torrance, California, under government contract came out with the Northill AIR LUNG Regulator, a well-built product with a cluster of innovations that in the long run appeared to be too complex for the general public. In 1955, the Davison Brothers under the name DACOR produced a double diaphragm regulator with a feature called dial-a-breath. By 1957, Sam Lecocq had come up with a replacement for the DIVAIR Regulator (that proved to suffer from electrolysis). Lecocq's new two hose regulator was called SCUBA. U.S. Divers wasn't sure how to handle this competition and even created more challenge to the Aqua Lung by selling the Aqua Lung internal mechanism inside a different cover by agreement with the powerful sports equipment company, W. J. Voit Rubber. U.S. Divers even tried to supply Sears with an Aqua Lung regulator, disguised to fit into Sears' J.C. Higgins line.

COUSTEAU AND MIKE NELSON

With exclusivity gone, René was receptive when Air Liquide's subsidiary Spirotechnique came up with an offer of about two million dollars to buy René out in 1957. Spirotechnique took over U.S. Divers, and with Jacques Cousteau as Chairman of the Board, began to capitalize on the Cousteau name and new-found recognition. America had a real-life French hero and with that image and U.S. Divers' large head start with the Aqua Lung unchallenged for several years, U.S. Divers looked like it would retain the popularity of the Aqua Lung. Even the entry in the late 1950's of a fictional TV series with an American hero, Mike Nelson, did not take away from the Cousteau magic, and it was the Aqua Lung that was used in the series.

MANAGEMENT CHANGES AND MISTAKES

These were enchanted years for diving and U.S. Divers right on through the late 1950's and early 1960's. Some of the magic was temporarily disrupted when a young French manager, Francoise Villarem, with a background in bowling, came to run U.S. Divers after René, who had grabbed his fortune, ran to the French Riviera to open a golf course and have a life of luxury. Villarem was a pleasant man and well-liked, but he made several errors according to people who worked at U.S. Divers at the time. A cheaply built one hose regulator was marketed in 1957-1958 called the Aqua-Matic and its low quality rubbed off on the popular Aqua Lung. It was a relatively expensive mistake. Al Tillman reported that Villarem asked him to develop a prospectus for a string of Aqua Lung Schools across America following the construct of the Los Angeles County Program but Spirotechnique suddenly replaced Villarem with Maurice Michaud as a "moonlighting Santa Claus albeit," a yeller. Michaud did a clean sweep of personnel, some left over from René's ownership, and U.S. Divers finally realized that it had to hit the pavement with company salesmen, follow Harry Rice's advice about how to sell sporting gear. The Aqua-Matic went with the sweep and apparently so did the idea of a chain of Aqua Lung Schools which, while most dive leaders who heard about the possible involvement of U.S. Divers in mass training sites, thought it a good idea; the feeling also was the move was too late as several strong training programs away from the manufacturers were already in place and emerging.

Some of the problem for U.S. Divers, some diving analysts recalled, was U.S. Divers trying to become a French Company with the major power in a one-man CEO. Some felt Villarem was too nice a guy to

René Bussoz and colleagues after selling the first ten Aqua-Lungs imported into the USA.

instill such an autocratic rule. He suspected that instruction was going to be the gateway through which equipment sales would flow, but he didn't take a hard stand on it.

Under Villarem, Harry Rice got to develop sales displays packaged for dive shops that were role models for the industry. The displays presented a complete diving package and changed the piece meal selling by retailers. Indeed, it was now an *industry* with competing manufacturers and Villarem really wasn't allowed time to figure it out. Actually, the Aqua-Matic was a first attempt at a one hose regulator and Al Tillman remembers when he had a team recovering a half ton nugget of Jade at 60 feet at Big Sur, California. "U.S. Divers, Villarem, gave us Aqua-Matics to test and although there was the wondering, "Where's the rest of it?", we all just forgot about the regulator in the hardwork and drama of the Jade-lift, and the regulators seemed to give us all the air we needed." When Al asked his brother, Don, who was on the dive, a Cal Tech Civil Engineer for Los Angeles for 30 years, what he thought (Never expect a short answer from an engineer but this time he was succinct.) Don said, "Sure beats a garden hose and bicycle pump." The Aqua-Matic didn't make it to the catalog, never sold, and probably took Villarem down with it. It would seem that French Corporate Heads didn't allow *one* mistake.

Francoise Villarem's replacement, Maurice Michaud, may have cranked up U.S. Divers internally with his replacement of personnel, but he didn't know diving nor how *U.S. business* functions. Michaud dismissed the competition as "little dogs nipping at U.S. Divers' heels." But little dogs grow into big dogs with new ideas. And so it was that Sam Lecocq went beyond his brawny regulator, scuba, to develop the first well-engineered and very effective one hose regulator called the Waterlung. (Why bother in thinking up a really new name so nobody would confuse it with Aqua Lung. Or was that the point?)

Don St. Hill, Los Angeles County's Aquatics Director and Al Tillman had an instructor's certification institute scheduled at the Rosemead, California, Pool in the Spring of 1959 where Dick Klein and Sam Lecocq showed up unscheduled dragging some of the new Waterlungs behind them. They were obviously well-made, had a substantial look compared to the prior Aqua-Matic or Rose Aviation PRO one hoser. Clint Degn was there, and Vince Van Detta, eventually big names in diving instruction. They joined St. Hill and Tillman in praising the Waterlung's performance. Don St. Hill, a pioneer diver from the 1930's, said something about, "Every time you get used to one kind of diving, like jumping in with just a big rock, a pair of sneakers and goggles, there's a piece of equipment that comes along and you have to start your thinking all over. The Aqua Lung sure did it and this one hose regulator will, too." St. Hill, besides being one of the great diving lifeguards of all time, seemed to also be a prophet. The age of the one hose regulator, with its streamlined and less intimidating look, with good supply/demand breathing performance, became a popular transition from the two hose regulator beginning in 1960.

The Waterlung spawned a new company, Sportsways, (as Healthways experienced financial difficulties) with Richard Klein and Sam Lecocq transferring to it from Healthways. U.S. Divers was forced into a whole new line of production. The one hose regulator had arrived. U.S. Divers met the one hose demand with the Calypso and other manufacturers followed. Harry Rice ended up at White Stag in Portland, Oregon, that had also entered the regulator field to go along with their wet suits. U. S. Divers had earlier handled Perelli and other dry suits, but got heavily into wet suits with a diver named Terry Cox constructing them. The first wet suits by EDCO had no patent. Vellarem divers still halfheartedly gripped their aging Aqua Lungs and wondered if they needed a new one; could they trade it in on a Waterlung? New divers took to the one hose enthusiastically. Dive instructors had to shuffle some of the taught skills, like clearing water out of regulator hoses. The two hose Aqua Lung would hold a shaky reign over the next decade. The manufacturers' catalogs still put the two hose in front of pages on the one hose until one hose finally pushed the two hose completely out of the ensuing catalogs by 1965.

While Sportsways spawned some dynamic salesmen such as Paul Tzimoulis and Ray Tussey under the Master Sales Manager, Dick Bonin, it too folded. Into this breech stepped Scubapro with a line of equipment, especially a regulator, that matched up with the best quality gear of U.S. Divers and the rest of the manufacturers. There running this powerful new company, destined to make large inroads into U.S. Divers sales, were Gustav Dalla Valle and Dick Bonin.

Although diving was still estimated to be a market of 1,000,000 divers, by 1960 the interest was plateauing as the brand new aura and mystic fascination with scuba diving generated by the Cousteau films and *Sea Hunt* TV wore off. The power of the training agencies, starting with Los Angeles County, then the YMCA, NAUI (National Association of Underwater Instructors,) and PADI (Professional Association of Underwater Instructors), was beginning to be realized. Convenient ways to learn and be safe under talented, passionate instructors were doing the marketing for the manufacturers. The manufacturers and retail stores were resentful of that power, didn't like the idea of instructors dictating the way diving was going. But competition is competition, and the companies and shops were automatic "enemies" of each other.

Dive leaders reflected back in evaluation that U.S. Divers was too content with what they thought was a big lead and of course, the powerful image of Cousteau at its figurative helm.

FRENCH INFLUENCE SUBSIDES

Air Liquide Spirotechnique would start thinking about withdrawal from the American marketing scene, one they never seemed to really understand. In addition, U.S. Divers was moved from Los Angeles to a 45,000 square feet facility with a 30 foot testing pool and decompression chamber in 1960. U.S. Divers had made five million dollars in 1959 and expected a 60% increase in 1960, and it was all done with a stagnant market in the early 1960's. Government money was headed into the outer space program, rather than the so called inner space of our oceans. Diving would suffer because of it.

THE AMERICAN CULTURE OF 1960 EFFECTS

As the 1960's evolved, America was in a state of domestic and international stress with the Vietnam War absorbing the young male market. Some of the young were drawn into the hippy-culture and drugs. Diving wasn't one of their favored activities. Sales dropped in the early 1960's and many wondered if interest would ever recover again to the level generated by Cousteau films and the *Sea Hunt* television series. The manufacturers had not yet realized that competing with each other was wasteful, that they would need to take on other sports like skiing. Nor had they foresighted the eruption of dive travel with the jet age.

At U.S. Divers in the mid 1960's, top job went to an American, Jim Carroll. He had a background in American business practices but none in diving. He moved U.S. Divers in the direction of diversification under the concept that the sport diving field would be the main market, but there would be a great surge in commercial, industrial, and military diving. Oil exploration and recovery and the Vietnam War created a new demand for underwater equipment. A division called *Surviair* was setup to answer some needs in fire fighting and related safety services. U.S. Divers was presenting a number of faces during the 1960's, but the diving economic attitude of the country was still on the wane.

THE SHOPS AND U.S. DIVERS

What Carroll knew was what Dick Bonin at Scubapro became the guru for, that the retailer was the direct link with the consumer, no matter what else you did in advertising, relying on the Cousteau image, more television specials or another *Sea Hunt*. (*Flipper, Aquanauts* and other attempts were made on TV in the 1960's, but none approached *Sea Hunt*'s impact.) There was nothing like grassroots-hustle by live people in the boondocks (where the young and middle aged wanted to escape humdrum small town life and seek great adventure). Diving shops were still basically a very small hole in the wall, low-inventoried outlets operated by divers who had not much business sense and could care less. Most of the shop owners were gung-ho-divers, elaborate storytellers, learned to teach diving according to the growing number of how-to-manuals, and barely held off creditors with day-to-day cash flow. But...they oversaw the rabbit hole that Alice went down for the great adventure.

Healthways and other manufacturers were going to challenge U.S. Divers with their own S.C.U.B.A. Dick Anderson, Gustave Dalla Valle and Randy Stone plan the attack.

Many of them sincerely hated the manufacturers who forced them to buy more than they could sell in a season, using "dating," a concept whereby a retailer commits to a big order a half-year before the "season" begins, and thereby merits discounts, depending upon how soon the shop owner can pay up. Go through the season and he paid full price, no discounting.

U.S. Divers loomed as the *major* faceless monster to shop-owners, even while the company was really trying to reposition itself and gain a better rapport with the dealers who sold their equipment. Up to this era, there was a sort of disdain for the little specialty shop and over production got dumped into the market place in volume deals with discount outlets and department stores. In some cases, U.S. Divers slapped a different nameplate on the basic Aqua Lung as it has already been related here about Sears, Voit, New England Divers, and shops like San Diego Divers Supply. The solid position of U.S. Divers from the 1950's became questioned. Its integrity in the industry came under scrutiny.

FIELD REPS

Fortunately for divers, a solid corp of "traveling salesmen" gave stability to diving. They were the field representatives who hit the nooks and corners of America where a dive shop owner was trying to make a go of it. U.S. Divers was usually "far away" in their eyes, and answers to questions and back orders were slow in arriving. So jobbers, "the middleman," warehoused large inventories for the manufacturers and distributed swiftly to regional dealers. In some cases, they supplied by mail order. New England Divers was a major example. Many shop owners who survived through the 1960's credit these dynamic representatives of the manufacturers with teaching them the business side of diving.

The representatives would stop in, observe the local situation by rolling up their sleeves and standing shoulder-to-shoulder with the owner/operator. The representative listened to questions, problems, complaints and showed the shopman how he'd do it. He showed the owner how to listen to an irate customer and listen and listen and not retaliate with defensive verbal abuse. Most of the factory spokesmen had been there themselves on the floor selling, getting to where they were in the 1960's.

The representative moved inventory around, got up in the store front window to put a lure-display in it, cleaned the dead flies off the sill, helped in scheduling instruction, and even drafted advertising and fly- ers. The shop owner was treated the way these master salesmen had

An early U.S. Divers ad from Popular Science.

wanted to be treated, if the roles were reversed. U.S. Divers hadn't yet uncovered their savoir faire to equal Dick Bonin of Scubapro in the early 1960's.

Dick Bonin knew the retail business from ground level experience and had great empathy for the dealers. He brought great credibility to the stores, being sure that Scubapro gear didn't show up any place but in the specialty store, even to the point of Scubapro carrying the financial burden in part, giving broad lines of credit. Bonin got across the idea that this manufacturer, Scubapro, was a "partner" with the store. U.S. Divers, in comparison, came across as a self-satisfied, self-serving monolith.

DACOR's Davison Brothers themselves went to stores the West Coast manufacturers weren't getting to, and resorts in the Caribbean, too. Sportsways did the job with ebullient Paul Tzimoulis and handsome, charming Ray Tussey and others. Of course, U.S. Divers had some pros out there taking orders (and trying to defend U.S. Divers position). Marty Conley in the Southeast Region was a good-natured uncle who helped pump air at a shop, and commiserated on problems. The superstar was U.S. Divers representative in the Great Lakes Region. He was the tough John Cronin, full of Irish charm and wit and a background of learning "on the street selling" from clever Jewish retailers in his youth.

CRONIN TO THE RESCUE

Cronin was a diver who knew what it was like behind the counter, and he taught his salesman-ways to divers who had stumbled into the business of diving. He wrote orders, lots of them, from guys who felt Cronin was one of them who would lead them out of the darkness. (Could he in reality part the Red Sea they wondered?) He was the first million dollar order-writer in the industry. (A million dollars was quite a significant amount in the early 1960's.) He was certainly U.S. Divers' star, exceeding output of all the other U.S. Divers' representatives combined. Year after year he posted up record breaking sales. He was a strong advocate of instruction, and along with Ralph Erickson, found fault with NAUI as slow-moving, diluted by branch approval for everything, and as a nonprofit corporation naive about the business of recreational diving. He and Ralph splintered off a new training agency,

John J. Cronin in 1976 while President of U.S. Divers.

Professional Association of Diving Instructors (PADI), with the door open to easily become a recognized instructor and truly oriented to the shops.

U.S. Divers was perfectly willing to let its star salesman dictate some of the company's direction. In fact, they finally pulled him and his ideas into the main headquarters where he became Sales Manager in 1969. The Cronin era for U.S. Divers was about to begin.

In 1968, U.S. Divers celebrated the 25th anniversary of the invention of the Aqua Lung, by producing 100 gold-plated Royal Aqua Master Aqua Lungs. (Did you get one?) They hosted parties for top salespeople and retailers. Cronin had brought to the "party" a new sparkle. He had a dynamic effect on the company, and he knew what was happening in the field, what divers were looking for. He relayed this to the research and development department, and new color and design products flowed.

PADI AND U.S. DIVERS

PADI began to grow "down the street" from U.S. Divers with Cronin there to advise. It was operating as a non-manufacturer aligned corporation and there was some question about it being nonprofit or otherwise. Ultimately, its status was determined by court action. PADI would be a for profit business but be required to support a safety/environment foundation.

Separate as they might be, no one in diving was naive enough to not believe that there were great benefits back and forth between U.S. Divers and PADI, both John Cronin domains. The question, in the year 2000, of which one helped the other more is still up for speculation.

Scubapro was certainly number two by 1970 and had gained much respect throughout the sport diving world. Cronin and Bonin were often compared, the two Irish guys and distant relatives as well. The dealers mostly felt Dick Bonin was personal and had a heart, was a friend, while they saw John Cronin as a commanding father-figure who could lead them into battle. Either one of them could charm the fur clothes off an Eskimo in midwinter at the North Pole.

U.S. Divers by the early 1970's was moving into instructional material. They brought in Commander Leslie Tommy Thompson, an ex-Navy diver and active leader in the Los Angeles County Program, to gain more leverage with instructors who had become the powerful influences in diving. Students followed their leads. They were trying to match-up with Scubapro's instructional videos.

U.S. Divers even was providing lesson plans which the training agencies already had. The agency leaders regarded it as "throwing more salt in the ocean."

SCALLI ARRIVES

Cousteau was still U.S. Divers' ace card but Cronin was the catalyst, and he moved quickly to make a difference. In 1970 he became General Manager and then President in 1974. He added personnel with great track records. Frank Scalli, who had done a masterful sales job in the Northeast Region, came into headquarters to be National Sales Manager. Beloved Scalli was a pioneer diver who had made a lot of promotional things happen over the years, could match Cronin quip-for-quip with his own sense of humor. Gordon McClymons, Vice President of Marketing for U.S. Divers, said of Scalli, "He talked the language."

Typical of the new humor brought into U.S. Divers by Cronin and Scalli was a feathered-quill pen award, a creative writing award, to John Murphy, one of five $l,000,000 salesmen in the early 1970's whose expense accounts "rivaled the talents of Jules Verne and Walt Disney for creativity."

DEMA

Attempts had been made in the past decade to bring the manufacturers together to share information and a Diving Equipment Manufacturers Association (DEMA) was formed. But trust was lost as the companies shared false figures. The DEMA idea went into a limbo until revived in the 1980's, and once again an effort was being made to unite to compete, not against each other, but against other sports fields that were drawing off large segments of the consumer pool, especially the risk sport of skiing. (Indeed, diving looked to how the ski industry was functioning for guidance.) "Look we're a very small piece of the gross national product, equivalent to selling velvet ribbons or something, a small voice in the commerce of this country, and we'd sure better fight like hell together to hold on to the market we have or add to it," said Mike Kelly of Voit and key founder of DEMA. Ralph Osterhout, President of Farallon Industries at the time, had compared it to "less than the peanut industry."

It was during the 1970's that this whole thing of making diving grow didn't and wouldn't keep growing in sales based on making minor technical changes in the equipment each year. Trying to get divers to appreciate cyclic plastic housings, tilt valves, special Venturi action wasn't moving them. Lifetime guarantees for regulators, new light aluminum tanks that would last for 273 years, and silicon masks helped sales to a minor degree. But, "They bought the box they came in or how good the product looked; they weren't engi-

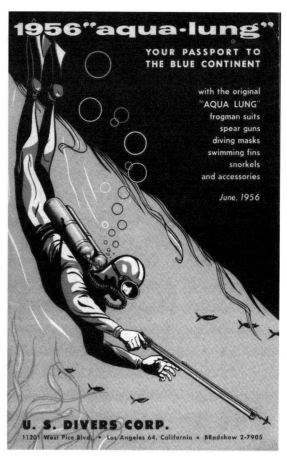

U.S. Divers 1956 catalog.

neers," recalled Bill Barada, who was promotion man for U.S. Divers back in the late 1950's and early 1960's. And so generally in America the sizzle took over for the steak. Marketing became the powerful force in directing companies. The art of selling exceeded the making of a better functioning product. Appearances drove the sales, the bright colors, the streamlined designs, how people themselves looked in the equipment. For example, shore divers would walk majestically into the ocean to an admiring gaping crowd of non-divers, only to come back to comically stumble over a jagged moonscape in the pioneer gear. "Cosmetics took over changes in equipment and fueled marketing," recalls John Gaffney who spent his career trying to glamorize the diving experience. DEMA itself changed its name eventually to Diving Equipment Marketing Association and brought in retailers, resorts, and training agencies as members (stakeholders). "It's all marketing now," said U.S. Divers Marketing ace, Gordon McClymons, who was the first trained marketeer non-diver brought into a top executive position with a diving company.

By 1975 the two hose regulator, the bulky, substantial, very visible piece of equipment, became almost extinct. U.S. Divers eliminated its top of the line Royal AquaMaster (sold at $124) as the slick looking one hose regulators in light, designer styles dominated completely. Nick Icorn, who worked as a U.S. Divers engineer in the demise days of the two hose Aqua Lung, pointed out that the original design of the Aqua Lung was setup to work with shorter French air tanks, and the longer ones in the United States pushed the regulator up in an awkward position, increasing pressure differential to the lungs and a variety of training techniques for clearing the hoses was taught (but actually unnecessary). "But the two hose," said Icorn, "provided a larger, more sensitive four-inch diaphragm, a smoother flow of air through the larger hose system than a one hose, a more comfortable mouthpiece due to buoyancy of the large hoses, and quieter operation with exhaust bubbles exiting behind the diver. The new people coming into diving, the non-water athlete types, especially in the 1970's and beyond, were less intimidated by the smaller, modern one hose regulator."

CATALOGS AND WILD COLORS

U.S. Divers went into a graphic battle with their rivals, and beautifully colored professional catalogs were the rule by the 1970's and beyond. As was previously indicated, the products themselves, Aqua Lungs, wet suits, mask, fins and snorkels were gussied up in flamboyant colors and design, especially the U.S. Divers colors of bright yellow and black. Some special attempts to be up with the times were red, white and blue striped fins, mask and snorkel. That was very *American* with a pitch on "joining the Olympiads." U.S. Divers touted itself as the world's largest and oldest manufacturer of sport, commercial and military diving equipment. A lot of print still went into complex explanations of why U.S. Divers Aqua Lungs all breathed easier than others but the others claimed the same thing in reverse. Marketing was in the saddle.

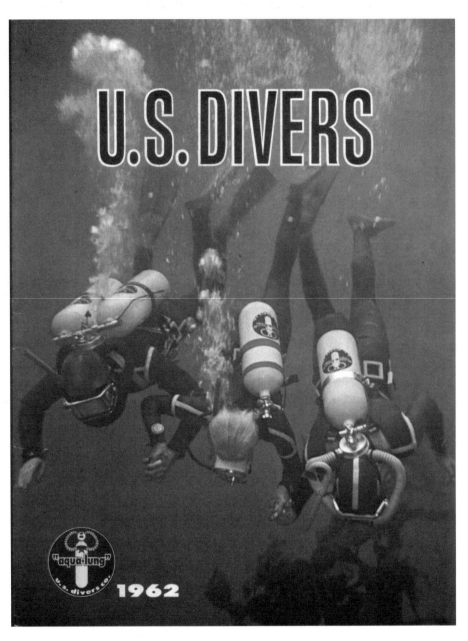

U.S. Divers 1962 catalog.

The 1970's catalogs were changing over from flotation vests to the new buoyancy compensator jackets (BCs) at high prices. The first BC by Fenzy and the next, Nemrod, sold from $120-$130. Expensive. Divers could buy a used life jacket (a Mae West) for $15-$20 and did. An Al Giddings Housing for advanced cameras was listed for $139.95, a Nikonos II camera for $198 and a Star Strobe Unit for $139.95. Spearguns were pushed aside with the arrival of the full-bloom of underwater photography.

COUSTEAU REVIVAL

In the 1980's, Cousteau's films were back on television, along with specials by other underwater cinematographers. U.S. Divers shamelessly overlaid their graphics with Cousteau's hawk-nosed distinctive face. Cousteau-appeal surged again as the exploration excitement gave way to saving *his* ocean. He had become a fanatical environmentalist and U.S. Divers followed along in support. The Cousteau Society, formed in 1974, was a strong link with the public, and U.S. Divers benefited.

DIVE TRAVEL STIMULATES SALES

Dive travel had arrived in a big way in the 1980's, and dive resorts became a significant market for dive equipment. You didn't go to an upscale resort with shoddy equipment. You went with top-of-the-line and a vast array of new accessories, not the least of which was the new dive computer, which was rapidly becoming a necessity and at a major cost equal to the new regulators that were selling for $200-$250.

New companies were again coming into prominence in diving with new looks in equipment, and they captured segments of the market. There were Oceanic USA and Sherwood. Sherwood was the company that made most all of the different manufacturers' regulators at one point including U.S. Divers. The company decided to make its own regulator and go directly to the market place. They did, and by year 2000 a great number of divers were praising the Sherwood regulator as the best of the modern pack.

By the 1990's, world trade was the thrust of the dive equipment industry. Huge markets arose in Asia, particularly in Japan, as more countries had populations with discretionary money and a hunger for the exotic recreation pursuits of America. Training agencies went international full-bore, and divers were traveling to far off isolated places, like Borneo, to dive off luxury liveaboard vessels.

NAME CHANGE

U.S. Divers became the *Aqua Lung Company* in 1999, with a full awareness that a lot of people still interchanged Aqua Lung with scuba, much as Kleenex; a brand name sat side-by-side with "generic" facial tissues. Aqua Lung would void the USA identification, as America itself lost favorable images of itself around a strife-ridden world. By year 2000, the world in many places and America in particular, had experienced a decade of a booming economy unlike any seen before. Two-job households with money to burn were ready to buy top-of-the-line exotic merchandise and travel experiences. They flashed their plastic credit cards and bought the big ticket items. U.S. Divers couldn't coast in this past decade. The pie was being split in too many ways. U.S. Divers' segment of the market had gone from 100% to 80% in the 1960's to 45% in the 1970' and 1980's having to share a lesser portion of the percentage-pie of marketing in the year 2000.

When Cronin finally retired in and Cousteau died in 1997, U.S. Divers (now Aqua Lung) had lost a great measure of its powerful direction and image. The playing field had become level as other equipment manufacturers put it, and this dominant company over the decades would have to play by new rules.

The U.S. Divers story is as much the story of sport diving in America as anything that happened. It was a mutual influencing. One company no longer with its original exclusive power, carried the responsibility like a father figure in explaining this new sport to Americans, primarily through the equipment it produced and the surrounding aspects of promotion and marketing.

In the year 2000, there is still a concern for safety and liability, and what is happening to the environment, for allowing these things to get out of hand can destroy the recreation culture of sport diving. But the concern after a decade of the 1990's of catering to an economic elite market now must contend with getting new people into diving - blowing bubbles underwater, as the old timer's tended to say disdainfully. More people are needed to keep all these equipment companies solvent. Easier entry procedures into the sport are still necessary but also to keep it safe, and not put undue stress and impact on diving places. Most divers think the year 2000 rebirth of the rebreather, the modern rebreather, with its computerized gas capacity to go deeper and much longer, will be intriguing, but the excessive expense and intense maintenance responsibilities will relegate it to special use by the commercial, the scientific and of course, the wealthy.

U.S. Divers, now the Aqua Lung Company, may have abdicated its golden years as major player in the direction of sport diving in America, but it's lasting impact is undeniable.

6
NAUI
NATIONAL ASSOCIATION OF
UNDERWATER INSTRUCTORS

DEFINING EVENT: 1960 NAUI HOUSTON INSTRUCTOR COURSE

The NAUI Bailout was first used in Houston in 1960 at the first Instructor Certification Course. The students above are seen jumping into the shamrock shaped pool at the Shamrock Hotel in Houston.   Al Tillman Collection

The single most influential event in the history of sport diving could well be the birth of the National Association of Underwater Instructors. The organization of NAUI is a multi-faceted process. But the high-profile moment in time would have to be the first instructor certification course that took place at the Shamrock Hotel in Houston, Texas in August of 1960.

Why? Even the writers of this history *Scuba America* experienced contention about this between them and certainly a majority of the one-hundred founders of sport diving, who have been interviewed would argue for a different ruling event. But Al Tillman said, "Of course I'm biased to the depths of my soul on this, but that Houston NAUI Course was when America became united in its goals for diver education. Divers needed a lighthouse of things to believe in to feel there were standards and could be safe following them. Some of the best instructors, divers and experts came together and showed the support for that idea. The course simply forged an authoritative foundation for a complicated sport which to that time seemed to be sprawling and unfocused."

NAUI was brewing in the innards of the Los Angeles County Program and the main architects of NAUI had been part of the Los Angeles County Program. National certification was being explored in other places as well. The Red Cross took a look at incorporating skin and scuba diving into their highly effective water safety program, but passed on it in 1958 as being too major an undertaking. The YMCA, through its central think tank developed a national program in 1958, a nice adjunct to its aquatics programs. The YMCA had an abundance of indoor pools across the country. The problem was each YMCA was stubbornly autonomous and in many cases resisted the YMCA instigated program. They chose to work with local dive shops and local instructional programs.

The YMCA also tried to get by with weekend training certification institutes to qualify instructors and perhaps failed in the beginning because their requirements fell far short of Los Angeles County's comparatively long and comprehensive course approach. Then later, the limited system of the YMCA did not measure up to the NAUI approach.

Everybody meant well but the time was ripe for a face-to-face summit course to bring together the best practicing dive instructors from across the country and forge a national standard criteria for certified instructors. Air travel, the jet, came in as a force allowing divers to leave home and try different diving venues. It meant dive instruction could no longer focus just on local conditions, but that instruction must enable a certified diver to function

The above booklet was issued by Los Angeles County to outline its proposed national certification course. Los Angeles County officials pulled the plug on the idea and Al Tillman used this program to design the NAUI organization.

effectively in a diversity of diving conditions and places. This would be enabled by confidence in a universal set of rules and skills.

On a hot August in 1960 just such a summit occurred. A fledgling organization calling itself the National Association of Underwater Instructors held a week long course in Houston, Texas, that would set the standard for professional instructor certification agencies in the decades to come.

The territorial animals of scuba had gathered at the water hole that week of August 20-26, 1960, in humid and muggy Houston, Texas, at the new state-of-the-art Shamrock Hotel. Jet travel, the Underwater Society of America Convention, and dueling instructor programs coincided to give birth to that fated certification course. Lodging was $3.50 per night and participants slept in four-man rooms. The course cost $75 and included instruction, tanks, pool, boat trip and graduation dinner. Course directors had originally predicted that 25 people would attend the historic course, but diving pioneers came from across North America to learn from the pioneers of diving instruction.

If you had been there, you would have seen the Chicago contingent lumbering across the lobby - big guys - Ralph Erickson (who later founded PADI) and Al O'Neil, looking like they'd come to wipe out a rival gang. They outwardly projected the belligerent, you'd-better-be-good attitude toward the course and its instigators that probably stirred within every one of the 72 candidates who had enrolled. This was serious - no fun lark. They had all paid their way there, as well as the $75 fee, but more important, they were risking a lot of themselves and their careers in diving by submitting themselves to measurement of their capacity to be instructors.

Dave Woodward and Eugene Winter, the group from the Northwest, had that indoor paleness that people from that part of America wore like a badge. They seemed prim and proper - pencils sharpened and neatly laid in a row, note-taking books open and at the ready, respectful front row eager beavers. They were the first ones in the classroom every day.

In contrast, the flaky guys from California flashed tans and a partying attitude. They talked easily to course mates from other parts of the country. They talked about movie stars taking up diving, sea lions and kelp and Garibaldi, big "goldfish" in the clear island waters of their coast. They were confident; after all, they had already had a top-of-the-line instructor training program.

The guys from New Orleans were smooth and laid back and silver-tongued charming. They talked about diving in the gulf like they were going to an oyster bar for polite conversation.

TOP GRADUATES

Captain Garry Howland, U.S. Air Force, was a chiseled, Lincolnesque-kind of guy who would be used as a military poster boy. Later he would emanate a kind of goofy enthusiasm that made him seem more like the captain of a space ship from another planet. But in this course, Howland would zoom to the top and set the standard for everyone who went through a NAUI Instructor Certification Course in the future. He would be the number one graduate of NAUI Houston.

A U.S. Navy dentist, Dr. Joseph Bodner, would walk off with best written test score and so the military provided a level of achievement that set the disciplined pace for the existing chaos of civilian diving instruction. See appendix I, if you want to see a copy of Part I of the written exam.

Florida's water rats were there, but they were more of the steady cracker/bubba types than the slick beach boys. They were dive shop operators like Joe Kingry, and they were privy to a lot of underwater territory, oceans, sink holes, springs, and caves, but they also had a small town shrewdness.

The Canadians - serious guys, prim and proper types who iron their underwear, showed up with serious intent. They represented a nation and they intended to be equal partners even though Canada's population would probably fit into Houston city limits.

Texas was there - guys from the enterprising Southwest Council of Clubs who already had a formulated instructor program. They were good old boys, drawling and twanging good humor throughout the course and holding their own even if they seemed to speak a foreign language.

Something special had to happen with these divergent forces as they came together - either head on collision of dissension or a tough amalgam forged from sweat, tears, and anguish. Each of these pioneers brought to this place, at this fermenting time, a real desire for a unifying power bred of synergism of knowledge and experience. There were a few confrontations and rebel yells heard, but when the pieces dropped in place at the end of the week, no one could really go away without a feeling of new power; no one would just go back home and do the same old stuff. They were America's first full-blown, nationally certified instructors, and if they were going to have to show any stinkin' badge ala *Treasure of Sierra Madre*, then it would proudly be the NAUI one. Some didn't make it, only 53 of the 72 enrolled received full or provisional certifications, but those that did, knew that they were the best of the best from across North America.

So what are some of the highlights of that Houston course? Perhaps we should step back in time and recall people and programs that gave birth to NAUI and its Houston Course.

THE ORIGIN

The original idea that Neal Hess had planned on was designing the organization as an offshoot from the YMCA program that had been founded in 1958 and implemented in 1959. Hess had suggested in a memo to Tillman on June 18, 1960, that the Board of Directors would consist of Hess, Tillman, John Jones, Jr., Bernie Empleton, Jim Young, Captain Albert Behnke, Jr., Cmdr. George F. Bond, Jack Whalen and Jim Auxier. Empleton and Young were the leaders in the YMCA program and Hess felt their association would be necessary to the success of NAUI. Tillman, Hess and Jones eventually decided that NAUI could stand on its own and use Jones' Broward County program and Tillman's L. A. County program as the foundation for building the NAUI idea. NAUI would also become the official training arm of the Underwater Society of America. Hess had been the Society's Training Director prior to NAUI's founding.

NAUI NAME

Many names for the fledgling organization were bounced back and forth in correspondence between Hess, Tillman, Auxier and Jones. Hess' original plan was for the National Diving Patrol to be the name of the organization. A group by the same name located in Boston and under the direction of Walter Feinberg refused to allow Hess to use this name for the organization. Hess then proposed the name National Association of Sport Diving Instructors. Tillman countered with using the term "Underwater Instructors" which was the term that he used when planning the national certification program for L. A. County. In a June 28, 1960 memo, Hess agreed and the name was adopted. The short form, NAUI, was perfect in an industry where the word MAUI brought visions of lush and tropical diving locations.

SKIN DIVER MAGAZINE SUPPORT

Jim Auxier and Chuck Blakeslee had a joint conscience about diving. *Skin Diver Magazine* subscribed to a clipping service which cut articles about diving out of newspapers and by 1959 many of these articles were "obituaries" about fathers and sons drowning while scuba diving. A magazine called *Skin Diver* saw that scuba had taken over diving and that it was a far more risky way to go underwater. They knew that something like NAUI had to come into being to protect the sport.

They knew about and supported local programs and had been especially supportive of the L. A. County program. But now something had to happen nationally. When asked why they supported Hess and Tillman's concept of NAUI, they said "because we felt we had strong stable people putting it together. Those guys had the courage and foresight, and there just wasn't anything else available." They didn't feel Mel Fisher's ads at that time - "Teach You To Dive In One Hour" - were any kind of answer to giving diving a future.

At the Houston course, four man teams were set up with a group leader assigned (see roster). This was an L.A. County device to pull and nurture leadership from the participating pack. It augmented the small staff and served as a liaison between those in charge and the candidates.

The First ICC - Houston, TX - August 26, 1960
Roster of Instructors and Students
* Designates Team Leaders

Students	Hometown	Team
Edward D. Ezekiel	Redwood City, CA	A*
Richard De Young	San Francisco, CA	A
Frank Liberatore	Farmingdale, NY	A
Thomas McGee	Redwood City, CA	A
Samuel Pick	Spokane, WA	B
Richard Kimball	Harlington, TX	B*
Bob Hollingsworth	Amarillo, TX	B
Richard Rogers	La Jolla, CA	B
Ray Pelle	Louisville, KY	C

NATIONAL ASSOCIATION OF UNDERWATER INSTRUCTORS

P.O. BOX 111, LYNWOOD, CALIFORNIA — c/o SKIN DIVER MAGAZINE

JAMES F. CAHILL   JIM AUXIER   NEAL HESS   GERRALD H. HOWLAND   JOHN C. JONES, JR.   AL TILLMAN

BOARD OF DIRECTORS

MR. JAMES F. CAHILL
Mr. Cahill is a former Lieutenant in the Naval Underwater Demolition Team 2 (Navy Frogman), Chairman of the Governors Committee to study Scuba and Skin Diving in Massachusetts. Member of the Massachusetts Marine Fisheries Advisory Commission and Senior Diver at the Texas Tower disaster recovery operation.

MR. JIM AUXIER
Editor, "Skin Diver Magazine"
Jim Auxier has been closely associated with divers and diving activities since 1944. Skin diving became a full time job for Jim in 1951 when he and partner Chuck Blakeslee founded Skin Diver Magazine.

MR. AL TILLMAN
Mr. Tillman is former Director, Underwater Activities, Los Angeles County Department of Parks and Recreation, Associate Professor Public Recreation at Los Angeles State College.

MR. JOHN C. JONES, JR.
Mr. Jones is Director, Underwater Training, Broward County, Florida, Red Cross. Mr. Jones pioneered the training of scuba instructors in Florida.

MR. NEAL HESS
Mr. Hess is instruction editor, "Skin Diver Magazine," and Director of Instructor Certification, Underwater Society of America.

CAPT. GERRALD H. HOWLAND
Capt. Howland, USAF, is an Air Force Instructor Training Officer at Randolph AFB, Texas. He was the leading student at the NAUI 1960 Houston course.

CO-SPONSORED BY
THE UNDERWATER SOCIETY OF AMERICA and SKIN DIVER MAGAZINE

The National Association of Underwater Instructors is a nonprofit organization whose purpose is to promote high standards of instruction, through sanctioned instructors, for non-military divers who use self-contained underwater breathing apparatus (SCUBA) and skin diving equipment. Through its objectives, NAUI ultimately hopes to open to all qualified people the science, wonders, and adventures of the underwater world.

NAUI is incorporated in the State of California and files State and Federal income tax forms and offers training and certification for instructor aspirants in North America. The governing body of NAUI, the Board of Directors, consists of a maximum of seven. These Board of Directors appoint the President, Vice President and Executive Secretary, as the executive officers of NAUI.

The Board of Directors meet once each year to determine NAUI policies and fiscal estimates. They also authorize the certification of all successful NAUI graduates. This Board certifies the training and teaching competency of NAUI instructors.

Current NAUI President is Mr. Tillman; Vice President is Mr. Jones, and Mr. Hess is Executive Secretary.

Certification as an instructor requires attending the NAUI 60-hour course in skin diving and scuba teaching, passing tests designed to demonstrate the applicant's qualifications for classroom and pool instruction and to assure that instructors possess technical knowledge of basic principals. A file will be maintained for each certified instructor at NAUI Headquarters, Lynwood, California.

The Board of Directors will select and provide instructor trainers for each official course. Courses will be offered at various locations in North America to meet the demands. Mr. Eugene Winter, Head, Dept. of Physical Education in Walla Walla College, will serve as instructor trainer for Washington, Oregon, Idaho and British Columbia. Mr. Frank Scalli, Maldon, Massachusetts for New England, Mr. Edward Ezekiel, Redwood City, California, for Northern California and Nevada, and Mr. John C. Jones, Jr., Ft. Lauderdale, Florida.

NAUI reaches its objectives by holding 60-hour instructor training, testing, and certification courses, and the production of diving literature, films, etc.

NAUI also compiles statistics on diving accidents so that hazards may be spotted before they become major causes of concern. Further, NAUI, through Dr. Andreas B. Rechnitzer, provides counseling to people who wish to make water sciences their lifetime work.

NAUI is financed by income from the training, testing and certification courses, sale of diving literature and generous grants from manufacturers of diving equipment.

CAPTAIN A. R. BEHNKE, JR.   COMMANDER GEORGE F. BOND   CAPTAIN J. Y. COUSTEAU   DR. ANDREAS B. RECHNITZER

BOARD OF ADVISORS

COMMANDER GEORGE F. BOND — Medical Corps, U. S. Navy
Commander Bond was Squadron Medical Officer, Submarine Base, Pearl Harbor 1951-1956 and Assistant Officer in Charge U.S. Naval Medical Research Laboratory, U.S. Naval Submarine Base, New London, Connecticut until last year when he was promoted to Officer in Charge of the same installation.

Commander Bond is a member of the American Medical Association and was Regional Consultant to the President's Commission on the Nation's Health for six years. Commander Bond is a Qualified Submarine Medical Officer and a Qualified Deep Sea and Scuba Diver, U.S.N.

CAPTAIN A. R. BEHNKE, JR., U.S.N. (ret.)
Captain Behnke entered the Harvard School of Public Health as a research fellow working with problems dealing with exposure to high pressure. Dr. Behnke was Instructor U.S. Naval Medical School 1937 to 1942. In 1939, he participated in the five months of rescue and salvage operation incident to the U.S.S. Squalus disaster. During World War II he carried on intensive investigations in the applied physiology of respiration under high

altitude, surface and deep sea conditions, and has been connected with the investigation work at the Naval Medical Research Institute since its foundation.

DR. ANDREAS B. RECHNITZER
Dr. Rechnitzer is the Scientist in Charge of Project NEKTON, using the most unique submersible, the bathyscaph, "Trieste." He is a biological oceanographer with his Ph.D. from UCLA. He received the Distinguished Civilian Service Award from President Eisenhower, February, 1960 and is a life member of the National Geographic Society.

CAPTAIN J. Y. COUSTEAU
Capt. Cousteau is first known as the co-inventor of the world famous "Aqua-Lung". The "Calypso" under his direction has sailed over the world doing general oceanographic investigation, making movies, doing research work and preparing material for the National Geographic Society and scientific groups. He is president of the World Underwater Federation and is author of the popular book "The Silent World".

The front page of NAUI's first newsletter showed the organizational structure that formed the foundation of NAUI's administration.

National Association Of Underwater Instructors Certified Instructors

DICK DOEHRING
Houston, Texas

DON E. BLOYE
Oregon City, Oregon

CHARLES M. CARROLL
Helena, Montana

JAMES K. CHAMBERS
Kenosha, Wisconsin

EDWARD H. BELL
San Marcos, Texas

RICHARD F. ROGERS
La Jolla, California

ROBERT H. SMITH
Austin, Texas

RAY PELLE
Louisville, Kentucky

ENGENE WINTER
College Place, Wash.

LUTHER SWIFT
Houston, Texas

DON E. BEER
Amarillo, Texas

DON J. EVANS
St. Clair, Michigan

EDWARD EZEKIEL
Redwood City, Calif.

R. J. CHAMBERLAIN
Omaha, Nebraska

DR. J. A. BODNER (DC)
USN, Bradford, Conn.

BRUCE C. BRADSHAW
Orlando, Florida

EDWIN D. TOWNSEND
Centerport, L.I., N.Y.

THOMAS H. McDONALD
Arlington, Virginia

RICHARD W. KIMBALL
Harlington, Texas

RALPH D. ERICKSON
Chicago, Illinois

BOB STAUNTON
Seattle, Washington

CHUCK GRISWOLD
Seattle, Washington

DAVID C. WOODWARD
Spokane, Washington

JOHN S. MILNE
Vancouver, B.C.

SAMUEL R. PICK
Spokane, Washington

THOMAS McGEE
Redwood City, Calif.

D. R. TUSSEY
Dayton, Ohio

ALBERT M. O'NEIL
Chicago, Illinois

WILLIAM GEBHART
Kent, Ohio

DONNIE B. WEEKS
Lubbock, Texas

JOSEPH R. DORSEY
Baltimore, Maryland

JERRY DZINDZELETA
Racine, Wisconsin

BOB HOLLINGSWORTH
Amarillo, Texas

R. W. LONG
San Jose, California

HARRY VETTER
Long Beach, Calif.

JAMES DREW
W. Palm Beach, Fla.

HERBERT INGRAHAM
Ancaster, Ontario

A. R. MISER
San Jose, Calif.

JACK RUDDER
Lake Jackson, Texas

RALPH POPLAR
Kansas City, Kansas

JAMES CANADY
Austin, Texas

RICHARD BROWN
Evergreen Park, Ill.

RUSSELL JACOBS
Brookfield, Wisc.

JOE KINGRY
Pensacola, Fla.

JAMES BLACKMORE
Massena, New York

JACK HOWARD
Richmond, Mich.

EUGENE McDONALD
Pensacola, Fla.

DAVE LASKY
Kingsville, Ont.

TED ECKHARDT
Hulmeville, Pa.

ERWIN HUTCHINS
Massena, New York

(No Pictures) — ARTHUR E. CREASE - Fort Lauderdale, Fla.   WM. R. HYATT, JR. - Orlando AFB, Fla.

The back page of NAUI's first newsletter showed the graduates of the first ICC.

David Laskey	Ontario, Canada	C
William Gebhart	Kent, OH	C
Ralph Poplar	Kansas City, MO	C*
David Woodward	Spokane, WA	D
Richard Case	Tucson, AZ	D
Garrald Howland	Biloxi, MS	D*
Don Santesson	Puerto Rico	D
Richard Brown	Oak Lawn, IL	E
Albert O'Neil	Chicago, IL	E
D. R. Tussey	Dayton, OH	E
Ralph Erickson	Chicago, IL	E*
Chuck Griswold	Seattle, WA	F
A. R. Miser	San Jose, CA	F
Jerry Dzindzeleta	Racine, WI	F*
Arthur Cresse	Ft. Lauderdale, FL	F
Crew Schmitt	Phoenix, AZ	G
Don Evans	St. Clair, MI	G
Luther Swift, III	Houston, TX	G*
Edward Bell	San Marcos, TX	H
Richard Long	San Jose, CA	H
Jerry Stugen	San Jose, CA	H*
Donald Bloye	New York, NY	H
James Drew, Jr.	West Palm Beach, FL	I*
Donnie Weeks	Lubbock, TX	I
Eugene Winter	College Place, WA	I
Charles McAughan	Sun Valley, CA	I
Ted Eckhard	Hulmeville, PA	J*
Charles Grogan	Levittown, PA	J
James Blackmore	Massena, NY	J
Erwin Hutchins	Massena, NY	J
Robert Smith	Austin, TX	K*
Charles Carroll	Helena, MT	K
Eugene McDonald	Pensacola, FL	K
Dr. Joseph Bodner	Bradford, CT	L
Robert Michaelis	Sioux City, IA	L
Russell Jacobs	Brookfield, MD	L*
Joseph Dorsey	Baltimore, MD	L
Richard Chamberland	Omaha, NE	M
Bruce Bradshaw	Orlando, FL	M*
Richard White	Orlando, FL	M
Joe Kingry	Pensacola, FL	M
Edwin Townsend	Long Island, NY	N*
Clinton Christianson	Minneapolis, MN	N
James Chambers	Kenosha, WI	N
William Hyatt	Orlando, FL	N

Jack Howard	Richmond, MI	O*
Thomas McDonald	Arlington, VA	O
Jack Rudder	Lake Jackson, TX	O
James Canady	Austin, TX	O
David Van Buskirk	Freeport, TX	P
Lewis Williams	Valparaiso, FL	P*
Herbert Ingraham	Ancaster, Ontario, Canada	P
Bob Staunton, Jr.	Seattle, WA	P
John Milne	Vancouver, B.C., Canada	Q*
Don Beer	Amarillo, TX	Q
Richard Doehring	Houston, TX	Q
John McGuire	Galena Park, TX	Q

INSTRUCTORS	**SUBJECTS TAUGHT**
Neal Hess	Introduction, Search Patterns, Pool Work
Prof. Albert Tillman	Teaching Techniques, Ocean Tests, Written Test
John Jones, Jr.	Life Saving, CPR
Capt. A. R. Behnke, Jr.	Medical Aspects
Hal Lattimore	Legal Aspects
Cmdr. George Bond'	Physics
Dr. Andreas Rechnitzer	Marine Biology, Oceanography, Graduation Speech
Harry Vetter	Equipment

One of the assigned leaders was Ralph Erickson, a really big Swede who looked as if he should have the nick name of King Kong and represent the pro-wrestlers union. Ralph approached, as if he were going to mug you, but it was a facade over a nice, bright, serious persona. On the second day of the course, however, Ralph bulked up at the lunch table to complain to Neal Hess that there was too much time pressure to meet all the assignments the course seemed to require. He was representing his team's Chicago divers, including Al O'Neil, a big Irishman who personified clout and who was an instigator of turmoil through others. Erickson had courage and he could be soft spoken but with a cutting edge. He'd just picked the wrong time and place to have his say. Tillman, at that point, decided that the course was for real and he wouldn't be satisfied with a diva role, nor be a figurehead. He figuratively stepped in front of Hess and took the bullet. "Wrong time, wrong place to discuss this," Tillman told Erickson, drawing a line in the dirt. The guys who were running this course were not going to be intimidated. They had a track record in diving to stand on. There was a physical air to this encounter and course candidates at surrounding tables were watching with great attention. Perhaps it was a test, but it did allow course admin-

The candidates in the first ICC were broken into teams. The teams are seen above in the Shamrock pool practicing scuba skills.   *Al Tillman Collection*

istrators a chance to publicly assert their full intention to run the course as they saw it and the inmates would not be allowed to take over the asylum.

There was the pressure of time for everyone. The staff found little time to sleep and the candidates were really hard-pressed to get their assignments ready on time, especially the oral presentations. Many couldn't sleep, even if they found a moment to try. It was just too exciting being part of a pioneer effort and hunkering down with many of the best divers in America.

Al Tillman is seen above evaluating the final written exams at the first NAUI instructor certification course.   Al Tillman Collection

Those who came under prepared and hadn't done their reading really had to scramble. They sought out the gurus, the guys who had a lot of knowledge and experience, and drained information out of them. Ray Tussey was a good example: ex-UDT, handsome, smart, an athlete, a role model and willing to help others less endowed. Candidates wolfed down notes wherever they could. A candid photo of very proper Herb Ingraham from Toronto - the kind of Canadian-English-type you would expect to say, "toodle-oo" when he leaves - caught him enthroned on the toilet pouring over notes. Many did the same; boning up while brushing teeth was routine. It paid off for Herb, who became NAUI #37.

It wasn't just the candidates who were scared about meeting the challenge. The staff wasn't all that sure of themselves, either. After all, who had ordained them to create the universe? Al Tillman had the whole L.A. County system, as his creation to lean on, but he knew he had to do more than shuffle papers and talk fast. "Yeah, but what can he do in the water?", was surely the thinking.

Tillman chose the newly introduced mouth-to-mouth resuscitation on a diver's float which in those days was an auto inner tube. He had devised the method with the new artificial respiration technique for divers to use for towing a victim back to boat or shore. It was showcased as a main event at the Race for Life contest at the Big L.A. Sportsman Show. Two women were lined up from local university swim teams and diving instructors raced against the clock in making the rescue, replete with drum rolls, spot lights and an excited announcer. Two shows a day for the 10-day run of the show got the skill perfected for use in classes.

Tillman was sweating some in the Texas heat as he slid into the outdoor pool which was shaped like a shamrock. But he didn't count on the Irish symbol of luck to get him through. He'd practiced this tube rescue over and over again before coming to Houston. Every possible thing that could go wrong was rehearsed into the practice. As a college professor, he knew you'd better be ready to get shot down if you weren't way ahead of the students and hadn't had a lot of hands-on exposure to a skill you were going to teach. The future NAUI instructors hadn't seen this one before and it's very newness caught their fancy. They would go back home with a brand new skill to teach. It was the case of a skill that really worked and which a learner could experience immediate success. Tillman knew from experience that he'd picked well and that the candidates had something to look at besides a guy in a suit acting like he was in charge.

Andy Rechnitzer was good. He was NAUI's official scientist-oceanographer as well as a talented guest lecturer. He had played the same role with the L.A. County program in the 1950's. Oceanography, everything one ought to know about water conditions, bottom geology, and marine creatures had become a cornerstone of diver training and no one anchored it in better than Rechnitzer. He had command of the podium and looked lean and chiseled and ready to physically dive into any situation.

Andy was no textbook diving scientist. His ears were wet all the time. He not only made the final course boat dive off the Flower Gardens in the Gulf but brought back some unusual coral whips to take back to his home base, Scripps Institution of Oceanography. So how do you get a bunch of three-foot gamey specimens home from Houston? You put them in your lap in a jet airplane and hope to charm the stewardesses. That jet probably still smells like the bottom side of a pier at low tide.

John Jones, Jr. was the kind of a Southern good 'ole boy you'd expect to meet at a small country store off a Tennessee highway. He was a smart and efficient organizer. He could put stuff on paper and have it make sense. He produced NAUI's official course outlines and that was only one of his main contributions at NAUI Houston.

John could drawl with the best of the Southern U.S. down home guys and he did a lot to pacify some of the restless and outspoken attempts to verbally have a shoot-out at the O.K. Corral with lecturers and staff. John wouldn't like to be called a father figure at the Houston course, but he was the best at talking away dissension among the troops. It also helped that he wasn't another hot shot Californian but pure south and out of Broward County, Florida...a long way from L.A. County.

THE BAILOUT

The bailout was the final testing exercise. The ultimate challenge at that point in time. It was still new enough that some of the candidates had not done it before. It represented just how at ease with equipment underwater a person could be. So at the Shamrock pool on Thursday afternoon, no one had practiced the routine to a point where it was just too easy for them. Eventually, the bailout version in open water replaced it.

The usual panic ensued and the old experienced diving instructors were busy explaining, encouraging and tutoring their roommates in the techniques of the test. More than any of the material used at that course, the bailout test got the most questioning. "Well, hell, that ain't any skill you use underwater. What fool would get himself in such a predicament?" paraphrases all the grumbling. Painstakingly, over and over, the staff patiently defended the bailout. Funny how those who criticized, but got through it with high marks, stopped being critics.

George Bond was a bear of a man not entirely comfortable in the full dress uniform of a U.S. Navy Commander. A gruff macho giant, he had been a country doctor before developing much of the Navy's submarine escape technology.

George Bond was a commanding figure who could impress both the candidates and the staff.

Al Tillman Collection

His storytelling in a deep, common-man articulation impressed the candidate instructors. Here was a real-life, American hero-type who physically did his own experiments. He was an example of a perfect figurehead expert which lent NAUI its aura of authority. He probably more than any other - even more than Cousteau, was a major foundation block on which NAUI was to build.

Albert Behnke, Jr. was a legend in 1960 - a kindly, rugged, soft spoken, godfather figure of diving medicine. He had to oversee the medical aspects of the U.S. Squalus Submarine rescue in 1937 and was the authentic backbone of much of U.S. Navy developed knowledge about underwater warfare and survival. He was also a key member of the team that founded the Naval Medical Research Center in Bethesda, Maryland. He, along with Bond, were bigger than life figures and the Navy diving activities were the birthing arena of what would transfer to civilian life and become a major American outdoor sport. The two of them provided the tone of authority and credibility for that Houston Course. Medical aspects were the scary and intellectually mystifying core of why diving needed well-trained instructors.

Hal Lattimore was a brash, diving, Texas lawyer, who was signed up to take about legal liability in diving to the instructor candidates. It was an excellent hip pocket course all by itself and worth the price of admission. Lattimore was confident and the perfect storyteller. His classic cases of people being sued are remembered to this day by graduates of NAUI Houston. One case was of a man causing a bear to roll garbage cans into a campsite which resulted in a miscarriage in a pregnant woman. Terms like "proximate cause" roll off the tongues of that course's graduates (with some referral to notes). The legal side of instructing is one of the areas that didn't get the coverage in the years to follow at NAUI courses and certainly would not be done as well as those two hours in 1960.

SOME CRITICISM

Not all the memories of NAUI Houston were positive. Donnie Weeks, still a NAUI instructor in Texas, thinks ordinary divers today exceed the 1960 candidates at Houston. "A lot of those guys just weren't prepared, hadn't done much diving or read anything." Donnie, an infantile paralysis poster boy in his youth, may have been the first physically challenged, handicapped person any of those divers in 1960 had ever seen. Donnie probably has a right to downgrade the quality of those pioneer NAUI instructors based on his own preparedness and conscientious effort during the course, and graduation as NAUI #17.

One of diving instructions most controversial issues was whether students should be harassed to determine their resourcefulness and instant reactions to emergency situations. Things like flooding masks and turning off tank air were the ways some instructors set up their boot camp-mentality reputations as tough operators. Some instructors encouraged "horseplay" - students doing dirty tricks to each other such as pulling a weight belt release, and many students hate those instructors for taking up formal course time with it. But those same students were also grateful for that class harassment later on in unexpected situations during which they were able to cope.

At NAUI Houston, there seemed to be an equal split of opinions on this matter. NAUI took a stand by not incorporating this loose emergency training into the Houston curriculum. What everyone has always agreed about is that it is more fun being harasser than harassee.

Al Tillman on NAUI Houston:

"We were really proud of the L.A. County program by 1960 and I was ready for a new challenge. My regard for Jim Auxier and Chuck Blakeslee and their Skin Diver Magazine made it easy for me to go along with the idea of the national training program that they were supporting. Neal Hess hustled together the logistics for the NAUI Houston course and brought me and John Jones, Jr. together. Credit Hess for the smarts to put New England, Florida and Southern California representatives in charge. Those regions were diving population hot spots.

The course itself was pretty old hat for me after the L. A. County UICC's, but I was impressed with the big names on the guest staff, the diversity of personalities and regional differences among the candidates, and the feeling that we were taking a very serious step in establishing how diving would be taught in the future. What bothered me, coming from a public service background, was the lurking commercial interests that were moving into instruction."

Bill High on NAUI Houston:

"I was the Underwater Society of America Director of Conservation and enrolled in the NAUI Houston course. I went to the course for three days but the government called me back home on a job emergency. I felt the newness, the excitement, that this was a major breakthrough in diving."

Garry Howland on NAUI Houston:

"Some 70 students arrived in time for the beginning of the week-long program. I arrived in Houston Tuesday night, while most of the candidates came in Friday. They were assigned to teams, given room assignments and a schedule for the program. We had been asked to bring our library to have available for study just as if there was going to be any spare time to read.

There was plenty of water work in the large hotel pool, with attendees role playing as individual divers, as diving students and as an instructors - heavy on the instructor part. The highlight of the diver portion was the famous NAUI bailout off the pool diving board into the deep end. As was the practice, you were to take all your dive equipment in your arms and leap into the water. That was to include your weight belt, if you wore one. In those days, as now, I seldom wear a weight belt, so I went in without one. Those who wore 10 and 20-pound weight belts cried foul because you had to tread water for 15 minutes after the bailout and recovery. They were dying, trying to stay on the surface without vests. So at the end of the exercise they insisted that I do the bailout over again to show I could do it with a weight belt. Piece of cake! I had been diving for a long time before coming to Houston and had graduated from the U.S. Navy Underwater Swimmers School, awarded Diving Supervisor rating with a Gold Graduate Certificate (Honor Graduate). I was the Training Director for the State of Mississippi Council of Skin and Scuba Diving Clubs. On the Mississippi coast, I had helped start five dive clubs in as many cities and helped to keep them going before going to Houston. I worked with Walter Feinberg of the Boston Sea Rovers in writing an instructor's manual and I had written the regulations for the Air Force regarding the use of recreational scuba equipment. All this meant Houston became a real fun week.

It was a long week, with long hours, deep into the night - sometimes past midnight. everyone worked very hard to succeed. A common purpose, team work, hard work and excellent leadership made the program successful - to form the core for what NAUI has become. NAUI came into existence on the basis of old-fashioned principles intended to have ladies and gentlemen serving ladies and gentlemen. We were guided by men of education from Boston, New Haven, Los Angeles, Biloxi and Fort Lauderdale, who made up a good cross-section of diving in America. Subsequently, being advised by divers from around the world rounded out a great organization.

The highlight of the week for me was all the people that I met and the friendships I made that have lasted a lifetime - and being selected for the Board of Directors. The NAUI Founding Board of Directors was Joe Bodner #9, Neal Hess, John Jones #2, Al Tillman #1 and myself."

John C. Jones, Jr. on NAUI Houston from an interview in the early 1970's:

"Our program in Broward County ran parallel to the L.A. County program during the 1950's and there was a lot of reciprocal correspondence between Al Tillman and myself. At Houston, it was very good to meet and work with Al and put our two programs together to create the new NAUI concept. We debated a lot of things but we were always friends."

NAUI Houston did adopt the YMCA physical fitness test which included chin ups, push-ups, and mile runs as part of instructor qualifying requirements. L.A. County never used it, but relied on swim and watermanship tests. There was a lot of grumbling about it being irrelevant, especially from guys who just weren't in shape to do it. It was a controversial issue, but those who got though it became big supporters.

Jerry Dzindzeleta, NAUI #5, in a letter looking back on the Houston course, wrote, "I think the greatest satisfaction was to have known, and in following years to have worked with, the men who conceived, labored and succeeded in bringing into reality the first nationwide organization devoted solely to training of skin and scuba diving.

Those men whose skill and organizational knowledge made NAUI happen were Mr. Neal Hess and Mr. Al Tillman." The fresh water instruction outline that would become the standard for NAUI was created by Jerry Dzindzeleta.

During the year to follow Houston (NAUI was basically on hold until the courses in Chicago, Toronto and Ft. Lauderdale), Neal Hess was wooing the manufacturers and trying to position NAUI as the training arm of the Underwater Society of America against formidable opposition.

Fred Calhoun, from the Northeast, in an abrupt, nononsense manner, was ruffling feathers in the Underwater Society of America. Calhoun's outlines for instruction were comprehensive and effective but probably ahead of their time. The Society was trying to bring together diving councils of clubs run by local politician types who were more into promoting the interest of home constituency than creating a meaningful directive force to unify all diving interest. Fierce pride in the superiority of the regional instruction programs springing up overnight kept the Society from moving strongly into instruction coordination.

Probably the importance of this chaos is that it allowed NAUI to move ahead, not bog down with politics. One problem that never quite got resolved in the early days was whether NAUI would be the ultimate high standard of certification or establish a minimum standard to be met for all instruction. Local programs in the YMCA and L.A. County went ahead with what they had. In some cases the instruction quantity and quality exceeded what NAUI required. The NAUI founders never intended to eliminate the high-level local programs and, in fact, encouraged the elite programs to reach beyond the minimum.

Candidates at the 1960 ICC studied where and when they could.   *Al Tillman Collection*

NAUI, as an ego thing with its leaders, found itself motivated beyond the minimum caretaker role and leaned toward being the best program in instructor certification. Some confusion always seemed to exist, ...do numbers, getting bigger mean "best"? This would be an important influence on NAUI's growth and development from this point.

WHAT HAPPENED AFTER HOUSTON 1960

NAUI, in its first year following the Houston course, faced an inevitable leadership crises. Al Tillman and John C. Jones, career professionals with Los Angeles County Parks and Recreation and the American Red Cross, respectively, were strongly behind the idea that instruction in diving should maintain a public service and nonprofit orientation. The original incorporation papers (signed by Tillman and Hess, as president and secretary,) that were filed with the State of California to form NAUI defined the organization's mission along those lines.

The articles of incorporation for NAUI stated that the organization was nonprofit and that "the primary purpose of this corporation is to promote and encourage through purposeful activity the education and training of the general public in the safety and techniques of participating in underwater activities.

Neal Hess, on the other hand, graduate of the Harvard Business School, saw NAUI as a business venture and solicited backing from diving equipment manufacturers. The first post-Houston Board of Directors consisted of Tillman, Hess, Jones, Auxier, James Cahill and Garry Howland. A separate Board of Advisors was also formed to involve experts in NAUI operations and add name credibility to the Association. The first members of the Board of Advisors were Capt. A. R. Behnke, Jr., Cmdr. George Bond, Capt. Jacques-Yves Cousteau and Dr. Andreas Rechnitzer.

The issue from the very start was whether instruction was a moral obligation to be assumed or another commercial product from which to derive profit. It is perhaps so in all sports, but risk activities place an added responsibility on those who promote it and derive financial reward from it.

There was no wrong or right on this issue. There was the opportunity to fuse both concepts and that was what finally came to pass. But in these frontier years, the early 1960's, there were-narrow minded, territorial power struggles going on and the field sought control by strong advocacy of one side or the other of the instruction issue.

Skin Diver Magazine was caught in converging tides, pressured from all sides, manufacturers, dive shops, the clubs and independent instructors. Auxier and Blakeslee had to look at both advertising revenues and subscriptions to survive; but they didn't roll over. Instead, they shifted even more support to NAUI as 1961 passed. *The Instructors Corner* was published for a final time in January of 1961 and the *NAUI Page* took over.

Neal Hess welcomes Jacques Cousteau to the NAUI Board of Advisors in Houston, 1960.

Al Tillman Collection

Hess had consigned the next NAUI course to Ralph Poplar in Kansas City, Missouri. Poplar had been the apparent active instructor there and had gone through the 1960 Houston Course with good results. Somehow the rapport between Poplar and Hess took a wrong turn and Poplar began a letter writing campaign criticizing Hess for failing to provide adequate guidance for running the course and pursuing his (Hess') personal monetary gains. Hess claimed Poplar just hadn't done the job and with only light sign-ups, the course was simply canceled. Garry Howland, who was to be the key assistant to Poplar on the course said that Poplar never communicated with him and he had no idea what was going on.

Due to the pressure exerted by Poplar, Jim Auxier had Hess release NAUI's financial records for 1960 and many questions arose. Course fees for the Houston course raised $4,950 for NAUI and Hess had raised $1,800 from manufacturers, $800 of which was supposedly refunded. Out of these funds Hess had paid himself $900 as a salary and covered all of his own expenses. All of the other instructors combined, including Jones and Tillman, received a total of $1,744.95, which included all expenses, including those of Hess.

Hess recovered from this sufficiently and set up three courses for the summer of 1961, one in Toronto, one in Chicago, and one in Ft. Lauderdale. The Toronto course would be Canadian controlled primarily by Ben Davis, who was a powerful force in the Underwater Society of America and considered by many to be the patriarch of diving in Canada. His involvement would help insure that NAUI would be recognized as the official training arm of the Society and get an early foothold in the Canadian diving scene.

The Toronto course, with 27 students, was held at the University of Toronto and was the first course for diving instruction held in Canada. The legal sponsor of the Toronto course was The Underwater Club of Canada (NAUI was only incorporated in the United States at this point). The Ontario Underwater Council and the Etobicoke Underwater Club also joined in as unofficial sponsors. Ben Davis was awarded NAUI #101 (numbers 1-100 were reserved for U.S. instructors). In a 1995 article, Larry Burden, Jr., NAUI #5251 (his father was in the Toronto course and was NAUI #127), discussed that first Canadian course with Ben Davis. Davis recalled, "most of the participants were pretty strong swimmers and we threw some things at them then that we sure wouldn't today. The participants had to tread water for 15 minutes with their weights on and they had to show us that they could breathe off of tanks without a double hose regulator, that is with no regulator at all, since single-hose units were not yet available."

The Toronto course also had its own Board of Directors. Members of this Board were Bruce Babcock, George Burt, Ben Davis, Ed Day, Herb Ingraham, Ken Lynn and Bob Smith. This group of divers represented the management of the sponsoring Canadian organizations and gave authority to NAUI in the local diving communities. Teachers at the course included Dr. Ed Lanphier, Neal Hess, Jerry Dzindzeleta, Ray Tussey, Al O'Neil, Cressy McCatty, Prof. Roger Dean, David Anderson and Ben Davis. Only 22 of the 38 candidates were certified as NAUI instructors and eight received provisional certifications.

Ralph Erickson was the force to reckon with in Chicago and had done well as a graduate of the Houston course; he would be the local director in charge with Hess and Tillman as standby consultants and administrative staff. John Jones, Jr. would head up the hometown Ft. Lauderdale course and bring the big diving population center of Florida face to face with the emerging NAUI.

Hess was setting the scene for the NAUI invasion of New England, which already had a strong instruction program history through the YMCA and the Boston Sea Rovers. Hess went for Jim Cahill, probably the strongest commercial force on the East Coast and a lovable, likable man. Cahill accepted a position on the NAUI Board of Directors. Ben Davis would also go on the Board which at this point in February 1961, was made up of Tillman, Hess, Jones, Howland, Bodner, Cahill and Davis. But no Board of Directors meeting was held at this time and none would take place until 1962.

The manufacturers finally did come up with some support, but no records exist to show that anything more than scuba equipment was supplied for the staff. Hess kept a tight, close cover on all these negotiations.

The Chicago course was running concurrently with the Toronto course. Hess moved between the two with Tillman serving as the chief overseer in Chicago during the August 6-12 course. The course was held at the Glenview Naval Air Station and most of the 30 candidates felt the facilities were adequate if somewhat Spartan. One of the highlights was the legendary, physical educator, Thomas Cureton, barrel chest and all. He stepped into the pool with only a bathing suit, nonchalantly controlling his buoyancy, and walked the length of the pool underwater, which left everyone there in awe. This was freshwater country, Lake Michigan, and there was new information such as learning what a seiche (waves created by winds across a lake) is, and limnology, the fresh water counterpart of oceanography.

Registration day was Sunday, August 6th and the candidates arrived at Barracks 26 of Glenview. Candidates and teachers alike shared the same quarters with the exception of NAUI's first female candidate, Nancy Gill, who stayed in the Naval Wave housing. The course was officially opened at 8 A.M. with a speech by Hess. The Chicago course trainers included: Hess (physics of diving), Tillman (teaching techniques), Dr. Walter Kirker (medicine), Hal Lattimore (legal aspects), Donald McNaught (sea life), Ralph Erickson and Jerry Dzindzeleta (pool work), Al O'Neil (equipment) and fitness expert and diving author Bill Barada. The week's course work lasted from 8 A.M. to 9:30 P.M. with three hours of breaks during that time.

The first female NAUI instructor, Nancy Gill (NAUI #92) graduated with the class. Twenty-four of the thirty candidates were certified as NAUI instructors. The open water check-out was in George Toberman's Racine Aqualand Quarry, 60 miles north of Chicago. Local, Jerry Dzindzeleta, who served on the staff, a Hess favorite from the days of mailing in course outlines to the *Instructor's Corner*, did a superb job.

One of the great stories is about graduate Hal Edick from the little logging town of Brookings, Oregon. Hal got more than his certificate as an instructor. He learned how to survive, barely, in a big city and he with Nancy Gill were an affectionate twosome as a result of meeting during the course.

Hal Edick had never seen a big city before and going to the NAUI course took a bit of courage. Hal got to Chicago a few days early. He went down to swim in Lake Michigan and lost some clothes. When he went into a bar to get a drink and break a $40 bill, the guy next to him grabbed the change and ran out the door. Looking for the suspect, Hal looked down an alley to see a man shooting at someone, then turn and point the gun at Hal...who ran, of course, almost all the way back to his room at the YMCA. But on his way he met his first transvestites at Washington Park. After this adventure, the NAUI course itself was a cake walk.

Hess and Tillman joined Garry Howland, Joe Bodner and John Jones, Jr. at the Ft. Lauderdale course the next week. An out-of-season luxury hotel, the Galt Ocean Mile Hotel, was the site. Ft. Lauderdale was magnificent in 1961, quiet and relaxing, a lush tropical paradise, quite a contrast to the sparse diving landscape of Chicago. Rooms were $3.50 per night with a four person occupancy. Among the 39 candidates who enrolled, two were women.

Hess had made an error in trying to keep control by a kind of secret negotiations approach. He hadn't bothered to consult Tillman or Jones on what was really going on. They were the point of authority that was the foundation of NAUI in those years of infancy and Hess was fueling NAUI's growth and development with the divers' respect for the programs that those two gentlemen had founded. In *Skin Diver Magazine's NAUI Page*, Hess would even write, "There is no question in my mind but that he (Tillman) is the cornerstone to safe diving in the United States via his work with Los Angeles County, the YMCA and NAUI." Hess didn't arrive from Toronto until the end of the course and meanwhile Tillman and Jones, along with Howland and Bodner, had a lot of time to discuss things. Notes were compared on Hess and a lot of questions arose on just what Hess was trying to personally build for himself with NAUI. Hess walked into some heavy dissension. He gave out equipment donated by manufacturers to try and woo the four Board members into his camp. It almost worked.

A late 1961 course was added to be held in Seattle, WA. The Seattle NAUI ICC was held in cooperation with the Washington Council of Skin Diving Clubs, Inc. and was held September 10 through 16, 1961. Graduates received certifications by both agencies. Housing was made available at the University of Washington for $2.50 per day and tuition still remained $75.00. Eugene Winters was the head instructor trainer with help from Bob Sheats, Dr. Shaw from the U.S. Navy, Dr. Fleming from the Oceanography Department at the University of Washington and Bill High. Al Tillman, assisted by Dave Woodward and Eugene Winters taught teaching practices and techniques and represented NAUI Headquarters.

Bill High recalls the 1961 Seattle Course:

"I was the only person to ever be the course director and an instructor candidate at the same time. I graduated number one from the course. Captain Dusty Rhodes (NAUI #176) was in the course and is still in Thailand running NAUI classes. Dr. Behnke was on the staff. Chuck Petersen, one of the great underwater photographers and Mac Thompson, who designed the Pisces Deep Submersible were enrolled. We did a 30 foot bailout off Alki Point."

Following the 1961 series of courses, Hess and Tillman, who both lived in Los Angeles were more or less the powering force at this point. On the drawing board were two courses, one in Gloucester, Massachusetts, and one in Los Angeles, California, a direct assault on the two major strongholds of sophisticated diving instructor programs.

At this point NAUI decided to break its affiliation with the Underwater Society of America. Tillman and Howland had stopped in New Orleans on the way to Los Angeles. Tillman recalls that he attended a Society meeting and formally announced that NAUI was breaking away from its role as the "official" training arm of the Society but that the Association would still work with them on an unofficial basis.

There are different versions on the relationship between NAUI and the Underwater Society of America. It should be pointed out that the Society was also born at Houston also in 1960 with its first full-fledged convention. Struggling to bring together a variety of personalities and geographical concepts, it was easier for them to recognize NAUI as its training arm, but NAUI would operate autonomously. Howland recalls that he was appointed Director of Training for the Society for three years and operated out of Biloxi, Mississippi. High recalls that NAUI did become the "official" training arm of the Society but that there wasn't any hands on connection. Other sources involved in both organizations report that the Society saw NAUI as better organized than they were at that point in time and felt it better to use their energy for other aspects of diving while supporting the NAUI operation. The whole relationship has been misunderstood for decades. As late as 1978, according to articles in NAUI News, some NAUI members and leadership were under the misconception that NAUI was still the "official training arm" of the Society.

Hess and Tillman were now dueling over what exactly the NAUI mission was and how much of the previous criticism of Hess' efforts to personally deal with the manufacturers perhaps needed to be questioned. The debate went before *Skin Diver Magazine*'s Jim Auxier, who still held the power to promote and keep NAUI alive. Somebody had to go and *Skin Diver Magazine* went along with Al Tillman's version of what NAUI should be.

Hess had done most of the hustling to put the NAUI courses together up until this point, but many questionable practices and allowances were uncovered. In a formal letter to Al Tillman dated October 20, 1961, Hess resigned all affiliations with NAUI citing "business pressures". *Skin Diver Magazine* set up a NAUI office at its headquarters and put Al Tillman on the payroll as NAUI's Executive Director and President, *Skin Diver Magazine*'s Director of Public Affairs and as the Executive Director of the International Underwater Film Festival. Garry Howland took over the position of Executive Secretary. The *NAUI Page* would be expanded and *Skin Diver Magazine* would become fully supportive of NAUI.

1962 REORGANIZATION

With January 1962 came a complete reorganization of NAUI. At the annual Board meeting in Los Angeles, directors Tillman, Davis, Howland, Jones, Auxier and Cahill unanimously accepted the resignation of Neal Hess and a new era began. The new officers were elected and Garry Howland became President, John C. Jones, Jr. became Vice-President and Jim Auxier became Secretary-Treasurer. Al Tillman became Executive Director. The actual operations of NAUI were transferred from the position of Executive Secretary to the newly reorganized position of Executive Director. This was the first time that all of the NAUI Board was able to be together at one place and time.

NAUI also moved all of its operations from Al Tillman's kitchen table into *Skin Diver Magazine*'s offices in Lynwood, CA. The agreement stipulated that SDM would provide management of NAUI (Al Tillman), office accommodations, clerical support, mailings, and news space for a token fee of $1500 a year. NAUI also offered a liability insurance for the first time to instructors for $10 per year.

The NAUI course in Southern California, Los Angeles County territory, was held in Santa Monica and drew 51 candidates (the second largest since Houston). A number of the top Los Angeles County instructors enrolled for the cross over certification. Larry Cushman, who was to become NAUI's Chairman of the Board in 1974 was a member of the course. Also Dewey Bergman, who pioneered dive travel with Sea and See went through with his long time friend, Roy Damron, who became the major NAUI leader in Hawaii. The course had a prime staff made

NAUI's Toronto course in August of 1961. This photo was taken following the open water checkout at Lake Simcoe in Northern Ontario. Among those pictured are Ben Davis, George Burt, Bill Meeks, Glen Graham, Ray Tussey, Trevor Meldrum, and Jerry Dzineleta.
Trevor Meldrum Collection

up, in part, of the current Board of Directors (Tillman, Jones, Cahill and Howland).

The Pacific Southwest course, as it was called, presented a session on the psychology (a first) of diving conducted by one of Tillman's colleagues at California State College in Los Angeles named Dr. Ronald Kalish. Legal aspects were taught by NAUI's incorporating attorney, David Jacobson, and Jim Stewart covered dangerous marine life. These subjects were given expanded attention in this particular course and were well received. Psychology, in particular, had been overlooked in earlier diving curriculums. Thirty of the 51 candidates were certified at this course.

NAUI had now successfully invaded the Southern California scene and L.A. County leaders decided to just accept it as an added, geographically broader recognition. Neither replaced the other and what appeared to be shaping up as a battle for power in the region between Tillman's current project and the program he had founded before never took place, perhaps to the confusion of some instructors who wanted a final authority to be left standing and pull everything in instruction together.

The East Coast course at Swampscott (Gloucester, Massachusetts) was the NAUI passport into the cluster of fine instruction programs already maturing in New England. Frank Scalli, Paul Tzimoulis, Frank Singer, Walt Hendrick, Fred Calhoun and the leader, Jim Cahill, were destined to become historical figures in diving over the years to follow and the course epitomized their great talents and potentials coming together. For NAUI, the Pacific Southwest course had just ignored the local regional giant (L.A.County) and did its own thing; but the New England course went into action with a perfect regional support team, a YMCA stronghold at the time, and NAUI came away a big winner.

After two years of operation, NAUI had conducted six instructor certification courses of real substance, supervised standards and drew in the leading instructors across North America. At this point, it was the most popular and effective national instruction program, and had the strong foundation which would carry it though the years. NAUI was established.

NAUI was a firmly entrenched in the *Skin Diver Magazine* offices by 1963 and joint operation identity benefitted both. Jim Auxier and Chuck Blakeslee had their fingers on the pulse of diving overall and guided NAUI with their wisdom. The "*NAUI Page*" and a NAUI Newsletter recruited new candidates for courses and reinforced the growing corps of certified instructors.

The procedure at that time was for an instructor to send in a list of trained students after a class's completion along with the class outline. Certification cards (later to be referred to as C-Cards) would be sent out by return mail. There was some grumbling over not having the Cards for the last class session, so most instructors just submitted their preliminary course roster to circumvent the problem. A lot of trust was placed on the instructors not to issue cards to unsuccessful students. The course outline submitted was often just a copy of the NAUI recommended minimum course outline devised by John Jones, Jr. NAUI was becoming wary of its liability in endorsing student certifications.

QUALITY CONTROL

As complaints built up over questionably-trained students showing up at diving venues, some type of policing was needed. The L.A. County system of sending questionnaires out to most of the students on each roster was adopted. The questionnaire quizzed the graduates on course content and left open ended space for other feelings about the instruction received. The many returned questionnaires - over 80% were returned - were positive endorsements of the instructors in most cases. Here and there a disgruntled student would use it to "get revenge". Unless additional complaints were received about the same instructor, the returned questionnaires were simply filed at NAUI Headquarters. If a number of returned questionnaires showed that a specific course left out certain diving physics topics, especially, those related to diver safety, the instructor would be notified. If the flawed teaching continued to be reported, a warning would be issued to the instructor stating that the instructor could lose certification if the area under question was not retroactively corrected. In some cases master instructors with good reputations were asked to sit in on courses and observe. Standardized instruction was thus monitored and protected as a major role of NAUI administration.

In January of 1963, John Jones, Jr. and Al Tillman also put together NAUI's first instructors manual. Jones did most of the work on getting this manual put together and Tillman oversaw the project. The book was designed in a "loose leaf" style so that the contents could be supplemented and updated as time passed. The manual included: Part I, General Procedures; Part II, Basic Course Procedures; Part III, Instructor Course Workbook Section; Part IV, Teaching Aspects; Part V, Medical Aspects; Part VI, Reference Reading; and Part VII, Membership Roster.

NAUI's Instructor Training Manual set the standards by which NAUI instructors were to conduct courses, and themselves, as representatives of the association. A code of ethics was established that was part of the teaching standards. This may seem like just another step toward taking away the individual nature of these pioneer instructors that were part of NAUI, but in every copy sent out was a note from Al Tillman: "The Association is fully aware that in some areas and for specific teaching situations the above standards are not feasible. NAUI exists to serve individual instruction and not to create unrealistic obstacles. By the same token, we are a professional rather than commercial organization. Standards can be waived (if unrefutable justification is presented), but never lowered!" That simple statement told the membership that they had the power, but that nothing less than the best would be accepted.

Some 600 NAUI instructors were out there in 1963 expanding the role of NAUI into the student population. The NAUI membership number that each successful graduating instructor received turned out to be a matter of pride to many. Strangely enough, Al Tillman in his role as Executive Director was on the verge of abandoning the NAUI number (he holds NAUI #1 himself), when he realized that letters from instructors always signed off with name and NAUI number. It looked as if some of the fierce independence that typified instructors in past years had yielded to instructors who enjoyed recognition as an official member of an institutionalized and respected organization.

RECERTIFICATION

Meanwhile the concern for ensuring instructors were kept current and maintaining a high level of teaching skills was growing. The need for recertification called for another program. The L.A. County approach of seminars, workshops and encampments was attempted but only a regional participation was possible. One such effort was a Santa Catalina Island encampment in 1964. Eugene Winters directed it with Al Tillman at Camp Fox. Jon Hardy (NAUI #1002), who would eventually head NAUI as Executive Director (Manager) in the 1970's, was the camp manager, and Pat Laub, who would marry Jon Hardy, was in attendance as the NAUI headquarters secretary.

More instructors were needed to meet the growth of scuba across the continent. It was time to put on courses in Miami, Florida, the Northwest, Northern California and San Diego. San Diego was the home of two organizations that were the building blocks of diving on the West coast, The Bottom Scratchers and Scripps Institution of Oceanography.

There was no question that the instructor certification courses were the strength of NAUI as the major instructional influence in the diving world. The formative years of the early 1960's were filled with criticism. It took some strong self-assurance for the leaders to march straight ahead on their mission, even though, as they told themselves, "You'll never hear your name mentioned if all your life you aren't criticized." It was especially tough because there were strong differing opinions even among the key NAUI shapers and movers and so the criticism was often internal, and perhaps deserved. This criticism was also vital to help the organization grow and mature.

By the 1963-65 era the manufacturers were still sitting back taking a neutral stance. They were getting static from the certifying dive shop owners and their demands. John Gaffney's NASDS (National Association of Skin Diving Stores) was the key challenge and the manufacturers probably didn't want to create more alienation by jumping in fully behind NAUI. NAUI, struggling in the first years, could have used some commercial support, for it was doing the industry's job of training people to be safe. This, in turn, was a protection of the diving field from onerous legislation.

From the dive shop owners viewpoint, many of which had affiliations with NAUI as instructors or having hired NAUI instructors, the concept of instruction as a service was still in vogue rather than treating instruction as a saleable product.

The day-to-day operations at NAUI Headquarters expanded as more instructors processed more students. But besides the vertical growth in numbers, there was the diversification into new programs such as the Junior Frogman program for youths, the formation of new specialized training courses for cave and ice diving, underwater photography, rescue diving, and a NAUI research bureau. (The forerunners of the advanced specialty courses.) The core activity of NAUI, the Instructor Certification Course, also needed some re-tooling as NAUI's army of dedicated instructors became vocal about reforming and improving all aspects of the courses.

Much of this new programming was farmed out to regional NAUI leaders for tryout and development as pilot regional efforts. The clamor for improvement came from everywhere. It was certainly no time to sit back and be smugly complacent.

PETERSEN GIVES NAUI A NEW ADDRESS

Other challenges arose that slowed much of this expansion and refining. *Skin Diver Magazine* was sold to Petersen Publishing Company and a new corporate mentality took over in September of 1963. Jim Auxier was retained as Editor and NAUI was given new offices and secretarial help by the new owner. The new address was on Hollywood Boulevard in Hollywood, California.

Petersen executives looked at the bottom line fiscal aspects of supporting NAUI and weren't too interested in its public service values. Additionally, they may have listened to some bad advice from their promotion people in that supporting one specific instruction program could effect advertising revenue from diving's commercial interests involved with other instruction programs.

The effect of Petersen's takeover was that the friendly handshake relationship that allowed both *Skin Diver Magazine* and NAUI to grow together came apart in the publishing conglomerate. NAUI's Board was not too shaken by this for it did seem the time had arrived when NAUI had the strength and reputation to stand on its own. NAUI headquarters went back on kitchen tables and its branch operations took on greater importance.

The branch operation was put into effect at the 1964 Board meeting in Annapolis, Maryland, (where a NAUI instructor course was being held at the Naval Academy). There was to be an Atlantic Branch under John Jones, Jr., a Canadian Branch under Ben Davis and a Pacific Branch under Al Tillman. Branch managers received a $600 management fee. Jones was elected President and Ray Tussey, new to the Board, was elected Secretary-Treasurer. Al Tillman was reappointed Executive Director.

UNEXSO AND NAUI

Al Tillman was now involved in developing his idea of an Underwater Explorers Society (UNEXSO) that he envisioned would be housed in a state-of-the-art resort facility with all the diving amenities and be located in Freeport, Grand Bahama Island. Financed by a group of Canadian investors, the Grand Bahama Underwater Explorers Club would also serve, at no cost to NAUI, as its International Headquarters. NAUI was ready to go international at that time and Al Tillman, with the Board's approval, had even traveled to England to sign an agreement between NAUI and Charles Ellis of the British Sub Aqua Club advocating reciprocal recognition of divers and instructors.

As UNEXSO came into operation in 1964-65, three outstanding NAUI men were hired to staff this new James Bond-type of diving resort; Chuck Peterson, Dave Woodward and Jack McKenney. The first year of the club's operation was very NAUI oriented and an instructors' course was held there, the first outside of the United States or Canada. NAUI headquarters was officially opened in its Freeport site on December 12, 1965.

The first NAUI course held in Freeport was conducted by Hank Halliday (NAUI #504). The course was actually held at the Bell Channel Villas pool and in a local school classroom. UNEXSO was not quite up and running yet, but the success of the 51 candidates (nobody totally failed the course) affirmed that Freeport would become a major site for diving and a long time stronghold for NAUI. The outstanding graduate of the course was William Alspaugh, Jr. (NAUI #730).

The first NAUI ICC held at UNEXSO was in 1966 and directed by Garry Howland (far left) and Albert Tillman (far right). John Englander is a teenage student in the class - can you find him?   Al Tillman Collection

At the 1966 Board meeting, Tillman was reappointed as President and Executive Director until another candidate could be found. The scope of the UNEXSO operation eventually required Al Tillman to take a leave from his position as a university professor in California and withdraw from all administrative positions with NAUI. The NAUI Pacific Branch management went to Art Ullrich, the outstanding graduate of the San Diego NAUI course in 1964. The Executive Director position went to John Jones, Jr. NAUI Headquarters was transferred to Ft. Lauderdale with the plan of eventually moving it to Freeport.

At this point, with *Skin Diver Magazine* and Al Tillman out of leadership roles, and John Jones, Jr. soon to follow them out, the principal founders of NAUI would give the organization a different look and move in new directions.

The NAUI motto, devised by Garry Howland based on the phrase "Peace through Air Power," and prominent on the original NAUI patch designed by Herb Ingraham (Houston NAUI #37) was "Safety through Education". This was nothing fancy but went right to the heart of the NAUI mission. The scope of the changes made to NAUI very well could have rewritten the motto to read, "Safety through a lot more Education". Numbers, size and revenue started to be strongly promoted from a rising new NAUI leadership. More decentralization and more branches would appear to be the effective way to better meet regional demands and groom new leadership.

Daily operations continued on through this changing of the guard and venue. New challenges were arising in competitive organizations. New national agencies were formed and NASDS would go for a larger share of the instructors and change its name to National Association of Skin Diving Schools, replacing the word stores with schools. Local instructional programs were still hanging on with a fierce local pride and the Canadian Council of Clubs asked that NAUI only evaluate their courses and not actually run them.

THE AFFILIATE PROGRAM

Criticism of a special program called the Affiliate NAUI Instructor Program finally put that effort on ice. Designed to deter strong area instructors who hadn't made it to a NAUI course but could carry a whole region another way, it gave them a face saving way to come on board. About 30 excellent instructors joined the NAUI ranks before the program was abandoned. The requirements were extremely difficult and no one became a NAUI Affiliate that wasn't extremely qualified. Dissident factions develop in every organization that want to take it over or desert and begin rival efforts.

In the end of that 1962-65 era, Art Ullrich, a constantly harsh and exacting critic of the existing operation moved strongly to expand the Pacific Branch (still the most populous diving region) and advocate a new centralization back to the Pacific Branch. On the other hand, Ralph Erickson, disgruntled with the changing NAUI picture and having his Chicago course canceled without consultation, moved with John Cronin of U.S. Divers to put in operation the Professional Association of Diving Instructors (PADI).

NAUI, under the new leadership factions, decided to proliferate instructor courses and expand its ranks hopefully while maintaining the uniformity and continuity of its standards. So NAUI embarked on a sort of franchise program, letting instructor courses happen under new and different staffs everywhere. The result was more instruction and more students from them. More revenue resulted and NAUI moved into the computer world to handle the increased volume of business. Indeed, NAUI, by necessity had to move from a nonprofit public service role to a business operation to survive. A debate will still ensue among NAUI people as to whether NAUI then got better or just bigger and more complex. The term "card factory and souvenir shops" came into the vocabularies of the traditionalists who felt quality was being sacrificed for quantity.

It might help to understand the course of NAUI's development by looking at the students of these diving instructors. The country was in the middle of the Vietnam War and lots of young men were not around. The counterculture youth movement was challenging everything traditional. Risk taking could be done with drugs, jetting to other destinations for resort diving was just beginning, and two job families weren't as yet producing big discretionary incomes. Diving was still relatively inexpensive and instruction was the best bargain of all. The major issue that really affected all diving instruction was what came in as a criticism on a majority of student questionnaires, not enough open water time during beginning courses. The one dive finish to a course as a sort of party after the class would not be enough. Now all instruction programs would duel about having multiple open water dives, a necessity before C-Cards were issued.

By the end of the 1960's there were almost two thousand certified NAUI instructors and that number was growing at an incredible pace. NAUI had been born of a critical need as diving moved from the simplicity and naivete of diving in the 1950's into the 1960's where diving became a recreational activity visible and sought after by thrill seekers across the continent. The NAUI tree had been planted in those early years upon which new leaders would build over the next decades. Changes were to be made and programs expanded to incredible dimensions, but the basic idea of NAUI would remain a good idea as long as people venture into the unknown.

1966-1969

Garry Howland had arranged for Art Ullrich to receive one of the NAUI Board of Director's personal scholarships for him to attend the San Diego course in June of 1964. Art realized at that course that there was room at the top of NAUI. The curriculum and organization were still fermenting and Art was an organizer extraordinaire. He openly criticized NAUI materials and testing and the course administrator, Dave Woodward. This open attack of NAUI was the preface for his future move into NAUI leadership. In an interview by *Scuba America*, Ullrich said that he later "apologized fifteen times to Dave Woodward."

Al Tillman later took Ullrich's criticism and energy and had him feed tests into the March Field Computers to make them more effective. This became NAUI's first foray into the world of computers.

When the time came that Tillman and the Board decided to decentralize NAUI into branches and move the world headquarters to Freeport, Grand Bahama Island, Ullrich was appointed as Pacific Branch Manager and took over administration of over 50 percent of NAUI instructors.

Ullrich could see that "the Board was very conservative, split by personality conflicts, and satisfied to sit a rock on top of what had been established." He attended the 1966 Board meeting with Dave Podowitz. They were not there by invitation, but had gone to evaluate their chances of moving onto the Board. With support from Podowitz and Eugene Winters stepping aside to avoid a split vote, Art became a Board member by 1967.

The shift of headquarters from the West Coast to John Jones, Jr., on the East Coast brought on a period of stagnation for NAUI. Jones had to deal with numerous personal problems. Ullrich questioned the lack of active administration and felt there "were problems like liability insurance, part time administration, inferior record keeping that demanded the rock be pushed off." Ullrich felt that three instructor courses a year would doom NAUI and that the market must be expanded.

Some of the new programs were very promising. Tillman and Jones worked out a plan with Donald Higgins and E. E. Hoisington to make NAUI the official instruction agency for the Boy Scouts of America. Skin diving instruction was encouraged for all Boy Scouts, and NAUI scuba training was offered to Scouts over the age of 16.

In 1966, eight NAUI courses were held and the number increased to 24 in 1967. Real money was finally beginning to come into the NAUI account.

THE ULLRICH ERA

In 1966 Ullrich was named Airman of the Year for his work with NAUI.

The Air Force had supported him during these years of working on NAUI. They provided free air travel and allowed him the time to pursue his interests in the area of diving.

NAUI was experiencing rapid growth at this point. Numbers across the board were growing and Ullrich was the main architect of this growth. Some criticized NAUI for building an unwieldy bureaucracy, but most supported Art based on the numbers.

He eventually hired his wife, Gloria, as a part-time employee of the Pacific Branch and maintained the offices in his garage in Grand Terrace, California. This position eventually built up to 40 hours per week. The growth was too big and the NAUI Board moved to create a total of nine branches in 1968. Art left the service to go to work for Dr. Bruce Halstead in the private sector. He also rented office space and put his wife to work full time. The Branch gross went from $10,000 to $60,000. Based on this success Art was elected Vice-President of NAUI and was appointed Executive Director at a salary of $600 per year.

By 1969, NAUI had grown so large that a full time chief had to be found to manage the growth. Ullrich went to the Board and demanded a centralized NAUI Headquarters once again and creation of a full-time General Manager position with an annual salary of $12,000. The Board agreed to let Ullrich have what he requested and Art Ullrich became NAUI's first full time General Manager.

ICUE or IQ

NAUI instructors Larry Cushman (NAUI #206), John Reseck (NAUI #949), and Glen Egstrom (NAUI #937) joined forces to organize the First International Conference of Underwater Educators (ICUE) or otherwise known as IQ_1 in 1969.

1970 - 1980

In September of 1970, Glen Egstrom would move into the position of President, Larry Cushman was elected Vice-President, Dr. Joseph Bodner, elected Secretary/Treasurer and Frank Scalli was elected as a new member to the Board of Directors. The transition would be complete. NAUI expanded across the ocean by holding its first course in Japan in 1970. NAUI JAPAN was created in 1979. The international aspects of NAUI continued to grow. In 1972, NAUI CANADA was formed as its own independent organization. In September 1974 Mexico held its First NAUI International Conference Course.

On May 1-8, 1971, NAUI held its First Diving Medicine Course designed to teach physicians about the medical aspects of diving. The course was held at UNEXSO in the Bahamas. It was taught by Dr. George Bond, Dr. Edward Tucker and Dr. John Clements who were renowned diving physicians. The course was open only to physicians and basic scuba instruction was available to those who weren't already certified.

The next year, 1972, NAUI became the United States representative to the Technical Committee of the World Underwater Federation (CMAS).

The 1970's were a time of continued global expansion for NAUI. A NAUI Instructor named Dusty Rhodes (NAUI #179) had been living in Thailand for some time and teaching YMCA instructor courses. He couldn't teach NAUI International Certification Courses because of the policy at the time that a representative from NAUI Headquarters be present. While teaching YMCA courses, Rhodes had always remained loyal to NAUI and continued to petition NAUI to allow him to hold the ICC's in Thailand. When a new branch administration came in, Rhodes was finally given permission to hold the ICCs. Now a full and active NAUI THAILAND exists. This kind of expansion became a common practice.

THE NEW NAUI LEADERS HUMAN SIDE

Here Jeanne Bear Sleeper recalls an example of what fun-loving guys they were.

"One of the funniest situations I have ever witnessed involving diving types was during IQ_4 in Miami in 1972. At a party after the Saturday night film festival, John Reseck boasted that he could lift any three men with only one hand. Glen Egstrom and two others in the room took the bait. Reseck had them lie down side-by-side on their backs on the floor. Then he intertwined their arms and legs around each others so that they would "stay together". After a bit of ceremonial huffing and puffing, Reseck stood over Egstrom, who was in the middle, grabbed his belt, and like a flash unzipped Egstrom's fly and poured a drink in. And you know, Reseck was able to lift all three men with only one hand! I have never laughed so hard or seen Egstrom so flustered. I don't know if Egstrom has ever found the opportunity to pay Reseck back yet, as he promised. When he does it will be good."

Ullrich took NAUI in some risky directions from 1970 to 1975. Numbers were the new key and NAUI was ahead in the industry during the first few years of the 1970's because of its high reputation earned during the 1960's. Courses and materials proliferated in NAUI and the organization grew too big to successfully manage. The country was in a downward decline due to the recession and NAUI's reputation and numbers began to decline along with it.

Actually, in 1970 NAUI went broke. Bill High sent Ullrich $2,000 out of his own pocket to make payroll and keep the headquarters door open.

According to High, "NAUI was going broke with its low cost registration of students and failing to keep graduating students as customers for future classes and materials. They (NAUI) may have gotten into too big an operation, but then they really needed to expand, grow and change."

Four important staff people conjured up the idea of the NAUI Divers Association (NDA). They were Art Ullrich, Ed Cargile, Jon Hardy and Dennis Graver. The problem from the very beginning of organized instruction was how to keep divers diving after the first excitement of just being underwater wore off. It wasn't reliable to depend on one diver calling another and saying, "Let's go diving".

COMBATING DIVER DROP OUT

L. A. County had worried this one for quite a while and it had formulated an Advanced Diver Program. The same idea found a right time in NAUI because Ed Cargile, a versatile ex-SEAL, who crossed over from sport, to scientific, to military, to commercial in his experience and thinking, headed it up. NAUI proceeded to offer NAUI divers a chance to keep involved for a $20 annual fee. For this they got a four-color magazine, *Divers World*, an entree to a series of seminars all over the country, covering underwater photography, marine biology, wreck and night diving and just anything new in diving.

The branch managers initiated the request and in came Cargile with guest experts from all areas of diving, pacing every seminar with 300-350 NAUI Divers Association (NDA) and NAUI members. It was a bargain for divers and probably overall an economic break for NAUI in general. Cargile got it off the ground during his 1972-1974 stint with NAUI. NDA went on a level pace but was costly and proved an irreconcilable burden. Diver dropout still bothers the industry and NAUI especially.

1975 MANAGEMENT CHANGES

In 1975 the NAUI Board of Directors felt that NAUI's decline was the fault of management and made changes. Ullrich stepped down to a lesser role as Special Projects Coordinator and Jon Hardy was elevated to run the show. The days of managing NAUI like the old dive clubs had passed. The early organizers had to yield power to the new businessmen of the industry. Bill High replaced Glen Egstrom as President of the Board. The Board also decided to increase its number from seven to nine. Each member was to be from a different geographic region to increase local representation.

JON HARDY (NAUI#1002) ERA:

Jon Hardy was born in Glendale, California in 1938. At an early age, he failed his first swim test because he was a sinker. A lean, handsome man, he was an excellent skin and scuba diver since his teens. Jon would rather run out of air deep than get cold without his wet suit. As a kid, he memorized the narrative of Cousteau's *Silent World* with a flashlight under a blanket. That book became his scuba textbook. Oh yes, he did go beyond "don't hold your breath" by taking a Mel Fisher three-hour course in the Hermosa, California, Biltmore pool with a used DA-Regulator he bought from Mel's Aqua Shop.

As a long distance runner in track, Jon found in skin diving a parallel - agony and loneliness. But he loved it and

1970's Chicago ICC group photograph. Front row is Mark Novak, Don Pittan, Bob Foote, Marcel Lachenmann, Jon Hardy, Judy Shape and Claude Jewell. Back row is Wayne Fisher, Tim Briscoe, Ken Frisco, Jim Foley, Merritt Bartlett, Jeanne Bear Sleeper, Klaus Lindermann, Bob Sheridan and Dick Jacoby. *Jim Starr photo.*

became one of the leaders in the National YMCA Scuba Program as an instructor and instructor trainer. He pursued diving day-in and day-out as a young manager of the Camp Fox Y-Camp on Santa Catalina Island. A lot of the diving was to 130 foot depths without regard for the tables.

Jon, as a recreation management student, had classes with Professor Al Tillman at California State University in Los Angeles. He also became acquainted with the L.A. County Program and would become an L.A. County certified instructor at age 21 in the 10 UICC.

NAUI had outgrown its capacity to operate effectively. Jon, a Certified NAUI Instructor, having served a hitch as a U.S. Navy officer, was brought in as Special Projects Manager to form the National Divers Association in 1971-1972. Jon challenged what he saw as wrong management decisions and for awhile he left NAUI to just dive. His criticisms, however, were not unheeded. As had happened before, the critic got his chance to "do things". Jon went back into NAUI as General Manager from 1975-1979.

Jon gave NAUI consummate leadership. He was a role model for other leaders to follow. He changed the thrust of the program from certifying to training. As the best of instruction potential was creamed off in the early years, training became essential to prepare the less experienced and less qualified to instruct.

Jon Hardy came into NAUI Headquarters in the early 1970's to operate under the Board Chairman Egstrom and General Manager Ullrich. There was conflict at the leadership level and it had plagued NAUI from its very beginning. Jon Hardy recalls "the Board lived in a dream factory and that some at the top level had outlived their usefulness." Bill High saw conflict resulting from "each Board member pursuing his own pet project."

This was a tough decade for NAUI as it discovered that quality control wasn't easy as you get bigger and, quality was the core of NAUI's reputation. Hardy seemed to represent both a passion for diving and NAUI, coupled with "business savvy". "Lack of business sense" was a catchall phrase to explain any or all things that were failing with NAUI. Great ideas existed in abundance, but the budgeting and operating procedures to carry them out did not have a significant person to make them happen.

Jon Hardy faced a big deficit, but carried on valiantly. It would seem that NAUI had been underfinanced since it started unless the nonprofit status with use of volunteers was strictly adhered to. Many felt, nonprofit or not, you couldn't survive without operating "like a business". The competition in diving instruction seemed to be all business in their approach. Each succeeding NAUI "manager" tends to explain each NAUI failure by saying "dedicated nice guy, but he wasn't trained to manage" about his predecessor.

In 1972-1973 NAUI certified 83,000 divers. Larry Cushman came up with the idea that NAUI should be selling continuing education to those divers. It could be a NAUI money machine.

Jon Hardy had done one stint with NAUI in 1971-1973 then left until the Board brought him back in 1974. He had been an ardent critic of Board decisions about "NDA as a rip off" and a half-million dollar contract made by the Board with Jeppersen to produce training materials. NAUI revenue was only $400,000 a year at this point. Jeppersen defaulted and NAUI lost money in the deal.

TOO MANY PROGRAMS-TOO LITTLE MONEY

During the 1970's NAUI had trouble getting a proper budget in place, taking on projects to produce revenue that ultimately put NAUI further in debt. The industry was also faced with legislation in key venues such as L.A. County and Florida that forced some dive shops out of business. Fighting this legislation cost NAUI and other organizations a lot in resources and money, but aided in bringing the instruction agencies closer together with the goal of self-regulation.

Another key issue arose in the 1970's over where certified instructors should be teaching. The YMCA advocated a 1950's approach through dive clubs, while NASDA (National Association of Skin Diving Association) and PADI (Professional Association of Diving Instructors) saw dive stores as the appropriate venue. NAUI, under the influence of university oriented Dr. Glen Egstrom, Dr. Lee Somers and John Kramer decided that instruction should outlet through the schools which could hold onto things when everybody else was in trouble. It was an honest miscalculation in hindsight. Certainly there was dignity and guaranteed quality in the school concept, but NAUI had taken a wrong turn at this point. The dive shop was geared toward the daily walk in public off the street and the average person felt it a stable and less threatening presence. The dive shops were an easy way to offer instruction. NAUI demanded standards much higher than other organizations. NAUI continued to do the quality job of producing instructors that built its reputation, and the proud men and women who held NAUI certifications didn't want to see the program watered down. Many of these instructors, however, participated in crossover training that enabled them to teach under PADI or NASDS as well.

There were also some major changes in instructor certification in 1974. The Instructor Certification Course (ICC) was replaced with a two step Instructor Qualification Course (IQC) to certify Assistant Instructors (AI's) followed by an Instructor Training Course (ITC) to fully certify instructors. The main water skill testing was now done in the IQC, while more time was focused on training instructors to teach in the ITC instead of the time spent testing their basic skills.

The door to women opened a bit more in the 1970's. Pioneers like Zale Parry, Helen Drew, Nancy Gill, Noureen Rouse were ahead of their time. Jeanne Bear Sleeper came into NAUI Headquarters from 1975 to 1980 as Director of Instructor Training. She was motivated by *Sea Hunt* to become a diver and eventually began certifying at the University of Minnesota. In reality, Jeanne became the first female Instructor Training Course Director and managed the NAUI Midwest Branch. She established women as great potential leaders for NAUI. More importantly, diving in general would see women gain prominence and respect.

Dennis Graver came aboard NAUI Headquarters in 1974 to put together NAUI training materials after the Jeppersen deal fell through. He would soon leave to help develop materials for PADI, and NAUI would be left with no solid training materials that would appeal to the shops until 1985 when Graver returned to NAUI.

By 1976, when Bill High (NAUI #175) was elected President of the NAUI Board, there were almost 5,000 certified NAUI instructors. By the end of the decade there would be 5,704 and the age for instructor qualification was reduced from twenty-one to eighteen.

NAUI was still undergoing a lot of financial troubles toward the end of the 1970's. Many instructors were concerned about the future of the organization. In 1979 a group of NAUI instructors took the initiative by contacting John Englander (NAUI #1148), who had taken over UNEXSO. Englander ran for the Board unsuccessfully in 1979 but returned the following year to win the election and even be appointed President. John Englander would help turn NAUI around financially and probably helped save the NAUI idea.

During 1979, John Englander was with President Bill High and General Manager Ken Brock, (who had replaced Jon Hardy in 1979), overseeing the first NAUI Japan course, but nobody said anything about the organization being $200,000 in debt. In some ways it reflects the good and bad of a democratic organization that belongs to its members. Electing a Board prevents corruption of power, but it also means that sustained leadership and resulting continuity gets lost as well as accountability at times.

If the 1970's could be summed up for NAUI it might be said that this premier organization of diving instruction grew faster than it could keep up with in terms of money and leadership. Many would say in reflection that NAUI had no marketing ability. Good ideas from good minds were attempted - the NDA, the Jeppersen plan for an ultimate training system, the continued elevation of standards, the efforts to outlet through schools. But there were too many ideas, too many diverging opinions between Board and staff, not enough money for everything, negative legislation and fierce competition. In the face of it all, however, NAUI stood tall, new leadership arose out of the ranks, and the general public still envisioned "quality" when the NAUI name was heard.

1980 - 1990

At the Board meeting in March of 1980 John Englander was elected President of NAUI's Board of Directors. He ran for the position after being encouraged by several Board members, who felt that Englander had the experience and drive to turn NAUI's financial situation around. NAUI had been running at a loss and some believed that NAUI was on the verge of bankruptcy.

John Englander had earned himself a reputation in the diving industry as a top notch financial manger. Englander had been hired as manager of UNEXSO in 1979 and was able to build a highly successful business while maintaining many of the original ideas that Tillman had dreamed of for UNEXSO. By 1980, NAUI and UNEXSO were both similar in size with approximately one million dollar budgets.

The night before the election the current President, Bill High, shared a room with Englander. They discussed the future of NAUI and its current problems. Englander was interviewed on this and other subjects by Dennis Reeves Cooper for the book, *The Underwater Explorers Society: Silver Anniversary History.* Englander recalled that High resented the fact that Englander would get the credit for the financial turnaround of NAUI after the hard work that High had done to accomplish the task. (Remember earlier, Bill High was the angel who gave $2,000 out of his own pocket to meet payroll.) Yet, Englander pointed out that he (Englander) would also take the blame if NAUI went bankrupt over the next year. They came to an acceptance of the situation that evening and have apparently remained friends over the years since.

John Englander started the year by asking for one year to turn NAUI's financial situation around, but that it would only work if Englander had complete control. The full turn-around took Englander eighteen months, but by the end of 1980 NAUI financial statements showed a surplus of $90,000.

Englander really dug in as President, certainly "coming to live at the Headquarters for weeks at a time," examining every detail, doing cost accounting, and eliminating costly projects. Marshall McNott came in as Executive Director. McNott was the first manager to come in without a diving background. He had been a fund raiser for an Evangelist. Some hard-ball belt tightening seemed to do the trick. However, some NAUI leadership feels the turnaround had begun years before, as the economy changed. NAUI rebutted the PADI invasion with a more easy to use system. Recovery was inevitable. NAUI had a valued product.

NAUI needed a fresh start, a new look and a new Headquarters. In 1981 the NAUI Headquarters moved into a new building located at 4650 Arrow Highway in Montclair, California...and finally to Tampa, Florida, by year 2000. NAUI also wasn't adverse to borrowing ideas; after all, the other organizations had certainly not hesitated to use a lot of what NAUI had created. It is a little known fact that one of the largest competitors of the NAUI program held its first course using the materials and applicant mailing list for a NAUI scheduled course. NAUI materials merely had the name NAUI whited-out and the name of the new organization added in its place.

Larry Cushman (NAUI #206)

In an interview before his death for the book, *Scuba America*, NAUI President Larry Cushman looked back on his association with NAUI. "My careers in commercial diving were never as fulfilling as my involvement with NAUI. It was a great idea, pure and clean from the very beginning and came from a few divers with a real caring about people and protecting diving as a safe sport. Mistakes were made in trying to keep up with the competition and grow bigger, but it was easier to clear the air when we got back to the founders original idea of the mission of NAUI."

Although an attempt to bring NAUI into the computer age dates back to 1963, no real changes in this area occurred until 1982. The first two computer systems were a "disaster" and NAUI continued to operate effectively despite this. What everyone learns today in a growing world, profit or nonprofit, is you either pay to stay technologically in step or you're doomed. Somehow the bills got paid in the worst of times; sometimes the money came out of the pockets of personally-dedicated NAUI leaders, but organizations must continue to stay in tune with society. Ben Davis described it nicely when he said, "The NAUI light shines no matter how dark it gets...and, after all, we all came through the same machine and are proud of it."

In 1983, *NAUI News* was discontinued and the *National Divers Association (NDA) News* was created. The new *NDA News* was a joint effort between NAUI and its partner organization, National Divers Association.

In 1985, Dennis Graver came back to NAUI and did what he did for PADI in 1982. He put together a simple modular training program. The idea, born out of a meeting with John Cronin, Dick Bonin, Paul Tzimoulis and Graver, was spun out of a brainstorming session of "what's the easiest way to teach someone to dive?" It put NAUI in a new favorable position to better serve dive shops rather than just the independent instructor. Ted Bohler's Pro Manual for NAUI gave NAUI a solid universal text to standardize instruction, a map, so to speak, on getting a diver into the water quickly and effectively. Bohler also gave NAUI its first small specialty booklets on things like night diving, simple and practical. There had always been manuals and materials around, but a lot of it was too complex and needed another training class to understand and use it.

Unified training standards were brewing (pushed by the negative legislation attempts of the 1970's) and NAUI worked closely with the National Association for Cooperation in Aquatics to help standardize training across the United States. In 1985, the Recreational Scuba Training Council (RSTC) developed the minimum training standards for entry level certification. NAUI, as did most other agencies, adopted the Industry Training Standards in 1986. These standards required four open water dives and other minimum requirements for beginning certification.

Sam Jackson became Executive Director in 1987 to 1995. He epitomized the quality of leadership that NAUI produced for the diving industry. He came in to NAUI Headquarters with the promise of no Board interference. Sam Jackson gave NAUI another fresh start, inserted marketing acumen, got the computers in gear, and more or less, got NAUI ready for the Twenty-First Century. NAUI membership also elected Nancy Guarascio to its highest office in 1987 to become NAUI's first female president.

In 1989, the *NDA News* was changed to *Sources: the Journal of Underwater Education.*

In 1994, NAUI discontinued NDA and it was reorganized under the name *International Underwater Foundation* (IUF). This allowed even greater tax breaks and the original mission of continuing education and awareness for all divers continued on.

In 1995, Sam Jackson moved on to be the Executive Director of the Diving Equipment and Marketing Association (DEMA). It was a reward for getting NAUI in balance against the fierce competition of rival instructional organizations like PADI and SSI. A NAUI instructor in 1971, then President of NAUI Canada, Sam Jackson epitomized the very nature of NAUI as a member directed organization where anyone can rise through the ranks.

In 1994, NAUI introduced CD-ROM training materials to supplement the regular course of study. NAUI continued to grow technologically and its involvement in the computer world had come a long way since Al Tillman first asked Art Ullrich to use government computers to improve NAUI testing in 1963.

Mike Williams and Wally Barnes pioneered another first in the 1990's by being the first instruction agency to have a strong presence on the Internet and create an official World Wide Web site. Here's an example of a 1995 exchange on the Internet:

"It shouldn't be about who's a PADI-Waddie or a NAUI-Wowie, it's who just blew by his safety stop or just chipped a big piece of coral off the reef - I've seen new divers do it and I've seen Divemasters do it, both PADI and NAUI."

or

"I happen to be a NAUI Advanced Diver, and I like the agency, but what I've noticed is that regardless of certification agency, it's the instructor and students' attitude that make the difference."

NAUI had always grown through allowing a self-questioning from its membership; that communication was now speeded up and had a broadened exposure. Only a new strong leadership with thick hides would survive it.

As the Century ended, NAUI is proud of training some 20,000 instructors and millions of divers. It's new Headquarters in Tampa, Florida is closer to the new central core of its international role. The General Manager and President in NAUI's 40th year, Jim Bram, is a non-diver and business oriented. Incoming revenue supports a $3,000,000 budget and is primarily derived from its roster of 8000 active instructor members dues of $120 annually. The members also must have liability insurance and through NAUI, they pay $460 annually for a million-dollar-coverage. Back in the start-up days of the early 1960's dues were $10.00 annually and $15 for insurance.

PADI OVERTAKES NAUI IN NUMBERS

That NAUI was surpassed in the 1970's by rival PADI in terms of volume was probably due to the fact that NAUI often stumbled over it's own democratic direction by election and a few wrong management decisions. But a lot of good decisions to finish up by the year 2000 with dignity, respect and the potential to remain strong and true to its motto: "Safety through Education".

To some degree the easy crossover process that opened the door to collecting badges, allowed many instructors to become recognized under different instructional agencies. Loyalty and pride suffered a blow and NAUI especially suffered in a loss of prestige and exclusivity. Tom Hemphill, NAUI's Vice-President in its 40th Year, perceived that during the 1960's, a diver was asked if he had a NAUI Card. By the early 1970's, the question was if the diver has a C for Certification Card. And by the late 1970's, it was whether the diver had a PADI Card. NAUI ended up the Century somewhat smaller than its rival, but repairing itself from many bumps, set backs and changes of leadership, it stands with dignity , health, the original and still the guardian of high standards.

As we compare the divers today against those in the beginning, we now have everybody in a hurry to get it done, get diving and forget all the science and esoteric curriculum and watermanship. There seems to be a feeling with the new breed of would-be divers that all of this colorful, technologically trendy equipment will take them diving and take care of everything without too much effort on their parts. There's a whole lot of "I-don't-want-to-read-the-directions-just help-me-get-the-stuff-on" attitude out there. Tom Tillman recalls sitting on the shore on Catalina Island in the mid-1980's with his father and Zale Parry during an open water check-out trip. "I will never forget when Dad came up after teaching divers all day, sitting down and saying, 'You may as well send the equipment out by remote control. They just don't care about the adventure of diving. It's all color-coordinated snorkels and BC's and who has the most expensive equipment.' It was a profound observation in its simplicity coming from a diving dinosaur like Dad, but it said a lot about what diving has become over the years."

Who are these new people whom Chuck Blakeslee reports seeing fill the water of his old diving hole in Laguna Beach. Chuck says, "They had just used up all the space and were lined up to go in, like an amusement park. I just went to my favorite spot in Lake Tahoe and two hundred divers filled the parking area, gearing up to go in. Some of them looked pretty soft compared to the old time divers."

It seems to be a youngish market, newly affluent baby-boomers, college students, the usual risk-takers, people getting ready to travel to exotic places where diving is exquisite, and people seduced by films on TV. It's not an inexpensive, casual experience anymore.

Diving still lures lots of people into trying it out, but retaining them, giving them a long term interest that they can handle with expertise has continued to be the failing of all organizations. The quality of their training introduction to the sport will determine their passion for it and how long they stick with it.

The essence of NAUI in its 40 Years is that despite differences there is a deep sense of belonging to an organization with dignity and integrity. The pride in that belonging unites its instructors into a force that has greatly influenced and directed the recreational diving field. The mission of NAUI was clearly stated in its beginning that it would provide a nonprofit service to the public of the finest education possible and with which beginning and advance divers would be assured that their safety and well-being would be protected and uncontaminated by commercial influence. NAUI instructors would be the most effective device for learning diving that could be produced.

NAUI over the years always belonged to its member instructors. It bogged down at times because it followed democratic concepts and was directed by service to the public over the business of making money. It cared about people and not about how much they would spend to go diving. The rival training agencies that developed after NAUI were commercially motivated and presented fierce competition over all the years.

There were many who wondered if NAUI had served its original purpose and should dissolve and let the professional marketers take over instruction. Some felt NAUI never had any business sense and without profit as a motive what else was there.

Through all this criticism and some was justified, NAUI was always there with the public's best interests at heart and using psychic gain for people as its measurement of success. But perhaps more importantly, NAUI was there in the beginning to set standards that were never exceeded and gave integrity and order to sport diving.

As instruction became a major profit center in the retail business of diving, the full-time employment of instructors eliminated an army of part-time instructors who taught with a passion and zeal on an almost volunteer basis.

In its 40 year history, NAUI Worldwide has certified an average of 100,000 students in any given year (except, of course, the first couple of years). In the year 2000, there were 30,000 NAUI instructors. NAUI service centers could be found in 17 countries with 600 retail centers called affiliates which include universities and dream resorts in over 100 countries. Instruction materials are printed in 15 languages.

NAUI ANNIVERSORY 1960-2000

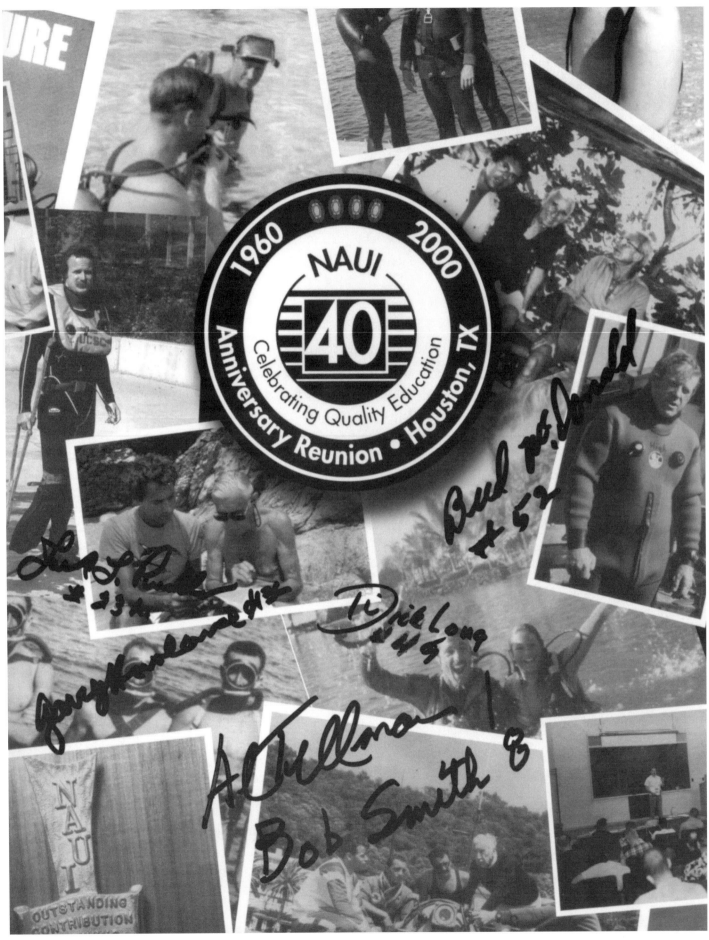

Naui held its gala 40th anniversary celebration in Houston, Texas on November 10-12, 2000. The event featured a gathering of NAUI men and woman from the past 40 years. The inaugural induction of 22 outstanding instructors was made to the NAUI Hall of Honor. The event also featured seminars, exhibits, special events, speakers and a behind-the-scenes tour of the NASA Neutral Boyancy Lab courtesy of it NAUI trained staff. The photo above and to the right is of five graduates and Course Director Al Tillman of NAUI's first Instructor Certification Course that was held in Houston in 1960. Top: Jack Rudder, Bud McDonald, Al Tillman, Garry Howland and Dick Long. Right: Bob Smith and Albert Tillman

NAUI ADMINISTRATION

Board of Directors President/Chairman

1960 - 1962	Prof. Albert Tillman (NAUI #1)
1962 - 1964	Garry Howland (NAUI #13)
1964 - 1966	Albert Tillman (NAUI #1)
1966 - 1968	John Jones, Jr. (NAUI #2)
1968 - 1969	Ben Davis (NAUI #101)
1970 - 1974	Glen H. Egstrom, Ph.D. (NAUI #937)
1975 - 1979	William "Bill" High (NAUI #175)
1980 - 1981	John Englander (NAUI #1148)
1982 - 1983	Larry Cushman (NAUI #206)
1984 - 1986	John Englander (NAUI #1148)
1987 - 1988	Nancy Guarascio (NAUI #5008)
1988 - 1990	Ken Heist (NAUI #1036)
1991 - 1992	Nancy Guarascio (NAUI #5008)
1992 - 1993	Robert "Bob" Brayman (NAUI #6058)
1994 - 1995	Bret Gilliam (NAUI #3234)
1995 - 2000	Keith Sliman (NAUI #3417)
2000 -	Jim Brown (NAUI #6186)

7
THE DIVING MANUAL
THE DIVERS GUIDEBOOK

DEFINING EVENT: SCIENCE OF SKIN AND SCUBA DIVING

At the hard-core heart of going diving with confidence has been the instructional diving manual. Forget learning by experience because diving is wrought with highly technical and mysterious conveyances that invisibly interfere with what you just go ahead and do. The Underwater Demolition Team under Doug Fane at Coronado, California had a big sign up in the classroom - "Before you have all the experience you need, you'll be dead".

Forget the classroom instructor because he forgets crucial things and tends to entertain with diving stories. Diving magazines for all their value and keeping divers motivated are maneuvered by equipment and dive travel sponsors.

The instructional diving manual had to target the vital things that a diver has to know to do it right and be safe. No froth and frosting, straight facts or the critics would swarm all over the author and publisher like summer locust. Knowing what the "experts" put down in writing gave sport divers a necessary confidence for entering this unpredictable and unknown separate planet of water, three times as big as all the land mass on earth on the surface and thousands of times as big beneath the surface.

The first instruction manuals for scuba diving were evolutionary outgrowths of manuals for hard hat diving. Physics and physiology and oceanography were deep subjects that could kill you if you didn't know them and whether helmet-hose-diving or self-contained, they were basically interchangeable. But even those "absolutes" were altered as research scientists disproved and reversed some of them for application in this new medium of depth. The classic example is the changing of advice on avoiding decompression sickness, the bends, by exercising and moving vigorously at scheduled decompression stops to get the bubbles out faster - which eventually was determined to be absolutely wrong and bubbles must be avoided by slow relaxed ascents and stops. This discrepancy probably killed a good count of old time helmet divers, but perhaps worst, the divers stopped believing the "experts and their manuals" and winged it, did whatever seemed to work for each individual.

As we examine the early manuals of pioneer days of scuba in America, we discover the embryo base in the manuals of the military designed for young, very fit men. The population going skin and scuba diving in the 1940's and 1950's were a mixed group of athletes and passive civilians and of varying ages. What worked for the military didn't always recognize the variances in the general population.

U.S. NAVY DIVING MANUAL

The first book divers turned to was the *U.S. Navy Diving Manual*. It's first issue in 1915 was prepared after extensive tests of deep diving were conducted and a definite program of development of diving in general was actively begun. It was addressing the scientific aspects that all forms of diving must be aware of. Beyond that the manual was by then addressing the arrival of scuba diving, primarily rebreathers. It was designed in a bureaucratic form, stiffly written like the directions for handling and maintaining an MI rifle. Each point of information was a numbered entry such as:

Part 2 Basic Principles of Diving————Articles 511-535

A. Physics of diving————————————Articles 511-522

B. Elementary physiology of diving—Articles 531-535

(Later revisions had one seeking the contents by chapter, section, paragraph and page. Chapter 8 would be found under 8.1. Titled Open-Circuit Systems. Page numbers. Search 8.1.1 to 8.1.9. Similar to the old and new testaments of the bible with headings, chapters and verses.)

It was a big 9"x11" book, with stiff gray board covers, about two to three inches thick. You could kill a rat with it. It was serious stuff not fun reading. But it was the authentic, official backdrop against which all the instruction manuals of the 1950's were written. The 1943 Navy issue and then its easier-to-handle revision in 1952 in beige paperback, became the serious divers' bible during those times. The 1954 Navy "Special Edition" was big time news for the entrance of scuba alone.

Unless one was privy to the American Medical Association publications with printed reports by Dr. Christian J. Lambertsen on *Problems of Shallow Water Diving*, based on experiences of operational swimmers by the Maritime Unit of the Office of Strategic Services using the LARU, Lambertsen's closed circuit scuba, or his printed "Predictive Studies" on the Effects of Respiratory Gases at Extreme Pressures in those early days of 1942, one would seek out the U.S. Navy Diving Manuals. We make note again that Dr. Lambertsen and his team devised the term scuba, back in the dark ages of the sport of diving. During World War II the Navy called the operational swimmers the underwater demolition teams.

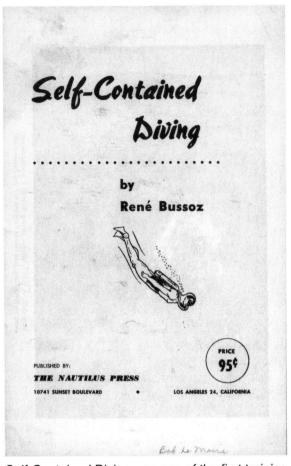

Self-Contained Diving was one of the first training manuals.

The Lambertsen Unit LARU (scuba) and its uses were well kept secrets. In October 1945 the "Secret" classification was removed. Only then were the publications and the apparatus revealed to the public.

The booklet (manual, really) *Problems of Shallow Water Diving* was very comprehensive in techniques, equipment, physiology, physics, and the "strangeness of the underwater environment". It covered marine life including the shark problem in underwater work. Unfortunately, this enlightening manual could not be found on the magazine stands or bookstores. It could easily be snatched up by divers in the medical field. And was.

Finally, on April 1, 1954 a Special Report Series: *Diving with Self-Contained Apparatus* was designed to fill in the gaps that appeared in the past printings. The forward read, "The spectacular rise of self-contained diving in recent years has left authoritative Naval literature far behind in the subject." It offered "anyone who found discrepancies either in form or in substance to submit his findings to the U. S. Navy Experimental Diving Unit, Washington 25, D.C., so that appropriate changes would be incorporated in subsequent issues." This special manual was prepared by Dr. Edward H. Lanphier (LT. (MC) USNR) and Jolly V. Dwyer, Jr. (LCDR USN). It was a joy to behold!

E. R. Cross's *Divemaster Skin and Lung Diving* home study training, 1955 published by U.A.S. Corporation, Chicago, Illinois was a manual in segments. The enrollment fee was $169.50. Each printed-bound-lesson with separate test sheet was sent to the student one at a time. The test sheet was mailed back and corrected by Ellis Royal Cross himself, then returned to the student with the next lesson. Zale Parry was certified Member No. 1303. The entire training program was planned to give workable knowledge to the student for the adventure with safety in diving and many opportunities to earn a living in the new sport.

Cross's book, *Underwater Safety* followed. It was put out by Healthways which was challenging U.S. Divers at the time with a regulator, the Divair, that worked but didn't measure up to the original Aqua Lung. The book was a small paperback 5 x 9 and followed closely the style of the *U.S. Navy Diving Manual*. And so it should, as Ellis

Royal cross was a well-respected U.S. Navy Masterdiver.

A thin booklet, *Skin Diving Safety* prepared by Bill Walker, Safety Director for The California Council of Diving Clubs sold in 1955. Walker was president of the Aqua-Guards, an organization established in the fall of 1954 along the lines of the National Ski Patrol, as the official Underwater Safety Organization for Southern California. As members of the AAU and selected by the Southern Pacific Amateur Athletic Union, the Aqua-Guards members handled the safety problems of the major spearfishing tournaments held on the Pacific Coast and National Championships. Scuba diving had not been recognized as a common expression yet. All of us, with or without the bubbles, were referred to as skin divers. *Skin Diving Safety* instructed the skin and the scuba diver, too.

Gilbert Abbe, Dr. William T. Burns, E. R. Cross, Bernard E. Empleton, Loyal G. Goff, Wallace B. Hagerhorst, Dr. Edward Lamphier, Richard Norris, Fred Schwankovsky, Capt. James Wren, and James Young in 1957 at Yale during one of the first meetings.   Loyal Goff

There was a pamphlet *Self-Contained Diving, The Aqua Lung*, by Rene Bussoz published in 1949, a token bit of first steps information about the equipment, recommended accessories (not included), a touch of physiology, and simplified tables of decompression for shallow water. It didn't go much farther than to say put the mouthpiece in your mouth, then breathe. Just let yourself sink gradually. Take your time. The price was 95 cents.

U.S. Divers with the help of Navships 394-0056, Bureau of Ships, Navy Department, Washington, D.C. published a fine looking, black leather-like cover for their twenty-page, 3-hole-page bound instruction book, *Aqua Lung Demand Type Diving Apparatus* in September 1954. It considered the management of the demand regulator from description, operation preparation for use, preventative and corrective maintenance with instructions, guidance with illustrations for putting on the Aqua Lung, regulating buoyancy, simple safety regulations and precautions.

Dave Owen had published a book called *Manual for Free Divers* in 1953 and another *Divers Using Compressed Air* in 1954 and it was at a level of divers at Woods Hole Institute of Oceanography. Somewhat esoteric but it was a well-written introduction to scuba that the next generation of manual writers turned to for researched information.

Bev Morgan whipped out a manual called *Underwater Safety Manual* that was closely constructed in the style of the *Los Angeles County Lifeguard Manual*. This was in 1954 when Bev and Al Tillman began developing the foundation of diving instruction, the public classes for the Los Angeles County Department of Parks and Recreation. This preceded the formation of the first Underwater Instructors Certification Program and only about 500 were printed and sold at a cost of one dollar each.

In 1955 Bill Starr and Al Tillman authored a new version of an instruction manual called *Underwater Recreation*, with content directed away from warnings and more oriented to diving as a fun experience - when you knew what you were doing. The cartoon-like illustrations by Jess Gruel and colorful cover made it a best seller in United States diving, and especially in the Los Angeles County region where it was the official textbook for all classes taught by Los Angeles County Instructors.

In 1955, Bev Morgan resigned from his Los Angeles County lifeguard position to become an initiator of dive

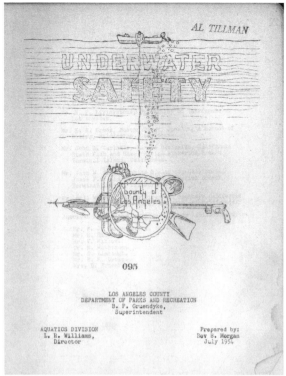

Underwater Safety was prepared by Bev Morgan and served as Los Angeles County's first text in 1954.

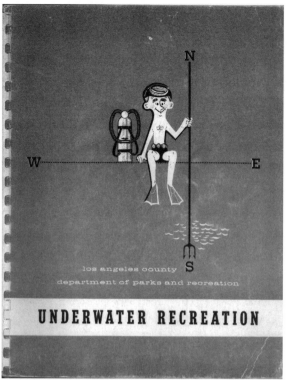

Al Tillman and Bill Starr wrote Underwater Recreation in 1955 to replace Underwater Safety. Underwater Recreation continued on as the official text for four decades.

businesses that would make him a legend. He produced a diving manual, a 5 x 9 paperback for U.S. Divers Company that had wide circulation. Many dive shops adopted it as their official text. Title was *Diving with Safety*.

Dive written by Rick and Barbara Carrier in 1955 had a lot of information and was an impressive "real" book with dust jacket and a major publisher. It got wide distribution through book stores. Written as a how-to-book, it contained much more entertaining information than was essential for a basic diving course. Some people probably learned to dive from it but the majority of would-be-divers were looking for an authoritative agency's instruction manual.

SOURCES OF FACTUAL INFORMATION

"How come you don't have anything on spearfishing in the diving manual?", asked Jim Christiansen, full of disdain for newly arrived diving with a bubble machine. He was hard-core, tough skin diver, who pushed sharks out of the way. He was big, Paul Bunyan big, when he jumped in the oceans waves broke on far away shores. It was 1957 and fish-sticking was getting some bad mouthing by a new generation of creature huggers.

Probably should, Jim, I told him. What do you think we ought to say if we did?, responded Al Tillman.

"It's something you do by doing. Maybe you can't write it down," says Jim.

Must be some technique, what's the secret of getting one of those big white sea bass? What would you say?

"Sure, first you hold your breath and go down 50 - 60 feet and sit there, go up get a breath, go down, up and down, up and down until you see one coming by....."

"Not many of the new divers, the scuba weaned divers can do that? I know, most of them get too tired just getting all their doodads on, couldn't hold their breath long enough to get done pooping in a construction workers road john."

It was decided to skip the mysterious lore of the bluewater hunters, the spearfishermen, from the diving manuals. The transition had begun to underwater photography anyway.

THE EXPERTS

Every manual needed a point of authority. The content has to come from bonafide experts on different aspects of diving. Diving medicine had a number of celebrated names such as: George Bond, Albert Behnke, Edward Lanphier, Robert Workman, Edgar End. Los Angeles County, being a West Coast diving region didn't have a good shot at recruiting advice from the big East Coast names. But West Coast Conrad Limbaugh suggested Dr. Robert Livingston from UCLA Physiology Department in the 1954 beginning and then in 1955, Dr. William Burns with some Navy background came on board. The rest of the Board was fleshed out with Limbaugh, E.R. Cross, Fred Schwankowsky, Roger Plaisted (LA Red Cross) and Dr. Feron Losee. All were steeped in Aquatics. Any question on manual material could be run past them if challenged. So the famed Los Angeles County manual had a strong base for its content.

The National YMCA Program came on line in 1957 and adopted the National Cooperation in Aquatics Conference Group pooling of knowledge from different aquatic agencies. A committee of good experts in their fields put together the *Science of Skin and Scuba Diving* which was not only picked up officially as a text by the YMCA but many other agencies. It was the best selling diving manual of all time and went through many printings over the years

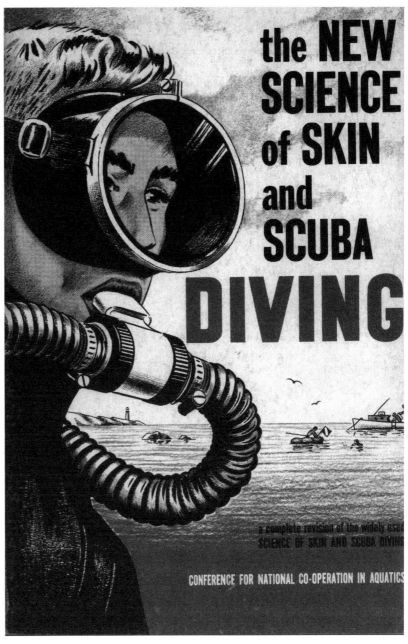

The New Science of Skin and Scuba Diving and its predecessor were landmark manuals for the infant sport of recreational scuba diving.

but not much revision. Because different individuals wrote each chapter, it had a varying style and a tendency to over-emphasize some topics.

The New Science of Skin and Scuba Diving was issued under that title in 1962 and ceased publication in the 1980's because the certification agencies had become large warehouses of cards, badges and instruction materials, and especially, vendors of their own identifiable diving manuals. *The New Science of Skin and Scuba Diving* never changed much, and adequate as it was for basic training, the writing remained that of a committee, somewhat colorless. The word "new" added to the title always seemed a selling device rather than a restructuring.

There is a great fear in writing and publishing a diving manual that people might stake their lives on. Liability was a constant demon that hovered over every point made. Instruction agencies tried to revise their manuals to keep up with new equipment, marine life behavior, physiology, and diving techniques.

Buddy breathing, the sharing of air with a partner from one regulator, was an accepted and necessary skill in the pioneer days and it was generally practiced in dive courses, pool and open water. It became highly controversial because every situation is so different and the panic possibilities had the potential of creating and did result in

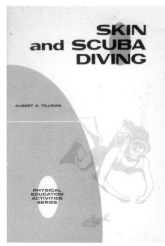

Al Tillman wrote this text for the college programs.

some accidents. Even in the pool let alone a 100 foot open water running out of air ascent, the reliance on someone else to share and execute the skill properly was tenuous. The practice of it was diluted down to just swimming around in the shallows doing it.

Then the "octopus", a secondary air supply hose and mouthpiece came into use, adding to cost but adding safety. UNEXSO which prided itself on safely providing deep dives may have been the first to use it on all guided dives. Dave Woodward gets some credit for its "invention". The auxiliary air supply, "spare air", a small second tank with separate regulator was showing up by the 1970's. Bob and Bill Meistrell at Dive N' Surf were among the first retail stores and schools utilizing it. Dick Anderson, as a workshop engineer at Healthways, used to job small spare units together in the 1950's.

Looking at all the manuals over the 50 years, content changed in a more evolutionary way, not radically. Fins took on all kinds of shapes, were made of more comfortable materials, got longer but the skills in using them remained basic. But buoyancy, always a diving challenge, took a momentous turn in sport diving, as the BC, the Buoyancy Compensator, graduated from the simple vest to a system with intricate controls to maintain divers without effort at a neutral buoyant state at any depth and even picking up anchors or other heavy objects to add to their weighting during a dive. New kinds of dry suits required special instruction and new information appeared in the basic manuals. This special instruction would ultimately lead to specialty diving manuals in the 1980's and 1990's.

Free ascent, buoyant or swimming was another controversial issue and much more was said on it in the manuals. The rate of ascent was the most traceable specific change with coverage in manuals. Little bubbles followed was and is still a good rule of thumb but as for numbers, the manuals followed the U.S. Navy's 25 feet per minute, then with new experiments and experiences, 60 feet per minute became the allowable by the 1960's. By the 1980's, there was a shift back to 30 feet per minute and then 40 fpm, with the final conclusion; "the slower the better". The "safety stop" came into vogue for any dive, the stop at 15 feet for three minutes. The Mexican diving guides back in the early days may not have been too wild in utilizing slow slant ascents to achieve a rule of thumb avoidance of the bends.

As we have noted, no one is going to get in very much trouble by using one of the pioneer manuals.

The 1960's were James Bond Years for diving with dive travel beginning to emerge as jet planes filled the skies. New minds of fashion designed equipment filled the oceans. As we noted, the basic laws of physics and physiology remained constant.

Diving manuals would try to keep up with this cosmetic change of diving and even suggest new skill things to learn. Swimming ability was given less emphasis for entry level divers; a lot of people, who became dependent on the equipment itself to rescue them in an emergency, slipped in. The techniques of manipulating the equipment became more prominent. More recognition of special behaviors in different types of diving became recognized, more on kelp and currents, unique territorial hazards. As we noted already diving was moving toward special classes for special types of diving and special manuals to cover each one. Some of the

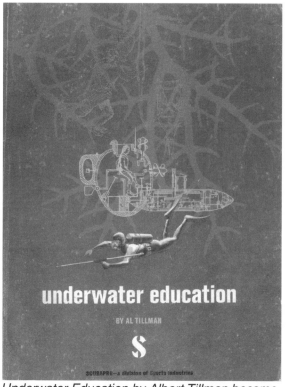

Underwater Education by Albert Tillman became a standard text in every diver's library. The above photo is of the first edition's cover. The book eventually went on to over 35 printings.

ominous edge, the warning and scaring nature of early manuals, got softened in keeping with the industry's concern that people's interest was not so much in hair-raising adventure as recreational fun.

The YMCA stuck with *The New Science of Skin and Scuba Diving* as a text.

The National Association of Underwater Instructors came into existence and wanted its own manual identification. Scubapro had come on the scene to challenge U.S. Divers dominance in the manufacture of equipment guided by the two veterans of Healthways and Sportsways, Gustav Dalla Valle and Dick Bonin. They contracted to publish the *Underwater Education* diving manual Al Tillman had written for the college market with Wm. C. Brown Company. *Underwater Education* came out under two different covers, one designed to make a splash in the commercial marketplace and in particular the dive stores that SCUBAPRO was wooing into their family of no discounting retailers. The developing NAUI organization in the early 1960's was under the management of Al Tillman and the Board of Directors who approved *Underwater Education* as the primary official text.

Al Tillman says that writing a manual in the early days was pretty much a paste-up job, getting your facts from the existing manuals like that of the U.S. Navy, Dave Owen's book and Cross's *Underwater Safety*. If all those books said the same thing about something like air embolism, it seemed like au-

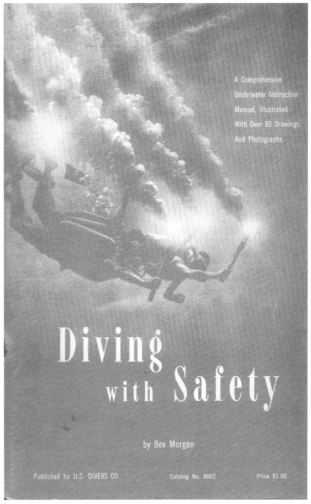

Bev Morgan's Diving with Safety.

thentic, documented information. Tillman had the Los Angeles County Underwater Program under his direction from 1954 to 1960 when he took over founding and running NAUI from 1960 to 1965. It embodied plenty of contact with top divers, instructors, and experts and served as substantiation for the few written sources.

It was a tough write and he wanted *Underwater Education* to be different and better than *Underwater Recreation*. He was involved in full time professorship at California State University at Los Angeles where he was the Chief Diving Officer, doing the media work for the Keller dive, producing an International Aquatics Exposition, staging the International Underwater Film Festival with Zale Parry, and sitting at night staring at blank paper with pen in hand while "drops of blood formed on his forehead" as Gene Fowler so cleverly metaphored it. But that manual emerged in two weeks while the publisher's son sat on his doorstep waiting for the original manuscript. It wasn't easy bluffing and saying "it's almost done", while staring at a page that only had the title written down.

At the time, Al wanted to put in case studies and stories that colored and reinforced the material - taken from first hand accounts of the outstanding divers of the time. The great lifeguard officer, Don St. Hill, who pioneered search and recovery for the Los Angeles County Lifeguard Service, largest in the world, showed Al how he held his breath so long while skin diving which he started doing in the 1930's.

"When you get on surface, don't act like you're trying to catch a train, relax, think of lying on the beach under a palm tree, then turn your head to the side and take deep breaths, in and out, about 3 or 4 times, then a half breath, then slip under with as little effort as possible, and glide down as effortlessly as possible." It was as good an explanation of how to hyperventilate as Al had heard and though he suspected Don didn't give a hoot about the physiological why of it all, it was certainly a working skill direction not as well explained from lab experiments.

125

While Al was interviewing Jim Christiansen, the Champion Spearfisherman, of the 1940's and 1950's, he took Al to his bedroom to show him how he trained for prolonged excursions under the sea.

"Sort of hulk over like this, all relaxed, then rear your shoulders back and fill your lungs to bursting, then relax forward letting it all out forcefully, 3 or 4 breaths, and I do it about 20 or 30 times before I go to bed." Jim then demonstrated, his enormous barrel chest swelling greatly and then he passed out on the bed. A few seconds passed and he looked up at Al -

"Oh yeah you got to be careful, blow out too much carbon dioxide and you get light headed and pass out - that's why I do it here by the bed."

KNOWLEDGE FROM ACTUAL EXPERIENCE

This gathering of actual experience was the way the Council for National Cooperation in Aquatics (began in 1951) took on setting up a model diving course in 1954-1955 and derived the *Science of Skin and Scuba Diving*. It pooled knowledge from experience of a dozen "experts". Conrad Limbaugh was probably the key source at that moment for the actual use of scuba - teaching others at Scripps Institution of Oceanography where he was the Chief Diving Officer.

Over the 50 years, debate was carried on about the necessity of good swimming ability, or what level of fitness, or how to test and know a diver was really ready to go on his own, or as noted before whether to engage in buddy breathing, or how to make the perfect free ascent. Setting hard and fast rules became questionable as equipment changed, as new safety was built into the equipment. Most of the early manuals could be picked up today if nothing else were available and guide a person along a fairly safe learning route to competency.

Diving for Fun, Joe Strykowski's manual for DACOR Corp. and its President, Sam Davison, was put out in 1971. We interviewed Sam a few years ago, after this book came out and asked, why Joe Strykowski? "Well, we're located in the Midwest and Joe's not just one of Midwest pioneer divers, but he's also one of the first instructors to be nationally certified by the YMCA in the 1950's and he knows our equipment and can write." But why another manual. "We thought the existing manuals ought to be stripped of all the 'sea stories' and other superfluous prose, and one written down to basics...but publication brings the diving manual up to date with the new exciting advances." Huh? The manual dismisses the rebreather concept (which emerged as a distinct possibility for deep long dives in the 1990's) and takes note of the Cryolung, mixed gases and even the artificial gill. It was a good working manual but didn't differ that much from what already existed.

One of NAUI's first instructors, out of Chicago, was Ralph Erickson. A solid aquatics professional, Ralph was destined to lead the way in pioneering diving instruction. This he did with John Cronin in founding the Professional Association of Diving Instructors, (PADI), in direct competition with the YMCA, NAUI and NASDS. Not satisfied there, Ralph authored his own diving manual. Erickson had written for and edited a number of diving publications to this point. So PADI which had U.S. Divers' backing through John Cronin supported his *Discover the Underwater World* in 1972. U.S. Divers was listed as publisher. But Ralph has integrity and although there are too many non-pertinent color pictures of Cousteau, it is a comprehensive well-written text. It didn't necessarily go beyond or replace the previous existing manuals.

A lot of good divers without more than their individual reputations were tossing their hoods in the ring of manual publishing. Usually the information fell in line with what had been printed before and so the public wasn't confused. Why did so many manuals get written? The writer-divers needed it as a credential, a passport to carry them to prominence and a larger role in leading sport diving thinking.

John Gaffney by hook and by crook put together the National Association of Scuba Diving Schools and he liked having his own materials to sell to his member dive shops. One of his important "products' was a diving manual called *Safe Scuba*. The manual was designed to fit into classroom modules with quizzes at the end of each section. John was taken with the way the ski industry did it and his overall approach was influenced by it. A scuba pioneer and a Los Angeles County Instructor and shop owner put the first manual together in 1971 but the 1978 *Safe Scuba* printing credits Richard Hammes and Anthony G. Zimos as authors. Leading up to Gaffney's ultimate concept of NASDS, were some very bright diving pioneers: Bill Hardy of San Diego Divers Supply, Bob Clark, who split off to form Scuba Schools International and Ed Brawley, who had one of the first diving stores in the world in San Francisco. *Safe Scuba* was well done and went into member stores' glass cases as a prime product. It deviated very little from the earlier manuals.

There is an attempt in *Safe Scuba* to present a different look at decompression tables but it is basically the U.S. Navy tables with better color graphics to aid in their use...and John decided to call them the "*Safe Scuba Diving Tables*". Computers eventually would almost eliminate the challenging task of manually computing dives on the tables in later years.

SSI under Bob Clark was looking for a good manual in 1975 that would be that organizations basic text. A company that puts out training manuals, Jeppersen was contacted and developed the *Open Water Sport Diver Manual*. No author is credited nor is SSI referred to. It was a well done manual but similar to its predecessors. NAUI had a deal with Jepperson about the manual that went sour.

Underwater Safety by E. R. Cross came out in 1954.

By the 1970's PADI had caught up with NAUI in the instruction field and NASDS was running a distant third. Bob Clark had left NASDS to set up SSI by 1970. All but NAUI had focused their main thrust for stability with the dive shop and the instructors aspect was integrated with the approach. NAUI lost some momentum by recognizing the instructor as the primary concern for its organization and trying to avoid the commercialism of dive instruction. None the less, NAUI began like the others to develop materials to sell to its members. The main saleable item was the C card, the official card establishing a diver is certified. Shops and instructors bought millions of these cards over the years but the specific official diving manual for each organization was a giant profit center.

The *PADI Open Water Diver Manual* had a polished, well-laid out look. Ralph Erickson still maintained a large writing role. Al Hornsby and Bob Wohlers were part of the production team and would be names to be reckoned with in future contributions to sport diving. NAUI moved its own text *The NAUI Instructor Handbook* strongly with its members at this time. SSI developed its own identity manual, *Open Water Diver*, by 1990 under Bob Clark's leadership and writing. NASDS was struggling in the competitive field of instructional organizations and would eventually merge with SSI which continued to grow in strength, mainly by requiring SSI stores to use only SSI instructors and SSI instructors could only teach at SSI authorized stores.

The basic beginning diver manuals were all looking very much alike. They needed very little change with time passing because series of specialty diving manuals joined the product proliferation. It was PADI who developed the first certification courses in Ice Diving, Cave Diving, Wreck Diving, and other specialized diving techniques. It didn't take long before night diving, dry suit use, computer use were among the topics of these books and divers were encouraged to build libraries for reference in the future.

Col. John D. Craig and Morgan Clint Degn put together a wonderful book, *Invitation to Skin and Scuba Diving* in 1965. It was a text for the late 1960's which served Los Angeles County after *Underwater Recreation*.

Independent efforts to publish popular training manuals outside the purview of the agencies was probably best achieved by Dennis Graver's *Scuba Diving*. Dennis had done much of the materials for NAUI and PADI moving from one to the other as training director. One of the most knowledgeable second generation pioneers around, he proved his expertise with the brilliant scuba quizzes in Skin Diver Magazine.

Another manual that emerged in the 1970's was designed for The National Oceanic and Atmospheric Administration, Manned Undersea Science and Technology Office, United States Department of Commerce, by many of the same smart diving pioneers, who played roles in consulting on all of the their manuals. NOAA,

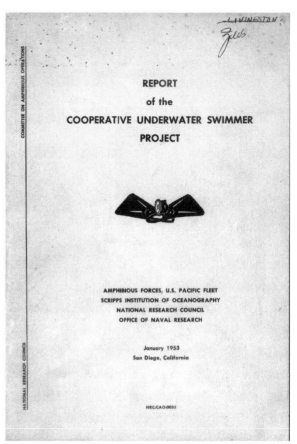

1953 manual created by the Office of Naval Research in cooperation with Scripps Institution of Oceanography. It is geared toward the UDT.

which took on many of the underwater projects of the National Science Foundation was prominent in providing diving scientists with habitat opportunities and supporting the creation of underwater parks and sanctuaries. Dr. Sylvia Earle is a prominent name in much of NOAA's best efforts for diving. The manual, *The NOAA Diving Manual: Diving for Science and Technology*, is slanted toward science divers and NOAA staff but it has an authoritative ring and did serve sport divers as well. It was a 9 x 11 publication originally available by 1975 through the U. S. Government Printing Office for $8.55.

The Complete Underwater Diving Manual was published by David McKay Company, Inc. New York and based on *The NOAA Diving Manual*. This book was much smaller in size and print font with same content. It sold for $8.95.

This history would be remiss in not recognizing, Owen Lee's *The Skin Diver's Bible* published in the early days and showed up on used book shelves over the long history of diving. Owen, a bright and excellent diver, was ubiquitous in diving, showing up at events and resorts and promoting every aspect of diving. A charming and sparkling personality, his *Bible* conveys all of that and was a well designed manual.

An Analysis of Methods Used to Teach Self-Contained Underwater Breathing Apparatus (SCUBA) Diving by Donald Michael Morrison in 1970 was distributed by Dive N' Surf, Inc. It truly was an analytical discussion on everything from literature, training techniques and skills, diving accidents, to safety precautions. Don scrutinized each progression in the entire teaching systems. As he summarized, "even within the 'recognized' training agencies, a lack of uniformity and confusion in systems of instruction has been found to exist." It was one of those "pick-a-little, talk-a-lot" inspections of what was already out there for the teaching tool and the safety of the student diver. Morrison didn't miss a beat with a lot of advice.

Hank and Shaney Frey's *Diver Below! The Complete Guide to Skin and Scuba Diving* with the Foreword by Dr. Joseph B. MacInnis, who expressed that the book is up to date (1969) in all aspects and respects of diving information. Skin diving, as well as scuba diving, are covered thoroughly for that generation. Because Hank loved underwater photography and did a fine job of it, the book is loaded with great photographs of divers in action taken by him and others. The drawings are by Shaney.

The 1957 *Complete Manual of Free Diving* was written by the members of the Undersea Research and Development Group of the French Navy which included Philippe Tailliez, Frederic Dumas, Jacques-Yves Cousteau, Jean Alinant, F. Devilla, R. Perrimond-Trouichet, and P. Cabarrow. The original book, *Diving in Diving Dress (Plongee En Scaphandre)* was done in 1949 and revised in 1957. The French origins for scuba in America are to be admired and respected. Although this book was translated, it never got wide attention. It's form and style did not seem to be appropriate for the American sport diver.

We suppose this chapter has little of the blood and guts, sex and excitement, political drama of most of the other chapter events but the diving manual was the rock in the wind for many divers, no matter who wrote it or sold it.

When Al Tillman met Tom Hemphill in the late 1980's, a highly successful dive shop and charter boat entrepreneur and key leader for a 1990's NAUI, instead of "Hello!", it was, "I learned to dive from *Underwater Recreation* and I still have my original copy."

A new generation diver in the Northwest encountered in the Puget Sound Region told us that she goes back to her SSI manual a lot, recalling how she had to show her husband, who had experienced vertigo on his first night dive, exactly what had happened in terms of spatial disorientation, (divers are fond of reciting the rare jargon of the underwater fraternity to the public. *Scuba America's* favorite has always been "caloric excitation of the vestibular apparatus" which would always turn heads.)

1952 diving manual published by the Bureau of Ships. Geared toward had hat divers.

In summary, we'll just tell you what we unlocked after all of our own experience, interviews and research. That some of the instruction manuals mentioned here had a shining moment for their time and some are still brilliant today.

And, so we end this chapter with our controversial selections. There are more astute, new dive leaders out there, who will take on the next 50 years by writing the "ultimate" great American diving manual that will be flawless and bring us completely up to date. (This history can afford a little fantasy conjecture.)

As Gustav Dalla Valle used to say, "You tella people what ever, but they only believea what is written down (in a manual)."

8

THE YMCA

DEFINING EVENT: FIRST INSTRUCTORS COURSE IN CHICAGO

The good old YMCA has been like a reliable and multi-talented uncle who seems to be able to do everything but is champion of none; who thought up new sports that others exploited into commercial successes. There was basketball, volleyball, fitness tests, skinny dipping and a whole lot of other worthwhile activities. The Y was there on the scene, programming, when the first breaths were sucked cautiously from the first scuba.

When the YMCA dipped its toe in the waters of this new activity of skin and scuba diving in the mid 1950's, it had about 700 swimming pools in America and around the world.

Those were mostly indoors and filled with children and adults learning to swim in heavily chlorinated water.

A lot of divers grew up in the YMCA programs and learned to swim in the nude back in the 1930's and 1940's. Al Tillman recalls how painfully embarrassing it was to many of the young boys who had not quite developed all their anatomy yet, and it probably retarded learning to swim for some.

The YMCA was a great idea generated in London, England to provide a pure and protected environment for young men who had left country places to come to the wicked city to work in factories initiated by England's industrial revolution... way back in the 1830's. Young men met to discuss Christian ideals but the idea of fitness through physical activity became important too with the exposure to disease and unsanitary conditions. Swimming pools were a much later development and primarily an American innovation.

Al Tillman was one of those boys who learned to play sports in YMCA Clubs. He recalls that the first level was for eight to ten year olds called "The Friendly Indians" (now "Gra-Y") and his club was the "Navajos". He led clubs and counseled at camp during his teens and was a locker attendant at the downtown Los Angeles YMCA. Eventually, he was assistant physical director at the Pasadena, California YMCA in 1949, got the physical Director Dave Daniels into skin diving which Al was deeply involved with then. Al says, "We took some of the Y boys to the ocean to watch us do it. From their enthusiasm, we knew that diving was going to be a big involvement for the YMCA down the line."

Why it didn't run wild with skin and scuba diving, solidify national control in America, was a repetition of how dozens of activities started by the YMCA have slithered away into the grasp of other more ambitious commercial organizations. First off, the YMCA has always moved slowly in changing its national profile and philosophy; speaking analogously, they debate what to feed the horses long after the automobile has replaced the buggy. As a national organization, it has been a large, unwieldy creature whose central headquarters could only suggest and philosophize, and then only after long listening periods and extended committee analysis-years dragged by.

The second reason for losing dominance over scuba instruction also explains its slow total organization reactions. Each YMCA operation in each small town or big city outpost is autonomous. Therefore, professional leadership varies in interest and abilities, and separate governing boards of each Y gives primary attention to local conditions and demands.

But if the Y as a total organization or association of branches failed to exercise a powerhouse follow-through in diving, it spawned an impressive number of graduates whose leadership has provided the thrust for other dominant projects and organizations over the past four decades.

THE YMCA SPAWNED LEADERS

There was Jon Hardy, who back in the 1950's as a teenager, got a good youth diving program going at the

Glendale, California YMCA. Glendale Y had Camp Fox over on Catalina Island and Jon got the diving bug there. The Glendale Y had an indoor pool, unique in that Southern California , because of its climate, tended to feature outside swimming pools. Hardy would eventually head up NAUI and be a major, professional consultant in diving.

Back in New England, the YMCA was very strong and featured indoor pools. In 1953, Frank Scalli went to the Huntington, Massachusetts, YMCA and took three lessons from an ex-navy frogman, Jim Cahill, and headed for the ocean. Scalli would set up the training program for the prestigious Boston Sea Rovers Club and in the late 1950's for all the YMCAs in the Northeastern United States. His training manual guided by the one from Los Angeles County given to him by Neal Hess, (Co-Founder of NAUI) was a main ingredient in composing the strongest YMCA contribution, *The Science of Skin and Scuba Diving* manual. Bernie Empleton recruited Scalli to serve on the new CNCA Committee on Skin and Scuba Diving in 1958. Frank Scalli became the first nationally YMCA Certified Instructor in New England by attending the First National YMCA Certification Course in Chicago in 1958.

Frank Scalli

Bernie Empleton, the Physical Director, at the Washington, D.C. YMCA had been appointed to head up the Skin and Scuba Diving Committee for the Conference for National Co-operation in Aquatics. CNCA had introduced the aquatics concern for this new sport at its 1954 meeting at Yale University. Meeting every four years allowed time for diving to evolve into a major recreational activity that demanded structured programming.

Local programs did abound, in particular the Los Angeles County operation and those of councils of diving clubs. The Underwater Society of America was just forming and politics kept it overwhelmed with bringing regional mentalities into cooperative effort. It was ripe for the YMCA to move aggressively into the opening.

THE CHICAGO INCUBATOR

Chicago was a powerful domain of the YMCA with the stronghold of advanced and very large skyscraper YMCAs. A strong leader, a Y Physical Director, Monte Topel, moved on the programming of a National Instructor Certification Institute for the YMCA. Empleton was deeply involved in getting out *Science of Skin and Scuba Diving* (which by the year 2000 had sold 2,000,000 copies) which he believed would be the unifying factor for diving in the YMCAs. But he was still listed as the Chicago Course's "Institute Director". Bernie, after returning from the 1954 CNCA Conference, had set up a prototype diving course that served as the foundation of the training manual.

It is probably a good assumption that Harold Friermood, the Executive Secretary of the National YMCA Physical Education Committee, realized that a wider involvement was needed to bring all YMCAs in support of the diving movement by the YMCA. Bernie Topel at the Chicago Downtown YMCA was probably a good move.

Chicago Y possessed over three-fourths of the indoor pools in the area during the 1950's and sucked in any and all new aquatic activities. Plus backyard Lake Michigan had all the attributes of a miniature ocean. Because of or in spite of the hard northern weather, Chicago saw the First YMCA Instructional Workshop launched there. Twenty-two out of the thirty-five in attendance were certified.

The Chicago program was the model around which the National YMCA program was built. A National YMCA Scuba Committee was formed and regional commissioners appointed. But in the Chicago area, where this Y program had its 1959 birth, there were dissenters. The Illinois Council of Diving Clubs had great numbers and the strength of an existing training program serving member clubs. Some of the dive shops were going their own way and independent instructors like Ralph Erickson, who would conceive PADI, were saying the YMCA screwed up diving training at the time and kept on doing it.

WEEKEND INSTITUTES

Monte Topel went on the road for the YMCA to provide a continuity in a series of regional weekend institutes staged to standardize, test and certify some professionals and a great majority of volunteer instructors.

At this point, the YMCA was barely ahead of the formation of NAUI and while both organizations were non-profit, the YMCA was a multi activity program while, NAUI was just for diving and independent instructors, who could teach anywhere. Revered and respected as the YMCA was, it had a certain restrictive aspect to it.

As Monte Topel moved about, the interest in the Y role in diving began to bloom. *The Science of Skin and Scuba Diving* with its copyright 1957 had been adopted by clubs, councils, and regional training programs everywhere. Many instructors drafted their personal course outlines from it. In Boston, Frank Scalli, who had gone through the 1959 Chicago Certification Workshop, directed the First National Certification Course in the Northeast attended by men like Jim Cahill, Fred Calhoun, and Frank Sanger.

The YMCA at the time was set up in 17 geographical administrative areas throughout the United States. Scuba program strength evolved at first in seven of them: New England, New York, Pennsylvania, Central Atlantic, Michigan, Illinois, North Central, and the Pacific Southwest. The Aquatics Commissioner in each of the areas appointed Skin and Scuba Diving Commissioners in turn to run certifying institutes and develop a YMCA instructor corp.

On the West Coast, the Pacific Southwest area, Aquatics Commissioner Fred Cope, chose as his Scuba Commissioner, Al Tillman. This area was heavily influenced by the Los Angeles County Program which already had four organized years of success in the training field. Many of the Los Angeles County's certified instructors used YMCA pools so dual certification became a status symbol, as well as, practical insurance for tenure at the Y facility.

Because of a visionary physical director and a strong in-house diving club spearheaded by Bert Fulwider, the Sacramento YMCA was cho-

Bernie Empleton

A 1960 YMCA Scuba Instructor Certificate.

sen as the site of the First West Coast Regional Certification Institute in 1960, strategically removed from the heartland of scuba instruction, Southern California. Monte Topel was on hand to represent the national interests and Al Tillman directed the institute. Two significant veteran dive instructors came through it: Jon Hardy and Bill Jeffs.

The next year, Tillman appointed Jon Hardy to direct the Y's invasion of the Los Angeles area with an institute at the Alhambra, California, YMCA. Dual Los Angeles-YMCA Certification became a desired status. There were several strong Y programs in the 1950's even before this national coverage: Rory Page and Harry Vetter at the Long Beach YMCA; Sacramento with Bert Fulwider; the Santa Monica YMCA with Eugene Poole and Dick Samp; Glendale Y with Jon Hardy; Pasadena Y with Bill Jeffs; San Diego with John Kenney; and the Hollywood YMCA with Bill Wilde and Al Tillman.

Elsewhere there was the Seattle YMCA, the San Francisco YMCA, Washington, D.C. Y with Bernie Empleton and Jim Young and New Haven Y with Paul Tzimoulis. These 1950's programs all gave strong foundation to the emerging National YMCA picture. Down South, especially involving Florida, the YMCA institute was hosted by Gene Vezzani at Atlanta, Georgia. Vezzani was a forceful political figure in the forming of the Underwater Society of America and various spearfishing competitions. A young Y professional and diving enthusiast, Ken Brock, came out of that institute. But it was Vezzani and the Atlanta institute that played a major role in eliminating Monte Topel from his strong leadership role coming out of the 1950's.

As the story goes, Monte, a suave yet virile handsome specimen of YMCA physical fitness, took advantage of Vezzani's housekeeper. Vezzani complained to higher authorities in the YMCA and in the interests of shielding the high moral reputation of the YMCA, Monte Topel was banished from his professional YMCA career.

Into the gap left by Topel, stepped Y professional Bernie Empleton of the Washington, D.C. YMCA and another Chicagoan, YMCA Physical Director, John T. Moloney. The National Scuba Committee was then composed of Frank Scalli, James E. Young, Bernard J. Empleton, and John T. Moloney.

But they exercised little control over the many autonomous branches with their individualized programs. Beyond the initial printed format of class procedure and standard minimum course content, the credentials and emblems were released like ad pamphlets dropped from an airplane. No central office was officially supervising the quality or legitimacy of any of the programs. In a few instances, cards were given away upon request of a local Y. In specific spots, a few we've mentioned, the YMCA with indoor pool facilities and ready made student interest from members of the Y, conducted blue ribbon classes in many ways superior to the more regimented and sophisticated courses machined for the almost robotized divers of later years. These very good classes are best identified by a criterion on longevity, scuba programs that ran continuously through the 1950's, 1960's and 1970's and beyond.

The YMCA's role in the national training picture got evaluated several times. Two dynamic leaders in diving training history reacted as follows:

Fred Calhoun in making a report as Training Director for the Underwater Society of America, and on the New

An early YMCA course.

R. Cahill

England Board for YMCA Scuba Instructor Certification along with Frank Scalli, Paul Tzimoulis and Paul Hennessy, said that the National YMCA Program of Instructor Certification suffered from a lack of standardization. He felt the diver training course was a good standard. But there was nothing comparable for instructor testing. He cited the problem of autonomy of area YMCA's with no quality control. Certifications of instructors differed...one YMCA to another. Fred pointed out there was no existing ties with the Underwater Society of America and he politely offered assistance to the YMCA program which he saw as "an honest and sincere endeavor".

A MODEL PROGRAM

A good example of a local YMCA, inland at that, was the program initiated by Ivor Thompson and Jay Hytone in Des Moines, Iowa. Ivor got his first SCUBA from a widow of a guy who had drowned in 1957 at the same time he arrived at the Des Moines YMCA as physical director. He went to a 1958 certification in Minneapolis but it turned out it was ahead of its time and there was yet no official national certification. But Ivor Thompson with the Y director, who taught him to dive , put out Des Moines Y C-Cards. The diving in open water was in a strip mine. He put through about 1700 people before he got certified to certify instructors and put on the first sanctioned Instructor Institute of Midwest at Cedar Rapids with 25 candidates of which half passed. Ivor was an appointed

Commissioner of the Y for the region during the 1960's and regrets that no records were kept. The National Committee asked for no reports. As a manual, Ivor had been using *SCUBA II* and *Let's Go Diving* but went with *The New Science of Skin and Scuba Diving* in 1962 Then Jay Hytone entered the picture and took over scuba for Ivor. The Y acquired a compressor and twenty-four complete rigs and more than 90% of students going through were not even YMCA members but joined for scuba. While some flew off to Cozumel and Hawaii, most put up with six-foot-visibility in local lakes. During this period, the Y leased an entire resort on a clear Minnesota lake some 500 miles away.

By 1966 there was a huge decline in interest, the impact of *Sea Hunt* and Cousteau was fading, and the Des Moines Y almost quit on the classes. Ivor and Jay went to the nearby university and got them to give Physical Education Credits. Attendance soared with thirty in a class and five instructors teaching. Jay discovered Cozumel on the map and went there, sending Ivor a postcard saying "clean up the pool". The clear water simply exploded interest that made dive trips to Cozumel an integral part of the Y diving in Iowa and Nebraska and also led to yearly caravans down to the Florida Keys. Amazingly, the only contact that this program really had with the outside world of diving was *Skin Diver Magazine*. A national reference point for information was never established.

TRIAD CERTIFICATION

Al Tillman recalls the impactful time he was YMCA Scuba Commissioner for the Pacific Southwest. "I loved the Y! It raised me as a kid and as a volunteer. I worked out of the old downtown YMCA for Fred Cope, overseeing the spotty YMCA programs we had at the time. Basically, it was to get some instructors certified. This was 1960 and I had just helped launch NAUI after a decade of Los Angeles County Underwater Program direction. I ran the only Los Angeles County/NAUI/YMCA Basic Scuba Course, certainly the first, at the Hollywood YMCA.

"I can't remember getting any direct communication about what to do from any YMCA National Committee, nothing. I liked Bernie Empleton, John Moloney and Frank Scalli a lot, but I felt they just wrote us off as too far away or something. So we just went ahead with what we felt was right for the Y in the Pacific Southwest. When NAUI decided to establish a base of instructor certification in Los Angeles region, taking on a program I'd started, we scheduled a local NAUI UICC (later called ITC) and joined it with a YMCA institute. Many excellent County instructors crossed over, and went through it to come up with a triad certification. Some important people, who went through it, were Larry Cushman, Gary Rubottom, Dewey Bergman, and Roy Damron.

"I'm not sure whether it enforced the Y's role or diluted it over the long course, but at the time it gave the YMCA status along with the two most

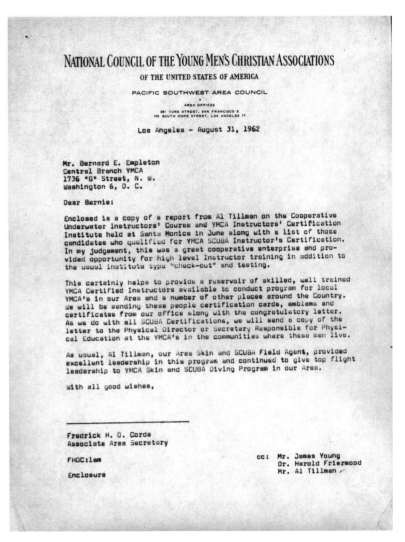

Letter to Bernie Empleton about the first cooperative certification course. The course was directed by Albert Tillman in Santa Monica in 1962.

powerful certification agencies in America."

The local YMCA scuba programs had impactful institutes and seminars all through the 1960's and a few held their own against the powerhouse of the time, NAUI. The arrival of two more commercially oriented programs were NASDS and PADI; both of which had established their positions through the dive shops. It is important to note here that dive shops and YMCAs in remote places often worked together effectively.

The Y's influence in scuba spread beyond the United States. In faraway places with great diving waters, the Y director with a diving interest would run a training program. In the Bahamas, about the same time as UNEXSO was emerging in the mid-1960's a new YMCA was started up in a trailer. The Y decided to run a diving program for the locals while UNEXSO serviced the tourist crowd.

The Y program actually took away a market portion from UNEXSO, the locals, which the resort needed to operate during slack tourist times. But the Y was doing what it should have been doing. "UNEXSO just has to do it better," said Bill McInnes, an owner/partner of UNEXSO.

FINALLY A NATIONAL DIRECTOR

Enter Ken Brock, who had gotten interested in diving as a little boy in Pensacola, Florida, where "fascinated, he'd be able to sit and watch peculiar behavior of one little fish." Ken took over the YMCA operation at Grand Bahama in 1969 and built a strong program and expanded the diving involvement. He felt the lack of a national point of reference, a National Headquarters and Director. The same year, he attended the Fourth YMCA Aquatics Conference in Ft. Lauderdale, where they were still discussing the idea from the 1967 Conference of turning the National Program over to NAUI...the Y Program seemed to be going down the tubes. Brock says, "John Moloney, the National Aquatics Committee Chairman, said that they were going to take a major step by setting up subcommittees to spawn ideas and the YMCA would do them. Out of it, came a National Headquarters and a National Director. Frank Scalli, Chairman of the National Scuba Committee said, "It's about time. Let's find somebody good." It took until 1972 before they did, appointing Ken Brock over Joe Strykowski.

By 1976, Frank Scalli, who had been on Advisory Boards for the Y, NAUI and PADI, dropped off the Y Board as did Bernie Empleton. The new Board of Robert Smith, as Chairman, Joe Strykowski and Tom Mount came on with full support of what Ken Brock had been doing over the preceding four years.

Brock had moved around the country to Y's and seminars and conventions with exciting display exhibits touting the YMCA scuba program. He got out a unifying newsletter, *Ascent Lines*, and developed all new certifying materials. He served on the National Scuba Committee and helped draft a reciprocal agreement on minimum standards. He elimi-

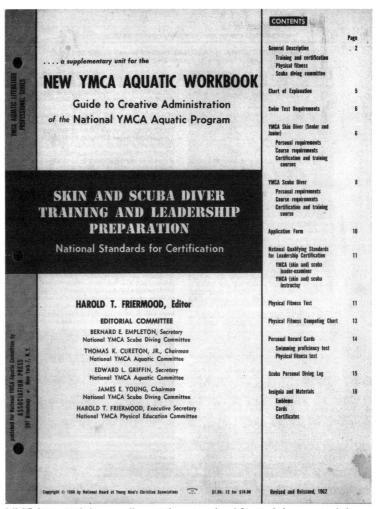

YMCA materials usually set the standard for training materials.

137

nated the Y's weekend certification institute and put in seven-day-courses.

Despite the long overdue National Center for local YMCA diving programs, the future came too fast for, as we have said, the YMCA is a cautious, slow moving operations. Ken Brock wanted to do it yesterday and he made his superiors and elders in the YMCA hierarchy nervous. But PADI and the new SSI Training Agencies were charging ahead, running neck and neck with NAUI and NASDS by the mid-1970's. To some extent the rank and file out in the field, those local YMCA's were making very little input, being politically oriented to what was happening in their communities right there in front of them.

The YMCA involvement in diving in the pioneer years brought a strong, revered institution that had always had a strong aquatics program into the diving field. It might have had the momentum to capture the overall dominance over diving training except for several things:

1. Despite having a lock on indoor pools everywhere, many of them were old and uninviting. Dive shops put in their own training pools, private fitness clubs with pools sprang up and parks and recreation departments constructed many new ones.

2. The YMCA is a nonprofit Christian institution and not attuned to the high-powered marketing of commercially oriented rivals.

3. The YMCA was just too spread into autonomous facilities that had to respond to local conditions and made up their own rules. There was no official national director or headquarters to turn to. Bernie Empleton was a much admired guru for the YMCA Program and his leadership in developing *Science of Skin and Scuba Diving* certainly provided a high profile symbol of YMCA's role in diving but grass roots contacts were ephemeral if not non-existent.

4. The regional areas of YMCA were each protective of their own way of doing things. Y certified instructors from one area had to process through another institute in any new area they went to.

Jon Hardy in 1976 as General Manager of NAUI and representing the newly formed National Scuba Training Council through it's National Scuba Advisory Committee (Sometimes over-organization and a proliferation of agency and committee names served to confuse bureaucrats and the public.) prepared a comprehensive document to show how diving was self-regulating itself through the various agencies involved with training divers. It was a biased but well thought out presentation. He identified the National YMCA SCUBA Program as officially starting with its First Instructor Institute in California (Sacramento). He lists the Y at this point in time as having certified 2600 instructors and 99,000 students. He notes that the Y's mission is to give people a new possibility through SCUBA to enjoy as full and complete a life as possible. The Y is not driven by profit motives was Jon's conclusion.

The YMCA diving survived through the 1970's 1980's and 1990's but it must be remembered that the YMCA is made up of a large diversified menu of programs, some long established over the century and diving was a new thing in aquatics demanding special equipment that often chipped sacred pool tiles. Scuba air had to be obtained from diving shops, some seeing the Y as competition and were uncooperative.

It is often asked, why the YMCA got into a parallel swimming/aquatics program with the Red Cross? It just happened because people in each case decided that there was a calling and they moved to fill it. Why didn't the Red Cross move into diving in the early days? There were places where the Red Cross took charge and programmed skin and scuba diving. A pioneer leader was John Jones, Jr. in Fort Lauderdale, Florida. John was a director of the Red Cross Chapter there, primarily in charge of water safety and swimming. His senior and junior programs had well constructed outlines that served as models for NAUI's first basic training courses. The Fort Lauderdale Red Cross diving was up and running closely behind the Los Angeles program and John and Al were in close touch in those years exchanging ideas. When Neal Hess and *Skin Diver Magazine* decided to sponsor a national program, it was to Jones and Tillman they turned.

The two set up the curriculum and testing for the First NAUI Course in Houston, Texas, which in a way closed off Los Angeles County's guiding role and John Jones' Red Cross efforts which might have been the igniting spark for the Red Cross full involvement nationally.

Al Tillman looking at the Los Angeles Program that was the forerunner of all public training programs says, "I taught Water Safety Instructors for the Red Cross back in the 1950's and I incorporated some diving into the classes. I think the Red Cross, nationally, felt that was sufficient coverage at the time. It might have been enough except for the equipment which made it complex. I saw it as a brand new sport and needing special classes. So we put it into our overall sports program for the County of Los

YMCA course held at Catalina Island in 1972. Ken Brock pointing the way - the Y way.

Ken Brock

Angeles. It could easily gone into the Red Cross Aquatics Program as it did with the YMCA. But I remember Red Cross people investigating the possibility, meeting with me and the Los Angeles County Lifeguard people but they decided they had their hands full already. The commercial interests pushed diving into a different realm, akin to skiing, lots of special equipment and special places needed to do it. Personally, I like the YMCA being involved but they peaked out, missed too many opportunities, and the future is being scooped up by private, profit-making entities."

Another important reason the YMCA would pick up a national and worldwide program in scuba diving was its recognition as the largest nonprofit community service organization in the world. In contrast to the Red Cross which had no aquatics facilities, the YMCA had 2200 YMCAs in America (by the year 2000) and 1700 swimming pools. The public could trust the YMCA.

If we follow up in more detail the reign of Ken Brock as National Director, we find the advent of computers creating a fast communications link with the spread out YMCA Branches. In 1976, the National YMCA Scuba Underwater Activities Program (whew!) was established in an office in Key West, Florida. The YMCA now moved into advanced diver training following the lead of NAUI, PADI, NASDS and SSI. It operated a national college there for YMCA diving instructors.

Some other firsts credited to the Y at the time was putting together a Scuba Lifesaving and Accident Management Course technology that went into a 1978 publication. In 1978 the first International Hockey Championships were conducted at the YMCA Scuba Convention in Miami, Florida.

CMAS EQUIVALENCY

In early 1980, the World Underwater Federation (CMAS) granted equivalency to YMCA SCUBA instructors and divers. CMAS is composed of 12,000 diving clubs and 3.5 million divers from around the world. The same year, a Bernard E. Empleton Society Award was established in order to preserve a living testimonial to the work of

Bernie Empleton in developing the YMCA Diving Program. Additionally, the YMCA has a lifesaving award (1981) to recognize an act of heroism in saving a fellow diver.

In 1985, the YMCA became part of a national committee to develop standards for training for entry level scuba certification. The YMCA joined PADI, NAUI, NASDS, SSI on the Recreational SCUBA Training Council (RSTC) which oversees The ANSI (American National Standards Institute) SCUBA Instructional Standards. In 1990, the YMCA conducted a full scholarship Instructor Course at Ball State University in Muncie, Indiana with thirty-six YMCA's represented.

THE MODERN YMCA SCUBA PROGRAM

In 1999, the YMCA Celebrated its 40th Anniversary and its role in expanding the opportunities to learn and go diving beyond the dive shops and other more profit-oriented outlets. The Y's national online website says that the Y will enter a new century with a continuing mission of providing SCUBA diving opportunities to YMCA members and the public of their various communities.

The modern YMCA National Scuba Program has taken on the current issues of diving and has shaken off its early years image of slow, plodding, locally controlled and general old-fashioned thinking. By year 2000, the Y worries about extreme diving: the mixed gases, staged decompression, deeper and longer high-tech diving which is being pushed upon the general diving public as the recreation diving of the future. Generally, the YMCA sees the casual sport diver being intimidated out of sport diving as it has been for almost 50 years, safe and simple. The YMCA could be the last protesting philosophy to retain sport diving as it has been for a half-century and more. The YMCA will continue to be on hand to perhaps prevent a monopoly by any one instructional agency and provide an environment to learn diving with concern for body, mind and spirit. Maybe it can all be summed up by Bernie Empleton, who told us, "Trust the Y, it's the place where I'd want to send my family to learn."

APPENDIX

• The National YMCA Headquarters in year 2000 was in Norcross, Georgia.

• THE BERNARD EMPLETON AWARD

The YMCA recognizes Bernie Empleton who died in 1980 as "the father of recreational diving instruction. The award in his name is the Y's highest scuba award. He was the major force behind the most popular manual, *The Science of Skin and Scuba Diving*. A typical recipient was Bill Athow who was inducted into the "Empleton Society" with the award in 1998. He spent thirty years, four nights a week teaching scuba at several YMCAs. He served on the YMCA National Committee and the Recreational Scuba Training Council in the 1980's. In the 1970's, he spearheaded the YMCA's Crossover Institutes which recruited instructors from other training agencies into the YMCA Program.

• A newsletter *Currents* is a current comprehensive coverage of what is happening in diving and the YMCA role in it. It is part of the reason the YMCA Scuba Program survived the decades.

The following is the roster of persons who attended the First National YMCA Scuba Instructor Institute held in Chicago, Illinois, during August 1959. The institute was directed by Bernie Empleton with associate, Monte Topel.

Mary Alice Brennan
Leo Darwit
Jerry Dzindzeleta
Bernard E. Empleton
Covert G. Franzen
Loyal G. Goff
Gerald F. Harris
H. J. Keithline

June Kieser
Roy Kieser
Rev. Edward H. Lanphier, M.D.
Dr. Paul G. Lineweaver, Jr.
Richard W. Malpass, Jr.
Jack Mountford
Al Mueller
Wallace Mundell
Elmer Munk
David M. Owen
Frank J. Scalli
Monte Topel
Dan Wagner
R. G. Wasson
James E. Young

YMCA SCUBA PROGRAM COMMITTEE CHAIRS
James E. Young
John T. Moloney
Frank J. Scalli
Robert W. Smith
Joe Strykowski
Spencer Slate
Thomas R. Leaird in 2000

YMCA SCUBA PROGRAM DIRECTORS
Ken Brock
Robert Smith
Robert Freeman
Millard D. Freeman, Jr.
Frankie Wingert
Craig S. Jenni
Thomas E. Clark in 2000

BERNARD E. EMPLETON SOCIETY
Bernard E. Empleton
John T. Moloney
Edgar End, M.D.
Joe Strykowski
Jay M Hytone
Loyal G. Goff
Albert L. Pierce
James A. Horstman
Rev. Edward Lanphier, M.D.
Frank J. Scalli

David Brittig
James E. Young
June M. Kieser
Thomas R. Leaird
Millard D. Freeman, Jr.
Ron Nelson
William Naughton
Frankie Wingert
Harold L. Maples
Joseph R. Dabbs
Frank Best Thompson
William Athow
Spencer Slate

YEAR 2000 COMMITTEE MEMBERS
Thomas R. Leaird - Chairman
Peter Plocher
Rena Bonem, Ph.D.
Ellen Keller
Spencer Slate
Dr. Duke Scott
Kenneth Nemeth
Samual Scott
Glennon Gingo

Approximate total of divers certified since 1959: 800,000 divers.
Estimate due to the lack of many certifications on a computer database.

9
LOS ANGELES COUNTY: CRUCIBLE FOR AMERICAN DIVING INSTRUCTION

DEFINING EVENT: THE FIRST UNDERWATER CERTIFICATION COURSE - 1955

What was that one bright and shining moment, volcano spewing event, that defines the impact of a long term happening in diving? Many of us can't or just refuse to be that specific. Which brick in the building holds it up?

The Los Angeles County Program of diving instruction brought the arrival of scuba into an orderly perspective. In the early 1950's there was a slow, ragged weaning of skin divers through this transitional technology.

In 1952, a memorandum arrived on the desk of Norman S. Johnson, the CEO of the Los Angeles County Department of Parks and Recreation. We are printing that memorandum here in its entirety because it laid the foundation for all public diving instruction.

****

June 10, 1952

To: Paul Gruendyke, Director LA County Parks and Rec.
From: Al Tillman, Sports Director
Subject: Skin Diving Classes

A new sport - skin diving - is becoming popular in the area. Recently while diving in Palos Verdes, I ran into several divers in the water with me who didn't know what they were doing. One had one of the new underwater breathing units that allows divers to stay under for long periods of time. I have purchased this equipment for evaluation.

The Palos Verdes area in question is not covered by the Lifeguards and serious problems could arise if an accident occurs and if the County doesn't act proactively. This activity falls into the sports category and I propose that my department get involved in this sport and provide training classes. I believe that diving will grow in the future and we have an obligation to make the sport as safe as possible.

Let's get together soon to discuss the possibilities of a County sponsored training program.

cc: N. S. Johnson
    Chuck Bollinger

Los Angeles County's first instructor certification course open water exams. Al Tillman (far left) is evaluating and Bill Starr is on the far right. The course was loaded with pioneers such as Bev Morgan, Bob and Bill Meistrel, Chuck Sturgill and Paul McComack.

E. R. Cross

Just a memo that could have been absorbed into a stack of idea memos that were coming across an administrator's desk. It was the year of a momentous transition of one of the world's largest parks and recreation operations. Los Angeles County was being balkanized into a checkerboard of small incorporated cities. Citizens wanted more local control and ambitious others saw the opportunity to rule over their communities.

The County recreation operation to survive, as a major department of County government, had to reach out for a new role. It went from a line organization with employees on recreation areas with a hierarchy of supervisors going up the line of authority to a predominantly staff development with specialists in a central office providing programs of a regional scope—therefore, programs such as adult softball leagues on a large center serving several cities and unincorporated areas.

The County could afford at this moment of change to experiment, actually had no alternative but to take on a more sophisticated functioning. What could LA County do that the smaller cities couldn't do for themselves? In addition, these challenges were still in the pre-commercial-era of recreation before the explosion of amusement parks, travel, resorts and fitness centers.

So the memo directed from the then acting Director of Sports to his boss suggested two new program areas to pursue. No question bicycling could have been organized into a broad, popular addition to what the department had to offer but scuba diving was more exotic, a startlingly new sport and certainly made the most of LA County's prime territory, the shoreline and beaches.

Unquestionably, an individual pushes hard for a personal passion in his work venue. Al Tillman, as sports director, was motivated to inject a new look into the existing traditional program he inherited from Chuck Bollinger, who had moved up into the number two spot administratively in the department under Norm S. Johnson, who became the Director of Parks and Recreation. Both Bollinger and Johnson were relatively young and open minded and gave strong support to Tillman.

It is necessary here to delve somewhat into the politics of a government agency. There is a unique separation in this department between a division called The Lifeguard Service and the downtown "rekeration guys", as the beach situated lifeguards referred to the parks and recreation divisions in downtown Los Angeles. The lifeguards strongly felt they were a safety operation like sheriffs and firemen which provided grander perks such as early retirement and hazard pay. They saved people from drowning primarily, and programming activities was a secondary aspect. They wanted to stay at the beach but the various swimming pools, mainly summer outdoor facilities, were under their jurisdiction. All of this would change in the years to follow and lifeguards would get their wish.

The complication was that skin and scuba diving was a sport but it was based in the water environment. So where did it belong? The lifeguards were to a man, all divers of course, and powerful politically with LA County's top elected officials...who were often wined and dined at spaghetti-abalone feeds in the company of the rugged and glamorous lifeguards. (Los Angeles County Lifeguards would eventually serve as the model for the popular television show *Baywatch* forty plus years later.)

Anyway, that bright and shining moment for diving instruction could well have been that one memo in 1952 that opened a big door to a brand new way for government to guide a new sport into orderly existence. The Lifeguard Division insisted that one of theirs should physically spearhead the setting up of classes in diving instruction but the Department wanted the original memo writer and the Sports Director to represent —let's say the "downtown office" and sports— as a consultant.

The memo was important just as the original writings, the Federalist papers, suggested creating a country, like America. Or perhaps we might imagine, Orville writing a shop note to Wilber Wright in their bicycle shop— "people are going to try and fly, Will, maybe we could design something that would do that." Anyway, what triggered that memo?

BASIS FOR "THE MEMO"

Sports director, Al Tillman, back in 1952, was living by the ocean in Redondo Beach, California, where as a kid he'd had his first experience in diving. Every morn-

Instruction on the proper use of equipment is presented by Bill Walker at Los Angeles County's first instructor certification course. Course Director Al Tillman is on the far left with other pioneers such as Bill Starr, Rusty Williams, Herb Barthels, a sleeping Bobby Meistrell, Paul McComack, Bill Jeffs, Julie Arenstein and Johnny Josephs.

E. R. Cross

ing before heading into downtown Los Angeles to his office at the LA County headquarters, he'd be trying to fill his passionate lust for exploring underwater by wading through the shore rocks into the cold mysterious world off Palos Verdes. It was a premier world diving spot, congested with marine life and beds of kelp and clear water. It was also a great wild, unpopulated slice of watery paradise right on the edge of a highly developed urban region. Tillman went diving alone simply because there wasn't anybody else available or he knew that lived close to him.

One day out in the water off Flat Rock, Al Tillman came face to face with another diver for the first time on one of these mid-week morning dives. Oh no! There goes the neighborhood, the wildness, the exclusive private "rights". Worse- —he was facing not just another diver but one with a loaded speargun pointed directly at him. "Hi!", this careless intruder sputters, "did you see that weird fish on the bottom down there?" "Please! Point that gun some place else," grumps Tillman, who is thinking that there is some village missing an idiot and he's trespassing in my ocean. "Yeah, okay, I'm going to spear that fish" and this stranger in a flailing of fins and himself splashes under and clumsily bicycles his way down. He jams his spear point into the guitar shaped fish and fires.

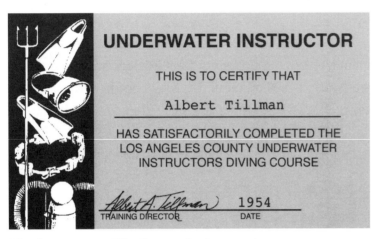

First instructor certification card.

Immediately, grasping the shaft of the imbedded spear, he reacts by being thrown backwards then comes pawing desperately to the surface.

He holds his hand in Tillman's face and wide-eyed burbles, "that thing shocked me or something". Okay, moron, it was an electric ray. One of those marine hazards that we'd all have to learn about in the ensuing years. At that point, Al Tillman realized that his ocean was going to see a lot more "idiots" trying in ignorance to become divers. He thought, "Well we teach baseball and basketball and we'd better teach people how to dive, too." That very day, he sat at his desk and scrolled off the memo that began the long odyssey toward the multi-million dollar sophisticated private instructional programs that would guide and direct diving for millions, upon millions, of addicts worldwide.

At that point, LA County got double lucky—first in getting a passionately motivated diver in a main office administrative position to push and support the Department's involvement in a new sport; and second, in a brilliant waterwise, beach lifeguard assigned to put together the program.

BEV MORGAN

Enter Bev Morgan talented, intelligent, flowing with ideas. Bev shook the sand from between his toes, not easily, and applied himself to the challenge, (on the days when the surf wasn't up; he was a top-notch surfer as well as a diver). Morgan and Tillman had both come off of the Los Angeles mean streets and were compatible, another great break.

Sample of one of the first Scripps Certification Cards.

It was mutually decided that a point of authority was necessary to give the classes credibility. Where did you go to get that? Los Angeles County approved Bev and Al going to the highly respected Scripps Institution of Oceanography in La Jolla, California and taking instruction under Conrad Limbaugh, who oversaw the diving activity there as a graduate student. Limbaugh, another brilliant rebel (not very tolerant of those "suit and tie guys") had been putting on scientific diving classes, not well structured but effective for getting budding oceanographic types underwater to really see what was there. Connie and Bev were instantly kindred souls and in that decade of pioneer diving, would be mutually inspiring to each other.

Bev and Al brought back a sort of "seal of approval" for themselves and to use to hoist the sails of the LA County instruction program. Even more authority evolved through a Board of Advisors made up of Limbaugh, E. R. Cross, Dr. Robert Livingston, and Fred Schwankowsky, all pioneers of diving in the early 1950's. Bev designed the first diving classes with Al to follow a pattern similar to the Red Cross Water Safety Classes. There were three classes: Beginning Skin Diving, Advanced Skin Diving, and Scuba Diving. It was expected that everybody would fill the skin diving classes which required little equipment but the big surprise was the interest in scuba was soaring.

Classes were given in Lakewood, Arcadia, and East Los Angeles in outdoor LA County pools in the evening during early summer. They filled up with people coming to the scuba class with borrowed equipment. The classes were heavily based on safety.

Guest VIP divers were invited to talk to classes, including Mel Fisher and some of the old time diving lifeguards. Bev was Chief Instructor aided by another young 21-year old lifeguard, Ramsey Parks, who would go on to become another diving legend.

Bev did his research and produced the LA County's first diving manual *Underwater Safety* patterned after the LA County's lifeguard manual, well illustrated in cartoon style. It sold nonprofit for $1.00 per copy and took a simpler approach than the E. R. Cross's *Underwater Safety* or Dave Owens *A Manual for Free Divers* all of which were key research resources at that time.

LA County was seriously into programming diving by the end of that 1954 summer. Then tragedy struck. In the physical exam Bev and Al had to take to go to Scripps, the Civil Service Unit picked up on a deficiency in Bev's eye exam and ruled that he was not qualified to be a lifeguard. Bev's appeal was that his eye sight was hurt by staring into the afternoon sun, a hazard of all Pacific Coast lifeguards watching swimmers in the glaring water. The appeal failing, Bev felt betrayed by LA County and left to begin a long commercial diving career that is now legend. It was a serious loss to the newborn Underwater Program but not a death blow.

The Lifeguard Service at this point, the fall of 1954, lost interest and the Underwater Program went directly under the Sports Division and its director, Al Tillman. Administration did not really want a division head traipsing about teaching classes and so Al Tillman decided that LA County could get out of the public class business, always an unpopular idea, that was competing with commercial enterprises. The dive shops, especially, wanted dive classes in their hands where the sale of equipment could be influenced by loyal employee instructors. It was time to move into the "regional mode", that of the County training instructors who would adhere to standards and ethical practices. And so for 1955, a series of Underwater Instructors Certification Courses (the UICC's) were planned.

TRAINING INSTRUCTORS

At this point, Al's diving partner since 1953, was brought into a part time position to do a lot of the planning and leg work leading up to the 1UICC at the new Lynwood Natatorium. Bill Starr was a passionate diver, bright and a good organizer. He was meticulous about details; you could watch the careful way he took care of his equipment, the powdered, folded-proper Bel Aqua suit coming out of his rubber pack looking like it had been pressed, told it all. He had gone to the first public class with a borrowed scuba unit from Al Tillman. Bill Starr pitched in with Al Tillman to set up a curriculum for the Lynwood Instructor Course, and to develop a new diving manual that had a more positive fun approach, moving from Bev's black covered *Diving Safety Manual* to a colorful upbeat publication. Al Tillman surveyed leading name divers of the era for a nominated new Board of Advisors retaining Cross, Limbaugh, but adding many new names to give broader perspective and support. Such a board cleared away any opposition.

A lot of concern was given at the time and since as to whether this was truly a training course or just a testing device to hand out certifications. In some movement away from the original concept the "Certification" designation was replaced with "training". Actually, the first courses were a combination of training and testing. It should be remembered that the candidates in the One UICC were for the most part a bunch of experienced, if not formally trained real divers.

Al Tillman's 1955 Impression of the First Los Angeles County Underwater Instructors Course (1UICC):

There wasn't a pretty face in the lot. The weathered and lined faces of the twenty assorted water-type men who sat hunched forward on the damp aluminum bleachers in the Lynwood Natatorium in April 1955 were screwed up in unaccustomed attentive thought. They were to be the avant wagon masters of an explosive trek West of West, taking millions of Americans safely into and under the Pacific Ocean off the California Coast.

At that moment, however, they were midway through the first of 47 consecutive UICCs or Underwater Instructor Certification Courses to be held over the next 45 years by the year 2000. They were straining water-thickened eardrums to hear about the "new fangled machine" that had suddenly arrived to become an odd member of the aquatics family of pool and beach activities. These were old water dogs for the most part, even the kid, 23 year old Faye Fletcher, was already a veteran of fifteen years of around-the-water jobs. Most all of what aquatics was to this point had to do with brawn, experience and discipline - and a lot of masculine pride. Surviving close calls had graduated them as survivors and experts.

But what they were hearing in this underwater thing was much like school learning, academic, scientific, somewhat mystical. This was beyond conquest by sheer physical extra effort; bubbles they couldn't see were waiting to kill them if they deviated from the rules. My God, each was thinking, the speakers were talking about physics, physiology, the technology of valves and orifices.

There sat a bunch of gruff, fish-like people who rabidly and stubbornly guarded their water surfaces like personal kingdoms and defied any new trespasser who would change the way of things. They were sitting like school children and they were realizing that the old era was giving way to a new one, that suddenly there would be people beyond their vision, under their surface domains, operating a highly technical cluster of paraphernalia and they must either learn and join the descent personally (or at least officially through programming) or relinquish some of their power and control.

In a sense, the men who sat there, somewhat ill at ease, were like a primitive tribe being exposed to the first samplings of the machine age - their fluid grace in the water wilderness, their jut-jawed extra stroke overcoming of obstacles, their awesome breathholding deep dives for fish and lobster, looked crude rather than dashing in the sudden flash of the breathing machine. The ability to make fire by Stone Age man was not unlike this scuba transition, as the ability wasn't required to be carried in one's muscles and tribal procedure, the instant lighter had arrived and was available. Scuba made its first inroads into removing the special personal control as individuals that these men had always had over the water medium. It was evident as they slipped eel-like into the Lynwood pool and moved in, over and under the water almost in spite of the new encumbrances strapped to faces, backs, waists and feet.

1UICC LOS ANGELES COUNTY UNDERWATER INSTRUCTORS - 1955

Julius Arenstein	Herb Barthels	Leonard Chapin	Kaye Fletcher
Chuck Fremdling, Jr.	Harold Guthrie	John Hawkins	William P. Jeffs
John J. Joseph	Robert Le Maire	Richard Luippold	Robert Luippold
Paul J. McComack	Frank McGregor	Robert F. Meistrell	Denny Miller
Bev Morgan	James Norris	Ramsey Parks, III	Thomas Rice
William Starr	Charles Sturgill	Bill Tannehill	Al Tillman
Phil Udell	RustyWilliams		

Open water checkout ot the 1963 UICC at Surfers Cove in Palos Verdes.

A number of diving pool mangers, such as Johnny Joseph, Kaye Fletcher, Julie Arenstein (Head of LA County Swimming Pools), and Paul McComack, Manager of the Lynwood Natatorium enrolled. Bobby Meistrel was there, Bill Starr, Al Tillman, and a few manufacturers representatives. Course "instructors" were Limbaugh, Cross, and Bill Walker (President of California Council of Diving Clubs). There wasn't a great deal of teaching methods disseminated as such but everybody learned from the master faculty and each other. No one can be certain that the very first underwater instructors anywhere in America had been processed, at least as far as their being fully prepared instructors following a definite set of techniques and standards, but it was probably a group that could match up with any instructors processed anywhere in the following decades.

The content of all courses, instructor and speakers, were in that rich stew of UICC. The course material, outlines and such were processed into printed instructor manuals and newsletters. Two more UICC's were launched that first year's summer, 2UICC and 3UICC, both held at the Belvedere pool in East Los Angeles at night. New important divers showed up. Dick Anderson, Chuck Blakeslee and a roster of people who would go on to carry the LA County operation far afield. The enrollees from the various manufacturers were essential to the LA County program's acceptance; the industry knew instruction was essential to progress and growth. It perhaps did the industry's job for them and made liability for accidents and deaths much less of a costly worry. Would standardized instruction happen with the LA County Program? A big maybe in a sport fraught with unpredictable happenings and hazards. It wouldn't have come as soon and could very possibly have come too late. For Al Tillman, he felt he may have saved himself from a spear in the eye from another stranger in the water with no sense...or training.

Now it was time to establish a Board of Directors that would be made up of instructors directly trained in the LA County Program. The Board of Advisors was perfect for authority and certified knowledge. A Board of Directors would plan courses based on actually being a part of them and suggest new directions for the LA County Underwater Program (as it was now being called). It was time to go beyond just teaching people how to dive and find new recreational uses for the newly learned skill. The first members of the Board were selec-

Divemasters Ed Peterson and John McNichols packing their gear up hill from Surfers Cove in Palos Verdes (1963).

Clint Denn

tively picked because they were critical and had constructive suggestions or were highly respected by other divers. A "sweetheart" choosing would have been easier to operate the program, just rubber stamp what the County staff representatives wanted, but the difficult mix insured the program would improve, get tougher and better, and survive against any competition. The top graduate from each course would henceforth be invited to serve on the Board.

Some true leaders came out of the Board in the 1950's. The ones Al Tillman recalls as top contributors were Vince Van Detta (a Covina pool manager), Harry Vetter (a long time YMCA instructor), and Paul McComack.

The UICC course had a few changes along the way. A major one was actually having candidates teach something in the classroom, poolside, and in the water. Staff evaluated each performance and candidates did it for each other. They had to submit lesson plans and essays on subjects they were given and felt comfortable with. Top graduates from underwater certification courses started showing up on course staffs.

Bill Starr blew an ear drum cocking a spear underwater, holding his breath with scuba, so Al Tillman lost his diving partner of several years. The LA County program also lost Bill as he moved up administratively in the Los Angeles school system and got involved in youth clubs. Al Tillman pulled Dottie Frazier, (LA County's first woman instructor or perhaps anywhere) and Big Jim Christiansen, (Champion spearfisherman and fireman) out of UICC courses to work part time on programs and courses for the LA underwater program. Paul McComack became Al Tillman's diving partner and a valued member on the Board and staffs of UICCs.

That was in 1956 and a crucial transitional time for the fledgling underwater program. Al Tillman decided to accept a full time teaching position at California State University at Los Angeles in the Recreation and Leisure Studies Department. He had just obtained the first masters degree in the subject from CSULA but would stay on with LA County as a specialist overseeing the Underwater Program.

The LA County Underwater Unit tentacled out to do lectures, presentations, workshops, film festivals, underwater photography clubs, recertification for instructors, and the Junior Frogman program. Jim Christiansen moved on after leaving a strong positive mark on the program. Dottie Frazier becomes the program's poster girl, starring in the first official diving training film, *Introduction to Skin Diving* and doing the tank shows at the big Los Angeles Sportsmen Show. Vince Van Detta becomes a top graduate of a UICC and sharing rides to classes and beach tests with Al Tillman impressed as an ideal instructor that can inspire others. An excellent water performer and school system educator, as well as, small town pool manager, Vince typifies the grand role model that LA County wanted to put forth. He eventually chaired the Board and was a popular leader at UICC courses.

The County Department had created a position of Aquatics Director corresponding to Sports Director, partially in hopes of diverting Tillman from leaving for a college teaching career. The position was filled by Don St. Hill, a veteran lifeguard lieutenant, a handsome craggy pioneer diver who set up and captained the Lifeguard Search and Recovery Team.

Don was a King Neptune of a man, who gave enormous credibility to the program. He was there in the very beginning of diving and even in his late 40's could out do any of the hot dog candidates. He and Al Tillman worked well together, respecting each others special talents. Together they went to educational workshops and introduced the new sport of diving. Eventually by 1958, the effect of putting shoes on to go downtown and operate the Underwater Unit with Tillman got oppressive and he went back to the beach he loved...but not until he'd left indelible contributions that set solid blocks in the foundation of the program.

JUNIOR FROGMEN

The continuity of the program was sustained by Al Tillman, who brought in young people like Glen Lewis and Paul McComack to work part time on staff. Tillman put the Junior Frogman program together to get back to skin diving classes that had essentially been dropped by the surge of scuba mania. People were bypassing skin diving to get right into scuba. The age of 16 was set as a minimum qualification for scuba training so there was nothing available for those younger. It was important to establish future adult divers from earlier generations - a farm system. Frank Roedecker's Frogman Club which Sea Net Company sponsored in 1940's gave membership materials through a mail-in coupon with their fins and mask sales. But it wasn't a programmed action operation. The 1950's Junior Frogman Program went to the various swimming pools, primarily with Al Tillman teaching the first classes and conducting a Junior Frogmen Olympics Competitions. The significant new program became popular and provided youth with an introduction to diving. Financial support for it came from surplus funds from UICCs that could only be held by the department if the money were put in a special fund for youth div-

The Junior Frogman Program was the first of its kind. Above, Clint Degn instructs Gary Ohanion, Jeff Huebner and Douglas Smith in the Rosemead pool.   Los Angeles County

ing. Many of the Junior Frogmen got to go on a bus trip to the Underwater Demolition Team Base where Commander Francis Douglas Fane put on an action show in the water with his men. Many went on to learn scuba diving after good preparation as Frogmen.

Other programs involved underwater photography. The County supported the formation of the first specialty club, the Los Angeles Underwater Photographic Society, which conducted contests and field trips, all of which helped diving move out of killing things to taking pictures of them. The County also sponsored film festivals and the beginning of the International Underwater Film Festival that showcased all of the young upcoming underwater photographers. There was effort made to house a diving museum at Zuma Beach and marine interpretive Shore Stations at key diving areas.

But producing instructors remained the core of the Underwater Program. Here are the course outlines for: The Fourth UICC and...1957 UICC (and a picture of the candidates).

TILLMAN MOVES OUT TO NAUI

When Al Tillman moved on to found the National Association of Underwater Instructors (NAUI) in 1960, Morgan "Clint" Degn moved out of managing LA County Swimming Pools to become the new Aquatics Director. Degn had graduated high in the 5UICC and worked with Tillman on college water safety classes, Junior Frogmen, and was well qualified to take over direction of the Underwater Unit.

During the early 1960's the UICCs continued as a major annual diving event in Los Angeles County. Chuck Petersen and Pete Manos were hired as part time staff under Clint Degn. Vince Van Detta played a significant leadership role on the Board of Directors carrying over the founding concepts and philosophy. Prestige and knowledge came into the program with Board membership of Colonel John D. Craig, and Dr. Glen Egstrom.

The concept of an advanced divers seminar and field program was introduced. (ADP)

The following content is covered over a three-month summer period on weekends:

Oceanography and Marine Life

Underwater Photography

Physics

Equipment

Skill Development

CPR and First Aid

Rescue

Search and Recovery

Altitude Diving

Six sessions are Open Water Dives at places like Catalina Island, other Channel Islands, Cabrillo Beach and Castaic Lake in the Los Angeles mountain area.

Anatomy for instructors was brought into dramatic focus by UICC course sessions at the LA County coroner's office. Candidates eye-balled cadavers with lung tissue exposed and much more...a few had to be removed and revived...the candidates that is.

When Clint Degn left LA County in 1968 to operate a photography store specializing in underwater photography, he also picked up a lec-

Women have played a very important role in diving and Los Angeles County certified the first female instructor when Dottie Frazier graduated. Joan Gillen and Jean Van Dyke are shown above.
Homer Lockwood

ture circuit following in John Craig's footsteps. Tom Ebro was recruited from Oregon where he had been overseeing aquatics at a lake. Ebro was tall, handsome, self-confident, and ambitious. Ebro served as Aquatics Director from 1968 to 1973. He polished what already existed but the LA County program was by then whatever it was supposed to be, a well-done regional program that was able to stretch an instructors course over three months. The NAUI certification in 1960 was the big national emergence that swallowed up local efforts at creating instructors. Some good programs for training instructors had climbed out of the club movement, the Southwest Council Instructors Program (SCIP) was a solid effort, the Boston Sea Rovers were building one, and of course the YMCA's program was a spotty national program that had strength here and there.

NAUI moved into prime diving areas and recruited strong leaders in each place. LA County had to contend with NAUI in 1962 coming into the Southern California area with a course in Santa Monica. The County wanted to work out a crossover deal whereby LA County Instructors could all be recognized as NAUI instructors but NAUI had a special affiliate status designed to pull in key well-experienced instructors by requiring ten letters of recommendation from important diving and aquatic agencies in the applicant's locale. The affiliate status also asked for records of classes they'd conducted and some testing administered by a local official.

In the 1950's, similar type of by-mail certification allowed the County to step beyond its boundaries and recognize out-of-the-area people such as Dave Woodward in Spokane, Washington, and Phil Bayouth in Oklahoma. Mail order certification was not supported by LA County regulars but this LA County effort helped diving instructors unable to come to LA County gain some authority and be exposed to a standard of a recognized agency.

The NAUI Santa Monica course drew good LA County certified instructors. Neither NAUI nor LA County suffered any damage from the competition. Many of the divers just wanted dual recognition but while the 1962 NAUI course introduced the national status to the Los Angeles Area swimming pools and dive shops, and established a foothold, the LA County-only instructor remained accepted and highly revered.

One of the major problems that arose in the LA County program in the 1950's was how to evaluate instructors after they'd been certified and so a system of contacting a representative sample from classes was done by survey. The idea of recertification seminars was also programmed to be sure instructors were keeping current.

The first acceptable one hose regulator, the Waterlung was introduced at such a seminar by the inventor, Sam Lecocq, and Sportsways Company CEO, Dick Klein. The switch over to mouth-to-mouth resuscitation was introduced at a recertification seminar by its developer.

During the 1960's, LA County continued to see its program of certification of instructors grow along with the Department of Parks and Recreation changing its role in serving the public. The idea was introduced of incorporating the LA County Instructors Association as a nonprofit entity to carry on the courses. The County would serve in an advisory capacity and provide services to the Association. The control and power began to shift and personality and politics combined to cause some confrontations.

It is important to note here that the LA County program was the pioneer incubator of diving instruction everywhere. In the beginning, the innocent years, it led the way for all to follow. NAUI was based on the materials and processes developed in LA County. Neal Hess, an LA County certified instructor in 5-UICC and Al Tillman just took the works and put a new face on it...nationally and worldwide.

The following list cites people who were major contributors to developing the LA County Program of Instruction:

Pioneers ~ 1950's

Al Tillman	Bev. Morgan	Conrad Limbaugh
Dottie Frasier	Jim Christiansen	E. R. Cross
Ramsey Parks	Dr. Andreas Rechnitzer	Clint Degn
Vince Van Detta	Don St. Hill	Roger Plaisted
Herb Barthels	Bill Starr	Paul McComack
Dr. Robert Livingston	Fred Schwankowsky	

TIMELINE OF MAJOR HAPPENINGS

1952 The Catalyst Memo Proposing Underwater Instruction by a Public Agency

1953 Bev Morgan of the LA County Lifeguards and Al Tillman Sports Director of LA County Department of Parks and Recreation assigned to develop a program.

Bev Morgan and Al Tillman assigned to gain background and training from Conrad Limbaugh at SCRIPPS. Ramsey Parks attended, too.

Nine skin and scuba classes were presented with Bev Morgan as instructor for the public in County swim pools. About 100 attended with the surprising major interest in SCUBA diving.

Bev Morgan writes *Underwater Safety Manual* as one of the first diving manuals designed specifically for public classes.

Bev Morgan receives bad news that the physical exam by Civil Service for Scripps training showed his vision was inadequate for lifeguarding. Bev leaves for commercial diving career.

1954 A strong Board of Advisors was officially founded with important diving persons such as: Conrad Limbaugh; Rechnitzner; Dr. Kenneth Norris; Roger Plaisted; American Red Cross, Ferron Losee; E. R. Cross.

Al Tillman takes over Underwater Instruction under his Sports Division in cooperation with Lifeguard Service Division Head, Rusty Williams.

Bill Starr is hired part time to assist Al Tillman. Together they structure the first Underwater Instructor Certification Course (UICC) in the world. The first course is held with 25 candidates at Lynwood Natatorium, Lynwood, California.

Two more UICCs are conducted to meet a popular and growing demand.

Bill Starr and Al Tillman write a new manual *Underwater Recreation* that fuses safety with an upbeat recreation approach and works well for public beginning diver classes.

1956 The UICC becomes a 3-month long annual production and 30 or more candidates are the pattern. Full certification is given to about 65% at end of each course. The majority of candidates have dive shop connections or will.

Al Tillman accepts a University teaching position at CSULA but is retained as a specialist to help continue the underwater program.

1957 Don St. Hill brought off the beach as a Lifeguard Lieutenant and Chief of the Search and Recovery Team of the LA County Lifeguard Service to serve as Aquatics Director. Tillman and St. Hill are very compatible and cooperatively polish the program.

The Junior Frogmen Program is introduced with great success but a Diving Museum and Interpretative

Glen Egstrom instructs at a UICC in 1965.   Clint Degn

Shore Stations don't get budgeted. A recertification seminar program for instructors is put into operation. Diving is promoted widely through various shows and demonstrations. St. Hill and Tillman stage the diving tank shows at the hugely popular Los Angeles Sportsmen Show. They take Braille Institute children "diving" for touch and feel experiences.

St. Hill, Tillman and Dottie Frasier produce a first training film *Introduction to Skin Diving* with technical assistance of USC Cinema Department.

Skin Diver Magazine, Jim Auxier and Chuck Blakeslee (who enrolls and graduates from 2UICC) throw extensive support behind the County Program.

1958 Requests to be recognized by the LA County Underwater Unit come from across America, from organizations and individuals. An affiliate by mail program is introduced to help highly qualified and experienced instructors achieve some sort of official status. A certifying one week course was announced for the summer of 1959, billed as a National Association of Underwater Instructors but the County officials stepped in and discouraged any more movement or programming beyond County boundaries.

UICCs grew strong with enhanced curriculum. A Board of Directors was formed made up of outstanding graduates of previous UICCs.

Seminars on Marine Cooking, Search and Recovery, Marine Biology, and new equipment were introduced to help in recertification but opened door to regular divers coming to advance their skills and knowledge.

The first convening of an Equipment Committee under the program. Representatives all manufacturers joined to make recommendations on instructions and hear input about improvement of equipment from instructors.

1959 The program is generally stable and achieves great National and Worldwide recognition even with the YMCA introducing a National Program and NAUI advertising a 1960 course at the Houston USOA Convention.

1960 Al Tillman departs LA County Program to found NAUI with Neal Hess.

1960's Under Clint Degn and Vince Van Detta's leadership, the LA County Program introduced a multi-specialties Advanced Diver Seminar to keep basic course graduates diving. Enrollments would often exceed 100 for the three-month annual course. It was the forerunner of Advanced Specialty Courses eventually programmed by all training agencies by the 1970's.

1970's - 1990's In 1970 era prior to the infamous LA County Ordinance that mandated government supervision of rentals, air fills, instruction, certification and charter boat operations, the Underwater Program was still in a strong position to attract instructor candidates despite the strong rising of several national training agencies. A brochure entitled "Our Underwater Program at a Glance" boasted that it had been borrowed and copied since its 1954 inception. At this point LA County claimed to have certified 507 instructors and 156,000 divers. It listed as programs the Junior Frogman, the Adult Skin Diving, Adult Skin and Scuba, Advanced Diver, Junior Frogman Instructor, Underwater Instructor Courses. In addition, LA County was extending out of sport diving to include training for underwater police, firefighting, and technology courses. And so the first two decades of diving were big growth years with a quality reputation. NAUI was the most serious competition but PADI, NASDS, SSI, and the YMCA were looming large.

The LA County Underwater Instructors formed a Non-Profit Association by 1974 to conduct the UICC's and Advanced Divers Courses with LA County serving as a deeply involved consulting force. The UIA provided all the manpower for any of the programs offered. The staff came from the outstanding instructors and divemasters as volunteers. Their remuneration was only a free graduation celebration dinner.

LA COUNTY RIFTS AND ACHIEVEMENTS

1992 Frank Gonzalez was the official LA County Department of Parks and Recreation liaison. Bill Lidyoff was President of the nonprofit private Los Angeles County Underwater Instructors Association. The joint coordination led to a conflict of power. David Ellman, a resigning Board Member, recalls how "the best of friends turned into the worst of enemies. The main issue evolved out of which of the two parties had the power to staff the 39th UICC." Jennifer King, who went on to form The Women's Scuba Association, was the course director. ...the first woman director.

Ellman's protests were in official letters to the Board and indicated LA County (the government agency) stepped in and over-ruled Jennifer King. He claims graduates were disappointed in the "lowered watermanship requirements," especially dropping the free ascent exercises from significant depths. Ellman protested the letterhead on program flyers saying "Los Angeles County Underwater Instructors Association sponsored by The Los Angeles County Department of Parks and Recreation." 'Have we lost our independence completely?" asked Ellman.

Certified LA County instructors were invited to participate in a YMCA and NAUI crossover. Recertification was required for UIA membership. Recertification requirements were to require current CPR, ten students or two classes per year, and a medical exam every two years in over forty years olds. Jennifer King was officially reprimanded for by-passing the Board and going directly to the membership with her written grievances.

The Board concluded that instructor certification is a County Program and UIA was to serve as expert advisors. There was a strong feeling that Ed Petterson, as an instructor and diver, contributed greatly to smoothing the relationships between LA County and Underwater Instructors Association.

LA County by the year 2000 had survived the usual politics and confrontations of a Democratic Institution and although reduced in scope maintained a quality reputation.

The year 2000 47th UICC graduation banquet was held at the Los Angeles Athletic Club and was well-attended and had great dignity. Zale Parry introduced Al Tillman, who was the recipient of two significant achievement awards, One being in the name of his friend and mentor from the 1950's, Conrad Limbaugh. It was the 45th Anniversary of the instruction program that set the pace for all instruction everywhere over all those years. David Golden, President of the LA County Underwater Instruction Association, cited the veterans there - Vince Van Detta, Glen Egstrom, Paul McComack, Nick Icorn, Frank Fleidner, John McNichols, Don Morrison and the new faces of quality leaders who were carrying on the grand traditional programs. Dave said, "Al Tillman, see what you have wrought and it lives on. Awesome!"

Hall of Fame

CONRAD LIMBAUGH MEMORIAL AWARD

Vince Van Detta 7 UICC
    1965
Tommy Thompson 10 UICC
    1966
Dr. Glen Egstrom 13 UICC
    1967
Morgan Clint Degn 5 UICC
    1969
Norman S. Johnson Dept. Director
- retired   1972
Otto F. W. Gasser 16 UICC
    1973
Dick Fitzgerald Director of Beaches
    1979
Ron Merker 13 UICC
    1981
Ed N. Petterson 11 UICC/Dept. P&R
- retired   1988

Vince Van Detta becomes the first recipient of the Conrad Limbaugh Award. One of the first female instructors, Barbara Allen, does the honors.

James Stewart Scripps Institution of Oceanography	1989
John McNichols 14 UICC	1990
David Bunch 13 UICC	1993
Nick Icorn 13 UICC	1998
Albert Tillman LA County Program Creator	1999

By 2000, LA County was recognizing their upcoming leaders with the following awards:

Outstanding UICC Graduate: Norton Wisdom

Outstanding Year 2000 Instructor: Tom Wetzel

Presidents Award: Joe Takahashi

Golden Snorkel Award: Brad Johnson

The issues being discussed at Board of Director's Meetings:

- Advanced Diver Program
- Recognizing volunteer staffing at UICC and ADP
    Long timer - Ed Petterson
    LA County Liaison - Tyrone Brown
- Divemasters: Joe Takahashi - Bill Lidyhoff
- SCUBA 2000 Booth Coverage
- Luggage tags promoting LA County Underwater Instructors Association

The year 2000 President of the Los Angeles County Underwater Instructor Association was Dave Golden who started diving in 1952 and graduated from 18UICC. He was certified as a "Moss Back" (divers with a great measure of experience) with LA County and with NAUI in 1967. Dave is typical of the program's leadership over

the decades - providing a multitude of writings for the UICC's and Advanced Diver Program with titles like, *Teaching Marine Life to Beginning Divers and Beach Oceanography for Divers.*

One of the LA County mottos: *Diving is safe and enjoyable with proper training, proper attitude and good physical condition.*

FOURTH UNDERWATER INSTRUCTORS CERTIFICATION COURSE
WINTER 1955
Monday - November 14, 1955
7:00 TO 10:00 P.M.
Lynwood Natatorium

		Instructor
	Course Orientation	Al Tillman
7:00 - 7:30 P.M.	Water Safety	Fred Schwankovsky
7:30 - 8:30 P.M.	Skindiving Equipment	Bev Morgan
5 Minute Break		
8:35 - 8:50 P.M.	Artificial Respiration Exercise	Herb Barthels
8:50 -10:00 P.M.	Water Tests	Al Tillman
	Swim - 4 Lengths of Pool	
	Weight Dive - Treading	
	Submersion Methods	
	Tube Rescue Exercise	Fred Schwankovsky

Monday - November 21, 1955
7:00 to 10:00 P.M.
Lynwood Natatorium

7:00 - 8:00 P.M.	Diving Physics	E. R. Cross
8:00 - 9:00 P.M.	Scuba Equipment	E. R. Cross
9:00 - 9:30 P.M.	Deck Exercises	E. R. Cross, Bill Starr, Al Tillman
	Buddy System	
	Unit Assembly	
	Unit Mounting	
	Clearing Face Plate	
	Clearing Unit Tubes	
9:30 -10:00 P.M.	Pool Exercises	
	Run Course - No Problems	
	Clearing Face Plate	
	Clearing Unit Tubes	

Monday - November 28, 1955
7:00 to 10:00 P.M.
Lynwood Natatorium

7:00 - 9:00 P.M.	Diving Physiology	Dr. William Burns
	Physical Requirements	
	Conditioning	
	Physics as Applied to Body	
	Divers Diseases	
9:00 - 10:00 P.M.	Pool Exercises	Al Tillman, William Starr
	Clearing Face Plate	
	Clearing Unit Tubes	
	Buddy Breathing	
	Underwater Removal and Replacement of Unit	

Saturday - December 3, 1955 (See Alternate)
9:00 to 5:00 P.M.
Shipboard

9:00 - 9:30 A.M.	Equipment Transport	
9:30 - 10:30 A.M.	Marine Biology	Ken Norris
10:30 - 12:00 Noon	Water Entry & Exit	
	Scuba Run	
12:30 - 1:30 P.M.	Submarine Topography	Lt. Don St. Hill
	Currents - Tides	
1:30 - 3:00 P.M.	Scuba Run	
3:00 - 5:00 P.M.	Specimen Preservation -	
	Ocean Chemistry	

Saturday - December 3, 1955 (Alternate)
9:00 to 5:00 P.M.
Torrance Beach or Cabrillo Beach
TORRANCE BEACH OR CABRILLO BEACH

Monday - December 5, 1955
7:00 to 10:00 P.M.
Lynwood Natatorium

| 7:00 - 8:00 P.M. | Review of Course | William Starr |
| | Evaluation of Ocean Class | |

| 8:00 - 10:00 P.M. | Scuba Equipment | |
| | Lecture, Demonstration and | |

Participation by Manufacturers

U.S. Divers	Chuck Frembling
Healthways	Arnold Polk
Scott Hydropak	Dick Noelck
Northill	Robert Kimes
DESCO	Leo Unger

Saturday - December 10, 1955
9:00 to12:00 Noon
Lynwood Natatorium

9:00 - 10:00 A.M.	Written Test	Al Tillman
10:00 - 12:00 Noon	Practical Test	William Starr

Monday - December 12, 1955
7:00 to 10:00 P.M.
Lynwood Natatorium

7:00 - 10:00 P.M.	Teaching Techniques	
	Group Dynamics	Dr. Feron Losee
	Visual Aids	

Saturday - December 17, 1955
9:00 to 5:00 P.M.
Marineland of the Pacific

9:00 - 10:00 A.M.	Evaluation of Tests	William Starr, Al Tillman
10:00 - 12:00 Noon	Underwater Photography	Conrad Limbaugh, Don Ollis
12:00 - 12:30 P.M.	Lunch	
12:30 - 1:30 P.M.	Movies	Conrad Limbaugh
1:30 - 4:00 P.M.	Ocean Practical Test	Conrad Limbaugh
4:30 - 5:00 P.M.	Graduation Ceremony	Tech. Advisory Committee

There was only one Underwater Instructor Certification Course during 1957. The curriculum read as follows:

All applications will be evaluated as to the applicant's intent to instruct, opportunity to instruct, and diving experiences.

Final acceptance to the course will be based upon Los Angeles County Scuba Certificate of a Practical Skills Pool Test on February 2, 1957 involving the following:

1. Swim 200 yards
2. Tread Water
3. Underwater swim - 25 yards
4. Clear mask (using scuba)
5. Clear hoses (using scuba)

6. Buddy Breathe (using scuba)

7. Swim with weight belt (12 pounds)

DATE/TIME/ PLACE		SUBJECT	INSTRUCTORS
Feb 2 Sat 9-12:30 PM	L.N.	Entrance Tests	Staff - Paul McComack
Feb 5 Tues 7-10 PM	C.L.A.	Introduction to Program and Equipment	Staff
Feb 9 Sat 9-12:30 PM	L.N.	Skin Diving Techniques	Herb Barthels - Staff
Feb 12 Tues 7-10 PM	C.L.A.	Equipment	Bob Kimes - Staff
Feb 16 Sat 9-12:30 PM	L.N.	SCUBA Techniques	Staff - Roger Plaisted
Feb 19 Tues 7-10 PM	C.L.A.	Physics and Physiology	Dr. Bateman, Dr. Johnson, Dr.Burns
Feb 23 Sat 9-12:30 PM	L.N.	Equipment Seminar	Manufacturers - Staff - E. R. Cross
Feb 24 Sun 9-5 PM	Marineland	Practical Ocean Work	Ken Norris - Staff - Capt. Dwight Crum
Feb 26 Tues 7-10 PM	C.L.A.	Recreation - Teaching Techniques Class Org. & Adm.	Dr. Ferron Losee - Staff
Mar 2 Sat 9-12:30 PM	L.N.	SCUBA Techniques	Jim Christiansen - Dottie Frazier
Mar 3 Sun 9-5 PM	Catalina	Practical Ocean Work	Staff - Dan Ryan - Conrad Limbaugh
Mar 5 Tues 7-10 PM	C.L.A.	Written Test	Staff
Mar 9 Sat 9-12:30 PM	L.N.	Practical Pool Tests	Staff
Mar 10 Sun 9-5 PM	Palos Verdes	Practical Ocean Tests	Staff
Mar 12 Tues 7-10PM	Roger Young Auditorium	Graduation Dinner	Staff

Staff: Don St. Hill, Training Director - Al Tillman, Coordinator

L.N. = Lynwood Natatorium   C.L.A. = Central Los Angeles

The success and soundness of the program was due to the efforts and cooperation of the following Technical Advisory Committee:

Medical: Dr. Robert B. Livingston, School of Medicine, University of California at Los Angeles. Dr. William T. Burns, Medical Diving Consultant, Long Beach California. Aquatics: Capt. R. Williams, Aquatics director, County of Los Angeles, Dept. of Parks and Recreation. Water Safety: Mr. Roger Plaisted, Director of First Aid and Water Safety, Los Angeles Chapter, American Red Cross. Mr. Fred Swankovsky, Director of First Aid and Water Safety, Long Beach Chapter American Red Cross. Mr. Bill Walker, Safety Director, California Council of Diving Clubs. Equipment: Mr. E. R. Cross, Author, Lecturer, Master Diver, Wilmington, California. Oceanography: Mr. Conrad Limbaugh, Chief Diver, Scripps Institution of Oceanography, La Jolla, California. Recreation: Mr. Albert Tillman, Supervisor of Sports, County of Los Angeles, Dept. of Parks and Recreation. Organized Diving: Mr. Homer

Lockwood, President, California Council of Diving Clubs. Inquiries: Mr. Bill Starr, Public Classes and Certification Program Coordinator of Underwater Recreation, County Dept. of Parks and Recreation, Los Angeles, California.

Candidate Program for Year 2000
Underwater Instructors Certification Course

Bill Lidyoff received the credit for reprogramming the entire course in the past few years. The following shows the brawn, brains and fortitude one needs to become a Los Angeles Underwater Certified Instructor.

Preliminary Requisites
Certified Diver with at least 50 logged dives
Diver Rescue Card (CPR and First Aid Water Rescue Level)
Current Medical Exam (within one year)
Pre-Test/ Written Exam, Ocean Beach dive (Entry and Exit)
Pre-Test/ Pool, 400 yard swim under 10 minutes time
Underwater 75 foot swim without aids
Course fee is about $900

Program Overview
20 Sessions, 14 Weeks, (including 6 Sundays)
Sign in - 7:15am Start - 7:30am End - 5:30pm (unless otherwise specified)
67 hours - classroom, 36 hours - pool, 52 hours - ocean = 155 hours +

Attendance
Only 2 absences allowed in the course (I per quarter)
Sessions missed become incomplete and must be made up for certification
Maximum grade that can be received on makeups for an incomplete is 7
Being late is not acceptable, and will be reflected in the grade received for that day
Each candidate will receive a log book, which must be filled out and signed by the Divemaster after each session. This will be checked at the end of the course.

Dress Code
Shoes, shirt, and pants, must be clean and neat. Dress as if you are teaching a class.

Attitude
All Candidates are expected to act professionally at all times. Remember you are being evaluated as if you were teaching a Los Angeles County Basic class. You need to demonstrate an attitude that reflects the high standards of a Los Angeles County Underwater Instructor.

Dive Teams
Candidates will be grouped into dive teams. Staff for each team will consist of a Divemaster and team leader. These two staff members will be responsible for hands on training of the team.

Candidate Team Leader
Each week one candidate from each dive team will be assigned by the staff to be the team leader. This person will be responsible for making sure the team is setup and ready to go for the day's activities, and organizing the

team to assist in any special setup for the program (room setup, assisting speakers, etc.)

Equipment

All Candidates' equipment must be in good working order, and meet minimum requirements for both RSTC standards and the Los Angeles County Ordinance. Each Candidate must have their equipment approved by the Divemasters. Date is designated.

Classroom and Lecture Sessions

During UICC, lectures will be given covering a wide variety of topics. These lectures will be given by some of the top experts in the diving industry. Much of the material from these lectures will be used in the 4 graded written exams given during the program. Note taking is recommended. During the lectures please give these speakers your full attention. Do no bring food or drinks into the classroom during the lectures. Make sure that when we start the lectures you are in your seat on time, and do not leave during the lecture, except for designated breaks given by the speaker or staff.

Areas of Grading

Pool teaching - Must maintain a minimum average of 70% (5 graded sessions)

Ocean teaching - Must maintain a minimum average of 70% (5 graded sessions)

Oral presentations - Must maintain a minimum average of 70% (5 graded sessions)

Watermanship and Equipment handling skills - Must have a minimum of 70% in all skills

(5 graded pool skills) (5 graded ocean skills)

Academics - 70% required in all topics (4 graded exams)

Teaching technique, Equipment, Physics, Medical aspects, Physiology, Dive tables (11 segments including dive computers), Emergency procedures, Oceanography, Marine life, Fish and Game laws, Legal aspects, Diver fitness, Navigation, Deep diving, Continuing education.

Speakers: Dr. Jean Hawkins, Medical Aspects - Pete Haaker, Fish & Game - Carl Hungens, Dive Table Theory, Dr. Glen Egstrom, Diver Fitness - Nick Icorn, History of Scuba Diving and Equipment, Jim Stewart - Scripps Tour, Santa Barbara City College Legal Aspects

10

CLUBS

DEFINING EVENT: BOSTON SEA ROVERS OR LOS ANGELES NEPTUNES

In the beginning days of diving both skin diving and scuba diving clubs brought everybody together. The clubs gathered the loner individuals of which diving was comprised and created a warm and friendly second family.

They came together in meetings and elected a president and a vice president and set up bylaws. They planned weekend trips together. They shared equipment, usually a scuba unit belonging to the club, told each other fish stories, and the experienced members taught the novice divers the tricks of diving.

Through the club it was possible to work out deals on diving equipment discounts, charter boat trips and air. Competition was now possible and intra-club spearfishing meets were scheduled regularly. Clubs had exhibits in booths at local shows and made contact with the rest of the public, getting special attention for their involvement in an adventuresome, mysterious new sport, and recruiting new members along the way.

When the pioneer divers were interviewed, they usually talked about diving alone in the prehistory era of the 1930's and 1940's. The lucky ones found a diving buddy as soon as they could, although diving solo had a special and different thrill to it. Going alone into the unknown was no church picnic. It was necessary in finding a partner, to have two relatively equal in skills. Men with parallel enthusiasm meshed for a quality buddy team - and they had better have liked each other. (The women, with a few exceptions, were shunted out of what men considered their manly male domain.)

Al Tillman recalls those days, "I guess I started serious diving with my big brother, Don, the engineer, and some of his co-workers from Los Angeles City. I was leader of a couple of YMCA teenage clubs in the late 1940's, and sometimes one of those young guys I got started in diving was my partner. Bruce Graves was a good example. Later he'd come to work for me in the Los Angeles County Program. It was the spearfishing meets that pushed us in declaring ourselves a club. You had to be a club to qualify. It was a very informal arrangement. We'd just call each other and see if anyone wanted to go diving.

"By the early 1950's, I was loading the station wagon and going diving by myself whenever I could, mainly because no one else was available.

"Actually, I had joined a club, probably the classic big club, the Los Angeles Neptunes in 1948."

The Los Angeles Neptunes represents the historical prototype of the open membership when the club out-grows its effectiveness. The Los Angeles Neptunes met at the Los Angeles Police Academy during those late 1940's, and the membership boasted some big names of that diving era: Jim Christiansen, Woody Dimel, Bill Barada, Jim Miller, Doc Mathison and Ralph Davis. There would be 50 or 60 members at a meeting which usually involved discussion of where the big fish had been seen in the previous week, a show-and-tell of new homemade equipment and inventions, spearfishing meets, and plans for a club dive (just show up). Actually, the club was a fireman's club at the start because half the divers in those days were firemen because of their great day-on, day-off work schedule.

Jim Christiansen recalled, "We had a main core of really good divers and some of us were labeled King Neptunes if we got three abalones on one dive, speared a big fish and caught a ten-pound lobster. We were all in great shape, with some of us diving to 100 feet for three minutes. We lived and breathed the giant white sea bass; getting one was probably the ultimate skill in diving. There were a lot of new divers joining the club, but they sort of sat around and sucked up our stories."

The Los Angeles Neptunes had 300 members at one point and Bill Barada said, "We had members as far away

The May, 1958 issue of Skin Diver Magazine showed the patches from most of the major dive clubs across the country at the time.

as Fresno, California, because if you joined the club, you could get a pattern cut out of newspaper to make a dry suit. Trying to get warm, finding something, baby oil or long johns or this dry suit made out of a fragile, brown, surgical rubber was the holy grail."

Woody Dimel thought the club stopped being a club when it got so big. A good club doesn't exceed twenty members, or the individual loses his identity, doesn't get a chance to have his say. Under eight members, and there isn't enough variety of personalities or power to make deals, like getting a boat charter. With a big club that the Los Angeles Neptunes got to be, special interests started splitting up the group. Ralph Davis, who made the keeping of fish records happen and was impresario for the big spearfishing meets, and should get credit for staging the First National Spearfishing Meet, made pitches for support, but most of the members were bored with it. The ungrateful attitude seemed to be, "Just do it, Ralph, and we'll do the diving."

Jim Christiansen and Al Tillman, reminiscing of their early days with the Los Angeles Neptunes, felt the commute into Los Angeles for the meetings was a burden. Christiansen said, "It was 50 miles round trip, no freeways from Long Beach. I could hear fish stories closer to home." He pushed the program of recognizing branches of the club to be geographically more convenient. There's no record of how many branch clubs spun out of the Los Angeles Neptunes, but Tillman had a small club, the Santa Anita Neptunes far out in Duarte, and Jim Christiansen formed the purists' free-diving-spearfishing Long Beach Neptunes, which by the year 2000 was going strong as the flagship club of free diving. Names like Doc Nelson Mathison, Dr. Omar Nielsen, John Lockridge, Terry Maas, Al Schneppershoff were legends on the roster.

One of the prideful symbols of being a member of a club, was the jacket patch. The Los Angeles Neptunes had a colorful one that members wore on light blue denim jackets with knit cuffs, the outdoorsman's fashion of the day.

Belonging seems like a basic human need, and divers wanted to show they belonged to this new fraternity of "daredevils." Before the graphic evolution of the "C" Card, divers showed their qualifications as a diver in jacket patches.

When *Scuba America* was being researched in the early 1970's, a formal list of reasons for the early diving clubs was:

1. Direct reinforcement by others for the results of one's diving - game, artifacts, even treasure
2. Manufactured audience
3. Create pressure group to extort special deals on equipment and boats
4. Social contact and interaction with others with like interests
5. Limited time and limited money meant one had to combine social time and special interests
6. Have a ready stable of potential diving buddies available
7. Fulfills the need to be stimulated and feel needed by those who are not by nature inclined or capable of initiating their own activities as an outlet for their interest.
8. An arena for competition in getting game.

SKIN DIVER MAGAZINE *- THE GLUE*

Clubs proliferated rapidly in the 1950's. Nothing did more to bind the clubs in exchange of information and give them status than *Skin Diver Magazine*. Jim Auxier and Chuck Blakeslee, who created the magazine, believed in clubs. Both were members of the Dolphins, a very competitive spearfishing club. All a club had to do was send a short article about what it was doing - contests, instruction, putting on exhibits, cleaning trash out of lakes.

Looking back at the early clubs, one can see there was a fun attitude - just look at some of the names and activities. Mixed in are some serious efforts to maintain safety and protect the diving environment.

THE CLUBS

1. Wild and Crazy Names of Clubs

Jacksonville Jelly Jumpers

Pacific Grove Loony Goonies

Aquaholics

Kelptomaniacs

Neisi Kelp Tanglers

New Jersey Aqua Dunkers

Grouper Gropers San Diego

Hawaiian Coral Gypsies

Southern California Sons of Beaches

Hollywood Aqua-Nets

Snorkel Snoopers

2. Most Well-known Clubs Over The Decades

Bottom Scratchers

Los Angeles Neptunes

Boston Sea Rovers

Puget Sound Mud Sharks

3. Best Club Achievements in the Past

Boston Sea Rovers' Clinics

Underwater Photographic Society's Competitions

Los Angeles Neptunes' Preserving the Pure Art of Free Diving and Spearfishing Club Instruction Program

Puget Sound Mud Sharks' Octopus Wrestling (A new activity that didn't kill the creature.) They swam with and helped the Aquarium with Namu, the captured Killer Whale.

4. The Big Club Year - 1955

What were clubs doing? We will skip the endless accounts of fish and their weights. Spearfishing was the major activity.

Rhode Island Spearfish Club experimented with rebreathers and found them unstable.

Long Island Dolphins were concerned over two deaths. They formed the East Coast Safety Council with ambitions for a National Safety Council. Their main thrust was to be an instructors' SCUBA course. Club members Barbara and Rick Carrier wrote one of the classic general public how-to books, *Dive*, a hardback.

New York Bel Aqua Club worried about members going down with faulty scuba and being liable.

Island Diving Association of Fort Worth club members were into homemade camera cases and favored diving Possum Kingdom Lake.

California Aqua Familias was based on family diving, and member, Dottie Frazier's son, Donny Gath (12) broke into skin diving by getting an 8 1/2 inch abalone on the charter boat *Herbie Too*.

Chicago Aqua Venturers spent winters patching leaky rubber suits and playing underwater hockey in the high school pool.

Chicago Submarine Exploration Group's Vern Pederson reported that members checking out wrecks in Sturgeon Bay, building a decompression chamber, a tow sled, a 4-hour type rebreather, and shooting underwater movies on vacation in Florida.

St. Thomas Virgin Islands Blue Mantas entertained Mel Fisher and Doc Nelson Mathison from California and actor, Bill Holden, who was filming The Proud and The Profane.

The San Diego Bottom Scratchers was the first club. Glenn Orr, Jack Prodanovich and Ben Stone founded the club in 1933. Jim Stewart and Conrad Limbaugh were young members.   Lamar Boren

Michigan Treasure Unlimited Club was laying out a compass course.

Long Beach Junior Neptunes reported diving the wreck of the Valiant at

Santa Catalina Island. There was only a barren hulk. So they dived for pennies from the tourist steamer and collected $15. All the members completed their own brass camera cases with member, Jack McNeal, already exhibiting fine color slides.

Sharks Underwater Adventurers report spearing a 500 pound Manta Ray and three members Chuck Vallance, Joan Gillen, and Mel Fisher were certified as instructors by Los Angeles County. Kathy Conley was rescued from rip current by lifeguards. (Kathy Conley became Club President in 1963.)

Wisconsin Midwest Amphibians had movies of Key West vacation by member, Fred Roberts. They were diving the old standby Racine Quarry, but there's a parking problem.

Long Beach Neptunes' motto is "Never take more than you can eat."

Montgomery, Alabama Skin Divers helped the Highway Patrol search for a body.

New York College Point Underwater Club cleared out 60 starfish from oyster beds.

Washington Puget Sound Mud Sharks led by Gary Keffler recovered bodies from an airplane crash that ended up in 110 feet of water in a sunken forest lake.

California Aqua Guards led by Bill Walker were trying to create a diving lifeguard group.

California Kelp Worms were sharing two Aqua Lungs and an underwater camera. They have made spearguns from fire extinguishers.

The Bottom Scratchers' Wally Potts reported an exhibit of early diving equipment at the Crippled Childrens' Fair.

Ohio Skin Divers were collecting fish under the ice for Cleveland Aquarium.

Bakersfield Frogmen had an exhibit in the lobby of a theatre showing *20,000 Leagues Under The Sea*.

Five Fathom Club (teenagers) of Roslyn High School were saving their money from lawn mowing and baby sitting for their Florida Keys skin diving and spearfishing trip over Easter Vacation. Summers were spent diving in Long Island Sound.

Sea-Farers for men and the feminine contingent Sea-Fairs, University of California at Berkeley, California's news declared, "Stuart Mackay was duly elected President with Dave Garbellano as Vice President. Other officers are Fred Jenkenson as Secretary and Carter Collins, Treasurer. Club officially launched on July 25, 1954 with about 25 members." Dr. Parry Bivens and Dr. Hugh Bradner were members.

MILITARY CLUBS

A coterie of divers surfaced at the United States' military bases near an ocean or a lake far from America's mainland. Service men and women formed scuba clubs. In the 1950's and for many years after, Kwajalein Scuba Club's newsletter from the Marshall Islands in the Mid-Pacific was sent to Zale Parry and her husband, Dr. Parry Bivens, as an insert in Christmas greetings from friends, Bud and Gladys Weisbrod. Membership in the Club granted individuals privileges. Excerpts from a 1963 club newsletter announced, "Bud Weisbrod and Herm Scherer would be available Friday Night from 7:30 until 9:30 for anyone who wants to place an order for any scuba gear. Sportsways and U.S. Divers equipment are featured. Free advice will be given if you need it. Another note said that the Scuba Club 35mm Calypso underwater camera was available to members. Just call Paul Walter to make a reservation."

In the 1970's, American Northrop Aircraft Corporation and other American companies' scuba diving employees stationed at the Damman, Saudi Arabia, Air Base joined the American Northrop-Arabian Scuba Divers Club. The club was put together by Cliff Robotham for

Bill Barada, Homer Lockwood and a guest from the Puget Sound Mudsharks enjoy the catch after a day of friendly spearfishing.   Homer Lockwood

Clubs would frequently get together to compet and socialize. The gathering shown above was in 1956. Among those pictured are Woody Dimel and Doc Matheson. Center in light coat is Jim Auxier of the Compton Dolphins.

Homer Lockwood

American employees only. Members were warned by Dr. John Burchard of Aramco Marine Biology Laboratory about the undersea creatures, especially sea snakes, when diving in the Arabian Gulf in a club news bulletin. Another directive came from Dee McVay, representing a Saudi Diving Service, citing the fact that on one of the diving expeditions a scuba diver poked a snake with his spear. In a lightening-like response, the snake attacked. Fortunately, the diver was equipped with face mask, rubber gloves and wet suit, and escaped without harm.

The fun-names mostly came from California. Everywhere else clubs showed more reverence for involvement in diving. One presumptuous Detroit, Michigan, Club named itself Champion Divers.

That's just a small example of club activity that enjoyed its zenith when America was getting out of its neighborhood contacts, out of the cohesiveness of family and joining special interest groups, expanding their interaction with other people. Fully supported by *Skin Diver Magazine*, clubs in 1955 celebrated a banner year. The lone wolf diver and the permanent buddy teams of early years were made to feel left out.

The club had an identity in a national magazine, the only magazine, *Skin Diver*, (and probably worldwide to a degree).

But first of all there was ... well ... the first club. There have been many old-time divers that have claimed that they were diving way back in the 1930's. Once in awhile four or five of them did get together socially and underwater. They all mused, "Guess you could call us a club." A bunch of diving firemen in the station house making plans to go diving the next day may or may not have been what would constitute a club, the structured and organized concept. If we accept the first as being the one identified by the media as such, it would be the San Diego Bottom Scratchers. The May 1949 issue of *National Geographic Magazine* had its first complete article about free diving.

The club's activities in *Goggle Fishing in California Waters* was written by David Hellyer, with photographs by Lamar Boren, a club member.

The Bottom Scratchers, the original three guys who came together, were Jack Prodanovich with his Charles Atlas-Schwartzenager-build (on sight other divers' mouths hung open,) Glenn Orr, and Ben Stone. It all started in 1933 with very athletic, competitive divers. Membership was held down to accept only the best of divers. Legendary names like Bill Batzloff, Lamar Boren, Ron Church, Don Clark, Jack Corbeley, Emil Habecker, Professor Carl Hubbs, Bill Johnston, Conrad Limbaugh, Tucker Miller, Earl Murray, Wally Potts, Harold Riley, Rob Rood, Beau Smith, and Jim Stewart were stingily added.

They did socialize, really liked and respected each other, and brought their families together for cookouts of sea life on the beach. The crux of what the Bottom Scratchers were was plunging in after game and, in particularly hunting the big fish. They set many "biggest fish records." They were bringing game home for the table when there were tough economic times.

The Bottom Scratchers survived into the year 2000, primarily in the form of two originals, Wally Potts and Jack Prodanovich as a bonded buddy team. Hearing impaired they can be seen shuffling down to the ocean every day and still loving diving.

SUPER STAR CLUBS

In those early days of diving, the prehistory 1930's and 1940's, Southern California probably had 80% of the divers in America and most of the clubs. There were the Muirmen, North American Sea Sabres, Sharks of

The Bootom Scratchers enjoy some early publicity in Esquire Magazine.
Lamar Boren

Inglewood, and the list goes on and on and on. Bottom Scratchers and Los Angeles Neptunes set the mold for others. By 1955, half the members in a club were skin divers, the other half had gone to scuba. Most of these clubs were concentrated on competitive spearfishing, at least spearfishing, but had also taken up the instructional role in diving, more formally taking over the casual, random way being shown how by a friend or older relative (Tillman called them "Uncle Charlies" in his writing about the origins of diving instruction.) While some shops served as the cracker barrel hangouts for some divers, the club membership gave them a place to really belong and feel in control of their own destinies.

An early Boston Sea Rovers certification card signed by Nea Hess.

Clear across America, in the Northeast region, specifically New England, divers were starting to proliferate to dive the cold Northern Atlantic and to dive in Florida on short vacations. The exposure suit accelerated diving's growth in Massachusetts, Connecticut, Maine, New York and Rhode Island. Like divers everywhere, there was an inventor or two, maybe a dozen in each club trying to find better ways of going diving, more convenient equipment. Something to wear to keep warm was at the top of the list of challenges. Walter Feinberg, the Boston Sea Rovers' second President, told of Jerry O'Neil coming into meetings with some gizmo to improve equipment. Walter wasn't sure if it was Jerry who brought forth pa-

Gathering of clubs in Boston to form USOA in 1959.   *Skin Diver Magazine*

jamas coated in a rubberized paint (the first wet suit?), but O'Neil was the Boston Sea Rovers' member, who came in with the super bug-bag, a backpack, a gadget to fit onto the exhaust hose to allow a diver to breathe another diver's air without sharing his mouthpiece, and he developed the Portalift.

It is the Boston Sea Rovers that became the prominent club in New England, although it wasn't the first. It ranks right up there with the Los Angeles Neptunes and the Bottom Scratchers as the super star clubs of sport diving history.

Scuba America had plans to do a special chapter just on the Boston Sea Rovers, one entitled *Clubs With Brains*, but old time divers guided us into a better way of thinking. There were so many clubs out there that got no publicity yet achieved impactful things for sport diving development. Equal treatment for all clubs seemed to be called for.

Walter Feinberg told us that Joe Cortese put the Boston Sea Rovers together. Walter had received Cortese's name from a 1954 *Frankie the Frogman Club Newsletter* distributed by the Sea Net Company. Frankie the Frogman Club had 60,000 members at one point and was the invention of life-guard Frank Roedecker. This particular newsletter issue was about diving clubs forming in Boston. So Cortese, Feinberg, George Gorman, Gordon Holloway, and Jim Shad got together to be The Boston Sea Rovers at Walter Feinberg's home. For twenty years Walter had been snorkeling, but he only had goggles and flippers. Cortese and Gorman had the works, Aqua Lungs and dry suits , purchased from a Lawrence, Massachusetts, camera store. Feinberg got a ten minute-lesson on using the Aqua Lung at Cape Cod and simply borrowed one to use from the others. Soon he rushed to get his own, "whole works," he said.

One of the Sea Rover's most unique traditions involves filling the Annual Diver of the Year Award Bowl with a secret elixer, in order to "Baptise" the Diver of the Year, and other lucky Rovers and friends. Here, Frank Scalli gets a little help from his friends.   *Frank Scalli Collection*

Feinberg said that no one thought "Boston Sea Rovers" was much of a name but no one came up with a better one.

The name proposal instigator was Joe Cortese. Cortese immediately proposed doing a clinic. (Feinberg's wife, who hated diving as if it was a wanton mistress of her husband, told him, "A clinic was where sick people go.") Cortese was President of course, Feinberg was Vice President and Gorman was Secretary. Five members kicked it off, and the club had never exceeded 20 regular members, although visitors were welcome at meetings and on dive outings. (Frank Scalli claims 79 members during his reign as president.) It had a steady existence through the year 2000. Over the years many associate members were "appointed," from Jacque-Yves Cousteau to Dr. Harold E. Edgerton to Dr. Eugenie Clark. A few new people came in slowly because, as Feinberg related, "Difficult to get into the Boston Sea Rovers, but easy to kick out. If we liked you and you were a nice guy, those were the only qualifications, plus our dues were only $2."

The Long Beach Neptunes were a spinoff of the Los Angeles Neptunes. L to R is Dick Jaffe, Herb Sampson and Dock Mathison.   Homer Lockwood

Joe Linehan and his diving partner Frank Scalli breezed in. Feinberg, Linehan, Scalli and Dan DeSanctis were long-time members from the beginning of 1954 through 1976 and beyond.

The Boston Sea Rovers were always safety conscious. Members would bring equipment to meetings and if it was decided it was dangerous equipment like "homemade airplane regulators," they were told to destroy them or quit. In fact, the whole idea behind the Clinic was to promote safe practices and never to raise any money. They were having three diving fatalities a year in New England. The feeling was a treasury of size leads to arguments.

The First Clinic in 1954 was in the basement of the YMCA where Jim Cahill and later Frank Scalli taught diving classes. It was a booming success with 200 attendees. All they really had was a display of members' equipment, some old U.S. Navy training film, Dr. Harold Edgerton and Jim Cahill as speakers. It was a social good time, "a clam bake." Cortese left for California never to be heard from again, while Walter Feinberg moved up to be President. He "managed meetings," he said, "by invoking the Feinberg Law, which read: Anyone who proposes an idea is in charge, whether it be a raffle or a dive or whatever. It stopped loose talk." Walter became the victim of his own law and had to oversee the Second Clinic in 1955.

The speakers over the years ranged from close-by significant people in diving, such as Dr. James Starr from the New London Submarine Base, Dr. George Bond on saturation diving, and Hannes Keller on curve decompression. "Much of the time," Feinberg relates, "the divers had no idea what these advanced thinkers in diving were talking about, because most of them were still trying to figure out how to clear their ears."

Most of the original Boston Sea Rovers agree that it was the Fourth Clinic in 1958 that elevated the Boston Sea Rovers into a world-class power in diving and national prominence. Interestingly enough, it was a Californian, Neal Hess, who was getting a Masters Degree at Harvard, who brought the significant change about when he joined the Boston Sea Rovers.

Hess said, "Get Cousteau."

Walter Feinberg said, "How?"

Hess said, "Stake me to a long distance call."

Walter did. Hess was connected to U.S. Divers by telephone and booked Cousteau for that 1958 Clinic. "Twelve hundred divers showed. It was a clinic that was heard around the world," said Feinberg. The clinic was already a success in cooling down local divers who had been "Going around like heroes who dive 400 feet with a knife between their teeth and slit open sharks when they encountered them." All of this knowledge coming from experts at the clinics humbled them.

Feinberg retired on that success. He appointed Frank Scalli President (Sea Rovers never practiced democratic ways.) Now Neal Hess and Scalli took a look at an instruction course that Hess proposed should be standard for the club, perhaps for New England Clubs in general. Hess had come out of the Los Angeles County Program certified as an instructor and everybody in Boston was impressed with his diving knowledge. The Boston Sea Rovers were turned down by the Northeast Council of Clubs who felt the Sea Rovers were getting too "almighty arrogant with their Clinics and such" and the Council went so far as to try to boycott the clinics. Unfortunately for them, the next clinic was the Cousteau one and divers weren't about to miss it.

Scalli and Feinberg convinced the New England YMCA and then the National YMCA leaders to adopt the Boston Sea Rovers instruction program. "Nobody knows the YMCA invented basketball, the Y lost lifesaving to the National Red Cross (who has no swim pools) so don't lose SCUBA diving," said Feinberg to them. And so, Los Angeles County to a Boston Club to the National YMCA and another linkage in the great family of diving.

Jerry O'Neil took over the Boston Sea Rovers presidency from Frank Scalli, and a succession of great leaders were spawned out of the Sea Rover ranks. This club and its clinics provided the launching experience that allowed divers to soar. As a matter of course, clubs have been the base jumping-off sites for a great majority of leaders in sport diving.

There is no clearly defining rationale why clubs lost their momentum or influencing power in diving over the decades. Clubs were always a matter of socializing individual divers.

They were also incubators of politically-minded divers. Laws against diving, restricting and limiting taking of game in particular, and a resistance to scuba as an unfair advantage, brought fishermen to the sides of their boats screaming for legislation.

COUNCILS OF DIVING CLUBS

The diving politicians created the Councils of diving clubs in the 1950's. These Councils were instrumental in persuading legislatures to see "the other side" and were effective in keeping diving from being bureaucratically bogged down. These Councils had a lot to do with regulating competitive spearfishing and, in some cases, they set up competent instruction programs. They exercised a power that was objectionable to individual clubs made up of people who went diving to be free of worldly restrictions. Bill Barada (He formed the Greater Los Angeles Council.) remembered how Council organizers insisted that, "Either we discipline ourselves or government will do it." The clubs, member divers, were really too busy diving to get worked up about the issues the Councils were posturing.

The Councils were all looking regionally at control, but in the periphery, was national power. That would come in 1959. Once again out of one, with those forceful club leaders, Dick Meyer of the Worcester (Massachusetts) Frogman Club, came up with the idea and production of a National Convention of Divers. It happened in Boston and out of it came the formation of the Underwater Society of America. The Boston Sea Rovers were assigned to get Cousteau for the Convention. They did it by going through Cousteau's ghost writer, James Dugan.

Clubs now had a national voice, it seemed. Certainly the power was there, all those Councils representing thousands of clubs. When the Underwater Society of America (USOA) spoke by 1960 and had its Houston Convention, people had better listen. Unfortunately, USOA spoke in too many voices, bickering voices. It is this

The wives of club members played an important role in the social aspect of club membership. The Sharks Club Banquet, pictured above, was hosted by Dolores Fisher and Dorothy Lockwood, among others. Homer Lockwood

questing for power even at the lower level of the club that slows and stops action. It eventually erodes an organization into oblivion. Strong, articulate leaders clash head-on at Council level, then collide at a national level. Everyone represents a constituency, a region that has different issues and problems and needs from others. While much is agreed upon through compromise, an equal amount never gets beyond an argument. The infrequency of executive meetings allowed little time to resolve things. Like most big complex assimilating of parts, the Society didn't get back to the clubs and the member divers.

Clubs yielded the instruction standards-control to the proliferating, and growing in power and influence, training agencies by the late 1960's. Competitive spearfishing was being viewed negatively, and legislation had tamed down as diving stepped out of the limelight. Clubs and divers wondered by 1970, "Why have a Council or an Underwater Society of America?" Sometimes a false sense of "being needed because we exist" does not justify staying in existence.

SHOP CLUBS

Meanwhile by the 1960's and 1970's, divers were being picked up in new designs of grouping divers into shop clubs, college clubs, special interest clubs, training agency clubs, and even resort clubs. The diving stores/shops could either ignore clubs or absorb them. Many shops had successful "club operations." A good example was the Squid Diddlers Club of the chain of Ski N' Dive Shops in Southern California which was a pre-1970's approach. Each shop had a club branch, but they all came together for big charter boat dives, barbecues on the beach and much partying. The idea was to keep customers and certified divers on the premises, plant the leaders, control the newsletter, and sell equipment. Failure to fully control a club that a shop organizes may mean, "It will come back and bite you in the ass," as Mike Kevorkian in his Hialeah, Florida, shop warned us. "A club will come at you eventually wanting discounts, free air, special treatment. The members will try to boycott you by going to a store across town. They have the loyalty of wild goats. It's one of the reasons there weren't many clubs in Florida. And," Mike continued, "the weather is so good, the divers don't waste time sitting around in heated rooms trying to organize everything like they do up North."

Al Tillman remembers that they organized a local diving club within UNEXSO (Underwater Explorers Society) and they met there. Jack McKenney was assigned to guide club members and keep them loyal to UNEXSO. "Unfortunately, Jack joined the club rather than being UNEXSO's objective representative. The club bought its own boat, compressor and began inviting UNEXSO's off-island customers to go diving with them, thereby taking away UNEXSO's primary revenue."

Another aspect, a club would loan equipment and sell-off used equipment to each other, which is a great thing for clubs but terrible for retailers.

Colleges and universities were excellent places for diving clubs to originate. Universities had swimming pools, instruction potential, the right age in the students, and the school could often buy its own SCUBA equipment and run their own air compressors. Several classes every year birthed certified divers who were eager to be in a club about a new interest. "I think in 1955 we had one of (if not the first,) state college diving club in America at California State University at Los Angeles," relates Al Tillman, who was The Devilfish Club's advisor. "As many as 50 members would trek down to Mexico, as well as to Catalina Island and to local beaches." Zale Parry remembers Stu Mackay, Hugh "Brad" Bradner and Parry Bivens' avid activities with the University of California at Berkeley's diving club which was a cohesive diving group for several years before the official thrust with election of officers July 25, 1954. The college club lost members on graduation, so the change-over in such clubs caused instability, especially when the catalyst leaders move on and aren't replaced.

Company clubs follow the same lines, but employees don't graduate out. Most companies supported the idea and provided facilities. The company often spotted administrative potential in the club leaders that wasn't evident doing their "assembly line jobs."

Special interest clubs rose strongly during the 1960's and 1970's. Photography, particularly, cultivated a club approach and the Underwater Photographic Society (UPS) Los Angeles Chapter is a good example. Organized in 1957 by Al Tillman and Earl Sugarman, with Zale Parry as an early President, the Society/Club went beyond socializing to a greater process of exchanging technical information, providing the competition (once the domain of spearfishing), and staging elaborate film showings and Festivals. The underwater photography club beat the spearfishing club, whereby only one member gets to spear a specific fish. Camera people can all get film of an individual fish and let it go on to be photographed another day. But spearfishing survived the decades and in club-form, with the free diving/spearfishing addicts. The Long Beach Neptunes club was a prize example into the year 2000. There has been evidence that diving is moving back (even as it goes forward with high-tech) to free diving. Skin diving only clubs have been appearing, perhaps a desire to really be free once again in diving.

One big reason dive clubs in general lost their lure was that as more and more divers showed up at diving sites (and one had to practically get in line to get into the water), divers were forced into a congested diving area, with the fish scared away, the bottom stirred up, the sense of wildness dissipated, and your own fellow club members becoming an annoyance. Better to sneak off alone or with a buddy, have a secret spot all to oneself. The pure club was losing its appeal and a "sort of club," at least it was called club, was an open joining to anyone and everyone serviced by a training agency or a large diving retailer like Sports Chalet with its twenty-three stores in Southern California, owned by Norbert Olberz. Again, it is important to define a club as a containable small group of 8 to 20 people who interact well, have face-to-face gatherings and are compatible. These big entities weren't really clubs.

In the early 1960's, *Skin Diver Magazine* made a diligent effort to support the club idea by setting up an award and recognition program within its pages for achieving clubs. Clubs submitted "scrapbooks" of their activities, service to diving and community projects. Write-ups in local papers, photographs, awards, instruction programs, starfish mop, underwater trash removal and even things like the Boston Sea Rovers' raffle to raise $10,000 for a room for a school with crippled children. All were evaluated and recognized. The presentation folders were archived and available after coverage in the magazine to interested club organizers. It was a good idea, but it didn't stop the lessening of clubs.

Herculean efforts were often required to keep clubs going by the end of the 1950's. A prime example is the Treasure Hunt and Competitive Games of the Cleveland Skin Divers Club. In an area not blessed with clear water or plenty of fish, it was difficult to remain enthusiastic about diving. All the Ohio Area had to offer was "muck diving" and plenty of water. The club acquired ideas from other clubs and sent out 64 invitations to other clubs to compete in the 1959 Underwater Games. The events were the weight retrieve, compass course, relay race, and depth guessing. Manufacturers pitched in to help. Even Mike Nelson/Lloyd Bridges attended.

Another factor that gave clubs less appeal to divers was the attitude of spouses. During clubs' ruling days in the

The California Council of Diving Clubs celebrated the opening of Marineland of the Pacific.   Homer Lockwood

1950's, 1960's and 1970's, clubs were "good ole boy" oriented, very male, and although invited on outings, divers' females felt left out, as diving became the all-involving "mistress." When women did arrive full force on the diving scene in the late 1970's, 1980's, 1990's, they spiced-up the club membership. Where wives or husbands didn't dive, liaisons could be expected between the sexes, as they were thrown together in common exotic interest.

The research of the history of sport diving seems to indicate that sport diving was shaped in many ways by the club movement in the 1950's and 1960's, then to some lesser degree in the 1970's and 1980's and took on a larger, different shape during the 1990's. Clubs enabled better opportunities, especially in the use of charter boats. Clubs have also generated many of diving's best leaders. It was where they had a first chance to shine.

The club generated competition, information exchange, politics, invention and finding friends and diving mates. The overall impact on sport diving was to create a family of divers where common concerns could be discussed and group action taken.

Nelson "Doc" Mathison, a Champion California Spearfisherman and renown underwater photographer, could easily have gone his own individual way in diving but he was a member of the Long Beach Neptunes and the Underwater Photographic Society. He said, "Join a diving club, you'll never feel lonely and you have an audience for your fish stories."

11

PADI

PROFESSIONAL ASSOCIATION
OF DIVING INSTRUCTORS

DEFINING EVENT: PADI'S MULTI-LEVEL SPECIALTY PROGRAM

A young couple went in the door of a diving store/school in a small town in middle America; the year was 1999, and asked the man at the desk, "We want to become scuba divers, learn to dive. What do we have to do?"

"This is the right place; we can make you both Basic Open Water Divers, PADI Certified. Why, my friends, you've come to the biggest and best diving instruction program in the world, and it's all over the world. This is a PADI Dive Center; you couldn't do better...as for Irish, well, there's a bit of connection there. Let me tell you how PADI started."

The store operator sort of knew the origins of the agency with which he had affiliated, and for sure, he knew that PADI was a big business in the diving industry, operating on a $50,000,000 annual budget in the last year of diving's 50-year history. Thirty-three years after it started, it could boast 101,000 (Over 46,000 of these total are Divemasters) PADI Professional Members Worldwide. In 1999, PADI Members issued 810,000 dive certifications, giving PADI a cumulative total of more than 9.3 million divers since opening its doors. The PADI Trade Association represents more than 3300 retail facilities and over 1300 resorts worldwide.

In 1966, when PADI (Professional Association of Diving Instructors) was forged from the unrest of two men, NAUI was the dominant and respected training agency, and people were proud to say they were NAUI divers as a NAUI C-Card was a passport to diving anywhere. NAUI was a bit arrogant and over-confident and saw no challenge to their ruling position.

The NAUI leaders might have been thoroughly shaken if they'd been able to be flies on the wall at a Morton Grove, Chicago, Illinois, restaurant when in 1966 John Cronin came storming in after calling to say, "Ralph, we've got to talk."

John Cronin was a tough, hard hitting salesman representing the U. S. Divers Company at the time in Chicago, seven Midwestern states and Canada; Ralph Erickson was a tough, ambitious, professional, educator specializing in aquatics.

John Cronin tells us he met Ralph the first time at a divers' association meeting. They mutually agreed that the way diving was being taught was wrong. They chase people away. "They take a doctor or an attorney, and he's got to swim Lake Michigan before they'll teach him to dive."

Yes, John and Ralph agreed. You had to make people safe, but make it as easy as possible. At a point in time, when diving was at a peak in its popularity, the early 1960's, Cronin felt the training was unpleasant and uncomfortable.

Cronin got involved with an ITC (Instructor Training Course) with NAUI, hoping to help change the training approach, renting the banquet room for the course, but the NAUI people never showed up.

Ralph Erickson describes the dive instruction situation in the early 1960's:

"The entire Midwest had a great number of Dive Stores, each one with Instructors who were teaching diving.

Dick Bonin and John Cronin.   PADI

Most of these Instructors were never certified as divers, much less Instructors. It was a problem, as far as I was concerned, for the cost of a course was $18.00. The course didn't require any open-water training, and if they had a dive with an Instructor, training was not very much, if any.

"Interestingly, the state of the art for these dive stores, was to make an assistant instructor out of any diver completing one dive with them. After about ten dives, they made them Instructors.

"The Chicago YMCA, had Certified Instructors. To become one, the individual had to sit at the feet of an Instructor for about three years. The Instructor would periodically let loose small gems of wisdom, which were the heart of the Instructor Certification.

"One of their gems was, 'What are the twirley bends?' That's the only one I remember, and I could never have passed their course, for I would not have memorized all the laws of physics or known the little gems of wisdom. I would never have learned their complicated formulas for computing amounts of air used on dives at various depths."

Cronin recalls sitting in a hotel room for two days with a group of Midwest Instructors to draft an eight-week course under Ralph's academic guidance. U.S. Divers thought John was wasting company time and told him to keep it *separate.* He tossed in $30.00 to start PADI, got an *Undersea Journal* printed at an orphanage by trading a bottle of booze and seconds-masks and fins for the kids.

Ralph packed up his courage and pride and went to the first NAUI Instructor Certification Course in Houston in 1960. He felt he was the most ignorant of diving theory of anyone there, but no one outshone him in water work. His background of life guarding, coaching championship water polo teams, and diving put him near the top of that class.

Ralph recalls:

"I had never had any training, just merely went diving in Lake Michigan when the Chicago Park District Lifeguard Service bought two complete sets of Aqua Lungs. As a Captain of lifeguards, I had immediate access to the equipment and spent a lot of time on the bottom of Lake Michigan looking for wrecks. Of course we could only dive in the summer time, for we didn't have any means of insulating ourselves except for a sweat shirt.

"When I returned with my NAUI Certification, I taught a lot of diving with a mandatory open water dive for NAUI Certification. I also increased the price to $40.00 for training. The YMCAs in Chicago would start with a class of about twenty students and would physically disqualify all but three or five. I took the disqualifiers and made them divers. Word seemed to have spread through the YMCA underground that if they failed the YMCA course, go to Erickson since my students were diving successfully long before those from the YMCA.

"I'll never forget a time at a diving convention in Chicago when a YMCA Instructor, whom I didn't know, asked me if I got paid for teaching diving. I told him that I did. He then proceeded to tell me that I was lower than a snake for teaching diving for money. I asked him what he did for a living and he told me that he drove a bread truck. I asked him if he got paid for it, and he replied that he did. I then told him that he was lower than a turd for taking money for driving a bread truck, and he responded that he had to eat. So I told him that I taught diving and swimming for a living, and I had to eat so I had to be paid. He left shaking his head but I guess he didn't know what to say. Needless to say, I was on every YMCA Instructor's shit list."

When John Cronin called in anger and told Ralph, "We've got to talk," it was a boiling point for Cronin's dissatisfaction with the weak instruction and resulting diminishing interest in diving. The Midwest with limited diving waters or a diving season was coming off a boom-time when diving interest was peaked by the movie, *Silent World*, and television show, *Sea Hunt*.

Ralph Erickson was one of those early diving pioneers who reluctantly joined up with NAUI, but served as a harsh critic.

Al Tillman remembers Ralph driving up to the *Skin Diver Magazine* office in Lynwood, California, in 1961 with a long list of ways NAUI ought to do better:

"Ralph was a big man and he didn't have time for pleasantries. I always felt I was in the ring and a big, mean, burly, wrestler was coming at me. But he was right about a lot of things, and I could see his smarts and leadership were going to have to be absorbed into NAUI. I worked with Ralph to put on a roadshow Film Festival at McCormack Place in Chicago in the next year. He had directed our 1961 Instructor Course at the Glenview Naval Air Station outside of Chicago. I assigned him another Chicago Course in 1965, but when I left to run UNEXSO and gave up directing NAUI, somebody just cancelled it. That's all I know about it, but I always felt Ralph should have been on NAUI's Board of Directors from the outset, and I felt we could work on things together."

EVENT'S MULTI-LEVEL SPECIALTY PROGRAM

Jumping back to the genesis at that Morton Grove Restaurant, Ralph relates:

"One night, John called and told me that he was giving an equipment lecture to a NAUI Instructor Certification Course at Western Illinois University. WIU is the hardest place to reach from Chicago. To Peoria is easy, but from Peoria to McComb, Illinois, is an impossibility. It's an eighty mile trip and took three hours on a two-lane highway used exclusively by farmers and their equipment.

"John arrived and there was no course. He was furious and called me and asked if I could meet him in a restaurant in Morton Grove five hours later. I met a very angry Cronin, and he kept telling me that it was time. 'It's time, Ralph, it's time,' he growled.

"I told John to sit down and relax. Once he was seated and calmed down, I asked, 'What in the hell is it time for?'

'For a new diving agency.'

That was the birth of PADI."

"We met at my apartment the following Tuesday night. John brought a bottle of Scotch with him. I was in one of my phases of not drinking, so he took care of that side of it. Ever since, John has been fond of telling people that we kicked in thirty-five bucks a piece to get PADI started and that I still owed him for that and for half a bottle of Scotch.

"We got our meeting started by my declaring that we should have a name for this new organization. I suggested that we could write down about fifty or sixty names and then, maybe pick one or put a couple together. Incidentally, I was only interested in the lower half of the Western side of Lake Michigan.

"John said that he didn't care what we called the organization, as long as, we had "professional" in it. I suggested that we could then be the Professional Association, because we would be an Association of Diving Instructors. John said, 'That's it, that's it, PADI!'

"I said, 'John, you SOB, you sand-bagged me.' He never admitted to it but it turned out to be a good Irish name, catchy and had a certain ring to it. The name apparently appealed to the macho store owners of the 1960's. We've had a lot of fun with the name and its being Irish through out the years. And John always counters with, 'If Ralph had his way, it would probably be a Swedish name like Viking or something.'

"We needed a logo and once again John came to the rescue by saying, 'All I want in the logo is a world similar to the one on *National Geographic*,' which immediately changed my concept of our new organization and conceptually, where John had been all along.

"Since I had two years of mechanical drawing in high school, I would draw the logo with the world. Drawing the

John Cronin, Ralph Erickson with others.   PADI

world with longitude and latitude was the hardest thing I have ever done. If it hadn't been for the U.S. Navy Navigation Manual, I would never have accomplished it.

"I drew two circles - one inside the other and started using press-on letters to get our name into it. I worked on this eight hours a day for two weeks and John would call and ask how everything was going. I always had bad news, for I couldn't get the letters to fit. Finally, I succeeded, and I was elated and called John.

"We decided we would have a diver with a torch in the center of the world. The torch was for education - lighting up the world of diving. John had a copy of a catalogue by U.S.D. whereby the outer cover showed Cousteau divers with torches underwater.

"Neither John nor I could draw a diver. So we asked a diving friend of mine if he would do it. I told John that we might have to pay him twenty-five or thirty bucks for his work. Keep in mind, we only had $35.00. We met him (diver) downtown for lunch and John suggested that we might not have to pay him anything. We might possibly be able to 'knight' him with a snorkel.

"When I broached the subject to our guy at lunch, he said he would do it. When I asked him how much it would cost, he hemmed and hawed for a while and then he asked, 'How about my getting an Instructors Card instead?'

"John kicked me under the table. I said that I didn't know and asked John what he thought? He fiddled and pretended to be thinking and then said, 'Ralph, I guess its okay. What do you think?'

'It's a deal.'

"We all left the restaurant happy. When we got away, John chuckled and felt that we had knighted the guy with a snorkel. Within a couple of days we had the diver and torch (logo) and we were ready to go. When we got the patches and decals, John sold them to all of the dive stores in his territory and enlisted them as PADI Instructors for $85.00 each. I sold it to all the swimming coaches that I had taught scuba to. They in turn, were teaching in their respective locations. We soon had sufficient money to do or create anything we desired or thought to be appropriate for diving."

A lot of pioneer dive leaders from the 1960's felt PADI just jumped in, copied NAUI, and gave away instructor certifications. The other agencies didn't feel threatened by this new organization. Many felt it would just be another weak attempt at a sort of mail-order certification. Many people under-estimated the abilities of Ralph Erickson to put together material in a professional way; nor did they realize that John Cronin driven as he was, would rise out of the Midwest portion of America and become the successful architect of the most powerful diving manufacturing company despite burgeoning competition."

Cronin says that on his sales tour over seven states, he signed up the shop owners. "Dues were $15.00 a year and $2.00 for a diver's C-Card." John built an office in a basement of his home and typed out C-Cards on weekends. He was dyslexic and spelled a lot of names wrong.

To raise money to keep PADI going and pay a part-time secretary who wasn't dyslexic, John and Ralph put on a film festival and raised $2,000.00. Harry Shanks and Tim Mankey Smith, (who replaced John for U.S. Divers, when he went West in 1969), took it over the next year and it became Our World Underwater.

Ralph changed the way people would be certified and explains it here:

"I had always been dissatisfied with merely one course for certification. I was keenly aware that LA County played with an Advanced Course and so had NAUI. I think that both organizations tried to make it an all-encompassing course so it didn't work.

"We had Certified Diver, with a mandatory dive for certification. An Advanced Course with not much in it, and no one pushed anyone into it. I then had written a Master Diver Course but Frank Scalli, in talking with John (Cronin), thought that it would alienate Navy Divers. We changed Master Diver to Divemaster. In retrospect, we should have kept both. But, what the hell did we know in those days!

"I was used to the Red Cross swimming program of Beginning Swimmer, Intermediate Swimmer, Advanced Swimmer, Junior and Senior Lifesaving (Course) followed by certification of Swimming Instructors as Water Safety Instructors. I was also well aware of the Boy Scout System of movement from Tenderfoot, to Second Class, First Class, Star, Life and Eagle. So I think a lot of what we did was based on those two organizations.

"I also played with Merit Badges but didn't quite know how to incorporate it into our program. We had Specialties but not in name. It wasn't until Dennis Graver became our National Training Director that Specialties came into being." Nick Icorn, Director before Graver, by giving it its titles pushed its creation, too.

Jon Hardy, who took over NAUI management in the 1970's, saw PADI as watching other agencies, taking what works, and "borrowing it". Jon felt NAUI was creating instructors and PADI would pick them up because it was easier to use PADI material. NAUI would tighten standards and instructors would go to PADI. Then PADI went after the dive shops, which upset John Gaffney, whose NASDS had 380 shops members.

Ralph Erickson didn't think PADI was any carbon copy of NAUI but had some new needed features. Ralph expressed himself this way:

THE INSTRUCTOR MANUAL

"Early in 1969, I wrote an Instructor Manual which was never accepted by any one too much. I think it was too far removed from the thinking of Instructors of that era. Each Chapter had objectives for diving based on similar format for flying by the U.S. Air Force Instructor Manual that Garry Howland had given me.

"Nick Icorn rewrote the Instructor Manual and did away with my Advance Course. Dennis Graver rewrote Nick Icorn's work, and my Advanced Course was gone. John Stewart rewrote the Manual, and my advanced Course was missing. But with the advent of Drew Richardson, a new era of Education came into being, possibly the finest Education System in the world. No school, college or university can compare. Drew reincorporated my Advanced Program, with changes, of course. It was a new day and we knew much more about diving and education. The Advanced Course became broader in scope and is used extremely successfully in 1999."

THE LOGO DONE PROFESSIONALLY

"Incidentally, a year and a half after we started PADI, John was now Marketing Manager of U.S. Divers and he got a call from one of our Instructors, who told him that in our logo, Professional had only one s in it. John sort of wondered what we should do about it. I thought we had enough money to have it done professionally. I had been so engrossed in those press-on letters, over the two-week period, I unconsciously left out the one s and at this stage of the game, I wasn't about to try it all over again."

THE UNDERSEA JOURNAL

"John wanted a JOURNAL for Instructors in our new business. I guess in talking with his dealers (Instructors), he found that was what they wanted most. He told me the only thing, he wanted it called was 'something Journal.' We quickly agreed on the name, *The Undersea Journal*.

"I knew some people who would write some articles, and I wrote on anything I could dream up. At a meeting once, Ben Davis asked me where I got the articles. I wasn't about to tell him, so I merely said that I got them from all over.

"The *Journal* would be in black and white and never have any advertising, which was true for about twenty years. I even wrote all the articles for one issue and put names of Instructors that I knew well, as authors. I put my mother's maiden name as one of the authors, and got a letter from a guy in Canada wondering if that author and he were related. It was a Swedish name.

"We had my secretary type the *Journal* in columns. We paid her $25.00 and both of us were happy. I made a paste-up and we went to a printer who was doing good, inexpensive work. As it turned out, John got the first issue printed for a bottle of Scotch."

THE PIC PROGRAM

"In about a year's time John came from a National Sporting Goods Association Show in New York and told me about having dinner with Paul Tzimoulis. Paul suggested a card with the student's picture on it. We accepted it, and another integral part of an association fell into place.

"Cronin saw the PIC-Card as a major PADI innovation that gave it a big push forward. Instructors told John that they weren't about to chase ten students around for pictures. 'You're crazy, John.' John just packaged an envelope, the instructor signed and gave it to the student to send in."

PHOTOS

"I didn't have a source of underwater photos, so I went to the manufacturers and begged photos for the cover of the *Journal*. They would only give them to me as long as no other manufacturers' equipment was in the magazine. Such was life at that time, quite narrow minded or I guess, a better phrase would be 'tunnel vision'."

PADI was a part-time operation headquartered at Ralph Erickson's; Ralph was teaching at Loyola University full-time. Using 1967 as the actual starting point or birth year for PADI, the idea of a new training agency was slow to catch on for the next three years. It provided an easy way to become an instructor by just putting up $85.00 and filling out an application.

Many divers just didn't want to face up to NAUI's tightening standards and there were disgruntled shops and instructors disenchanted with NASDS, NAUI and the YMCA. Sometimes a new offering can come along, ease up on entry requirements, and copy the ideas the others have already worked hard to prove out.

But by 1970, it was time to pick up the pace. There were only about 400 PADI members and the financing was still out of Cronin's and Erickson's pockets for the most part. It was operating as a nonprofit corporation. John Cronin had been pulled into U.S. Divers Headquarters in California, and rapidly moved from Sales Manager to Vice President, and then President and CEO. From this power position in the industry he was able to guide and promote a separate but close-by PADI operation. "Space with a lot of cardboard boxes," was what Nick Icorn encountered when John Cronin pulled him out of U.S. Divers Engineering Department to direct PADI in late 1970. Nick was an early pioneer and got involved in all the training programs: Los Angeles County, Scripps Institution of Oceanography, YMCA, NAUI and then, PADI. As National Director, he more or less replaced Ralph Erickson in over-seeing PADI's development. Ralph stayed with teaching in Chicago, as PADI now rooted itself in California in 1970. Nick loved instruction and he brooded over the questionable reputation of PADI with its crossover certification that took anybody, (The rumor went around that, you could certify your pet duck with them if you did the paper work.) Nick had trained employees at U.S. Divers, and of course, since U.S. Divers had become John Cronin, he did it as a PADI convert.

Dennis Graver, who would replace Nick after six years, saw PADI being supported by U.S. Divers, if not in actual financing, at least being able to ride coattails in getting printing done and other joint purchases. Nothing illegal, they remained separate operations. Nick, more or less, agrees that a sprinkling of U.S. Divers' dust greased the way for PADI in the industry. Ralph Erickson gives Nick credit for picking up on his concern that divers needed a hierarchy of achievement, a ladder to progress up, in order to keep their interest continuing. Yes, the Boy Scouts Merit Badge System played a large role in the diversification and expansion of dive instruction. Nick Icorn was four merit badges short of Eagle Scout and Dennis Graver raised rabbits for one of his merit badges. They've got the badges to prove it.

The training agency leaders in the early 1970's were watching an 80% per year dropout rate loom bigger and bigger. The basic course left divers without any real introduction to special kinds of diving and highly inadequate to jump into instructing. They needed to be locked into an interest like photography or collecting specimens, it seemed. Dennis Graver felt that by the 1970's, instructor training and certification had pretty well skimmed off the qualified skin divers and water athletes that had, to that point, been fairly qualified to move into an instructor role in diving. Unfortunately, the new breed was coming along, enthusiastic but without good, basic skills or experience.

A major area of concern was that checkout open water dives were being done in

PADI marketed itself everywhere. Here Al Hornsby is making a donation to Jerry Lewis' telethon.

PADI

a fixed set of skills-testing or just an in-the-water-together experience. The feeling was that at least one open water dive should be integrated in the basic course. (The agencies in the 1950's and 1960's were leery of liability that might ensue with mishaps in the unpredictable open water environment.) Al Tillman recalls the 1954 campaign he and Bev Morgan waged to get Los Angeles County legal advisors to agree an open water experience could and should be tied into the first public classes.

PADI went for this required one open water dive, NAUI followed, but it was John Gaffney's NASDS (National Association of Skin Diving Schools) that upped the ante. NASDS was pouring it on, making the basic course longer, more complex and designed an open water basic class that would be mostly open water dives, seven or eight.

It forced the industry leaders to look closer at this instruction expansion. Retailers liked the idea of instruction as a profit center product, and lots of required dives could mean significant revenue from sales and rentals. With that big an investment, a basic diver would be around for awhile. But the counterpoint to this new extension of entry instruction also became a deterrent to new people coming into diving, who saw this new time and effort imposition as too burdensome. What was gained in retention was lost in diver start-up disenchantment. The National Scuba Training Council was just coming into being and represented the various agencies. In a rare and refreshing agreement, it was put forth as a standard that four should be the expected and minimum supervised open water dives required in a basic scuba course leading to certification as an Open Water Diver.

NASDS had made a big mistake with its Gold Program, as it was called, packaging an elaborate course program for its member shops that went beyond what they could promote. At the same time, the premiere training agencies were for a lesser expectation that sold better to the public.

Let's look back at the specialty areas of diving as the other major factor in changing what was to be offered to divers to hold them into diving. Giving them a variety of outlets for diving and a hierarchy of achievement. Ralph credits Dennis Graver and Nick Icorn with putting in specialty courses for PADI which would pick-up where basic classes left off. The basic courses for most agencies tried to incorporate these specialities in an introductory way in the basic diving courses. "We were doing it in the 1950's classes in Los Angeles County, a little bit on photography, even cooking the catch, but it was a rush job and pretty well left up to the individual instructor to do what he would with it. The tendency was, because the basic course always felt rushed, that the referral to specialty clubs and seminars was the best procedure. It was generally felt that creating more kinds of classes would look too burdensome and costly for the new entry divers at that stage in sport diving development," recalls Bill Starr, a Los Angeles County Program Coordinator.

But PADI, under Nick Icorn and then Dennis Graver, stuck them in place as follows:

Underwater Photographer

Cave Diver

Ice Diver

Wreck Diver

Search and Recovery Diver

Deep Diver

Research Diver

Equipment Specialist

They seemed to work. The interest was there and instructors were captivated, enticed into new training and certification, in order to teach the specialties. But Dennis Graver, looking out NAUI's window and then as PADI's Director of Training in the late 1970's, saw that interest in photography and night diving. And those types of specialities were thin in comparison with the interest in divers moving up a pure diving ladder from Advanced Diver to Senior Diver to Divemaster to Assistant Instructor to Instructor and then, Instructor Trainer. Later Rescue Diving and Paramedic-type categories would become popular.

NAUI had shot itself in the foot with an expensive project, The National Divers Association, a personal passion of NAUI President of the moment, which tried to hold trained divers into the sport with a membership concept. Where it had been the question in the 1960's, "Are you a NAUI diver"? the tide was shifting to, "Are you a PADI Diver?" by the end of the 1970's.

PADI had 4,000 instructors in the fold by 1974 and the many crossovers recruited were increasing rapidly. Nick Icorn left because of conflict in the directions that PADI seemed to be pushing. Dennis Graver, who had been let go by NAUI, after designing much of their new training materials, put sense, order and polish to the outdated and existing publications. PADI picked him up to take over Nick Icorn's position as National Director of Training. There he did the same job developing professional written materials about training courses and the specialty program. PADI was starting to emerge from its quick and easy image to a training agency with bonafide standards.

In an interim between Icorn and Graver, Cronin brought in a woman, Sonna Whisnand, who became an Operations Manager, a good editor, office organizer and did orderly up-to-date, day-to-day public and industry relations. Cronin credits Dennis Graver as PADI's first Ambassador and a key person in PADI's growth in late 1970's. He was followed by Al Hornsby, Jeff Nadler, Alex Brylske and a lot of young Turks, as Cronin saw them, tossing in new ideas and enthusiasm to keep the PADI pot boiling.

They were still picking up the best ideas of other agencies and moved to recognize dive stores as PADI Training Facilities in late 1970's and early 1980's. They brought in outside-the-industry consultants in marketing and bor-rowed the existing restaurant rating systems of "stars". They listened to advice on how to capture the market. A five-star facility would have trained and certified PADI Instructors, all the course levels and specialties, broad inventory, and dive charter boats. This was the old Boy Scout Merit Badge Program again at a higher level in the world of business.

Indeed, PADI , which had started as a nonprofit corporation, was moving toward a for-profit status. There would be some legal challenges by the State, but when John Cronin retired from U.S. Divers and became CEO of PADI, (He'd always been the Chairman of the Board of Directors), the PADI Corporation became a full fledged business. NASDS, which had stalled by this point, partially due to the unwieldy and bulky training program they were

PADI instructor on the beach with students for an open water dive. PADI was the first instructional agency to push multiple open water dives in a basic course.   *PADI*

pushing on member stores, couldn't handle the mushrooming PADI movement. Gaffney came up with some new ideas, but some of his talented colleagues over the years had split off to start new training organizations. The stall turned into a continuous weakening and by the end of the Twentieth Century, NASDS with John Gaffney gone, deceased, would merge with SSI, (Scuba Schools International).

By the late 1970's, some of the industry's power figures such as Cronin, Dick Bonin of Scubapro and Paul Tzimoulis of *Skin Diver Magazine* were meeting to sound an alarm that diving training had to be simplified. What had evolved was discouraging neophytes. One of the outcomes of that was a simple concept of letting people try scuba, the Discover Diving Program, in a couple of sessions without getting certified for open

water. A step before taking the basic course...something added on, rather than taken away from the multi-leveled menu of courses. NAUI, resting on its laurels and dignity, was slow to catch on to where diving was headed; political in-fighting led them to try to protect a status-quo that would not work in a changing world of sport diving. PADI, as a commercial entity directed by a continuous strong leadership in John Cronin, raced ahead. PADI got into the travel and resort business...dive resorts became PADI starred centers. PADI divers would feel secure in being referred to a PADI-endorsed resort facility.

PADI just continued to grow to become the mammoth training agency internationally, and various leaders passed through to leave their mark. Al Hornsby came to PADI to push that direct-dive-store involvement and clashed with Dennis Graver, who moved on to other challenges. PADI, finally, put together what the majority of divers seemed to want and were willing to support. Competitors still felt PADI was a Frankenstein monster assembled from the parts gathered from other agencies, but then what large business isn't created that way?

If results are the way we measure success, then PADI certainly deserves a great deal of credit for changing the face of sport diving, in particular. Its popular smorgasbord of specialty classes is probably the major event to launch its rapid rise to King of the Training Agencies. As the fifty-year diving history ends, to the best of our information, PADI International operates on a multi-million dollar budget, services over 176 countries and territories around the world and provides training materials in 24 languages. John Cronin was still around, unshaken by Y2K, as 2000 was rung in - still serving as titular head and guiding a PADI financed nonprofit environmental foundation which gives back to sport diving.

A FINAL SUMMARY

Al Tillman who founded NAUI, the original national training program devoted exclusively to diving, reacted to the evolution of the mega growth of the rival PADI which dominated the training business by year 2000.

"NAUI was a noble and an effective idea and probably still is. Unfortunately, the very essence of it belonging to divers and the instructors, who trained them, created a critical membership who pressured its leaders into stretching and reshuffling its shape and programming. And NAUI was so busy wondering how to change to meet the competition, they slowed to a crawl trying to sort out everybody's input.

PADI, on the other hand, was able to move fast and act on any new idea taken from the hard-earned successes of other training agencies. That comes with a one-man-rule which was always John Cronin with Ralph Erickson at his side in the beginning shaping and polishing Cronin's ideas for taking over diving instruction. PADI got into operation because John Cronin and Ralph Erickson just sold instructor certifications to anyone and especially to dissident dive shop owners or non-aligned instructors or instructors who wanted to cross over and get another badge to wear. Not very "professional".

PADI divers training underwater for specialty courses that expanded divers total training experience and held them in the sport. PADI

Reacting quickly to the trends in particularly, the specialty courses, putting out Photo C-Cards, and finding a lot more things that the diving business could sell to divers. PADI grew and grew. The other agencies were wrestling with in-house political turmoil and financial set backs.

NAUI was loaded with idea-people with pet projects that weren't always in the best interests of the organization. The ideas often collided and when resources and energies were put into some of the ideas, it was difficult to retreat even as the idea failed in various ways. PADI picked up a lot of thoughtful and ambitious talent along the way and they executed what John Cronin wanted to happen.

I think NAUI lost a powerful person in Ralph Erickson through perhaps an arrogance in ignoring the force of regional differences and local leaders. PADI jumped right in with dive shops pushing NASDS and (later, SSI to the side training agencies that operated in the dive store/school centering of the sport diving industry). PADI picked up on resort diving as well, and made it so much easier for stores and resorts to identify with PADI and get flooded with services, saleable programs and materials.

All the other agencies have survived the last half of the century. Many, supposedly different ones, came into being. None met the fast action of PADI on the battlefield. None had a titular head, a street fighter, who ran diving's biggest equipment company, U.S. Divers, and directed PADI's emergence at the same time. The general feeling with observers of the past is that Cronin and U.S. Divers were to PADI in the start-up days as Cousteau's name was to U.S.Divers' staying power.

We used to say a big growth company was the General Motors of its field and now we suppose we say it's the Microsoft.

Like all giant corporations, they often make even bad ideas work and gain acceptance. PADI deserves much credit for keeping divers into diving, shutting down the alarming dropout rate (averaged 80% over the first two years after certification) always the disturbing issue and reality of sport diving. Even with cutting corners to get established and relying on support from the manufacturing world, in particularly U.S. Divers, I think PADI had earned its fountain-head position and John Cronin must be recognized as the Czar of sport diving by year 2000. But I hope that the other agencies survive because they do good things beyond just being big and marketing the public into submission."

Dennis Graver, the author and editor of PADI's and NAUI's best written materials during the 1970's and 1980's, in the year 2000, said that the reason for PADI's rise to the top could be explained best in one word, "marketing".

Nick Icorn, who had leadership in all the training agencies and was PADI's National Director of Training for six years, would explain his retreat from PADI with a simple, "I could see by the end of the 1970's that PADI was going in different directions, too commercial, too concerned with making money than my own beliefs."

How to become a PADI Open Water Scuba Instructor in year 2000.

The PADI Instructor Development Course prepares the instructor candidate to function as a PADI Open Water Scuba Instructor. The program further develops leadership and teaching abilities to the instructor level and prepares candidates to teach PADI courses.

PADI Open Water Scuba Instructors are qualified to:

Conduct the entire range of PADI experience programs and PADI courses from Open Water Diver through Divemaster (except for specialties and PADI Medic First Aid, which require specific Specialty Diver Instructor and Medic First Aid Instructor ratings).

PADI Divemasters training is the first leadership level in the PADI system of diver education. The rating denotes an individual who:

1. Has a high level of personal diving skill
2. Has instructor level knowledge of diving theory
3. Has had significant training in how to assist an instructor during training activities
4. Is able to assume appropriate responsibilities that benefit the welfare of other divers.

Student certifications issued in:

1970 - 47,500
1980 - 732,000
1990 - 3.3 million
1999 - 9.3 million

Year 2000 total list of SPECIALTY COURSES
Altitude Diver
AWARE Fish ID
Cavern Diver
Boat Diver
Deep Diver
Diver Propulsion Vehicle (DPV) Diver
Drift Diver
Dry Suit Diver
Enriched Air Diver
Equipment Specialist
Ice Diver
Multilevel Diver

PADI materials are considered some of the best in the industry.

Night Diver
Peak Performance Buoyancy
Project AWARE
Rebreather - Dolphin/Atlantis
Rebreather - Ray
Search & Recovery Diver
Underwater Naturalist
Underwater Navigator
Underwater Photographer
Underwater Videographer
Wreck Diver
(Total 23 in year 2000)

12

NASDS
National Association of
Scuba Diving Schools

Defining Event: The Red Book - Teaching on the Same Page

No training agency is more identified with a single person than the National Association of Scuba Diving Schools (NASDS). The person was John Gaffney, an ebullient and sometimes raucous man of Irish Ancestry, who took a stand against the powers of the sport diving industry back in 1960.

The specialty dive shops of the 1950's were owned and operated by passionate divers, who in too many cases, were inexperienced in business matters. The manufacturers of equipment at the time seemed to dictate the way the retailers would do business by controlling the terms of buying inventory.

Large discounts were available to any dive store that could buy $100,000 or more worth of equipment to stock their shelves. Tough terms of credit were imposed. The lone store sitting out there with a minute bank roll was struggling with the obstacles of establishing a new business - in a new industry.

The worried shop owner didn't have any place to turn for solace, advice, or support. In walked a confident, cocky guy, who knows the industry and can talk diving because he was a real diver, who as a teenage kid rode his bike to spear halibut under a Long Beach, California, pier.

"You gotta stop fighting with the shop across town, he's not the enemy." "Gaff", as he was fondly called by the dive shop people, was about to unite them into a union of common interests in order to direct their own destiny. At the time, 1959, Gaffney was getting around the country as *Skin Diver Magazine's* advertising sales manager.

"Your enemy is making the equipment you need to sell, but we don't treat them like enemies; we show how much they need us and how they need to bend and keep every retail shop in business because that's where people buy their equipment." A decade later, Gaffney would be identifying other recreations - skiing, surfing, golf - as the competitive enemies that dealers and manufacturers should unite against.

As he traveled the country, John Gaffney, was forming an association in his mind, going from store-to-store, and manufacturer-to-manufacturer. But the manufacturers saw what was brewing as a threat to their controlling power. They put pressure on John's employers, Jim Auxier and Chuck Blakeslee, whose magazine depended on the major manufacturers' full page advertisements to carry the cost of publication. For this reason, the magazine and Gaffney parted ways.

Gaffney wanted more than an association of the stores; he felt he knew the magazine business and could publish his own. So along with getting a store front headquarters, he incorporated NASDS, as a commercial entity in 1964, (In some publications Gaffney credits 1962 as the birthdate of his organization), published *Dive Magazine*, and pulled in some of the more successful store operators to fuel the enterprise with ideas and money.

Al Tillman recalls that he and John Gaffney had friendly verbal clashes about nonprofit instructor training versus instruction as a product to sell. "I was following John's exit from *Skin Diver Magazine* and going on staff at *SDM*, as Director of Public Affairs, overseeing NAUI and the Film Festival - and physically sitting at John's old desk that was made from a door on top of two file cabinets."

John Gaffney and NASDS had some real loyal followers but animosities were incurred from various sectors. Suddenly, the manufacturers had to contend with the power of dozens of dive shops, some of them major customers of the manufacturers. One of the new Manufacturers was Gustav Dalla Valle and Dick Bonin's Scubapro that launched a major threat to U.S. Divers in 1962. Scubapro introduced a fair trade practice; there would be no dumping of merchandise in discount stores, no underselling by Scubapro dealers, and this new direction was just the edge NASDS members would find. It gave them dignity and an incentive to work together. Gaffney and Bonin hit it off well at this point in diving history to the extent that Scubapro was a prime supporter for *Dive Magazine* with its stylized advertising, mainly crafted by John Gaffney and his in-house artist, Roy Brizz.

What really made NASDS succeed in the 1960's was the easy access to the main-man, John Gaffney. Gaff lived with the phone to his ear consulting, consoling and advising the isolated dive shop owner. Al Tillman and Jim Christiansen, exchanging Gaff stories, recalled how Gaffney would be on a phone talking to a dive shop owner in some Southern swamp-town and manage to tell the owner how Al Tillman, Jim Christiansen and Sir Robert Marx were "sitting in front of me right now, talking about the same thing we're talking about." He was a talented name-dropper. Gaff could take on any problem called in, would humor, cajole and promise he'd take care of it now for the dive shop caller.

He'd settle feuds between two dive stores and he wasn't above profanely cursing the dive manufacturers and training agencies in a loud voice, a very loud voice, for he did dearly crave an audience for his cleverness and furor.

NASDS had picked up key successful shops and their owners right from the start up. He found a leader owner in each of the diving population centers. Bill Hardy and Bill Johnson in San Diego, Bob Clark in Nebraska, Ed Brawley up San Francisco Way, Bill Hogan in his headquarters hometown, Long Beach, Hal Watts in Florida, Roland Reviere in New Orleans, and Chuck Buchanan, the Meistrell brothers of DiveN'Surf in California, as well as the Brauer brothers of Ski N' Dive. He set up a Board of Directors from that roster.

It is important to recognize the necessity of *Dive Magazine* here. NASDS needed a voice and the reigning publication, *Skin Diver Magazine* wasn't about to support this new approach. *Dive* had two lives. Its first attempt was a good attempt to challenge *SDM*. The first issuance had lots of color, lots of 1960's modern reverse negative illustrations, and artistic graphics. Its verbal content had pieces of quality to match *SDM's* accidental publication of competent writing at times, but the stories were results of old crony favors from Robert Marx, Dick Anderson, Jack Prodonovich, and Bev Morgan writing articles.

The magazine was a direct violation of the good, small dive business principle that NASDS religiously espoused - don't plunge under-capitalized. Gaffney did, half vendetta inspired in a pique at *SDM* and half an attempt to go for broke. Only the new Scubapro line was willing to place top rate advertising. About $1200 were roughed together in putting out the first *Dive* issue in Gaff's mother's garage. It went six issues in an erratically scheduled issuance over two years before the bottom of the bag gaped open. It would come back by the end of the 1960's with new financial backing and the growth of NASDS.

Shop owners kept a low profile as they joined up with NASDS letting Gaffney be the target. The shop owners had their philosophies and criticisms of the industry, and practical field wisdom that Gaffney was able to articulate as a kind of a lyrical "dock fight", garment industry, union boss. He had verbal confrontations on behalf of NASDS with the establishment powers of diving - U.S. Divers, *Skin Diver Magazine*, and NAUI from 1964 on. There was heavy-handedness, underhandedness, and sheer, crude chutzpa on occasion. Those silent member supporters found in John Gaffney the representative street fighter, gladiator, to enter the arena for them and challenge the lions of sport diving. He was a mercenary combatant who seemed to ask little personal monetary tribute. He seemed to relish the center position of the battle ground, the power to face crisis continuously.

SECOND CHANCE - NEW MONEY

John met Bud Smith on a diving outing in Baja California and sold him on becoming the new financial support for the second life of *Dive Magazine*. It was only the magazine and not NASDS or Gaff Productions, separate business entities. So in 1968 and 1969, NASDS picked up new steam with a magazine that tried to be more about fun and adventure, the best way to sell diving to the American culture that was being reformed at that time by the Vietnam War, Civil Rights Movement, the counterculture generation, and walking on the Moon. Al Tillman, just back from developing UNEXSO in the mid 1960's, met with John Gaffney to restate his position on instruction and the future direction of diving. Tillman was con-

Mil Clark, Howard Patten, Paul Hos, John Gaffney (center with trophy), Ernesto Geraso, and Ralph Davis at the 1955 Inter-American Championships in Mexico. NASDS had a solid pioneer diver as its founder.   John Gaffney

vinced that resort areas were where diving was going to happen in the main, that the dive shop was the conduit through which instruction and travel would have to flow. This pleased Gaffney, who said, "See Al, I told you the shop has to control diving."

"No, John," Al corrected him, "the shop is the central communication point and a continuing one for divers, but the independent instructor has to exist to keep them honest and acting in the best interest of the diver."

The meeting did not exactly result in a fusion of the minds. Al felt NAUI wasn't going to move in this direction of the shops and resorts, rejecting his concepts when proposed. Gaffney was enthusiastic to have NAUI's founder join up with NASDS.

Tillman, who had run philosophically in the opposite direction from John Gaffney as to the role of diving instruction, (Gaff had always cheerfully sneered at the Los Angeles County and NAUI programs that Al had founded) was now working with John because as Al Tillman pointed out "He was an up-front villain, no deviousness, his views, good or bad, were right there on his sleeve or coming out of his mouth as he eye-balled you." NASDS represented a new concept for Tillman that he came to realize, after operating a dive store as part of developing UNEXSO in the Bahamas. He saw the independent instructor, who could go anywhere and teach, might be doomed.

He could see that where you went to get equipment, get air, exchange dive talk seven days a week was a nerve center and the glue to hold diving together. It was a physical presence where the weekend warrior type of instructor was basically invisible. NAUI and PADI were late in coming to this thinking, but eventually, they'd develop store programs.

Al remembers John Gaffney had that hungry animal look in his eyes when he was about to out hustle you on a deal, and that he saw Tillman as a NAUI rebel, a born again convert or something, and he loved to exploit that. Al became *Dive Magazine's* unsalaried Editor of Travel and Education in exchange for large ads pushing his *Underwater Education* book. Tillman wrote articles on Deep Diving and Blue Ribbon Resort Guides for DIVE, serving as Editor of Travel and Instruction, and participated on the lecture staff for the dealer-only NASDS seminars and in its instructional sales clinics steeped in creating instructor/salesmen. The first such instructional sales clinic was held in 1967 in Denver, Colorado, with twenty-seven member stores sending their instructors "to learn a revolutionary new way to teach diving." The "new way" was not to qualify divers by seeing how well they stood up to the ordeals or tests conducted by drill-instructor-mentality individuals but to make the learning fun.

NASDS under John Gaffney was inventively trying to introduce new ideas to give them a profile of being progressive, whereas, the "other agencies" seemed bogged down in status-quo procedures and growing on basis of numbers. Over the years NASDS would claim introduction of the VIP Program (in 1964), whereby, tanks are to be inspected every year for interior corrosion - by NASDS member-stores, of course. A CIP program came later, in 1976, where Certified Inhalation Protection checked regulators and hoses on a regular basis. Both of these programs carried a fee and profit for the stores.

NASDS claims to be the first in 1967 with a plastic certification card, putting computers in the stores to control inventory, a Code of Ethics that prevented sale of equipment or air to consumers not certified to dive. NASDS's plastic cards went to photo cards with a dotted-on blood type, medical history. Rival agencies and their leaders felt NASDS copied or elaborated or glossed up the materials from other organizations, rarely gave credit for anything. But in some cases, there is no doubt, NASDS led the way in innovative safety and upgraded instructional practices.

NASDS went into the 1970's with a new name, same acronym. Gaffney recognized that more than just a product, teaching diving was the most controllable adhesive in the commerce of diving. So he changed "stores" to "schools". With the name change came a sort of mock

Gaff works behind his desk at NASDS Headquarters with NASDS President Chuck Buchanan.   *John Gaffney*

conversion to motherhood, church and safety. A fanatical construction of elaborate instructional systems were energetically assembled from diving manuals to more graphic C-Cards. From a kicking-dog role, suddenly NASDS consumed a massive portion of the who-cares-what-badge-lets-dive public entering the sport. NAUI found itself in the early 1970's desperately and precariously holding on to its number one edge in the instructional field after a series of monster gaffes with bankrupting, over-expansion efforts. The YMCA continued to flow erratically, never establishing a figure-head-leader nor full control over its network of pool facilities. PADI, bludgeoned along by John Cronin, made it easy to join PADI with a lot of giveaways, and benefited as NASDS had from the experiments of the pioneer instructional agencies; doing and imitating those things that showed successful shelf-life. By the mid 1970's, there were the big three-NAUI, PADI, and NASDS controlling the major roles in diving-instruction.

What made NASDS different at that time from the others was being shop-centered. The only doorway to any NASDS class, program or trips was through a bonafied NASDS shop. Shops became NASDS designated facilities by paying $100.00 a year dues and contracting to buy instructional materials exclusively from NASDS - and use only NASDS Instructors.

The enforcement of that familial loyalty was daily and continuously reinforced by Gaffney by telephone bull-shitting and no mercy evictions from membership for violations. It was all sutured across the continent by the brash pie-in-the-sky optimism and big brothering of the Gaff, who encrusted himself in a plushly red vinyl chair around the clock with his mouth incessantly flogging the mouthpiece of the telephone.

All this time, a series of talented dive store pioneers floated through NASDS's life. They were a Senate to Gaffney's Caesar, a Central Council to his Godfather approach, and over the years a number of those supporters defected to exploit ideas and contributions they'd made to NASDS but had not received adequate credit for. They were honest breaks, the need to be identified away from the organization's imposition of anonymity, to be more than Gaffney Guys, to try to create bigger-than-a-dive-shop enterprises of their own. But in the beginning they were family, united against common demons, some real, and some figments of Gaffney's spell -casting. In those start-up days, it was exciting to see ideas executed on a stage broader than their local bailiwick and because there was nowhere else to go for representation of their needs and problems.

MUTINY IN THE RANKS

Chuck Buchanan, who was President of NASDS for awhile and a strong force during its building years, had this to say, "Off and on, there was mutiny brewing in NASDS, the Board of Directors turning on John when he'd made an audacious move without consulting them. Unplugging John wasn't the answer; he was vital in the worst of times and the really outraged NASDS prime movers just left for other involvements."

Ed Brawley broke off after he started the first PDIC (Professional Diving Instructor College) in 1969 in Northern California. NASDS was to recruit students for it and get $250.00 from each candidate's $1,450.00 tuition. Actually, the college was to be called NASDS Dive Instructor College. The California State Vocational Section approved it, and Santa Clara College assigned the course-giver there seven units credit. A quick summary of what then happened is that several NASDS chains of dive shops, San Diego Divers Supply, and the Bamboo Reef sent employees to the PDIC as students. They took notes from Brawley's copyrighted lectures, which Ed felt must be given word-for-word. According to court records, Brawley sued NASDS, John Gaffney and his Club Aquarius for taking the notes when Gaff had come up to the College to give a lecture and purloining them into an instructional manual called The Red Book. The court found that The Red Book plagiarized Brawley's lecture notes and material from Brawley's Green Book, which preceded NASDS's Red Book. What a mess!

Gaffney in cooperation with Bill Hardy set up rival NASDS Instructional College in San Diego. The employee he sent to Brawley's PDIC came back with materials to start the new NASDS College. Brawley gave a free ride to Hardy's employee because "When your employee comes back, he'll be so good you'll enroll all your employees." Brawley at the time was listed as Secretary-Treasurer of NASDS and didn't resign membership. But he would never come back into the fold.

Another valued leader, Bob Clark, became disenchanted with where NASDS seemed to be going and started up a copy of NASDS in Colorado called Scuba Schools International (SSI).

Gaffney's and NASDS's miseries about this time, 1969 and 1970, were topped by a disengagement of Bud Smith and John Gaffney. According to court records, Gaff got Bill Hogan to help him in the middle of the night to transport NASDS materials to another location. Smith retained Dive Magazine and Dive Industry, another Gaffney production, changed the locks and hoped to publish without NASDS. It just didn't work out without John Gaffney. In bitterness and disappointment, Smith took residue NASDS materials that were overlooked by Gaffney and gave them to an amusement park operator. You could have gone to Nu Pike Long Beach and have a fast talking huckster try to guess your weight and if he failed, one of the choices of prizes was a genuine NASDS C-Card saying you were a diver. This was not a Hallmark moment for diving.

John Gaffney always had his eye on teaching diving and he knew that ultimately NASDS could not depend on any outside instructors - he knew he had to create his own to survive. His training program was well in place by

John Gaffney and two of his favorite divers - writers Bob Marx and Dick Anderson in the late 1960's.   John Gaffney

1970, but to many, it seemed a whole lot like NAUI's, except it was profit-oriented and store-centered. PADI's Ralph Erickson always said after trying to operate a Chicago dive store in the 1950's, "You can't sell equipment without teaching diving."

Gaffney never saw teaching diving as a noble calling. His philosophical motto, to anyone naive enough to believe serving mankind was motivation enough, was "Money is the way you keep score." He was constantly looking for a new idea from other industries that would help his member stores. Remember the plastic photo card? Beyond that, he pushed the buoyancy compensator in as necessary equipment and designed new plastic tables for sport diving. Gaffney would fly all over to visit a store in trouble or a diving convention where he'd rant and rave about - "Giving away instruction." While flying, he'd read the airline magazines and from that reading he developed a respect for the ski industry. He brought in the marketing top guns from skiing to look at diving. NASDS paid out big fees to High Yield Management, and a Dr. Steinmetz, their consultant for five years, to get customer attitude studies. When NASDS went to DEMA (Diving Equipment Marketing Association) talking about joint efforts on such research, according to John, they were asked to leave DEMA.

The best result was that the outside consulting taught NASDS about target marketing and demographics. NASDS, through Gaffney, had been seeing the public "as people he flew over," when he went from California to Florida.

Gaffney knew how to recruit talented people to carry out the ideas he uncovered. Effective store owners were brought on his staff for training seminars which brushed past classic teaching methodology to cover fully the selling of equipment and diving instruction.

He got veteran diver and shop owner, Bill Hogan, to write his *Safe Diving* Instruction Manual. It was graphic, gaudy, much like the flamboyance of *Dive Magazine*. Gaffney gave credits and royalties, making little known people celebrated in the diving community that NASDS served.

Other diving agency leaders were highly critical of NASDS and John Gaffney, his loud, aggressive manner, his sneering bombast about how "the others were driving people out of diving with excessive standards." At conventions, one might find the Gaff in the hotel lobbies working the magazine racks, performing the cunning trick of shuffling *Dive Magazine* to the front and better display position. There were lots of rumors and accusations that NASDS, through John Gaffney, cut corners and played dirty tricks to get ahead of the field. But the member stores found in Gaffney their protective white knight, and almost everybody was glad to see him in person, hear his gossip and humor, and booming optimism for NASDS. Gaffney could quell troubled hearts by assuring store owners that, "We'll get even." Gaffney's excitement and hearty good- fellow treatment didn't always hold up and occasionally went against NASDS. Some, as we have mentioned, began to desert NASDS but not the idea of it. Competition would continue through the 1970's and 1980's as diving's devil incarnate and Jim Christiansen, diving's gentle giant, would observe, "Maybe, if Gaff had joined the Boy Scouts, he'd have more character."

Resentment against NASDS practices rose to a point where Los Angeles County, reportedly through ambitious employees of its Underwater Program, drafted an ordinance that would place excessive safe practices upon diving stores, instructors and charter boats. A few diver deaths got picked up by the Los Angeles Times, notorious for inflating small incidents into major epidemics, and a series of articles pushed Los Angeles County government officials into this intrusion into private enterprise. The training agencies had been riding out an early 1970's recession at the time, and they certainly didn't want any more restrictions imposed. NASDS may have been the first agency to take action to stop or at least temper the writing of the ordinance (which may have been because it was supposed to be the primary target). Gaffney claims to have spent $16,000 to fight it. He also claimed that he brought the training agencies together to form the National Scuba Training Council, a coming together for self-protection of NAUI, PADI, YMCA and NASDS.

These big four agreed to follow standards that met or exceeded that of the American National Standards Institute and its 1972 Z86.3 - a minimum course content for *Safe Scuba Diving Instruction*. No doubt the ordinance was an over-reaction, but it forced a minimum standard for all agencies and in the long run sold a lot of things, such as log books and open water dives.

After having to set up a new headquarters due to losing Bud Smith's backing, Gaffney had gotten NASDS back on track with a new track. NASDS would now be joined by Gaff's Club Aquarius, which would book travel and operate diving resorts exclusively for NASDS. Once again, John Gaffney got inspiration from an airline magazine. He had attempted to establish a swinging, diving resort with a charter boat in Ensenada, Mexico, but it was not a major success...then he read about time shares.

Aha! Why not buy a resort by selling week-long use to NASDS's dive stores. Throw in a boat and a charter plane, too. It was a grand plan but never reached full glory for NASDS. What looked good on paper got smudged in the execution over the years, as nothing lived up to the Gaffney hype, and individuals and stores made too many individual demands and were having enough pressure to pay their bills to keep the store operating. The other part of it is, how fickle the public was in the 1970's and 1980's, as a huge smorgasbord of choices in resorts and liveaboards made the latest development and offering more desired.

By 1975, NASDS was claiming to have certified over 500,000 divers since its inception with 1200 full-time NASDS instructors teaching in 389 stores. A big jump from 51 dues-paying members in 1969 reported in court records of the Brawley vs NASDS case.

John Gaffney and friends on a dive trip. The Gaff surrounded himself with famous divers. Bill DeCourt, Bob Marx and David Doubilet were on hand here.   Bill DeCourt

NASDS held on to its contender status among the training agencies but saw much of its power drained off, as Bob Clark blueprinted his SSI into another NASDS, and PADI grew strong. Then NAUI finally got into dealing directly with the retail stores. Gaffney pulled out to a retirement in the mid 1980's and NASDS dwindled. By 1998, its strength diminished considerably. It merged with SSI. The impact that NASDS had on sport diving in its formative years was both good and bad. While NASDS was held in disrespect as diving's "evil empire" and Gaffney as everybody's demon to fight, innovative programs that kept up with the partying mood of the country gave NASDS a special place in a business that gets too serious about itself at times. While NASDS was promoting Dive-Ins with

Hal Watts NASDS shop displays Mammoth fossils found in an underwater cave. John Gaffney was quick to exploit exciting discoveries by his NASDS member shops.   John Gaffney

treasure hunts, wet T-shirt contests, and clean-up-the-bottom dives, its leaders were leading the way in instituting new safe practices.

The *Red Book* (and then a *Gold Book*) which put instructors on the same page, controlled exactly what was to be taught, made sure most divers got exposed to everything they should know.

NASDS gave the dive stores an opportunity to have dignity, respect and power. Its founder and leader was audacious and ruthless on behalf of his member stores. Sport diving got a lot of its direction over the years from NASDS's member stores/schools and NASDS was the greatest influence in turning instruction into a product, for better or for worse. Without NASDS, the dive stores could still be the pawns of the big manufacturers.

13
THE INTERNATIONAL
UNDERWATER FILM FESTIVAL

DEFINING EVENT: SANTA MONICA, CALIFORNIA IN 1962

On October 16, 1962, President John F. Kennedy was reading the newspaper in his bedroom. Nothing exciting. Suddenly the door flew open. There standing in the doorway was National Security Advisor McGeorge Bundy waving photographs of Russian missile sites in Cuba. The Russians could nuke any place in America in a surprise attack. America blockaded the island and the Soviet Premier Khrushchev blinked and removed them. The possibility of a world nuclear holocaust, the major international crisis in the post World War II era, was dissolved.

The coordinators of the Underwater Film Festival were stretching their international wings at the same time, putting the final touches to what would be the shining ultimate event of all such Festivals and Shows. The two night program at the December 1962 Festival included presentations by some of the greatest names in underwater photography. The Gold Medal Winners that year were Dimitri Rebikoff with *The Timid Octopus* in the Amateur Division and Don and George Brauer with *A Slurp Gun in Bimini* in the Commercial Division.

The Festival and Underwater Photography were fueling the diving fervor in America. It was at that moment in time much more than a Southern California thing; exhibitors, honorees and spectators were coming from far away places. It was probably the first cultural, social occasion where dedicated divers could dress up and see the filmed record of the current expeditions, explorations and discoveries. It was educational and entertaining. It was diving's Superbowl. It was diving's Academy Awards.

Al Tillman and Zale Parry, the principal founders of the Festival recall the thrill of standing outside the new, elegant Santa Monica Civic Auditorium, where the Motion Picture Academy Awards also took place a few nights earlier. Looking up there at the lighted marquee that read "INTERNATIONAL UNDERWATER FILM FESTIVAL SOLD OUT". The first sell out the auditorium had ever had. It was the key rewarding moment for all the time, effort, labor of love put into it.

The idea of film festivals had been around long before 1962. The Cannes Festival started in the 1950's. It is the most famous of grand flamboyant social happenings along with showing new unreleased films. That element of premiering film before it is let out for general public viewing was the

Paul McComack, Andy Rechnitzer, Zale Parry, Parry Bivens and Al Tillman at the 1960 Film Festival.   *Bab Jones*

197

basic intent of California's original Underwater Film Festival which meant showing footage before it was commercially packaged. It allowed Festival goers the only opportunity to view "raw footage," often unedited, with live narration, as the underwater experience actually was. It was as close as you could come to being there.

SKIN DIVER MAGAZINE

Skin Diver Magazine was a major factor in the success of all the Film Festivals everywhere. They worked with Los Angeles County in showing Dimitri Rebikoff films to Southern California divers in 1955, Stanton Waterman in a film showing in 1956 and a National Spearfishing Team fund raising showing of a potpourri of diving film in Hollywood in 1956 (the Boston Sea Rovers put on a broader event since, but films were an aspect rather than the core of the event). Some great films and photographers showed up and premiered there...e.g., Jacque Yves-Cousteau, Ron and Valerie Taylor, Philippe Cousteau, Dimitri Rebikoff, Ron Church, Ben Cropp, Stanton Waterman, Dr. Nelson Mathison, Al Giddings, Peter Gimbel, Jack McKenney, Ramon Bravo, The Brauer Brothers (George and Donald) Mel Fisher, Burton McNeely, Mart Toggweiler, Peter Stackpole, Chuck Nicklin, Col. John D. Craig, Coles Phinizy, George Benjamin, Dick Anderson, Jordan Klein, Dr. Hans Hass, Paul Tzimoulis, LeRoy French, Chuck Peterson, William DeCourt, Lee Tepley, E. R. Cross, Conrad Limbaugh, Dr. Wheeler North, Luis Marden, Dr. Andreas Rechnitzer, Lamar Boren, David Doubilet, Victor DeSanctis, Roberto Merlo, Ludwig Sillner, Flip Schulke, Ernest Brooks and Sir Robert Marx.

The Underwater Film Festival got its start as a free showing of local underwater photographers at the West Hollywood Park Auditorium in California. The idea had taken shape as a natural progression in the Los Angeles County Underwater Program. The organization of the Underwater Photographic Society in Los Angeles was a concurrent development evolving out of a close relationship between Earl Sugarman and Al Tillman, who were working on underwater cameras and producing underwater films as friends sharing a hobby.

It was Zale Parry's arrival on the scene as a founding member of the Underwater Photographic Society that helped elevate that First Film Festival into a respectable event. Zale dressed up the institutional look of the park auditorium by going to Ivan Tors Productions and *Sea Hunt* producers at Ziv Studios, (the *Sea Hunt* television series was just underway.) and Zale borrowed a red carpet for exhibitors to walk up when introduced by Master of Ceremonies, Al Tillman. Zale, as a well-known motion picture and television actress/stunt person, one of the first female divers, knowledgeable in operating an underwater camera, too, provided a presence with fashion that gave the whole evening credibility.

Earl Sugarman had worked a deal by trading a paint job (Earl had a small building-painting business in industrial Los Angeles.) to a printer for a small printed program. There was no source of funding and everybody was an unpaid volunteer. They were working on a logo that would symbolize underwater photography the night before they had to go to press.

The next morning Al Tillman drove down to Abalone Cove in Palos Verdes, speared a kelp bass, and right there on the beach inked it by pressing tissue paper to it and came up with a fish print. Driving to the printer in East Los Angeles, still in wet bathing suit, Al cut a picture of a Rollei Camera out of a magazine ad and pasted that picture over the eye on the print. Garcia, the printer, nodded OK and put it into the last minute process of printing the program. The only thing Garcia said was, "You just made it but mind not dripping on my floor."

The West Hollywood Festival-and Festival is a bit of a presumption-was a start even with a small auditorium that was only half filled. Al Tillman's diving partner, Paul McComack, had come aboard, responsible and conscientious, he took over the vital projection supervision and did so for the next fourteen years.

In the projection booth Doc Nelson E. Mathison,

Mel Fisher, Jack McNeal were part of a confusing turmoil trying to jockey 35mm, 16mm, 8mm, slide projectors into the projection window at the right time. Doc had to bring his own 35mm projector and the 16mm Al borrowed from California State University, Los Angeles. "A grand gathering of the innocents, we thought it was a small start. It was a defining moment for what was to come," recalls Tillman.

Al Tillman had gone to full time teaching as an Assistant Professor of Recreation Management in 1958. The Underwater Film Festival was scheduled at California State University at Los Angeles along with a cooperation of Los Angeles County-Underwater Photographic Society-*Skin Diver Magazine* photo contest.

It was again a free affair and the small auditorium was a better presentation facility,

Doc Mathison and Jack McNeal pioneered underwater photography in the 1950's with homemade housings.   Homer Lockwood

had its own red carpets, and this time filled up. Underwater Photographic Society members helped a lot in ushering people, giving out programs, recruiting members and most importantly standing on the maze of roads with flashlights and trying to direct divers to the right parking lot for the Festival. Some stuck to the job even missing the first part of the show, until batteries in their directional flashlights gave out.

At that Second Annual Underwater Film Festival, it was difficult to come up with a glamorous name to match that of our First Underwater Photographer of the Year but we settled on Lamar Boren, who was the leading American Underwater Cinematographer of the era. He did *Underwater* for MGM with Jane Russell; *Namu The Killer Whale*, a United Artists production; *Flipper* Feature for Ivan Tors Studios; *Old Man and the Sea* for Warner Brothers; *Underwater Warrior*-MGM; *Thunderball* - EON productions (England) and many more films including the *Sea Hunt* television series. An original Bottom Scratcher, diving's first club, he was a talented mountain of a man who seemed to breathe through the camera, indestructible, unflappable and reliable.

Connie Limbaugh arrived with wife, Nan, and dressed as if he'd scraped his wardrobe together from friends, with a tie that hung unfamiliarly from his neck like a garrote. He was uncomfortable away from the water it seemed. But this was Limbaugh, who at that time was recognized as America's foremost diver. Zale Parry and Al Tillman were now overseeing the Festival production as Earl Sugarman had moved to other interests in the diving field.

It was time to make the Festival pay for itself. The principal organizers had borrowed, begged and dipped into their own pockets for the Festival to this point. An auditorium would be rented and the San Gabriel Civic Auditorium was rented for $150 for one Saturday night in 1959. Zale and Al were by now writing to every underwater photographer with a recognizable name. The impossible happened, they enticed Hans Hass to come and receive the Award as Underwater Photographer of the 1959! Hans Hass was on par with Cousteau in significant contributions to diving's beginnings. Exposure on worldwide media had left him a mysterious myth in America. He came, graciously, at his own expense, and wowed the audience. Tillman, as Master of Ceremonies of the Festival again, suffered various abuses as projectors and sound systems had breakdowns and a diver audience, complete with club jackets festooned with patches of speared fish and sharks, hooted and tossed peanuts on stage.

In keeping with trying to show raw documentary footage, they showed Wheeler North's and Connie Lindbaugh's sand waterfalls, entitled, *Rivers of Sand*. The film was an extraordinary record of a new discovery. Then a very, very long fifteen minutes of manganese nodules on the deep bottom of the ocean taken with an unmanned camera was projected (always review film ahead of time). The film would show more manganese than had ever been mined on land in history of the world. It promised a great future in mining the sea. It sounded exactly like the kind of real discovery, you-are-there-viewing, the Festival was based on. Unfortunately, every single nodule was shown, from a distance, up close, from middle range and they just sat there like stones. Two minutes into the film the audience was shuffling, then grumbling, getting up to stretch. There was an air of the villagers amassing to storm the castle. Ten minutes into it, profanity and curses were being showered on the available targets, the MC and the narrator, whose narration went, "...there's a big band of nodules, there's another one, there's a big one.... ." MC Tillman was trying to hand-gesture a signal to projectionist, Paul McComack, to cut off the film, as there was no telephone connection to the projection booth. Paul did get the signal. The audience was won back with the awesome black and white footage of Hass' film. The scenes showed a fleet of giant Manta Rays coming unexpectedly out of no where. The Mantas were hovering over a rock outcropping in a vast barren sand plain, as small fish demonstrated divers' first viewing of a grand barber shop-cleaning station based on the concept (a Conrad Limbaugh discovery) of symbiosis. It is classic footage. Nothing in the ensuing decades of underwater photography have matched it...the *Citizen Kane* of underwater cinematography.

The San Gabriel Auditorium was more than packed. The tickets were printed as general admission, no reserved seating. Innocently, the Festival coordinators didn't keep a close count on how many tickets they put out to various dive shops to sell. Mel Fisher's Mel's Aqua Shop, got a double order and sold all of them. Without an accurate report from shops as to the number of tickets sold, the tickets being sold at the box office and tickets given away to the media, the accurate count was a mystery.

Tillman was in the box office with Lee Berger, who had come aboard, as associate producer in 1959. Both were trying to secure the money that was pouring in to figure when they should stop selling tickets. The best clue was when someone came running up to say, ..."there is a fist fight over seats in the balcony, the last few seats left."

It was finally settled when Tillman went up, reseated people to free some single seats. The show started thirty minutes late. By that time, the audience was making paper airplanes out of pages from the program.

One other sad note about the 1959 Festival was the failure to give Honoree Peter Stackpole proper royal treatment. They were so overwhelmed with getting Hans Hass, the coordinators were surprised when Peter Stackpole actually showed up the afternoon of the Festival in the lobby with a portfolio of 8"x11" black and white prints. The pictures were probably photographic classics representing America's first underwater photojournalist, who pioneered the field through *Life Magazine*. There was no provision for small black and white prints, but somehow Peter took it upon himself, found a wall and some scotch tape to put up a display. It didn't get a lot of attention and the divers passing by didn't realize that there taped on a wall were museum quality artifacts of underwater photography's beginning.

Zale had the task of hostess for visiting dignitaries and being one in her own right, the experience always sent VIPs away fulfilled and charmed. Zale drove Hans to Marineland, met Al Tillman and Doc Nelson E. Mathison, who were waiting there. Marineland of the Pacific had just come into being in 1955. Hans, our Photographer of the Year, was impressed. There seemed to be agreement that despite the flawed event, it had arrived, as a required experience, for the divers going into the decade of the 1960's, that it was time to move "uptown".

Now the ugly intrusion of money had entered the picture. Tickets had been sold and there was a profit after rentals and other bill's had been paid. The box office security and accounting were chaotic.

NONPROFIT INCORPORATION

Lee Berger ended up just stuffing bundles of bills in his pockets and going to Al Tillman's house that night after

Gustav Dalla Valle. The Festival's International Ambassador.

the Festival saying, "What do we do with all of this money?" Never again would the Festival not utilize a professional box office service. Some of the Underwater Photographic Society members felt the Festival had slipped away from their direct involvement and began questioning. Who owned the Festival and the profits? Tillman incorporated the International Underwater Film Festival as a nonprofit corporation in the State of California with a Board of Directors of Jim Auxier and Norm Robinson with Zale Parry as Secretary/Treasurer, Paul McComack as Vice President and Al Tillman as President. The Executive Planning Committee consisted of Paul McComack as General Manager, Lee Berger as Administrative Assistant, Zale Parry-Communications, Norm Robinson-Exhibitions, Mr. and Mrs. Gary Pietila-Evaluation, Gustav Dalla Valle-Foreign Relations, Al Tillman as Program Director. The Underwater Photographic Society would henceforth have the Festival to participate in but would not be involved in its operation. *Skin Diver Magazine* would eventually take on a greater involvement. With Al Tillman's departure from the Los Angeles County Program in 1960, it would participate but not be in any official sponsoring capacity.

There was an aftermath of some bitterness, accusation of self-serving interests, money ownership because some principals overlapped in other competitive diving projects. The Festival held up as a nonprofit corporation and the majority of money from admissions went to fund grants to photographers and seed other Festivals.

Putting the Festival together was a year long job. It was an event that promoted the diving industry at no cost to the manufacturers. Because it was self-sustaining, it didn't have to answer to the directions of any outside forces and could create its own destiny. The public never paid more than a $2.50 Admission Fee.

The California based Film Festival was stoking the furnace of interest in underwater photography. *Skin Diver Magazine* was giving it broad exposure and reaping the benefit of readily available photos for the magazine. The Petersen Publishing buy-out was a positive uplift for the Festival with a separate headquarters office on Hollywood Boulevard. Jim Auxier was retained as editor/publisher to keep the magazine firmly behind the show. The office served as NAUI Headquarters, as well, with Tillman serving as executive director for both enterprises.

ROAD SHOWS

Other areas of America were not getting direct access to the dramatic atmosphere of the Festival so Zale Parry and Al Tillman decided to take it to other places as a roadshow of the Festival. It was necessary to recruit a local mover and shaker in each locale to pull it off. It was George Burt in Toronto, Ralph Erickson in Chicago, Paul Tzimoulis in New York, Bob Morgan in Dayton, Ohio, Mike Kevorkian in Miami, Don Pablo Bush Romero in Mexico City and Fred Calhoun in Boston.

The Chicago Festival came up first and it was almost an all Jack McKenney show. Here's what happened. Al Tillman tells the story:

"One thing I learned about going out of town with your act is you have to have a local guy with clout to be successful. It was so when we took the Underwater Film Festival on the road.

"It was importantly so in Chicago. There's a feeling that if you come from out of town and try to do it on your own, not only will nobody show up, you get the feeling a guy named Luigi will come by and break your knee caps.

"So I lined up McCormick Place as the "theatre" and Ralph Erickson as our local front man. I liked Ralph a lot and I planned to push him into a top leadership role in NAUI. When I stepped down in NAUI, those that followed missed the boat in not getting Ralph onto the joint drivers seat and so Ralph went on to put together an overwhelming rival organization, PADI.

"But for this time and place, 1964, Ralph Erickson was the Chicago honcho to count on. He did the job.

"Jack McKenney flew in to help with the Festival - I'd just hired him for UNEXSO. So Ralph, Jack, and I met on the day of the Film Festival to go over all the logistics. Yes, the tickets had been sold; yes the projector and projectionist were set; yes, McKenney was set to present his films; yes the other films were...oh, oh they had not arrived. I'd parcel posted them a week earlier and the train should have brought them. I figured if something detoured me from being there, McKenney could do the MC job and narration. I hadn't thought sending the films would be any problem.

"Ok, Ralph, how do we check parcel post arrivals. It was Saturday and the train freight yard was closed. I felt a bit of panic creep through me. Ralph was cool, 'I'll call a friend that works there, but it might cost us.' In Chicago, it's very union and the bite gets put on for anything out of channels, special favors.

"Yes, Ralph's friend could meet us at the yard, but he was giving up a good extra job opportunity he had on the side to do it, or so he said.

"I think I had to shake hands with a twenty dollar bill in my hand when I met Joe who had keys for the wire fenced freight yard. Inside the compound Joe wasn't sure about the system exactly so we fanned out and began the search, not knowing of course if it had even made it out of Los Angeles yet. I was thinking, OK, Albert, Mr. Impresario, the films won't be found and you're in for tar and feathers or worse if you try to skinny by with just Jack McKenney's films.

"I was thinking I should have some kind of attack right there and go hide in the hospital and let Ralph and Jack have all the fun that night when this guy, Joe, calls, 'Hey, maybe these are it, they're film boxes.' "Yes! Yes!" I whooped, "that's them," and ran greedily to them. But as I grabbed them I could see the American Red Cross labels on all of them. Not our films.

Ten minutes later, McKenney was holding a pack of film boxes over his head and grinning. 'Got 'em.'

"An what did we learn? Carrying those films with you at all times even if a change of underwear and whatever else has to be left at home. Incidentally, we had a full house and the tough Chicago crowd seemed to be grudgingly impressed."

From there it was on to New York and the Hunter College Auditorium. John Schuck, Cougar Sports, and Paul Tzimoulis were the local coordinators using the Festival production guidelines we had mailed them. It was not a full house but the New York crowd we expected to be demanding turned out to accept and respond with satisfaction. A Teddy Tucker Treasure Film was a good local addition to the films we carried with us. We flew Roberto Merlo representing Italy and Mrs. Eizo Tanabe representing Japan from California there, so the International flavor was strong.

BOSTON FILM FESTIVAL

The Boston Festival was an invasion of Boston Sea Rover territory and Fred Calhoun, who has always been a controversial character, was the local coordinator-with our fingers crossed. The one thing known about Fred was that he was responsible. When Al Tillman arrived the day before the showings, he ran into Fred on the street by the Boston Commons. It was almost as if they were enacting a daily occurrence.

"You're here," says Fred.

A 1975 Jack McKenney Skin Diver Magazine cover. Pat McKenney appears in the picture - one of five SDM covers that she has graced.

The International Underwater Film Festivals were always a sold out event.

"I'm here. Is everything okay, the auditorium, the projectors?"

"Yes, Brother Tillman, don't worry...I've added David Doubilet as a part of the program...his slides."

And it was indeed ready to go although there was still the matter of the projector but not to worry, Fred would arrange for it that afternoon. He did. The show came off efficiently. Calhoun did the Master of Ceremonies chores. Tillman had to narrate some of the films that were still just packaged into a story format but without sound.

The kid, Doubilet, was a blockbuster revelation. His slides were as good as any we had ever had at a show or contest. A star was born at least for those of us from elsewhere seeing his work for the first time. That night Fred had the accounting done and turned over a major share of proceeds after paid costs to Tillman to be used for the International Underwater Film Festival grant fund. In addition, air fare from foreign lands and accommodations for the honorees had become an expense of the festival ceremony.

The way the grant fund worked for the road shows was whatever length of time a film was shown represented a parallel percentage to go to the film maker as a grant of money to pay for future films. The Festival had paid for the copy. There were hopes of building an archival film library from them, but after Al Tillman moved on to develop UNEXSO on Grand Bahama Island, no one came forward to carry on the roadshow idea. Actually, the roadshows were seeds from which sprouted many independent underwater film festivals that were operated by established divers' clubs and organizations in the various major cities.

Film festivals that had good runs and have even continued until the present seemed to happen because highly

Norm Robinson, Fred Roberts, Mart Toggweiler, Doc Mathison and Jim Auxier judging the 1958 Festival entries.

Zale Parry presents award to Nan and Conrad Limbaugh at the 1958 Festival.

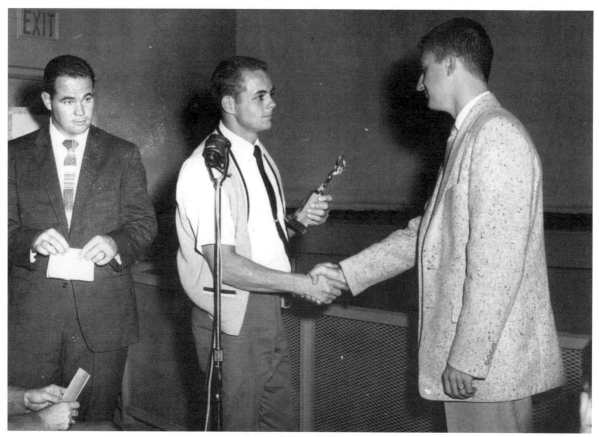

Al Tillman and Glen Lewis present an award to Jack McNeal at the 1958 Festival.

Gary Boren, Dan Ryan, Nan Limbaugh, Conrad Limbaugh and Homer Lockwood in the Honors Circle at the 1958 Film Festival.

Al Tillman and Dave Woodward working with National Geographic Staff Photographers on the 1966 Film Festival.

Andy Rechnitzer presents Stan Waterman with his Underwater Photographer of the Year Award in 1962.

motivated people who succeeded with other diving enterprises stepped forward.

CHICAGO'S OUR WORLD UNDERWATER

The Chicago OUR WORLD UNDERWATER was the combination exposition and film festival. It was conceived by Ralph Erickson and John Cronin who put on a Chicago Film Festival to raise money to keep PADI afloat. They'd been dipping into their own pockets so the $2000 they made helped a lot. Harry Shanks and Tim Mankey Smith picked up the film show, added some seminars and exhibits and called it OUR WORLD UNDERWATER which became a continuing annual event in the Mid-West. It all happened in the 1960's when Civil rights, Vietnam protests, a counterculture and the feminist movement had people looking for something more stable and less revolutionary - the show became that for divers.

SAN DIEGO FILM FESTIVAL

San Diego, California always a solid center of diving activity with resident Scripps Institution of Oceanography, the home of the Bottom Scratchers, the original dive club in America, the Coronado Island U.D.T. Base Unit 1 commanded by Francis Douglas Fane and glorious diving waters, all came together in a San Diego Film Festival in the mid 1960's following the format of the Parry/Tillman event. The local chapter of the Underwater Photographic Society formed late in 1961 was behind it. Chuck Nicklin and Andreas Rechnitzer were two prominent names that gave it a high profile attraction.

The local dive store, The Diving Locker, presented an impromptu film night. People gathered to view underwater films and slides. Those present were Ron Church, Chuck Nicklin, Bill DeCourt, as well as others who founded the San Diego Underwater Photographic Society. This small gathering was the incubator for the successful San Diego Film Festival. They achieved maturity quickly with the wealth of extraordinarily talented underwater photographers who live there.

The prime movers for the Film Festival were: Chuck Nicklin - President, Emil Habecker - Vice President, Ron Bazewick - Treasurer, Barbara Allen - Secretary. The festival committee included Chet Tussey - Presentation, Emil Habecker - Facilities, Ron Bazewick - Tickets, Tom Harman - Publicity, Charlie Ricketts - Display, Pat Howard - Advertising, Don Williams - Program and Royce Johnson - Master of Ceremonies. For the 25th anniversary, in 1989, Chet Tussey was the Film Festival Chairman, thirteen people were assigned as Committee Chairs, sixty-seven people were Committee Members and Jean-Michel Cousteau was the Master of Ceremonies. The San Diego Underwater Film Festival remains strong and continues to share skills as underwater photographers.

OAKLAND/SAN FRANCISCO CALIFORNIA-UWFF

Al Giddings and Dewey Bergman of Sea & See Travel put together a Festival in Oakland, California in the 1960's. It, too, followed the format of the original International Underwater Film Festival of Santa Monica, California.

This Festival and others that spun-off tended to diffuse the motivating force of the one "Hollywood oriented" opportunity to premiere film. No longer did the excitement of getting ready all year long for the one grand opportunity to showcase the previewing of film. Exhibitors were becoming more demanding for remuneration for attending a Festival over receiving an honor and award.

Television was devouring films as the public stayed home while viewing commercially polished, structured films on their sets.

By 1970, the International Underwater Film Festival was becoming one of many. The little sponsorship it got from the industry was being spread around. John Gaffney's *Dive Magazine* had come into a sponsorship role filling the gap left by *Skin Diver Magazine* under Petersen Publishing's withdrawal. An attempt was made to add broader interest with support for the Festival by combining it with an Environmental Exposition and Underwater

Photography Clinics. *Dive Magazine* put color into the printed program, turned Roy Brizz, then graphics artist, loose on its appearance. It was arranged for Bob Marx's treasure trove under guard to be displayed. Arthur Godfrey was on hand to receive the First Environmentalist of the Year Award. But times were changing and the fresh, first look at underwater photography achievements couldn't be recovered by tacking on something like ecology. Like safety, both important issues of diving development, they were not popular audience attractions.

The International Underwater Film Festival was dissolved as a nonprofit educational incorporation and the Film Festival's kleig lights would not fill the Santa Monica/Hollywood skies again. The year was 1970.

The legacy left by it is seen in the many world renown underwater photographers who were feted and often discovered through the opportunities provided by the Film Festival. Encouraged and recognized, many of the photographers have remained to became the main talent of the Hollywood film industry, television documentary series and magazine photo contributors.

Ron Church, whose death triggered the writing of *Scuba America*, usually acerbic and critical, had this to say after being honored at the Festival in 1959, (The same year Hans Hass was honored.) "Having all those people all in one place, looking at your pictures and praising them with applause made me want to get back in the water with my camera the very next day. Nobody else had ever done anything like the Festival before."

Ron Church (1961) in Hawaii with underwater camera equipment. From Calypso to Hasselblad.

Shirley Richards

PARTYTIME MEMORABLE MOMENTS

There was always a party after the International Underwater Film Festival after it set up Santa Monica Civic Auditorium as its venue. The best ones were held in a room at the Santa Monica Hotel around the corner from the auditorium. Honorees and Festival Staff would finally have a moment to relax and relate in an informal setting. Their films would be recovered there which was always an important cleanup responsibility...especially to avoid Customs and mailing for foreign visitors.

Lee Berger, the Associate Producer over the years, was a professional part-time bartender and stretched the budgeted booze over a lot of people. He'd put a heavy shot over a glass of Seven-Up and everybody sipped away thinking they were getting a legitimate drink. About half the people would opt for root beer, given the choice, and walk around looking like they were soundly drinking with the rest. Pan dulces, Mexican sweet rolls, were always on hand having been picked up at an East Los Angeles bakery next to the program printer's shop. They were a big hit.

Once in awhile a serious argument would break out when an honoree would suggest another exhibitor's scenes were faked. It takes one to know one often seemed the case but the "friendly" bit that is remembered best is: Ben Cropp from Australia suggesting that Dick Anderson's gold was phony. There were some snide remarks about pulling dead sharks about on a wire from Anderson and Cropp saying that the pancake-size gold nugget Anderson was carrying about to show off wasn't gold. "You can bite into gold," Ben said, and proceeded to do so. A tooth broke on the lead lump that Anderson had gold plated. "Let that be a lesson to you," Anderson said deadpan. "I keep my real one in a vault at home." It was a lesson in something, for as far as we know, Ben Cropp never bit into gold again.

Gustav Dalla Valle was a great host and let his home be used for several after-festival-parties, the last really intimate ones before Petersen Publishing and *Skin Diver Magazine* decided to host a bigger affair which was just noisy and too large to really settle down and bond with anyone. Gustav would be at the Festival early greeting everybody in his great, booming accent, mustache flowing over corners of his mouth, and an ascot twisted about his neck. He loomed big and was like a living international logo for the event but he'd never stay to see any films but instead disappear to setup his house for the later get-together. Asked about a film, he'd shout, "Gud, Gud...want anuder drink?" Gustav created an atmosphere of foreign flavor that embellished the Festival in the best of ways.

The Festival was diving's grandest celebration of itself and diving's most pleasing social event in the early years. It provided a showcase for divers where their hidden adventures could be feted to friends and public that might never go down under to see what they had seen or might see in the future. It was inspiring to divers and preserved historical moments.

The Sixth International Underwater Film Festival

Programs from the Film Festivals are popular collectors items since they featured the best photography from each show.

Al Tillman, the Executive Producer of the Festival chose his favorite film: Elgin Ciampi's *Silent Spring*. It needed no narration to witness life and death through a fish's eyes. A fresh water pond was the setting and the black and white footage was textbook perfect with dramatic angles, contrasts and shadows, and all of the best of cinema style and tricks. It had a simple touching storyline and yet was as perfect a documentary as could be. A diver had to be setting on the bottom observing over many hours to film it. It was the epitome of what a great diving film could reveal and move emotions without bells, whistles, bright colors and huge dangerous creatures. It didn't take a trip to Fiji and a ton of bloody chum to get it.

MOONING THE FESTIVAL

It was the 1960 International Underwater Film Festival. Luis Marden of National Geographic Society was to be honored but he had to be off on a photo expedition assignment. So wife, Ethel, came to receive his Award. The gracious and dignified lady arrived a day early and the Festival always tried to escort such VIPS about the Southern California area to places of their choice.

The Festival lucked out this time giving the staff needed time to check the nuts and bolts for the eminent film festival. Andreas Rechnitzer, America's most renown oceanographer, generously offered to play escort for Mrs. Marden and began a drive down the Pasadena Freeway toward a destination of Ethel Marden's choosing. Five minutes into the ride a rickety, big sedan pulled along side of them and strange bulbous objects were pressed against the windows. Rechnitzer used to looking out deep submersible windows at strange sights wasn't shaken and the car stayed under control at 55-miles per hour. A few minutes later after the car with the "monsters" staring out the windows at them, Ethel looked over at Andy and asked, "Did you see what I saw?" Andy grinned back at her and said, "I think they were bare bottoms!" It was probably Andy's and Ethel's first mooning, a new prank just starting to show as a questionable way for teenagers to shock people-and indirectly, the first mooning of the Film Festival.

WERE THE FILMS THAT GOOD?

Another balcony upset moment was to see people getting up from their seats in one section and exiting toward the aisles. They looked disgusted and rightly so. Lousy films? Nope. Some guy was moaning and-masturbating-during the showing of the slides. There were no signs up that said you couldn't, such as: "No-Smoking" or "No-Masturbating". But after the removal of the pleasuring person, the Festival moved on with more decorum.

COUSTEAU THE SHOWMAN

Jacques-Yves Cousteau knew how to make an entrance. Event producers were never sure if he'd actually be there. He entered from the back of the auditorium and with an entourage strode up the aisle. A grand murmur swelled from the audience and stage whispers were heard, "It's him, it's him, Cousteau!"

When Cousteau finally showed up in person at the 1965 International Underwater Film Festival in Santa Monica he was...well, here's associate producer Lee Berger's take on him:

"I'm thinking, good Lord, this is Jacques Cousteau, it was like here was Napoleon or Mahatma Ghandi standing next to me back stage and asking me what he was supposed to do. He seemed confused, not at ease, so I told him exactly what to do, and brushed dandruff off his dark suit shoulders and I thought here's this unbelievable legend with human problems and I felt a real sense of power in being in charge of him."

Masters of Ceremonies added a polish to all the Festivals. When things went wrong, a projector breakdown, a nervous tongue-tied narrator, they had to have the professional ability to step in and smooth it over. The Santa Monica International Underwater Film Festival, at this location for the first time, had to bring in a special master of ceremonies to match the new glamor. Al Tillman had presided over the stage and introductions for the first three and back in Boston, Fred Calhoun would find his stage voice and do the honors.

It was important to have the show's main producer back stage and ready even with a show business veteran. Lloyd Bridges couldn't MC without a script and a show staff member at his elbow to whisper pronunciations and spontaneous changes in his ear. It was good to have real divers handle MC duties and the two main masters of ceremonies for the International Underwater Film Festival were Bill Burrud, who had a television adventure show and Tom Franzen, a smooth, unflappable charmer who had coordinated many talk shows on local television. Burrud was a fun guy and found humor in situations but he'd often make fun of the "keystone cops" when things went wrong (they always did in some minor way) and he "protected" himself at the expense of the show. Franzen didn't try to save himself but assured the audience with explanations of how the films were fresh out of the cameras and just edited for the show that night and glitches could be expected. Bill and Tom were both excellent but it was a good rule to have someone who knew the presenters, diving and the intricacies of the show back stage and on call to step in. And, the fame and personality of the MC shouldn't outshine the content of the show. A Dick Anderson, Mike Kevorkian, Andreas Rechnitzer, or Stanton Waterman could and had done the job from the stage but they shine too brightly in their own diving acclaim and there's a chance that might diminish the program itself.

Here's a contrast in styles: When the lights went out in the auditorium during an introduction of the next on the program, narrator Bill Burrud would say, "Oh, Tillman, you forgot to pay the light bill. We got to get better organized next year." That's funny but it lightly disparages the Festival. Tom Franzen in the darkness would say, "Relax, folks. We'll just keep talking and...you can watch this footage of inside a dark underwater cave."

In a final analysis, The International Underwater Film Festival that came out of the Los Angeles-Hollywood area was the bell-ringer major event for sport diving. From its meager beginning in 1957 with its numerous pratfalls, it evolved into a prestigious and professional social and cultural event that brought great dignity to the newly formed rough hewn recreation. It heralded the changing of the interest guard from game taking to underwater photography. From it were cloned many other underwater film festivals but the big original one that reigned over a fourteen year period pioneered the format. It brought together the world's greatest underwater photographers in a show case before the opportunities arose on television. It introduced to the public the unknown divers who were just beginning to conquer the underwater world with a camera and in many cases financially supported their efforts with grants from the event's proceeds. In particular, film (before editing changed it into less authentic entertainment) was usually shown for the first time, as close to reality as possible. Sport diving took on an attractive and much more sophisticated image directly and indirectly because of that specific founding underwater film festival and the other festivals that emanated from it over the five decades of diving history.

14
THE CAMERA GOES UNDERWATER

DEFINING EVENT: PRESSURE COOKER HOUSING

In those good old days of the late 1940's and early 1950's, pioneer divers would come stumbling out of the water sputtering, "Yyyou sssshoulda seen...." Shaking with excitement and perhaps cold as well, their awe came tumbling out in half sentences.

Many times they would have seen what <u>might never happen again</u>. Unbelievable things. A great octopus and a giant lobster in a fearsome duel, perhaps. Ah, if only they had been able to take cameras down.

It was predictable that after years of slapping together the gear needed to go diving on garage work benches and the old kitchen tables, they'd try to create an underwater camera. But the majority of efforts went into constructing watertight underwater <u>housings</u> for the family camera or in a few instances, for expensive land cameras like the classic Leica or the Hasselblad.

The time had arrived for a great new sport and recreation to emerge for mass consumption and because it took place in the hidden environs of the sea, the only way to really get an audience was to bring back pictures.

It was certainly scuba that played a major part in paving the way for underwater photography (along with a waterproof way to shoot the pictures). The difficulty of holding a camera steady in the movements encountered in the water, buoyancy and currents and holding one's breath, could be overcome with the stability of having an air supply down there with you; it allowed time to adjust and hold a fixed positioning.

A lot of pitfalls are inherent in shooting pictures underwater over land exposures. You can't change film without surfacing nor make adjustments as easily. There's the water itself, always there trying to get at the internal mechanism of a camera. It required constant vigilance to avoid the corrosive touch of trickles and drops.

UNDERWATER PHOTOGRAPHY - ROUGH INTRO/HOW IT BEGAN

It is important at this point to recollect the historical moments in the development of underwater still photography. Some of those moments paralleled what was going on in the technological development of land cameras and lighting accessories. It was a shaky start until the arrival of scuba and even then, the steady unmoving physical freeze required of human control of the still camera was still a challenge far beyond that experienced on the land.

Holding position in a current, maintaining neutral buoyancy, holding one's breath (a serious taboo in scuba diving) for steadiness, coping with water's magnification and suspended matter, the paucity of light made taking a good picture difficult. The eye of a diamond cutter, the coordination of a juggler and the fierce concentration of a lion tamer were traits to be desired in the beginning. The talents and traits multiply when we add shivering from cooler than comfortable water temperatures.

The participation for the majority of divers was usually that they went diving to look, and experience the sensation of being underwater, breathing under, then to hunt, then to take pictures. Even the most awesome wilderness with its creatures and visual scenes get boring and the "tourist diver" eventually wearies of the sights. Taking things from the sea, fish, lobster, abalone, treasure was the next step in sustaining divers' interest. The environmental movement came along in the 1960's and created a new consciousness about depleting the oceans and lakes of life; many fish-stickers semi-converted to preservationist photographers. But the taking of game and other items through diving is inherently imbedded in the sport and will always be a prime motivation for some divers. It is part of American's rugged pioneer past of living off the land and taming the wilderness.

But underwater photography presented divers the opportunity to have an audience and visually back-up their fish stories. Now the one that got away could be verified. The 1950's began the transition of diving heroes not from hunting but from taking pictures.

We need to go back and consider the early efforts in all photography then underwater. There always seems to be another, earlier story arise just when the research historian thinks the real beginning of something has been nailed down. Who did take the first picture and with what?

Somewhere way back in time, the first persons to walk the earth, saw a lot of water everywhere. It was the surface area and little did they suspect that beneath it was a vast wilderness teeming with life, and canyons and mountains exceeding what they could see on land.

Some of those cave people probably looked down through a clear spot in that water and could see strange things were down there. Some wished with all their hearts that they could get down there amidst the unknown and see it up close. They wished they could show others somehow but the best they could do was scratch pictures on cave walls with burnt sticks.

We've come along ways from burnt stick to the modern underwater camera and computer enhancement of pictures. But the desire to share our experiences and encounters with the wild unknown remains deeply in the core of our psyche.

Basic photography started in 1790's when Thomas Wedgwood, son of the English pottery magnate, silhouetted profiles by the agency of light utilizing the light sensitivity of silver nitrate. Then Louis Daguerre and Joseph Niepce (Frenchmen again) collaborated to produce a negative and a direct positive in 1827. So, it was almost two-hundred years ago that the capturing of an image in a permanent form, on film and paper opened the gates to a possible vast sharing of underwater exploration. But how to make this happen immersed in water was mind boggling.

Those early inventors didn't have means to go underwater, or fast film or even film, for they used glass plates. Nor did they have cameras that wouldn't leak or corrode nor any extra light source beyond the natural.

Photography was the elusive grand climax lure of going underwater and many trials and tribulations would ensue for almost a century before it would become the most popular activity of scuba diving.

The divers, who owned good land cameras, wanted to take them down with them but most experiments with water tight housings were fueled with cheap cameras, strips of chamois and sheets of toilet paper. It took plenty of trial runs to get the leak-bugs out.

Here were the problems to be solved:

1. The housing had to be as light and compact, as streamlined as possible to hold and maneuver in the water. A sphere would be best-like a submarine.

2. The unit had to be balanced to a slightly negative buoyancy so as to be held steady and so that if released, it would not float up and swept away by surface currents.

3. The air in the housing needed to be pressurized to withstand possible implosion and resulting leaking at increasing depths.

4. Working the levers and buttons to trip the shutter, advance the film, adjust the focus, and set the exposure time were all difficult considerations with the varying conditions underwater.

5. Changing film could only be done with difficulty by surfacing and finding a dry and shaded spot-especially in a boat in a rolling sea.

6. Available light underwater rapidly loses its intensity and in unclear water particles can catch some of the light and send it in other directions than the subject. Artificial lighting had to be introduced into the process.

7. Colors rapidly disappear underwater at as little as six-feet, first red then orange until at twenty-feet every thing is blues, greens or murky shades of those colors. The camera would see what the divers eye would see.

8. There was the securing of the camera when hands were needed by the free swimming photographer.

9. The concentration needed by an underwater photographer left them vulnerable to hazardous marine life or

other dangerous conditions inherent in being out of the normal air-breathing-world above.

10. Composing a picture had to be done with an external sport finder, gun sight type because of the difficulty of getting the mask close enough to camera viewfinder.

All of these challenges were the great restraining wall that the sport diver would eventually face beyond the historic efforts just to lower a camera on a cable, fix it in one spot, or take it down in a submersible to shoot out of a window. Continuous controversy erupts as to how important it was to have a free swimming diver unencumbered by lines, down underwater, subject to all the potential dangers to human life when a robot procedure could be used. The arguments in favor seem to be centered on the value of human intelligence, decision making, and adjustment to changing conditions that could be achieved by a diver at the spot of picture taking.

We can see that in the early years leading into, particularly, in the first part of the 20th Century, experimentation would be expensive and only the military joined with science with government money could afford to take chances with new underwater camera systems. We suppose, if you took away from the bureaucracy, the chance to build giant, complex systems and said, "Make a camera for a diver to take underwater," such a simple device would have been invented much earlier.

There is not a lot of information of the specifics of the varied attempts around the world to develop underwater photography.

LOUIS BOUTON - FOUNDING FATHER OF UNDERWATER PHOTOGRAPHY

Back in 1893, a Frenchman, Louis Bouton, bored with "not knowing" got hooked on the idea of getting pictures of the mysterious and unseen underwater world. Jules Verne in his *20,000 Leagues Under the Sea*, the foremost science fiction of its day, could imagine a strange world and Bouton may have been inspired by the book to want to take a picture of it. So how was Louis able to go underwater to do it?

If only Bouton had scuba available to him. He was 100-years too soon and must have agonized over the remoteness of trying to expose film underwater. A biologist/scientist, he was an ardent advocate of observation and study in the field. He surely must have drooled on the surface of the water when on a great visibility day he could see down through the water from the side of a boat.

The early pioneers took some big chances. If Matthew Brady in the battlefields of the Civil War was stressed by lugging heavy equipment and shooting with slow exposure glass plates, imagine Boutan trying to operate in the rugged condition of an alien environment which water certainly was.

Louis must have scrounged about among Paris junk shops scraping together the fixings for a huge metal box to hold a glass plate camera to be set on the ocean floor about fifteen feet down. He used a barrel full of air topped by a glass dome protecting a flame. Then a bulb and tube to spray magnesium to create crude artificial light. He got down there with it by means of a hardhat diving suit with surface supplied air.

Others went down in cable suspended sphere like Beebe in the Bathescape and shot pictures through a small window. While others just sent the camera enclosed in huge water tight cases and on a line let it shoot automatically and mindlessly. Cinematographer J. E. Williamson in 1913 built a huge cylinder or caisson in shallow water with a window and merely climbed in and out of an open-to-surface vertical tunnel. He shot pictures through the window and we guess gets credit for making it possible to shoot the first movie version of *20,000 Leagues Under the Sea*.

All of these efforts were clumsy. The results murky and crude. But these men solved problems in procedure that would eventually let all of us get underwater with a camera.

World War II (1940-1945) was probably the greatest affecting period of time when the greatest changes happened socially, economically and inventively. Here are some of the ways things trickled down and eventually had impact on sport diving and thereby underwater photography.

1. Plastics were forced to new quality and uses, as the availability of raw resources, were decimated and

restricted by the vortex of war. Metals and rubber even wood were not available.

2. Cameras, lenses, film, other photographic materials got upgraded and improved to solve the special needs of fighting a war. The innovations spilled over into the civilian commercial world.

3. Science got support with financing from the military to do the research and development of devices to explore, observe and record in special places where the military would now fight wars-underseas for example. That symbiotic relationship flowered with World War II. It remained an institutionalized reciprocal union throughout the 20th Century.

4. The Underwater Demolition Teams (that evolved into the SEALS) later on were organized during World War II. Equipment developed for them found its way to civilian use later, as it was distributed through mushrooming Military Surplus Stores.

5. Experimental Diving Unit (EDU) was the research bureau of the U. S. Navy and from it flowed knowledge extracted from experimentation that eventually reached the civilian sport diver. They provided the guidelines for diving so the underwater photographer could concentrate on taking pictures.

6. Cousteau and his colleagues got the opportunity to tinker as German prisoners when doing salvage work in Toulon Harbor. No war-maybe no Aqua Lung. Cousteau had a chance to design equipment for taking pictures underwater as a grand accompaniment to using scuba.

7. Of all the things invented, the Atomic Bomb created a fear than transformed our thinking worldwide. It perhaps created an ease in taking risks like going into underwater wilderness when the whole world could blow up any minute.

8. World War II gave us some impressive diving sites led by Truk Lagoon and hundreds of other places where war sunken wrecks went down. The A Bomb tests at Bikini Atoll in the 1950's may have destroyed some of wild nature but the relics left, emerge as prime historical diving places.

9. With the War, the world and especially the American economy turned around. A large middle class was initiated as millions of people saw good wages for the first time following the Great Depression of the 1930's The war machine of production converted to civilian consumer needs, houses and cars and other transportation. By the 1950's the majority of Americans were not only paying for basic needs but discovered there was money left over-discretionary money to do with whatever they wanted. With the slowly dwindling fear of a nuclear war happening, the new philosophy was to live now after almost two decades of austerity. And so they bought into the new toys and recreational activities. New sports and pastimes were invented which required equipment.

10. Magazines like, *Life* and *National Geographic* showed the planet and its places, people and events in dramatic photos. A demand for unusual pictures of strange places erupted. Underwater was certainly one of the most mysterious.

The equipment could be homemade but as the demand grew from the busy wage driven American public, entrepreneurs saw visions of new industries. Among which was this idea of diving, in particular scuba diving. The hunger and desperation of the depression era, war rationing times in the past, divers hunting for food was now not a legitimate need; they could afford to get it at the store. The changing economics set the stage for adding expensive photographic equipment to the basic diving outfit.

We all may abhor war for it's destruction of places and human lives, but we take advantage of the fallout that allows new activities to emerge. Americans, in particular, seemed to need more fun and entertainment on the bumpy road through life, and were capable and willing to buy it starting with the 1950's decade.

PETER STACKPOLE PIONEERS MODERN SPORT DIVING UNDERWATER PHOTOGRAPHY

Peter Stackpole was perhaps our premier pioneer underwater photographer. He was an ace photographer topside and down under, for the greatest photo journalism magazine of all time, *Life*. In 1941, the first year of World War II, he got the assignment to take pictures of a reigning movie star of the time, Errol Flynn.

Here's his account: "Actually my real interest (underwater photography) started when I had to do some underwater pictures of Errol Flynn spearfishing off his yacht in Catalina in 1941 and I had to rig up a plastic box for my Leica. I did it using Flynn's wooden goggles which he brought from the South Pacific and we had no fins, as they weren't on the market yet. A diver named Al Hansen stood by with his diving helmet, but I didn't know how to clear my ears so all I could do was hold my breath, but I did manage to get some pictures before too much water reached the bottom of the camera. I did some more camera housing building using metal after that event." *Life Magazine* had him do all their underwater assignments from 1941 to 1961.

Peter Stackpole's camera recorded finding Spanish Treasure with Teddy Tucker, the Hope Root fatal deep dive, the filming of *20,000 Leagues Under the Sea*-all in early 1950's (and the 1948 introduction of the Aqua Lung in the Los Angeles area). His *Life* pictures of these events created an enormous awareness of this new sport.

Immediately following the war, in the late 1940's homecraft time for Americans was popular. Work benches and kitchen table time. There weren't any real demands for underwater pictures, except for an occasional notice by *Life* or *National Geographic Magazine* stories.

Jacques-Yves Cousteau showed up here and there with some black and white movies. (In 1948, he was at Los Angeles Neptune Club meeting at Los Angeles Police Academy with some blurry footage.) Cousteau was developing underwater photo equipment even as he was developing the Aqua Lung. Probably trying to give the yet unheralded Aqua Lung an introduction into the market place.

• Hans Hass was just starting to be recognized through still black and white photos he had taken as a traveling adventurous youth. His best outlet

Peter Stackpole in Bermuda in 1973. Stackpole pioneered underwater photography while working for Life Magazine.
Peter Stackpole

turned out to be his own books which created much of the pioneering foundation of diving that stimulated the first generation of divers.

• Dimitri Rebikoff was engineering sophisticated photographic equipment and shooting movies to give the gear a showcase in the late 1940's.

We were lagging a bit in America. Inventively, we were putting cameras in plastic bags, using a rubber band to create the seal at the neck of the bag, then trying to work the camera by pressing the plastic against the controls. Awkward at best.

We made wooden boxes sealed with resins, and fixed a glove into the side to reach in and manipulate controls. "It was the Voit Aqua Eye that claimed my first 35mm camera. The camera we bought originally to take pictures of our first purchased home. Yes, I tested it with a rock and toilet paper but putting the camera in was the jinx. I guess. It didn't flood but the camera did get wet and some of my pictures ruined-not that a color slide of a starfish sitting on a rock was any great loss," declares author, Al Tillman.

The home crafted efforts went through many cheap cameras and rolls of toilet tissue. It took numerous trial

Chuck Peterson created his earliest housing out of his mom's pressure cooker.   Chuck Peterson

runs to get the leaks out if ever. Mom's old pressure cooker got replaced by a new one as the retired kitchen item got converted into a tough somewhat heavy housing. It really helped to be handy with tools, nuts and bolts.

Tillman remembers Chuck Peterson, one of the great relatively unsung diving athletes, an underwater photographer, and top notch instructor. Chuck was the main photographer for the Los Angeles Fire Department and was one of the original blue ribbon staff at UNEXSO, along side of Dave Woodward and Jack McKenney. Chuck was handy. He could cut the metal and seal a glass port in, drill holes and gasket in levers. The great attribute of the pressure cooker was a sealing lid already built in through which the camera could be inserted. Chuck's invention could enclose both a still or movie camera. He had many award-winning pictures with it.

Jordan Klein in Miami put out a fixed focus self-contained underwater camera called the MAKO in the 1950's. It was the "Brownie" of underwater photography. One bought off E-Bay on the Internet for the Scuba America Historical Center in year 2000 still works.

Plexiglass really was the popular homemade housing material. It cut easier than metal, outlasted wood, and the camera and workings could be observed through the clear sides. It also allowed the diver to quickly spot leaking. It was not as tough in taking a clanging around rocks and such but repairs were easier.

"Earl Sugarman put together my first plexiglass case for my 240EE Bell and Howell Camera. It sported the new electric eye that read like a light meter and automatically set the shutter speed. It worked first time out and shot many of Los Angeles County UICC, Underwater Instructors Class Course, footage and several Film Festival movies," recalls Tillman.

Zale remembers clearly her first underwater camera involvement. It was 1953 after an exhausting fun weekend of water skiing and diving from end to end of the North shores of Santa Catalina Island when on the drive home from the Wilmington boat docks, spouse, Parry Bivens, decided to create a housing for a battery-driven military gun camera he had acquired. Somewhere on the road between Wilmington and Torrance, California, Parry stopped at a commercial junk yard. The place had acres of stuff of all sorts. Exhausted, anxious to reach home, I could not believe he had the energy to search and find exactly what he wanted. Parry found a heavy cylindrical steel pipe about fifteen inches long. It had

Divers discuss ownership of a Jordan Klein plexicase housing.

Jordan Klein

a good sized hole to arrange ledges inside for the camera's unrattling security. Being an engineer, he had the entire movie-camera-housing designed in his head before we arrived home that evening. It had a glass window-port, a steel circular hatch with permanent bolts, specially ordered o-ring for the lid that had the holes to fit over the bolts, an orifice with unique water tight seal for the gun camera trigger. All drawn on paper, he delivered the idea to Butane Tank Company in Los Angeles to do the welding. The job was completed in a week. Here was a happy camper! I mean diver! He took excellent pictures with this heavy monster. Sold footage to Disney, Hal Roach Studios, and a few others, who were looking for underwater material for television programs. Soon he purchased the "hot" 16mm housing designed and manufactured by Sampson-Hall. His father's Bell and Howell with fancy lens worked just fine in it," recalls Zale.

The pioneer great photographers such as: Peter Stackpole, Luis Marden, Rory Page, Jerry Greenberg, Jordan Klein, Chuck Pederson, Conrad Limbaugh, Nelson Mathison, were using both metal

Jacques Cousteau and Luis Marden discuss photography.
Charles Dierchsmier

and plexiglass. The entrepreneurs among them were thinking public consumption, a whole new diving sub-industry if the right housing could be manufactured to handle most 35mm cameras. Remember the incentive to shoot pictures for reasons other than personal satisfaction were few in the late 1940's and early 1950's.

But the 1950's ushered in well-crafted commercial housings - Herb Sampson in California, Jordan Klein in Florida and the Fenjohn Comany developed the underwater camera for movie makers such as, Lamar Boren. Then by 1960, Cousteau who had always been passionate about underwater photography and was a great incentive for him to develop the Aqua Lung, came up with the design of a completely self-contained underwater camera - no housing. It was called the Calypso and it became the Nikonos when Japanese interests took over the manufacture. The Nikonos discussed in a separate chapter in *Scuba America* was like walking on the moon for diving. The Nikonos became almost a basic piece of diving equipment. The gateway to underwater photography had been thrust widely open.

15
UNDERWATER PHOTOGRAPHIC SOCIETY

DEFINING EVENT: FIRST UNDERWATER PHOTO CONTEST - 1958

A picture might get sold to an agency like Black Star to fill in on an assigned magazine story. Other than publishing your own book to showcase your photos, there just wasn't much publication demand in the pioneer 1940's and early 1950's. The original, all influencing magazine for the diving population was *Skin Diver Magazine* and it was years before it got past guys holding fish they had speared ("...or me in first issue holding a prize lobster," mumbles Tillman), or paid for a picture. *Skin Diver Magazine's* policy was get articles and pictures free and let the contributors bask in the vanity of exposure.

There were no photo contests or film festivals or specialty underwater photographic clubs until the late 1950's.

The first real recognition of underwater photography came with the 1956 issue of *Skin Diver Magazine* that was a special Underwater Photography Issue. It probably ushered in the new diving interest in a slow evolutionary changing of the guard away from the reigning interest in spearfishing. At the same time general interest magazines, *Argosy, National Geographic, Life,* were starting to do more underwater stories creating a demand for accompanying photos.

Cousteau's film, *Silent World*, and *National Geographic* films were hitting the American public via their new parlor entertainment, television. Television was visual and the first sights of an unknown world were rousingly popular.

It was also the time of major entertainment movies such as, *Underwater* and *20,000 Leagues Under the Sea*. There was *Sea Hunt*, the television series coming up. The underwater world had not yet become a new sport icon of the popular culture of the new affluence for the masses.

UNDERWATER PHOTOGRAPHERS GET TOGETHER

It was a time to draw together the recreational and commercial underwater photographers in an interacting group. The pros were independent-minded and generally kept their own counsel. As it was with general diving clubs, there was a sharing of information plus a sharing of equipment. More importantly it would appear, all clubs joined the original Los Angeles Underwater Photographic Society in getting their pictures out of shoe boxes in a closet to be appraised with approval by peers. The best way to do this was the photo contest.

PHOTO CONTESTS AND UPS

The competitive aspect of diving provided by killing fish had many dissenters in the general public and with divers, too. The "save-our-wildlife" was just starting out of the gate as part of the environmental concern in the United States. The Photo Contest was a popular new approach for competing without destroying or diminishing the water wilderness.

Note that the contest was actually proceeded by the film festival. The film festival emerged from the Los Angeles County Underwater Program, as did the Underwater Photographic Society, which was in essence a club of divers whose main interest was shooting pictures. Each of these happenings will be covered in depth as special sections of this history.

The Los Angeles County Program, which was initiated as public skin diving classes for the general population in the interests of safety expanded to instructor certification then to recreational activities for divers. Underwater photography was the major development.

The Underwater Photographic Society in 1958. Norm Robinson, Jim Auxier, Al Tillman, Mart Toggweiller, Jack McNeal, Doc Mathison, Robert Kendall, Bob Figueroa, Fred Roberts, Paul McComack and Zale Parry among others.

Howard Kennedy

Al Tillman was sitting at his film editing table in his home in El Monte, California, in 1956 with Earl Sugarman, who had just brought Al's first plexiglass housing. A conversation ensued. Earl had been one of Al's diving students in a class at the Hollywood Athletic Club. Earl then became a sort of personal assistant for some of Al's projected ideas for diving.

Tillman: "Earl, maybe we should pull together all the underwater photographers into a club."

Sugarman: "An underwater photography class or a club?"

Tillman: "No, we'd start with divers already taking pictures or movies, learn from each other, have contests, and rather than Club call it a Society...."

Sugarman: "How do we get the underwater photographers?"

Tillman: "We already know a few, some of the underwater instructors and we can get *Skin Diver Magazine* to put in a notice."

Sugarman: "I can get the Community Center at Monterey Park (California) for a meeting."

And so it happened that Underwater Photographic Society, UPS, emerged with help from Los Angeles County as an autonomous nonprofit group. With Earl Sugarman, as President of UPS, Al Tillman, as Technical Consultant and a celebrity, founding member in Zale Parry, they put on a First Underwater Film Festival in 1957 at West Hollywood Park Auditorium. They just arbitrarily picked people to honor making Jacque-Yves Cousteau the First Underwater Photographer of the Year.

By the next year, moving the Festival to California State University, Los Angeles, an Underwater Photo Contest was initiated through the Underwater Photographic Society to provide more interest and exhibitors for the Film

Festival. As Earl Sugarman moved on to other things, Al Tillman and Zale Parry became the production team for the Festival and the Photo Contest with Underwater Photographic Society taking a support role. The International Underwater Film Festival incorporated as a nonprofit enterprise and Underwater Photographic Society continued on as a self-interacting Club and eventually took charge of the photo contest. The Festival was strongly supported by *Skin Diver Magazine*. The two joined forces to provide a powerful double show-casing for the contest winners and underwater photography in general. Underwater Photography had arrived to open the gates to new kind of diving.

Diving would eventually burst into a shower of special interest activities like: wreck diving, cave diving, ice diving, aquarium collecting. There would be special training. Underwater photography would be the brightest and most sophisticated of them. The camera would be a tool for all of the other special interests.

The camera-carrying diver was a small minority in the mid 1950's, in fact, most general diving clubs could boast one in-club underwater photographer, if any. Feeling isolated with no club member divers to discuss the intricacies of taking pictures underwater, the underwater photographer sought ways to associate and interact with other photographers.

The concept for the first Underwater Photographic Society was to draw together photographers already shoot-ing underwater...in America...or anywhere. But the need to have face to face contact dictated a more local devel-opment and so the first members in were from Southern California where a substantial amount of diving origi-nated. But out of the area people joined, too. Ultimately, the nucleus club became UPSLA, Underwater Photo-graphic Society of Los Angeles. Then a San Diego Chapter, followed by others. Today there are numerous chapters...perhaps twenty-five.

The roster of founding members was Al Tillman, Walt Nash, Anna Saudek, Earl Sugarman, Manuel Novak, Charles Frankel, Dick Bartlett, Karl Remmen, Mike Mirano, Bill Jeffs, Ed White, Ken Tillman, Lillian Kemble, Sandra McCandliss, Dick Bartless Jr., Bill Lynn, Zale Parry, Jim Auxier, Virgil Mirano, Mart Toggweiler, Joe Marshall, Gene Waldo, Leon Paddock, Ralph Davis, Mike Allen and Arnold Sugarman.

A logo for UPS took up time and effort at first. Member Bob Figueroa, the only 8mm movie shooter, came up with most of the early meetings were held at the Union Ice Company Ware-house in industrial downtown Los Angeles and arranged for by member, Ed Nelson. Mem-bers showed each other photos, slides and movies. There they planned dive shoots on charter boats.

The first Underwater Photographic Society boat outing was in 1958. UPS went to Santa Catalina Island's Ship Rock, Eagle Reef and the Isthmus. All were popu-lar dive locations for one-day outings. There was a hodge podge of cameras aboard, home made housings, a couple of Rolleimarins. Doc Nelson Mathison, Al Tillman and Bob Figueroa were shooting movies. Ed Nelson had brought his girl friend in a leopard skin bathing suit to be the blonde underwater model for the day.

We anchored near a big herd of sea lions, who were teaching their young how to swim and maneuver under-water yielding some impressive film footage. Dan Ryan was along to get some shots for the slide lectures he gave Junior High School Classes. Dan had a 35mm camera in a plexiglass case. He expressed the same fervor as his boyhood chum, Connie Limbaugh. He even managed to tape sea lion sounds to back up the slides although his bull sea lion roar was manufactured from the sound of a seasick member throwing up over the side of the boat. Dan Ryan's post cards featured his prize-winning underwater creatures . They were sold commercially. Frequently one would find a Dan Ryan post card on the twirling rack-holders with other post cards for tourists.

Doc Mathison was a celebrity member along, a champion spearfisherman, and professionally shooting 35mm movies along with all other film media. Tillman was coming back from filming seals when he spotted a platter-size halibut in the sand, nicely displaying its outline for camera shots. Members on board the boat were alerted to load-up, come on down for the perfect film shoot setup. It was at a twenty-foot depth, bright sunshine, light sandy bottom, clear calm water...the works. Well, guess we can rummage an old saying about and come up with, "You can take a man out of spearfishing but cannot take spearfishing out of the man." By the time a half dozen UPS members got down in the area, Doc Mathison had already been there and speared the halibut. He later said that he already had fish pictures but didn't have his dinner for that night.

The Underwater Photographic Society worked very well as a local club for photographers. No formal classes were sponsored but more experienced members taught new ones informally on ocean dives. Meanwhile, the Los Angeles County Underwater Unit already had done some "film festivals" with Dimitri Rebikof and Stanton Waterman, Gustav Dalla Valle and an appetite for producing them was fermented. Earl Sugarman, Zale Parry and Al Tillman in cooperation with UPS staged the First Underwater Film Festival in 1957 at West Hollywood Park, California. It was the original that would emerge over the next fourteen years as the International Underwater Film Festival, the flagship for all underwater film festivals thereafter.

The festival was a showcase for UPS members: Mel Fisher, Doc Nelson E. Mathison, Jack McNeal, Mart Toggweiler and Jacque-Yves Cousteau. But to do another Festival, it was realized that a contest

Gene, Nancy and Laura Parker preparing for a photo expedition.   *Times Union*

was needed to provide some of the material for future years. UPS had been doing informal "contests" in its own midst but now an underwater photographic contest was put together at California State University, Los Angeles with sponsorship and support from *Skin Diver Magazine*, California State University, Los Angeles (CSULA), Los Angeles County and, of course, UPS.

No one was really knowledgeable about the criteria for judging any kind of photography contest. So after researching the rules and structuring of topside contests, they devised their own first underwater photography contest guidelines. Originally, the categories were prints, (mostly Black and White), color sides, both 35mm and 2 1/4 x 2 1/4, 8mm movies never did amount to much. Most divers were not spending the amounts of money cameras and film cost to shoot 16mm movies. Today video categories dominate the movie category. Computer enhanced color prints are a main attraction.

Jim Auxier, Mart Toggweiler, a veteran diver/photographer, and Al Tillman were the judges for the first contest in 1958. They worked off criteria they developed almost as they looked at entries. What's "composition?", was a question to be answered and about which they had to educate themselves. Visual impact, some kind of "ooh and aah" arousal that came instinctively on first look became important. There was also clarity, color, subject, story told, rare and unusual sighting, still or action. The neophyte judges were laying a serendipitous pattern for what a good picture was but in the final analysis, no exacting objective measuring scales really worked. Finally, it evolved to going back to a picture that just knocked your socks off without much artificial values or dimensions. Jim Auxier, as Editor of *Skin Diver Magazine* had to pick pictures for publication. He had great influence on the final selections. *Skin Diver Magazine* would fete the winners, an award better than the plaques given out. Premiere magazine exposure was always a giant recognition.

So was there a picture or film that really rocked the judges? Are there any from those first contests that stick in the pioneer diver minds?

Jim Auxier recalled a striking transparency by Mick Church of his brother, Ron, suspended in blue space. Jim put it on the cover of *Skin Diver Magazine* and most people, when they see it, think it stands up well against top slides being shot 40 years later. Mick was an unknown talent until that contest. Ron Church was experimenting with dying slides at the time and critics suspected the vivid coloration of Mick's transparency was lab enhanced. In the year 2000 of computer-improved pictures, it seems a minor complaint.

Al Tillman thinks Jim Houtz caught the essence of what diving is all about - exploration - with a slide of a diver penetrating deep into Death Valley's Devil's Hole. It's black and white but the light tones are pure art. Al put it on the cover of the 1963 International Underwater Film Festival and the posters for the Film Road Shows.

Zale Parry remembers her favorite winner...let's say winners. The delicate nudi-

Don Ollis on a poisonous fish expedition holding a 16 mm Cine Kodak Special movie camera with a custom made lucite case. Jaluit Atoll, Marshall Islands, 1954. Ollis was a charter member of the UPS.

branch in the iridescent, electric hues were eye catching. The slides of benign, colorful creatures that would make perfect wallpaper, if repeated in a pattern, were tops.

UPS played a smaller role with the contest and the Festival over the next few years, as the two events stayed closely allied with the Los Angeles County Program. Ultimately, the Festival incorporated as self-contained non-profit corporation. The contest eventually was taken over by UPS to administer with the Festival and *Skin Diver Magazine* as an outlet for the winners.

By 1963, the UPS roster boasted many famous names: Ron Church, Burton McNeely, Don Ollis, and Flip Schulke. Jordan Klein was on the Festival Board of Directors.

Underwater Photographic Society, Los Angeles, survived and grew more sophisticated along with diving in general. Diving was no longer the average wage earners sport and a chance to make your own equipment, especially with Underwater photography. UPS, in year 2000, is predominantly made up of professional career people in medicine, law, dentistry, high tech business. The cameras with accessories are expensive to add on to general diving gear costs. The costs of travel, especially the live aboard luxury dive boats of the 1990's are a great financial burden except for the upper level incomes of America.

UPS was a good idea for diving in America and remains the best possible way to sustain an interest in shooting underwater pictures.

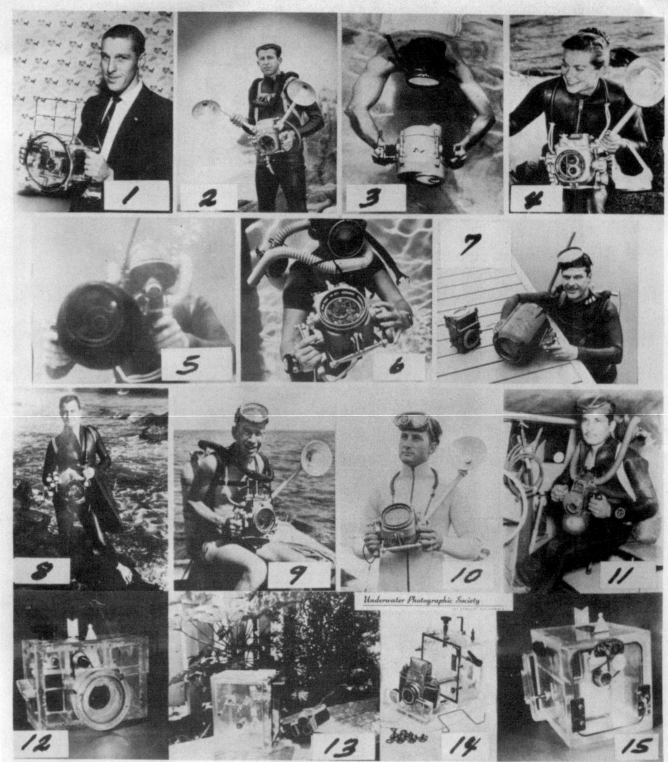

SOME OF THE UNDERWATER PHOTOGRAPHIC SOCIETY MEMBERS AND THEIR EQUIPMENT

1. Ed White, homemade housing for Minolta Auto-Wide 35mm.

2. Gary Blockley, Rolleimarin.

3. Dr. Nelson E. Mathison, Fenjohn housing, 16mm magazine load.

4. Zale Parry, Rolleimarin.

5. Paul McComack, Sampson-Hall housing for 16mm Bell and Howell.

6. E. M. Babs Jones, Rolleimarin.

7. Bob Retherford, Sampson housing for 16mm B&H and Ondiphott housing for Rolleiflex.

8. Jack McNeil, Kalimar Reflex in molded fiberglass housing.

9. Don Ollis, Rolleimarin.

10. Ron Church, Rolleimarin.

11. Bob Figueroa, 8mm Keystone Olympic, homemade housing.

12. Praktica housing, 35mm, homemade housing by Norm Robinson.

13. B&H Electric Eye 16mm EE housing, Al Tillman.

14. Exa 35mm housing, Fred Roberts.

15. Tower T92 8mm with full controls.

   At left: Marshall Ross, Bolex 16mm with Bolex housing.

16

NIKONOS ERA

DEFINING EVENT: COUSTEAU'S CALYPSO - 1959

With all of this energy expended, nothing pops up on the screen of history, at least no underwater camera set up, that can easily and inexpensively be picked up to use by the general diving public. It took the 1930's arrival of free diving or skin diving to ignite a small flame of desire to take pictures of sights they were seeing and show the dead things they were taking out of the ocean alive and kicking.

So while some of the skin diving era pioneers were fashioning spears and such, a few others were trying to fit a camera into a wooden, aluminum or plastic box. It helped a great deal to have some mechanical or engineering aptitude-and some basic photography know-how.

Perhaps the affluence of the post World War II era had reached a point where getting something to bring home for the dinner table was simply not enough justification for taking life as a sport.

How many times does one have to kill fish before the repetitive act becomes boring? Perhaps when the task of cleaning the take surpasses the joy of eating it and the limp beginning-to-smell corpse is forgotten in the trunk of the car or corner of the back porch. Wives didn't want it, neighbors didn't want it, and the final outcome is fertilizer for the rose garden.

Could taking a picture of the living sea creatures in the scenic sea substitute for the thump of a speargun hit? It was the doorway to the exciting new application of diving.

And so it was. Almost suddenly, the new heroes of diving were not the breathholding spearfishermen but bubble blowing men with housed cameras in hand. Scuba had arrived.

The inventive genius of early divers was called forth. Good pictures came from good cameras with good lenses. How to create a water tight housing that would permit shutter tripping, film advancement and speed and distance setting from outside. It is to be remembered that in those early days, money was still scarce in most households and commercial interests didn't see a justifiable market to research, develop and manufacture such products.

So it was back to the garage bench and kitchen table where plastic bags, pressure cookers and plexigass were cut and fitted around the family camera.

But there were expensive cameras going underwater in the hands of professional journalists and scientists. Cases were custom made for top of the line cameras such as the Hasselbad and Bronica. Hans Hass had a large role in the development of the self-contained Rolleimarin. Author, Zale Parry, recalls her first Rollei and why every diver didn't have one:

It opened the door to underwater photography. The Nikonos V was a state-of-the-art evolved Calypso.   Nikon, Inc.

"As a winning contestant on Groucho Marx's television show, *You Bet Your Life*, in 1954, I was asked, 'What are you going to do with the money?' My answer was to take a trip to France to swim with Cousteau's menfish. What I really did was purchase the first Rolleimarin that arrived at the Santa Monica Camera Shop. It was costly! The sophisticated camera housing complete with a f: 3.5 lens Rolleiflex camera price was $659.00. I had a lot of experience with a Ciroflex camera using a Weston II light meter, but this set-up could not go underwater. The Rolleimarin came in a dim- green, zippered, canvas carrying case. It's shape and size compared with a bowling ball. Weighty to lug along with diving gear, but it was neutrally buoyant in the water and worked easily."

Dr. Harold Edgerton, Jacques Cousteau and Sam Raymond examine a Calypso camera - the breakthrough from the homemade housings.

Underwater photography could only become a mass public undertaking in the sport of diving with the concurrent development of scuba and related diving gear. Forget the diving bells, submarines, robot devices-great underwater pictures had the best possible chance of artistic achievement through direct human contact. A diver with camera in hand free swimming in the water in direct contact with the subjects. The volcanic eruption of diver interest in taking pictures underwater had to be the historic moment when the Nikonos Camera was introduced in 1959. Historically, underwater photography was dependent on putting a land camera into a water tight housing. Now a relatively inexpensive self-contained camera was available.

Aboard a research vessel in the Red Sea in the winter of 1951-1952 Jacque-Yves Cousteau and Jean de Wouters talked about a camera that they wished they had. Over the next eight years, the camera eventually was developed by Wouters, the Belgian aeronautical engineer, who worked single-handedly on the camera that was to be called the Calypso-phot.

In 1959 the first cameras were made in France by Spirotechnique with Som Berthiot Flor 35mm f:3.5 lenses. The potential of this camera with fantastic capabilities caught the interest of Nippon Kogaku K.K. of Tokyo (Nikon, Inc., in the U.S.) Nikon Incorporated in the United States acquired the license to manufacture and distribute the Calypso underwater camera worldwide. In Europe it was called Calypso/Nikkor. The rest of the world called it Nikonos and still do.

In 1963 through the mid-1960's U.S. Divers sold the Nikonos I as the Calypso at the cost of $160.00. The carrying case, accessory bag, sport finder and flash adaptors could be purchased at an extra cost. A self-contained quality camera with high grade mechanism and lens, utilizing the popular 35mm film format, the Nikonos was a piece of diving equipment compact and easily operated.

The Nikonos was a franchised product. Dealers got exclusives in various areas and they had so designated the camera store at Freeport, Grand Bahama. UNEXSO couldn't get the cameras in 1965 without paying full retail prices. It was an item UNEXSO had to have and important as a profit center. Ways were found to get "bootleg" Nikonos Cameras at a wholesale price through Puerto Rico. Nikonos sent its security force around to trace UNEXSO's source after a complaint from the camera store. But UNESXO owners, who did not approve the pirated import, went quickly to Ernie at the camera store and made a deal. Ernie would sell the cameras, UNEXSO wouldn't, however UNEXSO would be able to buy wholesale for their rental service and would refer interested potential buyers to Ernie. In turn he would sell a Nikonos diving trip-lesson with every camera sold and UNEXSO would collect for the lesson. Once UNEXSO got the camera buyer to the club, there was film and processing that could be sold to him - and lots of trips out to the reefs.

Cameras are much more delicate than other diving gear. Rental cameras took a beating, water flooding after a tourist tried to change film, banging on the rocks, and forcing the film advance lever at the end of a roll. The cost to take a look at a busted camera before repairs was $50, a significant amount thirty-five years ago. Over the decades, Nikonos would improve the basic camera, mainly through the quality of the lenses and put out a number of new editions over the years. New attachments for macro shots of a nudibranch's "eye" and fish eye bubbles would allow greater artistic achievement. Video cams are almost as prevalent in year 2000 as still cameras. The digital camera is on the way. High tech promises to make impossible shots...possible. There will always be a need for the eye and mind of a human diver.

BEYOND THE NIKONOS

Another great leap in underwater photography has to be in the evolution of artificial lighting underwater. When *National Geographic* photographers exploded, in 1924, magnesium on the surface to get the first underwater color pictures (autochromes), it seemed a long journey to Dr. Harold E. Edgerton's (Papa Flash, Cousteau's crew called him) strobe lights. In the interim, bags of flash bulbs in little net bags or stuck in belts like so many eggs drifted behind divers. The light given off often overexposed a close-up shot or was wasted on anything more than five feet away. Bulbs imploded on occasion and once used were let float away and be flotsam in the sea - before we cared about a pristine ocean.

The strobe underwater permitted greater depth of field and froze action with fast shutter speeds. Multiple strobes on long extension arms could light up the colors of fish and corals to amaze divers who had never realized those vivid colors even existed.

Faster film, new high density digital equipment with precision lens, all could allow masterpiece photography by any diver. A diver would still have to hold the camera steady.

17

SHARKS
THE ULTIMATE VILLIANS

DEFINING EVENT: THE PAMPERIN ATTACK

Shark!

That one word is probably the most chilling disinclination effect to the majority of divers. The literature, fact and faction, carry the most terrifying stories of men being eaten alive. For most of us, there is a shudder and a scream suppressed at mention of sharks. There are so many of them out there, probably out numbering the world population of humans.

Nothing set human teeth on edge for centuries like the nightmarish vision of TEETH-the serrated, jagged rows of sharks teeth that await anyone who would fall or jump overboard in the sea. Divers, especially scuba divers, laid that horror legend to partial rest by invading "shark infested" ocean hot spots without serious incident. American diving areas seem to be especially safe from man-eating shark attacks and divers in their voluminous tale-telling depicted sharks they encountered as turn-tail cowards.

In the pioneer days of the 1940's and 1950's, divers were going into a mysterious and unknown environment. They were a risk-taking small segment of the population and the threat of sharks, created for them a daredevil image and exciting sensation of danger.

There was a large body of folklore to fan the fires of possible encounters. But divers were not

John Perry brought in this 16-1/2 foot shark for the championship at the 1970 U.S. Open Shark Tournament in Florida.

John Perry

seeing sharks except on rare occasions. Perhaps with the sights being so new, they weren't paying enough attention. The attitude that prevailed was certainly not one of great concern.

The generations of divers that followed the Golden Years have seen miles of film of divers, particularly underwater photographs, swimming with schools of sharks, facing them down. Jacque Yves-Cousteau said that a blast of Aqua-Lung bubbles will send them off. Hans Hass told us that yelling underwater made the shark the frightened one.

Shark billy-sticks with nails on the end, were carried by Cousteau's team and resort guides during the 1960's. Nobody during this time was being too brazen in the vicinity of sharks except a few daredevils like Francis Fane.

A lot of close encounters and non-fatal attacks get covered up to avoid a panicky attitude that might destroy the diving business.

"Look," the leaders of diving were saying to each other, "sure there are sharks down there, lots of them, but more seem to run away than otherwise. The sharks are part of the excitement of going under just as wolves and lions and snakes are, as we go into any jungle or wilderness."

The stories that were recorded as authentic were quite gruesome but they were so rare that divers felt no immediate worry in those days. That lots of sharks were out there in the ocean and could attack with horrendous results were dramatized by the fate of the USS Indianapolis aircraft carrier.

In July 1945, the Japanese sunk her and 900 men went into the water. For five days, screams recorded the horror as bands of sharks arrived to pick off floating men until only 317 remained when they were rescued five days later.

In 1942, the S.A. Nova Scotia sinking set the record with 1,000 being taken by sharks.

In 1916, the same great white shark took five victims in a one-hundred mile region around Matawan, New Jersey, within ten days. Caught two weeks after the first victim, the shark's stomach contained fifteen pounds of human flesh and the bones of the second victim. It was the idea basis for Peter Benchley's *Jaws*.

In 1952, a Sea Otters Skin Divers Club member, Barry Wilson, was attacked in Monterey Bay. His buddy saw him jolted out of the water to his thighs and while five club members surrounded his mangled body and tried to get him ashore, the shark bumped and fought the rescuers to get at Barry but didn't bite them. Barry died on shore of shock and blood loss.

In 1946, a large shark was found on a sand bar near Tampico, Mexico, with two legs protruding. A fully clothed man was stuck in the shark's gullet.

World War II in the early 1940's was the real starting point for interest in sharks. The war put plenty of bodies in the water and the military wanted protection. The need to know spawned a new generation of marine biologists to study sharks. The names of Dr. Perry Gilbert and Dr. Eugenie Clark were bandied about by divers and their discoveries about sharks informed but didn't lessen the divers' wariness. Perry Gilbert in one test found he had to measure a shark's bite not in pounds but in tons per square inch. California lifeguards were suggesting that half of unrecovered drownings were probably shark attacks.

And so as the fifties drew to a close and scuba diving had entrenched itself as a popular American sport, there wasn't enough evidence - stories, facts, or sightings to dim divers' enthusiasm. After all, wasn't the reigning cliché, "You're more likely to be killed by lightening or a bee sting than a shark attack?"

WHAT MANUALS ADVISED

The diving instruction classes at the time and the manuals that gave them substance, were very sketchy when it came to sharks. Sharks were sharks and differentiating the 350 species was to be a thing of the future. Generally, the leading advice was, "If you see a shark - GET OUT OF THE WATER."

Shark!

Feel a little twinge? If you were around in the start-up days of sport diving you were getting a lot of warnings about sharks, how they circle you, constricting the circle before closing in and bumping you before taking a bite. And, how you could tell an attack was coming when they made erratic movements and hunched their backs. Commander Francis Douglas Fane of Underwater Demolition Team fame reminded us of the fact, that sharks "sniffed us like dogs."

Taking a look at the early day manuals, here is what divers were told about sharks:

1943   *Bureau of Ships Diving Manual*

Navships 250-880 By U.S. Navy Department, Washington, 25, D.C.

(First Revision 1 July 1952)

This was the point of authority-diving manual on all technical matters for scuba diving for a least the first decade, even though, the manual was written for the helmet diver with plenty of "Don'ts and Nevers" in the instructions. Equipment, mental and physical safety control were greatly stressed. Accidents were caused from A-for Air Embolism to S-for Squeeze. The first manual was prepared and issued in 1915 with the establishment of the Navy Diving School at the Naval Torpedo Station at Newport, Rhode Island. In 1926-27, the Deep Sea Diving School, the Experimental Diving Unit, the Salvage School were established under the auspices of the Bureau of Mines then organized under the Naval Gun Factory, Washington, D.C. <u>Nothing is written about sharks or marine creatures</u>.

Sharks were a real fear in the early days of spearfishing but pioneer women divers tamed them.
Ron Taylor

The U.S. Navy manual, *Shark Sense*, in 1944 advised personnel encountering a shark:

"Remember that the shark strikes with his mouth opened wide, and his vision blocked. If you can avoid his mouth by moving a foot or so out of his path, it is a miss for the shark...if you can attach yourself to him by grabbing a fin, when he turns for another attack, you aren't there; you are riding with him, behind his mouth and out of danger from his teeth. Hold tight and hang on as long as you can without drowning yourself." This was accompanied by cartoon illustrations depicting the shark as a buffoon.

Sea Frontiers in 1969 notes such shark handling as Japanese fishing people wearing a long red sash to protect them or Ceylonese pearl divers using the exorcism by a shark charmer before going into shark waters.

Very few of these things worked in practice and pioneer divers were afloat in a claptrap of erroneous information.

1945   *The Complete Manual of Free Diving*
By Philippe Tailliez / Frederic Dumas / Jacque Yves-Cousteau / French Navy
Nothing on sharks.

1946   *Guide to the Underwater*
MCMLXVI   By Bill Slosky / Art Walker
Great controversy over danger of sharks. Leave if present. No splashing.

1955   *The Complete Book of Skin Diving*
By Carrier Rick and Barbara, Wilfred Funk, Inc.

(Revised later 1963 by Gene Parker)

Although this book was not picked up officially as an instructional manual by any certifying agency nor by a manufacturer it was a well-done comprehensive book/manual. Neither the original nor the revised version mentions sharks although many pages are devoted to spearfishing and mythical sea monsters. There is a half and half content devoted to skin and then scuba diving.

1955   *Underwater Recreation*

By Al Tillman and Bill Starr

Los Angeles Parks and Recreation

Plenty "Do's" of wisdom about sharks. Do avoid large sharks at all times. Belief that the diver on the surface is a better attraction for a shark. Raw meat or blood will attract sharks increasing the likelihood of their attack. When carrying bleeding fish, do leave the water immediately, if possible. Stay submerged if sharks are in the area and appear aggressive. Cases of sharks attacking fully submerged divers are virtually unknown, (to that point of TIMELINE).

1956   *Underwater Safety*

By E. R. Cross, Los Angeles, California:

Healthways

"In writing, I stayed away from sharks. Don't get me wrong, in the water they are there and unpredictable," E. R. Cross. When the public would ask about sharks at his lectures, Cross would say, "What sharks!"

1957   *The Science of Skin and Scuba Diving*

Council for National Cooperation in Aquatics
(Next Version arrived in 1980)

Sharks a holdover from prehistoric life. Villain of many sea stories. Hand-drawn (opposed to modern computer generated) illustrations with detailed definitions. Because of the variety of species and their unpredictable behavior, manual explains that no hard and fast rules for handling an encounter will apply in every case.

It devotes six pages to the shark with two of them colored drawings of the dangerous ones... This is justified because non-divers and new-divers find it a most popular topic of conversation. (Experienced divers do not think it worthy of much space.)

Smithsonian's documented account of shark attacks numbering 1000 over a 50-year-period is noted. Nothing new is revealed and the emphasis is on "few authenticated <u>unprovoked</u> attacks that have occurred involving divers. Cousteau is quoted as saying, "Every species of shark...is anatomically a formidable source of potential danger..." The usual tank-banging, bubbles- shouting-prevention measures put forth up to this publication are "questioned by authori-

Shark research has allowed us to learn much about these mysterious creatures. Cages allowed divers to go amidst sharks but Peter Gimbel pioneered diving with sharks without a cage.

Brooks

ties". A shark billy should be used to push the shark away not wound it. The usual precautions about buddy diving, keeping the shark in view, face it, swim smoothly, don't carry speared fish close to body are presented but there is the warning that because of unpredictability there are no hard and fast rules. Not much new here but it does go beyond "get out of the water". It says there are 250 or more species of shark; other manuals and shark books take that number up to 3,500! There is a danger in a book written by a committee.

The shark section of this manual goes two directions saying don't worry on one hand but perhaps you'd better worry on the other...The drawing on page 231 didn't soothe learning divers.

1962   *Let's Go Diving*

By Bill Barada U.S. Divers Co.

This "Condensed Instruction Manual" attempts to keep divers in a recreational frame of mind. The shark coverage has the usual about no blood, the novice spreading stories about "close calls", no way of determining a shark's intentions and - defensive tactics of splashing, shouting, diving at them have no more success than similar tactics used on a dangerous looking dog.

1962   *Skin and Scuba Diver*

By Lil Borgeson and Jack Spoliss

Fawcett Publications 1962

States - "Any diver goes in water with preconceived idea that sharks are not dangerous, is well on way to becoming a first class statistic." It says don't worry about the whale shark, the biggest, because it has "less teeth than Whistler's Mother". But a big Great White can cut a man in two with one slashing bite. The usual precautions are given but there is suggested if the shark moves in too close, use the spear as a cudgel and clout him on the snout - don't use your hand. The Shark Research Panel of the American Institute of Biological sciences said "the shark is awfully good at his business and his business is being a predator."

1962   *Underwater Education*

By Al Tillman, William C. Brown Co.

NAUI's first text book and designed for universities. It was Scubapro's first venture into an instruction/manual. The shark coverage went beyond existing manuals at the time and its content would probably hold up well for diving at the close of its 50-year-history.

SHARKS

There is no doubt at this time that sharks have a cruel and vicious potential. Unfortunately, fact and fiction have been fused at various times to create mass panic. Even the veteran divers who have never seen a formidable shark in their long careers find themselves tense and spinning like underwater tops in such times of group hysteria. It is indeed a disservice to diving if not downright criminal to fan the fire of fear with any fantasies or even authentic gory stories.

The argument may be that new divers should be warned. New divers have enough trouble with a more common and hard to defend against foe-panic. "Sharkphobia" badly weakens the wall of nerves. This text is going to point out what seems to be the general schools of thoughts by great divers who have authenticated experiences with these monsters.

1. Sharks, like people, are completely unpredictable from one area to another, from one species to another, and even from one individual shark to another.

2. Sharks have attacked men and eaten them but the causes for such tragedies are vague and complex. The occasions are rare when compared to the millions of water

experience units recorded each year.

3. Certain areas of the world seem to possess sharks with a greater inclination to attack than in other areas, e.g., Australia. The reasons may be similar to those resulting in conflict on land - lack of food, climate, or perhaps just a general neurotic attitude.

4. Consider sharks on an individual basis at first. He may be protecting "his" reef, after your catch or feels trapped. There are also "rogue" sharks that can no longer forage for food in a normal manner due to injury or old age. This creates a "psychotic personality" dangerous to anything in its path.

If sharks come in groups, don't delay your exit from open exposure.

5. A surface exit appears to be quite hazardous with sharks in the area. Attempt to keep sharks in your vision at all times with your back protected by rocks or growth. Exit on bottom into shore if possible. Most reported experiences indicate it is best to face the creatures under water if possible.

6. There are some relatively harmless sharks but let years of experience be your guide on such relationships. Any shark that moves swiftly through the water can usually expose some devastating teeth. Even those in holes or lying on the bottom may turn and remove a pot roast if disturbed.

Some of the worst damage reported has been from the abrasions caused by brushing against the sandpaper hide. Don't ward off with bare hands but use some sort of projection if available.

7. Those in tropical and subtropical water should be the most aware of sharks and especially during the summer. Deep water close to shore appears to be the most frequented areas of encounter. Speared fish are prime targets for sharks. They seem to come out of nowhere.

8. Sharks' behavior is always strange. They are often only seen as dark images in the periphery of vision (now don't start seeing things) and will probably stay there. A circling shark is up to something but not necessarily attack. Erratic swimming movements seem to indicate a type of frenzy just before a running charge. Sharks do not have air bladders as fish so they must make a swimming approach. They do not have to turn over to bite.

9. At this time, the best advice is to stay out of the water where sharks are known to frequent. If no "graceful" way of escape is available face the creature. Make a bold, threatening movement toward the shark, this has been successful for many. Yelling in the water has had some positive results. Most of the repellents leave a lot to be desired at present and seem to have limited capacity and duration...although they have been tested with good results.

10. Sharks can smell, see, hear, and feel. We are just now finding out to what extent under different conditions these various senses are employed.

The existence of sharks cannot be denied nor can the presence of bears and other wild animals in areas where we go camping. Once in a great while, a bear injures somebody but we haven't let this interfere with our camping fun. If we decide to go camping in the middle of the Amazon, then we'll take special precautions. Know the shark potential of the specific area by talking to respected veteran divers.

The event that finally moved sport diving back a number of spaces, and generated a conscious layer of fear of

Sharks have increasingly become a popular subject for underwater photographers.   *Uwe Fund*

Dr. Lanny Cornell of Sea World inspects a great white shark that he and biologist Ray Keyes prepared and put on display for the public at the marine park.   *Sea World, Inc.*

sharks, was the Robert Pamperin attack of 1959 off La Jolla. The media jumped in and sensationalized it.

The Pamperin attack was a real media event and *Life Magazine* put out a story that petrified the diving community which resulted in the suppression of diving activity as we have already described. Divers of some years of experience and officials of various diving programs went on radio and television shows to talk about sharks and how "they were rarely seen and there was a much greater chance of being hit by lightening than being attacked by a shark and more people die from bee stings than shark attacks..."and on and on. It did help turn around the general diving public's timidity. It was said *Life Magazine* tried to get shark photos for the story in a hurry and failed. So they used old stock photos.

This time there was an eye witness to the attack, Robert L. Pamperin's diving partner, Gerald Lehrer. Skin diving off a cluster of rocks near La Jolla Cove, California, about 100 yards out, hunting abalone, Lehrer saw a dorsal fin moving toward Pamperin. "Robert rose high in the water, his arms flailing." When Lehrer looked underwater, he saw a twenty foot shark swallowing his friend, head without face mask, wide eyes looking up, and hands and arms sticking out, and a cloud of blood. Forget taking a bite, this was a devouring. "He just cruised off into the kelp and that was the last I ever saw of Robert." Search parties failed to find the shark or Robert. Experts determined from Lehrer's description it was a Tiger shark.

Nothing shocked the diving community and intensified the image of the shark like the eye witness account of Robert Pamperin in the Jaws of a Great White Shark being carried off through the kelp beds of LaJolla...and never to be seen again. There was some speculation that Pamperin showed up in Mexico to meet his wife, who had the insurance money. Real or faked, the publicity of it sent a thunderbolt of renewed fear through every diver. Divers quit diving or if they went in the water, they spun like dervishes watching in every direction fro that voracious "wolf-of-the-sea." Nobody wanted to be eaten alive! People, who had just taken a diving course, decided not to take the newly learned skill out of the swimming pool. Orders for the new bright colored neoprene suit were suddenly canceled. Yellow as too visible and suits already half-made got dumped on the market at very low prices. For years after, the less afraid divers were sporting a yellow bottom, black top or visa versa and they were quite dashing in the two-color sports look.

Up to this point as previously noted, there had been very few deaths from shark bites, or event reports of attacks. Frankly, divers just didn't see any sharks except for a careless spear fisherman who let a dying fish flap and bleed into the water. Even then sharks didn't seem aggressive toward divers.

THE MEDIA HIGH PROFILES SHARKS

The Pamperin attack was a terrific story and the media made the most of it. It scared off a whole generation of novice enthusiasts and even made the old timers shake their heads and have second thoughts. *Life Magazine* had to scrounge about to get any shark pictures. They dredged up old fish tales, legends, those of extracting whole bodies from the big sharks. The Tiger, the Great White and the Mako were top of the list as killing machines and all the talk about attacks and mutilations were fully within their potential.

We noted before that the thing most divers thought in those days was that a shark was a shark was a shark. Now with Pamperin, the Great White, Tiger, Mako, Ocean Blue, Lemon and a dozen others were being designated as dangerous, (or potentially dangerous) which was a more euphemistic label than the media's "man eating". The wrong words can give divers the shivers. Old ones, too.

In Los Angeles, dive shops had a sudden drop in sign-ups or instruction in the wake of the Pamperin devouring. The Underwater Unit of the Los Angeles County Department of Parks and Recreation reported a drop-off in professional people; doctors, lawyers, dentists; but a sudden new infusion of blue collar types and clerks. Something to do with a quick- macho-fix for some and 'I'm too valuable to die for others'.

Colored wet suits were just then available and custom orders for yellow and orange were rapidly cancelled - the assumption of the time being bright colors would draw the attention of vicious predators.

"I got my first yellow wet suit on a cancelled order, half price, from Earl Sugarman, but I'll have to admit every time I went diving in it, I did more whirling dervish maneuvers looking out for a yellow hating shark," said Al Tillman, who ran the Los Angeles County Underwater Unit.

Tillman recalled that he and a group of respected diving leaders went on a number of television diving shows and general talk programs to try to disparage the Pamperin story and the shark scare. "Hey, we don't see them and we're taking thousands and thousands of dives where they're most likely to be," was the general statement of these experienced divers...Jim Christiansen, Zale Parry, Don St. Hill, Mel Fisher and Al Tillman.

SHARKS EAT REPELLENT

As usual, opportunists sprung forward with all kinds of devices to dispel shark attacks, One of Conrad Limbaugh's best stories is about an expedition to Gulf of Cortez, Baja Mexico to check out a chemical shark repellent. They had a good shark infested spot; they could see them swimming around the boat. They tossed the little sacks of repellent in the water and started to suit up to dive in. The sharks gobbled up the repellent bags like sardines and swam around in tight circles, either waiting to feed on more repellent or the divers.

It was mainly World War II that pushed the development of shark repellents. It was discovered that sharks will eat every bit of helpless flotsam and jetsam about but sharks won't eat decaying remains of their own generic species. They will of course, eat other decay and for that they get exalted support from preservationist groups. They eat diseased fish and keep the disease from spreading. For some reason they're immune and don't get cancer or have heart trouble. And, so decayed shark was put with copper sulfate and dye, packeted and introduced as Shark Chaser. It worked infrequently but stayed around because it provided a sort of false courage to divers who believed in it and didn't ever have to test it in a real attack situation.

THE BANG STICK

The U.S. Navy tested an electric barrier that a diver could carry and create through a hand-held zapper. Someone pushed striped wet suits but most all of these test expeditions ended up going back to the bang stick, a shotgun shell or .44 caliber cartridge loaded device that exploded into a shark when bumped with it.

A guy named Slaughter in Florida, one of many divers who developed a bang stick, received a good amount of attention using it. It seems he was mad at sharks for stealing fish he had speared. He was out to eliminate all the sharks in the oceans which was quite ambitious considering we eventually found out that the seldom seen shark existed by the billions and probably outnumbered human beings on the planet. And the number had probably been the same millions of years ago, 300 million years ago, when sharks probably came into existence. Anyway, Mr. Slaughter went out to notch his weight belt with shark killings, sort of like the records flyers set shooting down

Zeros in World War II. Slaughter got to 37 and apparently lost interest. He hardly made a dent in the vast population off Florida and the Atlantic Coast which seemed more heavily infested than the Pacific United States Coast. Later more and more sharks appeared in the West and when more and more divers traveled to places 30 degrees either side of the Equator.

As we said sharks were part of the thrill of going diving in the 1940's and 1950's. Movies and books heated up the fear of them with some gruesome accounts. That risk factor probably seasoned every diving experience, whether sharks were sighted or not. They were part of this mysterious "life" we all enjoyed but opponents contend sharks make the environment we want to dive too threatening. A shark attack could just be around the corner for any diver if the wrong circumstances prevail.

The public has a favorite question for divers, always had, "What about sharks?" The best answer may just be, "They haven't gotten me yet!"

At UNEXSO in the Bahamas during the 1960's, the policy was to play down sharks. (Later by the 1990's, UNEXSO would lead the way with shark feeding programs for the consumer-diver.) No one was to spear fish or try to feed sharks. Actually, the thing the guides did, if they spotted a shark, was to try to get their diving charges to look the other way which required some inventive dramatics on the guide's part. "I saw my first in the water 'dangerous' sharks while I was putting together UNEXSO in the early 1960's just after the Pamperin jolt," recalls Al Tillman. He goes on to report that though they didn't see many sharks during the day; at night native fisherman pole-fished large dark shapes onto the beach every time a line was cast. Those piles of dark shapes were reef sharks with teeth.

The Pamperin event generated both positive and negative attention to diving. Rumors went around that it all might have been an insurance fraud and Robert Pamperin was in Mexico and the wife was busy pursuing the life insurance claim.

In later years, Great Whites have been sighted on many occasions in the California and Mexico waters. THEY WERE ALWAYS THERE, and still are, but to this day, we have no concrete idea of how many there are out there nor very much on their behavior or attitudes.

DIVING SHARK-INFESTED WATERS

The 1960's and especially the 1970's unveiled a broad and intensive attention to sharks as photographers got pictures and footage to feed television. Books and manuals went into depth on differences in shark species and how individual creatures acted in confusing ways. The whole anatomy of sharks began to be part of the conversational jargon of divers. *Jaws*, the book, and in particular the Speilberg movie, exploded a fiction somewhat based on the Matawan, New Jersey "shark massacre". (See Chapter JAWS.) The 1960's ushered in the jet age. Divers were moving out of local diving spots to exotic tropic waters with clear waters and extensive, visible shark populations. The shrug of "We never seen them.", became a cry of "Let's go see them."

Here's a continued chronology of how diving instruction manuals of the late 1960's and 1970's were handling the shark issue.

1968   *The Golden Guide to Scuba Diving*

   By Dr. Wheeler North, Golden Books

The usual about blood in water, infrequency of attacks and staying calm. One unique line says, "sharks are a minor menace to divers compared to such hazards as fatigue".

1969   *Diving for Fun*

   By Joe Strykowski, Dacor

Two paragraphs given to sharks. Million to one chance of a shark attack. Accord shark respect you'd give a strange dog. Sharks totally unpredictable. Misinformed divers are increasingly thinking shark is timid.

1971   *The NOAA Diving Manual*

Diving for Science and Technology

By Manned Undersea Science and Technology Office - Includes a list of prestigious individuals in committee in collaboration representing the United States and Territories. National Oceanic and Atmospheric Administration, U.S. Department of Commerce

Two sections in this manual tap the shark with an honest and sensible approach. Recommends that divers carry some form of shark defense; devices designed as security mechanisms such as the "Shark Billy". A power head can be used if the diver desires discouragement by death to the shark. Gives a thorough explanation in treating a shark bite wound, such as a large chunk of flesh missing. Quick necessary steps to be taken to control bleeding by stopping the flow then treating the victim for shock. Obtain qualified medical aid immediately.

1972   Discover the Underwater World

By Ralph Erickson (PADI President)

U. S. Divers Company

Warns against specific sharks: Great White, Tiger, Hammerhead. Seldom attack but unpredictable. Use spear only as a probe to ward off.

1973   Scuba Diver's Guide to Underwater Adventures

By Judy Gail May

The Stackpole Books, Harrisburg, PA

A direct approach to sharks. She lists the voracious species. Explains that sharks have a highly developed sense of smell and extremely sensitive lateral line system that detects vibrations in the water. We chuckled when Judy, the author, mentioned Lloyd Bridges (*Sea Hunt* television series) looking good stabbing sharks with a knife. Her Dangerous Marine Animals section possesses merit.

1975   Skin and Scuba Diving

By John Cramer, Bergwall

Few recorded scuba diver attacks. Less than lightening strikes. Precautions in shark waters include: have a buddy, avoid murky water, keep visual contact, use shark billy or shark dart.

1976   Scuba Diving - How to Get Started

By William Koelzer, Chilton Books

Nothing on sharks.

1977   THE ALBUM OF SHARKS

By Tom McGowne, Rand McNally

This would be a good text for those special advance classes that diving instruction has evolved. It pretty well sums up what we knew by the late 1970's, the end of the first 25-years of sport diving history. He adds a few precaution points:

(1) seek local advice; (2) avoid shiny jewelry of equipment fittings attract, looking like sheen of fish scales; (3) porpoises don't mean no sharks, both are predators and feed on same prey.

It's the sharks home, the ocean, and divers must avoid those places where they frequent or back a campaign to kill and remove them. Which is doomed to fail as being too expensive and against the end of the Century mind-set to protect all species of everything.

A cute note on the abandonment of repellents. One scientist said best way to prevent shark attack is find a dry desert and lie down in it. Most of what we know about sharks is from ones in captivity where they get fat, are well fed and don't hurt anything.

1978   Safe Scuba

By Richard Hammes / Anthony Zinos

NASDS

States no records of sharks attacking a <u>submerged diver.</u> Bang tank with knife handle to scare if you can't avoid them.

1980   The New Science of Skin and Scuba Diving

(First published 1957)

Council for National Cooperation in Aquatics

This most popular of all the manuals was first put out in 1957 by the principal grouping of pioneer diving leaders. This 1980 version had added two significant dive luminaries to the crew that wrote it - Jon Hardy and Ken Brock. Nothing new on sharks in the new 1980 edition.

1990   Open Water Diver Manual

PADI

Nothing on sharks.

1993   Scuba Diving

By Dennis K. Graver

Human Kinetics Publisher

And so by the 1990's, sharks are almost disregarded. This fine manual says attacks on SCUBA divers is almost non-existent. That Hollywood has greatly exaggerated the danger of sharks...that it is rare to encounter the few that are aggressive especially in diver-visited waters. Most divers would be delighted to see a shark because they usually retreat from diver infested water. This is all, paraphrased, the manual has to say about sharks lumping them in amidst a laundry list of other potentially dangerous "aquatic life". It warns about feeding any of them.

1995   Adventures in Scuba Diving

By Steven Barsky

NAUI

This follows a long string of manuals recommended for instruction by NAUI over the years. It says, "most fish swim away from divers...humans are the most fearsome creatures underwater." Lumping sharks with barracudas and killer whales, it says encountering a large shark that would bite you is less chance than a traffic accident on way to dive. Diver's pay big bucks for special trips to get to see one.

SUMMARY: Looking at the manuals overall, not a great deal of radically new information was disseminated over five decades. Basically, it seemed the only advice anyone wanted to give was avoid them, get out of the water for any shark, big ones and little ones. Sharks are sharks. By the 1970's there had been a number of attacks and diver encounters and solid precautions were set forth. Repellents were pretty well abandoned and the shark billy or probe was only the device that seemed to work. By the 1980's, manuals were doing more identifying and differentiating so divers could recognize sharks and act accordingly. The Great White Shark took a special top of the ladder fear role. The "avoid them" remained the final solution, but it ran in the face of the year 2000 shark feeding programs.

FEEDING SHARKS

By the 1990's manuals got almost indifferent to diver concern for sharks although scientists and diver encounters had built up a large lexicon of new information. We had begun to know so much about sharks, see so many films that they seem to become part of the family. Not only were they dismissed as dreaded danger in going into the ocean, the attempt to feed and pet them became a saleable product in resorts everywhere. The grand effort to protect the species was the latest designer fashion going from hugging trees to loving sharks. Whether this was a ticking time bomb waiting to explode as divers became less cautious and more brazen, we shall see. The sharks are there, always have been, by the billions we guess, with huge killing teeth but we end the fifty year period still puzzled by them, still calling them unpredictable in our manuals of diving instruction.

Great White Shark encounters loom as the most frightening of the shark attacks. In the early days of diving there weren't many reports of white sharks being seen underwater but they were there, always there, and fishermen had many legitimate sightings and catches. When a really big one was caught, it could be sold to traveling road shows or roadside attractions where the public could come see the killer monster on ice. Sea World, San Diego, California, had one on exhibit.

Shark stories were all we had to go by in the early days and even to this day, they bulk out our shark knowledge beyond scientific studies. This may be because a wild creature is in another dimension compared to dead sharks or ones in captivity. Taking a look at the stories, we should begin with those patron saints of diving, Jacques Yves Cousteau and Hans Hass. Jacques and Hans learned the hard way - by doing the things that divers were warned not to do later on. Both are great story tellers and accepted as truthful in a sport that is noted for its exaggerators.

In 1939 Cousteau met sharks for the first time while "goggle diving" off Tunisia. "They were magnificent gun metal creatures, eight feet long." They made Cousteau uneasy but his diving partner wife, Simone, was terrified. The sharks haughtily passed on by.

Cousteau kept a casebook of shark encounters but gave up recording, overwhelmed, when he went to the Red Sea in 1951 where great numbers of sharks appeared on most dives. Summing up his casebook, Cousteau concluded at that point that: "(1) the better acquainted we become with sharks, the less we know them; and (2) one can never tell what a shark is going to do."

Silent World says the shark has existed for over 300 million years without evolution - indestructible and armed to kill. Some experts disagreed, feeling the pelagic sharks have <u>evolved</u> into the perfect swimming, killing machines they are today.

In the Red Sea, Dumas and Tailliez, Cousteau's main partners in the early days, had to pull sharks' tails to get them out of caverns so Cousteau could film them but the sharks immediately vanished swiftly into the distant blue. Dumas tried to spear one 15-foot nurse shark with a super explosive-head "harpoon gun" but the shark shook the shaft off and swam away - tough guys these sharks.

During one movie sequence, Cousteau and Dumas "were galvanized with ice cold terror... What we saw made us feel that naked men do not belong under the sea." There appeared from the gray haze the lead white bulk of a 25-foot Great White Shark, the only species that all experts agreed is a confirmed man-eater. "Then the shark saw us," says Cousteau, " in pure fright the monster voided a cloud of excrement and departed at incredible speed."

It was typical of all Cousteau's shark encounters and he was ready to state flatly that all sharks are cowardly. Then the day arrived where they harpooned a small whale in open ocean, which Cousteau excuses with it "being part of a serious shark study". Confident, Dumas and Cousteau went in the water to film sharks and this time a gray shark showed, of a kind they had not seen before, an eight footer, that did not retreat when they swam toward it. The shark circled with its pilot fish and then two 15-foot Blue sharks came up under the divers.

Cousteau says he and Dumas "ransacked our memories for advice on how to frighten off sharks"...gesticulating wildly, a flood of bubbles. Hans Hass's shouting loudly didn't work. "We hooted until our voices cracked. The shark appeared deaf." Cousteau released cupric acetate tablets, the so-called shark repellent, but the shark swam right through it without blinking. His black beady eye watched the divers. Then the shark came at them head on and Cousteau banged it on the snout with his camera. The shark brushed past and resumed circling. Cousteau wondered why this shark was picking on them while a hurt juicy whale was nearby.

The Blues joined the Grey and were making a direct attack as Cousteau and Dumas went to the surface to signal the rescue boat. They dove and faced the sharks who resumed a circling maneuver. Cousteau felt that they were in the worst possible position with head out of water, legs dangling to be "plucked like bananas". The sharks finally just disappeared with the approach of the main boat.

Outside of this apparent attack by the Grey and Blues, no sharks ever attacked Cousteau with any resolution...and this attack they assumed was because of being on the surface. A diver down under is an "animal they may sense to be dangerous". Aqua-Lung bubbles may also have been a deterrent.

Finally, in *Silent World's* "Shark Close-Ups" Chapter, Cousteau advocates a protective shark billy, a four foot broom stick with a couple of nails in the end, maneuvered like a lion tamer's chair. However, Cousteau says he never had occasion to apply the billy and it may just be a psychological defense against a creature which has eluded man's understanding.

SHARK STORIES GALORE

Hans Hass in his first book *Diving to Adventure* had a large share of shark encounters while skin diving and spearfishing. He told the 1950's generation of divers to expect sharks to come after speared fish but he advocated shouting into the water as the best deterrent. Neither Hass nor Cousteau was ever attacked or bitten and their books and films alerted divers of the time that, yes, there were sharks out there, lots of them. A diver, especially divers, the more the better, shouldn't be bothered by sharks underwater.

Generally, divers were not happy to learn that there were so many sharks and started turning to watch for them. Along with this new fear, they had the Cousteau/Hass conclusion that sharks were not interested in taking on a functioning diver, who would face off with them. But if you speared fish, you greeted danger.

Al Giddings has been in many shark alleys with his movie camera. Big, fearless and tough as any shark, Giddings listed as one of his memorable shark dive incidents the one that occurred in the Virgin Islands during the 1960's. The "three stooges dive" he called it. With his eye to the viewfinder and unbeknownst, a big shark was behind his head, the other divers speared a nice fish, left it, bolted for the surface, pointing vigorously at what was behind Al while Al gestured impatiently for the ascending divers to come back and hold still for a picture just as the shark knocked Giddings into a somersault to swallow the fish and spit out a bent staff. Everybody then scrambled up a coral head on the surface, and there sat, cut and bleeding from the coral, waiting, and waiting and a bit petrified.

The stories of sharks told out of the Pacific Region generally indicate a kinship between native population and the creatures. The children play in the lagoons with sharks. Sharks contain the spirits of their ancestors. There seems to be some sort of religious overtone to it. On close examination of native divers using only goggles, they seem to have experienced the same realizations that modern scuba divers have - sharks are curious but unless they sense a helpless prey, they won't directly attack someone underwater. It is interesting to note, there seems to have been a different shark philosophy in the Caribbean: More fear in the native populations of the man-eating capacity of sharks.

A side note: In 1999, the world's greatest basketball player, Tim Duncan of the champion San Antonio Spurs, was intent on being an Olympic Champion Swimmer until a hurricane demolished the only swim pools in the Virgin Islands. Lot of ocean there available for swimming but Tim was deathly afraid of sharks so he switched to basketball. Guess the NBA gives thanks for the existence of sharks.

Pulp fiction and cheap adventure books created an excess of the dread concerning sharks...mainly in the 1930's and 1940's. Dramatic covers sensationalized big toothed sharks guarding treasure, gnawing on helmet-hardhat divers, attacking surface swimmers. These were vivid pictures that projected a terrifying image to young-sters who would grow up to be the founding generation of sport divers. Movies over-dramatized the vicious attacking behavior of sharks in films like *Reap the Wild Wind* and South Seas island film stories. Then along came *Jaws* in 1976 which is a Chapter in itself. The pictures are imprinted in the mind even if divers knew they were far fetched. Often it was an especially gory cover that flashed in the mind's eye when a shark was just passing by.

DON'T ADVERTISE SHARKS

The diving industry almost came tumbling down over an advertisement that pictured a - Oh, no! - shark. Hard on the heels of the Pamperin tragedy, there was a push to sell a shark repellent. John Gaffney as advertising manager pushed *Skin Diver Magazine* to carry a shark swimming through what looked like blood half page and in a first use of color in the magazine, make the ad blood very, very red. Wham! The big equipment manufacturers turned white and red, threatening to withdraw all their advertising. In those years, they didn't want customers to be reminded about sharks and especially how much blood could be spilled if a shark bit a diver. It was a faulty product anyway (as Limbaugh could have told them from his tests where sharks ate it and wanted more).

Rodney Fox of Australia, the poster boy of shark attacks, got hit without seeing it coming. Rodney was gobbled half up by a big White during a spearfishing meet. We know now, that dying fish are a big lure for sharks of all kinds. "It hit like a freight train and the teeth cut like a surgeon's scalpel," he expressed. Rodney was falling apart from the bites. He was a mass of train track scars but he survived after they took 1000 stitches up and down his body. He went back in later and has been the world's most famous guide for going Great White Shark watching. The pictures of Rodney's attack, at least the aftermath surface shots were brought to the USA during the 1962 International Underwater Film Festival in Santa Monica California. Ben Cropp was being honored and when he arrived and reviewed the films with the Festival producers, there was shark material besides the Rodney Fox footage that might make Festival-going-divers return their diving gear - and would certainly alienate manufacturers.

But truth and curiosity won out and Cropp showed his film intact. It was certainly a deviation from pretty fish and coral and in some ways it boosted the stock of those who like to bask in the "danger" of being a pioneer diver before loved ones and friends. "But Ben," we asked, "what is that line running across the screen, a scratch? Should we stop the film?"

"No, No, not to worry, Mates, sometimes we just had to wire-up a dead one to get our closeups."

FEEDING THE FEARS

Was it a disservice to diving and sharks, like with the pulp fiction magazines? The desperation to get shark footage, clusters of sharks, feeding frenzies, snout in the lens led the best of the "documentarists" to arrange and stage exaggerated depictions of the way it is with sharks when one went underwater. Rodney Fox's scars aren't easily forgotten and many divers lie down to sleep even now with nightmares of being eaten alive. The danger felt through shark films at the early 1960's International Underwater Film Festivals and later on television was both a fascination of fear and a lure of risky adventure. Hey folks, it was saying to the public at large, there's a forbidding wet jungle out there with death machine creatures, so aren't we the brave ones?

Most of the real encounters were about sharks seeing us, the divers, panicking, defecating in our faces and running away scared of us. Most of the divers in the early days took solace in such stories when they looked down at herds of sharks flitting about beneath them prior to a dive or when one cruised into a bucolic scene of sponges and corals, and there cruising at them from the other direction was a big shark. Funny how huge and menacing a shark can look, when its just a "you" alone down there.

There were divers who never flinched at the sighting of a shark. Fearless Francis Fane, Doug or Red Dog, as he was affectionately and variously called by admirers, and more profane things by the military athletes he commanded in the U.S. Navy's Underwater Demolition Teams was the ultimate. He was the kind of leader who led the charge up the hill against the enemy. Ivan Tors got the first shark footage needed to excite backers for the *sea Hunt* series when Fane jumped in the water with a fish in his hand to play bull fighter with a pack of hungry sharks. Bold and brazen in the 1950's long before others with bodyguards would film television's documentaries on sharks. Fane was awesome driving his muscled troops through "shark infested" surfs off the Coronado, California U.D.T. Base and took up the tail gun position coming in to shore so he could visually sort out who would become one of his frogmen and who wouldn't. One day as he churned through the breaking waves and bellowed at a few "sissy swimmers," he felt a tug at one of his fins and he kicked out at what he thought was a prankster testing him. When he stormed ashore he roared, "OK, who's the wise guy...?" Then he looked down to see a crescent-carved half piece of his right fin was gone. Only a shark could leave such a signature bite. Doug Fane would be heard to growl when the media asked whether he worried about sharks - that is was like swatting mosquitoes.

Peter Gimbel was a hard-core diver who famed himself beyond his family's department store recognition by giving diving it's grandest divable shipwreck coverage, the Andrea Doria. Beyond that, he mounted expeditions staffed by the best divers in the world to get fantastic footage of sharks. His Atlantic Blue shark film got honored at the 1962 International Underwater Film Festival in Santa Monica, California. But he wanted more, much more; he wanted the big one, the Great White Shark. The grand thrust was in the making of *Blue Water White Death* where he put Stanton Waterman, Ron and Valerie Taylor into a black sea 200 miles out, over 3000 feet depth, amidst chum, bait and a killed whale. Peter himself dove through a churning shark frenzy to get cheek-to-gill with a huge shark tearing chunks out of the whale. He wanted it on film whatever he had to sacrifice to get it. He didn't ask anybody else; he just did it himself.

In the interviews for this history, few divers cited a shark experience as one of their three most exciting dive experiences. The few that did, usually looked up to see a huge submarine shape "about 17 feet long," passing overhead and disappearing.

Everybody had a shark story or two. Many of the stories seemed like they involved a "shark attack" but since no one got bitten, there might have been some misinterpretations.

A lot of shark fear arose from just listing what has been found when their stomachs are cut open.

A roll of tar paper 40 feet long

Keg of nails

Three overcoats

A chicken coop

A reindeer intact

Binoculars

Front half of a bulldog

Rear end of a horse

Sheep bones

A man in full armor (from a Fifteenth Century account)

54 stingers from rays

A man's arm with wristwatch (solved a murder in Australia per Valerie Taylor)

HEY, IT'S A WILD ANIMAL

It is a wild animal searching for food. Although it can go months without eating, it must be ready to take food when any opportunity arises. In a mob feeding, the famed frenzy, sharks will eat anything in the water including their own spilled organs. The general conclusion was drafted over the years that sharks do not swim around looking for humans to eat but they will if they come across a weak or crippled one. The Zambezi Shark found in African rivers has an acquired taste, it has been surmised, from feeding on the many corpses that have been dumped in the Zambezi River. Hungry and mean, it has been observed that sharks will give birth to fully formed babies and if they come across them later will eat them.

The 1970's found a lot of divers going on expedition to faraway places to study marine life. Dr. Bruce Halstead, who was the leading expert, who wrote the book, *Dangerous Marine Animals*, and top underwater photographer, Don Ollis, were on a project in the Marshal Islands when they found themselves surrounded by Gray Reef Sharks in an open lagoon. They had to swim back-to-back pushing sharks out of the way to get back ashore. The same team of Halstead and Ollis were driven out of the water at Eniwetok when a big school of sharks followed us "like a pack of blood hounds over a reef in six inches of water, snapping at our heels."

Bev Morgan tells the story of the shark expedition he and his colleagues experienced off Coco Islands, Costa Rica. The boat had slowed to a stop into perfect position at the dive site. As the anchor with metal chain reeled into the water's depth, everyone on board heard crunching and grinding metal noises from beneath the boat. As they leaned over the bow, in amazement they watched a school of sharks biting and gnawing the chain as the anchor made contact with the sea bottom. It was a heads or tails coin-kind of decision to learn which team would enter the water first. The final judgment was one team worked on the intended assignment, the other team had shark sentry duty. There was never a day without a pack of mean sharks in their midst.

Jim Stewart has occupied a high llama post in diving over most of the 50-year history. Outstanding pioneer diver and knowledgeable. For 40 years, if any question arose about diving there was a tendency to go ask the Chief Diving Officer at Scripps Institution of Oceanography. That was Jim Stewart. Jim liked to lecture in short sleeve shirts because he had a wonderful battle ribbon to display as a teaching prop.

A long pink scarring wrapped around his arm down to his elbow. He'd been with a lot of sharks but one finally bit him in 1961. He was on a tracking station maintenance project with Ron Church off of Wake Island. After first going to Canton Island, "the sharkiest place he'd ever seen, where they got chased out of water several times so they moved onto Wake. At Canton, they worked as a threesome with one playing shotgun with a lead pipe. "We alternated so no one would get an ulcer." At Wake Island, which only had a few sharks, they relaxed. Coming in a surging Channel but riding its reef walls - because of the outgoing

Valerie Taylor on the Great Barrier Reef was fearless and led many divers out of their fears and phobias.   Ron Taylor

current, a 5 1/2 foot shark started buzzing Ron Church and Jim. Both of them, just skin diving, dove at the shark as it approached each of them.

This shark did the S-shaping, the humping of the back that Jim had never seen before. "Geeze," Jim thought, "What's the matter with him? Then he dropped his pectoral way back and got this big hump in his back and started to bite in the water...lot of sharks do that before they attack...like a dog with a bone...shake until their teeth are in position, grab and saw a chunk out."

Jim is holding his breath at five feet underwater, when the shark suddenly comes straight at him, like a bolt out of the blue. "Just like that," Jim slaps his arm hard and calmly describes "Raising my arm to protect my face and...he got my elbow, set his teeth twice, and with me raising and him hanging on, we just rotated this whole chunk out. No pain just slight tearing. Shark turned and swam off." Jim looked at an exposed joint capsule with impression, "that sure is a shiny joint," then he shut off the bleeding brachial artery just in time. Ron got to him to get him up on the reef. Jim thinks the shark didn't hold on because he was an unfamiliar taste.

So what was Jim's feelings about sharks from that incident? "I had spent an awful lot of time in the water with sharks...made runs at me but turned off...but from then on, when I saw a shark, I didn't just say that's nice." Jim thinks it's a good idea to carry something, a pole spear, and feels he might have not gotten bitten if he'd had something in his hands at Wake. He finishes talking about the attack by rubbing his scarred arm and remembering when Vern Fleet got bit in the ass spearing fish off La Jolla. Vern felt a clunk in his rear end, reached back. A nine foot long animal swam around to look him over. Then Jim says, "If sharks ever decide that they do like the taste of man, then we have a problem. Because obviously, we are the slowest thing that ever went back in the ocean. It's probably a matter of being in the wrong place at the wrong time."

The 1980's accelerated the jet stream long diving vacation to places hard to get to. Virgin diving territory was opened up and dive operations popped up on the shores of remote diving paradises. Divers, who had missed out on the golden years of exploring their own regions when they were untouched and wild, were able to experience some of that first on-the-scene feeling.

Where they went was to clear water tropics - where they also could expect to see sharks. The dive industry analysts were claiming that 98% of scuba divers would never see a shark. In actuality, the sightings were somewhere between always and never. The advanced specialty classes that grew from the basic scuba course were producing lay experts on sharks with knowledge about sharks and how they differ in looks and behavior.

Television was loaded with documentary films which familiarized the public and divers, especially, with the shark. The unpredictable creature of the 1950's and 1960's and 1970's was becoming - well, almost predictable.

FEEDING SHARKS

In some places, at resorts, dive guides and divemasters were recognizing individual sharks and gaining confidence that these sharks were like the neighbors dog, that you might even be able to reach out and touch. Those dive trips out to feed fish graduated from Angel fish to Morey eels and even to sharks.

A lot of this was "stunting", as guides strived to find more dramatic contacts with sealife to entertain the customer divers. Some of this feeding had been going on from the early days of diving. El Gitano, the fearless guide from Cozumel, considered by some Mexico's best ever, came to UNEXSO in 1966 to learn more about guiding and ended up showing the UNEXSO pros some macho acts, such as, removing his mouthpiece and letting a Morey eel take a piece of Conch from between his teeth. He would do this with "his friends, the Tiburones", the sharks of Cozumel's Palancar Reef. UDT's Doug Fane back in the 1950's was handing out fish to sharks for film and just for the hell of it.

Art Pinder, considered by many senior divers as the greatest spearfisherman of them all, has been reported to fear nothing underwater and would push eels and sharks around. One of his prodigious fetes was to be hanging on surface with some ace divers, when they saw one of their pals, Murray, being stalked by a very big shark as he speared a fish. Pinder dove the 70 feet down in time to spear the predator as it was moving open-jawed 12 inches from Murray's calf.

The Taylors, Valerie and Ron, put together the first chain mail suit that could sustain a shark bite without injury to the diver. Inspired by butcher's boning gloves, Valerie Taylor went in with six foot Blues and big Grey sharks, held out a fish to the sharks, one then snatched it away and shoved her arm into the gaping mouth of another one. Her metal-net-glove caught on the snaggletoothed beast. Action recorded on film. No penetration and no blood. Valerie shouts at the surface something about "that one got my glove!"

The welded steel-ring-suit moved on to other divers and places. UNEXSO at Grand Bahama was one of the first dive sites to dress up their guide shark feeders and provide shark feeding experiences for their visiting, and paying divers. They were charging extra to sit on the bottom and watch dinner time in shark alley.

The shark in the wild is...it's wild. But attempts were continuous to try and maintain them in captivity. But they were short lived in holding tanks for various reasons; they were hunters and handouts of food made them fat and lazy and a lesser creature than counterparts roaming free hunting, being pelagic.

In lab tests, sharks could be conditioned to respond to a "dinner bell", identify a sound with food. Beyond that they appeared to be untrainable.

Their brain seems to be programmed as it has been over these millions of years to seek and take food. The shark has to be on the move to get water past his gills and as he has no air bladder like the other fish, he would sink. This constant movement creates a powerful killing machine capable of destroying anything it encounters. Strangely, the shark will feed on what's easy to come by, the weak and the dead. They will not eat other decaying dead sharks but diseased fish are partaken keeping the disease from spreading to other fish. The shark is immune. This service has gained supporters for the preservation of sharks.

We can read of Cousteau's crew and divers laying into sharks with axes and hooked gaffs, with fierce hatred as a mob of sharks devoured a whale tethered behind the Calypso. And into the 1980's and 1990's we find divers have become not just tolerant and accepting of the sharks rightful place underwater but are trying to become friends with them.

Perhaps the New Century of diving will open up a new interaction between sharks and divers, as we have done with other large creatures of the oceans. Many divers would say that's like saying we'll never have wars again.

The shark has shaped sport diving in a pronounced way. In its full impact, the presence of sharks, despite the relative infrequency of attacks, turned a corner around which divers over the past fifty years encountered and established their threshold of fear.

Millions of years ago there was a really giant toothed shark called Carcharodon Megalodon. A book, *Megalodon*, fictionalizes the appearance of one in modern times; in the deep recesses of the sea they may still exist. Fifty feet long, six people could stand within the jaws. Meg needs to be noted here because bigger and bigger sharks are showing up. The British Museum has a 40 foot specimen shark. Perhaps a deep submersible will locate one - and they better hope they aren't mistaken for bait. Banging rocks together probably won't do much to scare one of these monsters off. And, <u>forget</u> <u>Tarzan</u> <u>riding</u> a shark and killing it with a knife - that won't work on even the little ones.

THE 1990'S A CLOSURE TIME FOR THE 50 YEAR HISTORY FOR SPORT DIVING

In the 1990's, the end of the fifty year period of scuba's rise in the American culture, the USA divers were flaunting a booming economy that put them in luxury diving off liveaboard charter dive boats in exotic places where they dressed to the nines in designer custom rubber suits, BCs with a proliferation of bells and whistles, space age double regulators, jewelry laden with slick gauges and computers (Hello! Is there a diver in there?). It was a once-a-year shot for most, the cost being budget-bending but the diving venues were see-forever clear and the big pelagics were cruising by for sure. Sharks became routine and if divers weren't trying to get real close, feed them, pose with them like an old buddy at a reunion, they were pushing them out of the way with their state of the art underwater cameras. The strobe dazed sharks lumbered about wondering what happened to when they were king of the ocean domain, they were the masters and they scared everybody. Indonesia became the hot spot to label on your dive bag for serious divers. New places were used up and the ancient wonder of discovery and exploration gave way to re-examining where others had gone before - the matching up of what had been seen on the Discovery Channel and the satisfaction of being able to say, "been there, seen that". It was all a civilized way to tour the wilds, and encounters with sharks, who had made diving a thrilling and risky adventure, were relegated to the pest category.

The Great White Shark could be petted from a cage, if you wanted to spend $5000 or more dollars and perhaps, the new millennium of diving would feature out-of-cage, in-the-water riding them, a sort of underwater pony ride.

The 1990's moved divers' thinking into the environmental consciousness that we'd better save everything or the planet would be denuded of natural things. Saving whales was transferred to protecting the billions of sharks, those tough guys of the sea, stop the fishing for and decimating them. Perhaps, the physical sensation of shaking loose of gravity, and flying through liquid space and scenery would sustain much of the diving interest as it always has and the virtual reality of wildness, the ho-hum presence of tame sharks could be as mild as walking by the neighbors dogs. Or the computer composed sharks would satisfy our quest for the mystery of it all. We would be able to dive vicariously.

By 1998, Petersen Publishing Company went beyond the more placid content of corals and Angel fish to put out a *Shark Diver Magazine*. Ads for shark dives and feeding opportunities, resorts that pulled back the curtain and touted themselves as shark infested venues. Had diving become less of a wild adventure and more of an amusement ride?

There is the chance that the unknown mystery can be recaptured by deeper and longer penetrations of the sea by habitats, submersibles, mixed gases and new types of rebreathers. It'll cost us to do it and the average person will be hard pressed to buy into it. It's a big ocean and if we don't pollute it into submission, turn it into a beaten down stew of the obvious and routine, there is hope for diving. Sharks ought to remain ominous, preserved living dinosaurs to strike awe and manageable terror in divers. The wild can't become too mild or be replaced by artificial special effects.

It is good to look at a few other pioneer diver stories, a last look down as we ascend from this shark chapter, so to speak.

It is hard to dispute that the pure storybook warriors of all diving are those phenomenal athletes and adventurers, the deep breath-holding divers, who spear record breaking denizens in the open ocean, the so called Blue Water Hunters.

Carlos Eyles, perhaps diving's poet Laureate, in his 1985 book, *The Last of the Blue Water Hunters* captures the heart and soul of it all. He addresses sharks as unthinking, unfeeling, and unkillable animals; mention of death and shark carry the same impact. He says probably 99% of scuba divers won't see a shark (which may have been so in the pioneer days) but Blue Water Divers have the shark as a reality...that we are all conditioned to react with terror at the sight of a shark. To be a Blue Water Hunter, with or without scuba, requires "an exorcism to rid oneself of the psychic weight of fear of sharks." Carlos refers to sharks as "eaters", prehistoric beasts that divers can't really flee or hide from or protect against. Race car drivers, he writes, expect and accept accidents may happen and the adjusted diver has to accept a vulnerability in the ocean.

Carlos achieved this epiphany, this riding of constant shark expectation after a dive where he speared a large grouper at 60 feet that holed up. While figuring how to extract the fish, he felt a presence, turned, at 20 feet away was the largest shark he'd ever seen until then or since - 18 feet, a yard wide, maybe 2,000 pounds hanging motionless. So Carlos went to the top, looked down to see the shark swim lazily off. A second dive to tug at grouper, same presence felt, and there 10 feet from him was the same shark. Carlos made a threatening pass at the giant which didn't move. Kicking up, the shark moved into him, then under him. The next time down Carlos took a shotgun crew to protect him but the shark only swam by and fled. From that time on, Carlos had a confidence that sharks' unseen presence gave off strong signals and he could pick them up in the right frame of mine. Concentrate on the task, the blue water and the attitude will influence the shark encounter. This trust in himself was a bit shaken when Al Schneppershoff took his place on a spearfishing trip to Mexico's Guadalupe Island. Schneppershoff by himself, but near the boat, was surveying the area when the other divers on the boat heard him yell "tourniquet". Pulled aboard the boat, his calf bitten off, he died from blood loss right there. An imbedded tooth indicated a very large Great White had done it.

It was a first fatality for Blue Water Hunters and the tribe, as they called themselves, realized that it could happen to the best of them, which Al Schneppershoff was, but they all had to shake it off and get back a mind-set of confidence.

Mel Fisher was another fearless guy , who put together one of the first clubs, The Sharks , in California and wouldn't let anybody join before he caught a shark with his hands (Okay, so a harmless Horn Shark counted). Fisher later, ablaze with gold fever, became America's premiere treasure diver and was willing to fight sharks to get it.

At Silver Shoals, Mel and diving partner, Mo Molinar, were trying to retrieve an anchor when they were covered by a ceiling of sharks. Mel surfaced but Mo went back down to get a dropped shark billy. Fisher used his tank to bang a shark off the boat transom but one pulled him back in, he got a cramp and sank to the bottom where Mo brought him up with the billy. Was Mel finally frightened by sharks. "I forgot all about doubloons so you know I was scared."

Dr. Eugenie Clark is the shark lady. A world expert. In 1955, she set up the Cape Haze Marine Laboratories in Florida supported by Vanderbilt money. Turned on to sharks while catching some for Dr. Heller of the New England Institute of Medical Research, she retrieved big specimens from fishermen's nets. The sharks all died in the transfer from ocean to holding tanks. Dr. Perry Gilbert of Cornell University, the pioneer shark expert arrived on the scene with an anesthesian process that rescued the sharks. A long colleague relationship...that greatly benefited diving, ensued.

Genie, as she is affectionately called, has papers and books she has written exclusively on sharks. She has a 1969 book, *Land and the Sharks*.

Thor Heyerdahl didn't have a lot of concern for danger. Off the Kon-Tiki Raft, he pulled big sharks by hand in an unusual sport. Grabbing the tail, he hauled them aboard. Without tail power a shark can't do much and up-ended out of water, the stomach sank down toward the head and paralyzed it. Letting them go might have put a mean revengeful shark back in the ocean for divers to contend with. Thanks Thor!

The Florida Mote Marine Laboratory Center for Shark Research started in 1992. It epitomizes the huge focus on sharks. It even runs a catch and release tournament for anglers, tagging the catch to trace migratory patterns. Dr. Samuel Gruber at the University of Miami has spent decades studying the Lemon shark, using radio tags to trace its movements. The studies have spent much time with the biting aspect, determining that sharks are usually seeking something else, that they are looking for fat sea lions not humans, and the biting takes two forms: bite and spit out or kill with first bite to lessen chances of a fight.

The most terrifying shark attack stories seem to follow that first biting premise. The wonderful horror story of diving's history concerns two pioneer divers, who were close friends, college roommates, and eventually business partners. Both are paragons of courage.

It was a cold, foggy day in February 1963. They, with a group of divers, were diving off the Farallon Islands, twenty-five miles out of San Francisco in sea lion and shark infested waters. Al Giddings was getting on the boat returning from a dive, when he heard a piercing scream and looked out to see his pal, LeRoy French, in a sea of red blood and a monster triangular fin pass just behind him. LeRoy standing on the dock at UNEXSO years later, his body a mass of scar tracks from 317 stitches, told us in an interview that he saw Al coming for him and he thinks he yelled, "Al, he's eating me." Even while the total shock was settling in, LeRoy, the ultimate documentary photographer, was hoping in the back of his mind that Giddings had brought his underwater camera - let's not waste a perfectly good shark attack. Then, the Great White Shark, for that's what is was, took LeRoy for the second time. The shark took him down about 40 feet then let him go. Al got him at the bloody surface and swam him to the boat, expecting the shark's jaws to close on the two of them at any time. The shark disappeared and LeRoy and Al made it. LeRoy was a lacerated mess but they saved him so he could stand on the dock at UNEXSO ready to go into "shark infested" Bahama waters. Al and LeRoy may retain vivid memories of that attack but they never stopped diving and, of course, each went on to become great diving legends. "You get back on the horse" was what they both seemed to have conjured up as a philosophy about sharks.

Certainly all these relatively few attacks considering the large populations going into the water have been sensationally exploited by the media and victims become celebrities. Divers return to the ocean with a paradox of fascination, a love-hate attitude, fear and awe, the need to see these prehistoric sleek killing machines close up and have a moment of truth to thrust diving beyond scenery watching into an awesome adventure.

Sharks - can't live with them, can't live without them. They have always spiced up the experience of diving.

OTHER DANGEROUS MAINE LIFE PIRANHA / BRUCE W. HALSTEAD'S CREATURES

Piranha!

Fortunately although this word froze a lot of divers in mid-entry, it was easy to shake off because these small fish with scalpel teeth live in the rivers and lagoons of South America. The little ones can nibble away until in a few minutes, there's nothing but the skeleton of a cow trying to ford a stream. The big foot and a half variety can sever a finger trailed in the water without the victim even feeling the razor sharp bite. A school of Piranha working together are big enough to constitute a "monster".

Sea snakes, fatally venomous exist in few areas of the world but they do populate the oceans. They were not too well publicized until the Australians, Ron Taylor, Valerie Taylor and Ben Cropp put them on film and they became stars of National Geographic Society films and magazines. As with land snakes, they aren't considered aggressive unless violated. But deadly, they existed and it put an ominous burden of thought into the heads of divers heading for tropical locations where sea snakes prevailed.

Almost every body of water in those days of early diving seemed to be yielding up its roster of dangerous things to watch out for while diving. Florida, Mexico and tropic waters had barracuda, sting rays, fire coral, needle spined urchins, morey eels and the stinging Portuguese Man-of-War. California divers had morey eels, urchins, sea lions and sting rays and entangling kelp forests. Northern waters had wolf eels and different kinds of toothed sharks. Almost any fish could prick you with a spine covered with toxic mucous and cause serious infections and kill you. And those were only the things we knew about in those days when divers were diving in home waters rather than jetting off to strange foreign water venues where...Whew!...there were deadly stonefish, lion fish and even a shellfish, a cone shell with a stinger full of deadly venom.

Were the pioneer divers scared? Yes, they were but in a way, once again, this was part of the risk excitement, the draw of the mysterious and unknown, the lure of danger and our curiosity about it.

Here are some stories of famous divers and their handling of the hazards of the alien underwater world.

Sport divers in those pioneer days enjoyed heroic daredevil status with the general public because they went where dangerous creatures lurked. The underwater world was dark and foreboding and unseen by everyone except the person in the face mask. The scars from brushes with these dangerous creatures were badges of the brave and adventurous.

Dave Doubilet's *National Geographic Magazine's* December 1995 photo essay on the Manta Ray and its behavior during feeding and cleaning behavior was visual and literary prose but a huge area of mystery still hovers over these "dreamlike creatures" as they themselves hover and swoop "elusive and harmless as shadows in the sea." Doubilet notes that giant Mantas are found world wide but their breeding, birthing and life span remains poorly understood since they were first described in 1798. Not much more has been revealed in the forty years since Hans Hass filmed photographed, and wrote about this flying phenomenon in his book *Manta*.

A favorite photo to get is of a diver riding a giant Manta Ray. Dangerous only if we get close enough to get swatted as they maneuver - sort of like petting a dinosaur.

FINAL WORD ON SHARKS

People like to be scared, test themselves. It's why they go to horror movies. The biggest and badest villain has always been and remains the shark by year 2000. Divers have been lulled into a dream-state by seeing a film of an avalanche of hundreds of big Hammerhead Sharks swimming overhead; but it's probably the little 5 foot individual shark that'll come along and have you for lunch. Even Peter Gimbel would say among close friends, "Sharks...they scare me."

Dr. Perry Gilbert, the shark expert, gives us a final sign off - "Sharks will be around to say goodbye to the last man."

18

TREASURE OF NATURE - BLACK CORAL, PEARLS AND GOLD

DEFINING EVENT: BLACK CORAL IN HAWAII

Discovery of Black Coral added a new dimension of inspiration for the majority of the divers motivated by the lure of sunken treasure. Black coral is a natural treasure of great monetary value. An actual living and growing substance that would eventually take its place with older more classic precious gems. It filled a gap in the intrigue of diving in all forms that was left with the exhaustion of the wild natural pearl oyster beds.

Today in elegant shopping areas, there are stores devoted to exhibiting and selling black coral exclusively. All kinds of jewelry incorporate it. Large specimens of unusual design, polished to a glossy sheen are sold for prices in the thousands of dollars. As the supply has dwindled, the prices for available material spirals upward.

Jack Ackerman had made the Hawaiian Islands his home in the pioneer days of diving. His tough and difficult career was living off the ocean, earning his living as a diver. There were no shipwrecks for salvage nor sunken treasure yet more divers in Hawaii than anyplace in the world. There was diving there in the ideal climate and clear water by the Polynesians long before fins and mask.

Jack Ackerman made his living spearing fish before he created the black coral industry.

Jack was highly respected for his diving prowess in this place where diving was a way of life. He was one of first to introduce scuba into the arena. He wanted to just make a living in underwater photography but...here are his words taken from his personal account of those days.

"Our primary objective was underwater movies which were extremely expensive and troublesome, in that there were no underwater cameras to be bought in those days. The trial and error of having to make everything yourself was a constant drain and financial problem. Our eating habits could not wait for any eventual income that might arise from such a long-range program so we relied on commercial fishing as our main and immediate source of revenue. Meanwhile, we could only hope to pursue a future later on in this new field.

To us, commercial fishing meant (1) Picking up lobsters, (2) Searching for turtle grounds, (3) Spearing fish or catching them in nets and traps and, (4) Selling shells, corals, etc... We eventually hoped for underwater movies of these various activities to be of some monetary value."

Deep off Hawaii's island of Maui, Jack Ackerman, was down deep at 120 feet chasing fish with his spear gun and scuba in 1956. In a forest of seafans and coral trees, he made his first encounter with the soft squishy branches of a black coral tree. He tried to break off a large branch, hacked at it with his diver's knife but couldn't extricate it. He'd been diving with scuba deep for several years and had seen many corals but this was unique. Here's an excerpt from Jack's own account.

"Larry Windley and I signaled each other to go ahead and follow the fish. We reached the edge of the cliff and saw that it dropped off about 20 feet and then the bottom tapered off slowly or gradually into the abysmal depths. This 20 feet drop formed a ledge that had a cave and we could see this large school of Ulua circling all about the outside of this cave. As soon as we approached the whole school disappeared slowly into the cave. And then we became aware of another spectacle. Black bushes, like miniature trees, were growing off the side of this 20 foot ledge. I tried to pull one loose but it was firmly implanted in the coral bottom. This was an impressive sight to see so many trees for I remembered seeing a few off Kauai while diving with Lee Ohai. That was in 1956 and our friends eagerly received these trees as gifts for decorative objects in the homes. Now here was a whole forest of them! I thought maybe we could sell these instead of giving them away."

Jack goes on to describe more dives to specifically recover this black coral.

"I picked up the camera in one hand and the hammer and chisel in the other while Larry grabbed his powerful arbalete spear gun. Once again we paired off into the blue water. This time we swam down a good 50 feet before the bottom became visible. We guessed the depth to be between 160 and 180 feet deep. As we neared the bottom, we looked for a blue void. Sure enough! There was a cliff or drop-off about 70 feet to our left. We could already see black coral trees growing straight up from the ocean bottom. We kicked our swim fins vigorously and headed toward the cliff. As we reached the precipice, we were struck with a sight never before seen! Enormous, black, branching animal growths, eerie and graceful, spreading out in forests of trees growing out of the side of this cliff. Larry saw me adjusting the camera controls so he signaled he was going over the cliff to investigate. I nodded my understanding. Larry looked at his depth gauge and peeled off the top of the cliff looking pretty much like a sky-diver as he glided toward the bottom with a few effortless kicks.

"I took movies of these black coral trees from every possible angle just to make sure some of the footage would turn out good. Then I laid the camera down and proceeded to hack off a selected black coral growth as a sample to be analyzed later.

I noticed two big Ulua coming toward me that were probably attracted to the metallic "clink" of my hammer and chisel. I had no spear so ignored them as they circled me once and then disappeared into the forest of black branches jutting out off the cliff. I broke off my black coral tree and started looking for Larry's bubbles. I saw Larry was quite a distance from me. I started my long swim back to the surface with both hands full carrying the camera, hammer and chisel and the coral tree."

As Jack continues this narrative, the fierce pride of the hunter in his sport, the deeply ingrained challenge of spearing great trophy fish seems to override the pleasures of finding underseas treasure.

"Larry bobbed to the surface and we went up alongside to relieve him of his spear gun and make it easier for him to unstrap his Aqua-Lung in the water. He handed the Aqua-Lung to me and chinned himself into the boat. When Larry fell into the boat he yelled, 'I saw two of the biggest Kahala (Amberjack) I've ever seen in my life! They came right up to me and I hit one square in the gills! He swam off with my spear as if it were a toothpick! Boy, that certainly would have been a world's record if I could have grabbed him.' Then Larry looked down at the small coral tree and added, 'You know the cliff I went down? Well, its straight up and down for 90 feet and full of big trees. Out on the bottom close to 300 feet some of them are 15 to 20 feet high!' And so another day of excitement closed behind us as we headed back home wondering what to do with our black coral tree.

"Bringing the black coral to the surface, it appeared reddish, the color of the soft animals which lived in a plant-like skeleton. When it dried and the sheath of now brownish skin was rubbed off, the underlying substance was dark and when polished by buffing it, shone a gemlike black - similar to ebony wood or jet."

Jack Ackerman writes in his *The Black Coral Story* account:

"Now our tree looks like a small stunted little growth without any leaves. It closely resembles the Japanese art of stunting or miniature trees so frequently used as decorative objects. Also, the fact that no two trees grew alike, makes them originals in design and gave us reason to believe they could be a marketable item for interior decorating.

"We placed a tag of $35.00 on it and sold it a few days later. This gave us incentive to go out and bring in several more of these trees. Some of them appeared scraggly and unkempt. We improved their appearance by cutting off the undesirable branches to create nice looking designs. The hardness and texture of this growth was such...that it required a hacksaw to cut off and trim the branches. This hardness fascinated me. We knew jewelry was made of red and pink coral and other semi-precious stones, so it didn't take much imagination to launch experiments with our discovery of Hawaiian Black Coral.

"First of all, we wanted to know the scientific name and all information possible on this black coral. So we sent a piece to Dr. Edwin Bryan of the Bishop Museum in Honolulu. Dr. Bryan reported they were unable to identify it and requested two more samples. One sample to go to the Smithsonian Institute and the other to Cornell University. The Smithsonian Institute was indefinite as to it's proper identity. Dr. John W. Wells of Cornell University was recognized as one of the world's foremost authorities on corals and he sent back a report that we had found a species of black coral identified as Antipathes Grandis. Prior to our find, the only other such coral was dredged up off the Island of Niihau, Hawaii, fifty years ago by the United States Fish and Game Division. (From the authors date of interview, the year would have had to be in the 1920's.)"

As Jack says, black coral had been found before, brought up by accident in fishing nets. Probably native divers had gone deep enough to get some over the centuries preceding because black coral showed up in fetishes and amulets.

Black coral was a good discovery, a natural treasure, at the right time. Other gem quality corals, especially the red coral that had been harvested by Mediterranean sponge divers for many years. Red coral was designed in the gold jewelry of the Romans and Greeks. It also was a second favorite to turquoise in fine crafted Indian jewelry.

Jack Ackerman initiated a full blown industry in Maui producing black coral for the tourist market. He had teams search deep with hatchets and a systematic harvesting ensued off Kauai Island in 1956. As the supply diminished at the shallower depths the divers went deeper. They worked the dangerous edge of the tables that protected them from the bends. Jack, himself, went over the edge in 1957. He took a bad hit, was out of the water for a few years, but returned in 1960. He stayed out of the deep water stuff, he told us, but persevered with the fish and lobster capturing. Jack was struck with the bends three times. After that his partners continued the harvesting, while he took care of the black coral enterprise.

His divers remained on Maui. They were Jack Ackerman Maui Divers. The partnership, which was run by what Jack called 'sharpies', separated from Maui Divers but wanted to use the name, "Maui Divers", when they opened fancy shops in the Waikiki hotels. Jack said, no way did he want to share his Maui Diver name. Added to all this disenchantment, there was a discrepancy of $83,000 debt at the time of the split. His associates chose the name Pacific Trader which didn't fair well. The legal decree in settling the debt was forced to be shared by all partners. With the partnership indebtedness, Jack said, "Okey, let them use the name Maui Divers of Hawaii."

So Jack remained Jack Ackerman Maui Divers on the Island of Maui. "We were happy diving on Maui. We were the homesteaders. The 'sharpies' went worldwide as Maui Divers of Hawaii. The big money? It came. Approximately $6 million of it. Clifford Slater, a smart non-diver from London, operated the Maui Divers of Hawaii. In the 1970's Honolulu got the two-man submarine (submersible) to harvest the red coral 1,000 to 1,200 feet. How big did the business grow? It's still growing."

Black coral now discovered was looked for in other diving areas of the world. Small forests of it were found off Cozumel, the Bahamas, Philippines, New Zealand and the Sea of Cortez of Baja California. Generally, everywhere in the world with deep ledges nurtured by swift deep water currents there was the black coral. The depths all appeared to be from 160 feet to 300 feet. Why that particular zone? The answer seems to have been: Black Coral likes shade and sought out ledges and crevices in deep walls dropping into the abyss.

A coral rush took place for awhile in 1960's and 1970's with exploiters utilizing deep submersibles to collect specimens. Governments moved with legislation to outlaw the removal of this endangered marine life.

Jack was explaining how the laws of the State of Hawaii limited the size of a black coral tree that could be harvested. Then the environmentalists got into the picture and wouldn't allow the removal of any already depleting forests. When Hawaii ran out of coral at reasonable depths, Jack moved his location search to the Kingdom of Tonga. There the royalty and ministry in charge required that Jack provide his qualifications. He took all of his valuable records, papers and book he published for proof to open a coral export business. It was very complicated with a requirement that the open partnership would include the Tonga businessmen. If he had procured a dual-citizenship for $10,000, he would not have needed the Tonga partnership. This marriage didn't last long. When the money came in, there was a horrible disaster of a flood that wiped out Jack's own personal records that he lent to them, drowned the partnership and his side of the profit. Search went to Indonesia, Maldives, and Fiji. Until one day he read in a periodical that China is manufacturing artificial human eye balls out of coral. It is a white coral and works so well that the human eye can move like the naturally born eye. Jack has his license to import white coral because it is for medicinals. The coral for human bone transplant is remarkable with no body rejection. He explained Interpore International of Irvine, California had the patent on the white coral as it is the supplier for the medical human transplants.

Jack Ackerman's largest black coral tree was 7 feet in height and 3 feet in width...a trophy indeed. In his spare time he finds great joy in gardening his fruit trees, plants and vegetables on his three acre plot. He expressed life is good to him!

PINK, GOLD AND BAMBOO CORALS

Dr. Richard (Rick) Grigg expressed his research and experiences exploring the precious corals. "I and other scuba divers off Maui and Kauai often worked to the depth of 250 feet while collecting black coral. Navy divers using highly specialized diving gear dived to 340 feet. No black coral scuba diver, except for one, has ever been so bold as to expose himself to such danger on scuba. My friend Jose Angel, one of those legendary black coral divers, would one day attempt this superhuman depth and drown.

"I'll never forget September 9, 1971 when Maui Divers launched the first dive in history to explore a precious bed of coral at a depth to 1,190 feet with a submersible, because a year before (1970), I had viewed this area through a TV camera on the University of Hawaii's research ship. But this was the first time that I or any human had viewed it first hand. There were pink corals everywhere. It was a coral reef that wasn't really a reef but rather a hard, limestone pavement with solitary coral trees growing about randomly. Like treasure spilling from a pirate's chest. There was bamboo coral coiled like the writhing snakes from Medusa's head, pink coral, and the rare angel skin coral, in ancient times worth twenty times its weight in gold, all in abundance. The gold coral trees were unequaled in beauty. As we headed for the surface the gold coral trees blinked with a thousand eerie blue lights. The tiny polyps making up the coral colony created their own light called bioluminescence. One more of nature's miracles."

By 1973, Rick Grigg worked with Maui Divers, Boh Bartko and Claude Brancart, scuba divers from the Makai Range at Makapuu. He has acquired 30 new records of coral for Hawaii and 11 species that haven't been described. He located the gold coral off Koko Head but no pink coral there. Most of the deep diving was done with a submersible equipped with a cutting blade and a wire basket for selective harvesting.

In 1974, gold coral was retailing at $40 up to $5,000 depending on quality and size.

By 1977, Dr. Grigg published *Hawaii's Precious Corals*, a book about the joint venture, research project with Maui Divers and the Sea Grant. Almost all corals grow at agonizingly slow rates, about 3/8 of an inch or so per year. But black coral is a fast grower about 2 inches per year. Thus, the largest coral trees are very old. Interestingly, he continued to explain that the average life span of pink coral is about 20 years. By harvesting a maximum sustained yield, Maui Divers would take whatever would die anyway in that time. There's an exciting future not just with pink coral but gold, bamboo, and of course the black coral.

The authors had their trip in exploring black coral, too, as many of the sport diving hunters quickly learned the value of the oceans treasure chest. In 1965 Zale Parry had her black coral tree plucked by diving buddy, Richard Adcock, while plunging off his Marisla near Los Animos, Baja California. Found in 120 feet of water in a slight current, it is no museum piece but a sentimental treasure from the sea on display in her living room.

Al Tillman first encountered black coral on the UNEXSO special dives to 250 feet off the ledge (wall) of Freeport, Grand Bahama. There seemed to be a band of it there extending the length of the island but nowhere else. Except in a 60 foot deep sink hole in the bottom that dropped another 30 feet, a place called Zoo Hole for its abundance of teeming marine life. There on one side of the hole near the bottom, that branched out into a set of caves that seemed to be going back into the island, was a giant six foot black coral tree. UNEXSO attempted to keep this special diving spot a secret but failed. On one of the rare trips back not six months after being discovered, the hole was invaded by unknown parties, who took the great black coral tree. A huge tragedy.

Dr. Richard Grigg discovers Paragorgia, or Gold, Coral in deep water in 1971.
Grigg Archives

We'll look at some of the other natural treasures as scuba and then submersibles increasingly invaded and probed the world underwater. That invasion has not been kind or careful of these natural treasures. They have become rare and scarce, lessening the potential pleasures of finding things that don't quickly or ever replenish themselves. The beginning golden years of diving are a sacred memory because of these natural prizes.

THE PEARL

Scuba diving arrived a little late to be in on diving for pearls. The natural beds of oysters were dived for centuries by native divers without equipment. The pearls found in those natural oysters were among the first gems to be used as adornment.

The natural beds were worked heavily and by the 20th Century a scarcity of pearls inspired a new development. In Japan in 1905, a man, Kokichi Mikimoto, discovered the concept of the cultured pearl. By inserting a piece of shell into a living oyster, protective coatings are secreted around the foreign material to form a "cultured pearl" of almost the same quality as a natural one. The difference is that cultured ones have a shell bead nucleus with a thin pearl coating; naturals are pearl clear through.

In 1920's there were still over 300 United States natural pearl dealers and now there are none. The supply disappeared. With cultured, only five out of a hundred oysters implanted yield gem quality pearls.

Even when natural pearl oysters were being found in quantity, thousands had to be collected to get a yield of a handful - even of those, few had a depth of color or were round.

The famous divers, Japanese women called AMA, once dove for natural pearl oysters and then dove for just the oysters to be implanted but then they weren't needed as the farms grew baby oysters.

In the warm waters near the equator in the South Seas, the grandest pearls are nurtured. So rare are these white and black pearls that one can be valued at $40,000.

But with many countries, especially China moving into cultured pearl farming, the competition was pushed into a fast production with poor quality pearls flooding a growing market for affordable jewelry. There is a thin layer of nacre over the nucleus shell insertion and dying taking place to create a variety of hues. Mikimoto controlled this eight decades ago by buying up inferior pearls and ceremonially burning them to be sure his pearls were known as the best.

Traditional Ama diver searching for oysters.   *Tillman*

E. R. Cross trained pearl divers about safety while in the South Pacific. The above photo shows him in 1947 holding the first underwater camera housing that he built.

Scuba and free divers are used in modern times to scrub algae and fungus off the farmed oysters on huge floating rafts. Divers have become tenders, rather than seekers. While diving in 1970 with the scrubbers at Aguinaldo's pearl farm at Davao in the Philippines, Al Tillman was shown small groups of natural pearl oysters still growing in the nearby depths. But here and there natural pearls are recovered not from beds but often a single specimen oyster living isolated and untouched. Some of these live for 20-30 years and are gigantic. While scuba diving off of Fuga in the Philippines and escorted by free diving natives, a foot in diameter oyster with a black lip was recovered from an old wreck in 50 feet of water. It yielded a perfect black pearl that the divers turned over to the owner of the island.

E. R. Cross while in the South Pacific in the 1950s worked with native divers to instruct them about the bends and shallow water blackout. Many were getting into serious trouble trying to go deeper and deeper to find pearl oysters as they became an endangered species and then disappeared.

Black pearls were once a grand bounty for divers off of LaPaz in Baja California. Foreign ships, especially from Japan invaded the oyster beds in the 1920's and 1930's and suddenly they were gone. Whatever was the full cause, they never reappeared.

California divers had a bottom stacked with abalones, one on top of another in the pioneer days. Beautiful "blister pearls" were cut from their shells and occasionally a round or baroque bluish pearl like a bead was found in the folds of the abalone flesh. Indian children in previous centuries are reported to play marbles with them.

It is possible that a great discovery is probable in some isolated, remote atoll yet undived. Could the granddaddy oyster of all time be waiting some diver poking under a virgin reef - and produce a glorious huge pearl that only a Cleopatra could afford and wear.

RARE FISH

People who maintain aquariums take great pride in having a rare fish that no one else has. It's probably so with all collectors. Salt water tanks offer a huge diversity of possibilities all over the world. In Manila, Philippines there are courtyards filled with bubbling plastic boxes that hold a milky way of exotic colored fish fluttering about. They have been collected by teams of scuba divers spread over the Philippines' seven thousand islands. Hand collected with jars and small nets, they represent a huge industry that earns millions of dollars.

Sometimes a rare fish is not the norm in the beginning of owning and maintaining a home seaquarium; the population is usually common neighborhood tidepool critters .

Zale Parry and husband Parry Bivens enjoyed watching the interaction and beauty of their home aquarium in the 1950's. Aquarium stores did not have salt water animals for sale so they had to scuba dive out and catch their own. But in Florida, rare reef fish were collected and sold by Ed Fisher (the scuba diver, who lived underwater in 1954 for a record 24-hour period). Scuba diver and ace underwater photographer, Jerry Greenberg of Miami, was one of the first fish gatherers and paid his way into photography selling rare specimens to collectors and the Florida Seaquarium.

In Zale Parry's diary notes she recalls aquarium fish not living long and replacing the deceased with fish caught with plastic probes, bags and jars on weekly dive trips to the California Channel Islands.

Pioneering in this hobby was not always easy or enjoyable, it was plenty of not easy work. After two years, Zale returned all the survivors (and some quite valuable in the collectors market) back to the big house ocean. Having a rare, costly gem-of-a-fish needed 24-hour nursing care. Zale's final thought on it: "Praise to those hardy scuba divers who own and 'manage' their pricey, precious rare fish."

During the early 1960's, when conservation and killing things with a spear were in the forefront of new thinking by divers, there was two directions the sport was to head. One interesting pursuit was the popularity of the salt water aquarium and collecting for it. The other route was underwater photography, which won out. But during that short era divers added a new piece of equipment to their arsenals - the slurp gun. It had the look of a gun made of clear plexiglass but in essence it was a large hypodermic needle which sucked water in, fish too.

The slurp gun required some skill but it never managed the macho image that came with a speargun. It was exciting to be able to populate a salt water aquarium on your own and not have to pay hundreds of dollars some rare specimens were priced. But aquariums took up a lot of time maintaining them and in addition, watching caged creatures just didn't have the wonder of encountering them in the underwater wilderness. But interest in aquariums always seemed revivable. Showing off a baseball-size Purple Tang from the Red Sea, (worth $150.00 each) or a Bright Orange Brazilian Sea Horse (worth $70.00-$80.00 each) seems like it should have been a potent lure. But most rare fish don't fair well. They have selective specific foods. Fragile. Less common to find in your aquarium store. And, there is a fair chance they will die no matter how much care is given. They are vulnerably out of their natural wild element.

One diving story relates how a very intense underwater photographer was getting a chance to shoot his first models underwater. Every time he thought he had a great shot, a pesky fish would swim in front of the lens and he had to shoo it away time and again. When he got home and had the pictures developed, he showed them to his diving friends expecting them to ooh and aah over the pretty model and the excellent exposures despite the presence of the weird fish in most of the frames. One of the guys was an amateur ichthyologist and he yelled, "Look, that's a Coelacanth! I've seen pictures of it but they say it's extinct." Sometimes we step over treasure we don't recognize because we don't just know and limit ourselves to only what we are looking for. Divers seemed to have done this repeatedly.

GOLD UNDERWATER

Eureka! It hit California diving with a great impact. Why not? All those descendants of the 49ers had heard all the stories of great gold nugget finds by old timers sluicing and panning the river beds.

Dick Anderson with a pan of gold laden gravel extracted from an underwater crevice.

No one person ever emerged like John Marshall at Sutters Mill as the first gold diver. Dick Anderson, one of America's most versatile commercial divers, did it as a sport and made humorous movies about it. He had his own claim in the gold country and he worked it underwater. He picked gold out of the crevices using scuba and hookah. He panned and sluiced. He found enough gold to show around at gatherings of divers and send them into the rivers.

Mel Fisher, the grandest promoter in diving's history, could seduce a cadaver into buying a ton of gear including a gold dredge back in the 1950's just by grinning mysteriously and holding up a vial of gold dust or better yet of platinum. "Now here's this platinum and it's worth ten times what gold is." Mel eventually found a richest treasure wreck ever and by-passed the work of dredging up all that gold the hard way.

Gold diving sparked some new activity dimension for scuba and the romance of prospecting certainly was a part of the American character. But it was hard work and too often long distance expeditions yielded nothing. The good sites got picked over and shallow fresh water didn't maintain the wonder of the vast ocean playground.

JADE COVE

The Big Sur area of California is a place of steep rugged cliffs, crashing waves, pebble beaches, monster bull kelp beds and very cold water. Awesome!

To dive it, one had to let his heart jump into his throat, lock his jaw, and then yell "Geronimo" while leaping into the swollen white outgoing water of a giant wave that just broke over the rocks in front of you. Timing is all. Once you are swirled beyond the breakers, there is kelp and more kelp. You are in a special place. This is where the forces of nature come to roost.

This is also where in the beginning of this planet, enormous pressures forged wide veins of a hard, soapy, glistening gemstone called jade. There are two kinds of jade - jadeite and nephrite. The first is rare and quite valuable. The other, nephrite is found in large quantities in different places around the world. It usually is in shades of green and polishes up into fine jewelry. It has value when cut into slabs and then cabochons. At Jade Cove in Big Sur there has been a very large amount perhaps tons of jade over the years.

Al Tillman and Paul McComack raise a large boulder of jade in 1956.

The Chinese, who came to America, revered jade and they snuck down to Big Sur to pick for it in the beach rocks and the cliffs. It is said they'd find it and rebury it in the cliffs to avoid being robbed but with intention to come back later and recover it. Most of the jade was on the beach and rock hounds, who went there, suspected it was washing down from some deposit higher up in the mountains.

Al Tillman was interviewing some men from a rock club on a Los Angeles County radio show back in the mid 1950's. When he heard about the jade, it seemed there might be some in the water beyond the beach.

Al packed up his scuba gear and with Dick Bartlett, a diving partner, trekked to Jade Cove. The cliffs and the roaring sea were beautiful but terrifying at first view. But they went diving and pushed through the kelp beds under the kelp canopy. The water was gin clear and the bottom a bumpy carpet of reef mounds and green pebbles. There was soapstone, serpentine and maybe jade.

No maybes. Al Tillman plucked an apple green ten pound nugget out of one pebble bed. It turned out to be the best specimen the Los Angeles Natural History Museum's jade expert, Dr. Tom Clements, had ever seen. Fueled by this find, and more jade collected, many trips were made. Six months after that first trip, Tillman entered a cave 50 feet down and there it was. A half-ton boulder of dazzling green jade.

Over the next two years, Tillman would return to look at the boulder and figure how to retrieve it for the Museum that wanted to feature it in newly developing mineral display hall. But it played hide and seek, sometimes it wasn't there and Al thought someone else had gotten it. Then it would be back on the next trip - its disappearing act was caused by it sinking deep into the pebble bed of the cave and being rocked to the top during big storms.

With a team of diver friends and his brother, using a desert water bag and cargo net, Al parachuted the jade boulder to the surface, through the surf and up on the beach - not without some crunched fingers and toes.

The team pushed the chunk of jade 180 feet up a trail full of poison oak. There was grumbling and near mutiny but the big jade went into the Los Angeles County Natural History Museum to become one of its most impressive specimens. The Museum named it the Tillman Jade and over the years since 1957, it has been polished to a spectacular glow by thousands of little visitors hands. It will never be cut up as jewelry and is considered one of the finest specimens of nephrite jade in the world.

LOGS

Scuba divers find things that nobody else even gets a chance

Homer Lockwood supervises a jade dive at Jade Cove in California in 1961.

to look for. In the great Lakes Region during the 1990's, divers came across some logs on the bottom that the cold had preserved over a hundred years. They were cut from old growth forests of the region and the wood, oak and maple, had wonderful character when cut and was in great demand by builders and decorators. Each log was worth in the thousands of dollars.

EBONY

When two great underwater photographers of diving's history get together, they don't always talk about film speeds.

Ron Church and Lamar Boren were both members of the famous Bottom Scratchers Club of San Diego. Lamar told *Scuba America* that Ron had just told him of shooting deep pictures of black coral in Hawaii and getting some pieces while he was doing it. He gathered natural treasure and got award-winning pictures at the same time.

"Well, Ron," Lamar said, "when I was in Africa with Ivan Tors shooting footage of crocodiles, there I was watching a big croc swim by the legs of some prop-man cooling himself by sitting on the bank and dangling his legs in the water. I thought I'd let the camera run off some footage before I warned the dangler or else shooed-off the croc. Then I noticed these shiny black chunks on the bottom (It turned out to be ebony, a dense black heartwood that polished like gemstone and had significant value.) so I gathered up some with one hand while holding up the running camera.

"I was stuffing my swim trunks full of these pretty black souvenirs until my swim suit had sagged to my thighs. When I looked up and saw the crocodile swimming off and no legs dangling, I did a big Oh! Oh! in my mind.

"When I walked backwards out of the water, mooning the crew on shore, Ivan Tors was shouting at me, 'Lamar you don't have to sacrifice dat big butt to lure crocodiles.'

"Even the dangler, who had pulled his legs up when he looked down at the croc sizing him up, was forgiving when I passed the black ebony pieces around to everybody. I think when we got around to looking at the dailies on the big screen, they say the dangling prop-man gasped and fainted."

SHELLS

Some of the finest shell collections in the world are in the hands of scuba divers - who had the grand thrill to find them themselves. What's a sea shell? It's any of the 300,000 or more species of sea animals belonging to the zoological order of Mollusca. It may be a tiny periwinkle or a giant squid. Collectors gather "true" shells. The two varieties of the true shells are bivalves and univalves. The color and sculpture changes the closer they live to the tropical zones. Their art is the spectacular shapes and beauty.

In the early 1950's A Murex Argo collected 600 feet by dredging in waters off the British West Indies was valued at $1,000. Conchologists could fetch $1,500 for other glories. Some of the greatest rarities are truly valueless and are not for sale...museum pieces. Since 1952 the world's leading authority on the Terebra, a family of shells, is Twila Bratcher. Twila is one of the first women to take scuba diving lessons from Conrad Limbaugh. Later she completed E. R. Cross's diving and safety course at his Sparling School of Diving in Wilmington, California. She was an avid traveler especially tropical places and picked up pretty shells as a mementoes of the diving trips. That's when she became a scuba diving shell collector, "really shell shocked", she told us. That led to an interest in the mollusk that makes and inhabits the shell. "I was fascinated by the ecological niche in which different species live; what they eat; their camouflage; how they reproduce. I became a malacologist specializing in the molluscan family Terebra and was made a research associate of the Los Angeles County Museum of Natural History. I identify species of Terebra for museums and universities in the United States and other countries. Twila wrote a Sea Shell Column for *Skin Diver Magazine* for a number of years. A sea shell is a valuable sea treasure. Twila presented ninety-five percent of her shell collection to the Los Angeles County Museum of Natural History. It is on exhibit today.

E. R. Cross, who literally lived underwater working the Standard Oil pipelines at Barbers Point, off Oahu, did a masterful job but he was always on the watch for an unusual shell out of the corner of his eye. If any collection illuminated and reflected the finest application of scuba in conjunction with an acquisitive hobby, it was his shell collection. It capstoned his elaborate and diversified diving career and contained the Cross shell, Chicoreus Elliscrossi, a new species and some of the world's rarest and most valuable shells. One of his best finds was a Golden Cowrie worth approximately $7,000 in the 1970's. At one time Cross was the President of the Hawaiian Malacological Society and kept up with the Shell News internationally by writing in the *Hawaiian Shell News*, corresponding and trading with collectors. Schools were gifted with his duplicate, common varieties for their permanent displays.

When a specimen is recovered from deep water and finally identified, it becomes big news. In the 1970's the Maui Divers of Hawaii collected precious coral with a two-man submarine. Several times in addition to recovering coral, the submarine brought up shells that were either new to science, or previously were not known in Hawaiian waters. According to the *Hawaiian Shell News* March 1974, one such specimen had been identified by HSN Science consultant W. O. Cernohorsky in Auckland as Ceratoxancus teramachii Kuroda, 1952 - previously believed to be endemic only to deep water off the south coast of Japan. Though we mention here deep water and submersibles, the excitement of shells brings together another community of which the majority of the people are scuba divers.

During the early days of scuba diving, the Golden Cowrie had always been a holy grail of shell seekers. But some divers learned too late. Handling live creatures in shells was a hazardous pursuit. The infamous cone shell with its sabre-like defense emits a venom causing death. Some shells are attached and encrusted; their recovery can lacerate flesh off fingers. Al Tillman encountered a giant green abalone while harvesting brown cowries off the Point Fermin Beach area near Palos Verdes in California water. When he gripped the shell to pull it off a rock reef, the old shell in the polluted water crumbled and shards surgically sliced off some bits of fingers. As he held his bleeding hand high swimming ashore, he experienced the most pain, psychic pain, from the record breaking abalone that "got away".

In the 1970's the Hawaiian Puka Shells were designed into necklaces. Saks Fifth Avenue advertised them as the jewelry created by the natural rhythm of the awesome waves of the Pacific rising off Hawaii's fabled north shore. The ad explained that once a year the waters become just right to swirl these exquisite, chalky white, baroque shells on to the beaches to be hand-gathered and meticulously matched in nature's loveliest necklaces. Legend, it continues, has it that Queen Liliuokalani treasured her Puka shells over all the diamonds in the world for good fortune and happiness. The prices started at $150.00 and up from their exclusive collection of one-of-a kind Puka Shell necklaces. The Puka became so plentiful through scuba diver collecting that in no time at all the prices dropped to $17.99.

From nature's shell jewel box, diving collectors were finding breath-taking beauties all over the world on their dive trips. The Philippines had the White Rock Oyster tinted with rose. The beautiful and bizarre Royal Thorny Oyster is from the Pacific. The East Indian Rose-Branch Murex looked flower-like and rosy.

The West Indies and the West Coast of Africa were the residences of the Cypraecassis testiculus. It's the shell the Italian artisans place in a vice to carefully hold while they carve the delicate-see-through cameo pins and charms. The carving is always the depiction of a young girl or woman. These shells are highly valued by cameo carvers.

The appreciation of treasures from nature, especially those from underwater has been there since the beginning of human history. Greeks, Romans and Chinese emperors sent out fleets to scrape the bottom with grappling hooks and nets. The materials, pearls, jade, coral were often damaged using this crude gathering method.

Although divers using scuba were gentler with beds of these precious and semi-precious materials, it seems they have harvested them to a point of extinction. For the early generations of divers this was a thrilling discovery and motivated many divers to keep diving. However, it was a sport diving event that quickly used up the source materials and sounded another warning that divers could destroy their underwater world and its natural treasures.

19

ARTIFICIAL REEFS

DEFINING EVENT: DIVE N' SURF TOILET BOWL REEFS

When things are put underwater with the intent to create a gathering place for marine life - we have a pure artificial reef. Such created habitats have given sport diving an added new world and dimension. Divers have really felt involved and in charge when they have been in on the construction and ultimate use of them.

Some diving places that jut from the underwater floor happen accidentally. Ships sinking or an airliner going down are disasters but with the sunny side being, if in the right place at a divable depth, can sometimes turn out to be unintended artificial reefs.

Oil drilling rigs and breakwaters, abandoned or still operating have evolved into terrific diving areas. The planned creation of structured "islands" on barren ocean floors has been a challenge to sport divers. As natural diving spots deteriorate and become overused by the growing number of divers, the slow process of nature in replenishing the supply, has been inadequate.

For all the whooping it up, celebrating three-fourths of the planet's surface being water and a vastly unexplored bottom, there are immense areas that do not host anything but a flat, desert-like environment. Creatures need outcroppings that nourish plant forms, nooks and crannies and holes to hide from predators.

Some of the motivation for divers to build artificial reefs was an effort to establish private, secret "fishing holes". Fishermen and hunters like to brag-up their big trophy conquests but are shy with the whereabouts of their successes. A natural place use

Sunken ships make some of the best artificial reefs for both sealife and recreational divers.   Jack McKenney

to be the "secret place" in the pioneer years when the whole underwater terrain was the private world of a few divers. One of the worst sport diving experiences, perhaps exceeding that of facing up to a Great White with a speared fish in your hand, is to return to a secret diving spot only to find several boats flying the Diver Down Flag anchored over it.

So saying goodbye to a secret outcropping can be very hard especially when it's the only such oasis for miles and miles of barren bottom stretching out over a sand and rubble plain similar to the Sahara. Throughout sport diving history, ambitious divers designed their own outcroppings and plunked them down in desolate places in monotonous terrain.

Until the 1980's and 1990's, there has not been any organized, unified movement to develop artificial reefs. It has been very much the efforts of ingenious private individuals. Keeping them secret provided the exclusive payoff of a game that motivated the builders to work so hard in the first place.

A criteria for such builders has been:
- 1. Find an unlikely spot that gets little attention and is not much traversed by boats, fishermen and divers.
- 2. Strong currents to provide a constant flow of life to settle there (but, unfortunately, also sweep away and bury pieces of the structure and thwart food sources that might grow there).
- 3. A divable depth, say 50 to 60 feet to avoid surface storms yet yield a reasonable no-decompression dive.
- 4. A building material that won't erode, rust, float away or pollute.
- 5. The transport; equipment for moving and placing material at the spot.
- 6. The reef must not be an obstruction to interfere with ship navigation.

Reef designers have the paradoxical tasks of hiding their reefs and yet making them reasonably accessible to themselves. Sharing such artificial constructions with friends may require staying below on the way to the secret site or an oath taken in blood. But, as the diving population grew, divers were everywhere, boats followed the reef designer veterans out to sea. Word does get around. The secret private reef gave way to open-to-the-public built and managed by the government. Eventually, "no-take rules" about the creature life on them, froze them into just theme park-like scenery. The era of the preserves and sanctuaries replaced exploration, discovery and recovery of souvenirs and game.

While the private and semi-private artificial reefs were in their golden years, divers of some fame and talent had great personal stories to tell. Here are some of them:

The U.S.S. Palawan was one of many liberty ships that are now artificial reefs. The Palawan was sunk of Redondo Beach, CA in 1976.
Los Angeles Times

It was a 5:30 a.m. rendezvous in the late 1950's. Zale remembers meeting twins Bob and Bill Meistrell at a coffee shop in Redondo Beach. One hour later, the three of them were placing their gear in an outboard motor-equipped rowboat. Bob sat at the bow facing the shoreline. Bill ran the outboard heading out to sea. Zale was placed in the best seat of all but the rule was that the guest faces out to sea, too. All Zale knew was that Bob told Bill, "Slow down, I think we're just about on it". They were on one of their Toilet Bowl Reefs. It was like magnetic clairvoyance! This way, Zale learned years later, there would be no way to know that Bob was lining up the sights of a palm tree and church steeple on shore. The ingenious twins' were generous and unselfish in sharing of the catch but always kept the locations stealthfully sequestered. And, that was "my shortest fill-your-bag-to-the-brim-with-lobsters-dive," Zale said. A day to remember!

Leave it to the Meistrel twins, Bob and Bill, to design the perfect artificial reef. Bill tells the story:

"It was 1956. Our friend, Kooki Keeler and another diver were diving for lobsters off Redondo Beach on an old sunken fishing vessel, called the Sea Witch. They were diving alone when Kooki realized he was missing his buddy. Kooki came out of the water to get me. Our Dive N' Surf store was nearby on the waterfront and I went out to help. As we were searching and found the body, I observed two urinals intact on that sea Witch. There were two bugs in each one of those urinals." Troubled over the loss of a diver, did not deter Bill's mind from the thought of where some old toilet bowls could be possessed and owned free-of-charge. An open mind never quits working!

Bill continued, "Dick Holmes, a friend of mine, worked at the factory where they made toilet bowls. And I asked him, 'Dick, what do they do with all the toilets that have a little crack in them?' Dick answered that we throw them out. That they got guys, who come in and haul them out. So I asked him, 'Why don't you bring some down to us once in a while? We'll make a little reef out of them. The lobsters love those things.' So Dick started bringing reject-toilets to us in loads each time he came to the beach. We had a couple of thousand toilets in a couple of years. We had a supply of them in the lot next to our shop that you couldn't believe! We had to get them down to the boat. Every time we went diving, we would take about fifteen (15) or twenty (20) toilets. I don't

Commerically manufactured reefs unit are available. This one was made by a Japanese firm in 1980.

know how many of them we put down there, but eventually, they amounted to thousands of them. I don't know how many thousands of toilets are out there! It must be as illegal as hell!"

Bob resumes the story:

"We were placing toilets underwater for artificial reefs for over twenty (20) years. They're right out in front and along the Redondo City breakwater. The toilets are strung out in other areas, too."

Harry Pecorelli was in on the planting of the lobster pots (toilets) for the artificial reefs with the Meistrell brothers. Harry tells his side of the toilet tale:

"The unfortunate part of this scheme was that there was no tactical approach in the placement of these commode-reefs. Bob had an idea where it would be the best place to put the bowls, where there would be more lobsters. Bill had a good idea where to put the bowls where there would be more lobsters. And of course, I had a good idea where to put the bowls where there would be more lobsters. So, instead of taking all the bowls and placing them into one area, they were strewn out where each of us wanted them."

Bill said, "They're all over the South Bay. Then another time, we took about two-hundred (200) of the reserve water tanks, that connect to the toilets, and placed them underwater for a separate artificial reef. These were all in one area. We stacked them up fives (5) and then fours (4) and then threes (3). We made a very big circle. It was a court yard. We made places where the lobsters could get in and out easily. We never took any lobsters out of that spot. We only kept that reef for guiding sight-seers and special-guest-tours. There must have been five-hundred (500) lobsters living in those toilet water tanks. It was a happy spot until somebody found it, took a rope after putting holes in the tanks, tied the tanks, then dragged them out to the sand. I couldn't find the spot again."

Pecorelli said, "The interesting facts about porcelain toilets are: The bugs would not go to the toilet while the bowl was clean. They only moved in after this algae or moss grew on it first. We'd see new bowls empty. Next to them the old bowls with the growth would be occupied. Also, there is no obsolescence with porcelain. It does not disintegrate. The toilet bowls are good forever."

In the same conversation Bill Meistrell added, "Unless somebody drags an anchor on them."

There is another factor, too, Pecorelli explains. "There are sand-shifts underwater. The bottom actually moves with the current. And, some of the toilets got buried. There are areas where it is almost like quicksand. We found this by trial and error. We put the bowls down and they would magically disappear."

THE TROLLEY CAR CAPER

Back in the 1958 the California Department of Fish and Game was being pushed by sport fishermen to

Many of California's early trolly cars were turned into artificial reefs.

develop more fishing spots, as the burgeoning population threw more and more fishing lines into the water. About this time the era of the electric street car was coming to an end in Southern California, as it sprawled out in every direction making the previous network of rails obsolete. Buses took over. The trolleys were stacked down at Terminal Island near Fish and Game Department's headquarters. The alert eye of John G. Carlyle spotted them and put two and two together. The street cars would make wonderful habitats, lots of nooks and crannies. Just barge them out and crane them in place on the bottom off—guess where?—Torrence Beach close to good old Redondo Beach. Recognized in the Fish and Game printed bulletins as the key divers, who put them down were John Duffy, Ron Stratton and Charles 'Chuck' Turner and of course, John Carlyle, who was the overseer of the project. The street cars were placed fifty (50) feet down at a site where fishing boats and fishing barges converged for the largest catches of fish found anywhere. They did a wonderful job of putting frosting on the cake the fishermen already had. But for divers it was a special treat for many of them had sat in those old Red Cars, as they were called, to go to school or ditch and ride to the beach. Along with the nostalgia was the curiosity aspect of a large vehicle on the sandy bottom. A weird and spectacular apparition and full of marine growth, fish and lobsters.

Bill and Bob Meistrell were very close to the Red Car project, friends of the Fish and Game divers. Bill recounts some memories. "I remember we would skin dive through the doorway of the street cars. The surge would make the door swing back and forth, eery, ghost-like. The last time I went there, there were people (scuba divers) sitting in the seats. There was a diver pretending he was the conductor. We regret we didn't take pictures of that scene."

Alas, the metal trolleys were no match for the devouring ocean. They rotted away too fast. Then right after a colossal storm, they crumbled into rubble until they were mere rust spots in the sand and eventually even that faded away.

Whenever the Department of Fish and Game puts out a reef, notes Harry Pecorelli, they have to mark it. The marker meant that nobody could dive on it because they were counting creatures. Divers would ruin their survey. It was these markers that persuaded Chuck Turner from the Fish and Game to ask us if he could dive on one of our secret reefs...the toilet bowls, so that he could do his survey. That's how the study was done undisturbed. That's how we became aware of the reef program, which began in 1958.

After the Red Street Cars, the reef program included submerging car bodies, huge rocks and cement blocks. The car bodies deteriorated right away. The cement blocks lasted for a number of years. The rock seemed to work the best. After that test, they came back and planted big rock piles all over the South Bay. These are still there. They worked. They're all marked, Artificial Reef.

OLD TIRES

Old tires could be found in every vacant lot in America in the 1950's pioneer days of diving. While their insides, the old inflatable tubes, patched, made up the ubiquitous basic float device for divers everywhere, the blow out, thread bare tires themselves just sat there and slowly, very slowly, rotted away.

We're not sure who threw the first tire in the water and came back the next day and found three lobsters staring out of the casing. We all tried it, littering the bottoms from Puget Sound to Key West to New England. Names were even painted on tires to thwart poachers (Oh yeah, like that would do any good).

Many contruction barges are now artificial reefs whether sunk on purpose or by accidental sinking. The entire armada of earth moving machines used in building the Panama Canal are on the bottom of Lake Gatun.

The best set up we know of was Jim Cahill's in the 1950's just off his home on a jutting finger of land at Beverly, Massachussets. Jim was building that revolutionary diving gear supply giant, New England Divers. There wasn't much time to boat up and go way out for lobsters. The Cahill Tire Farm was laid out over several acres of his watery "backyard". Placed at fifty (50) feet intervals in a sort of spoke-pattern, he could take a quick gathering-dive around the circuit, harvesting the army of lobsters that would seek out this swell new housing provided for them. Jim had it made for a longtime, lobsters dripping butter turning up for most meals in the Cahill household. Ah, what a great life! But poachers finally broke the code, so to speak, and the morning treks to the "lobster traps" were luckless. Lobsters know when they're being overly harassed and the word gets around. They just disappeared after that.

The tire reefs began in Southern California, when the initiators of the toilet reefs, ran out of toilets. The tires worked great, was the proclamation from the Meistrells. The only thing they had to do with the tires was to cut holes about three or four inches apart. The holes helped to control them when they sent them down.

Then Harry Pecorelli's account about tires was that the first time they put tires in the water, tires went floating off with air trapped on top. They stayed on the surface...whole strings of 'em. They put out about 50 tires one time, truck tires, all kinds of tires. That's why they drilled the holes.

Bob Meistrell was saying that tires would last forever. Probably a hundred years. But they get buried and they disappear.

Eventually, tire reefs were everywhere but the water surrounding them was absorbing toxins from decaying composition rubber. It brought about a closure on putting any toxic potential materials in the ocean.

The line-up sights on shore got removed. There was the palm tree with the church. The next thing you know, somebody cut down the palm tree and they built a new church. They tore down the old Fox Theater. There went another ten reefs. Down went the old Riviera Hotel and that screwed up everything. Development and progress on shore changed the sightings to locate the many artificial reefs.

Another memory by Bill Meistrell was an unusual reef. They use to see a coil of barbed wire on the ocean floor. For some reason a pair of Levi's came through and hooked on it. The jeans waved in the current. They use to get two and three lobsters from it every time. The jeans proved a flag for the diver to easily find the crude trap. Lobsters need the clutter to feel comfortably at home. Little did Levi know that lobsters would be wearing their jeans underwater.

More than lobsters are attracted to artificial reefs. It starts with algae. That's the bottom of the food chain so to speak. Then anything up the food chain, fish, snails, crabs, you name it. They all come to these man-made reefs.

TETRAHEDRONS

There were many serious institutional efforts to make reefs out of the usual building materials. The big granite rocks used for breakwaters, jetties and moles have been a staple for holding back the power of the sea for centuries. They do work and enough of them carefully placed are quite substantial. A big, big storm will do them damage, break them down, but we're talking BIG. They're not cheap. The transport and handling of the huge rocks is a gigantic task. Unfortunately, placed out to sea, as an artificial reef, they get pushed around, sink in the sand and lose their integrity as a unified reef. If they could just lock together better...

Somebody watching his daughter play jacks noted that the pick up stars locked together. That tetrahedron design led to casting concrete pieces six feet across that could be interlocked on the bottom in stacks, allow the force of storm waters to pass through them but hold solid. They were diffused with openings and sheltered spaces for marine life. An experimental reef of them went in off the Santa Barbara region with reasonable results. It all seemed to die off when costs were figured plus they came along as the furor and craze for artificial reefs were tapering off.

THE MIRROR REEF

Al Tillman always wanted his own personal, private reef. He wanted to make one, still does. One of his ideas for an artificial reef evolved when he first began putting together the Underwater Explorers Society on Grand Bahama Island. While first scouting the area in 1964, he had to dive the territory by himself. In shooting familiarization pictures of underwater sites for trips, he came across a giant stand of pillar coral. In order to get a "person" in the picture, he procured a hand mirror and set it in the coral towers. So he shot a picture of himself shooting a picture. He also found out that there was a herd of large barracudas behind him watching...their presence, until the pictures were developed, he had not been aware of.

In the excitement of the dive, Tillman left the mirror in the heart of the coral. Two years later in an effort to find that special stand of pillar coral (He'd not done a shore fix on the spot.), UNEXSO offered a reward to anyone who found it. one of the UNEXSO members found it and mirror encrusted in coral was still there. The mirror glass surface itself was not encrusted and fish were bumping noses with it.

Aha, Tillman thought, what if a reef were created mostly of mirrors? What effect would it have on fish? Would their own image comfort them or frustrate them? It seemed like an interesting experiment to pursue. Perhaps, the mirrors would generate a herding instinct and fish would swarm the reef.

Mirrors, bands from diving tanks, and other metal throw away material was hoarded with the idea of putting the "reflection reef" at the ninety (90) foot ledge dropping off into the abyss. The materials were boated out to the remote spot with the decision to drop it in a natural pattern rather than placing it on the bottom.

Over the side it all went, glinting and fluttering in a snowfall downward. Suddenly, sharks came flying out of everywhere, (They rarely saw any sharks in the thousands of dives from UNEXSO in the Bahama waters.) bumping and inspecting what must have seemed to them a school of dying fish. As the tourist season enveloped the resort, the reflection reef project got tabled. The first drop of materials slithered over the ledge with the attrition of currents and tides.

"We still wonder if somewhere at 2,000 feet, in a forest of black coral, there's a created reef driving deep water fish crazy," muses Al Tillman.

Some dumb ideas were a lot of fun.

ARTIFICIAL TREASURE REEF

Art McKee rebuilt the shipwreck reef just off his museum in Florida Keys. After hauling it all ashore, the treasure, timbers and ballast stones, he took it all back so a movie could be shot of it. He added a few touches that weren't at the actual site. It looked so good he decided to keep it that way for guided trips to a shipwreck reef. We're not sure if this qualifies as a pure artificial reef, but it is reconstituted and it certainly would be great if more wreck sites could be rebuilt with actual materials. A new generation of sport divers could at least get a semblance of what exploration and discovery used to be.

FAUX SHIPWRECKS

Almost every diving venue has tried to put a shipwreck artificial reef down even when there is already a natural plethora of reefs and a bonafide shipwreck.

Putting a big ship on the bottom purposely to be an artificial reef is a major undertaking. It takes a lot of effort by a lot of people.

Probably the most expansive and organized efforts is by the Canadians in British Columbia. Here is the on going history of their meritorious ship sinkings.

A special foundation was created to raise money, purchase decommissioned Navy ships, destroyers in most cases, and prepare them for sinking. Hatches and doors had to be removed so the sunken ship would not trap divers exploring it. Diving areas with minor reef formations and generally sparse marine life were chosen.

The sunken ships work well as artificial reefs and corals and algae as well as fish take it over in only three months.

In the year, 2000, a San Diego Foundation spearheaded by Dry Suit Czar Dick Long paid $350,000 for a Canadian destroyer, The Yukon. They planned to have a grand celebration, fireworks and all, when the ship was sunk. But the night before, it rolled over and lay on its side on the bottom. They'd hope to sell off opportunities to be the first people to dive the sunken Yukon. Unfortunately, instead of upright, the preferred positioning, the new "artificial reef" was much less safe on its side.

The U.S. Navy has turned down countless requests from groups in many parts of America for old, obsolete ships to sink as artificial reefs (There was strong support from the line fishing sportsmen and fish and game departments but there mixed reasons - sentiment, value of scrap metal, the possibility such ships mothballed in retirement might be needed for war.). For a requesting agency there was the cost of making one safe and getting it on site. Time will tell as to how good an idea this was. The question always remains, do man-made intrusions take away the wildness.

Artificial reefs were events that were private endeavors before they went public. They kept diving interesting. They intrigued the inventive and engineering spirit in all of us. Cousteau played with a Mechano Set of building pieces as a child. Perhaps that was the forerunner of inventing the Aqua-Lung and designing the Calypso. And so many divers, who played with Erector Sets, Tinker Toys and in recent times, Legos, were directed to eventually build the artificial reefs that have served sport diving and may well be the most important way to expand sport diving in the future.

20
CAVE DIVING

DEFINING EVENT: CHALLENGING MOTHER NATURE

Arthur Barada penetrates a Florida aquifer with early cave diving gear and lifeline. Bill Barada

The "Point of No Return" is a soft term for what is often one of the most terrifying experiences in life. You're halfway into a cave and you think you'd judged you had enough air to make it out the other end. Suddenly, you're not sure and you want to go back the way you came in. If the air comes hard, there's panic gnawing at you and you sense you're going to drown.

Al Tillman remembers a cave in the Philippines off Fuga Island that native divers told him had another opening at its far end. Looking at a pinpoint of light by himself, his scuba breathing in a hissing whistle, the feeling of aloneness, the thrill of the unknown, the sudden impact of his claustrophobia, there was the sudden realization that his short air-fill just might make it all the way, but it was longer in than planned...this was "the point of no return". Had the locals only thought there was another opening or the language cross over miscommunicated?

It had been a long way in and he'd already used up more than half his air. What if that pinpoint of light was much farther than it looked? (It usually is when you're worried.) The sense of exploration and adventure had swept him into one of those taboo situations of diving protocol; diving alone, no safety line, a tiny flashlight, a short air supply,

Science Magazine cover showing artists rendering of Little Salt Spring in Florida.

to name a few dumb violations. Now I'm going to die, went his thoughts as the sour taste of panic seeped in.

But if he was going to die, and because he was supposed to be a role model in diving instruction, he wanted to do it with the same dignity Conrad Limbaugh displayed in his final dive in a cave in France.

He slowed his breathing and stroked smoothly toward the small light ahead. He did make it, bursting through a very narrow opening to the surface, the sun and the air. No more caves or tunnels; he was not psychologically equipped to go somewhere where you couldn't see the surface or at least the light of the surface. A rock ceiling is the evil empire to scores of divers. Cave diving is a very special kind of diving and for special people.

The BIRTHPLACE of cave diving is probably Florida with its twenty major springs and sink holes. But caves are found around the world especially where the land is actually an ancient ocean bottom, a limestone of Swiss cheese texture. The Yucatan Peninsula and the Bahamas are that way. Rain has percolated down through the porous limestone, dissolving into labyrinths of underground passages. In some cases, underground rivers carve their way to the surface and roofs over cavities cave-in creating sink holes.

By the 1950's scuba was available to allow many divers to go down in these sink, or blue holes and enter caves that branched off from them. Cave diving was born. NAUI set up a committee under instructor and cave diver, Dave Desautels to develop instruction for this speciality diving. A National Association of Cave Diving was eventually formed. "Killer Caves" took the lives of many divers who lacked technical procedures; negative legislation loomed with the possibility of all caves and springs being closed.

Even the best of divers have squeaked by cave diving close calls. Here's first cave dive account by Garry Howland, top graduate of the classic first NAUI instructor course in Houston.

Garry Howland in the 1960's was probably as fit and well trained a diver as we'll ever have in the field. He could dive anywhere with anyone under all kinds of conditions. He had a chance to go with a couple of Florida divers into one of their revered sink holes and figured "a piece of cake", go in and come out. Everybody didn't have a light, Howland didn't and not many bothered with a directional safety line in those days. Who, me get lost?

Garry Howland did, looking at the formations on the cave wall back in a side passage, suddenly the light from his buddies lights got dim and disappeared. They were gone and he was in the dark and close to being on reserve. First time in a cave, first time being in the dark, almost out of air and probably down 100 feet. Was that the metallic taste of panic he was sensing? But Howland was thinking that someone with his experience and diving skills, no way, was going to be taken by a dumb hole in the ground - still, fresh water at that.

He felt his way along the side of the cave, calculated if he'd turned before at any time, and then thought his way to the shaft where there was light filtering down from 100 feet overhead. The air was coming hard by this point but his heart beat went from racing to strolling and he easily surfaced. "Hi, Garry," called the other two cave divers, "we ran out of air," sitting on the ground munching sandwiches. "You sure make a tank last a long time."

Howland would dive the caves and sink holes again but never with just a confidence in his general diving skills. From then on he learned the special skills and took the special equipment.

The American cave diving enthusiasm was preceded by divers in England. Techniques were pioneered by a British Cave Diving Group founded in 1946. This evolved from two young Englishmen Graham Balcombe and J. A. Sheppard, who in 1934 dove the pools of caves in Somersetshire using flashlight, homemade goggles, bicycle pump, garden hose, and a respirator out of old bicycle frames. The prime cave dive was Wookey Hole which divers described as like being in "green jelly" and "awe inspiring" but not terrifying. The Americans lagged behind in this specialty form of diving but rapidly caught up in the 1960's and extended the boundaries with clubs, organized procedures, courses of instruction and manuals.

The Cousteau group was into cave diving early on, too. In 1946 they arrived in the French city of Avignon to solve the mystery of the Fountain of Vaucluse. During the year this placid, clear pool sits calmly but in March a violent torrent of raging water boils out of the mountain for five weeks. No one had been able to trace the source of this sudden eruption; not by using hard hat gear or floating dyes. Somewhere there was a secret room where this hydraulic phenomenon resided.

Cousteau and especially his partner, Frédéric Dumas, had misgivings about this dive, something ominous, an instinctive dislike for going underground, hung in the air.

Fossils from a Florida Spring headed for for a museum in the 1950's.

Bill Barada

Lots of hazards in a tough test for the new scuba. Jacque Yves Cousteau and Frédéric Dumas made the first dive into the unknown; Cousteau loaded down with a homemade constant volume suit, triple tanks, mini Aqua Lung, mask, dagger, fins, two flashlights, weight belts, and an ice axe—Dumas, too. Using reports of hard hat (helmet diving) explorations preceding, the team found great discrepancies, probably the result of dramatic imaginings to impress the people observing.

A 400 foot guideline had been dropped with a weighted end. There was a 30 foot rope tied between Cousteau and Dumas. A system of tugs on lines would tell surface tenders to clear, play-out or pull-up-line. Oh, Oh!

Cousteau and Dumas had gone to a depth of 200 feet and 400 feet into the caves. Nitrogen narcosis hit and Dumas lost almost complete control while Cousteau felt he was thinking and doing idiotic things. Misinterpreted signals brought down more rope.

The tender tied on more rope when he reached the end of the 400 feet and Cousteau encountering the knot as the rope piled up behind him felt a bit of panic as he realized he'd have to let the guideline go and climb the wall dragging Dumas with him. He fell back with Dumas' weight to the cavern floor, vomiting into his mouthpiece. He felt Dumas was now dead and so would he be if he didn't cut loose from him. But, he tried once more to give the

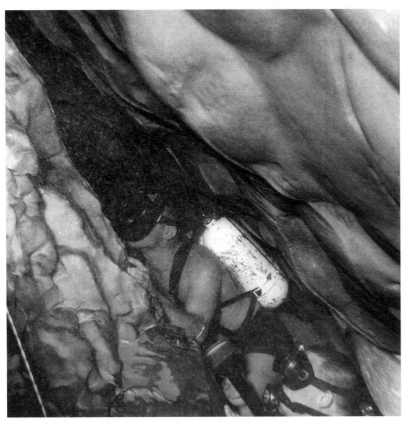

Merl Dobry and Jim Houtz inch their way through a narrow passage of Devils Hole in Death Valley. *Brooks Foundation*

six tugs on the guideline which would tell the tender to pull them up. The tender had no idea what was happening but finally decided to pull them up just in case.

As the bodies of the two-man-team broke the surface, others jumped in and revived Dumas on shore.

A second team of two led by Philippe Tailiez went down with no exposure suits and less equipment...no depth gauge! They also ran into trouble, feeling the strange exhaustion Cousteau had felt, and they had probably only been down 130 feet.

A third team went down but not deep. Later it was found "the strange feeling" was the result of carbon monoxide in their air from the compressor sucking in its own exhaust fumes. Yes, even our icons blundered at times.

In 1955 a diving expedition army sponsored by the French Office of Underwater Research descended on Vaucluse to solve the riddle. Truck loads of special equipment were on hand. But the mystery was never solved...it is only suspected that breaks in an upper plateau over the River Sorgue fill and eventually run off causing the surging.

The Americans once again learned some scuba lessons from the French. And Cousteau probably learned that cave diving wasn't his favorite scuba thing.

Americans got prominently into cave diving by the solo experience of Jon Lindbergh, son of Charles Lindbergh (who opened up aviation with his solo transatlantic flight in 1927). In 1953, twenty year old Jon made a cave dive, probably a first in terms of public awareness. He volunteered to swim alone into California's Bower Cave on an expedition set up by speleologist, Raymond de Saussure. Saussure believed this Bower Cave spa was fed from a huge underground chamber. Lindbergh, a marine biology student at Stanford, had the same great curiosity of his famed father, and his courage. He went in alone with a thin nylon line tied to his waist, one flashlight, a rubber dry suit and a single tank Aqua Lung. Over a series of dives he discovered a large inner chamber with a bottomless lake. His last dive was to inflate a raft in the chamber and shoot pictures. He had a lot of difficulty because he took a dry land camera wrapped in plastic bags and the raft filled with water. He had to take off his gear, put it in the raft and bale with his mask. The mask broke hitting his scuba tank and Jon expected the glass to puncture the raft and send it with all gear down, down, down. But he got his pictures and almost blind without a mask barely snuck out guided by a faint blur light from the mouth of the siphon. In modern cave diving, this would be considered a dumb dive but aren't all first dives a bit flawed. Ask Cousteau.

DEVILS HOLE

Devils Hole in Death Valley, California was the entry to a huge cave system that attracted a young underwater photographer, Jim Houtz. Here was a watering hole in the heart of vast heated desert, its waters moving with oceans tides suggesting a connection to the sea, and its surface hosting a school of fossil pupfish that had mutated down from three foot long prehistoric species to this small three inch long species. Prospectors and pioneers had bathed in it over the past century, refreshed and awed by it.

What other curiosities about this unusual place, were there? Houtz was determined to dive into it and find out. He mounted several expeditions and received a grant from the International Underwater Film Festival to make a film of one of his expeditions there. But, as well organized as Houtz was with all of his diving experience, tragedy struck with the loss of one of his best divers. They had penetrated to a depth of 284 feet and discovered a gigantic chamber. The death caused the custodians to close Devil's Hole and restrict access.

Another side note on reasons for closing this cave system to the public was the loss of many of the pupfish. Some snorkeling teenagers partied there and decided to have a fish fry.

BENJAMIN'S BLUE HOLES AND SINK HOLES

When the entrance to a cave system is a massive Blue Hole, it is beautiful lure to divers. After all a Blue Hole doesn't put a roof over a diver, the surface is iridescently in view, unless one decides to take a peek into a branching cave.

Most divers can handle a Blue Hole, no matter how deep, without being affected by some phobia. These holes, when in the ocean, often harbor schools of fish, unusual coral growths and large predators.

They are in a way the entree to cave diving, sort of vertical caves with a view of the surface.

Dr. George Benjamin, probably, did more to popularize Blue Holes than anyone else in the pioneer days. It was said that George would probably push a treasure wreck aside to get at a new Blue Hole. His addiction was strong. He led many expeditions with famous divers and his filming crew to explore and document these deep hole amusement parks drilled by nature into the sea bottom.

He was especially taken with the hundreds of Blue Holes just off shore of Andros Island in the Bahamas. George described what it was like to dive one of the submarine pits in National Geographic, September 1970. These holes can plunge to 200 feet and appear cobalt blue in the pale shallows. By 1970 George Benjamin, a research chemist from Toronto, Canada, had spotted a couple of hundred blue holes and dove fifty-four. These holes had mysterious strong currents, often counter to the tides, like none other in the world. The Great Bahama Bank is limestone, more than 14,000 feet thick, and once stood above the sea at which time rain eroded the labyrinth of holes. Andros, as an island, sits on top of that geological phenomenon.

George describes his first dive made near slackening tide and swam with partner, Tom McCollum, against the slight current into the dark opening. At 80 feet a grand chamber widened and branched off into tunnels. Above them silver schools of fish swarmed, snappers fed in large numbers, and some fish swam upside down where there were rocky outcrops.

George Benjamin had started in 1960 exploring these underwater holes and prior to that had been a dry cave spelunker. He had to develop safety procedures, such as, three-men teams, one diver remaining outside a tunnel with the end of a lifeline, diving for the twenty minutes of slack tide. As for dangerous marine life, only an occasional nurse shark had brushed by and through them...trying to get away.

George was drawn to ocean hole diving by the usual desire to go where no one has gone before...the unknown. The sensation of being the pioneer explorer can be seen in the analysis of it by Sir Edmund Hillary, who went to the top of Mt. Everest in 1953. Referring to the commercialization of climbing Mt. Everest, where people with a whim and $65,000 are taken to the top by guides, Hillary says, "Wherever they go, they're following in the footsteps of others...they're never pioneering." Today, helicopters can take you in and out, up and down. When Hillary climbed in 1953, no one knew if it was humanly possible to withstand the lack of oxygen and reach the summit. Hillary removed the psychological barrier for everyone else. In some ways though, he felt it might be more dangerous today; with all the new equipment and skills, the new breed is not as cautious, takes more chances. And, so it may be with diving.

Cousteau, the great documentarian, followed Benjamin into these blue holes after seeing one of his pictures of a vast opening in the wall of Andros at 200 feet. So in 1970, Jacques son, Philippe, was led by George's son, Peter, 100 feet into the largest underwater cavern they had found to that time. Cousteau called it, "Benjamin's Cave" in honor of the pioneer, who preceded him there.

This same cave took the life of a first class cave diver demonstrating the Hillary warning that those that follow may stretch the pioneering role to a dangerous point. The Diver, Frank Martz, with a buddy entered a passage at 280 feet that was too narrow to back out of once in. They went on to 320 feet on compressed air to a large silted cavern where they lost each other. Martz's companion squeezed his way out the narrow tunnel but Martz's body was never recovered.

Benjamin, ultimately, discovered back 1,200 feet in this same cave some amazing sights; the Roman Gate, three stalagmites that rose from the floor of the cavern with a limestone arch across their tops. Benjamin took Tom Mount, President and Training Director of the National Association of Cave Divers; Jack McKenney, Editor (at that time) of *Skin Diver Magazine*; and skilled cave diver, Ray Hixon, loaded with equipment to see the Roman Gate. Robert Burgess in his book, *The Cave Divers*, described it "like a midnight tour through a deserted art gallery", as Benjamin pointed out unusual rock sculptures to his companions.

At 1200 feet into the cave, they came into a cathedral-like room filled with stalagmites and stalactites as if a grotto of statues.

But mysteries still remain. Why do slack times of currents differ hole to hole? Some are veracious and some so weak that they have silted. It is suspected that the miles of tunnels create the varying effects. Cave-ins may alter the currents and also create new and changing dangers to divers.

Cave divers insist that these holes are not subject to the old "seen one, seen them all" description. There seems to be something unexpected in each one. Benjamin's favored goal was to find two blue holes linked by a tunnel so he could go in one, come out the other.

George J. Benjamin had staked his claim on these caves; he had permanent lines running, over one and a quarter miles, to different parts of the cave. Took a bit away from feeling like explorers for other divers to follow later.

Jack McKenney, who suffered no claustrophobia, just the opposite, he likes crevices. He felt less nitrogen narcosis deep diving in caves probably because of this. He described this blue hole dive as most like flying...into a sort of Grand Canyon. Some passages were so narrow their tanks would clank against the walls. McKenney had the feeling of being in a horror movie and that Boris Karloff would pop up at any moment. But shooting film in murkiness caused by silt dislodged by fins and bubbles proved to be the worst part. Generally, the water deep inside a cave is very clear unless sediment is disturbed.

While dry land blue holes and Cenotes have provided spectacular experiences, the ocean holes, those totally submerged caves offered a greater living and changing environment for divers.

WAKULLA SPRING

In 1954 Gary Salsman, a student at Florida State University, with some friends got a chance to scuba dive into one of the deepest and largest springs in the United States. One hundred and eighty three million gallons of water a day gushes out of it to form the Wakulla River.

The private owners of the Spring never allowed scuba diving. Salsman had skin dived it along with glass bottom boats and public swimmers. In the shadows of a towering limestone cliff is a 100 foot wide fissure, a yawning maw that would have lured any cave diver who saw it. It did Gary, and with his friends he practiced in other places for the day he'd be able to SCUBA into that dark cavern. They prepared by three-member-team buddy breathing from 100 foot depths in the dark.

The great break came when a movie company filmed in this extraordinarily clear water. Their air source broke down and there was Gary Salsman with an Ingersol-Rand Compressor on a trailer. The deal was that Gary and friends would be able to dive the deep cavern.

They got down to 180 feet where nitrogen narcosis hit and Gary felt as if he were swimming in clear molasses. It prompted Gary to reread *Silent World* to recall how Cousteau had faced the narcosis. Feeling more secure after this first experience with nitrogen narcosis, and understanding it, the next dive was a clear headed one and a huge mastodon bone, four feet long, was found. The Spring manager was really excited seeing the publicity in it and gave permission to Gary Salsman to continue diving there. Over 600 fossils were recovered in 1955 through 1956. Over two hundred dives of short 15-minute duration (to avoid the bends) were made.

A lot of speculation ensued from geology experts and paleontologists as to the reason all fossils were found at the 200 foot level. Salsman's dives eventually revealed that these huge caves with sloping entry passages were subject to landslides. Ancient man probably didn't kill and sort the bones of creatures in a dry cave area. Salsman noted this sliding of materials from above when on a dive. They looked below them and saw a great mass of white water surging up at them and coming out into the Spring...the result of an avalanche deeper in the cave system. Despite the strong outgoing current, fossils could and did slide down with overburden letting loose down the slopes.

A funny note is when the Salsman team discovered markings on the wall at 220 feet...petroglyphs from prehistoric people? But suddenly one of the divers waved the bottom of his fin which had the same two concentric circles that looked like suns. The diver with the guilty fins had pressed them against the wall silt while taking a photograph. Salsman went on to become a professional oceanographer but his heart remained at Wakulla.

Salsman in the 1970's felt his dives into Wakulla Spring were the fantastic voyages of his youth akin to the great sailing expeditions. To him Wakulla would remain an uncharted ocean, its specific source yet to be discovered. Why in 1964, on the night of the monster earthquake in Alaska, was there caused a large fissure in the side of the Spring with rumblings and white water coming up out of the Spring. To Gary Salsman there always would be something sacred about Wakulla Spring.

Many of the founding circle of divers relate one of their most memorable dives to a cave experience.

ANDY RECHNITZER, who commanded the U. S. Navy's Deep Submergence Program in the early days, is one of the few individuals who has been to the deepest points of the ocean. But diving the caves in Capri excited his imagination even more. "Perhaps because it was more mysterious," he reflected.

JEANNE BEAR SLEEPER, one of the pioneer lady diving writers, is eloquent on the subject: "The most challenging, adventurous, dangerous diving I have ever done is in the Blue Holes of Andros, Bahamas. These are certainly the most intense, life-endangering dives I have ever done. The power of the ocean surging in and out of the holes, the layers of fresh water that drop you through seemingly empty space, the caves, stalactites, human bones on deep ledges and the blackness of the bowels of the ocean are imprinted in my memory forever."

Andy Rechnitzer explores a cave under the Isle of Capri, Italy in 1957.
A. Rechnitzer

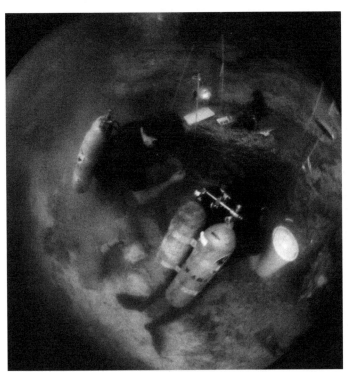

A 10,000 year old early man site was discovered in this Florida Spring.   Carl Clausen

<u>DR. CARL J. CLAUSEN,</u> marine archeologist, Director of Little Salt Spring Research Project for the General Development Foundation, involved in underwater archeological investigation of submerged prehistoric sites in the Gulf of Mexico/Caribbean area and member of the Monitor Foundation's Board of Directors, was asked in our interview with him in 1975: Carl, your favorite diving places?

"The Florida Keys are nice. I also enjoy diving in springs although I no longer go in for deep dives in caves. I was in at the first of it when safety lines were a novelty and lights were a length of wire connecting a 6-volt battery to a small sealed beam light. The battery was taped to your belt and rubber cement covered the connections on the back of the light."

The springs with their caves and tunnels are the Mother Lode for archeological excavation of ancient human and animal bones. Carl's reply to our inquiry revealed that he and Gordon Watts, the underwater archeologist of North Carolina, who participated in the discovery of the USS Monitor, "excavated a test sight 45 feet below the surface in Warm Mineral Springs, Florida, in which the more than 10,000 year old remains of an approximately six year old child were found in January 1972. The find represented the oldest closely dated occurrence of human remains yet discovered in North America and marked the first time that standard archeological techniques had successfully been adapted to the underwater environment."

Dr. Clausen pioneered controlled-excavation and photographic recordings in prehistoric underwater archeological sites. Bates Littlehales, *National Geographic* photographer, and Denny Bowman, a Dive Officer at the University of Texas, were key resource partners on many of the dives.

Tom Mount, one of the world's most experienced technical divers, developed a safety program especially for cave diving and began teaching cave diving courses in 1963. Tom is one of the founders of the first cave (technical) diving training agencies and America's oldest cave diving organization is the NACD (National Association of Cave Diving). He is the Chief Executive Officer of IAND Inc./IANTD, (International Association of Nitrox and Technical Divers) the first certification agency to offer a full array of Nitrox mixed gas and technical diving programs. Patti and Tom Mount with his son, David, explained to Zale Parry that cave diving is not a casual activity. There are cavern divers who never leave the daylight of a cavern. It takes more than special equipment to be a true cave diver. There is proper training with specific textbooks and workbooks. Most important is having a mind that isn't easily confused 'climbing' upside down, wiggling through sometimes tight passages, sans-claustrophobia and having the comfort and presence of knowing your bearings at all times. Here are a few of the many books authored by Mount: Basic Cave Diver co-author with Dr. Lee Somers for NAUI, *The Cave Diving Manual, Safe Cave Diving,* and *The International Association of Nitrox and Technical Cave Diver Encyclopedia.*

Cave diving and, in particular, blue holes were immediately a most intriguing interest with the coming of SCUBA. Just Skin Diving had allowed very shallow penetration to that point. It perhaps ranks along side of treasure diving as the exciting fulfillment of childhood adventure reading and dreams. It's forbidding aura, the double impact of going underwater and into black holes aroused both fear and longing. It separated the brave-risk-takers from...well, the brave-risk-takers, who required clear, sunlit waters of the unknown. It was a diving thrill apart from all other underwater experiences.

MODERN CAVE DIVING

The Cave Diving Section of the National Speleological Society by the year 2000 had created a hierarchy of different level classes. They propose that there are several reasons for going cave diving: (1) The challenge of traversing caverns of great scenic beauty; (2) the technology for cave diving requires more high tech equipment, a lure for equipment junkies; and (3) the scientific study of geology, biology and hydrology of underwater caves.

Scuba America found out through interviews with cave divers that the "mystery of the unknown" has been the

Braulio Garcia, Paul Bush and Emmett Gowen explore The Sacred Cave that was discovered by CEDAM at the Cove of Xelha, Mexico in 1960.   Pablo Bush

overwhelming attraction from the beginnings in the 1950's. In those pioneering days, as it was in all types of diving, people learned to cave dive by going cave diving. There were no advanced specialty courses and except for major cave diving regions like Florida, dive classes gave it little coverage.

By the 1970's, a cave diving specialty course showed up in the offerings of most training agencies. By the year 2000, there was a hierarchy of cave diving classes. The Cave Diving Section of the NSS requires that a diver must have advanced open water certification before training as a cave diver. They feel that it is very important that false pride and a macho ego be put aside and a dive aborted whenever things start to go wrong.

The first level course is Cavern Diving which covers elementary skills for limited penetrations. The Introduction to Cave Diving is next and seems to cover more skills and deeper penetrations. There are four cave dives in two different locations. There is air sharing for exit from a cave, buoyancy control, and eyes-closed line following. Penetration is limited to one-third of a single diving cylinder, a linear swim, 100 feet maximum depth, and no decompression.

Equipment required is a 2,000 psi cylinder, a second single hose regulator with 5 foot to 7 foot hose, a third battery-powered diving light, a safety reel with 75 feet of guideline, watch, depth gauge, slate, pencil, submersible dive tables, three line markers, and one primary cave-diving-reel with 400 feet of guideline.

The third course is Apprentice Cave Diver where emphasis is on dive planning and skill perfection. Four cave dives are included. Penetrations are limited to three of twin cylinders, 130 feet maximum depth, 20 feet minimum visibility.

Additional gear added to basics aforementioned are a compass, a dual valve manifold, 25 watt light with 60 minute burn time, and a gap reel with 50 feet of guideline.

The fourth course in the series is the Full Cave Diver. Covers four cave dives utilizing three locations. Minimum age is 18 years old. More perfection of skills.

The four courses take 8 days, 15 cavern or cave dives in at least six different locations.

The NSS-CDS address is P. O. Box 38057, Tallahassee, Florida 32315-8057. This nonprofit organization is the largest cave diving operation in the world. Florida has the most active members. A publication, *Underwater Spe-*

leology, is put out bimonthly.

It's TIMELINE history cites 1948 as NSS divers making first cave dives using scuba. In 1953 the Florida NSS sub-section conducted the first diver training course with written standards. In 1968 an NSS member wrote the first cave diving manual . In 1973 the Cave Diving Section for NSS was established. The Cave Diving Section became independently incorporated in 1983. By 1987 official nonprofit, tax exempt status was granted - as a scientific and educational organization.

More than 6000 cave divers have been certified. Some 500 Cave Diving Rescue and Recovery Specialists have been trained.

The NSS-CDS has installed safety/warning signs at the more popular underwater caves. It has created a "No-Light" rule for open water divers which prohibits divers from carrying a dive light which naturally limits their penetration by lack of daylight.

Cave diving is a very special kind of diving and is not for all sport divers. It has adds an additional risk factor to sport diving and has taken the lives of many divers - especially in the early years. By the year 2000 most of the caves have already been explored to some degree and outfitted with permanent safety lines and stringent rules to allow novice divers the cave diving experience.

21

THE LIVEABOARD

DEFINING EVENT: THE AGGRESSOR FLEET

The liveaboard dive boat was on every dive entrepreneur's wish list through most of the early decades of diving. Pioneer divers of the prehistory 1940's and 1950's made their own equipment and had to save up their loose change to pay for a trip beyond the local beach or quarry. In those days only a few owned and trailered a boat; a few more could maybe rent one but most camped and dove from shore.

Private and wealthy people have always been able to go buy the ocean. They could live aboard their yachts and dive perfect places the general public couldn't get to. The general public, during the past half century of sport diving, have had to struggle for equal affordable access.

TRAVEL EMERGES

The Charter Boats for a day came on the scene in the diving population centers, primarily, Southern California and Florida followed by New England, the Northwest and the Gulf of Mexico areas. One-day-trips were about all the general population of divers could afford to support. Then in the 1960's and 1970's, the land based resort emerged with clear warm water, superb visibility underwater, creature abundance, and exotic locations proliferated by the Jet Age. The jet airplane had exploded the travel industry ...and diving followed along.

The diver, who operated like a golfer in the early days, went diving every weekend, locally, and any other day, he could ditch work.

Jim Christiansen had this to say in interview:

"I was a firefighter, a lot of the divers were, which gave them plenty of off duty days. There was good diving off California back in the 1940's and 1950's but when I got to see some other areas during World Spearfishing Championships, even went to one of the first Club Meds, I could see divers would want to see these different places."

A few divers watched Cousteau's shows and heard the tales of the exotic diving places. They said, "to heck with being a weekend diver, feeling the way around in a cloudy lake or quarry or even a rocky ocean floor." They decided to not be butchers anymore or to replace mufflers or teach school. They decided to move to where the water was crystal clear with tons of sea life and see places where no one has ever been before.

TIMELINE

1950's - Dick and Mary Lou Adcock's Marisla operated in LaPaz, Mexico, Baja California. Bare essentials. Comfortable. Warm water showers. Diving oriented with one day hike to historical spot on a Sea of Cortez Island. Delicious gourmet meals on top-deck outdoors. Astronomy of night sky or a movie.

1960 - Skeet LaChance's Highlander operated in Bahamas with diving the main activity.

Mid 1960's - Bill Johnson, member of the oldest and most exclusive dive club, the Bottom Scratchers, named his first sport diving boat in honor of the dive club. Very spacious. Diving the primary activity. Operated out of San Diego, California.

1960's - The Reef Explorer in Australia.

The American culture in general was in this mood by the 1960's, young men wanting to change lifestyles, pursue careers of their dreams of adventure. These divers were responsible for the diving-designated resorts and diving boats ...and, yes, the ultimate liveaboard dive boats.

Dick Adcock's Marisla was the first liveaboard.

Dive resorts, even the grandest, like UNEXSO on Grand Bahama or Pablo Bush's Akumal in Mexico, had the limiting factor of featuring only the good diving off their local shores, as excellent as those diving conditions might be. The next step had to be something like the modern cruise ship, the mobile resort, the "ship board resort". That was the liveaboard dive boat.

Liveaboards though rare did exist in the beginning days of diving. But, as we have said, there were but a few people who could afford what the cost of a week of total service and quality diving would be afloat. It took an expanding middle class in America, a booming economy, an increasing discretionary income.

At the Grand Bahama UNEXSO during the 1960's, several charter liveaboards would dock at the club and come ashore. These were not pure dive liveaboards for they were not designated or designed for hardcore diving. Snorkeling, swimming, sunbathing but not the five dives-a-day with scuba divers. Skeets LaChance, a lake diver from Chicago, came by UNEXSO with his boat, his passengers touring the club and buying some accessory diving equipment, a snorkel or a mask, and swap stories at a real diver level with the UNEXSO pro divers. Skeets would say that he wished there were more real scuba divers on his charters because he'd like to try some of the great spots he came across. The liveaboard dive boat can do that, get you to virgin territories. The UNEXSO staff, who had to make many daily routine dive trips with customers over and over to the same closeby sites, always looked glum when LaChance sailed off to mysterious places.

THE CALYPSO INSPIRATION
Certainly Cousteau's Calypso was the dream liveaboard dive boat that divers envied as they watched films and

television shows of Jacque's dive team attack the world underwater. Of course, the Calypso was a converted mine sweeper designed to be a state-of-the-art oceanographic vessel. Its operation geared around scuba. It was serious business, not recreation (Or how else would he get those sponsors and grants?). Nevertheless, the Calypso had all of the features the liveaboards of the 1990's would strive for.

By the mid 1960's, Bill Johnson, had the boat, Bottom Scratcher. Another boat, the Sand Dollar, would be added within the next few years. It was big, spacious and livable for a week's stay off San Diego, California, coastline including Mexican waters and islands. Bread, breakfast, fruit, salads and drinks were purchased and stored at the beginning of each trip. The main meals were acquired by-capture from the sea by the divers during the day's play. Or Bill Johnson, himself, would dive for and cook the meals for his guests. Then, friends and food made up for the lavish luxury of the true liveaboard demanded thirty years later.

While divers watched Cousteau and Dumas and Falco cruise around to fabulous, untouched dive spots, they wondered if they'd ever have enough money to buy some of that kind of diving. It was that impending trip to the moon on a spaceship for wealthy consumers; that was how divers saw it in the 1950's and 1960's. Those divers were buying a house, a car, a refrigerator, and then what. By the 1980's, there was the full power of the credit card in the land of a new philosophy of not waiting for the big rewards - do things now. Women were filling top echelon jobs and drawing big paychecks. Couples were urged on by two paychecks. The 1980's belonged to the newly affluent divers ready to buy that most desirable diving experience - the week or two just diving night and day, a smorgasbord of going under at virgin spots, fully supported by luxury amenities.

TIMELINE

1972 - Paul Hunann's 86 foot liveaboard in Caribbean was Spartan with one bunkroom for six plus three two-person cabins. Two heads and one shower for entire boat. Water was rationed. But Hunann claimed good diving, good spots, and good food all came before luxury. He sold it in 1980 while only two more liveaboards had appeared in Caribbean. It looked like a dead-end for the liveaboard.

1972 - Skindiving Hawaii is the oldest and largest diving company in Hawaii. In 1972 it had the largest fleet of dive boats with custom designed dive packages.

1974 - Roy Hauser's first of a fleet of luxury boats, the Truth, was custom-designed especially for scuba divers.

1984 - The economy heated up. The nouveau riche were ready to buy a top diving experience. Enter the Cayman Aggressor. It was a boat converted from an oil platform-supply-ship into a luxury dive yacht with air conditioned staterooms and a huge dive deck. "It was 'crude' compared with 1990's liveaboards," says Wayne Hasson, President of the Aggressor Fleet, Inc. "It also had a large camera table on deck and on-board E-6 processing."

Local diving suffered to some extent, hardly competitive with the exotic venues of the liveaboard. Divers had to save their money to go on these $2,000, $3,000, sometimes $5,000 trips. It was never going to be cheap. But, ah, the memories from a liveaboard experience ...they last a lifetime ...and they wanted more. Nobody expected repeat business to the extent it happened ...for resorts, too. Because of the high cost of this kind of diving, people tended to go back where they had a great experience. The cruise business is dependent on those who repeat. By the late 1980's, this new segment of the dive industry had truly emerged.

LUXURY AND MORE

But it wasn't a given that the liveaboard would take over. The land resort could offer a lot, space and things to do between dives, more for a non-diving spouse. Divers wanted more than just unlimited air on deck and access to virgin dive spots. The demand for luxury accelerated. The divers wanted private rooms, private bathrooms, hot water showers, television, videos, personal lockers for cameras and computers, rinse-tanks, knowledgeable staff, personal one-on-one attention, photo processing and fresh gourmet food.

The costs went up and up. The prime demographic went up so high that the liveaboards had to cater to an upper income population. Diving in general became more expensive. Gone were the days of do-it-yourself, buy it with change out of the pocket, the freedom of choosing a spot close to home so you could walk in the door with the catch, get an ooh and an aah from the family - it all faded along with the old water dog divers who could dive in spite of any equipment hanging on them.

There have been more claims on innovations throughout all of sport diving. People are sure they were the first to invent this or organize that, but as history shows often, the same idea was arising in many places at the same time. Perhaps because the time was right.

The Bilikiki Cruises Ltd. operation in the Solomon Islands had two large liveaboards. It was started in the late 1980's by a pro dive shop-couple and ship builders. Two ships 125 feet by 24 feet with interesting provenance. They once served as fish processor, ferry and even a brothel before conversion to diving liveaboards.

Some trips feature celebrity divers like Steve Frink, underwater photographer. The crew amuses the guest divers with entertaining stories and are always at standby to help with gear, exit and boat entry, rinse gear and courteously see to the divers' comforts. Five dives a day, two forenoon, two afternoon, and a night dive. An eleven-night trip is around $2,475 a person, deluxe, by end of 1990's. There is free use of air tanks and weight belts. There is air conditioning and meals are served on time. The Solomon Islands feature Guadalcanal and the Iron Bottom full of sunken ships from World War II. Trips are varied as to locations of diving to lessen impact on the environment.

TIMELINE
Early 1990's - Celebrity divers, especially, underwater photographers dressed up liveaboard diving vacations. Close cooperation with certifying instruction agencies meant professional instructors and divemasters made up the crew. Liveaboards get on famous dive sites like the Cayman's wreck of the Rhone before the crowd of day-boats arrive.

Peter Hughes' Dancer Fleet and the Aggressor Fleet began two giant liveaboard chains that added ships and world locations almost yearly. Special markets were catered, families, seniors and specialty divers, even the handicapped diver.

Mid 1990's - Liveaboards found an affluent dive market ready to go far and to formerly isolated places. The liveaboard divers were often repeats, perhaps 50%. Over half were women. Specialty dive certification was offered.

Late 1990's - Liveaboards were everywhere you'd want to go in the world. Only foreign country politics clouded the industry but with land contacts at a minimum, conflict and restrictions were less than for the land-based resort. Prices between dive liveaboards and dive resorts were on a par. Luxury perks had maxed and upgrade innovations weren't being as easily found. Nitrox and rebreather diving became standard amenities.

The Solomons recently became an independent nation of some 900 volcanic islands and saw unrest over migrants coming to take jobs during the 1990's, a hazard the liveaboards face by operating in third world paradises of political edginess.

Mike Burke was selling barefoot-vacations on his Windjammer Cruises as far back as 1947. In 1955, he was putting out a fleet around the Caribbean featuring the former

Onasis yacht, Fantone. His deck cabins then were $690 per night per person. He pushed diving all the famous reefs - scuba was not mentioned in his literature or concern for certification. By the 1970's, Burke's Windjammer Cruises were showing signs of what was to be the dedicated dive liveaboards.

Skindiving Hawaii is the oldest and largest diving company in Hawaii. It boasted the largest fleet of dive boats, a professional staff with many years of experience, and store locations on the three major islands. Offering custom designed dive packages: "You tell us what you want to do and how much you want to spend and we'll do our best to put the package together for you and make all your arrangements." By 1976 the superboat Hawaiian cruise package was offered for three, seven, ten or fourteen day trips on the Spirit of Adventure. The 87 foot all aluminum "Super" cruise boat was a precursor of the future liveaboards with plush live-in accommodations, air conditioned staterooms, complete with piped in music and oversized beds. Add to that gourmet cooking, complimentary wines, salad and coffee bars included in the fare. Rates: Three nights $299 per person. One week $595 per person. Ten days $885.00 per person. Two weeks $1175 per person. All rates were plus air fare.

John Gaffney tried to field a fleet of dive boats, working out deals with boat owners to fly the Club Aquarius Flag, a membership club for divers who would have access to not so luxurious liveaboards and resorts under the aegis of NASDS and its 300 store/schools. Gaffney tried to turn the store/schools into full service travel agencies and the idea was a good one. But NASDS had battles going on a number of fronts and not all of the member schools wanted to be tied down to exclusive places nor were some of them capable of handling a different and more complex facet to their diving businesses. It was a $25 dues and $20 per year renewal for privilege of buying your dive travel through NASDS.

Pacific Sportdivers of Long Beach, California, was offering "Dive Cruising" in the mid 1980's to just about everywhere - from Micronesia to Red Sea to Cozumel and Bahamas. Fourteen days deluxe was $2595 on an average exclusive of air fare.

THE DANCER FLEET

Peter Hughes claimed a lot of firsts over his diving career, finally developing the Dancer Series of diving liveaboards. Hughes grew up in Bonaire and bounced around developing various dive operations from shops to resorts to charter boats. His motto seemed to be "no two dives are ever the same". He was in Bahamas, Caymans and Honduras and in particular got vast experience at the well-known Anthony's Key, Roatan. He built up the Bonaire dive shop, sold it, and went to work for the buyer, DIVI resort properties.

In 1986 Peter Hughes launched the Wind Dancer for DIVI. After fulfilling a five-year-contract with DIVI, Hughes bought the ailing Sea Dancer in 1990 from the company. Hughes knew that luxury was the key to the liveaboard business. He looked to the cruise ships and he refurbished every Dancer liveaboard in grand style, carpeting and wood panelling throughout. By 1994, he had added the Sun Dancer, then Wind Dancer in 1995, Sun Dancer II by 1996, and the Star Dancer in 1997.

All of the ships were conversions costing $800,000 up to $3.5 million by 1997. The bare bones dive charter boats had been left far behind in the Hughes approach. China dinner settings, instead of plastic, and coffee delivered to the cabins in the morning. He put in free Nitrox for diver safety and not for longer time down. He believed future Dancers would have to be built from scratch and the Galapagos Islands beckon him for the new century.

Hughes takes credit for putting moorings at diving sites for the Dancers to protect the reefs (just as Captain Don Stewart installed for the Bonaire resort dive sites in the 1960's). His guests never have to wait for an air fill. He has a 15 foot hang bar under the exit platform for the recommended safety stop. The last night on board, guests get to see themselves diving on video. Guest divers get quail and wine for dinner and bed turn-down service with a mint on their pillows. Onboard are specialty instructors who can certify guest divers. Oh yeah, there were hairdryers in the cabins.

CALIFORNIA CONVERSIONS

In California, the Channel Islands could be liveaboard- dived on three luxury boats operated by Roy Hauser's Truth Aquatics, Inc. The first boat, Truth, was custom-built and launched in April 1974. The official concessionaire of the Channel Islands National Park has all of the expected amenities from wet suit drying room to good reading lights on all berths.

It featured "No Wait For Air" with two air compressors that filled two standard single tanks every 3 1/2 minutes, flush deck side and flush bow exits for easy entry and a completely waterproof galley, allowing divers to come in and warm up between dives. They operated year-around during the 1990's.

The Truth was launched in 1974.

NOTHING TO DO BUT DIVE AND DIVE

The liveaboards were devoted to dive, dive, dive through the 1990's. Five dives everyday was the pattern and divers were given freedom to determine their own limitations. Those, who didn't have dive-computers or didn't do their own table calculations, often got into decompression trouble, especially, when they depended on some cursory directions from onboard divemasters. Divers seem unending in their wants for more and more luxuries. There will be state of the art dive-computers available and probably more entertainment. Some liveaboards were hiring crews that doubled as entertainers similar to cruise ships.

THE AGGRESSOR FLEET ULTIMATE

The final word in liveaboards by the end of the 50 year history of sport diving goes to the Aggressor Fleet. It represents the epitome of what might be called fantasy diving. The liveaboard diving of year 2000 would certainly have been a fantasy of most of the divers in the preceding decades.

By the end of the Twentieth Century, the Aggressor Fleet had thirteen luxury liveaboards. They were operating in Bay Islands, Belize, Caymans, Fiji, Galapagos, Kona, Okeanos, Palau, Red Sea, Solomons, Truk Lagoon, the Turks and Caicos. Like children of the modern age choosing Disneyland over the neighborhood playground of swings and slides, the modern diver now looks to the liveaboard experience that the Aggressor Fleet provides. It has discounts for divers over 65 years old. There is equipment loans as standard operating procedure on all boats if equipment breaks or is lost in travel enroute to their destination - regulators, computers, cameras, the works. There have been celebrity cruises year round with emphasis on top underwater photographers, such as, Stan Waterman and Jim Church. An example of a celebrity cruise would be on the Truk Aggressor II with photo courses involving both Jim Church and Stan Waterman for seven days in the Solomon Islands for $3095. Other cruises put divers on board with Jean-Michel Cousteau. There are Atlantic I rebreathers and rebreather certification, Nitrox, air conditioning and photo processing. Often there are movie and television stars on board, such as, David Hasselhoff on the Truk Aggressor II in 1998 working on his NAUI Advanced Wreck Diver Specialty certification.

The Aggressor state of the art marketing has CD Roms and videos that cover all their liveaboard dive areas. They pitched going to the last pristine areas in the undersea world. It invited divers to come and be pampered with high-staff-ratio to a "load" of twelve passengers. The Aggressor Fleet enjoys the 60% of business being repeat divers in keeping with the overall trend of the liveaboard industry.

UNEXSO HAD LIVEABOARD IN MIND

Here are some other attempts at creating the ultimate dive experience by taking the resort idea to sea. In 1967 according to Al Tillman, founder of UNEXSO, the company was ready to expand to a new location, part of a long-term plan to place Underwater Explorer Clubs around the world. The best idea at the time was to work with Pablo Bush Romero who was developing the Akumal Dive Resort in Yucatan.

But the foreign country politics were a real burden. Tillman tells how in Freeport, Bahamas, the police would commandeer the Club's diving boats to chase down some whim. Dodging that high-handed coercion meant hiding the gas supply or disconnecting a wire. The government tended to force hiring of unqualified locals. It meant at times hiring several Bahamians to sit around and watch one illegal Haitian refugee do all the maintenance of the Club.

The idea at the time was that, when the politics and interference got too much, a liveaboard could be moved to another place, another country to avoid such conflicts.

LIKE GOING TO CAMP

Divers prone to seasickness may find a 24-hour-day at sea for a week could mean no diving at all ...so much is dependent on the weather with a boat. The liveaboard gets itself in isolated, unsheltered venues and can find itself on the edge or in a typhoon or hurricane. But even in the worse conditions and perhaps because of it, the people on board the liveaboard are drawn close into a family more than in any other situation. It is a lot like going to camp where participants cry when its over and they have to leave each other - after only a week or two. Nothing like wetting your beds together for deep bonding.

Dr. Joe MacInnes, perhaps Canada's foremost pioneer diver, told Scuba America about an early liveaboard trip put together by dive travel developer, Dewey Bergman, off the Gulf of California. A fierce storm dropped on them without forewarning, a near hurricane, and the divers and crew huddled together expecting to sink any minute. But they weathered the night, sharing intimacies and praying and saw the sun come up for a new day. Joe said it left a deep feeling of the fragility of life and a special fondness for those who shared it with you. In the spirit of the Titanic and other near disasters, people tend to want to capture that remembered closeness and set up anniversary reunions. That's what happened in Joe MacInnes' case and sometimes it did with a liveaboard experience even without a storm.

THE FIRST LIVEABOARD - THE MARISLA

There will always be controversy about which was the first recognized liveaboard dive boat. Scuba America in interviewing divers, who were involved in the 50 year history, seemed to favor Dick Adcock, who had a not-so-luxurious liveaboard dive boat. Zale Parry remembers taking the opportunity to dive in another world in May 1968 off the Marisla with an invitation from Sue and Clint Degn to join them. Included on board would be: Millie and Colonel John Craig, Carol and Ron Merker, Pete Petersen, Mike Graf, Lynn and Keith Chase, Dr. Omer and Pat Nielson, Audrey and Chuck Rockwell, and 8 year old Margaret Bivens, Zale's daughter.

It was exciting but a lot of trouble. Have you ever wanted to take a child out of the U.S. to go to Mexico the legal way? Oh, dear, it took two seals of approval, a notarized letter and a health certificate. The group flew on a wing and a prayer on Aeronaves De Mexico to La Paz, Baja California. On afternoon arrival, Mary Lou and Dick Adcock met the group at the airport to help slip through Customs for the ride to the beachhead where the liveaboard was tied to their dock. At first glance, this floating house looked very much like a enormous shoe box with square holes cut on the sides. It was painted Spanish pink and a ladder to the top deck outlined in bright white. Immaculate. The upperdeck measured almost the size of the hull. Here was a large open area for all the entertainment and where regular-time meals took place. The uncanopied design of the foreword upperdeck had the lounge chairs for sunbathing or reading during the day, movies and star gazing at night. At the center of the deck was the wheelhouse with a slot machine and wet bar on the backside of it. From the center to stern, the upperdeck was totally covered by a roof that protected a long picnic table used for meals and camera preparation. Roll-down screens shaded the table from the sun's direct hit during parts of the day. Nearby, a sturdy barbecue stood on the port side. The hospitality and courtesies were outstanding. This early liveaboard was indeed a role model for what was to come.

We assembled as a family on the upper foredeck for the formal welcome and explanation of diving rules. Margueritas and hors d'oevres were served while Henry Mancini's music filled the air. Mancini and his group were guests the week before we arrived and left tapes.

In the 1950's Dick Adcock left his position as a bank executive in Los Angles and established La Paz Skin Diving Service, Mexico's Sea of Cortez cruises in 1956. The Marisla was a 60 foot by 20 foot floating liveaboard. Powered by two GMC diesel engines with 225 HP each. The pamphlet read, "7 knots", but Zale's recollection was that it went much faster when on the waves going down wind. The lighting was very ample, a 12 volt system plus 110 volt 60 cycle outlets for your own shaver, recorders or hairdryer. The staterooms were 8 foot x 8 foot double or single bunks. The bathrooms were shared with the connecting room. There was a washstand with fresh water and flushing toilets, and a hot and cold fresh water shower, too.

A former U.S. Navy LCPR (Landing Craft) towed by the Marisla was the dive boat. The front of the LCPR dropped open into a ramp for easy access in and out of the water. On board were an air compressor for refills, tanks and weight belts. We brought our own regulators, mask, snorkel and fins. The dive boat crew-of-two had every piece of equipment attached and lined up for us. By the second day, they knew who belonged to what and helped us into our gear. We walked off the ramp, stuck our head underwater and went diving. Another boat in tow was a 16 foot Glasspar water ski boat powered by an outboard motor. An easy lift to lower two smaller skiffs with outboard that were used for fishing or going to shore for non-divers.

Spearfishing, photography and eating were the games of the day. Breakfast at 7:30 a.m., two dives, lunch at 12:00 noon. A one hour siesta was required. Nothing happened. At 1:30 p.m. we were back in the water for two dives. Dinner was at 7:00 p.m. After the last dive of the day, we had plenty of time to shower and get dressed for the evening. John Craig remarked about fancy hairstyles created by Sue Degn, "You'd think the women were going to the opera." Night dives were divers' choice if we were not traveling in the dusk of day.

Mary Lou did all of the gourmet cooking. International cuisine, the best steaks, roasts, seafood with a beautiful presentation.

Trolling for billfish or skeet shooting, as we traveled through the Gulf of California, diving in the largest natural aquarium, the Las Animas pinnacles, photographing the big fish, sharks, the colorful reef fish, hiking an island to visit 1697 mission grounds, clamming in shallow water with bare feet for delicious pinna clams for seafood cocktail, night dives for rare seashells, having only to brush your own teeth, hold your own drink and being with competent divemaster/owners bonded all of us together forever.

In 1969, Dick Adcock replaced the "shoe box" with a 121 foot former U.S. Coast Guard buoy tender. This fancy liveaboard became the Marisla II.

More recently there are adventures on the high seas on Northeast liveaboards. They may not be spacious or lavish as their Caribbean counterparts but are well-equipped, are quite comfortable, designed to travel longer distances, and are prepared to handle a variety of ocean/weather conditions.

Captain Howard Klein of the 53 foot Eagle's Nest in Freeport, New York, and Captain Steve Bielenda of the 55 foot Research Vessel Wahoo in Captree, Long Island, operate their vessels for the joy of wreck divers, especially, those interested in historic war ships and submarines. Both captains are highly qualified for their sea credentials and multi-agency scuba certifications. The Eagle's Nest caters to the divers who wish to explore a wreck from 10 feet down to the Texas Tower at 190 feet, while the Wahoo includes an annual expedition to the legendary Andrea Doria which sank in 1956. These liveaboards offer another dimension to the diver's seasoning and usually attract the hardier, experienced person.

The Agressor Company has a large fleet and does extensive marketing.

THE BAD AND THE BEAUTIFUL

The liveaboard arrived on the diving scene full bore in the 1980's and 1990's with all the luxury of the grand resorts and cruise ships. They enabled divers to go beyond the diminishing resources of local diving areas and the stationary dive resort, and search out unpolluted virgin dive places.

By 1993 most dive travel advisors were touting Liveaboards over dive resort boats. The resort boats were having divers spend more time in boats than in the water. Following the recession in 1991-1992 divers were able to afford the $600-$800 weekly rates in Cozumel and Honduras as opposed to the upscaled rates in the Caymans.

Undercurrent, a watchdog publication put out a "Divers Speak Out" review of reports on dive operations from their readers. While Liveaboards were generally recommended, some terrible, horrible, very bad experiences were encountered. One young lady diver had three days of faulty rental equipment, leaky BC, no camera table or fresh water rinse and the crew handled photography gear like a toy. Divemasters and crew were rude, no lookout assigned on deck, long surface swims and strangers of the opposite sex had to share a cabin. But the food was good!

Other reflections that pointed up both the negatives and positives:

• Hey, this is diving, diving, diving and food, food, food. The only responsibility you have is to dive safely. Worth every penny.

• Great night dive on a wall; 60 minutes of critters. Tasty desserts afterwards. Captain told great shark stories.

• Traveled alone, couldn't find anyone compatible to dive with so crew said they recommend not diving alone but if you insist ...I did five or six solo dives a day, down the wall, complete freedom, no looking around for a buddy, no hurry, no worry about air consumption.

• Diving unsupervised, snotty crew, worked only with favorites, and dumped sewage where we were diving.

• Computers pushed over tables, fresh-baked bread and cookies, warm towels after night dive. Treated like royalty.

The old pioneer divers, who curled up in a sleeping bag on a clammy beach in order to travel and dive some new place, look at the end of an era modern liveaboards, shake their heads and walk off muttering, "...a mint on your satin pillow at night?"

Dreams did come true but at a price.

22

Diving Resorts:
Every Man a King and
Every Woman a Queen

Defining Event: Underwater Explorers Society

America by the late 1950's was in the mood to break the monotony of every day life. Divers, especially, were looking at the horizon and envisioning clear, warm, virgin waters. Local diving holes had gotten mundane and over explored. It was time to load up and go to the Keys or Mexico or the islands just off shore.

Here and there were resorts that featured the new diving thing as an exotic programmed activity. Resorts have always been a concept back to the Romans. A place where the cares and worries of jobs, bills and other obligations are left behind, to frolic at a special place set up to cater to the guest visitor, treat him/her like royalty. 24 hours a day; the resort goer would live for fun and exciting experiences, not make their beds or have to fix their food. They could try an activity out at a resort or in the case of experienced divers, jump into excellent water to fulfill their fantasies. There were activities for everybody of course: swimming, boating, fishing and much more. But diving was especially blessed to have resorts in superior water locations, abundant with coral reefs and multitudes of marine life, places where few divers had been before.

The resort lodgings that offered diving, as a key feature, were often a local beach boy who had the diving concession. A first contact with this superficial diving service was observed over a week period by Paul Tzimoulis and Al Tillman during the preliminary investigations for creating the Underwater Explorers Club (UNEXSO) at Freeport on Grand Bahama Island. The beach boy at the Lucayan Hotel there in 1964 was a hustling smiling charmer named Jimmy. It was strictly a snorkeling experience he offered, thank the Gods, for all Jimmy did was stick some gear on overweight, out-of-shape tourists and point them in the direction of the breaking surf. "Out there," he said, bypassing any tryouts in the pool that he "lifeguarded". The poor would-be-divers tumbled into the swirling surf, clutched at their masks and snorkels and filled their swim togs with sand. "So that's diving! Well, I've done that," spit out most of the returning tourists, often missing a fin or a snorkel for which Jimmy would have to bill them and they'd pay in their embarrassment, blaming themselves.

All along the resort hotel belts in the Bahamas, Miami, Hawaii, Mexico and elsewhere of lesser fame at the time, similar affronts were being enacted. Some of those people never tried diving again.

On the other hand, there were conscientious, high quality resort diving offerings. Gardiner Young and Stanton A. Waterman in the Bahamas were highly regarded tourist diving services in the late 1950's and early 1960's. They did teach people enough to create an enjoyable and relatively safe experience. Bob Soto was doing the same in the Caymans and scuba was becoming the primary interest exceeding snorkeling. Down in Mexico the Arnold brothers were doing a reputable job of guiding at Acapulco. Good divers and certified instructors were leaving home to establish high calibre dive operations in faraway paradises often forcing local populations involved in servicing tourists with diving to "clean up their acts". Bob Retherford and Ken Taylor, two outstanding dive leaders out of Southern California went to Hawaii and then Micronesia. Roy Damron, Reni Phillips, Roy Calcote and Denis Kirwan established their diving instruction in Hawaii to please the tourists as well as the locals. All of this time that diving was offered as one of the recreations at resorts, the concept of the diving resort was fermenting in several minds at once.

The 1960's ushered in the jet age. The fast jets allowed people, and divers, to go to far off places without taking weeks out of their lives to do so. As landing strips were built in the wilds, on islands and shorelines never easily and quickly reached before, tourists with deep pockets of disposable income arrived. Divers saved up, sometimes through special "Christmas plans" developed by the banks and bought the expensive airplane ticket for their traditional once-a-year vacation. After spending so much to travel, they weren't about to scrimp on the things to do there. Those 1960's traveling divers were primarily professional people, doctors, lawyers, dentists and wealthy business people. Not necessarily the rich who could buy the island, buy the airplane, but instead a sort of upper middle class.

America of the 1950's and 1960's was a place where the middle class was invented, while before then, there was only the poor and the rich. By middle class, we are identifying it as people coming out of the Depression of the 1930's and World II of the 1940's with more than enough money to just survive; by this era they had disposable income, a chance to buy the leisure consumer goods rapidly being created, especially those adult toys of adventure.

America was deep into the cold war with Russia, racing to control outer space, get to the moon (which we did in 1969), recognize and resent a new youth counter-culture challenging the idealized traditional family oriented culture of the adults. And, we were at war, a very unpopular war in Vietnam disguised by the government as assistance to people to stay free from Communism. It was a turmoil people tried to escape from, those who could afford to. The Beatles, couldn't sing it away; the civil rights marches, burn-baby-burn riots in the big cities, bra burning feminists just heaped anxiety upon two-job families. They took the prosperity of the times and went to exotic places with fancy resorts. Some of these resorts were embryo diving resorts where the major theme and activity was going underwater. They were where divers escaped to and went scuba diving until they were saturated with nitrogen every day and then went back in at night and talked about diving the rest of the time.

The Club Med (as in Mediterranean) generated waves of prime attention because it represented the sensual and sexy nature of the times. You could romp on the beach, nude if you chose, and not be taken for a hippie or psychedelic druggie. And, you could dive, oh, could you dive, learn to on the spot and try it with pretty, charming activity directors. They were your hosts and hostesses, sports instructors, tour guides, entertainers and trained child minders as the Club Med called them.

The Club Med eventually expanded its entry level diving offering to include Specialty Diving, Advanced Deep Diving. Some of the Club Med Resorts worked with CMAS (Confederacion Mondiale des Activites Subaquatiques) and PADI (Professional Association of Diving Instructors) on their diving programs. But *Scuba America* never turned up any Club Med ads in diving magazines.

Club Med rose to a series of prominent resort destinations around the world from being the Mediterranean humane recovery camps in thatched huts for refugees from World War II. By 1960's the plan was to put money in a fund and the bill for everything would be paid in advance. You wore a bikini, made famous by Club Med, and with no pockets had to wear a necklace of snap-together plastic beads, the currency, if you wanted to buy a drink, the only item the visitors had to pay for. Dive at no extra charge to your heart's content. Today the bead- system has disappeared in their nirvana vacation plan.

Jim Christiansen came back from a 1950's World Championship Spearfishing meet and said about one of the Club Med Resorts the team went to: "...that's a really fun place, they'd play games, blindfolded with tin buckets like a bunch of kids and they made diving an easy thing, a fun thing, and maybe they're doing a better job than we are, we're too serious and scaring people." He was close on the track of what many of industry leaders were beginning to think, led by NASDS, John Gaffney, and the Brauer Brothers (Donald and George) of Ski 'N Dive, who wanted diving to be fun, a party. A lot of diving instructors were hammering away at the diving diseases and physics with a kind of military drill mentality. We'll teach you but you'd better not smile.

SMALL HOPE BAY LODGE

Was there a first pure 'diving is our business resort'? *Scuba America* believes that Dick Birch's Small Hope Bay Lodge in the Bahamas at Andros Island was the first identifiable one. The Lodge was built in 1959 by Birch a former Canadian and started entertaining their first patrons in 1960. It's rustic facilities, not far different from the Club Med's earliest set ups, sat on the edge of one of the world's finest dive locations, with plenty of coral reefs, fish and the plunging sea wall dropping sharply into the Tongue of the Ocean Abyss. Wall Diving and Blue Hole Diving began here in 1960, remarks son, Jeff Birch, who added that Small Hope Lodge Diving Resort is the world's oldest, built and owned-consistently by his family, dedicated to diving entertainment.

In 1960, at the Houston NAUI Course, a devoted diving instructor candidate out of Toronto, Canada, Herb Ingraham, couldn't say enough about Small Hope Bay, that you hadn't really been diving, knew what great diving could be until you went there, a virtual diving Shangrila. The staff remembers young David Doubilet coming by UNEXSO, the premiere full service diving resort, in the mid 1960's and giving his comparative evaluation: "...nice place, nice reefs, but Birch's has real atmosphere for serious divers, and superior diving geology to anywhere else." We're not sure David would change his concept 35 years later after he'd been diving everywhere making masterpiece photographs for *National Geographic Magazine*.

UNEXSO

That leads us to describe what UNEXSO really was and why this chapter recognizes it as a major influencing event for sport diving. Ahead of its time, avant of the great resort and travel boom of the 1970's, it was the pro-

UNEXSO provided diving and training opportunities for all skill levels.

Sports Illustrated

totype of what the ultimate diving resort could be.

It all came about because three Canadian businessmen were moving assets to Grand Bahama Island to take advantage of tax breaks of a free port area called, what else, Freeport. They were moving fast to avoid heavy new corporation taxes being levied by Canada. The three: Bill MacInnes, a stock broker; Frank Stream, a theatre magnet and popcorn king; and Sam Shevsky, a tire manufacturer, were seductive and enterprising entrepreneurs.

Frank Stream had a cousin, Art Arthur, who was a producer and key writer for Ivan Tors television show *Sea Hunt*. Stream and partners had a holding company licensed by the Port Authority in the Bahamas, which operated without competition: a lumber yard, bakery, supermarket, sit-down and drive-in theatres, and a hotel among about thirty other businesses. They were approached by a couple of Canadian divers living there, who wanted to setup a wet suit manufacturing company. They also suggested a diving operation to cater to tourists. This was in 1961 when *Sea Hunt* was exploding interest in the new sport of scuba diving. Stream, thinking of his cousin, wondered if a Sea Hunt Village could be created, a diving resort to take advantage of would be Mike Nelsons, the fictional star of *Sea Hunt* played by Lloyd Bridges.

When Art Arthur was contacted, he referred Stream to Al Tillman, who at the time, 1962, represented leadership in instructional programs, film festivals, was public affairs director for *Skin Diver Magazine*, as well as, technical advisor on *Sea Hunt*. Tillman felt using *Sea Hunt*, as a lure to get divers to go to Grand Bahama Island would be a quick fix but down the line would not sustain a real diving resort. So Stream and partners told Tillman to dream up, Carte Blanche, what would work. Tillman already had a longtime dream - a place that would have everything a civilian private sport diver would want at a prime diving region and glamorous enough to draw movie stars, monarchs, astronauts and famous divers, which it ultimately did. The Pioneer Bahamas, Ltd. did not put a price limit on the dream, they wanted a resort that would transcend anything so far offered as a diving resort.

Tillman's idea was to have the finest diving facility possible, that anyone could come to and be king or queen for a day, a diving king or diving queen. It would be a membership organization, the kind James Bond would want to join but no elitism, the average working stiff could afford it. It would fulfill what diving was really all about in the early years - exploration and discovery. The name of the organization would be International Underwater Explorers Society and the Bahamas facility would be called the Grand Bahama Underwater Explorers Club, the first in a series of such clubs planned in other exotic diving places in the world.

This was not to be a roughing it on the beach in huts, as Club Med started out with and maintained as a low cost "resort experience" for its first couple of decades of existence. Ultimately, the title UNEXSO was coined as an acronym and encompassed both the facility and the membership society.

In 1963, Al Tillman was invited over to Grand Bahama Island by the pioneer partners to see what the island was like after he'd just directed a Miami NAUI Underwater Instructors Certification course. Until Stream had come to see him in Los Angeles, he had never even knew there was a Grand Bahama Island. He looked at three choice pieces of land where UNEXSO would be given one site at no charge from the Port Authority.

The general implication was that this would be a lure attraction for getting worldwide publicity and not intended to be a profit machine. Down the line there would be some dissension among the owners as to that interpretation and Al Tillman, as a 50% owner of UNEXSO (for his ideas, design of the facility, programming and use of his influence in the sport diving field) would have to argue the point with his partners over the four years of his involvement.

UNEXSO was closely tied in with the building and operation of a new hotel called Oceanus and new money was brought in primarily from the Power Corporation of Canada. The separation of the Club from the hotel would be a contentious point for a long time.

Al Tillman was expected to promote membership in UNEXSO in the two years leading up to its opening. The dream really seemed like a dream and Al Tillman couldn't believe it when the concrete was being poured and his ideas became a physical presence.

One thing Tillman knew was that this was a resort like no one had ever seen or operated before. It was a scary challenge and Al knew that it would work if he could get the very best versatile divers as staff. While he was introducing UNEXSO to the diving world, there had to be good people down there putting the physical property in working order.

At that point in 1964, Tillman had crossed paths with the very best people in the diving field from his *Skin Diver Magazine*, Los Angeles County, International Underwater Film Festival and NAUI contacts. In fact, his intention was that UNEXSO would become the NAUI world headquarters without cost to NAUI (but politics directed against it).

Picking the staff was the big challenge. Tillman set up a grid of twenty desirable traits or talents assigning them values in descending order of importance: outstanding diver, NAUI quality instructor, physically attractive and fit, people oriented, photographic ability, honesty and integrity, careful and safe, mature-age 28 to 40, family oriented, diving equipment repair ability, boats and outboards knowledge, neat and orderly and writing/promotional ability. Knowing the territory, the local diving conditions, wasn't on the list because learning the reefs and water doesn't take long; plenty of mediocre divers with beach boy mentalities were around in the Florida/Bahamas area but scored low on the vital aspects. A list of about twenty divers came up high in scoring.

At the very top was Paul Tzimoulis, a sales representative for Sportsways, who was smart, ambitious and had a comprehensive background although only 28 years of age. Tillman praised Tzimoulis at *Skin Diver Magazine*/ Petersen Publishing Offices, where NAUI and the International Underwater Film Festival were headquartered. Paul's writing and photography had been making an impression there for several years. Tillman would have liked Paul Tzimoulis to manage the Underwater Explorers Club but *SDM* snatched him up to replace Jim Auxier, as Editor and eventually, Publisher and a Vice President in Petersen Publishing. UNEXSO was an untried experiment in diving and Tzimoulis chose right to go with an established business.

High on the list was Dave Woodward, who had helped Tillman direct a number of NAUI instructors' courses and they had a close respectful relationship. Woodward was a fine diver and instructor, ran a dive shop and school in

The professional staff at UNEXSO consisted of Guide Ben Rose, Al Tillman, UNEXSO Ambassador Lloyd Bridges, Dave Woodward, Jack McKenney and Chuck Peterson.

Spokane, Washington. Dave was an all-round good person. He was available to uproot his family and move to the Bahamas, as was Chuck Peterson and Jack McKenney. The three would represent a high level staffing backed up by some locals in Freeport.

Tillman felt he could oversee UNEXSO, the club in the Bahamas, and promote the membership with a world-wide chain of clubs from Los Angeles, where he was a Professor of Leisure Studies at California State University at Los Angeles. The breakdown came early as the staff of Dave, Chuck, and Jack really had no background running a resort and they were "available" because they were ready to run away from some personal problems in their lives where they lived.

Unfortunately, the Club opened without the kind of leadership needed. The staff wasn't paid enough and had no participating incentive in the Club, as Tillman had as an owner. What the staff decided they had were a lot of perks and the Club operated as a kind of personal country club for them and their families for six months.

Al Tillman takes the brunt of blame for those first six months which proved to be an expensive operation with a soaring deficit. Tillman tried to keep up with what was going on by taped communication and a few quick trips to Freeport. It just didn't work. Tillman's Canadian partners finally came to him and said the Club was proving to be a bad business investment, a different look from the idea the Club would be a loss-leader attraction along the lines of the Statue of Liberty or Great American Mall. "Tillman, you have to get down here and run this place or we're going to close it," said the partners. Al took a two year leave from the University, turned NAUI over to others, got LeRoy French to help Zale Parry, produce the International Underwater Film Festival and moved there in June of 1965.

The Underwater Explorers Club was posh. It had facilities that surpassed what most people had available in the big cities back home. There was a complete color photo lab, a marine biology lab, a crafts center, a diving museum, research library, elegant lounge with bar, health spa with workout equipment and saunas, swimming pool and a deep 18 foot scuba training pool with viewing windows and much more - a glamorous country club theme around diving. The motto was "Where Great Diving is a Way of Life".

Beyond the Club lay multiple series of reefs, creatures galore, warm, clear water and the ledge which dropped off into the Tongue of the Ocean Abyss. There were also lush gambling casinos, bazaar shopping, skeet shooting, yachting, golf, the works. The Island itself was an ugly flat island with scrubby pine trees until Wallace Groves, a wheeler-dealer, discovered a lens of fresh water down in the limestone just under the surface. During the 1960's Freeport, Grand Bahamas, exploded onto the resort scene outshining its older famous counterpart a few miles across the water, Nassau on New Providence Island. With Cuba closed down with arrival of Castro, the Bahamas beckoned the tourists. For divers disgusted with the growing tackiness of the Florida Keys, the new place was close enough to switch their vacation venues to it.

UNEXSO offered everything a diver could want and treated everybody like family. A diver could try 6 foot deep snorkeling for the first time or advanced divers could work their way down to the ultimate dive of the era, 250 feet on compressed air. It took some turning around, time and motion efficiency studies, tightening the loose bolts of budget and pricing, but the Club righted itself and became fiscally feasible the end of 1965. The staff lost some privileges to accommodate - no more taking a boat and equipment for families on a day off when Club was peak-loaded with members and tourists. No more taking out the Club's prime customers on a friendship basis, no charge, on days off and more or less giving away the business. No more creating personality cults where customers wouldn't go out with anyone but their favorite guide. No more spending the day in the photo lab developing personal film and letting the less attractive chores slide. Tillman found that part of failure in first six months was poor economics, taking a trip out with one customer and two staff members on long jaunts down the island. Trips had to be run with at least three customers to break even and executed to, from, and recycled for next trip within a two hour period.

The staff under the new, efficient system felt a little put upon but they were pros and no one will ever surpass them in taking care of client divers. They were safe, careful and never lost a diver. Al Tillman became less a friend in their eyes, more of an arrogant, ungenerous boss. But UNEXSO over the next two years was diving's Camelot. Divers would come there and be awed and want to work for free, just to be there, hang around. The clientele was made up of movie stars and high level executive types and what the place was really designed for, the average middle class diver, who didn't have clear, warm water at home, nor so much marine life, or much of the glamor the complex of the facilities exuded.

A St. Louis, Missouri, doctor and his family could show up, join, all learn diving, go shallow or deep three times a day with expert diver-guides, explore treasure wreck remains, hand-feed fish, collect specimens, take pictures underwater and have a slide show of them in the evening in the Club's recreation room. Fish tales were swapped over billiard tables and the next day's dives planned after looking at the chalkboard specials listed in the entryway: Papa Doc Wreck, fish feeding, 100 foot ledge dive, Zoo Hole, or the all day picnic dive to Peterson Cay where all the movies were made.

You could join the Seven Mile Club and have your name put up on a plate besides Jacques Cousteau's, Woodward's, McKenney's, Tillman's, if you made enough dives, logged them with UNEXSO, that added up to seven miles underwater. There was Marty's Model Agency operating on UNEXSO premises where you could rent a diving beauty to go out with you on a photo-shoot or you could borrow a turtle or grouper to take on a dive from the holding pen next to the docks. Spearfishing was not allowed on trips but special runs to get a trophy could be booked to go out of the usual diving area. Take pictures was the push. If you got a trophy fish, you could avoid the big fee of having it stuffed over in Miami and instead participate in UNEXSO's craft speciality, fish printing, where your trophy fish would be inked onto imported rice paper and framed much in the manner of ancient Japanese fishermen did recording their exotic catches while long at sea.

DIVING WITH CELEBRITIES EVERY DAY

Your trip out to dive could well have been with a group of Astronauts, Lloyd Bridges and his family, a team of *National Geographic* photographers, Miss America Contestants with Jack McKenney, as your guide. If you wanted a set of slide pictures taken while diving, a guide, like Chuck Peterson, would show you how to gently lift a triggerfish from its hiding place and pet it, and be sure you had a full roll of award winning pictures developed and ready for you that evening, or at least the next day.

Dave Woodward might take you to a secret reef where you could take a prize coral specimen, where it wouldn't show and bring it back to biology lab, identify it, treat it and have it in a box of preserved specimens and sunken ship square nails to take on home.

Al Tillman might be taking you out with an intern guide, or a top guide from Mexico learning how UNEXSO did it, help you locate conchs, bring them in, clean them with you so you'd have shells to take home, - and conch chowder, if you'd charm the hotel cook.

UNEXSO had the best of equipment and kept it in top condition, the staff under Dave Woodward having become expert repairmen. The SOS Decompression Meter was used at UNEXSO, the first computer and the Octopus double-air-supply setup was used on the dives,

Walter Cronkite, Dave Darrow and Al Tillman at UNEXSO.

credit Dave Woodward for that.

You could have been included on dives that went out to film movies and commercials or have been part of some important diving experiments. Prince Rainier could have been sitting next to you on a dive that looked on while Orson Wells filmed the nude European version of a film that required diving; or watch Jordan Klein lie on his back on the coral and film a Kotex Commercial.

Chuck Peterson was the top inventive member of the staff, (He made the first pressure cooker camera case.) and figured out how to create neutral buoyancy for a Sealy Mattress for a naked lady to lie on, and you, as a visiting UNEXSO member, could have been shoulder-to-shoulder with Chuck as he put it together at Peterson Cay. Chuck was quick figuring how to suspend the mattress half way down but he took a long time teaching the nude model how to hold her breath, swim down, look comfortable and happy resting on the mattress.

UNEXSO was always scouting for special diving places off shore that could be reached quickly and even offered rewards to members who discovered and reported any that became one of the Clubs menu-trips. (Incidentally, the two-hour dive trip in a luxury Evinrude with all gear was only $17.50 in 1965.)

Orson Wells and Al Tillman going out for a dive on the Ama.

When Dave Woodward and Al Tillman scouted good dive locations before the Club opened, they accidentally found a huge stand of pillar coral (which UNEXSO claimed was the largest in the world, taking license, since nobody had come up with anything to beat it) and they shot pictures of a beautiful Queen Angel Fish, orange and astro-blue, nesting in it. Dave's slide won a lot of contests and Al's, because it was vertical, got the January 1963 cover of *Skin Diver Magazine*. Tillman made dives alone to the spot and used a hand mirror sitting on the pillar coral to include himself using the camera. He discovered looking at the slides, large "logs" hanging suspended behind him that he hadn't noticed on the dive and so he realized his first encounter with the giant barracudas of the Bahamas.

Wernher von Braun and family at UNEXSO.

The pillar castle of coral wasn't found for over a year until a member rediscovered it and got his $50.00 bounty; the mirror a bit encrusted had grown into the coral and many small fish were psycho from trying to make contact with their counterpart reflections.

UNEXSO supported numerous experiments and testing while allowing the members to participate, too. They tested new kinds of paint underwater, diving regulators and gauges, rods for divining gold, diving systems like the Cryolung, propulsion vehicles and staged a successful record breaking free dive by Jacque Mayol. UNEXSO supported Ed Link's SPID City Habitation Program which brought Walter Cronkite, Werner Von Braun, Jon Lindbergh, Robert Stenuit and more altogether at the Club. Later on in the 1970's when John Englander, who had been a teenage member at the Club, came on board to manage UNEXSO, the swim-with-dolphin-program was initiated that had been in the original plans for the Club. John got a ship, Theo, sunk off the Club for an artificial reef and eventually UNEXSO went into the 1990's with the most efficient shark feeding dive trips in the world. Ben Rose, the marine biologist guide, was top gun at managing this dressed in a Ron and Valerie Taylor-type chain mail suit.

Ben Rose is a perfect example of a good island born diver with a native sense of the local marine life, who was nurtured into an excellent guide. Ben was very shy, small in stature, and tended to be more absorbed in the marine life than the clients on a dive. Under the influence of the imported staff of Woodward, Peterson, and McKenney, Ben Rose bloomed and stayed on with UNEXSO right up through the end of the Century.

But the best bet for a top guide was to import great diver-instructors, who already had experience dealing with different kinds of people. Another UNEXSO staff member came on duty early even before UNEXSO's opening knowing the ways of a resort, schmoozing the guests, and knew the islands, a NAUI instructor, and knew how to build boat docks — no one else did. Chuck Hepp was single and free, an island hopper, but he was almost too smooth and tended to be too familiar with the visiting lady divers, a behavior that eventually on occasion erupted in antagonism toward the Club. A resort dive operation can not allow personality cults to develop. Professional usually means impersonal, just do the job. UNEXSO went through an army of instructor guides over the decades but that original staff was a dream team and laid the foundation for a role model, civilized diving resort that would survive for 35 years and is still going into the 21st Century.

The intent was to open other dive resorts under UNEXSO at which the manager/owner positions would go to Dave, Jack, and Chuck. Many things happened: the government changed from Anglo-Saxon English domination to a new black Bahamian rule which caused money to go elsewhere, scared the tourists and resident Anglo population at first, and there was a general recession falling in place in the States. Tillman's partners wanted to sell UNEXSO and move assets to the Caymans. UNEXSO was a successful idea where it was and it had only been in full operation for two years, and most businesses take at least that long to get in the black. There was also the failure of the Port Authority to enforce the license UNEXSO had to operate the only diving business. The big hotels had power and they got their pool boys into the diving business; UNEXSO had to pay off activity directors at the various hotels to get people referred for diving instruction and trips. If you're the only resort diving service in an isolated island location, competition is not one of your problems. But competition kept springing up at Freeport and UNEXSO at one point saw Fred Baldasare bring a huge glass bottom boat in and take people diving on the side. It was an attention getter

Jacques Mayol at UNEXSO following his record deep dive.

with a blonde curvy beauty sitting on the bow, a Miss Bahamas, by the name of Kitty.

Tillman sold out his half ownership to his partners. Dave Woodward stayed on to manage UNEXSO under several new owners, who bought it in the next couple of years; McKenney went on to be Editor of *Skin Diver Magazine* and one of diving's celebrated underwater cinematographers; and Peterson joined the Ed Link project team and the Naval Undersea Center in Hawaii; Al Tillman went back in 1968 to being a college professor, consulting resorts, and introducing the first resort management curriculum into the University.

In 1970, Al Tillman took his expertise to the Philippines and set up South East Asia Underwater Service with Dick Bartlett, Jr. and laid the plans for a China Seas Underwater Explorers Club on the Island of Fuga, which meant converting a former fly-to-retreat brothel into a family diving place. Everything was in place, the most sophisticated gear, a virgin coral reef setting, an island privately owned by one of the partners - when Ferdinand Marcos declared Martial Law and more or less confiscated the Island. Tillman learned more about operating in a foreign county - that you can lose everything on a change of power, or a whim. Businesses paid off "the bite," an annual protection "tax", Marcos expected, usually $50,000, for which the business got a box of cigars with the presidential insignia cigar band on each. *Scuba America* has one of them in its Museum of Diving display.

The early 1970's were a fruitful time for resorts and the travel industry. NAUI ran its first Resort Course for Instructors at the El Conquistador Hotel in Puerto Rico where Walter Hendricks, a top NAUI man, who would later be its training director, operated a diving service. It was typical of such operations where it was a major program offered by a resort hotel but not exclusively so. Joe Vogel was a key NAUI man doing something similar in the Virgin Islands. In 1957, Bob Soto had established his diving company in the Caymans. It's considered the oldest diving company but not consistently owned by same founder as is the Small Hope Lodge. Today legendary Soto's SSI/PADI 5-Star facility is operated by Kathie and Ron Kipp. Captain Don Stewart, owner of Captain Don's Habitat on Bonaire, was the first resort to organize each dive site with permanent buoys for the dive boats to tie on, thus preventing the ocean bottom turning to crumbs from anchors there in the paradise of coral fields. Places available by car like the Florida Keys were not quite as glamorous with old fish camps converted to diving resorts.

HAWAII

In Hawaii, there had been a strong military presence and many Americans got their first exposures to diving as servicemen and women on their time off. Many of the dive shops and instructors in the 1950's and 1960's came out of the military people who got discharged and stayed on. Jack Ackerman is a good example of a diver who pioneered not only the Black Coral Industry but servicing tourists' interest in diving. There was an ever increasing number of dive shops, charter boats, diving activity from a hotel. But a diving resort in Hawaii was established by Reni and Roy Damron high school teachers, who were teaching diving in all major YMCA and YWCA scuba courses. Roy became a 1962 California NAUI Instructor Course graduate and soon after a partner with George Magoon in the first and only true Hawaiian scuba diving resort. It didn't have the tourist trappings of shops, stores, bars, restaurants or night clubs. Kona Dive Lodge/Resort became a name with fame for the years that it lived.

Here is Reni and Roy Damron's brief summary of the Mahai'ula later changed to Kona Dive Lodge:

"George Magoon inherited Mahai'ula after his father (one time legal advisor to the Queen of Hawaii) died in the mid-1960's. It was a 1930's two-story farmhouse-style building along with a two-seater outhouse, slightly salty water system and outdoor shower. Magoon, a scuba diving, boating and underwater photography enthusiast, established Kona Dive Lodge but he needed scuba instructors. At this point, the Damron's were certifying 500 scuba students a year. Magoon contacted the Damron's for a visit to see the Lodge and exchange ideas. It was a two hour-five mile jeep trail-trip one way to or from the Lodge/Resort or Kona Airport."

Roy and Reni began taking local dive groups to the Kona Dive Lodge Resort in 1973. At that time Roy was on the NAUI Board of Directors and when he attended meetings or events showed photos and told of great diving off the Kona Dive Lodge. Word spread rapidly. A steady flow of dive groups, some included Bill High, Jim Hicks, Glen Egstrom, Dewey Bergman. Scuba Instructor and Scuba Assistant Instructor Courses were held at Mahai'ula's Kona Dive Lodge. Soon Naturists, the nudists, heard of a beautiful place, weather, beach, palms and isolation. Clubs and families arrived. Popularity grew and people came from the Mainland, Canada, Europe, Australia and the world knew of Hawaii's first and only sport diving resort.

The brochure for the Kona Dive Lodge/Resort at that time beckoned the nudist scuba divers as "The Paradise of Naturist Vacations...Year Round". A unique vacation at a daily cost of $52.50 or weekly cost of $335.00. Clothing is optional at all times. (Naked scuba divers?)"

In the late 1980's, George Magoon died and the family sold Mahai'ula to the State of Hawaii to become Kona

Coast State Park. Much of the original construction is still there, but the Kona Lodge Diving Resort is history.

THE CARIBBEAN

Sam Davison told *Scuba America* how he broke into Florida with the DACOR Equipment by riding a Greyhound Bus, staying at YMCAs and seeing dive shop/resort people person-to-person. Eventually, he did the same in the Caribbean with Jamaica and Bonaire his favorite spots. They had the beginnings of pure diving resorts by the 1960's and with *Skin Diver Magazine's* shift into high-gear travel coverage in the 1970's solidified the resort offerings in that region. Davison said that he could chart the growth of the resorts through all the islands as the orders for DACOR's scuba started coming in daily. Mexico wasn't far behind.

ANTHONY'S KEY

A popular, pioneer resort, Anthony's Key, established in 1968 is located in Roatan, one of the Bay Islands off the coast of Honduras. Owner, Paul Adams, had about a half dozen rooms in wooden cabanas to accommodate the early-day, traveling sport divers. Adam died in 1976 and his manager, Julio Galindo, became the owner/operator. Julio's son, Samir, talked with Zale Parry over the telephone. She heard his young male voice and asked if perhaps he was just a baby at that time his Dad went into the resort business as proprietor. "That was the year I was born!" he said. Father and son work side-by-side.

Anthony's Key has been around for a long time and beckons anyone who wishes a dream vacation in the middle of a hillside tropical jungle that expands to palm-lined sparkling lagoons. It's a PADI Gold Palm 5 Star Instructor Development Center. A full array of Specialty Courses including NITROX diving are on the menu plus the thrill of diving with dolphins. The Kids Dive Programs are the newest twist in getting children acquainted with the sport of diving. Anthony's Key offers the SASY (Supplied Air Snorkeling Youth) program for children 5 years and up, the Bubble Maker Program for children over 10 years, and the famous Dolphin Discovery Summer Camp for kids 8 years and up.

In 2000, Bob Talbot was there photographing the IMAX film, *Ocean Men*, about the free diving experts. The clear water location has been used many times for television commercials and motion pictures. It's one of the diving resorts that had a recompression chamber and staff to operate it by the year 2000.

John Gaffney got into the diving resort picture in the late 1960's. John had an opportunistic eye and was probably as close to P.T. Barnum as diving has ever gotten, with a concept that "money was the way you kept score in business". Barnum, of course, felt there "was a sucker born every minute".

John's National Association of Skin Diving Schools (formerly Stores) was hanging on the ropes with fierce competition from NAUI and PADI. He needed a new hook and he found it more or less reading the airline magazine on a trip. There it was - "Time Sharing". John knew how to take somebody else's ideas and convert them to serve diving. He had done it in developing NASDS in the 1960's by studying the ski industry. He pushed computers into the shop operations. He'd even tried to get into the resort business by having his organization buy into or lease a run down hotel in Ensenada, Mexico, and have his member shops rent it and the diving service he'd installed.

The Time Share Idea took him into the Caymans and then down to British Honduras. NASDS would buy a resort, jack up its diving infrastructure and sell ownership time shares to his member shop, which paid for the purchase of the property and insuring full usage and future maintenance expense. The next step was to get an airplane and sell time shares in that. Time shares proved to be a difficult business venture and while still an idea afloat in resort property sales, it became generally criticized as a no brainer investment. John Gaffney never got his time share resorts into full flight because the dive shops didn't have the cash flow to get beyond sales inventory at that time...and they didn't want to get committed to only one diving place every year.

Gaffney's magazine for NASDS was called *Dive* and in 1969 Al Tillman was serving as its Education and Travel

Editor. The February 1970 issue of DIVE has an article by Tillman on Diving's Foreign Legion covering some of the top resort pros, who emerged in the late 1950's and through the 1960's decade. Before them and around them, peroxided beach boys fawned over fat ladies with their oil bottles, jacks of all trades - diving included - masters of none. The pros were excellent divers, knew how to relate to people, serve them without the patronizing insincerity of beach boys. They helped people develop confidence in themselves, stepped back and let the customers be center of the stage. They sought excellence in themselves but accepted achievements less than their own standards in people they took diving.

Why weren't these pros back being urban executives, college professors, successful mainland businessmen? They were. In many cases, resort pros were a mature, mid-life, second career bunch. Some had been tourists and had been disappointed with the shallow, meaningless, dive offerings being mishandled at resorts around the world. They vowed to change the picture...and they did.

We've already mentioned several resort pros but to understand what resort diving was like in the first decades of sport diving history, we'd better describe them in more depth.

LeRoy French, who took groups from California to many of the dive resorts says, "Bob Soto of Grand Cayman is the best. Mr. Unnervous, we called him, free diving with us after getting us to a dive spot fast, all tanks and gear ready to go. He never imposed himself on my group, but always there ready to help, helping me manage the different levels of divers."

Jim Brown of Dayton, Ohio, said, "Soto never gets rattled and it influences everybody else. He knows what's coming next and exactly what to do about it." Soto was Cayman diving for many years and wherever he was stationed was a diving resort. A refugee from Cuba when Castro took over in 1959, he became a pillar of the community and diving icon.

Gardiner Young knows his beat too, like Soto, every inch of the territory. The territory was Nassau in the Bahamas through the 1960's where he knew every underwater crevice and crook. In a way, he was the patriarch of the blooming profession of resort manager/instructor, guide. A bearded bull of a man, he moved onto the tropical scene fleeing the snow drifts of Massachusetts and created a diving place that attracted celebrities and movie stars, who were willing to buy the very best, something better than a quick fling off the shore with a bored beach boy.

Young had a system based on standards he'd set up and incorporated them under a Bahamas Underwater Guides Association. Such things as requiring one guide for every two diving clients, which meant Gardiner trained native guides from the islands, which the isolated resorts followed as a normal, economical practice. The native guides under the system, snorkel supervised scuba diver customers, which urban instructors criticized, feeling on-the-bottom supervision was essential.

Joe Vogel of Caron's (actress/dancer, Leslie Caron's parents) at St. Thomas in the Virgin Islands, an exUDT whiz, felt strongly about learning while doing. Tourists figuratively used real bullets from the start. They learned to dive by diving in the open sea. Spit and polish order ruled all the diving, all tanks were carefully cradled, straps uniformly crossed in a pattern and each faced inland. His diver clients were told any deviance from the dive plan would abort the dive for all. Joe pulled a float with a divers flag around a circular underwater tour while another guide took a rear guard position. This kind of care and seriousness made new resort divers feel their lives were in professional hands.

On a clear day, Joe Vogel could almost see Walt Hendricks in action just across the channel at his El Conquistador Resort diving operation. When Havana, Cuba got sealed from American diving tourists, Puerto Rico joined the Virgins and Bahamas as the new jet-set destinations. Walt, a prized YMCA and NAUI instructor joined Jim Thorne, a pioneer of the resort diving business there in early 1960's. He required training even for the advanced divers, a well-organized system not unlike that of UNEXSO.

There was a cluster of outstanding resort manager/guides in the Caribbean: Big John Hamber at St. Thomas,

UNEXSO also made sure that members and their kids had educational opportunities aside from diving. Lloyd Bridges and Laura Tillman work on fish printing during a break between dives.

Greg Korwek of Miami and Puerto Rico, John Gruener at Grand Bahama, Charlie McCarthy at the Caribe Hilton, and the 1950's pioneer, Bruce Parker in the Caymans. If the 1950's paid tribute to the basic diver, the instructor in the 1960's, the 1970's its love affair was with the resort pros.

The 1960's ended with the first NAUI resort instructor course in Puerto Rico under the direction of Walt Hendricks and Joe Bodner. Standards for the resort diving business were formulated into a consensus compact course to cover the training of any average beginner for his first supervised underwater trip in the open sea.

NAUI authorized a Resort Branch which Al Tillman coordinated in Los Angeles upon his return from the Bahamas. A survey by Tillman indicated that the divers showing up at the resorts often already had NAUI training in hometowns, and the resort pros were mostly NAUI instructors. Unfortunately, NAUI let the opportunity to dominate the resort field get away and PADI moved into it with more vision. Politics again changed the course of sport diving history.

The 1970's was the boom decade for diving resorts. More and more divers from mainland USA, flooded Mexico, the Caribbean, Hawaii, the Florida Keys, the Netherland Antilles, arrived to present diving center proposals to existing resort operations, or bought a floundering resort outright or just picked up a motel and started one.

One diving resort that was the culmination of a great amount of research and effort was Akumal in Yucatan, Mexico. Don Pablo "Paul" Bush was the driving force for much of the good things that happened to diving all over Mexico. Indeed, he laid the groundwork for the Cozumel diving scene which would ultimately be a major diving destination with a host of diving operations "resorts". But Akumal was what Bush wanted to create after visiting UNEXSO. He created his own Underwater Explorers Society called CEDAM International, (Conservation, Exploration, Diving, Archeology, Museums) that had an official status in all of Mexico and eventually, internationally. Sanctioned to protect Mexico's reefs and archeological artifacts, its members went on expeditions out of Akumal and gathered information on wreck sites, fish populations, Mayan Caves, Cenotes and provided items for several museums. Akumal was carved out of a nineteen mile shoreline of a copra plantation, a jungle full of lagoons, and a sandy shoreline kissed by the equatorial current. Al Tillman trekked with Pablo Bush through the wilds of Yucatan in 1966 and remembers Bush saying, "...this is nothing but jungle now but in five years maybe less, the finest diving resort will arise." Akumal ran its diving under the management of ex-military divers from the United States and some well-trained Mexican guides. When Al Tillman returned to Akumal ten years later in 1976, he re-interviewed Pablo Bush, who said, "Don't you think we've matched up very well with UNEXSO? We might even have more to offer." Tillman picked up a huge dead scorpion off the floor of the thatched dining hall and good humorously said, "You do, Pablo, like these fellows." Pablo Bush built up Akumal on a serious basis of letting people join expedition projects, but there were some hefty dues involved. CEDAM and Akumal continued to serve diving through the 1980's and 1990's.

The impact of diving resorts was powerful in moving sport diving in a new direction. Going diving became a save-up-for-it special event. Local diving outings shrunk accordingly and divers had to periodically get fit, refresh their knowledge and abilities, and usually purchase new, more attractive, more technical equipment - or rent it at the resort. After diving warm, clear almost virgin waters on a concentrated basis for a week or two, local diving had a difficult time measuring up. The weekend diver became an endangered species. While dive resorts gave the diving population a new door to walk through and find veritable Eden, it gave the uninitiated a first opportunity to try scuba under almost ideal conditions and professional supervision. The downside may have been that as the resort element moved into prime locations, the untouched wildness of these places eroded. Dive Resorts did in a few cases, very few, take the long view. The made efforts to protect their natural assets, without which they wouldn't exist. The bans on spearfishing, taking of coral, wreck excavations, the setting aside of preserves are arguably positive efforts but they also represent a restriction of what had been a complete experience of freedom.

As the 1970's and early 1980's closed out as an era of dive resorts, interest swung to the new device that would allow the traveling diver to roam far and wide - **The Live Aboard Dive Boat**.

But despite the "new" popularity of the Live Aboard, there are many divers who like the stability of a land resort with diving mixed in with other activities, and more space, and less dependence on divemasters to structure the dives. Wherever a resort is, the imposition of local politics in the exotic places will always provide some precarious circumstances. The impact of the dive resort appeared to be to create a dissatisfaction with mundane local diving and cater to the growing affluence in America. The do-it-yourself, jump-in-your-car-days were gone forever.

23

DECOMPRESSION METERS AND COMPUTERS

DEFINING EVENT: THE 1983 ORCA EDGE

After a decade or more of scaring entry-level-divers with gruesome pictures of people bent over in pain holding their joints, a potential magic elixir popped up to ease the fear. Instructors enjoyed a kind of smug power in describing the "bends", decompression sickness (DCS) and explaining the tables to use in calculating prevention of the malady. Saying "don't" stay down too long or deep, "do" plan only no decompression dives, was ultimately ignored. Divers were too curious. It was in their nature to explore the forbidden. And so the decompression meter, the SOS, and, eventually, in the full glory of high tech, the tell-all multi-functional dive computer arrived as a "magic" instrument to inform the diver, defeat the bends and dispel fear. It became a basic item of diving equipment. Most divers would not go under without one. For the new generation of 1990's divers, it became a major attraction of the diving experience.

DIVER CALCULATIONS

The Golden Years of diving were also the dark ages of diving. The pioneers plunged in with a basic minimum of knowledge about the technology of the available equipment nor really knowing the physiology that made their bodies a bubbling cauldron of the effects of pressure and gases.

Even while early divers were enjoying the basic attitude of "keep it simple", a few of the diving lab nerds were questioning everything. They wanted to measure, know more, and create devices and methods to make diving a more controllable and safer experience...and more profitable.

While training agencies acted to promote a 130-foot no decompression diving rule in 1960's and set safe limits, divers from the old days had strong individual views about restrictions. They were strongly opposed to losing the carefree, exploratory, curiosity-driven freedom they enjoyed - the vary essence of what going underwater was all about to them.

When the Aqua Lung scuba arrived into American sport recreational diving, divers were mainly breath-holding skin divers with a few hose and helmet people, who dabbled in commercial activities, such as, salvage and game taking for profit. Nobody was talking much about decompression sickness (DCS). There was much bigger concern about ear clearing and air embolism from holding your breath on ascent.

There were United States Navy Decompression Tables designed by the Naval Experimental Diving Unit (EDU) which were primarily to guide hard hat divers but applicable to scuba divers as well. Yes, there they were but with a caution: The tables were designed to accommodate young and fit military personnel. The weekend warriors of sport diving were in part a healthy tough lot, fully capable of qualifying for the demanding Underwater Demolition Team (UDT) frogman units. But a lot of divers, who had not cut their teeth on the rigors of skin diving as a lead-in were less physically in the tested levels of the navy men.

No one was going really deep in the pioneer days. Although the early instruction programs covered decompression, as thoroughly as possible, the general feeling and in actuality, few divers were going to go deeper than 60-feet, a relatively safe level. The books and the agencies said: "Everything there is to see is in that zone no deeper than 60-feet."

But, as we found out, and especially because there were shipwrecks deeper, the lure of "forbidden territory", just the idea of someone trying to restrict them, drove the divers deeper. There was no underwater policeman watching and, surprisingly, any signs of decompression sickness were not reported. Perhaps the symptoms weren't recognizable, but nevertheless, no red flags of incidents were raised in the 1950's.

The action of pressure and time, the in-gassing and out-gassing, were so invisible to divers, that attention to the tables was more of an exercise in demonstrating that diving was a sport with special scientific concerns and participants were somehow flirting with greater risks than other physical sports. It impressed non-diving friends to explain the mysterious diving diseases. Being able to calculate a decompression schedule from tables elevated divers, said to the public, "Hey, we're not just jumping into the water and paddling around!"

Decompression sickness was like the giant squid; we hadn't caught it yet, but it's there...and it's dangerous!

Suddenly, probably in the mid 1960's divers everywhere began going deeper. A lot of possible reasons are suspected. More divers. Private dive places, "secret dive places" in the shallower waters were experiencing "heavy traffic". Al Tillman always felt territorially challenged when another diver showed up on "his beach", in his cove, taking "his lobster". To get away from this assumed impact, new diving places were sought-deeper. Stories of new and unusual sightings of big fish, unknown reefs and shipwreck sites were being told around the campfire.

There were no laws or authorities that had jurisdiction over a diver doing whatever he wanted. Cousteau always said in the beginning, "Divers using the Aqua-Lung to go deep, to set records, were imbecilic, akin to someone jumping off a ten story building headfirst." Cousteau didn't know that a sport called Bungee-Jumping would come along nor that his "over-exploring the oceans" might push the intrepid explorers of the future to go down beyond the regions that he had perhaps over-exposed in his zeal to share and persuade the public to protect the underwater world.

The diving tables on decompression took on a great importance as all this happened. The tables, as discussed in another Chapter in *Scuba America*, had its own evolution as efforts to construct a safe sport diving compatible set of calculations were designed around the world.

ENTER THE COMPUTER AGE

Surprisingly, we keep discovering that many things were happening long before we thought they'd been invented or introduced. The Chapter on the United States Navy's Committee on Undersea Warfare and Underwater Swimmers (1951), discussed the various ways to deal with the proliferating use of scuba in the military and by civilian divers. Scuba had just come on the scene and with it a need for more accessory devices to make it more effective, convenient to use and safer. The 1951 Committee at Scripps Institution, La Jolla, California, yielded a listing of ways to deal with decompression.

The 1953 report of the Committee said, "In ordinary diving (hard hat), the tender aboard ship keeps a log of depth and time history of the dive but the untethered free swimming scuba diver has to keep his own log underwater and computes decompression, or he follows a prearranged dive plan, or he guesses at it...none of which are satisfactory." The report suggested the need for a two tissue group pneumatic analog computer which simulated nitrogen uptake and elimination. The gauge would record the entire dive, different times at different levels and residual nitrogen from other dives. There was even a design for such a gauge in the 1953 report.

In 1956 the Naval Experimental Diving Unit pushed the need for a small portable indicating apparatus to be used to connote proper decompression in ascent.

Civilian dive manuals of the period contained nothing about dive computers. The most widely used manual, *The New Science of Skin and Scuba Diving*, in it's 1972 revised edition still gave it no mention.

The sport divers of the Golden Years probably slept through physics class in high school. What a shame the teachers hadn't explained it in terms of diving. But then, their passions for going underwater hadn't yet risen either.

Actually, the main player in all of this decompression meter and dive computer bluster is nitrogen. It's a gas that couldn't be seen and makes up 79% of the air breathed. It's a gas that just lies there, inactive, harmless and unneeded by the human body.

But, it is the cause of decompression sickness. It has to do with nitrogen being dissolved into the tissue and not being used by the body. The more pressure, going deeper, the more passes into the tissue. It is spread by the blood stream with oxygen which is used by the tissues. Nitrogen forced into solution goes into the tissues and just sits there.

When a diver comes up and the surrounding pressure is reduced; nitrogen starts coming out of the tissues. If this doesn't happen at a controlled rate, the pressure outside the body drops too fast and instead of solution, nitrogen forms bubbles that lodge in blood, joint or tissue cells. Ouch!

The exact balance of pressure and its effect on nitrogen differs from person to person. Different tissue types are faster or slower in elimination of nitrogen. Age, sex, fitness, body fat, blood circulation, medications, body temperature and exertion all effect the individual's rate of nitrogen elimination. Most dive computers only calculate decompression status on depth and time.

There are slow absorbing (bone marrow) and fast absorbing tissues (lungs) and plenty in between. To handle this variety, tissues are theoretically classified into "compartments". Compartments allow the mathematical break-down range of tissue types into different rates... tissues in gas and out gas nitrogen. This is not an absolute happening in each diver's body but provides a fairly safe theoretical range. The more compartments (0 to 12) a computer covers, the more effective it is.

The tissue half-time or tissue speeds has to do with time it takes for a tissue to fill with nitrogen. Well, this is all presented here in a dumb slept-through-physics-diver perspective.

There was no question that this appeal to Yankee ingenuity would produce an instrument to automatically deal with figuring decompression. There were a number of early attempts as there were with scuba before Jacques Yves- Cousteau's invention of the Aqua Lung in 1942. The first on record was the Foxboro Decomputer that was submitted to the Navy Experimental Diving Unit. It was similar to the one in the 1953 report. It used a combination of bellows, springs and porous resistors. EDU sent it back to be modified because it showed inconsistent readings within the United States Navy Dive Tables. It was never modified or resubmitted.

THE SOS DECOMPRESSION METER

In 1959, the first, most well-known decompression device became commercially available. It was the SOS Decompression Meter manufactured in Italy. Healthways began its United States distribution in 1961.

In 1963 Scubapro obtained distribution rights in the USA. A one compartment, pneumatic device based on average body tissue. At UNEXSO where deep diving was provided for the qualified civilian sport diver, the SOS was worn by the guides on all decompression dive depths as a backup to a regular prearranged dive plan based on the tables. It was not trusted to be accurate by the UNEXSO staff divers...for after all, it was a piece of equipment that could malfunction. Unquestionably, a greater quantity of bottom time was lost by adding on the hand-done calculation of the tables.

More attempts to build the ultimate dive computer came along in the 1960's. There was Tractor, an electrical analog computer in 1963 that the Navy's EDU rejected because different temperatures resulted in different values for the same dive schedule. By the late 1960's the Defense and Civil Institute of Environmental Medicine, (DCIEN) developed the MARK VS, which was good but it proved to be too expensive for sport divers at that time.

General Electric in 1973 came up with the G.E. Decompression Meter. It used semipermeable silicon mem-branes. This meter was a more complex four-chamber-mechanism, but General Electric never brought it to mar-ket. Once again the cost exceeded the budgets of divers.

Farallon Industries, a new diving products company that spewed out new ideas and designs, got their Decomputer before the public in 1975 by jumping on the semipermeable membrane technology. Scripps Institution of Oceanography killed it with an evaluation saying that it failed to approximate the United States Navy decompression limits. The Australian Navy said that it was too permissive. That there was mechanical deterioration with use.

Modern technology with the coming of pressure transducers and microchips took the decompression meter into the grander world of pressure. These activated diving minicomputers use mathematical formulas to calculate nitrogen absorption and release based on theoretical models. DCIEM followed up its MARK VS with several models. The most effective seemed to be the XDC-3. It was the first micro-processor based, diver-carried dive computer. But its power requirements, four-hour batteries life, was its major problem.

In 1978, a diving company, DACOR Corporation of Illinois came up with the DACOR Dive Computer. It also had short life battery power. Microchips were in short supply at the time, as the toy industry boomed and gobbled up what was available. Canada produced a Cyber Diver Device that was used by a few sport divers prior to the dive computer explosion in 1983.

In 1983 the <u>Orca Edge,</u> first successful dive computer, based on the Haldanean model and the Deco Brain I, based on Swiss Tables was introduced. The EDGE was fondly called "The Brick" by first buyers who stuck with it as new, smaller computers rolled off the assembly line over the next two decades. It was also the year that Oceanic (formerly Farallon) and U.S. Divers Company put together a 1.5 million dollar research effort - a first wherein two diving manufacturers cooperated on a product. The result was in 1987. It was an introduction of a series of inventive attempts that filled the 1980's with dive computers. There were leakage problems, power restrictions and failures to stay close to U.S. Navy Tables.

Orca Industries set a milestone in computer development in 1987 by coming out with a successor to its <u>Edge</u>. It was the <u>Skinny Dipper,</u> user friendly and less costly. It had a first in

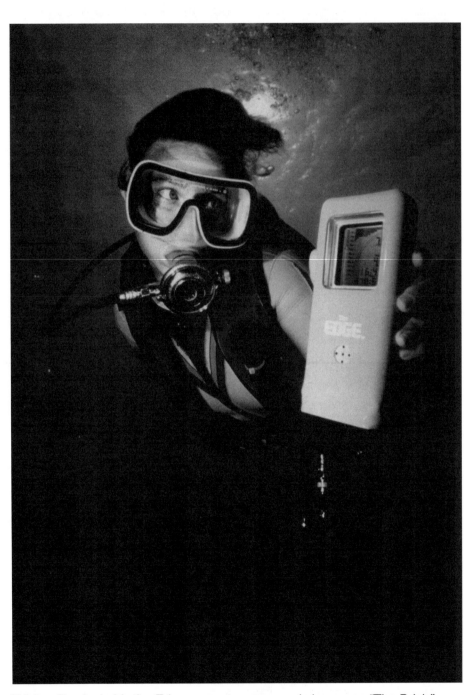

Kristine Barsky holds the Edge computer, commonly known as "The Brick."
EIT, Inc.

having a red Light Emitting Diode (LED) warning light with its Light Crystal Display (LCD) screen ...and it was a simple no-decompression dive computer.

Sea Quest came out with dive computers with the first dive recall feature, enabling a diver to recall an entire dive profile showing the divers maximum depth every 3-minutes. ORCA Delphi and Scubapro DiveVu had the same feature by 1990.

Another, step in late 1980's was OCEANIC's incorporating the air pressure gauge into the display.

The 1988 Diving Equipment and Marketing Association (DEMA) Convention showed DACOR's new Micro Brain, a Swiss Model multi-level dive computer. This one gave time and depth for up to 6-dives within the previous 48-hours. The Sherwood Sigmatech was out in 1988 with a console integrating the submersible pressure gauge.

The year 1989 saw a flood of new or redesigned computers arrive. Most improvements had to do with battery door leaks and better read numbers on the LCD. Depth capabilities were increased along with expanded tissue compartments. The Aladen Pro scrolled no decompression limits between dives allowing pre-dive planning and an audible ascent alarm. A number of computers had gone to the full decompression function and utilized the conservative BÜHLMANN Model.

That same year 1989, also had Orca with its Delphi introduce air consumption information calculated by remaining air time and a dive profile recall interface with a personal computer.

In 1990 dive manufacturers were becoming more sophisticated and adding features. Nothing radical except the back-lighted display and increasing the number of tissue compartments.

Generally, sport divers were confused with an industry flurry to put a "new computer" on the market which in many cases were attempts to keep things simple, design appeal, compactness and clever names. Overall, there was no dominant computer and in many cases divers were dealing with the same computer selling under a different brand name. (Remember when they had a Voit lung that was actually an Aqua Lung to be sold by Sears?)

Divers, by this point in time, were beginning to accept the Dive Computer, as a basic piece of equipment and comparatively affordable to other dive equipment. The new divers were computer nursed since infancy and they easily by-passed the hard work of table computing and embraced a "machine" to do the work. During the 1990's, divers prepared to spend a wealth of money to be part of diving and be a diver in the modern age. They made long distance dive trips to dive six hours a day (and night) or on live-aboards in wild places like Papua New Guinea at package costs rivaling half the cost of a new car. New cars got put aside to make sure the latest and best equipment would go with them on trips. So much diving all compacted into a short time meant stretching bottom time to the max. Outside of being in great shape, fit, a dive computer provided the safest way to get the most multi-level diving in possible. It became as reasonable to have backup computers (let alone spare batteries) along as spare regulators. The computer became the electronic dive log and a profile record of your diving history could be down-loaded onto a Personal Computer (PC). The print out was perfect evidence to be shown to dive masters policing dive tourism wherever a diver went. The arrival of the dive computer meant greater safety in one respect but it also meant another device to encumber the diver and steal away some of the fluid freedom felt in the beginning days of diving. Some divers have been seen with up to three dive computers strapped on "just to play it safe" or perhaps to just look really "high tech".

The 1990's also saw diving testing labs proliferate and dive computers submit to wide and varied analyses. Debate bobbed to the surface as to what if you got to the great diving place of your dreams and you forgot your dive computer, or the batteries were dead, and there weren't any to rent, and...Well, did you bring your tables, so that you could go back to the "old fashioned" way by your own calculations? What if you forgot a depth gauge, a watch, just how much diving can you have the courage to take on? You might have to "Mark Twain" it, lower a line to determine depths and time yourself by the sun's position in the sky.

The decade of the 1990's still did not produce the ultimate dive computer to take all of our diving worries away. Can it get better? Of course, it can and will. We have always accepted more equipment and expense to go diving even while the debate rages as to whether we have made a nice basic sport more sophisticated or more complicated.

The computers most easily taken up by divers were ones based on tables, the United States Navy's, and tables produced by experts like Haldane, Albert Bühlmann of Hannes Keller-Dive fame, Dr. Walter A. Hahn and Dr. Bruce Wienke. There is a maze of names of different people, models and computers to grope through for most divers. All of this new technology can fail, as it has in flying airplanes, but divers have had to trust the industry on this one over the years.

Dive Computers, the book by Ken Loyst, Karl Huggins and Michael Steidley, sums it up like this:

1. Use information from a dive computer to make an educated decision.

2. Dive computers do not make the dive...they provide information to the diver, who executes the dive.

If dive computers had not come along would diving have gone on as usual? We could compare that query to the original Aqua-Lung...if there had been no changes or alterations to the original scuba, would sports diving have had a different history?

Without the dive computer, divers would have been much more restricted on their diving: Multi-level diving would be a chaotic calculation. Repetitive dives essential in diving travel would have been greatly limited. To be safe divers would have gravitated toward conservative decompression tables and sacrificed a lot of bottom time.

• How were sport divers responding to the dawning of the dive computer era? Here is the experience and reaction of a leading-edge sport diver.

• Tom Hemphill, a second generation diver, impactful NAUI leader, and architect of Emerald Seas a five star dive center in the Northwestern United States, came into diving in 1971 but just did not trust this new instrumentation in diving. It wasn't until 1989, when he could believe that the computer was a major piece of equipment. He obtained a U.S. Divers Monitor One, which served him all through the 1990's without failing. In 1990, he introduced the use of the computer into his diving classes. In 1990 about one out of 30-divers were using computers; by 1999 three out of five were diving with one.

THE FOLLOWING IS A TIMELINE OF DEVELOPMENT OF THE COMPUTER:

1951 National Research Council with The United States Navy Committee on Undersea Warfare and Underwater Swimmers at Scripps Institution of Oceanography met and stressed the need for instrumentation of decompression calculations.

1953 The Committee issued a report that suggested a design for a pneumatic analog computer which simulated nitrogen uptake - and actually showed the design.

1956 The Naval Experimental Diving Unit in Washington, D.C. pushed for a small portable indicating apparatus to be used to show proper decompression in ascent.

1959 The first and most well-known decompression device, the SOS Decom Meter, became commercially available. It was manufactured in Italy.

1961 SOS Decom Meter distributed by Healthways in the United States by 1961.

1963 Scubapro took over United States distribution rights of SOS Decom Meter.

1965 The Underwater Explorers Club (UNEXSO) in the Bahamas used the SOS on all its decompression diving. All guides wore an SOS Decom Meter but they did not trust it completely.

1970's A gang of companies: General Electric, DACOR, Farallon tried to introduce to the public computers based on pressure transducers and microchips but limited power sources, high costs and short supply of microchips, (Toy companies had bought them up.), doomed them in a market not yet believing in them.

1983 The Dive Computer explosion happened! In particular the Orca Edge was introduced and in one form or another, under different brand names, lasted effectively through the 1990's. The price was $795.00.

1987 Sea Quest came out with first dive recall feature computer enabling a diver to recall an entire dive profile.

1988 Oceanic incorporates an air pressure gauge into the display.

1990 Many computer problems solved e.g., leaky battery doors and hard to read numbers (solved through back-lighting). Dive leaders were accepting the computer as a basic piece of equipment and influencing others.

1992 Long distance dive travel to off-beat places and the expansion of live-aboards made dive computing by instrument a boon to getting more bottom time (BT) and dives...therefore, your money's worth.

1993 Computers become electronic dive logs and the ability, in 1994, to download onto a Personal Computer (PC) upgraded record keeping.

1995 Scuba testing labs sprung up and dive computers were widely tested and given "Seals of Approval".

1998 More divers "wouldn't go in the water without one". The estimation was at three users out of every five divers. The new dive generation born to computers are fanatics. They may wear as many as three on a dive! Integrating with a PC becomes a growing demand. More buttons to push for more functions under-water and the new breed talks to the diver. They become increasingly affordable, under $400.00 but super micro-computers with elite functions will be around the $1000.00 range.

1998 The Orca Edge, the first successful dive computer, was carried over to the Marathon, the longest track record of all computers. It was a liberal computer with good warnings and penalties if not heeded, but no lockout of diver, if violated. It was diver controllable.

2000 New software in the programmed dive computer provides extensive and expanded information about almost anything you would want to know.

DIVING MANUALS ON DECOMPRESSION METERS AND DIVE COMPUTERS

Adventures in Scuba Diving, Steven Barsky, NAUI 1995

• Points out how all independent instruments divers use are combined into a single instrument...the computer. They record one or more previous dives and plan ensuing dives. Unload to a Personal Computer (PC).

Discovering the Underwater World, U.S. Divers, Ralph Erickson, 1972

• No mention of Decompression Meters or Dive Computers

Dive, The Complete Book of Skin Diving, Rick and Barbara Carrier, Wilfred Funk, Inc., New York, 1973

• No mention of Decompression Meter (DM) or Dive Computer (DC).

Open Water Diver Manual, Scuba Schools International, 1991

• <u>Dive Computer</u>. A data processor...used to plan dives, and to compute information about previous dives when planning depth and time limits for present and future dives. See your instructor and dive store about speciality training in computer diving.

Open Water Sport Diver Manual, Jepperson Sanderson, Inc., 1984

• The introduction of dive computers could revolutionize the way divers monitor and plan their dives...does not eliminate the need to preplan the dive and to plan repetitive dives with the use of the dive tables.

PADI Open Water Dive Manual. 1990

• Comprehensive coverage of function and use of dive computers. Advocates that divers learn to use the tables as no dive computer is infallible.

Safe Scuba, Richard Hammes and Anthony Zimos, NASDS, 1980
• Does not reference Decompression Meters or Dive Computers.

Scuba Diving, Dennis Graver, Human Kinetics Publishers, 1993
• Picks up for the abandoned *New Science of Skin and Scuba Diving* text and has best explanation of functions of a computer. Strong support for the programmed computer.

Scuba Safe and Simple, John Reseck, Jr., Prentice Hall, 1975
• The Decompression Meter which according to the directions and the advertisement of the manufacturer, supposedly puts an end to all of our worry about decompression. Unfortunately, this is not true. There have been quite a few people treated for bends, who were diving on the Decompression Meter...not saying the meter is no good. I dive with one myself, with great success...does not solve all problems...diver must keep his bottom time...and check his dive against the compression tables.

Skin and Scuba Diving, John Cramer, Bergwall Publishing, 1975
• The decompression meter...a guide for divers doing decompression and repetitive diving.

The Golden Guide to Scuba Diving, Wheeler North, Golden Press, 1968
• No mention of Decompression Meter or Dive Computer

The New Science of Skin and Scuba Diving, A Project of the Council for National Co-operation in Aquatics, Association Press, New York, 1980 (Cover by David Doubilet)
• Decompression Meter...considered by many divers to be an essential instrument when performing repetitive or deep dives...serves to double check preconceived dive plans.

In the year 2000 many divers consider that the dive computer has been the most significant invention to change diving since the Aqua Lung arrived. But just as diving equipment could not replace good watermanship, it is argued among divers that the dive computer should not be expected to replace comprehensive dive planning.

24

MAIL ORDER DIVING

DEFINING EVENT: SWIMMASTER CORRESPONDENCE COURSE

The postman used to deliver the ways and means to marvelous new adventures such as *Be A Ventriloquist Booklet*, *How To Start A Frog Farm*, the *Charles Atlas Course*, and a correspondence course on being a TV repairman. Through the 1930's, 1940's, 1950's, tongues were licking stamps and sending away for the instructions and equipment to become an exciting new trained-and-equipped person.

Why not add *Be A Scuba Diver* to the assortment? That's exactly what happened in sport diving. In the 1950's, a person could buy out of a catalog just about anything to do with diving. No questions asked, age, sex, health. Just lick the stamp, seal the envelop and the company will pay the freight. Mail Order was certainly a boon to those remote places in America not urban enough to support a retail dive shop.

A company called Swimmaster was a pioneer in the early days. They put out a flamboyant catalog, bright orange/red cover, that sold a variety of lines from Aqua Lungs to depth gauges. In 1955, Dick Bonin, a UDT officer,

freshly discharged, signed on with Swimmaster to oversee the operation. He'd already established his credentials while he was still in the service by editing a diving correspondence course entitled *Divemaster Skin and Lung Diving Home Study Training*, written by E. R. Cross.

Direct class instruction was not yet in full bloom, so any instruction, especially one that had been touched by two of diving's mightiest pioneers, was to be praised. Cross, of course, was teaching scuba at his Sparling School of Diving and his ground breaking book, *Diving Safety*, was out. The course that could be ordered for $5.00 was a landmark event. That money enrolled you in the Home Training Program with the advertisement's application. Then $5.00 each month until the full amount of $169.50 was paid. You would receive an 8 1/2" x 11" printed lesson of up to 40 pages, professionally bound with a test sheet by mail. When you were finished with lesson one, you sent the test sheet back to the company indicating you were ready for lesson two and so forth.

DIVEMASTER
Skin and Lung
Diving

HOME STUDY TRAINING

LESSON NUMBER ONE

U. A. S. Corporation
5637-43 West 63rd Place
Chicago 38, Illinois

Certified Member No. 1303
Zale Parry

DIVEMASTER
Skin and Lung Diving
Home Training Course
DIVEMASTER
5637-43 West 63rd Place
Chicago 38, Illinois

Copyright 1955 by E. R. C

The test sheet would be graded personally by E. R. Cross and returned to you. Cross told *Scuba America* that he corrected over 250 students' test sheets during the years the program was offered.

Middle-class America was experiencing prosperity in the 1950's, and the new concept of discretionary income meant new sports like diving, with lots of equipment to buy.

Any individual could order equipment from the catalogs, and some set up car-trunk shops selling direct to divers at diving sites or dive-club meetings. Bill Barada used to show up at abalone chowder gatherings, fund raisers for the Greater Los Angeles Council of Diving Clubs, and drag Bel Aqua Suits out of the back of his car and spear guns, too. Many a dive shop emerged from just such sparse beginnings.

The dive shops that had begun setting up small store front, hole-in-the-wall, retail operations moaned and groaned, complained to the manufacturers, and cursed the floating mobile equipment sellers. The catalogs that opened their order doors to the general public were an anathema to dive shops.

The manufacturers were out to produce and distribute as much gear as possible. They counted on the dive shops to move the bulk of their equipment, but they didn't turn anyone away in the beginning. Anyone out there selling their products was doing a great part of their marketing job for them.

Skin Diver Magazine in the 1950's was carrying a number of ads for direct mail buying. It was also supporting Neal Hess' program of mailing in a course outline. It would be approved and cited in the column, Diving Patrol, and indicating that the sender was a qualified instructor.

An Ohio company, Skooba-Skin offered two dry suits for $34.95. If you bought one from a dealer, you could send in the box label stock number and get one suit free from the factory or you could order both from the factory in 1958.

Central Skindiver's hodge-podge ad touts a catalog that's "more an encyclopedia of diving." Syron Divers in New York mail ordered all equipment with special prices if you joined their underwater club. Laguna Sea Sports refilled CO_2 spear guns by mail order.

By 1960, a benchmark year for many impactful events in sport diving, *Skin Diver Magazine* was still the key media force. The big companies were taking full page display ads to create name recognition and support but had pulled back from selling direct - there were U.S. Divers, Nemrod, Voit, Healthways, Dacor, Normal Air and Rose Aviation.

Dealer inquiries were encouraged, and catalog numbers and prices were given for specific products. During the 1950's and 1960's, *Skin Diver Magazine* carried one of the worst full-page ads ever printed. It made graphic artists cringe. It was the jumbled boxed conglomeration of small pictures and descriptive copy on everything from an underwater timer to a discounted single hose regulator for $26.50. It was Central Skindivers', operating out of Long Island, New York. An order form was right there at the bottom of the ad and a new 1962 catalog showing "thousands of items from all over the world" could be had for a dollar. Nothing about certification or instruction is mentioned.

Readers of some ads were being directed to contact a franchised dealer dive store, such as White Stag Manufacturing Company of Portland, Oregon. That, besides its swim suits and diving suits, had a White Stag Sea Lung for sale. NAUI instructors, Al O'Neil and Ralph Erickson, (Yes, PADI's founder) were mail ordering a diving manual, Under Pressure. Rose Aviation with its PRO Regulator was pushing its catalog but soliciting dealer inquiries. The magazine carried a new products page and gave the addresses of where to write the manufacturers to order from them.

New England Divers, Inc. owned and operated by an ex-Navy Frogman, Jim Cahill, had a fifty page catalog and a ten page safe diving guide available for 75 cents. It was available to the public and dealers. Small shops like Harbor Beach Tackle and Marine advertised inventory reduction sales by mail order. Small garage operations were selling direct by mail; there was a safety line for divers, camera housings from Al Giddings and LeRoy French at Northern California's Bamboo Reef Shops, regulator repair by Mac Synder Skin Diving Center in New York and

Swimmaster was still selling by mail the E.R. Cross Home Study Training Course. You could order the plans to build the famous Addict Gun for $2.00 from Underwater Sports in Long Beach, California.

There wasn't a whole lot of concern about product liability or liability for inadequate warning or instruction at this point in time.

Skin Diver Magazine was a good barometer of specialty diving interests as they occurred and the mail order ads highlighted those interests along with personal adventure stories. The August 1960 issue was all afire about gold diving. You could order your underwater mining equipment along with the original Farmer John-designed wet suit from Don and George Brauer of Skin N' Dive in Southern California - just put your measurements on the order form included in the ad. Mel Fisher would send you a $199 gold separator complete FOB from Mel's Aqua Shop in Redondo Beach, California.

Jordan Klein was shipping his MAKO Compressors and advertising one at $595 out of Miami, Florida. The Dive N' Surf Shop was selling custom suits by mail and Bobby and Billy were pushing their V-Design for women - but ladies had to send in additional measurements.

Even NAUI, which had established a strong instructors training program by the early 1960's was offering a mail order affiliate status in order to politically strengthen its position in various geographical areas and recognize highly qualified long experienced pioneer instructors (the so-called "Moss Backs"). Later in the 1960's, new instructor organizations would emerge and use mail order certification in order to carve out a piece of the instructor certification. And to a great degree, it was the rise to power of training agencies that helped close down the wild-cat selling through mail order.

Certified instructors needed direct, hands-on access to diving equipment, and the retail store was the necessary point of contact. Instruction was mostly about equipment and defining its quality without trying to advocate specific brands. The retail stores in the early days usually line up an independent instructor or the owner became certified. The larger retail stores could afford to have sales personnel trained as instructors but a divided loyalty often arose from this - the stores wanted the instruction to sell their inventory, to specify brands sometimes because they were greater profit items or slow moving products that needed help to sell.

Basically, the instructor profession did not advocate mail order acquisition of equipment. Instruction warned against the purchase of used equipment from a private party or picking up something at a swap meet. Nevertheless, much equipment changed hands in this manner. Mail order buying and private party purchases were a 50-50 balance with retail sales during the 1950's, but by the 1960's the full service dive shop was the prevalent supplier of equipment, probably covering 90% of the transference of equipment.

Mail order buying was a necessary way of life for the retail store that had no convenient access to examine new lines of equipment. Enter the manufacturer's salesman, or in some cases, a factory representative. Al Tillman recalls going on the sales route to various dive stores with U.S. Divers exclusive salesman, Forrest Dawn, and in contrast traveling with Jim Cassou, who represented the Northill scuba regulator and a line of anchors, among other things. Both of them carried samples of new products with them, showed and explained them to shop owners, and hopefully, wrote up orders. Someone specific, someone personal in sales could be pursued on any order foul-up. Not so with mail order. Sales worked, repeat sales worked, when delivery dates were met. Mail orders pitched exact date deliveries in their ads to maintain a competitive edge with direct salesmen but, occasionally, failed to deliver.

Something should be said here for direct-mailing lists. Such lists are often bought ...lists of newly certified divers or magazine subscribers. Catalogs or flyers may then be sent directly to the actual consumer, a personal and individualized contact, in contrast to the chancy exposure by a media ad. Another major development, the trade show, exposed retail shops to products available by all the companies with orders written on the spot at special show prices. Or at least printed materials, especially catalogs, could be taken away and ordered from.

Pressure from the industry, especially, the retail stores, discouraged magazines from carrying any mail order ads. Mail order buying tapered off in the 1970's and 1980's as retail outlets proliferated. And no matter where you lived, there was a diving store or diving department of a sporting goods store within driving distance. The impact of the large discount stores such as, Costco and WalMart carrying diving equipment also put a dent in mail order.

By the 1990's, the ads for new equipment were all directing readers to contact the dealer nearest you. Mailing costs, freight costs had soared, so direct mail order buying wasn't as big a price lure. Magazines were still putting in new product sections and giving 800-phone numbers for contacts on the equipment. By the end of the 1990's there were the computer inroads as a company putting out a new underwater light could be contacted at www.usphoto.com, an ordering website. Mail order was back with a click and a bang!

E-Commerce had arrived fully by 2000, and viewing products then ordering them on a computer was challenging the traditional way of direct physical contact with products selling much as mail order had done in the early decades.

If the world continues in its mad rush into a high tech way of doing business, then as Dick Bonin said away back in the 1970's, "the dive store is crucial to diving, to manufacturers, but if they don't do their job right, then another system for reaching the consumer will arise." Ordering by computer is probably going to be that new system, in spite of how effective the dive shops are. As a matter of course, the walk-in dive shop would just become a warehouse selling on the internet. The impact of mail order on the development of sport diving is significant because it got the land-locked, isolated public into diving and let the small one-product company get into the market.

QUOTES FROM INDUSTRY VIP'S ON MAIL ORDERS

John Gaffney - "You get what you pay for, Al, or I should say sometimes you don't get what you think you paid for and then who do you yell at, the postmaster? That's why I organized the dive stores."

John Cronin - "Mail Order? I don't know, but Jim Cahill was the biggest mass merchandiser diving ever had ...he had a smell for people. He used mail order, of course, but New England Divers was also a place they could talk diving and get a mask fitted to your face. That doesn't happen with mail order. Too impersonal."

Jim Christiansen, as a Vice President of Scubapro - "I'd been around the shops in a general way going back to the early 1950's when they first got started, but I didn't realize how much they were the bones of diving, holding it together in most places, until I went on the road to visit them as an equipment entrepreneur and seller. Mail order doesn't hold anything together."

Mel Fisher - "I never sold much mail order; I like to see how someone's reacting to what I'm telling them, my stories. Remember when I sold you the wet, encrusted pieces of eight out of my car trunk in Miami. That's how I like to sell."

Legend has it that Mel, like many of the pioneer divers, got lured into diving because of sunken treasure stories, along with get-rich-quick ads in *Popular Mechanics Magazine* and other pulp media of the 1930's. One of the "amazing" devices he sent away for was a $1.79 divining instrument for detecting gold anywhere. The postman delivered a gold plated arrow on a cord. It was supposed to be held over a spot and it would swing if there was gold below. Mel tried it off a raft in an Indiana river and it surely did swing but so did the raft. No, Mel did not find the Atocha with it, but he learned enough about the "selling of sizzle" through mail order.

Mail order was a dangerous practice putting complex equipment into the hands of uninformed, untrained people. Training without a live instructor is considered by many dive leaders to be equally hazardous. Videos can reinforce but not do the teaching-job complain many of the veteran instructors. On the positive side, sport diving was expanded by mail order taking it into the far isolated corners of America.

25
DIVING MUSEUMS - WINDOWS TO THE PAST

DEFINING EVENT: THE NICK ICORN COLLECTION

Don't throw anything away! The handful of divers who chanted that admonition as a mantra over the years often had disgusted spouses, cluttered homes and had to park their cars in the driveway.

These divers deserve an enormous measure of credit because they have been the visionary preservationists of our heritage. It's easy to say, oh, I'll remember, only to come up to a stonewall when someone asks where did you get your air when scuba arrived? Or how could you tell how deep you were? The diving museum preservers weren't taking any chances; they squirreled away every piece of equipment, things found underwater, old abalone shells, snapshots, magazines, catalogs, otoliths, Indian bowls, ship spikes, deadeyes and interesting bottles. And, some did journaling, kept diaries, old dive plans, log books and reminder notes written on the back of a receipt for a dollar fill of air.

Many of this handful of collecting divers had rooms in their homes, sort of in-house museums; some just left the artifacts in boxes and brought out their "museums" for special shows and meetings on request. Perhaps half of them were just collecting things because...the tremendous passion for diving they had was represented in owning a piece of history that later on would be rare, and only a few would have. The other half had grandiose visions of a sleek building erected to house the collection, permanently on display for everybody, especially future generations to view and say, "Things sure were different back then". The young new divers might be asking who the skinny dude is in the picture with that old fashioned two hose regulator...Cousteau, you say, where did he live?

Old timers will need to bring grandkids to someplace to see a Rebikoff Pegasus, a faceplate (mask) made from a coffee can, and a camera ready to go underwater in an old pressure cooker. As the saying goes, you can't really appreciate what you are until you see where you've been, what has come before.

Oh, there have been a number of diving museums over the 50 years of diving history and the stories about those that no longer exist, folklore that belongs in old, present and future museums. We're going to tell you about the museum efforts we know about. Many are specialty museums about one aspect of sport diving or military or commercial. Every effort deserves praise.

Museums are the graveyards of great expeditions and adventures. These viewing and storage receptacles for artifacts have not always been created in time to save all of the wonders of eras and explorations. scuba had a few praiseworthy attempts over its Golden Years. From one glass display case in the corner of a section of a general museum to small total facilities devoted to scuba or a phase of it, their life spans at maximum quality operating capacity were often of short duration.

Those that existed at various times did much to re-enforce scuba exploration, to perhaps justify taking things from underwater so that those many who would never scuba dive could at least see them in a real if shrunken state. The museums were a creditable alternative to backyard trash piles or a box in an individual's garage. The museums made found things important, interpreted their meaning, identified them and gave scuba a heroic image in the eyes of museum devotees.

In the 1950's, the Los Angeles County Underwater Program's founding days, Al Tillman, Bill Starr, and Don St. Hill packaged a mobile museum out of their own collections to take to hobby shows, sportsmen shows, school assemblies, dive club meetings and show on the new medium television. St. Hill, bonafide pioneer diver, who started in the 1930's tossed in the homemade goggles he had used, the gasoline can used as a float, a catch sack with quick opening bottom to outwit game wardens and a record red abalone shell. Starr put in some jewelry he had made from "sea weed", his surgical tubing powered trident spear pole, and starfish he had preserved in formaldehyde. Tillman came up with a pair of black surplus fins, the pattern for making your own dry suit from Los Angeles Neptunes Diving Club, and some Indian bowls he'd found offshore. It was a hodge-podge of obsolete equipment, bottom finds, pictures, and curiosities of nature. There was an abalone lamp in the collection, too, for every diver in California had made one to use as a light on top of that new piece of furniture in America, the TV set.

Even by the 1970's a boy would point a 12-inch bar of steel in a diving equipment display and ask, "What's that Dad?" The bar was a leaf from the old springs unit under old cars to cushion the ride. It was used to pry the flat tire off a rim and then by divers to pry abalones off rocks, thus, an ab-iron. The 1930's and 1940's and even into the 1950's were tough times for most people, what with the Depression, World War II, the scarcity of materials, products; any spare money was scarce to buy anything but food and shelter, and so everybody made do. Divers had to improvise their equipment out of scraps and stuff from the junk yards. Very little was made or manufactured for sport diving. A diving museum ought to show you how it was back then. As it was with the horse and bicycle being replaced by the automobile, the threat of scuba being pushed aside by a rapid technology that suggests computerized submersibles and a massive array of safety equipment, a great freedom of human unencumbered flying in the sea may vanish. Museums ought to not let us forget.

The underwater staff at Los Angeles County had a mixed relationship with the Lifeguard Section and the control of diving in LA County was always a bit controversial. Fortunately, respect and good friendships never let the program suffer. Bev Morgan was the lifeguard who designed the first public classes with Al Tillman and then, Don St. Hill joined Tillman two years later. So the input of the lifeguards was always there. But diving lost a museum when competition went on for a grand house on the beach at Zuma which became a Northern Lifeguard Headquarters, even as boxes were packed and layouts designed for it to be a Diving and Marine Museum.

Long before this time, in San Pedro, California, at Cabrillo Beach by the breakwater, a 1930's bathhouse was converted to an old time display case Marine Museum whose exhibits were mainly finds that divers brought in. A Los Angeles City Lifeguard Captain and fine diver, John Olguin, who was a kid on the beach there, took over and made the museum into an exciting "university" of ocean knowledge, especially about what was to be found under-water. Johnny would take kids out onto the beach, plant grunion eggs, pour water on them and little fish would be born wiggling. He could pick up a shell and explain how it was a nickel in Indian or native American currency. The Cabrillo Beach Marine Museum, a splendid modern one was finally built in the 1980's in John Olguin's honor and divers have continuously been educated on marine biology there ever since.

Scripps Institution of Oceanography and Woods Hole Institute of Oceanography seemed the most likely places for a pure diving museum to emerge. There were exhibits in the aquarium area and eventually in a special grand facility but the theme was more scientific, directed at oceanography and marine biology and very little of the development of diving, in particular, sport diving got any attention. Legendary pioneer divers like Dave Owen, Wheeler North, Conrad Limbaugh, Andy Rechnitzer, and Jim Stewart haunt those hallways.

The places that had perhaps the best shots at creating diving museums that would have been great added attractions, were the grand amusement park themed sea worlds and marinelands. None had more than token presentations of the ongoing story of sport diving history.

ART MCKEE'S MUSEUM

Art McKee's Treasure Museum unleashed the imaginations of an army of young visitors to the Florida Keys who for the most part were stimulated by what they saw to eventually scuba dive. Art started his museum in the Florida Keys in 1948. Art was the premiere treasure diver in the founding years getting into it as far back as the late 1930's. Art was the Mel Fisher of his day, and managed to make artifacts from the sea into a career for

McKee's Sunken Treasure Fortress on US Highway 1, 4 miles South of Tavernier, Florida.

himself. He constructed a living museum of a sunken ship underwater and took people to dive on it. Things he had taken to the surface previously, he took back and arranged a more orderly sunken shipwreck because he had contracted with a film company to use it in a movie. On land he took a barn of an old building and put the accoutrements of treasure diving in it to serve as a tourist attraction to families traversing the Keys on vacation.

Al Tillman was heading down the Keys in early 1970's to interview old friend, Mel Fisher, when he came across McKee's Sunken Treasure Fortress. It was in crumbling state and Art McKee, though still a tough old guy, sort of reflected the ageing of his museum. He was standing in front and was a bit gruff and abrupt at first. Then your heart had to go out to him for he had really been the first, after discovering in 1948, the remains of a sunken ship from the famous 1733 Plate Fleet carrying the annual output from the mint in Mexico, to hold onto pieces-of-eight, gold doubloons, jewelry, canons, muskets and cutlasses for a public display. Smithsonian's Mendel Petersen identified the wreck and took some of the find for display. But Art McKee pioneered the idea of a themed diving museum around the specialty aspect of treasure diving. He even recovered timbers and rebuilt the sunken ship in the courtyard of the Fortress building, highlighted by 17 feet high anchor. Art McKee died in the 1980's and his daughter, Karen, and son Kevin are still active in their father's business.

No one knows how much wealth Art acquired bringing up treasure over all the decades. The State, the Feds, no one was watching in those days. All we know, when we talked to him in the 1970's, was his cryptic and sharp retort - "There's my life, that treasure museum there, do you know anybody else that's got one?"

MEL FISHER'S MUSEUM

There's no question Mel Fisher got pushed into the benevolent role of museum curator. The hounds of bureaucracy tried to take it all away from him, trained their hawkeyes on his every dip into the sea. So he surrounded himself with bonafide archaeologists, documented and preserved things all the time he was marketing the finds.

All the old time dive shops had a corner where a seedling of a diving museum evolved. Mel's Aqua Shop near the Palos Verdes area of Southern California had its entry. Ask about an artifact and Mel would embellish it with an exciting story.

In the 1960's one of Mel's projects was to own and operate a treasure museum with finds on display. He hunted in Europe where he purchased an old ship in the 1970's, brought it across the Atlantic Ocean, and recreated a Spanish treasure galleon that was a floating museum and headquarters for his treasure operations. Everyone, who wanted to be a treasure hunter in America, got perked up on seeing it or the pictures of it.

Mel sought the ATOCHA. No one stepped in so many dog droppings, wiped his shoes and relentlessly moved forward. So many hardships. One of the times we interviewed him was on a Christmas Eve at Key West standing beside the Galleon Museum, which was loaded with real and questionable artifacts. The galleon was sinking in

Mel Fisher just thinking about a treasure museum in the 1950's.

the mud off its dockside berth.

He was having no luck in meeting his payroll that holiday moment, let alone finding the Atocha. But Mel said, "Merry Christmas even if it has to come next week, but it's a pretty good museum isn't it?" He was pointing at two googly-eyed young boys coming down the gangplank with their parents, jabbering non-stop about going treasure hunting. And so was Mel, when he was their age. For whatever other mercenary reasons Mel Fisher may have had, he gets a lot of credit for giving back, creating an exciting, motivating viewing place to display parts of his dreams that had come true.

Later, in the 1980's Mel purchased a huge former Key West Naval Station building to permanently house the nonprofit Mel Fisher Maritime Heritage Society Museum, its research center and conservation laboratories.

The Nuestra Senora de Atocha found, the Galleon floated, and by the 1990's the Mel Fisher Center, Inc. was opened in Sebastian, Florida, too, with traveling treasure exhibits planned and executed. Today, the Mel Fisher Family Trust carries on. The Center and Salvors, Inc. are showrooms guided by Mel's dedicated wife, Deo, daughter, Taffi, sons, Kim and Kane. Treasure objects can be purchased and fancied.

The Whydah Museum was set up in the 1990's by Barry Clifford to cover the discovery and excavation of the only pirate treasure ship ever uncovered. Barry called the "museum" the Whydah Sea Lab and Learning Center in Provincetown, Massachussets, near the wreck site. He felt archaeologists are elitists and the general public deserved a crack at the stuff and why not go commercial; nonprofit museums charge admission.

What sport diving has always needed was the complete picture of diving, not treasure or natural history or military diving but how it was over the years for the average American (and others too of course) recreational diver.

There have been earnest attempts over all the years but none have taken on the magnitude of a full blown facility properly endowed and financed. Some of the efforts have faltered and been abandoned; some have just been passionate diver/historians, who knew there wasn't failure if you didn't quit.

In Al Tillman's *I Thought I Saw Atlantis* book of reminiscences, he takes us back to the early day's of diving's junk yards. In it he restates the trials and tribulations of the collector as follows:

"Get this junk out of here, put it in the basement, garage..." A lot of us pack-rat type-divers have gotten that order from the high command. Wives have their own stuff with which to clutter up the house.

Doesn't she realize that this early diving gear is history...that I'm a conservator, a preservationist? You can dodge the bullet on that one but wait until you get ready to move to a new home. 'You aren't taking that junk, I thought you got rid of it,' she says. And it is tempting to finally dump the accumulation, damn nostalgia, damn trying to provide future generations with visual evidence of the way things were in the frontier days of diving.

She's not through yet... 'What are these wooden shingles with old tennis shoes bolted to them?' She now has opened a box and pulled out a smelly, rotting pretzel of sneakers and wood.

I snatch it away from her and growl, 'This is the way Bob Lorentz at Water Gill, you know the shop on 101 near Venice, (California) where I use to fill my tanks,...the way he started diving...back in the 1930's?' 'So,' she says, a bit scornful, 'Give them back to this Lorentz guy.'

'No, no these are mine. I think he told me about making his own fins, and I made up my own to try...' She had walked away in disgust.

The high command in another household never said a word about the gatherings of stuff and things, papers and books regarding the career of her diving, subservient spouse for 32 years. Until one day, he heard overtones of a conversation in jest to her friend that a match should be lit to all that junk he's collecting. Years later for other reasons, the wisecrack-arsonist permanently left the compound to never see that the justification for all materials was for a very good reason.

It was about at this point in a diving pioneer's life where he goes to the yellow pages to see if there's an underwater museum that would take these wonderful artifacts off his hands...out of his life. Back in the 1950's there was no such place.

Gustav Dalla Valle's widow asked *Scuba America* to provide a biography for a Hall of Fame. Could *Scuba America* look over Gustav's diving archives? Sorry, all those boxes of papers were thrown away.

By 1960, Al Tillman was getting involved and entrenched at *Skin Diver Magazine* with Jim Auxier and Chuck Blakeslee, through NAUI and the International Underwater Film Festival. They had a small museum of diving relics at this time that divers would drop off: A carved figure off Easter Island from Bev Morgan's diving expedition there, a brass cross from a galleon from Bob Marx, a piece of jade from Al Tillman, a porthole off the gambling ship, Star of Scotland, from Dick Anderson, and a piece of coral from Chuck Blakeslee and a bit more...it all sat on a brick and plank book case in the entry way at the 1950's *SDM* offices in Lynwood, California.

The diving clubs were peaking at this point in time and it was necessary to curry their favor to keep the Underwater Society of America from pushing *SDM* aside and publishing a strong, competitive magazine (Jim and Chuck avoided this by putting the Underwater Society of America supplement inside the pages of *SDM* and offered clubs a chance to have the *Skin Diver Magazine* Museum come to any major events as a mobile unit.

Al remembers best putting all the artifacts in boxes, loading up Jim Auxier's new Winnebago RV and heading up to the Sacramento Council's diving fair. They picked up Garry Howland at the Vandenberg Air Force Base on the way and took Gordon Chorpash, the diving hippie artist.

The four of them set up the "first museum" as a road show exhibit and manned it to answer questions. It was a hit! They were offered donations of all kinds of relics and old equipment. A large wolf eel skull was the most intriguing thing they took back. They didn't have those imposing creatures in Southern California.

The *Skin Diver Magazine* Diving Museum wasn't of any interest to Petersen Publishing, who took over *SDM* in 1964. So it ended up at UNEXSO in the Bahamas to become the Cousteau Museum. Housed in the two story glass and wood lobby with custom made display cases, it was a grand display of interesting historical items. Cousteau OK'd the use of his name and UNEXSO felt it was a fitting tribute as well as a promotional tool. After 1968 and a change in ownership, there was a break-in and some valuable items were stolen. Later owners were interested in marketing space and the Cousteau Museum diminished into wall decorations behind the bar.

Some of the things in that UNEXSO Cousteau Museum were a nail from the HMS Bounty courtesy of Luis Marden of *National Geographic*, a giant crocodile skull from Xelah Lagoon in the Yucatan, Al Tillman's Calypso Camera that Keller took on his 1962 thousand foot dive, a "gold nugget" from Mel Fisher, Jordan Klein's underwater vehicle prop used in the film *Thunderball*, prize jade nuggets and 1300 emeralds from diving expeditions all embedded in a huge wooden rudder from a galleon wreck, the entire collection of *Sea Hunt* scripts with Tillman's technical advisor comments in the margins, a gold chip off the General Winfield Scott wreck that Al Tillman had traded a Chorpash painting to Dick Anderson for - and a lot more.

There was a diving museum developing in Key West that the YMCA has some relation to.

Museums were started in a small way here and there over the 1980's and 1990's. The logical places like The Sea Worlds and Marinelands never picked up on it. Their mistake many divers felt.

The best possibilities as we end a 50 year history are in individuals, who have dedicated years to preserving old equipment and displaying it around at big events. But for such collections to continue, there has to be a new generation step up and carry on or it will all end up in garage sales or dumpsters. Bob Morgan of Dayton, Ohio with the help of Ray Tussey had a fantastic regulator display mounted in a basement but Bob and Ray passed on

Nick Icorn is recognized as the Guru of Diving History in museum form.

and the display disappeared - typical of hundreds of other efforts across the country and around the world.

Two passionate diver collectors came out of the 1950's putting aside everything they could get their hands on about sport diving. Dr. Sam Miller is the paper king with all the magazines, programs, catalogs - stacks and boxes full and he's still at it in the end of the century. But the other collector was Nick Icorn, and is the recognized Czar of gathering the artifacts. He has squirreled away diving's history and slept on top of it all these years, decades. Why? Why? The man loves diving and its' story and has been a part of all of it. Nick deserves a physical place, a grand museum facility. Perhaps the year 2001 will ultimately promote for us a final resting place for all these memories and artifacts in Santa Barbara, California, home of Leslie Leaney's Historical Diving Society.

The Smithsonian or the National Geographic Society seem likely sponsors for a full-blown in residence diving museum structure. The Diving Equipment Manufacturing Association ought to have pushed to support a real place.

Better than one museum, diving's history ought to be presented in key diving geographical locations, regional branches trading off duplicate artifacts with each other. It's going to happen as we move into the 2000's, we can feel it in the air.

On that note of regional museums to house sport diving's history, the specialty museums are worth examining for guide lines. The Naval Undersea Museum at the Hood Canal Nuclear Sub Base in Keyport, Washington, has institutionalized navy diving history with artistic presentations, and even has the premiere bathyscaphe, the Trieste, on permanent display. But by the time they get submarines filling the space available, there is little room or concern for sport diving. They have a very comprehensive library which every effective museum should have.

This is not the time to be timid or settle for a corner in large museums or "aquarium theme parks" - a sport diving

Nick Icorn has one of the best collections of dive equipment anywhere.

museum should stand on its own. The museum, a central one or regional, should have a traveling, mobile exhibit unit much as Smithsonian has had to do to broaden public interest. It ought to loan out duplicate artifacts, as many museums do, for school classes and public service television shows. Al Tillman remembers a TV quiz show he organized back in the 1950's where he pitted lifeguards vs divers bringing stuffed eels and shells from the Los Angeles Natural History Museum. Bev Morgan, Bob and Bill Meistrel were ace members of one team and answered questions like, why doesn't a shark need a dentist, or what is the danger of caloric excitation of the vestibular apparatus...and there'd be a shark's jaw there as a visual prop.

Museums can play a big role in refreshing memories or educating new generations about how it all happened. The ones we've had in whatever limited shape they were and are, have always ignited or re-ignited interest in sport diving.

If you want to get a sport diving museum started, here is a list we think every sport diving museum should have. Most of these things are housed now in the mobile Museum of Diving History that Tom and Al Tillman watch over and store in a newly built *Scuba America* Historical Center facility on Orcas Island, Washington.

A LIST OF SOME OF THE HISTORICAL ARTIFACTS
THAT REPRESENT THE HISTORY OF SPORT DIVING IN AMERICA

First Issue of *Skin Diver Magazine*

HMS Bounty Nail

Crushed Styrofoam cup from deep ALVIN dive.

Calypso Camera - Nikonos Camera First Models

Voit Aquaeye

Cousteau Shark Billy

Silver Piece of Eight from Mel Fisher's Atocha

Coffee-Can-Mask

Churchill Fins

Two-Hose Aqua-Lung

Waterlung One Hose Regulator

U.S. Navy Diving Manuals

Cross' *Underwater Safety*

Bev Morgan's, David Owen's, Albert Tillman's Manuals

International Underwater Film Festival Programs

Boston Sea Rovers Paul Revere Spike

NOGI Award

MAKO Underwater Camera

Arbolette Speargun

Photo and Brochure from First NAUI Course (Houston)

Original Brochure for UNEXSO

Mae West Vest - B.C.

Original Bel Aqua Snorkel

DEMA Award

New Science of Skin and Scuba Diving Manual YMCA

Jade from Jade Cove

Black Coral, Hawaii

First Wet Suit

First Dry Suit - Long Johns Underwear

John Steele Original Painting Cover

First Depth Gauge/Plastic Tube Type

Shingle Sneaker Fins

Cartridge Belt Weight System

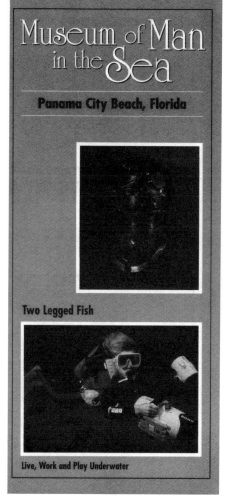

The Museum of Man in the Sea in Florida does a good job at displaying items.

First U.S. Divers Equipment Catalog

Silent World Book

Diving to Adventure Book

Andrea Doria Plate

Great White Shark Tooth

JAWS, the Book & Movie Poster

First Sea Vue Gauge

First Diving Watch, Rolex

Sea Hunt Script

Patches - First Diving Clubs

Pole Spear

Pressure Cooker Camera Case

Gauge from Keller Dive

Innertube Float Catch Sack

Gas Can Float

First Computer/Tables

Los Angeles County Certification Card

Diving Log Book, PADI, NAUI, SSI

NAUI Certification Card Picture

Native Goggles

First *DIVE* Magazine

Divers Flag

First Hand Signals Printout

First *Water Bug* Magazine, Florida

The Frogmen Book, Waldron/Gleeson

Special Issue- *Diving with Self Contained Apparatus*, 1954, U.S. Navy Manual, Lanphier/Dwyer

Underwater Photography and Television Book, E.R. Cross

Divers Using Compressed Air Book, David Owens, Pergmon Press

First Issues of *Fathom Magazine*

I Thought I Saw Atlantis Book

Exploring Deep Frontier Book, Earle/Giddings

Los Angeles County 1st Course Outline

Abalone Shell

Stuffed Lobster, New England

Slurp Gun

Cotton Gloves

Dry Suit, Baby Oil, Talcum Powder

Any Famous Sunken Ship Artifacts

Pictures of Artificial Reefs or Mini Models

Decompression Tables Wheel

Queen Conch-Shell

Purple Coral /Farnsworth Banks

Earbone from a Whale (Otolith)

Duck Feet Fins

Shark Chaser Packet

The children of the pioneer generation may be the best bet for preserving the history of sport diving. Tom Tillman, above with father Al Tillman in 1974, grew up around diving and manages the Scuba America Museum and writes about the history of diving. At the very least the children of the pioneers should donate the materials instead of throwing them out.

Boston Sea Rovers Clinic Program, 1950's and 1960's

Rubberized Pack Surplus (Dry-Pak) for Gear

Textbooks

Blue Ribbon photographs by top Underwater Photographers

Manatee Fins

All Equipment Development Stages over years to present

Photographs of Artifacts in use or being found to enhance their importance.

Hope-Page Non-Return Valve - Prototype

Hawaiian Tank Back-Pak

Thick Plastic Bubble with water seal-tight-glass removable port for small camera or light meter.

Original Air Pressure Gauge for tank-Medical-Type Tank Valve

Voit Fins used on *Sea Hunt* series

Treasure-Diving Holidays Book, Jane and Barney Crile

The "Key-Wrench" to attach pressure gauge and open medical valves on original air tanks.

Learn Scuba Diving in a Weekend Book, Reg Vallintine

Al Betters, an exUDTer of Korean vintage, contacted Zale Parry during the research of *Scuba America*. He has put together a small museum in the 1990's displaying UDT/SEALS items and wanted an autographed *Sports Illustrated* Cover with Zale on it for inclusion. He travels his museum around to schools and events. Many sport divers, the best, were exUDT warriors and became leaders in the civilian field, such as Jim Cahill and Dick Bonin.

Diving's real heroes, perhaps all of humanity's are those pack rat collectors of ancient artifacts and illuminating folk tales who stand firm against the wearing winds of organizing, cleaning up, moving on to act as watchdogs, prison guards, who will not let our memories escape. For those who might say, who cares, get on with life, the collectors say that what has past is the tough, gritty character and mystic of diving. It is wise to embrace the new but metaphorically it is only a splash of fresh paint over the seasoned wood of a grand old boat that has tested the unknown, the fury of storms, and the vast wilderness of the oceans. Diving needs those memories to give meaning to the present, without them we all have been just temporary holes in the ocean waters.

26

Jaws:

The Artificial Manufacturing of Fear

Defining Event: Nobody Went in Water for a Long Time

"...feeling in the blackness with her left hand. She could not find her foot. She reached higher on her leg, ...her groping fingers had found a nub of bone and tattered flesh."

With passages such as this, Peter Benchley created a classic monster in his novel *Jaws* to rival Mary Shelley's ersatz human, Frankenstein. Peter was a diver and a writer, who never got the 1916 Matawan, New Jersey, attacks out of his head once he read about them. The usual Benchley research resulted in a believable giant great white shark that attacked a number of times at a seaside resort.

The *Jaws* shark was created out of the reports, the catches, the attacks about the ultimate killing creature that had been seen and captured at lengths of 25 feet, so the 30 feet Benchley decided to make this one, is within reason. There is evidence that once there was a 50 foot shark with 6 inch teeth that swam the oceans, the Megalodon.

Peter Benchley put a young girl in the water at night, an awkward swimmer and set the stage for the shocking unseen attack - "...this time the fish attacked from below ...the great conical head struck her like a locomotive, knocking her up out of the water. The jaws snapped shut around her torso, crushing bones and flesh and organs into jelly."

The book presents a suspenseful story and has a factual and comprehensive foundation of shark information, especially about the big man eaters.

The book sold thousands of copies before it was snatched up for a possible movie, a potential *King Kong* in the water. Steven Spielberg took it on, putting his money into special effects, or effect, a giant mechanical shark, and it would be the star of the movie. The divers, who manipulated it from inside the body called it "Bruce" for no good reason...

The movie hit, like a nuclear bomb in the theatres, a block buster with box office receipts in 1975 on the all time earnings list, to an up-to-date re-release gross of $260 million. By year 2000, a special 25th anniversary collectors' edition was put out which is projected to perhaps double the total gross revenue. It's impact was astronomical compared to the minor tremor caused by the book. The shark seemed so real. People were staying out of the water everywhere that summer of 1975. It soared beyond the illusion on 'film' and struck terror in hearts of the bravest, and in particular the diving clan. The 1959 Pamperin shark attack off La Jolla, California, halted the rapid fire growth of the new activity of sport diving, but most divers shook if off in short time.

Jaws wasn't that easy to pass over. This was a believable good read as a book but as a technically crafted motion picture, it was a classic. Even hard core divers were showing reticence about getting back in the water.

Then a large number of sightings, actual shark attacks, fisherman coming across and capturing great white sharks in the range of Bruce's size. Was it illusory hysteria or had the wide public awareness through *Jaws* made people more observant and inclined to report all shark encounters. Sharks in general took on a fascination, research projects proliferated, while underwater film makers did dangerous things to get footage for the insatiable maw of television in the late 1970's.

Many of the interviews for this history were recorded about the time of *Jaws*. Al Tillman went across country, interviewing various diving pioneers. He hit Gloucester, Massachusetts, and sat down with old friend, Jim Cahill,

founding father of New England Divers Company. "How's business?", was a good leading question of the day.

Jim's answer was echoed everywhere in dozens of interviews: "*Jaws* has really put a hole in the side of our boat. Business in diving fell off 50% with that movie. I've sold New England Divers because if was time for me to retire not because of *Jaws*. But *Jaws* would be a good reason to get out of the diving business. Personally, it didn't bother me, I'm still going to go get my lobsters."

Diving entrepreneurs tended to shoot the speargun through their collective foot, wanting to wear the cloak of bravado, and yet, not wanting to scare off potential divers. Having it both ways wasn't possible. They had to be truthful in the end. They answered the question, "Are there sharks like that out there?" The answer given was a hesitant, "Yes," but with a modifier; "Yes, but we never see them." Unfortunately, some divers couldn't resist creating their own fictional shark experiences and an epidemic of fear pervaded the land.

Newspapers immediately, after *Jaws* first screened, were saying in bold headlines - **Shark Mania Is Sweeping The Country**. Quotes were received from experts like Thomas Lineaweaver III of Woods Hole - "People are scared out of their wits...people don't want to be statistics." Another headline said, **JAWS OF FEAR OPEN ON ALL SHORES**. Jim Holland, a Chief Lifeguard in Miami, Florida, reported - "Any fish in the water now becomes a shark. There are fewer divers and no long distance swimmers this year."

Bob Burnside, Chief of the Los Angeles County's 500 lifeguards, said, "My lifeguards are more effected than occasional bathers. They have to swim every day but all us had to force ourselves back in the water after seeing *Jaws*."

Ralph Osterhaut, head of Farallon Industries which markets a shark dart that injects CO_2 into a shark - "It's a $150 item top of the line and our sales have doubled."

As in the movie, *Jaws*, a lot of amateur "bounty hunters" boated out in search of big sharks. A 1400-pounder, 13 feet long was harpooned off Catalina Island and taken to Sea World to be refrigerated and put on exhibit. Al Tillman recalls seeing it, his first real great white shark and said - "Every dive I could ever recall I overlaid with this toothy monster possibly lurking nearby and it reinforced my fear of sharks as much as *Jaws*.

We asked Jim Christiansen, one of America's greatest spearfishing champions and diving legends if *Jaws* shakes even the mighty.

"You can't let a bunch of what-ifs spoil your fun. Danger is everywhere and facing it, doing something you want to do, need to do, well, that's how you find out if you've got mustard, at least, at some point in your life. *Jaws* maybe got me wondering what a bite would be like, how it would feel, then, I remembered it's just a movie and I've been down on thousands and thousands of dives without seeing any big teeth coming at me."

In the days following *Jaws* release, *Scuba America* prepared this original opening to a chapter on *Fear in Diving*. *Jaws* became a chapter in itself.

That the American public is vulnerably impressive has been perfectly clear since a radio program in the 1930's threw them into chaos over a dramatized Martian invasion. It took an unexpectedly and immensely successful movie of the 1970's to doubly reinforce the fact that they have not changed.

Just when diving was getting back on its feet and divers were learning to live and love the monsters of the deep as aquarium performers, and certainly not seeing them as vicious deliberate man eaters, a plastic and chicken wire shark in a move called *Jaws* set up a sense of fear that what was presented as a fiction in a very believable manner was certainly a possibility. It did not take an advanced imagination to visualize the horror of an attack actually happening. It swept many beaches clear of people that summer of 1975 and divers were as susceptible as anyone to transposing fiction to reality. Even the grizzled old mossback divers who had paid their dues with shark encounters seemed to revolve and glance anxiously around in the water.

For any new crop of divers already stimulated to try scuba diving there was a parallel chorus of parents and spouses who were convinced their loved one was about to make a human sacrifice to *Jaws*. Sales declined and so did student enrollments. People just were not as enthusiastic about sea bathing for the moment. And somehow

Jaws and the hundreds of spin-off man eating shark pictures and stories that there upon appeared, the frozen great white sharks on exhibit, the rash of shark frenzy footage on television, and special tours to meet and photograph great white sharks, reminded divers that the vicious propensity did exist and they were the endangered species underwater. It was a chilling fear genetically coded into humans and easily triggered by cues of much less impact than JAWS.

Equipment sales were off 50-60% with the arrival of *Jaws*, charter boat trips cancelled, and fewer people wanted to learn to dive. Later years saw inferior *Jaws* sequels but it was the original *Jaws* that panicked the nation.

TINTORERRA: A MOTION PICTURE

During the 1970's, diving's number one box office star was without question the Shark. Summer 1978 had *Jaws* 2 to set scuba divers teeth on edge and a Ramon Bravo low budget exploitation film, *Tintorerra*, to keep them on the beach. A giant tiger shark chews up some nubile beauties in graphic detail and the lead diver. The film didn't intellectually stump anybody. A few wires are visible pulling some of the "monsters" but there were some hard core real danger shots.

We all at once hated sharks and wanted authorities to get rid of them. Send out bounty motivated "posses" and exterminate those big killers was the mood. Over a year, sport diving worked it's way back into popularity probably because there was so much exciting environment underwater, thousands of other less ominous creatures to see. We weren't about to miss it despite the risk.

It would have been hard to imagine at the height of *Jaws* impact that later many would adopt an almost benevolent approach to sharks and make a massive effort to preserve them. Hopefully, we could all live in peace together. Cynics wondered how to get that message to a pea-brain-creature that hasn't grown much mentally in 300 million years.

THE UBIQUITOUS DICK ANDERSON

Scuba divers had a role in making the shooting of *Jaws* possible. Here are some of the behind the scene stories:

"There were several different fake sharks used on *Jaws*." Dick Anderson tells his story. "The main one was mounted on an underwater platform with hydraulic controls to make it do what sharks do. Another model was referred to as the 'tow shark'. It was fiberglass and about twenty-five or thirty feet long. It was the top half of the shark and towed by a tug to show it cruising the waters. We rigged-it up and took it to sea a trial run. Out in about two thousand feet of water off Nassau, we towed the shark at shark cruising speed. Too much of the nose was coming out of the water and the shark nose pull-point had to be readjusted. The easiest way for me to do this was to hop off the tug and tread water while the shark was being

Sharks became a major box office draw.

towed in my direction on the quarter-mile tow line.

"I hopped in and the tug kept going. The huge shark was coming right at me but I'm brave. - I got under the nose and raised the pull-point which would lower the nose. That completed, I left the shark and waved to the tug. The tug made a big circle and came back in my direction. It didn't stop. I heard a yell: 'Anderson, the camera chopper is coming out to make a shot. We'll pick you up on the next pass.'

"Well, here comes the shark - right at me. Here comes the chopper, door open, cameras ready. The shark's getting closer. The chopper swoops in for the shot. I should have dived under but what the hell! With the shark ready to attack me I pulled out my trusty dive knife and stabbed him a few times as he swam by. It was the first time I ever stabbed a thirty foot shark.

"That afternoon one of the film crew execs made a special trip out to The Shark Factory where the Special Effects were operated. He made the trip to tell me, 'Anderson, nobody gets away with that kind of crap. You'd better think about packing up your gear.'

"A lot of guys heard him say it. The rest of the day was filled with comments like, 'Hey Anderson, are you going in to see the dailies tonight? ' (Dailies are the review of the footage shot that day, or the day before.)

"I didn't go see the dailies but my friend, Pete Romano, underwater cameraman, did. It went like this: Various shark footage going on and on. Then there's this big shark cruising along the surface. He's heading right for a solitary diver. As shark approaches, the diver pulls out his big dive knife and stabs at the big shark as it passes.

"The director, Joseph Sargent, said, 'Hey, What the hell was that? Roll that back. That's the only good thing that's happened so far in this whole damned movie!'

"I never heard another word about it and didn't lose my clear, warm water job. And, that film sequence ended up in the party reel to celebrate *Jaws* with the title, *Jaws, The Revenge*. It does get a good laugh!"

Jaws, as a rerun and classic video, kept scaring people right up through year 2000. New films about sharks didn't get close to its impact on sport diving. A late 1990's film *Deep Blue Sea* starred newcomer actor, Thomas Jane, whose childhood nightmares were about *Jaws*.

Ricou Browning played The Creature from the Black Lagoon. It scared people out of the water also.

"The Shark was under my bed," he recalls, "and my sister thought it was going to jump out of the toilet." During *Deep Blue Sea* filming in the Bahamas, he was dumped into 30 feet of water to swim with real sharks...and the nightmares of *Jaws* came back.

Other films and books that scared a few divers out of the water for a short time were:

Creature from the Black Lagoon was shot in Wakula Springs, Florida, and starred Ricou Browning, another diving legend, who was Ivan Tors main technical advisor in the water for *Sea Hunt*, the *Flipper* series and this horror film. It required a lot of diving ability and knowledge and a wonderful costume. Ricou was flawless.

The film was about a hideous creature emerging from the calm but mysterious dark waters of a lagoon. It had a science fiction over-lay which kept it from being as believable as *Jaws* which was a projection of a real possibility and based on facts of nature. Nevertheless, beneath that vast ocean and lakes, ponds, springs, he's a panting beast ready to erupt and scare our exposure suit-pants off.

Jaws was a telling moment in time showing how fear could be manufactured from suggested ideas and how sport diving, like a sailboat, righted itself despite a stunning blow.

WITH JAWS OTHER UNMITIGATED FAKERY FROM 1940'S

Dr. Carl L. Hubbs, Professor of Biology, Scripps Institution of Oceanography, University of California, La Jolla, California, a scuba diver and mentor of famous divers, interpreted the authenticity of the book, *I Dive for Treasure*, by Lieutenant Harry E. Rieseberg. The book's first printing 1942 had a seventh printing by 1945. It was big reading for anyone, who was into skin and scuba diving.

When we began our research for *Scuba America*, Dear Dr. Hubbs gave his written report dated November 10, 1949 to us. You can well imagine the inquiries he received regarding the danger of encountering dangerous, giant octopi during diving operations. Hubbs general conclusion after examining *I Dive for Treasure* is that "I still retain, and will continue to retain the belief, until better evidence to the contrary is forthcoming, that fatal encounters with octopi are to a large degree myths of the sea... a diver might run into difficulty with a large octopus, if he happened to enter its lair, because the octopus like many other animals has territorial habits... and would defend such territory. Ordinarily, however, I think that even very large octopi would show fright and make efforts to escape rather than to attack."

Fakery makes the disbelieving believable. Dr. Hubbs further explains to all who ask, "Is this all possible?" Interpreting the pictures, he points out that a photograph taken showing the sunken remains of an ancient ship off Port Royal, in Jamaica shows a chain that hangs over the wreck with almost no corrosion after three centuries underwater. The plant unrealistically draped in the foreground is the giant kelp, Macrocystis, which grows abundantly along the California Coast, but not within 1,000 miles of Jamaica. Another photograph of the sinister octopus monster with a 24 foot spread is shown with a fresh water aquarium plant and with what are obviously medium-sized brook trout. The fearsome eyes catching high lights and protruding in the front of the head are obviously artificial, for they look totally unlike the flat eyes on the side of the head of an octopus. The octopus arm was curled giving a strong impression that a preserved specimen was put in a fresh water aquarium."

Rieseberg did well with excessively, imaginative and apparently imagined or fabricated sharks at great depths. "His remarkable vision could decipher 'triangular cutting teeth with their saw edges'." His fairy tale worked. It rivaled sex, blood and guts for that era. The book made good reading but added that ingredient of fear. His explaining of the myths of the sea erased the uneasiness early on that may have been felt in encountering giants that can devour divers. And Lieutenant Harry E. Rieseberg made a living.

On Location on Martha's Vineyard a book about the making of *Jaws* by Edith Blake is one of those behind the scenes books that matches the drama of the story being filmed. It didn't add to fear of sharks, more like fear of making elaborate special effects movies. A planned "small war" (as author Blake describes it) took five months instead of the scheduled five weeks. Things went wrong such as Hollywood people aren't nautical people and had no idea of how weather in the sea is more unpredictable and uncontrollable than sharks.

Divers spent more than enough of cold, rough water time recovering dropped objects, such as, panavision cameras and walkie-talkies. Universal Studios dropped $30,000 a day in expenditures in the town. All the crews carried libraries of everything there was to know about sharks.

Three mechanical sharks were needed because sharks aren't bright enough to be trained, the author reports and have a tendency to eat trainers. The mechanical sharks proved just as unpredictable as the real things although none of them ate any of the divers who had to clear, repair and bring them up when they accidentally sank - and kept the divers scared half to death. It cost $23,000 just to haul the sharks from California. The sharks had control panels out-doing the cockpit of a B29 bomber. The mechanical sharks had two sets of teeth; plastic for munching on boats and rubber for chewing up people - but sometimes that got mixed up and stunt divers really got bitten. The electric circuitry of the sharks was subject to electrolysis breakdown in salt water.

Some other tidbits about making the movie:

Special Effects Departments could make some very realistic looking sharks.   *J. Klein*

• Steve Spielberg, who rose to prominence with *Jaws*, spent a lot of time throwing marbles in the water to simulate bullets hitting the surface.

• A 12 foot dead tiger shark was flown up from Florida at a $12,000 cost, made up by Max Factor and used for dock scenes which required a real shark for some authenticity. Crew members back from a fishing trip said that they saw hundreds of them just off the island and could have brought one back for free. Rumor had it that the film people were bringing in these big sharks and releasing them into the harbor.

• Peter Gimbel and Ron and Valerie Taylor were hired to get lots of real great white shark footage to splice into the film. Only small sharks would come up to the cage, the big ones spooked. To get a 25 footer look, a midget was sent down and the sharks that would approach instantly grew 20 feet. *Jaws* needed the Taylors' shark footage to get audience acceptance. *Jaws* would have been sadly lacking without what those two great divers could provide.

• Directors kept track of where they were in the script during filming by who had been eaten: Christy, baby boy, man and the dog.

• In a scene where 400 extras raced out of the water fleeing the shark, one man was supposed to catch a finger in a pretty girl's bikini top and it would come off. One 10 year old extra, goggle eyed, stood up and stared - the water was supposed to be over his head with all extras on knees to give the "deep" impression - the whole cast of 400 extras had to do it all over again.

• Movie producers measure a film's impact by the sounds of the gasps and screams, of a preview audience or by the complete silent moments that indicated the viewers were caught up in the suspense. *Jaws* had more of those silent moments, no popcorn chewing or murmuring, than any film ever.

• John Williams music background won the Academy Award. Spielberg, the Director, thought it was a joke at first. Williams played it with two fingers at each end of the piano keyboard. It grew on Spielberg, who felt like he was tied to the rail and a train was coming. Ta Tump, Ta Tump, Ta Tump. The shark didn't have to be shown until the last half of the film. Until the sound was added, the film elicited small excitement.

In theatres, a rare thing happened, people sat glued to their seats, utterly silent, through all the boring credit lines at the end. Producers, Zanuck and Brown, were black and blue from elbowing each other during the premiere showing, saying over and over, "We did it! We did it!"

The demolition of the big shark eating the boat was carried off by experts from Woods Hole Institution of Oceanography. It only took a few days and all signs of *Jaws* were gone from Martha's Vineyard. But the terror and fear of sharks left by this fake shark movie would remain embedded in the psyche of every one who was involved in the production.

As the promotional blurbs ominously intoned - "This mindless thing lives to kill, will attack and devour anything...God created the devil and gave it jaws! Never mind the boat ride attraction at Universal Studios which hardly scares, (kids try to reach out and put their hands in its mouth). See the movie, *Jaws*, again and let your imagination go to work. It was and is a terrifying experience.

27

EXOTIC SCUBA

DEFINING EVENT: CRYOLUNG

How can a human unattached to the surface breathe underwater? A niggling question over the ages and a lot of our revered great minds and inventors took a crack at it - such as, Leonardo Da Vinci, Alexander the Great and Jacques-Yves Cousteau.

OK, implanted gills was the visionary answer, and with the advances in human anatomy research, it may yet arrive. But if we pick up from Cousteau's Aqua Lung as the final basic tool invented in 1942 and serving us well for over fifty years, the attempts to make it more perfect are not many. We have chosen to title all such efforts as exotic scuba.

We talk about the one hose regulator in another chapter, *The One Hose Regulator*, and certainly that innovation was perhaps the most impactful of three major changes. It streamlined the configuration of hose and mouthpiece; less bulky, more sanitary, and not as vulnerable to damage. It put the second stage at the mouthpiece where it diminished breathing resistance. It packed neater, too. (However, underwater photographers were put-off by bubbles erupting near their mouths on exhalations and disturbing focal setups.)

The Waterlung in 1958 was the first quality regulator of this type, developed by Sam LeCocq and distributed by a company called Sportsways, Inc. Was it "exotic"? It was if we accept the definition of exotic as excitingly different.

Around the same time, a young diver Rory Page, who was a diving instructor at the Long Beach, California, YMCA teamed up with a friend, Charles Hope, to create the Hope-Page Mouthpiece. The device could be put on any two-hose regulator as a substitute for the basic mouthpiece, which took in water and free-flowed air if it came out of the diver's mouth, a nuisance and a loss of air time. No one liked to stick a mouthpiece full of water in his mouth and either blow it clear or swallow the water. (Hmmm, that delectable salt water!) It was based on and worked by non-return valves that could be activated by a twist. The Garrett Corporation challenged the patent with a regulator called the Northill Airlung that utilized the same close-off feature, and in particular, utilized the Venturi Principle to force air and ease the effort of the diver. A diving engineer, Robert 'Bob' Kimes, put that one

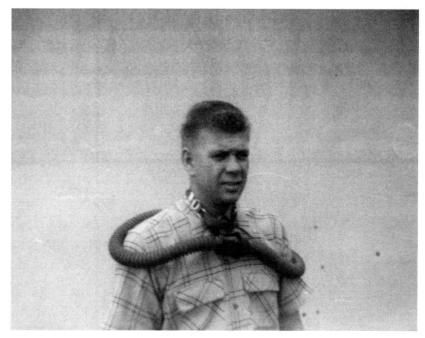

The first prototype of the Hope-Page valve. Rory Page was the inventor.

together. These efforts to create a difference were focused on the two- hose regulator.

Manufacturers advertised flamboyant claims in the late 1950's and early 1960's. A lot of pioneer divers reluctantly retired their two-hose regulators with regrets. Al Tillman recalls Bill Starr, a key developer in the Los Angeles County Program, saying in interview during the 1970's, "There was something substantial about those elephant trunks, those two large corrugated tubes coming around your head. The mouthpiece was always there, and it was actually a fun maneuver to roll around and clear water out of them...yeah, substantial that's what they were. I miss them."

And so the ads and catalogs slowly phased out the two- hose regulators in the 1960's, "dinosaur equipment," but later to be much sought-after artifacts by collectors. In the 1990's, a few collectors showed up at diving affairs with a two-hoser and startled the new breed of diver. The word "huh?" always seemed to be the reaction. By the late 1990's, two-hose regulators were being manufactured in Mexico in a sort of retro movement. The Nemrod Company never stopped production.

What else came along besides reduction in size, sleeker design, and shinier chrome and colors? We suspect the invisible inner workings were different, something about which manufacturers could persuade the general diving public. For example, "piston driven" was a term that came along in the 1960's and had an automotive sound that elicited a feeling of confidence in the ordinary group of non-technical divers. Only a diving engineer could get giddy over studying the exact process of a piston working to give one air.

By the mid 1960's, there were about two dozen regulators of different brand names available and split half and half between two-hose and one-hose. The holy grail sought by the regulator engineers was ease of breathing. This feature was a grand marketing device but most divers couldn't tell the difference. Mike Kevorkian, a pioneer shop owner in Hialeah, Florida, told us back in the 1960's as he looked around to see if a customer was listening — "Frankly, they all breathe the same to me. However, whatever I've got on my shelf to sell, that's the easiest breathing regulator."

Jim Drew, who ran a dive shop in West Palm Beach, Florida, during the 1960's and was a graduate of the first NAUI instructors course said, "You just confuse your students with trying to explain which regulators have easier breathing — it's a personal thing and depends on what you're doing. The Aqua Lung breathes easier, the beginning diver thinks, because it's the brand name he recognizes."

It is important to note here that the oxygen rebreather was fully designated as dangerous, as well as unpopular with civilian divers. Bev Morgan, who understood regulators as well as anybody in those early days, liked to refer to the other kind of scuba

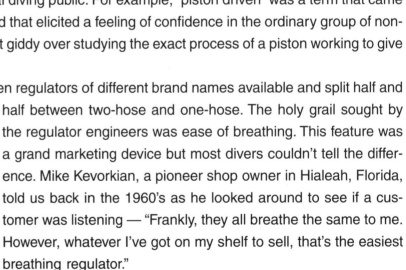

If it "breathes like a breeze"—it's a Northill!

(for a rebreather was a form of self-contained underwater breathing apparatus) as a CADBU or Compressed Air Demand Breathing Unit, but those initials were not easily transformed into a word as scuba had been.

When scuba is technically dissected to understand how it works, it is the regulator that is the heart of the process. The "demand" aspect was very important, or otherwise there would be the great waste of free flowing air which was the way many of the pre-Aqua Lung inventions were. The "demand" is what the diver needs in the amount of air, a small flow when at ease and heavy when working. For most divers that was all they needed to know; the nuts and bolts of it was designed by labs full of engineers and they could be trusted. (Couldn't they)? Otherwise, how could they sell it? (America, in general, still trusted authority and government in those pre-Watergate days). There was, of course, a certain pride among divers in being able to talk the engineering and design language. It gave one a sort of knowledge cachet.

Loyal Goff displays an exotic experimental S.C.U.B.A. at EDU in the 1950's

Here's a rolling list of terms the divers have had to contend with:

• <u>One stage-two hose</u> which means the high pressure of the air tank is reduced by one stage (valve) to a breathing air pressure equivalent to surrounding, ambient water.

• <u>Mouthpiece non-return valves</u> which allowed air to come through but kept water from entering the hoses.

• <u>Housing</u> is the case that holds the stages and valves and levers in a two-hose regulator. Most housings were chrome-plated brass to prevent corrosion but U. S. Divers tried a "plastic," cycolac housing for its Jet Air Brand, so tough an elephant could walk on it, said Forest Dawn to Al Tillman in the parking lot at the Los Angeles County Underwater Headquarters, then proceeded to demonstrate by jumping on it, at which moment it shattered in little pieces. Oops! As Bill Starr said, these heavy metal housings shaped like a triple sized hockey puck were "substantial."

• <u>Upstream</u> and <u>downstream</u> meant that "upstream" would open against the pressure of air and operate with a leverage provided by springs or by the Venturi Principle (air passing an orifice, automatically forces air into it). "Downstreams" open with the pressure of air and are help-closed by a spring whereby the mechanical leverage and the Venturi effect help open it.

Let's pause here because this is starting to sound like a directions manual which can be very boring. And divers were bored with a lot of such information, and they got heavy eyelids over eyes that seemed to ask, "Can't we just go diving now?"

James Lockwood testing an early SCUBA lung in 1938.   *James Lockwood*

But wait. There's more to clarify because each feature represents something the inventors tried to improve, to capture the exotic quality.

• The <u>diaphragm</u> is a round Teflon or neoprene disc that takes water pressure and pushes the levers that open the air flow, more or less, easing the amount of effort the diver has to make to open valves. (Remember pre-Aqua Lung breathing devices mostly controlled air flow by hand-turning a knob controlling air flow through a valve.) A diaphragm can be perforated and ineffective, causing hardship-breathing. DACOR had its Dial-A-Breath Regulator out in the 1960's with a double diaphragm (in case one got damaged), and a knob to adjust the flow of the Venturi process.

• Pressure gauge attachments were starting to be standard built-in-features of regulators, rather than special add-ons during the 1960's. The submersible pressure gauge (SPG) was joined to the regulator by an extra port.

Once again, it must be noted that, in general, many divers didn't want to know all of the technical complexities of a regulator. We can remember the impatient ones saying to the clerks trying to sell them the top priced regulator — "Hey, doesn't this one work, too? And it's cheaper, just wrap it up, I'll read the fine print later." Divers never did care to know that much about regulators. They just took off and went diving. But still, despite a general distaste for the explanations, divers did like the idea of getting the latest innovations and new features of regulators.

As diving instruction progressed and advanced training came on the scene in the 1970's, some of the traditional skills came into question. One of the tried-and-true methods of rescuing an out-of-air-partner was called buddy breathing, sharing air from one mouthpiece. But under panic conditions, the smooth transition of sharing air often got chaotic. The diver in trouble often wouldn't relinquish the mouthpiece and the result was victim and rescue diver having a "fist fight" over it on the bottom. Free ascent was the better alternative but a scary experience.

Why not just port an extra hose and mouthpiece into the first stage. The first noticed "octopus regulator" was high profiled at UNEXSO in 1964 where Dave Woodward introduced it as a necessary feature for the club's dive masters who guided people out onto the reefs. "Octopus" was the popular name, but it was basically an alternative second stage — the name came from the look the new hose added to others hanging from a diver, giving the vague appearance of an octopus' arms. Its popularity and effectiveness spread through the regular diver ranks. The training agencies picked up on it, as a required feature for the new cave diving and wreck diving classes.

James Lockwood demonstrating the "Lockwood Rebreather" that was used by the US Coast Guard.   *James Lockwood*

During the 1970's, some of the engineers, after their day jobs, ended up in their home garage workshops seeking to redesign a better regulator or amenities that would enhance it. Small companies sprang up, trying to market a new product for breathing underwater. A unit called the Divator 324 showed up in United States dive shops in 1974 after some wide use already in Europe, and especially in Sweden where it was developed. An undersea division of the AGA Corporation out of Melbourne, Florida, distributed it. Was it something really new at a steep price? Divers didn't really think so and were put off by the two upside down narrower tanks, (which most dive shops did not have capacity to fill at 4,400 psi). The easier breathing boast, heard over and over again, was the setup to use Divator SPM-1 full face mask. Even the use of "space age plastic material" failed to impress. It just wasn't different enough to make an inroad against established scuba, and the price wasn't truly competitive.

As the 1980's arrived, the buoyancy compensator (BC had replaced the old life vest and was custom-fitted to the diver's body and it could be adjusted to control buoyancy, actually to achieve neutral buoyancy). Rather than manual inflating, why not build a power inflator into the regulator? The regulator with all of these additions was becoming what manufacturers were calling a "system." Add to that an inflator for the dry suit, and we truly did have an octopus look.

Reviewing the diving manuals recommended by the various training agencies, the regulator did not grow in coverage. The most popular diving manual over the past half century, the *New Science of Skin and Scuba Diving* points out that divers don't select a regulator to breathe easy enough to take on arduous tasks — they seem to select on the basis of the pretty cases. Training agencies like divers to experience stress diving so they could move to a more intelligent choice of a regulator. It is easy to breathe when relaxed — the explanation example was to consider a person breathing through a straw and then trying to breathe through it on a run.

Units were made for 20,000 Leagues Under the Sea that needed to be both visually appealing and fuctional.

Now we move through the 1980's with a number of new pulls on the air from the tank and where "easy breathing" had been the supposed definer of one regulator from another, with more concern on how the diver comfortably wears this new encumbered regulator and has convenient control. All of these new attachments are going to draw off tank air pressure if used. So there was new concern about the quick and heavy using up of tank air.

When we were talking about this aspect with Mel Fisher back in the 1980's, he was concerned with keeping his treasure divers down longer when conditions were best. He said, "Hookah diving is the way to do it, plenty of air, but it gets you in trouble with decompression. I guess I was weaned on free diving and scuba diving and prefer it. Remember when we used to breathe directly from the tank, no regulator, just to impress them?" (And of course, if there was a gold doubloon shining on the bottom, Mel would have stripped off a defunct regulator and sucked air from the tank.)

While mainstream sport divers were restricted to the concept endorsed by training agencies, and in turn the manufacturers, regulators, over the decades, took on various shapes and adjustments, (much of it based on marketing concerns and some on safety) — the changes were made to perpetuate open circuit compressed air scuba.

341

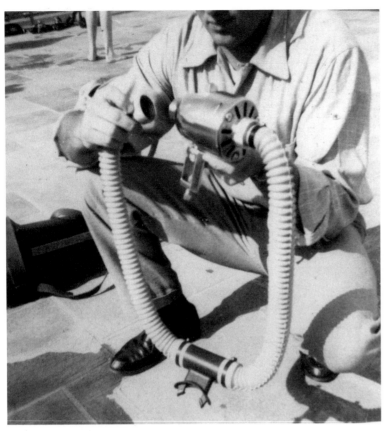

Eugene Poole and his no stage regulator.

But in the backrooms of the military and commercial diving interest, exotic equipment was being thought up, prototyped, and tested with no concern for recreational diving. Those two interests: needing to stay down longer, deeper, and get air easily, while working hard — and the military, of course, wanted no tell-tale bubbles as well.

Sport divers heard about this new scuba research mainly by rumor, and occasionally, by a brief article in a diving publication. Recreational diving had depth limits set for it, and deep diving was discouraged. The push was for no decompression diving at shallower depths where most of the color and marine life was. And there was still much virgin territory to be explored right in one's own "backyard."

There were several attempts to develop a scuba to satisfy the military and commercial and perhaps move sport diving into it as well. But for sport diving, costs of change-over could be prohibitive.

In 1939, Jack Browne, later of DESCO fame, developed a "Browne Lung," a rebreather that got good use in World War II going into areas inaccessible to helmet divers.

In 1963, the Emerson Company collaborated with Dr. Christian J. Lambertsen to mass-produce his LARU (Lambertsen Amphibious Rescue Unit,) serving as the Navy's MKG Unit. Emerson's Units were purchased by Westinghouse Electric Corporation by 1964 to add to its Men-O-Lung line.

All through the years the compressed air scuba served sport diving well but the military, oil explorers, and safety services were continuously pursuing a perfected rebreather system. Commercial companies had diversified by picking up smaller companies working on such units. While there was a large and attractive market, there was always a gleam in their collective eyes when the potential of sport diving consumers was considered.

In 1966, Jordan Klein brought a young inventor to the Underwater Explorers Club on Grand Bahama Island. He had a normal looking scuba unit with a 3-tank-bank on his back. The tanks were sharply cold to the touch; they contained liquid air — cryogenic air. Air cooled to a liquid. The supply of air far exceeded the normal compressed air-fill by three-to-five times. The regulator was the same, though. So the exotic change was only in the source of air. An inexpensive practical way to fill tanks was one major drawback, and the other was that there was no new equipment to patent and sell.

In 1955, the Scott Hydropak with its full face mask approach showed up. A beautiful green and chrome unit adapted from a firefighting dryland original. Dick Noelk brought it around while he was taking one of the first Los Angeles County underwater instructor courses. Dick Anderson grumbled that it was "too bulky." Dick Bartlett, in the same instructor course, bought one and brought it along while diving with Al Tillman.

Tillman recalls that the unit had the first stage mounted on an upside down tank and felt somewhat claustrophobic. "The worst thing was you couldn't exhaust all of the CO_2 (carbon dioxide) out and it built up — we both would end up with pounding headaches. We drank sauerkraut and tomato juice to shake it off. It was a shame because it was a beautiful piece of equipment. But it never caught on in the sport diving world."

The Meistrels of Dive N' Surf fame got into the manufacturing of a regulator as an added product to their booming Body Glove line of wet suits. It was the 1970's and the shops were all aggravated with having to deal with the reigning manufacturers' buying rules. A company called SAS (Submersible Aquatic Systems) was set up to service dive shops more fairly. The regulator, made of stainless steel with beveled washers, followed the existing open circuit scuba designs. It was called Mark X, but never really got off the ground.

Al O'Neil, a NAUI instructor in Chicago, took all the existing regulators on the market apart and developed the Demone Regulator but like the Meistrels, it had no significant innovative features.

By shifting the design slightly, regulators could be "invented" that violated no patent protection. They could look a bit different, but nothing came up exotic enough to bump the established brand names on the market.

In the late 1960's, a diving pioneer, one of diving's clever renaissance men, and who Bates Littlehales of *National Geographic* called a human encyclopedia of marine biology, Dr. Walter A. Starck II, was testing a device called the Electrolung. It was an electronically regulated, closed circuit, mixed gas unit. It was a rebreather, that kept popping up despite the early rejection of it as a dangerous device beyond thirty feet. Stark joined up with a Dr. John

Divers were always experimenting trying to find a better S.C.U.B.A.

Kanwisher, a biophysicist from Woods Hole Oceanographic Institution, Massachusetts, whom he met on a Bahamian expedition. Together they created a unit that electronically monitored oxygen into the system when sensors so dictated. Kanwisher made a close study of the physiological aspects of diving, was an expert in electronics and invented a special electrode used in breathing systems. He is also credited with having taken the first electrocardiogram of a whale. This was a brilliant team. No guess work. This was a smart rebreather that used helium and a chemical compartment to scrub out carbon dioxide. It is all in tune with a diver's physiological needs. But this was going to be an expensive unit if put into production. Things can happen and did when top underwater photographer and professional test diver, Bill DeCourt, (who grew up wanting to be Mike Nelson), had a failure of the system and drowned off Palancar Reef off Cozumel. DeCourt, had told us previously, "It's funny that I've always been satisfied and excited about the basic scuba diving equipment and here I am trying to find something better. But I guess that's progress and somebody's got to test it."

Beckman instruments bought the design and tried to sell the unit to the public at $2,975 in 1970 — but more fatalities happened with its use. Beckman beat a hasty retreat from the venture in 1971. It was the forerunner of the number of rebreathers that surfaced in the 1990's that would make an assault on normal scuba in an inflated economy.

About the same time as the rumblings of the Electrolung were heard, a unit called the Cryogenic Rebreather was being developed by a physicist, Halbert Fischel. Delayed by the inability of compressed air for scuba divers to go deep enough on an oceanographic project he was working on, Fischel could see the time had come to push the primitive Aqua Lung aside and find a way to control mixed gases and remove CO_2. As divers had always known, exhausting used air was wasteful and restricting; it had to be recycled, and if so, longer, much longer, bottom times could be achieved. A complex "regulator," a system was needed. The bug in the equation was how to adjust the gas mixture in relation to a diver's depth and maintain a safe concentration of oxygen. The old rebreathers were ineffective tools for that reason. It required oxygen in an oxygen/helium (helium to eliminate nitrogen narcosis) be cut down to a level which was not toxic at maximum diving depth, but the cut-down level of a pre-mix wouldn't sustain a diver at surface level. Sensors would have to automatically adjust the air mixture to diver's needs.

Jordan Klein with the Cryogenic Lung.

By 1967, Fischel had been joined by Tony Di Chiro, and NAUI diving instructors, Larry Cushman and Dave Joss. They put together a working unit on the floor of a lab in Inglewood, California. It was called Model S-6000G and was able to be a fraction of the size of the usual unreliable oxygen storage units by using liquid oxygen in cryogenic form. A company was formed - Submarine Systems, Inc. after 1,000 foot open water tests and several generations of improved cryogenic rebreathers ensued. Expectations were a unit that would weigh about one-hundred pounds and last for eight hours at 600 feet. It could also be equipped with a closed-loop water heating system, allowing a diver to work in comfort in the deep. The major basic premise is that the unit is a very efficient portable refrigerator and very cold temperatures convert CO_2 into a snow that is caught in a trap while the oxygen liquifies and separates from the helium going to a liquid oxygen supply tank. This coldness that operates the system, rather than sensors, is created by a LN_2 refrigerant bath.

Submarine Systems, Inc. was claiming the unit was fail-safe, because even if the temperature-controlled oxygen partial pressure approached toxic levels, there would still be an hour of normal breathing. The critics, who were questioning the reliability and start-up costs, set the production of this unit aside for several decades.

At this time, it would be wise if we took a look at the rebreather's history. For it was around long before the open circuit scuba that has been the primary toy-tool of recreation diving for five decades.

The rebreather is, of course, a self-contained underwater breathing apparatus. No umbilical cords. It is set aside by its recirculating nature ...and its use of pure oxygen rather than normal compressed air. The rebreather has the capacity to clear carbon dioxide from breathed air and replenish oxygen from a small cylinder.

It is compact and it is silent, very important features for military use. And used, it was, by the Navies of many countries during World War II, 1940 - 1945. Unfortunately, it also was limited to a depth of not more than thirty feet because of oxygen's toxicity at greater depths. Sport diving never embraced the rebreather for most of its fifty year history because the open circuit-compressed air scuba seemed to have less of a widow-maker potential. Open circuit allowed divers to go deeper and divers wanted to go to 100 feet, a sort of benchmark goal so they could say, "Been there. Done that."

But the rebreather arose out of other needs than recreational. In the early 1900's, the Draegar Works of Germany designed the first pure-oxygen closed circuit system for fire departments. The same system was adopted by miners, due to the unit's light weight. By 1941, Draeger had a small compact rebreather designed as an escape device from submarines.

Zale Parry recalls using the DESCO rebreather and the tedious job of refilling the baralyme CO_2 scrubber chamber and general cleaning of the unit with every dive. "Empty the canister of used 'little pills' and refill the canister with fresh/new little pills. Remember, do it slowly without breathing the dust! Phew! It didn't seem worth all that effort compared to the ease of the Aqua Lung."

The U. S. Navy in early 1990's was using the MK15 and MK16 after accepting it back in 1968. It was made by Carleton Technologies, but it is a unit that demands a diver's constant attention and is manually operated. It was heavy, too, required extensive training to use, had higher maintenance, had no redundancy, and cost up to $45,000 per unit. It had the same deficits as all the new generation of rebreathers standing in the way of recreation use.

By the 1990's, a number of tech companies were tossing their hats in the ring. Cis-Lunar Development Labs in Pennsylvania went to an electronic control system in its MK-3S unit, which has redundancy built-in and requires minimal maintenance. It mixes gases with on-board computers and allows a diver to stay up to 12 hours underwater. It can be used with air, heliox or trimix. The sports version of it weighed less than 40 pounds, offered a 10 hour dive at 218 feet of sea water. The cost was around $5,000. By the design, the MK-35 avoided the dreaded "Caustic Cocktail" — whereby the inherent design of rebreathers had always been that water entering the mouthpiece can reach the CO_2 absorbent material, which is disastrous.

Sport diving authorities are polarized on this issue of a rebreather-era emerging, or the simpler approach of sustaining conventional compressed air scuba diving, because its more manageable and already in place. Most leaders feel it comes down to a matter of need and how high tech-new divers will want to go, if they really have to dive deeper and stay longer to get the best possible underwater experience they seek. And, are they prepared for the hanging-off decompression stops required?

As more divers enter specialty areas, such as wreck and cave and photography diving, the rebreather may gather support. Out at the destination resorts and liveaboards, rebreather-diving is being put on the menu because it's a great profit center and there's time to learn how to use it.

But the innovators, who haven't given up on conventional open circuit scuba, keep trying for that perfect regulator. Rebreather-breathing is easy and constant and that raises the bar for regulators. The century ended with new materials coming into regulator construction. Divers, who now travel everywhere all the time, are faced with luggage weight problems by airliners, and a lot of convenient items have to be left behind if a diver wants his personal regulator along. The ultra-light regulator came into being, made of a marine aluminum alloy, bonded to a hardened Teflon-impregnated ceramic, and it reduces down easily into the corner of a carry-on bag. These new regulators talk about 25% reduction in inhalation-effort making use of a high travel-lever and exhalation ...well bragging goes on and usually passes over the head of the normal diver.

There are mixed emotions, as well, about underwater communications, the regulators that have been equipped with intercom. Many divers, who thrived on the "silent world", wondered if we really needed to talk to each other underwater.

There have been a number of exotic enhancements of scuba since the two-hose Aqua Lung arrived, but no major revolution had happened in scuba's fifty year history. OK, the return of the rebreather, a digital smart one, may turn everything around, but there also may have been too many accidents in the continuing evolution for sport diving to fully embrace it. Dive leaders were saying that divers get bored easily if they have to pay so much attention to their equipment while diving.

We end up the fifty years not a long way from the first basic scuba when Rene Bussoz, selling the first one in his Westwood, California, store told his customer, "All you do is put this in your mouth and breathe. ...and you'd better not hold your breath like you do skin diving. This equipment will do the rest."

And that it did!

28
PROMOTIONAL CONTESTS
AND DEVICES

DEFINING EVENT: CHOCOLATE ABALONE HUNT

Nothing ever beat somebody calling and saying, "let's go diving." The industry, the retail stores and the clubs often over the decades of diving history felt they had to do much more than that as divers dropped out periodically in great numbers.

The weather has always been the main influencer of enthusiasm. Divers waking to a dismal day, windy, choppy sea, whether the tropics or frozen north, groan, and think that getting back in bed is a good idea.

Wait, there's a scavenger hunt scheduled today, they remember. There's more than the same scenery, same creatures, the worry about clarity for photography, or having to clean and prepare any fish. Some enterprising organizers have scheduled something to give divers a new incentive, a change of pace, and the challenge of the game and competition. And there were often prizes!

The staged treasure hunt could be done in the murk of a quarry or the breaking wave ocean. It was a matter of the organizers, who were trying to keep divers in the water year round, coming to the dive site early to plant the "treasure".

One of the most imaginative events was the chocolate abalone hunt put on by a joint effort of clubs and dive shops in the Central California area. Chocolate was molded into the shape of the famous California abalone, actual size, put in plastic and hid in crevices on the bottom of Monterey Bay. Numbered tags in each unit entitled the finder to diving equipment, airfills, trips donated by manufacturers, shops and charter boats. It was an equalizer-kind of contest in that luck was perhaps more important than skill or knowledge. The starting site was a good family beach which gave spouses and children a chance to be part of the fun even if they didn't dive. Non-diving public got a positive view of diving and were lured into investigating, trying the sport. Conservationists were pleased because diving was not

This diver didn't find any Chocolate Abalone so he loaded up on the next best thing.
Lamar Boren

denuding the ocean.

The Chocolate Ab Hunt usually kicked off the Spring diving season, and Easter is a good themed timing. Oh, yes, you could eat the chocolate ab.

• John Gaffney got his NASDS shop members to stage regional poker dives. Plasticized playing cards stand up pretty well in water. Divers would collect cards until they got the best possible set of five cards. On shore, the hands would be compared, and prizes donated would go to the best ones. Carried further, the best hands could be set up in an actual draw poker game so everybody could watch. It was a popular event for NASDS during the 1970's.

• The scavenger hunt has been mentioned and this classic contest event has several forms, all easily produced. It has had a long life in diving, staged even in the 1950's when everything was virgin and surprising all the way to the blasé - 1990's with some liveaboards listing it on their dive program menus. The dive teams got a list such as an old tire, a sea urchin skeleton, an anchor or old bottle. Some things were planted on site, while the possibility of other things being there was a gamble. In the early days before the environment became so precious and the realization that the resources of the ocean were finite, scavenger hunts included creatures and flora and fauna. In the lakes, ponds and other more barren, mediocre visibility waters, the scavenger hunt was a well-accepted reason to go diving.

• Pumpkin carving at Halloween is a ubiquitous event that popped up for club activities in every part of the country. To avoid the mess and pollution, the timed event sends divers down with a gutted pumpkin and diving knife and they go at it. Some try it at night and then light all the Jack-O-Lanterns, or Jacque-O-Lanterns, with underwater flashlights.

• Christmas usually brought out one diver dressed in full Santa Claus regalia to sit on bottom and distribute waterproof gifts to club members who, of course, took pictures and got it in the local newspapers.

• Some clubs lined up underwater female models for photo shoots. One of the clubs dressed its model in a rented mermaid outfit two sizes too big and when it floated away in the current, everybody kept shooting, as the model shrugged and kept posing.

• One photography club was promised by its in-house-Lothario that he'd bring a beautiful blonde model, his own girlfriend to do the posing. After several dives and a lot of promises, the older Lothario in his 50's did show up with the very filled out, slightly rotund girlfriend in a leopard spot bikini ...who was also in her 50's. One of the younger shocked members recognized the "model" from another context. He stuttered out wildly, "Aunt Jane, it's you ...Oh, My God!"

• It seemed a shame to the purist admirers of the wild and natural scene that artificial events had to be staged to get divers in the water. But some divers really loved having a competitive experience and to dive with a group. Diving is a <u>hidden sport</u> with no playing field visible to a grandstand of fans. A lot of divers over the years resented all of the artificial devices to make the undersea world more appealing, from artificial reefs to camera shoots to scavenger hunts.

But if we're going to go after numbers and the manufacturers, retail stores, (and training agencies certainly did), then things have to be staged.

• In the beginning, taking game was the slam bang greatest appeal. America has an ancestry of hunters, it's almost in the genes. The power of taking, killing living creatures and then bringing the trophy catch home to the family was big-time joy all the way back to the cavemen.

TAKING PICTURES

• Because nobody was watching this element of diving happen, taking pictures of the game-taking rose in popularity. But before this the idea of finding "the best diver, the most effective spearfisherman, lobster grabber, and abalone taker was achieved by creating competitive contests." It was spearing fish that served as the best

Joe Dorsy with the Marine Honor Guard that served as the official timekeepers for his record duration dive.

measure of great athletic divers ...free diving of course. Scuba was seen as an unfair tool in stalking fish and an interfering one in that it's bubbles and noise spooked the game.

The clubs and the councils were the strong proponents of these contests. In some instances, these spearfishing contests were the major glue for keeping a club together. At first, the total aggregate of fish brought in after a timed half day of diving was weighed to find the winner. There was a biggest single fish category, too. But while the contestants stood amidst the dying and dead piles of fish filling the beach, the budding ecologists and non-diver public in general were aghast at this programmed slaughter. "Catch only what you can eat - don't get lazy and bury the catch in the rose garden," were moral guidelines conscientious divers tried to follow.

Abashed by the criticism, clubs and councils donated the fish to local orphanages and got positive publicity to counteract a growing resentment about the unlimited fish destruction.

It was from these local contests that the inevitable "super bowl" of diving arose. The National Championships were first put together by Ralph Davis of the Los Angeles Neptunes who had made himself responsible for the recording of record catches and having them on display at the Helms Athletic Foundation's impressive trophy room for all sports. The First Nationals were held at Laguna Beach, California, in 1950 and the winners were: Paul Haas, Keith and Kenneth Kummerfeld representing the Dolphin Club Team. Al Tillman was there on the Santa Anita Neptunes Team and recalls, "I didn't even see a fish worth shooting, but here came these divers who looked just like us, trailing clumps of fish on stringers, and we all came to realize that you couldn't compete by just jumping in the water with a spear. As the contests got more sophisticated and world championships evolved, the weapons got more complex, bigger and more effective. The pole spear gave way to the arbolette gun-like spear, some gas propelled or with rubber tubing, and then great long "canons" that had a long range capability and powerful piercing capacity. There were efforts to bring scuba into the fold and efforts to restrict the competitions back to just free diving with pole spears. Eventually, numbers were put aside and a limit set both on quantity and size.

The spearfishing contest held up into the 1960's when the environmental movement picked up steam. By 1969, when America landed on the moon and found nothing but the realization we'd better save

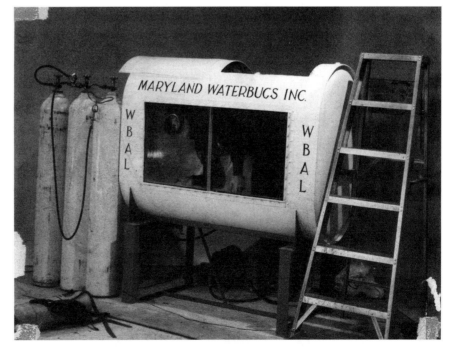

Joe Dorsy in the tank.

our planet, the open fish kill contest was on the wane. It gave way to the photography contest that took over diving in the 1970's and 1980's and 1990's.

Not a direct spectator sport, diving had to manufacture these competitive contests so that the general public would approve and admire diving. Diving always needed positive publicity. They held divers in and they recruited non-divers into the sport. Just going out and exploring what God had wrought, and as it was in the beginning of earth's birth, should have been enough, but it wasn't. The staged contest was a necessary, albeit ersatz, adventure.

Ed Fisher during his 24 hour endurance record in 1955. He camped out on the ocean floor in French Reef, FL.   Peter Stackpole

• The tank shows were a popular way for organizations and clubs to show off diving skills to the general public. Divers could bring family and friends to see divers buddy-breathe, clear masks and eat bananas underwater. Some shows could be done in pools with viewing windows for a very small audience, but the tank was superior. Some clubs made the building of a portable windowed-box to hold water a group project for the club.

One of the first tank shows ever was put on in the Los Angeles Sportsman Show at the Pan Pacific Auditorium in 1955. Buck and Morrison, the show producers, borrowed a ready-made tank from the Kingdom Of The Sea television studio for the two-week run. *The Los Angeles Examiner* was the key sponsor, and Al Tillman of the Los Angeles County Underwater Unit, was asked to develop and stage a <u>Little Wet School House</u>. Tillman lined-up the County's underwater instructors to man an information booth, and a few were the "actors" in the tank. Al Tillman recalls that every year over a four-year period of doing it, many days were spent in plugging leaks as the cold water dripped from the window seals. "I remember that I spent a lot of time repeating 'don't bump the windows!' for the 6' x 10' x 8' had a few tons of water that would spray glass and the divers over the audience if broken." I knew we needed something more 'believe it or not' than just the usual diving skills, so I hit on why not show eating underwater. So I went down to the ocean near my home in Redondo Beach by myself to see what was possible. I swam out with scuba and a mesh bag with apples, bananas and a Coke, then sat on the bottom at ten feet depth. I tried the banana first and it went down easily as I pulled the mouthpiece out and held my breath. The first time is a little scary, you expect to choke, but then it gets easy and you realize you could probably eat a barbecued chicken."

Al Tillman remembers that they did get around to a barbecued chicken when a film was made for the 1957 National Recreation Month by Ben Mintz who contracted to do it for the National Parks and Recreation Association. Tillman lined up Clint Degn, who was managing the Rosemead Pool at the time, to put together a diving family who would go picnicking on the bottom of the pool.

Tillman shot the footage and remembers the watermelon kept floating away and Clint would have to chase it. It was the kind of thing a Three Stooges Comedy is made of, but it swept across the country and played on every television station.

Tank shows have been a great promotional device for diving over the years to direct the phantom sport. One of the best tank shows was at the 1964 World's Fair in New York where a *Sea Hunt Theatre* was staged.

The World's Fair and the Lecture Circuit will be covered in depth elsewhere in *Scuba America*. Just like under-

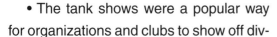

water photography, these are major happenings that stand on their own.

• A few more attention getting promotions are real weddings staged underwater that get great press and television coverage, especially, around June, the wedding month. At one such wedding, the best man dropped the ring in the sand and the entire gathering of divers spent a half hour gently fanning the bottom. At another, the bride tossed the bouquet (the legend being, catcher will marry next) over her shoulder, a grouper grabbed it and swam off. Some said diving ought to do a divorce underwater, too, ...using spear guns (in jest of course).

In 1997, the *Underwater News* was listing underwater weddings on par with dry-land couplings. One such described it as follows:

Sharks as wedding guests. The sharks were circling as Denise Koft and Jeffrey Aster tied the knot.

Twenty-four sharks and 1400 other aquatic animals swam around them in the Open Ocean Tank at New Jersey State Aquarium while the newlyweds took their vows. Each wore a wet suit and diving gear and Denise had a silk headdress, too.

Coles Phinizy, one of diving's founding fathers and a Senior Editor for *Sports Illustrated* magazine, wrote an article in 1965 about UNEXSO and introduced the coverage with this short story:

"Last fall, a mile off Grand Bahama Island, Robert Toll Jr., a laundry operator from River Forest, Ill., and his wife Nancy dropped off the side of a boat and swam 80 feet down into a labyrinth of coral, where spangled parrot fish grazed in soft, frittered shafts of light. Since the Tolls had never gone so deep on any of their five previous dives, they were accompanied by a California college professor, Albert Alvin Tillman, who in 20 years of diving has put more water through his sinuses than most people drink in a year. After the Tolls had inspected the residence of an irritable moray eel and Bob had stopped to pat an angelfish that tagged along, Tillman led them still deeper, until the meandering canyon walls fell away and only splotches of coral stood out dimly in the desert waste. When they reached a depth of 100 feet, the Tolls and Tillman shook hands. Then Bob Toll did a gracious thing. He tapped his wife on the shoulder, produced a petite diver's watch from his glove and put it on her wrist- a 10th wedding anniversary present, delivered two days late but in an appropriate setting."

This might be a reverse promotion but in 68 feet of water off Petoskey, Michigan, there's an eleven foot Crucifix placed there by the Superior Marine Divers' Club in 1962. Divers came from everywhere over the next decades on through the year 2000 to place markers with names of divers who have been lost in lakes and oceans throughout the world. In the winter, law enforcement officers from Northern Michigan cut a hole in the ice to visit it. A lot of media attention is gained whenever a special marker went down or a special group made the dive to this shrine.

It's perhaps a bit more eerie than the big Christ of the Abyss statue on Pennekamp Reef in

Zale Parry and Paul Coates on one of many television appearances that Zale made to acquaint the general public to the sport of skin diving in the 1950's.   Homer Lockwood

Early days of promoting equipment can be seen here at the 1957 Southwest Sport and Recreation Show. The diver is Sonny Logan andthe salesman is Jim MacCammon.

Florida. It gets periodic media attention, too.

Paul Tzimoulis, whose motto was always "go where the money is," was very successful taking slide shows to the Country Clubs back in the early 1960's. In the 1990's, when diving was seeking the broader middle class family market, a program called Discover Diving was being encouraged at all kinds of public shows and gatherings with the idea of letting people get wet and try breathing with scuba under the supervision of a certified instructor - before they took training. It was a big hit at DEMA's convention in 1986. Disney's Living Seas Exhibit had a grand opening during the same days that DEMA held its trade show. To promote scuba diving, DEMA's administrators hired brilliant underwater instructors to expose radio and television broadcasters from around the world to a wet experience in the use of scuba. Manufacturers provided the diving equipment. A hotel swimming pool near the convention center in Orlando, Florida, was used for the few hours' training. The objective to introduce the media at this time was the fact that these newly baptized divers could broadcast the evening news while seated on a coral reef, let the world know that their studio is underwater at the Living Seas Exhibit at Disney World Florida, and be exuberant with lively expressions that scuba diving is fun. For safety, four Disney's divers and the instructors held each announcer one at a time while sitting on this pile of coral in the main underwater tank. Out of camera range, the safety divers braced the announcer's back and gently held down the tips of each swim fin to control leg buoyancy during taping. Surprisingly, there was a good number of people from the television industry with spunk who performed well without previous scuba training. A lot of people visiting the exhibit were spellbound as they nosed-up to the huge windows to watch. Give credit to the Disney divers and instructors for their prowess in transforming the multimedia, there and then, into minute-made divers. It was a good promotion for scuba diving, too. Then in the year 2000, in Las Vegas, Nevada, DEMA provided a no-window scuba Demonstration Pool which was used often. The pool was a large portable one. Viewers stood around it to watch.

DUNKING THE MEDIA

Back in the 1950's, shops and training classes were smart enough to let media people go through a diving course gratis, and they'd have them rooting for them in their writings.

Getting a positive story into the newspapers and on television is one of the best promotional efforts. Divers who gave found-relics to museums got publicity not only for themselves but diving also. It could be an old sailing ship anchor or the huge rock anchors off "Chinese junks" found off Palos Verdes, California, by the Meistrel brothers. Al Tillman's ton nugget of Jade found underwater in 1957 sits on a pedestal in

An early promotional event turned sour when local dive clubs in California joined in to gather up all the starfish that were destroying the kelp beds. Unfortunately they were all taken to a local processing plant, chopped up and returned to the sea. Each piece grew into a new starfish and the total population of starfish ended up being 10 to 20 times larger.   *H. Lockwood*

the Los Angeles County Museum. Joe Dorsey gave up a few of the six-inch prehistoric sharks' teeth for the glory of diving. There have been many donations by divers everywhere, and they have breathed excitement into the general public ...divers, too.

• Healthways had an open cockpit submersible back in 1955 that they had Dick Anderson and Zale Parry ride in underwater on a Channel run to Santa Catalina Island. Gustav Dalla Valle, Parry Bivens, Al and Norma Hansen were in the guiding mother boat, *Hansen's Genie*. It took almost all day to get to Avalon's gas dock there where vast media attention was gathered. The following week at the parking lot by Healthways, more news people lined up as Gustav Dalla Valle announced the addition of Cressi products. Except for its bright yellow paint, the sub called Sea Horse II, identical to the little submarines used during World War II by the Italians, was not a mass-marketing item but primarily to have a large rare thing to photograph for Richard Kline's Healthways line. Healthways sold two of them.

TELEVISION SHOWS

• Local television shows did a worthy job for diving beginning with the mid- 1950's and early 1960's before the big primetime *National Geographic* and *Discovery Channel* shows. Mel Fisher had films of local Southern California diving, as did the Brauer Brothers, George and Donald, with their *Territory Underwater*. Fisher edited Al Tillman's *The Big Jade Film* for one of his shows, then had Jim Christiansen and Al Tillman come on to down-play the shark danger after the press had done a couple of attack stories. Back in Massachussets, a local television announcer and diver took his show underwater. He made his broadcast from the bottom, exploring what he saw and how he felt. These kinds of shows were out to recruit divers, and the intent was to show how safe, easy and fun it was. In those early days of television, the stations were open to expensive trade offs - put on a show and you could have the advertising time.

• Clubs and shops (later changed to retail stores) were very good about putting divers in booths to show off artifacts, equipment, and answer questions about diving. They went to home shows, hobby shows, sports shows and county fairs to toot diving's horn.

• The review of different promotional efforts over the years could go on and on. Diving has and will always need to have these hometown, backyard-kind of promotions to keep diving interesting ...that is, interesting in the sense of reminding and reinforcing divers, and getting public attention and support for this "invisible" sport. Postage stamps with Cousteau's image, "I'd rather be diving" bumper stickers, Diver Down Flag decals and the old club jacket patches and.........and interestingly, by 2000 all of the old promotional ideas were back. The industry was pushing the club idea that carried diving in its pioneer years.

Tom Fransen, Joan Gillen and Homer Lockwood on television showing off skin and scuba diving equipment and techniques.
Homer Lockwood

29

MINING NEW IDEAS
SPORT DIVING RESEARCH

DEFINING EVENT: NAUI's IQ

Nothing is more disturbing in any field of endeavor than to discover what you absolutely believed has been replaced by a new truth. Diving has its full share of epiphanies where old ways of doing things are often reversed by new ways.

One of the classic examples was the core belief of hard hat divers, before the turn of the Nineteenth-Century, that to avoid the bends, one should move about vigorously at decompression stops to rid the bubbles. Crash went that indelible training directive when scientists studied cases of the bends and directly related them to a new theory that divers were actually causing bubbles and the opposite behavior should be prescribed.

Sorely disillusioned with their teachers and text books, the helmet divers cursed and tossed all the old rules out the window - along with the new ones. The feeling was fooled once, shame on them; fooled twice, shame on us. It took a while before the divers got back to any standards they could believe in.

Scuba sport diving has gone through a few crises like that one. The change in the ascent rate from 25-feet per minute to 60-feet per minute and back to 40-feet per minute to...well, the changes could continue. So what has been the point of authority for any new ideas in the sport diving field?

Fortunately, and unfortunately, the sport diver has had to rely on the government and the military's scientific research conclusions and recommendations. It's fortunate that the military needs information for combat and rescue necessities and can pay for it; unfortunate because, none of it has been designed to guide the sport diver. Leaping extrapolations and sometimes miscalculations do not always give the sport diver any absolute guide-lines.

The old system of sitting around the campfires to tell stories and exchange information goes back to the cave men. Divers did it in the early days; in many cases in the 1940's and 1950's. It was the way to learn to dive. One diver would say, "I was just fooling around and I tried a dolphin kick instead of the flutter and I seemed to move smoother and faster through the water - and disturb the fish less." At one time it was a new idea, scoffed at, until tried and accepted as an alternative fin-kicking style. So thousands of ideas were empirically discovered and entered the lore and behaviors of sport diving.

But by the 1960's, there was serious effort to statistically substantiate theories. The scientific process was needed, at least a popular version of the scientific process.

NAUI (National Association of Underwater Instructors) in particular, the major force in instruction in the 1960's, moved to study and measure the diving methods, the equipment function, and effective teaching. A research committee was appointed from the membership to study such things as the desirability of practicing ascending with a partner using one "live" regulator, buddy breathing as it was called - the topic remained debatable to the year 2000 and beyond. A special committee was formed on Cave Diving under Dave Desautels, a NAUI graduate, and an experienced Springs and Blue Hole veteran.

Special topics split off from the general Research Committee to become other committees devoted to studying and proposing scientific research that needed to be done. High altitude lake diving or flying after diving were topics created by mishaps that needed to be explained. A dive is a dive is a dive, the just-do-it philosophy of the early diving pioneers, was just not good enough, not safe enough and a bit pig-headed.

And so, small dive groups of dive club members and instructors would replicate government and military research to try to interpret results in the parameters of sport diving. It was helpful when dive instructors, who were also college professors, keyed in and often were trained in research methods.

NAUI sponsored research encampments and seminars to achieve a specific result at a short weekend or week-long where concentration could be applied. One of the first such encampments was carried out at Camp Fox on Santa Catalina Island, California. Camp Fox is a piece of diving history for it hosted many Los Angeles County and NAUI programs during the 1950's, 1960's and beyond. It was a YMCA Camp and one of diving's founder icons, Jon Hardy, started to skin dive there as a kid, was Camp Director, then eventually, led NAUI as a guiding light for many developments in diving. Al Tillman recalled that his secretary for NAUI, one of his blue-ribbon university students, Pat Laub, came to the Research Camp, met Jon Hardy, fell in love and married him.

"Dr. Eugene Winter, out of the 1960 NAUI Houston Course, was the person I chose to direct the Camp and give it prestige. He had us squatting in tidepools, putting specimens in bottles, carrying identifying books and we all felt, hey, we're not just scuba divers, we can be amateur marine biologists. We can create knowledge. I think we all learned how to be patient and minutely observe, a way we'd carry with us later and forever in all our scuba diving. I kind of remember how we really learned about flight patterns of the smaller fish which would help us in collecting specimens for aquariums on a big scale. It was something we didn't learn or hadn't been taught in basic diving classes."

A lot of the "research" information was pretty crude. The scientific method wasn't perfect but it got everybody leaning in that direction. Some of it was just enough to ignite broader, better efforts. Some of it got into print in newsletters so that divers in different places could compare notes which synergized their interests.

Even in the 1950's, at diving club meetings the main topic of the meeting after planning the next dive trip, revolved around things like breath holding while using scuba and how to recognize a bad air fill. Divers were pooling information about their experiences. The ideas arising from these informal "research" discussions encouraged more structured approaches. Councils of Clubs sponsored seminars, brought in experts to answer questions about dangerous marine creatures or how to repair a wet suit.

The famed Boston Sea Rovers boasted a membership over the years of very bright and educated divers, Bob Ballard, for an example, (the Dr. Robert D. Ballard, marine explorer and discoverer of the R.M.S. Titanic (1985), U.S.S. Yorktown and much more.) and sitting in an advantageous site were able to attract the outstanding experts in various aspects of diving.

Los Angeles County, where public diving instruction began in 1954, was interested in research to expand the knowledge of their certified instructors and divers. The efforts to extend the training knowledge and keep current with discoveries was incorporated into a recertification program for instructors. Los Angeles introduced mouth-to-mouth resuscitation at such a recertification seminar, float rescue techniques and the one hose regulator. It was serious business as such topics as shallow water blackout while skin diving was bisected physiologically and pragmatically. Sometimes these seminars turned into social occasion reunions for diving instructors, and pranksters brought things like "new scuba ideas" in a form of a "rectalator" which had an enema hose attached to the tank outlet.

Most of the ideas and findings didn't get past the door at the end of these meetings and seminars. They might show up in a newsletter of a club or an agency but the exposure was narrow.

Credit NAUI with making the initial effort to bring together instructors from everywhere to exchange ideas. The attempt to work with the Underwater Society of America in the beginning of 1961-62 failed greatly. A coordinated effort to cooperate on the instruction program in 1961 did not jell. According to NAUI leaders, USOA wanted to take over. Many fields of study throughout human history have provided a stage for their members to express ideas and report on experiments and developments. The NAUI leaders on the scene for the First International Conference on Underwater Education, (original acronym ICUE got popularized into IQ) were as follows: Larry Cushman (cited in many places as key instigator of idea), Art Ullrich and Glen Egstrom, John Reseck, Leonard Greenstone. "Art Ullrich was the initiator of most of the fun projects we thought up. IQ being one of many. Abstracts from IQ_1 were prepared in hopes they would provide a buddy-line of continuity from one conference to the next and they worked," Dr. Glen Egstrom reminisced.

It seems that John Reseck, a NAUI Board Member at the time and a college professor at Santa Ana Community College in California was a prime mover and directed IQ_1 September 26, 27, 28, 1969 on his Campus. It might not have been a propitious time for NAUI to undertake such an ambitious endeavor. The Convention of the Underwater Society of America were costly affairs and their fiscal quicksands should have sent up a red flag to NAUI. NAUI had expanded broadly and rapidly with multiple instructor training courses each year with paid full-time headquarters staff and the budget was not balancing. The premiere national nonprofit training agency was having a financial crisis; individual members were loaning the agency money to keep it going. IQ_1 represented a major investment, but the Board decided survival meant staying in a leadership role among the agencies providing instruction.

John Reseck recalls that the First IQ drew regionally and had sixty-seven attendees. The revenue was less than the cost. But there was approval and enthusiasm from the diving world. PADI, YMCA, NASDS were supportive and gave it print space in their newsletters. And so more IQs were scheduled over the early 1970's, each growing bigger and taking on not only a true national participation, but international as well.

The registration cost for the First Conference was $12.00 for instructors and $7.00 for divers. The First ICUE rostered many big names: Jim Stewart, Paul Tzimoulis, Col. John Craig, Dr. Sam Miller, Dr. Eugene Winters, Bill High, Jim Christiansen, Sam LeCocq, Dave Woodward, Dr. Joe McInnis and even Jacques Cousteau.

Friday, September 26, 1969
The topics at the First IQ were:
- <u>Diver Certification and Its Implications - Panel</u>

Dr. George Rich

Arthur Ullrich

Frank Scalli

Dr. Glen Egstrom

Art Ullrich

- <u>Instructor Ethics</u>

Jon Hardy - YMCA

Chuck Buchanan - NASDS

Tom Ebro - Los Angeles County

Saturday, September 27, 1969

Glen Egstrom

- <u>Innovations in Teaching - Visual Aids</u>

John Reseck - Snorkel

Donn Gartrell - Visual Aids

Dave Bunch - Pool Kelp

John Gimbel - Portable Teaching Aid

Leonard Greenstone - Training Aids
Dr. Art Bachrach - Principles of Teaching
Dr. Lee Somers - The Role of the Instructor in Training the Research Diver
Ken Myers - Teaching

Dr. Lee Somers

- <u>Recent Developments in Diving</u>
Larry Cushman - Cryogenics in Diving
Jim Stewart - Man in the Sea Program
Jack McKenney - Subliminos

- <u>Underwater Photography</u>
Paul Tzimoulis - Underwater Photography
Col. John D. Craig - Underwater Films

Larry Cushman

- <u>Underwater Communications</u>
June Davis - State of Art Today

- <u>New Equipment - Modifying Diving Equipment, Care and Maintenance of Equipment</u>
John Reseck - Spear Guns
Dr. Sam Miller - Modification of Diving Equipment
Al Thompson - Care of Regulator

Sunday, September 28, 1969

John Reseck

- <u>Specialty and Advanced Diving Programs</u>
Clint Degn - Photography Class
Otto Gasser - Objectives of a Specialty Program
Tom Ebro - Advanced Divers Program

- <u>Resort Diving Instruction</u>
Dave Woodward - Freeport Diving Instruction
Dick Byam - Diving Instruction in Inland Waters
John Frederick - Lake Diving
Leonard Greenstone - Cave Diving

Jim Stewart

- <u>Why Certification</u>
Dr. George Rich

- <u>The Problem of Deep Diving</u>
Jim Stewart

Dennis Graver, who at different times was on the staff at NAUI and PADI, said, ..."It was just old stuff with a new twist, but it got those who taught diving together."

Many large national affairs, especially in diving, never had the professional staff with the knowledge of what it takes to market such an event nor the logistics of housing and staging for large numbers of people. Although NAUI

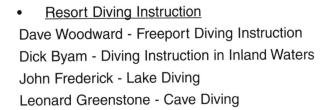

learned as it went, there was a turnover of people who produced IQ making progress and stability an erratic process.

Zale Parry remembers the First IQ Conference as a needed and effective gathering of diving teachers. Divers in general, but especially instructors, felt cloistered and left out of the main stream of information. It was like someone had turned on a light in a dimly lighted room. And that light was left on, used and made brighter as the instructor used his own ingredients in presenting the subjects as time went on. It wasn't only the brilliance of knowledge for the moment, but it spread like a good virus throughout the diving community's inner soul, a strengthening force toward improving the teaching matter in all phases of diving's know-how. Attendees were saying, "How are they going to top this for the next IQ?" They did! ...with a NAUI Industrial Orientation Course for a week's seminar August 22 - 29, 1970. Then the halogen illumination arrived with two NAUI Courses for Physicians in Diving Medicine given by doctors for doctors.

Al Tillman had delivered a presentation on diving resorts, how they were servicing divers with short courses. He'd just done a survey of the resort picture while serving as NAUI's Resort Branch Manager. (The Branch existed one year, but was dissolved to tighten the budget.) Tillman had a hard time remembering being at that First IQ and had this to say, "I could see NAUI needed to get different rather than bigger, do research events, get more involved in servicing dive stores and resorts more directly...keep up with PADI and NASDS."

The Third IQ was in Dallas, Texas, and was the first truly professional conference. IQ grew stronger and better. It was a good idea. In five years, by 1974, it took on the polished look of a top-rated conference. The research presentations were less ego trips and more sincere efforts to mine new ideas in a professional and scientific manner.

Paul Eisner deliveres a lecture at the secong IQ.

IQ_6 took place in San Diego. Art Ullrich, who had stepped down from General Manager of NAUI and was replaced by Jon Hardy, was still serving as Director of Special Projects. He edited the proceedings, which allowed those who couldn't afford attendance, access to all the information presented. Some people felt that there would be value in a selective choice of material and some critical evaluation written by a group of diving instructional experts.

Surveying the papers published, important names show up such as: James Cahill, Ben Davis, Dr. Glen Egstrom, Bernard Empleton, Lou Fead, Bret Gilliam, Dennis Graver, Jon Hardy, Tom Mount, Harry Shanks and Dr. Lee Somers.

Here are some of the topics:
- Woman As An Instructor
- Report of the Z-86 Committee
- The All Open-Water Course
- Decompression Meters - Another Look
- Dive Vessel Safety Procedures
- Minimum Standards For Courses
- The Changing Face of Air Embolism

- The Life Vest
- Teaching Buddy Breathing

One major addition to IQ was the influx of equipment manufacturers and resort offerings into the exhibit area. Where the Sportsman Show in Chicago had been the premier showcasing of diving products previously, the industry saw the value in special and exclusive attention to sport diving. It was a major support for NAUI's IQ and probably tripled the amount of learning over the formal presentation of papers and the ever-effective informal bull-sessions in hallways. DEMA would eventually supplant IQ with its own convention as the prime arena for the industry.

IQ designed for instructors in its original form opened up for sport divers.

By 1975, IQ_7 would be held in Miami and in many ways is considered by numerous dive leaders as its keynote Conference drawing thousands attendees and making money for NAUI. It stood as a strong weapon in holding off PADI, NASDS, SSI and the YMCA upward movement.

Lou Fead edited the proceedings with the papers presented by such recognized names as : Dr. Arthur Bachrach, Dr. Charles Brown, Fred Calhoun, Larry Cushman, David Desautels, Jon Hardy, Dennis Graver, Garry Howland, John McAniff, Al Mikalow, Dr Andy Rechnitzer and Jeanne Bear Sleeper.

Some of the topics were:
- Psychological Aspects of SCUBA Divers
- A NAUI Dive Shop Program
- Compression and Purification of High Pressure Breathing Air
- A New Approach to Cave Diving
- Report on Legislation
- Emergency Ascent Training
- Hazards of Sport Diving Free Ascent Training
- Ice Diving Safety
- Buoyancy Compensation

Some of the topics were a bit mind boggling and esoteric such as in "Theories of Learning," where diving instructors have to handle situations thus ..."the experimenter identifies and reinforces responses paired with stimuli so that differentiated responses and discommunicative stimuli form a desired path toward terminal behavior. In doing this, the response not to be attended (S^s) and the responses not desired (R^s) are eliminated from the behavioral chain." Mmmmm ...does that mean that we have to be sure we get student divers to do the right thing by teaching the thing that happens matches up with behavior you want or ....? Sometimes the papers talked science-babble, confusing, such as figuring the tables for repetitive dives into an underwater lake in an ocean volcano or something like that. On the other hand, some papers diligently followed the KISS method, Keep It Simple Stupid, to the point nothing is really said; read the title and you've got the gist. Some attendees felt that some of the topics needed screening such as: <u>The Four Ton Weight Belt</u> (somebody's diving story), <u>Microscopic Gas Bubbles</u>, <u>Nuclei</u>, <u>The Female Diver</u>, <u>Instructor In Hawaii</u>. As one curmudgeon put it, "You can slice baloney only so thin, then it ain't baloney."

But the exhibits were numerous and impressive. The trend toward resort diving as a major force in the industry of sport diving was apparent. IQ was on a roll and IQ_8 showed up again in San Diego with Jeanne Bear Sleeper, credited as Coordinator, and Lou Fead as proceedings editor again. New important names on the authors of papers roster were: Ted Boehler, Ken Brock, Bill Burrud, Roy Damron, William High, Richard Long and John Wozny.

Topics ranged from the sublime to the...well...not so sublime. Here are some in descending order:

- Teaching The NAUI Deep Diving Specialty

- Diving In The Dark
- What You Can Do To Help the Resort Instructor With Your Traveling Students
- Weight Systems
- Active System For Heating Sport Divers
- Fun And Games With Diving Physics
- Toxaemic Key
- Para-SCUBA

IQ_9 saw ICUE (International Conference on Underwater Education) changed to a shorter IQ. It went to the Eastern Seaboard to Miami Beach, Florida in 1977. A new feature was debates over issues. Not just for NAUI divers and instructors, divers from many agencies attended and participated. As usual, lots of socials and awards.

IQ continued on in a descending importance over the following years, losing some of its impact as regional seminars and symposiums popped up to cover the same research dissemination territory. After all, as the cost of travel soared, buying the proceedings for $15.00 covered the need to keep abreast of what's new in diving; magazines and newsletters were carrying duplicate information; and some of the local events did a smashing job. Fred Calhoun's Underwater Symposiums at Harvard Science Center in New England had the usual Calhoun panache. Fred had become a formidable NAUI leader by this time, 1978. NAUI CANADA was putting on its NAUI Conference Sous Marine, and Working Diver Symposium was being held at the respected Battelle Institute in Columbus, Ohio.

It was the upwelling of DEMA (Diving Equipment and Marketing Association) by the late 1970's that really drained off the momentum of NAUI IQ. DEMA knew how to stage a convention with flair, to entertain with learning. They drew in all the exhibiting commercial keystones of sport diving, most of whom could afford to do a first class job at only one show a year.

Another attractive feature of IQ's was the post Conference Dive Trips that allowed attendees to get wet together.

IQ moved on through the 1980's and into the 1990's with different organizers in different venues. The subject matter varied slightly and in general serviced new divers and dive instructors with the usual information with a "new twist here and there". As Chuck Blakeslee, Skin Diver Magazine co-founder, commented to us, "Diving is different from 1950 to 2000. Well, it's overcrowded...and it does seem they're reinventing the wheel."

IQ went to fully international in 1973 with Toronto, Canada IQ, as NAUI JAPAN, NAUI CANADA. NAUI AUSTRALIA splintered off from NAUI USA and sought recognition by bidding for sponsorship of an IQ. The one in Italy in the 1980's had a surprising large turn out representing the European Continent. Everybody spoke English, veteran IQ presenters held court, and the topics were familiar. No, Ezio Bartolli did not present a paper on How To Eat Spaghetti and Hyperventilate At The Same Time. It was all very serious and probably the most significant emphasis was on Cousteau's final warning, "If oceans die, so does Sport Diving. The environment is where we do diving, and without a good one, divers are just playing with a lot of equipment just for the sake of playing with equipment."

Besides the environment, there was the acute interest in marketing the sport. The NAUI IQ, originally meant for instructors, had to jump in and lure the salesman/instructor. They had been concerned with the drop out rate in all the Fifty-Year History of diving; divers suffered the same "been there done that" syndrome as the fickle leisure public.

IQ had its last United States territory Conference in 1995 and ends the Century unsure of where it goes. In 2000, Kapala was the site, certainly an exotic location. The topics had taken on the specialty resort and luxurious liveaboards. Most of the diving leaders feel IQ still has a necessary place. NAUI leader, Tom Hemphill, felt that there should be one in the United States every year with continuing leadership at the same site. Perhaps NAUI's Headquarters Tampa location, in the Tampa Aquarium. Tom says, "It's never over. We have to keep researching our own sport and talking about it together, or we could very well lose it. There's always more to learn; ideas and procedures change because technology and the environment is changing."

Sport diving research will continue to go on in garages, basements, equipment-testing labs, product research and development centers, universities and by instructional agencies. Many divers hope that there will always be events to recognize this research and share the ideas.

Looking back we can see how Los Angeles County tried to stimulate and recognize new ideas, to research results through a recertification program. Then, NAUI gave sport diving its full ceremonial illumination through its Conferences on Underwater Education. Sport diving has to be grateful to those who kept seeing more to scuba diving than just "put it in your mouth and don't hold your breath," as if that was all there was to it.

Long, long ago, back in 1962, NAUI did set up a Research Bureau to which the membership contributed. Interesting topics were published as a multi-paged newsletter edition. As much as IQ was a broad window, this original attempt at research information-gathering presented a peep-hole to new ideas that allowed the vision of a vast horizon of what could still be done. Al Tillman asked Jon Hardy (The two worked together on various instruction projects, pioneering the YMCA instruction on the Pacific Coast as far back as 1959.) to evaluate the NAUI Houston final written exam. Jon came up with great perceptions, but his overall response is worth repeating here. It is timeless:

"The biggest problem with these 'would-be-instructors' is a lack of varied experience, background, understanding, general education, research and general participation. They also seem to be unable to realize that how they dive personally is not the way to teach a beginner. There is too much of this idea that there is only one way to do things." (Jon Hardy went on to lead NAUI in the crucial years of the 1970's and operates the world-renowned Scuba Lab on Santa Catalina Island, California by year 2000.)

The NAUI Research Bureau was involved in all the studies and developments in providing a contact lens for divers. A doctor in Wheaton, Maryland, working with U. S. Navy, had come up with one to replace the divers' face mask. No fogging. NAUI got some and tried them. Supposedly they couldn't be lost because they float to the surface. Damned if NAUI didn't lose their tryout pair. They're probably still floating somewhere in the waters of the Rosemead, California swimming pool. Bill Barada tried a pair out in his hotel room while traveling in Florida. He spent a half-hour with lens stuck in his eyes. He could only see a blur, rolled on the bed in the struggle until he finally had to call two bellmen to come up and help him dislodge the pesky new invention. NAUI was even looking at studies that showed that among males, ten to thirteen year old boys float best. Or why sharks were causing an abalone shortage in California. (No, they didn't eat them. But after divers were driven to deeper, 50-foot water, due to an abalone shortage in shallows, they encountered sharks, and the market suffered its shortage because of the distraction.)

NAUI's Dave Woodward got the Research Bureau an Air Certification and the Scott Draeger Gas Testing Kit. It was a grand start in a small way but it certainly inspired everybody to take a new look at everything they knew at that point in the early 1960's. It could well have been the seed that produced the pearl of the IQ Conference.

It does seem that many divers stay intrigued with diving because of the chance to uncover a new idea. Most of the founders of diving we interviewed could claim to be the innovator of several new ideas to make diving safer and more fun. It will always be a strong factor in the growth, development, and continuation of sport diving.

NOTES

The authors of this history often found they had opposing views on the various elements and events in diving ...and they suppose there are thousands of different perceptions out there.

Just so you know this history had to wend its way through a battlefield, a 1976 confrontation of sorts of the authors is related.

Al Tillman returned from the 1975 International Underwater Education Conference, IQ$_7$ with the opinion the affair was a "tired one elephant circus, more spangles and sawdust than performance."

"Cut me and I bleed NAUI," says Al, "but I don't think IQ has any more substance than a three acre balloon." He saw it as a lot of old stuff, rehashed and a bunch of the instigators giving each other awards and charging to come see it. He sees it as a classic American rip-off. A bunch of one-line ideas at best, neatly folded, given in pseudo-academically packaged ego talks. Just read the titles and you'll be less confused.

There seemed to be plenty of all-of-us-together-gang party carousing - a lot of clay piled up at drunk idols' feet. The awards ceremonies were ludicrous; only the waiter and janitor failed to get one. The displays by exhibitors were colored lights and 21st Century stuff. Resorts staffed by tan, slim, bewhiskered hucksters dangling gold/silver loot from their necks ...but their fish stories were canned plastic.

Overall, was the Conference worth the effort, and cost to attend? Al paid his own way. It was worth about as much as a silk tie at a summer picnic tug-o-war.

Ouch, Al Tillman-Mr. Grumpy, let's be fair and hear the other view. Zale in counterpoint:

"You may be completely right in your judgement, Al, but all IQs haven't been the same or just enjoyed by the commanding few. I want to clarify by contrast that the IQs I had attended were put together with integrity, good taste, and long hours of planning.

If this IQ_7 didn't seem like an exhibition of extraordinary talent and innovation, did not seem to be a fountain of new knowledge, it may be scuba's age. Scuba, like the traditional age of the old maid, is beyond twenty-five years old. Scuba, like the old maid, needs some rejuvenating again. So what if there is a game-show aura for our tired tushies. It is only a few hours in our diving clocktime that we can rest side- by-side, cozied up in a giant gathering without being burdened with gear, spit in our mask, in preparation for our next water entry.

It is a near act of God and one to celebrate when one can get good attendance even in an ordinary family gathering. IQ is a family of diving get-together. As an instructor remembers: "Entertain them greatly while educating them immensely. I think IQ has done that."

Zale and Al's disparate viewpoints may not seem a healthy collaboration, but they are. IQ and all the rest of the sharing of ideas and the research over the years have given divers a feeling of the importance of diving, a large complexity of intriguing aspects that extends beyond most sports.

Sport diving can never depend on survival through other research programs for military, science and commercial interest. It has always needed its own exclusive inquiry.

30
THE GREAT DIVING PLACES

DEFINING EVENT: CATALINA VS FLORIDA KEYS - 1950'S

Once there were thousands of extraordinary places on the menu for the early divers. The challenging question of which was best was as it is today a very individual and subjective consideration. Here we hope to distill the best that have continuously been spoken of in awe. Not from the advertising hyperbole, but from the mouths of divers renown and some who just wandered through.

So much of what makes a dive place so wonderful is a matter of the moment. The day may come along with glassy surface, brilliant sun, unlimited visibility and a zillion creatures congregating from everywhere. It was for the pioneers many times somewhere where no diver had ever been before. Then it was a complete virgin opportunity for exploration and discovery.

Divers have all heard the refrain, "You should have been here yesterday." And when true, that one day at any particular moment, day or week or more, provides an unbelievable fantasy area. We have the dilemma of choosing the best.

We promised to do it and so from the hearts and memories of people who drained tons of water through their sinuses all over the world we give you the places and the reasons why they are the best.

CEDAM International, the organization started by Pablo Bush Romero and dedicated to conservation, education, diving and marine research has an ongoing project from 1989 to protect great diving sites by choosing the Seven Underwater Wonders of the World.

Their list is:

1 - Palau

2 - Belize Barrier Reef

3 - Galapagos Islands

4 - Northern Red Sea

5 - Lake Baikal

6 - Great Barrier Reef Australia

7 - Deep Water Vents

Some of these are very tough to get to; the average on-a-budget diver may just have to visit such wonders vicariously through the pages of *National Geographic Magazine*. It is indeed *National Geographic Magazine*, who published a coffee table book, *The Wonders of the World* in 1998 with Rick Sammon's CEDAM Report. The Report says CEDAM hopes to create an awareness by naming these which will extend protection to all underwater wonders. The criteria was apparently natural beauty, unique marine life, and its environmental and geological significance.

At Palau there are seventy submerged volcano islands hosting seven-hundred species of corals and fifteen hundred species of fish -the most biologically diverse coral reefs of the splendor of Eden and although most still exists, the impact of tourism, the progressive cattle rush to see the underwater world of Palau, has left some parts dead and barren. For example, where swift currents rush through Blue Corner, teeming with all kinds of fish, the coral is severely damaged by divers using a reef hook, a three-foot-line with hooks at both ends, used to hold a diver in place.

The Belize Barrier Reef has exceptional water clarity and is the second largest barrier reef in the world. It has the Blue Hole, the most famous crater in the world, 1,000-feet across and 400-feet deep. Corals trim the surface entry but at 125-feet there are stalactites formed during the ice age. The clarity of the reef is protected by mangrove forests which trap runoff sediments. Belize has been a divers paradise but it was popularly discovered by the 1980's wave of tourists and its relatively easy access to American divers may have a highly damaging impact.

Named for the giant turtles Darwin found there in the midst of uncovering his theory of Evolution, the Galapagos have no coral reefs but gigantic volcano rock formations instead, at this apex of our distinct major currents. The dull, arid islands host different creatures from various oceans brought by the currents amidst which are Whale Sharks, schools of Hammerheads and even Penguins. The sharks are shy, they say, in this 1986 decreed marine preserve. Always an expensive trip, it looms as the Mecca for deep pocket divers.

Eugenie Clark and David Doubilet, who have been everywhere, agree that Ras Muhammad in the North Red Sea is the best. The earth's most abundant coral reefs jut from the bottom in water surrounded by an unending desert of sand. Dr. Clark's influence brought about a national park

Al Tillman loved Southeast Asia, especially Fuga, so much that he joined up with Southeast Asia Undersea Services (SeaUs) to lead underwater expeditions to view the wonderful natural treasures in the area.

there in 1983. Special is the brilliant orange of the anemones covering the reef caused by algae in the tentacles - photographers haven't as yet captured the phenomenon on film. Probably the ultra laboratory for observing a vast diversity of creature behavior. The abrupt contrast between land and sea seems to have kept this place a "secret" until media stories opened the door to a diver tourist rush.

Once 30,000,000 years ago tectonic plates closed the southern end , then 20,000,000 years ago the north end closed and the southern end allowed Pacific species of life to join Atlantic species providing a great diversity.

The Great Barrier Reef is just an enormous natural amusement park for divers. Stretching 1,250-miles with 2900-coral reefs underwater and 900-coral islands, 135,000 square miles with 1500-species of fish. Lots of poisonous animals, such as, sea snakes, cone shells and the blue-ringed death-inducing octopus roam here so divers must be extra cautionary.

The Deep Sea Vents are like the planets, just too far away or deep in this case for the normal diver to have much hope of seeing as a scuba diver. It takes a deep submersible at $10,000 a trip to get to that two and a half-mile pitch black depth. Caused by volcanic or tectonic action, the vents take in sea water, heat it, then spew out mineral rich 600 F water. Amazingly, there is life there without oxygen or sunlight, strange 300 species, creatures of the deep, flourishing.

Other deep places to go in submersibles, are the Titanic for $35,500 a trip, Cabo San Lucas deep canyon at $9,000 for 5 dives and through a hole at the North Pole to 14,000 feet for $60,000.

All of these wonders listed by CEDAM are hard and expensive places to get to and the abyss is just a tease to the average sport diver. For pioneer American divers these places were not accessible.

When the Underwater Explorers Club in Freeport, Grand Bahama opened in 1965, a Seven Wonders of Diving

Places was posted, encouraging divers to go to these places and be able to wear a jacket patch signifying having made the dive. Here's the 1965 list:

1 - Puget Sound Giant Octopus Blakely Rock off Bainbridge Island, Washington
2 - The Ledge or Wall Dive off Bahamas Islands
3 - Kelp Forests of Santa Catalina Island
4 - The Coral Reefs of Florida Keys, Florida
5 - New England Giant-Clawed Lobster, East Coast, USA
6 - Black Coral Forests off Hawaii
7 - A Canyon Dive off La Jolla, California

Jet travel was just emerging in the early 1960's. The listing was designed to encourage and promote places to get divers on the move. Until that time, no major attempts had been made to discern the "best places".

During the 1950's, almost anyplace was a best place just by the virtue of being virtually undiscovered. The impact of divers was not yet felt. Divers had favorite, secret spots they were reluctant to expose. There was a fierce pride about local diving places. Besides most divers hadn't the money or need to jet off to special places. Even so, there was an Eden-like aspect to all of these local diving spots. Creatures encountered were undisturbed and humans appeared as another species accepted into the wildness of it all.

What do some of the pioneer and celebrated divers have to say to the question: What diving place do you consider was or is the best of them all?

Jacques Cousteau - "Each has its charm but the Indian Ocean may be the most amazing...and the Red Sea and even Port Hardy in the North West America. It's a very large ocean."

Hans Hass - "The Red Sea had been pristine when we dove it in the 1940's and we saw very large animals that no one had seen or photographed before."

Conrad Limbaugh - "The La Jolla Canyon is a vertical laboratory of marine life and it's easy to get to."

Al Giddings - "Truk Lagoon. More history in one place of biggest event in millennium-World War II."

Zale Parry - "The harbor pier at night Bonaire. The pilings are wide awake with with all kinds of delicate, colorful creatures."

Bill High - "The Hood Canal has been the Northwest's prime diving area and the San Juan Islands, too."

Al Tillman - "The sunken barge off Palos Verdes had lots of hiding places, lobsters, abalone, kelp, eel grass - not flashy corals but a real feeling of being in a fantasy ocean wonderland. Maybe it was just the time era and that I spent almost every day there in the early 1950's."

Michael Sleidley (Sea Quest, Inc.) - Writer and dive computer expert chose the Fiji Islands ten years ago before anybody got there. Hard to find anyplace left that hasn't been exploited. Indonesia may be the place of late 1990's. Divers backed by sponsors are going deep for periods of six hours on the new rebreathers and finding never before seen fish and getting to name the fish after themselves. Speculation is that half the multitude of fish off Fiji are unknown.

Carlos Eyles - Spending time underwater is like no other experience on this planet, Carlos writes in his book, *Free Diving*. Diving provides us with the opportunity of unlimited discovery. There are as many new and interesting sights and rewards in five feet of water as there are in twenty feet of water. Indeed so vast and varied is this marine world that it could easily keep the underwater explorer intrigued for a lifetime.

Colonel John D. Craig - Colonel Craig of *Kingdom of the Sea* and *Danger is my Business* never stopped talking about his experiences in the sea.

"I had been in thirty-five countries and had sailed on all of the seven seas and trod on all of the six continents. The bottom of the sea, covering four-fifths of the world, was the continent I finally chose. I was twenty-eight (1931) when I found it and I had looked for many years. It is like a mistress...dangerous, unpredictable,...one minute caressing and giving all it has, the next minute furiously trying to destroy with power and cunning and tricks that are endless in variety. But ever since the first day I went down to it, in fifty feet of water off the coast of Lower California, I have loved it more than any place I have ever been." John explained every place he dove was his favorite. The best - John tended to be especially fond nostalgically of the treasure laden Silver Shoals in the Caribbean.

Ernest Brooks II - Anacapa in the Channel Islands off Santa Barbara, California. Divers have been going there since the pioneer years and the Brooks underwater photographers have captured the best images. Great rock formations, kelp beds, clear water and large and small creatures. Gorgeous nudibranchs.

Two places existed in the golden years of the 1940's and 1950's that were the prize destination for divers. When any American diver could get a two-week vacation, he loaded up the family car, probably a Ford station wagon, and headed East or West or South.

Hanging off opposite edges of the United States were different but equally wondrous natural wildernesses that until those years, only a few local divers had dived and with slight impact. One was Santa Catalina Island, a volcanic island sitting in a jungle of giant kelp beds with frequently gin clear water, 20 miles off the diver-populated Los Angeles basin; the other was a long line of reefs and islands running South off Florida toward Cuba. Catalina was movie stars, movie sets, that cathedral-like kelp, and the protected bright orange Garibaldi (California's State Fish) and a vast zoo of large pelagic fish, lobster and abalone. The Keys were measureless acres of corals, exotic tropical fish in all colors, and big game fish, especially barracuda and a graveyard of shipwrecks. Divers saw both these places on movie screens, in magazine layouts, and travel agents in every city got plenty of help promoting them from regional visitors bureaus.

These two venues were like pitting Disney World versus Universal Studios against each other, each with different awesome lures. Divers saved for excitedly anticipated trips to each of these best diving places...sometimes for years. They went, were indeed awed, vowed to come back (maybe to live), and told stories back home that got green envy flowing.

Ask a pioneer diver, who managed to make it to both places in the golden years. Ask him which was best. Ask Dolores and Mel Fisher, who went back and forth and broke in these places, as they emerged as the two diving Shangrilas. Mel ended up living at the very end of the Florida Keys, Key West - because that's where the most shipwrecks abound. He might be living in Avalon, the main town on Catalina Island, if he hadn't stubbed his fin on the 1715 Fleet and the Atocha. Mel asked this question, would stall a bit, laugh his heh, heh, heh, and with a grin say, "I don't know they're both great places but I always get blinded by gold...but without the treasure, they're pretty equal...best in America maybe the world at that time."

Ask the spearfishing "fathers", the ones who were there in the 1940's and 1950's and hunted the big fish. Ask Jim Christiansen or Nelson E. "Doc" Mathison, or any of the competitors, who sampled the waters of both in competitive meets. "It all depends on what you're looking for, there are big fish in both places, but working the towering kelp stalks has a more challenging and mysterious aura, however, the skills needed to work the coral caves in the Keys are......... ."

Take a vote of all those who did both spots in those virgin days and it will probably come up 50-50. Most are sure glad they got a chance to see either of these places in those pristine times.

If you had been diving back in the golden years and Santa Catalina Island was your diving mecca, you might have got on Mart Toggweiler's Maray and putted out to Ship Rock, a pinnacle in deep water off the East end. On board a deck-hand named Ron Merker might have helped you into the water. Then he joined you, went deeper than you, and brought up a huge White Sea Bass. There were hundreds, swift moving armies of Yellowtail and White Sea Bass flashing by this great special dive place.

The next dive would be at Eagle Reef or the Isthmus. Places that were very clear most of the time and primed with kelp beds, a variety of fish and sea lions. Everybody got abalone and lobster. A few divers got a ten-pound Calico Bass or perhaps a seventeen-pound Sheephead. Once in awhile a diver got buzzed by a door-length curious Blue Shark.

Once in awhile a boat would swing way around to the lee of the island to get out to Cortez Banks, deep water pinnacles. The fish were there and hard Gorgonian purple coral branches. You were probably on the Vellron out of Newport for that one. But for most of the pioneers, their best memory seems to be of hanging suspended down fifty feet in window-clear water surrounded by amber stalks and fronds of giant kelp that soared up into a sun-glinted canopy like brown bottle glass. Cathedral-like it was, and some kind of awed spiritual feeling gripped them. No one ever described it as just that old Catalina kelp. It got branded into the left side of your brain, escaped over to the right. It was difficult not to wax poetic about the experience. In those wonderful days, all was fresh and untouched. Catalina was King of Diving Places.

And so the big event that changed diving was simply the grand contest between these two premiere diving places, Santa Catalina and the Florida Keys. It presented the dissatisfaction with hometown diving places and, indeed, we can see a true analogy here in the query - "How you going to get them back on the farm once they've seen Paree?"

Al Tillman explored and photographed many of the coral reefs of Grand Bahama Island before any other scuba diver.

Well not quite. The Florida Keys held a fat poker hand with a very special Ace card-the shipwrecks. With the Gulf Stream endlessly sweeping by its two-hundred miles of long barrier reefs and seasons-upon-seasons of ship bashing hurricanes, four centuries of the most prolific ship sinkings centered there. German U-Boats in World War II (1940-1945) contributed a fair amount. And, with the ships cargoes of embossed Spanish tiles to golden doubloons went down, too. Ballast stones and galleon canons spread everywhere, a lot encrusted into the coral reefs.

You couldn't go far without tripping over some evidence of a wreck. It was North America's largest coral reef system, the third largest in the world, just four-miles off shore. Not a shore dive but easily a trailered small boat's cup of tea.

They would zoom down in old cars with a towed ten-foot skiff from Chicago, New Jersey everywhere East of the Mississippi. They would jump in out of those boats to see a constellation of colored tropical fish and bizarre corals, conch, sharks and barracudas. They came down from Ft. Lauderdale and Miami, too. It was, generally, the case that divers had to go no farther than Key Largo with its Molasses Reef, Alligator Reef and Christ of the Abyss. No jet-set invasion, just weekend divers scraping the gas-money and air fill-money together, holing up in sleeping bags wherever, and eating peanut butter-jelly sandwiches they made themselves.

For those divers going over to Catalina or down to the Florida Keys in the late 1940's and 1950's diving itself was a new, emerging sport and those two places were the flexing giants, still mysterious and unknown, grand wilderness explorations where no rules, no certifications, no restrictions, no game laws got in the way of jumping anywhere with whatever knowledge or experience, and harvesting everything in sight. AND, the sight was breath-taking.

MORE DIVING CELEBS CHOICES

David Doubilet - "Been there, photographed that," is what you might expect from a diver, who has been everywhere. In the pioneer days David would choose the Wall at Andros. Then switched to the North Red Sea by the 1970's. In 1992 *International Wild Life Magazine* survey, he cited Papua, New Guinea's New Hanover Island, as a new favorite place. There he found "anemones big as a card table" and... "a supermarket of life instead of a single shop."

Jeff Rottman - In same 1992 article, Jeff picks the Red Sea, where he "finds a rainbow of diversity rich as a rain forest."

Howard Hall - In same article, *International Wild Life Magazine*, Howard would favorite dive Marisula Sea-mount in the Gulf of California, a peak that pushes up from thousands of feet to sixty feet beneath the surface. There he finds giant fish (but in dwindling numbers now) especially hundreds of sharks which seem scared of him.

Chris Newbert - Chris touts the Solomon Sea because you see reefs that "have never been seen by a human before". "Every tip of coral becomes precious because it's still perfect."

We have to put aside the moment-in-time determining aspect where an individual has had an earth or ocean heart-rending experience. There's no question that a place in one terrific rush of adrenaline caused by an encounter, a fleeting one, simply overwhelms us. But it may not be so much the place or perhaps not where you are at all. You come around a big rock in murky water to find you are nose-to-nose with ten Tiger Sharks, who brush past you without a sniff except for the last one which...well, you get the idea.

Scuba America distilled what seemed to be the reigning criteria for the best diving place from hundreds of interviews with the pioneer's and some from following generations, who had heard the stories.

THE CRITERIA

1. See-forever water, clear as the air, almost all of the time. No river run-offs, no boat pollution, no outfalls of storm water or sewage, no natural proliferation of floating matter or no upwellings.

2. Virgin. No diver has been there before or at the very least it seems so.

3. There is a wildness in the creatures, untamed but curious enough to not flee from divers. They virtually seem friendly but it just territorial and because they have not been touched as yet by the evils of man.

4. The terrain, kelp, corals, the sand has not been altered by any intrusions from land. No coke cans, abandoned traps, styrofoam molded-forms, snagged lures, scientist's markers or habitats. The exception here is finding an untouched shipwreck.

5. There are a lot of creatures, exotic ones, large schools, a multiplicity of things.

6. There is a profusion of sunlight coming down to a depth of about sixty feet, some colors still exist even without artificial light.

7. Things pelagic cross through the area often in a surprising changing of the sights so that it looks different on every dive.

Have you found such an underwater Eden? !!!

Finally, the pioneers agree it is the different places each with unique features that are essence of sport diving, the underwater experience. Without the views in these places, diving would be a mundane, swimming exercise while wearing a lot of equipment.

John Lockridge - (Pioneer Spearfisherman) - "Coronado Islands, five minute kelp, very big creatures there. But it's always a particular experience that endears a place. Over all up and down the coasts of California and

Baja, I guess. San Clemente Island, consistently stands out. Walls of Yellowtail and other pelagics."

George Bond - "Aside from some military diving, just for recreational purposes, I have a great fondness for the Virgin Islands. Very pretty water."

Undercurrents, the consumers guide to diving travel and resorts, publisher has volumes of choices which are reviews from Undercurrent subscribers.

Frank Scalli - "Cut teeth in cold fierce New England water and everybody should get eyeball to eyeball with the pugilistic face and lethal claw of a fairytale-ogre of a lobster coming at you out of a rock cave."

Gustav Dalla Valle - "I thinka the time I wasa in Haiti doing a tourista business. It let me explorea someplace no divers hada ever been to. It wasa a huge, cleara ocean teeming with fish and corals," he expressed in his robust Tyrolean/Italian embellishment.

E. R. Cross - "I suppose I like the Hawaiian Islands best, just off the entrance to Pearl Harbor where I found so many rare sea shells."

Jim Christiansen - "I was impressed with the coast off Yugoslavia when I went there for the World Spearfishing Championships. But it can't beat Ship Rock off Catalina on a clear day with White Sea Bass swimming by in schools."

Jack McKenney - "I always dreamed of the Great Barrier Reef in Australia when I was a young diver in Windsor, Canada, and only had the lakes and quarries to go into. I finally got there with some really good cameras and it matched every dream I ever had."

THE BAHAMAS - FLORIDA'S FRONT YARD

Many of the broad selections, such as, when some one chooses the Caymans or the Seychelles, may narrow down to one ultimate place, one reef or rock or wreck that by itself looms as the paradise dive location to satisfy most dramatically the diver's heart and soul.

Peterson Cay, six miles east of UNEXSO, a pocket one-half acre sand and rock island was surrounded by a variety of coral reef bottoms but in particular rolling westward from it was statuary field of orange Staghorn Coral that was filled with the full menu of colorful tropical fish. Probably more underwater movies and photographs for commercials got shot in its high clarity waters during the 1960's than anywhere else in the world. It was protected as a marine preserve (which stopped the native dynamiting for fish) at the instigation of UNEXSO. It never failed to please every diver who went there. For all the dive sites off UNEXSO, it was by far the favorite.

Assumption Reef

Jacques Cousteau probably saw more diving places, the special ones, than anyone in diving history. Wouldn't it be great if we could ask him right now which place was the best of all. As he passed through, back in the mid 1960's we had a chance to ask him that question. There may have been other candidates since that time but he did say, "Assumption Reef."

Where is Assumption Reef? In the Indian Ocean next to a little island called Assumption near Madagascar and the Seychelles. Cousteau and the Calypso were there in the mid 1950's making the movie, *Silent World*. Only an anchorage for the night, this pristine reef, which had never hosted a diver, dazzled Cousteau with a sloping pasture of massive coral domes, crimson sponges, beds of huge anemones, "that looked like a giant's tomato salad." A Black Coral Forest stood from the reef in 200 foot visibility clear water.

Cousteau said it was a dream fantasy, a glorious spot. Never had he seen so many fish in one glance. "We had found a wilderness where man is unknown." It was here that the Calypso crew discovered a three foot mascot, the grouper they called Ulysses, who stole the movie *Silent World* from all other actors. "It was Falco, who said 'we'll never in our lives see anything like this reef again' and all of us were silent in agreement." Cousteau's hooded eyes misted a bit and he was silent for a long time as he went inside himself and returned to Assumption Reef.

Bill High - One of diving's greatest leaders with involvements in NAUI, Underwater Society of America and

Catalina is an exotic island dive location located only a few miles from the home turf of many pioneer sport divers.

famous habitats. Funny thing, Bill, a professional marine biologist, told us back in the 1970's that collecting antique bottles in the harbor off Port Townsend (Washington) rises to the top - forget the exotic fish places.

Don St. Hill - The veteran diver, Don St. Hill, who had the Palos Verdes paradise diving all to himself back in the 1930's and 1940's, ended up in retirement back where he came from in the Northwest. He felt that nothing will ever beat Palos Verdes of the old days but Hood Canal where he has a home could be as good as it gets by the 1970's. Northwest divers are pretty much in agreement with him.

Jim Cahill - Jim felt the diving off his own dock, a promontory near Beverly, Massachusetts, was a sort of heaven on earth place. While the Virgin Islands are a pretty flash and he got to see exotic underwater places as an Underwater Demolition Team Officer, he liked the crisp muted rock reefs where the great Atlantic lobsters made their homes.

Garry Howland - Garry was always impressed with the Gulf Stream diving, just drifting over a vast area nurtured by the warmth of the Stream. Big surprise creatures always showed up.

Gary Keffler - Long time dive shop owner, Champion Spearfisherman and who spent more time with giant octopus than anyone told us way back in the early days: "I like our San Juan Islands, especially Lopez Island where I plan to retire. Everything you'll ever want to see in Northwest diving is there and you can take the family into the water if the currents are right. But it's Port Hardy for really giant octopuses, that's at the northern end of Vancouver Island. Even the Cousteaus listed it as a favorite place in all of the world."

In the 24K Golden Years of the early 1950's off the Southern California Coast, there were shore dives and there were boat dives. The more accessible shore dives fit the budget of most divers and the whole experience of warm rocks next to a blazing driftwood fire, eating a tuna sandwich, talking to a buddy about what had been seen on a first dive, getting ready for the next plunge, and sense of conquest after sinking under and sweeping excited eyes over the rocks and reefs in one breath-holding moment...that whole experience seemed more in keeping with the rugged pioneer spirit of diving. But the luxury of a boat dive can't be denied and it got divers to places as yet untouched.

Where were the best shore dives in those days. Palos Verdes, the largest marine terraces in the world layered from hillside down into the sea forming mighty fine reefs. Kelp beds bestrewed over glassy clear water. The Palos Verde place of places was <u>Flat Rock</u>. A giant rock pinnacle stood tall out of the water in the middle of a small cove. Being part goat helped you get up and down a clay and fossil earth cliff. You'd meet famous divers in muddy tennis shoes and with a gunny sack of lobsters and abalone slogging up as you went down. There was *Skin Diver Magazine* publisher, Chuck Blakeslee, with two kids and a diving wife (unusual in those days), Jeri, doing what he talked about in the heart of diving, the magazine *Skin Diver*. And there was Chuck Sturgill and his clan, all ignoring the bubble machine and free diving for their suppers.

More different things were being uncovered at Flat Rock, the most popular place of all, than anywhere else. Teak cabinets from gambling ships washed in from Santa Monica Bay, giant "Chinese Junk rock anchors" found by Billy and Bobby Meistrell of Dive N' Surf, Electric Torpedo Rays, 17 pound sheephead and record size green abalone. There was a cornucopia of abundance, enough for everybody, at least, while everybody meant two or three couples of divers. At some point by the end of the decade, as the diving ranks grew, Flat Rock was over-invaded and its carrying capacity for diving exceeded.

But once again, even its 24K gold lustre was tarnished by being embraced by too many divers. For those few golden years, it was as good a diving place, lying next to a dense urban greater Los Angeles region, as one could dream up.

Moving down coast from Los Angeles, there was Laguna Beach, and Dana Point (the abalone capital with abs stacked on top of each other), and then, San Diego with its La Jolla sandstone cliffs spilling into a vast kelp forest on the lip of the Scripps's underwater canyon, where Bottom Scratchers Jack Prodonovich and Wally Potts "dive ranched" scores of giant Black Sea Bass.

Then on to Baja California which was a hop and a skip down for Southern California divers. Lots of special places all along the coast but the creme de la creme was Punta Banda, a jutting peninsula of rocky shoreline forming Ensenada Bay. It teemed with big fish and a multiplicity of marine life because it converged subtropic warm water and colder northern currents. It was a crystal clear window into paradise.

Thousands of divers have cut their teeth in the shallows nearThe Casino in Avalon on Catalina Island.

In Northern California, divers from the San Francisco region drove station wagons to the La Jolla of the North in the 1950's and 1960's. The Monterey Bay south tip, Lovers Cove of Pacific Grove was clear and cold. It balanced on the edge of a creature loaded shelf extending to another submarine canyon. A grand shore dive off a white sand family beach. Cold water caused a diver to shiver even in his wet suit, but divers hated to leave this Underwater Eden. Today, one of the world's great aquariums monitors the vast ocean sanctuary there and a look-not touch restriction makes it just a viewing experience compared to the early discovery explorations by divers.

Great diving places have been wonderful in certain time periods. For reasons stated in this Chapter many have diminished in quality or completely disappeared. Divers are late in trying to save what is left but there is no choice. Sport diving has always been dependent on great diving places to maintain the passions of divers.

31

THE CAPTURED OCEAN
AQUARIUMS AND OCEANARIUMS

DEFINING EVENT: MARINE STUDIOS FLORIDA

A lot of people have been able to see underwater without getting wet. While scuba diving opened a big door to physically entering the water, going down and seeing and touching plants and creatures, the majority of people have passed on it to accept other ways of peering into the unknown.

There was the look box, a piece of glass in a box that was dipped into the water from a boat, and while staying dry, the viewer could see some of the underwater world - not all. Al Tillman recalls that when his brother, Don, and he started skindiving off Palos Verdes, they took along a look box in their war surplus yellow life raft to scout the underwater terrain before they jumped in - somebody said, "I don't want to get my ears bitten off by sticking my face-masked-head in." Fishermen in ancient times used look boxes to find productive fishing spots. Then bigger look boxes appeared at famous water resorts in Florida's Silver Springs and California's Catalina Island in the form of glass bottomboats. Any place that had clarity of water featured such an amusement ride for tourists.

Skin divers used glass bottom boats off Catalina Island to find shells before diving down for them.

Why not just take the ocean and its scenery and creatures and put them in a big bottle and avoid the boat ride on unpredictable seas. Aquariums with small glass cubicle tanks appeared in various seaside resorts everywhere, in dark, damp wooden buildings, often on the ends of piers jutting into the sea.

Most of the specimens were brought in after being caught in fishermen's nets. For the most part, individual species were separated and lived dreary, confined lives away from rocks, corals and plants they were used to in the wild ocean. Most developed diseases and didn't live long. Crude as the first aquariums were, compared to modern times' exhibit of sea life, millions were enthralled with these small peek-holes of things from the vast unknown world beneath the sea. Some wanted to see more; bigger windows, bigger tanks with mixed species and some, of course, were motivated to take up diving and go visit the ocean in person.

The paradox, that no one is sure of , is whether the aquariums and the oceanariums - giant outdoor exhibiting facilities of water - made it so people were satisfied with seeing captive species or drove them to want more without a window between them. In interviewing pioneer divers for this book, most of them took friends and families to see the wonders they talked about after going diving, but hardly any felt that the compacted abundance of hand fed fish inspired them to go scuba diving.

There is some indication that divers did learn about fish behaviors from window viewing and were able to apply this knowledge to encounters on dives. On the other hand, the behaviors of creatures in captivity may not really

Female divers/actresses were part of the underwater display at Weekiwachee Spring in Florida along with the fish.

parallel that of open sea living. Bill Starr, one of the developers of the Los Angeles County Underwater Instructors program, got one of the first chances to go into the big tank at Marineland of the Pacific after it opened in 1955. He was photographed giving Chuck Blakeslee, *Skin Diver Magazine* owner, his diving instructor graduation certificate underwater - a publicity photo shoot. Starr said after emerging, "I had the sensation of a rainstorm of fish...sawfish, sharks, moray eels, sheephead, like a Fellini movie set about the ocean."

Zale Parry, who has been in various oceanariums to film movies and ride dolphins, remembers her first entry into one of the big tanks during the opening ceremony of Marineland of the Pacific. She was joined by Col. John D. Craig, since the two of them were actively filming *Kingdom of the Sea* using the ocean. Both wore the Scott-Hydropak full-face-mask scuba with built-in microphones. "We could hear each other, and at the same time what we said was broadcast over a major national television network. Bubbles, the pilot whale had not taken residency in a bowl of water yet, but there were many common species of everything that treated us as though we were part of their ocean, too. Each of us would point or get close to the sharks, eels, opal eyes, big groupers and whatever swam by to express where these would be found in the ocean. The black sting rays had such cute faces under their black capes, but they were a little bit of a nuisance when they followed me everywhere to nibble on my light colored hair. Later, Marineland of the Pacific became a perfect place to fake the ocean scenes, with its location on the rocky cliffs off a beach head with a pier. It was used by all studios, photo shoots and scientific studies.

When Bubbles, the pilot whale, arrived the excitement

John Craig and Zale Parry during the opening days of Marineland of the Pacific.

to be captured in the same container with this huge creature was wonderful exhilaration! That whale would start speeding from one end of the tank to extend a welcome, then at the last second before creaming the diver against the wall, turn tail and swim gently away. It was full of mischief but very lovable. Many times Zale's work required no scuba gear. Safety divers were fish herders and babysat the whale to prevent the critters from swimming in front of the camera lens.

As Marineland grew older and beloved by thousands of school children and their parents, more special exhibits of ocean life were introduced until Orky and Corky, the killer whales, topped the programs. Generally, gentle but very capable of explosive tantrums, Orky, once nearly killed a trainer. Such was the attitude of many of these larger mortals, who brought joy to the hearts of all. Stolen from the sea, fed dead fish, their life span cut in half because of their captivity, yet they rendered or seem to supply a personal love for us. Or did we just think so?

The personalities of the dolphins were no different than people. A diver in the know could easily tell which ones were happily playful or give you an 800 pound shove to get out of their domain. Zale's favorite dolphins were those in Florida Seaquarium's fenced-off sea arena where *Danny and the Mermaid* was filmed. Highly trained to swim with people, these were the sweethearts of the sea. If the action was a block's distance away from the dock in this huge sea arena and ended there, Zale could slap the surface of the water with her hand to get the attention of any one of the dolphins. Instead of swimming forth and back again many times, the E-ticket ride back into close-up position for the director and cameraman was by holding on to the dorsal fin of the living-chariot that appeared from the dark water beneath her on command. Only in a captive situation could this act be done repeatedly.

After oceanariums opened everywhere and with everyone's love for *Flipper*, stories were told about wishes to have a pet dolphin in one's own swimming pool.

THE BEGINNING

A book by Miriam Cooper, who created the original *King Kong* movie in 1934 came up with an idea in the 1930's for an oceanarium by carving out a chunk of Florida's shoreline, netting it off, then filling it with captured sea life. There would be a natural flow of clear ocean water with the tides. On the face of it, a King Kong of an idea. Unfortunately, to depend on a uniform exchange of uncontaminated ocean water defied the natural order of things. Cooper found out before he undertook the creation of his confined ocean, that there would be impurities and unpredictables in the water exchange. There was also the problem of how the public would be able to see into the created lagoon.

Dr. Hans Hass visits Marineland of the Pacific in its early days.

MARINE STUDIOS

The idea was picked up by a W. Douglas Burden, a relative of the Vanderbilts, and Ilea Tolstoy, grandson of Leo Tolstoy, who visualized a natural oceanarium in a cliffside ravine, contained by bulkheads with glass in them so movie makers could photograph as J. E. Williamson had done with a tube in the Bahamas back in 1912. In time, they turned to steel tanks on the shoreline to create the Marine Studios where naturalists could make documentary films. Large and small species would swim together but the partners had no idea if they would eat each other. Cooper and Burden coined the title "oceanarium".

This first oceanarium processed and tested the ocean water and heated it as necessary. The partners hired a boy to count cars on the nearby roadway and in 24-hours only six passed by. But the 1938 opening saw bumper to bumper traffic and for the time a phenomenal 20,000 people showed up to crowd around the one inch thick glass viewing ports. The novelty aquarium, with its outdoor setting, was more of a success as a public attraction than as the intended movie production place. The oceanarium had indeed arrived.

Not for long. The World War II took its toll and gas rationing decimated attendance. The Marine Studios shut down in 1941. It struggled to maintain the facilities by doing scientific studies such as pursuing a shark repellent for the U. S. Navy.

MARINELAND OF FLORIDA

The Marine Studios did make a comeback in the 1950's as the Marineland of Florida. It was written up in the November 1952 issue of *National Geographic*; two years after this history of sport diving begins.

The story is by Gilbert Grosvenor La Gorce and the photography by the pioneer guru of underwater photogra-

Diver and Manta Ray, Marine Studios

Postcard of diver and manta ray at Marineland in Florida.

phy, Luis Marden. It begins, "Man has amused and instructed himself by watching fish in aquariums since ancient times. But only until today (1952) has it been possible to stand a few inches from the predatory shark, the vicious barracuda, and the malicious moray eel, and watch them together in surroundings like those of their natural habitat."

This Marineland was located halfway between St. Augustine and Daytona Beach and was primarily financed by public admissions. The old idea of a Marine Studios became a back shelf concept. The public saw two big tanks, 200 port holes, and 10,000 fish. Helmet and hose divers did the maintenance and feeding underwater - scuba was on the brink of arriving.

Fifty percent of the draw seemed to have been the porpoise show. They leaped in the air to take a fish out of an attendant's hand and that was their entire act in those days. Porpoises were collected by lassoing them from a boat. It took divers two weeks to tame a newly captured porpoise to accept food from the diver's hand.

MARINELAND OF THE PACIFIC

In 1955, the counterpart of Marineland of Florida opened as Marineland of the Pacific on a promitory in Palos Verdes, California. Divers had long faces about it because it took over a really wild place and great diving area called Abalone Cove, which up to then, had been a relatively little dived paradise of lobster and abalone. "It was off that point in 1949, after sipping Sake to get warm, with the congenial Neisi Kelp Tanglers that I swam out and banged my biggest fish to date, a 20-pound Sheephead. Then we used to buy a fifty cent lug of beef-steak tomatoes from the field where Marineland was built," Tillman sighed in memory.

Kenneth Norris out of UCLA, and trained by Dr. Boyd Walker, became its first curator, and the Los Angeles County's Underwater Instructors Program's main lecturer in marine biology during the 1950's. The General Manager, Bill Monahan, was very cooperative in letting Los Angeles County use the facility for instructor courses and eventually, serving as a "sound stage" for shooting *Sea Hunt*.

Dr. Ken Norris would always respond when LA County tried to thank him, "Well, we're recruiting and your underwater instructors have the potential to be staff here or at other oceanariums." Norris was an Ich (ichthyologist) and while at Scripps Institution of Oceanography working on his Ph.D., scuba dived with the likes of Conrad Limbaugh and Andreas Rechnitzer, super scuba heroes of early diving.

Limbaugh would say, at the end of the Marineland pier, while testing instructor candidates, "Ken never was one of those Nansen Guys (Nansen Bottle dragged from boat to capture and study underwater creatures.) - he always pushed scuba and helped make it the accepted new tool of oceanographers." Most curators at aquariums were scuba divers and hired scuba divers to do the feeding and care of animals, maintain the tanks and in some cases be part of the viewing entertainment.

The greatest need for competent scuba divers arose out of the collecting specimens process. Some independent divers such as Ted Griffin, who owned the Seattle Aquarium, got skillful at capturing and transporting Killer Whales and made a business out of it. Ted jumped in with a killer whale, Namu, at a time when they were considered the deadliest, most voracious monsters on the planet. The only behavior that we had on them was that they bit sea lions in two for the fun of it, and scuba divers in wet suits looked like sea lions.

Collecting is a delicate endeavor. The transporting after capture is more so. When nets, ropes and slings are used, creatures get roughly jostled in the handling. They injure themselves trying to escape. Scuba divers have played a major role in maneuvering creatures, big and small, safely to a transport device, often floating enclosures as big as dry docks.

Collector scuba divers such as the Marineland of the Pacific's crew under Captain Frank Brocato felt it was important for the diver-handlers to have a great love for the collected creatures, using their own bodies to bumper the big ones from hazards.

THE DIVERS ROLE

Some of the chief divers at the various oceanariums came out of the ranks of veteran hardhat (helmet) divers, and some were scuba sport divers as well. Jake Jacobs was Marineland of the Pacific's chief diver and his book, *Marineland Diver*, published in 1960 gave sport divers a close look at how a young diver "runs away to join the circus". Jacobs started diving for Gelidium, a plant that provided a gel that sets blood temperature and was needed during World War II in the 1940's. Divers got $75.00 a ton for it. But commercial California divers switched back to abalone after the war. Abalone was always one of the most expensive gourmet dishes in restaurants.

Jake recalls how you worked alone lifting the anchor and pulling the boat with the compressor pumping air along with you. He remembers holding onto eel grass to get into holes the surge pushed him out of. He figured his iron boots destroyed a wealth of marine life over the years. Once when he was lucky enough to have a tender topside, he used three pulls on the connecting line to signal "pull up", and two to "give slack". Get this - when he suddenly encountered a very big octopus with an attitude, he pulled three times to be pulled up - but the octopus had hold of the line, too, and would pull twice. Drove the tender crazy.

The Aquarium/Oceanarium was the next best thing to being there, the hired divers always said. Jacobs worked with Ray Cribbs, Jerry McLaughlin and Chuck Somar hand- feeding the fish five times a day, or the fish would eat each other. Circulating currents of water kept the fish on the move in the same direction. Each fish needed an average of 100-gallons of water.

Divers, who got to work on the collecting boats had the preferred jobs with scrubbing windows the worst job. The original Marine Studios had to lower its water level every day to scrub and remove killer marine organisms. The first curator Arthur McBride finally developed an antidote to alleviate that process. The disease and algae almost doomed the first oceanarium.

Marineland of the Pacific was nine years in the planning and traded stock with Marine Studios/Marineland of

1950's Chief Marineland Diver Jake Jacobs shown here with a co-worker on their commute to work.

Florida for knowledge and creatures. It operated from 1955 to February 1987. In December 1986 Harcourt Brace Jovanovich publishing conglomerate bought Marineland of the Pacific with a promise to keep it opened. Within two months time, the two killer whales, Orky and Corky were transferred to Sea World's operation in San Diego. Marineland closed. Its 300 employees fired. The entire situation was a disaster. The public protested. Harcourt received hate mail and pickets. Teachers refused to use their textbooks while newspapers wrote about big corporate selfishness and greed. Seven Marineland animals died because of the transfer.

The justification for big oceanariums despite their amusement park aura has always been scientific research. But divers at the aquariums provided the most natural observations of creature behavior and may have been at the core of all final scientific observations. They saw each fish as an individual and named each of them. They saw Sam, the shovel nosed guitar fish meeting the diver at the ladder to be first in line for food. A golden grouper, Charlie, wouldn't eat unless they removed the bones from the feed fish.

Oceanariums co-mingle fish but divers saw new arrivals get eaten while old timers were okay, even when the big predators were hungry. Fish that showed signs of being sick were gobbled up; it was nature's way of eliminating the unfit. New fish have to fit into traffic flow of the circulating pattern or they get eaten. When sharks first came in, they would snap at anything; even the ladder because it smells like food. Sharks don't last long. They swim in a straight line and with no distance sense, bang into walls. Divers had to jump in and put sharks under their arms and walk them around at first to get them to move with patterns, otherwise they gave up and suffocated. All these things were diver observations and built the lore of behavior to transfer to divers' understanding of behavior in open ocean.

Divers got nipped on occasion. Eels were night feeders and divers trying to feed fish would have an eel sneak from behind a rock and catch a finger - so they had to be moved to the porpoise tanks. The giant black sea bass could suck a diver's arm in and its small array of teeth would take the skin off. Ted Davis was a Marineland diver before he went with Los Angeles County Lifeguards and got his chest punctured when a 400-pound sea bass rolled over on him, using its spines as weapons. Turtles were bumbling food hogs and often nipped divers accidentally.

Don C. Reed was a professional scuba diver for Marine World/Africa USA in Redwood City, California from 1972 to 1985. He'd dreamed of living in the ocean as a child and so he did for a thousand hours every year in a tiny captive corner of it. In the thirteen year tenure, he spent about 12,000 hours underwater, much of the time in the company of sharks.

His book, *Sevengill - The Shark and Me*, is a grand fish eye view of being a chief diver for an outdoor aquarium. He selects out his most vivid encounter, his relationship with a massive female seven gill shark, a not often mentioned species that has a vicious predator's reputation.

Marine World got a big one from Steinhart Aquarium, almost eight feet long with a nine foot girth. This one that Reed was to name Sevengill had attacked, killed and eaten a live Great White Shark while at Steinhart.

Don Reed's first chapter on the birth and growing up of Sevengill until capture is an outstanding you-are-there narrative of how a shark views the outside world.

Putting Sevengill into the tank when it arrived was an adventure into the unknown. Reed was on the ladder after sliding the big shark into the water, when something clamped onto his leg. He kicked with what he hoped wasn't a stub of his leg, then a dark shape rose up - it was another diver assigned to protect Don's legs.

Actually there were thirteen sevengills put in the tank. Reed and his divers were quite scared not knowing what they would do. The sharks went weeks without eating until one finally ate a sick bass, performing the job all sharks do, devouring diseased fish, protected by their powerful immunity. The diver's hand fed them dead fish from then on although it seemed the sharks would rather catch their own, as in the wild. They also discovered that the sharks all had different personalities, an observation which is anthropomorphic (assigning human traits to animals) - it is thinking discouraged by animal behaviorists.

The sevengills would come directly at the divers at first but only brush by. An example of different behaviors was how a Garibaldi guarding its eggs would nip at the sharks. Shy, one of the sharks, would swim off in fright, while Crazy Jr. would turn and slam into a reef where the little fish had been. The big one, Sevengill, would cruise by, the Garibaldi would ease back in respect, and Sevengill would avoid the nest and eggs. Reed even tried feeding a fish to Sevengill held between his teeth, and the shark took it in a chomp and a bruising kiss - he did it only once! Reed felt he'd developed a friendship with Sevengill and the other divers got confidence in handling the shark to an unhealthy level.

No serious injuries happened over the years. But one day, Don Reed felt a tension in the water, a sixth sense of something about to happen, something he felt all divers experience occasionally. There was an electrical storm overhead and suddenly the sevengills all were in a frenzy and rushing at Reed, who pushed them off and fought them with his scrub brush. Reed's personal hero, Jacques Cousteau, came to mind and gave him direction with a remembered, "sharks can be handled".

Reed's long time coexistence with marine creatures in the tank, especially sharks, led him to conclude that one respects sharks, not fear them. Almost none of the millions of scuba divers in the world would even see a shark. Unfortunately, Reed lost his trust when Sevengill came up behind him one day and took his head in her mouth, exerting pressure, mouthing, but not chomping down. The torn red inner lining of an old hood had evidently incited the "attack". Reed punched Sevengill out but felt a friendship betrayed.

Reed's final considerations are exactly why oceanarium divers, better than anyone else, have the closeness and opportunity to evaluate captive creatures. One is, you must love an animal for what it is, not for what you want it to be. Sevengill, he felt, was no monster but she wasn't on this earth to be a pet. Reed said, "The shark is a force of nature, like a mountain or a storm. My perception of Sevengill had changed but she herself had not changed...she was neither my friend nor my enemy." Oceanarium divers have a multitude of stories that have given sport divers less fear of the unknown and the courage to go back in the ocean with expanded confidence.

THE INHUMANE SIDE

Many divers felt that watching creatures in captivity was not an example of real behavior. They saw in it less scientific value and an inhumane treatment. In 1861, it was P.T. Barnum of circus fame, who started the capture of large marine creatures for public amusement. His first two white whales were put in a shallow tank of fresh water and died in a few days; two more died in sea water. Barnum didn't have any idea of what to feed them.

Dave Brown, a curator at Marineland of the Pacific, told how Bubbles, the performing whale, first in the world, would butt divers which they determined was love making, but it hurt. Bubbles knocked out Marineland diver, Ray Cribbs with a "friendly pat." Divers, Marineland's collectors, got a big bull for Bubbles called Bimbo, who at 3000 pounds was then the largest in captivity in the world.

The Vancouver, Canada Aquarium opened in 1956 and Murray Newman, who became a scuba diver, was its director from then until 1992. Newman's book, *Life in a Fishbowl*, published in 1994 tells one of the most complete developmental stories of an aquarium over a period paralleling the fifty year history of sport diving. He traces the idea of the aquarium from Victorian England, as at first an amusement facility to one of learning and then as a device for stimulating public awareness about the pollution of the oceans. At one time we had assumed the massive oceans could consume all of our wastes and feed everybody forever. So outdoor aquariums have evolved to continuously ring the warning bell as perhaps a more vital purpose than amusement or scientific learning. However, their continued existence will need all three of those functions to survive. Jacques Cousteau gave the most ominous warning, "If the sea dies, we die." Rachel Carson's book, *Silent Spring*, published in 1962, was the most influential in creating concern for the finiteness of the sport diver's ocean playing fields. She dedicated the book "To Albert Schweitzer, who said, 'Man has lost the capacity to foresee and to forestall. He will end by destroying the earth'."

SMALL AQUARIUMS FOR A START

Many of these aquariums had starts in dank little spaces. The Vancouver Aquarium was just a couple of tanks in an old bathhouse where people had to wipe off the condensation to see in the tanks. The problems of chemistry and temperature wiped out creatures in a few days in the early days in a sort of put, remove and replace system. Fishermen and divers brought in the first specimens on a volunteer basis. When interviewing Bev Morgan, one of sport diving's celebrated pioneers, Al Tillman reminded him of the time they'd come back from training state lifeguards in scuba diving and stopped off at a place called County Line in 1954. Numerous movies were made on the beach there, but no one was diving it yet. "Oh, yeah," Bev laughed, "we got that big ten inch red abalone off that little reef, all by itself, took it to the little Hermosa Beach Aquarium to put in one of their tanks. Lifeguards used to catch a lot of things for the aquarium there...but I should have eaten it, cause it died a few days later." Without the divers voluntarily bringing in specimens in the 1950's, most aquariums would have had meager collections.

COMPETITION GROWS AND SPECIMEN DEMAND, TOO

By the year 2000, about 70 large aquariums will operate in America, up from 35 in 1990. Forty million visitors will probably pay admissions. More and more, the trend is to build them inland, away from the ocean, for people who rarely or never see the ocean. Technology has made it possible to create quality water and sustain creatures for long lives. Certainly that's a giant leap from when the Chicago Shedd Aquarium had to truck its sea water from Florida in the early days. State of the art aquariums use fog machines, eerie light, underwater tunnels with see-through floors and ceilings. But in an intense amusement market, a fickle public will demand to see more and more spectacular displays, and new exotic specimens may be required. Some things will need a Barnum touch, such as the Vancouver Aquarium calling a new specimen, "the

John Craig finds mermaid Zale Parry at Marineland in 1962.

famous mystery fish", publicizing it by asking, "What is it?," and eventually finding out it was fairly common in the wild ocean. Sport dives have and will play a major role in discovering and recovering new and exciting specimens if reinforced.

The aquariums can't get too scientific and scorn non-professional investigation. One diver complained about the indifference shown by aquarium staff when specimens were brought to them - "Just cause they've got some badge from the university doesn't make them the only ones who can identify and find the goodies." Competition between aquariums/oceanariums has been strong over the years and while competing for visitors, they also are very cooperative about sharing specimens. Breeding creatures to sell and share with other aquariums may be the backbone of their existence as more and more restrictions are placed on capturing animals in the wild.

These big expensive aquariums, $100 million for a world class one, can fail. The Camden, New Jersey and the Tampa Aquariums, opened in the 1990's, didn't meet the attendance estimates. Marineland of the Pacific closed down because new owners saw better value in other use of the land it sat on and the sale of the whales to another oceanarium.

There's big profit in selling off specimens. A killer whale was going for $1 million to $2 million, as bidding heated up during the Marineland of the Pacific/Sea World San Diego negotiations. Perhaps higher in 2000. The 1941 closing of Marine Studios saw their creatures released in nearby ocean only to have them try to find their way back where they were hand fed everyday by divers. To combat a "been there, seen that" attitude of the public, aquariums will have to stage events the way amusement parks have had to do when the existing parks proved to be not enough to get repeat business. Conservation as a cause and purpose has given aquariums momentum into the 21st Century, and people buy memberships in support and access for repeat visits. By the year 2000, the 1998 Long Beach Aquarium, replacing the demolished Marineland of the Pacific, will have over 50,000 members, many of whom are sport divers, who go to study behavior that might illuminate their dives in the wild.

There has been a trend more and more to allow civilian sport divers to actively immerse in the big tanks, swim with the fish for a fee. Diving classes are being allowed some access. We like the expression of a veteran old time diver, who "had seen it all," upon climbing out from his first dive in an oceanarium - "it's like having a zillion fish up your kazoo."

Within the ranks of divers, who collect big specimens for aquariums, there are a number of top guns. The fragility of the octopus, a favored specimen, has always made its capture and retention a delicate process. Octopus fight and kill each other unless separated and seem to have a three year life, dying after breeding. King of the Octopus collectors, a sort of legendary Paul Bunyan of the ocean, was John "Jock" MacLean, who captured giants off of Port Hardy, Vancouver Island. The 250-pound Jock was a major collector for aquarium expeditions in the 1950's and produced many big catches but hasn't been able to deliver the big one he'd seen that was 32-feet across. No aquarium has yet exhibited a giant octopus or monster squid or the living fossil Coelacanth. It will take the efforts of the divers'-catch, when it does happen.

We cannot forget the hundreds of volunteers, non-diving senior citizens, retired teachers, engineers and the still avid scuba divers, who take the training to spend time as docents for the aquariums/oceanariums. Lynn and Keith Chase, our long time diving friends, who spent their entire life's recreation on, around and under the sea, are two of over 700 dedicated docents at the Monterey Aquarium. In their Christmas letters in recent years, they have expressed their admiration of the rewarding pleasure being the guides with others in their same position as host and hostess, while sharing the sea with fresh enthusiasm. Each uniformed docent with name tag has a speciality and certain scheduled days of the week to usher school children and patrons through the hands-on exhibits or a gallery of separate tanks of unique specimens of the rich slice of the Monterey Bay of California. These friendly beacons of knowledge welcome, teach, show and give their time freely to support the establishments they want to perpetuate. Divers in the aquarium's Bay are computer connected to high tech equipment to talk about sea life with the young and older interrogators, who view them on a monitor.

Marketing and advertising policies are vital to keep turnstiles spinning. One advertising clip recently had a marvelous tag line - "We're serious fun!" Raising the awareness of the ocean's ecosystem is serious business. Yet, the programs presented are interesting, educational and sometimes irreverent when the advertisers can offer the guts of a mechanical shark with a quip "that visitors can get inside a shark without the hassle of being eaten". Public relations, marketing and advertising agencies are making great efforts to offer communication in other than English languages, too. This makes the tour unique, entertaining, educational and exciting.

Of course, it is difficult to leave an inspiring place without a souvenir. Every aquarium/oceanarium has at least one gift store or perhaps a theme gift store near the exhibit or show you had just visited. Toys, books, compact disks, videos, clothes and post cards are there for the purchase to seize that memory of your trip. The gift stores are another way to support the upkeep of the place and keep those super smart, colorful wonders of the sea alive.

One wonderful memory of recent years was the newspaper headline: "Sunfish Eats Its Way Out of Monterey Aquarium". Extremely cunning, this Sunfish, known as a Mola Mola, lives a longer life than most big fish. This one ate and ate and ate. Grew and grew so big that it didn't fit in the tank. The smart Sunfish knew that if it didn't fit, it would be released from "prison" and set free. Sure enough. At great expense, the aquarium hired a huge crane, designed and fashioned an exceptionally special sling to transport the smartie back to its wild ocean mansion.

SCRIPPS

Encouraging members with their year 2000 membership contribution brochure is the statement: "A visit to the Birch Aquarium at Scripps Institution of Oceanography (Authors note: Scripps is known to be the world's oldest, largest, and most important ocean research facility.) is a journey through the Pacific Ocean and its wonders. The brochures say: "See our giant octopus from the Northwest; our 70,000-gallon live kelp forest showcasing local waters; colorful fishes from Baja; the aquarium nursery with our newest baby arrivals; and our spectacular NEW jellyfish exhibits. Enjoy our exciting NEW family hands-on-discovery center in the museum."

Now the nice thing about Memberships, Passports, Voyager Team, Presidents Circle, or paying ahead to be an Active member, or whatever the title bestowed on you with your donation, it helps defray the awesome cost to keep the oceanariums/aquariums functioning. That donation becomes a reciprocal privilege to some of the other ocean exhibits elsewhere and is tax deductible in some cases.

About the Birch Aquarium, a post script on the brochure in italics says, "The aquarium must generate more than $2.6 million each year in gifts, grants, and earned income to meet its operating budget. Your membership is important to us." Sounds as though that $2.6 million is big money, but can be 'small potatoes' in comparison when the giants, such as, the Sea Worlds plan their yearly budgets.

More years will reveal whether oceanariums/aquariums have been a value to society beyond just amusing the public, promoting a love for animals, dispelling fear, promoting conservation. Or have they inhumanely caged wild creatures, stolen away some of the mystery of the ocean, and with the proliferation of them, over-exposed creatures to a point of boredom with it all?

For sport diving which grew along side of the oceanarium movement in the same period of years, it remains controversial. Divers seem to be saying in retrospect that the aquariums were a great way to share with family and friends who didn't dive, but on the other hand, they did seem to steal away the excitement of the unknown. Some sport divers did find career opportunities for their recreational diving interests. Undoubtedly, the development of sport diving was significantly influenced by the advent of large open air Aquariums...the Oceanariums.

AMERICA'S AQUARIUMS

Aksarben Aquarium and Nature Center in Louisville, Nebraska

Aquarium of the Americas in New Orleans, Louisiana

Aquarium of the Pacific/Long Beach Aquarium in Long Beach, California

Center for Stingray Biology in Santa Barbara, California

Florida Aquarium in Tampa Bay, Florida

Maine Aquarium in Saco, Maine

Marine World Africa USA in Vallejo, California

Minnesota Aquarium Society in Roseville, Minnesota

Monterey Bay Aquarium in Monterey, California

Mote Marine Aquarium in Sarasota, Florida

National Aquarium in Baltimore, Maryland

New England Aquarium in Boston, Massachusetts

New York's Aquarium for Wildlife Conservation in Brooklyn, New York

Oregon Coast Aquarium in Newport, Oregon

Point Defiance Zoo and Aquarium in Tacoma, Washington

Sea Center - Santa Barbara Museum of Natural History in Santa Barbara, California

Shedd Aquarium in Chicago, Illinois

Scott Aquarium in Omaha, Nebraska

Seattle Aquarium/Salmon Hatchery in Seattle, Washington

Sea World/ Busch Gardens in Cleveland, Ohio

Sea World in Orlando, Florida

Sea World in San Diego, California

Sea World in San Antonio, Texas

The Living Seas in Orlando, Florida

The Seattle Aquarium in Seattle, Washington

Sonoran Sea Aquarium in Tucson, Arizona

South Carolina Aquarium in Charleston, South Carolina

St. Lawrence Aquarium in Massena, New York

Stephen Birch Aquarium-Museum in San Diego, California

Steinhart Aquarium in San Francisco, California

Tennessee Aquarium in Chattanooga, Tennessee

The Cold Spring Harbor Fish Hatchery and Aquarium in New York, New York

The Okeanos Preview Aquarium in Riverhead, New York

Virginia Living Museum in Newport News, Virginia

Waikiki Aquarium in Oahu, Hawaii

32

SANCTUARIES, PARKS AND PRESERVES

DEFINING EVENT: PENNEKAMP

The name of significant underwater areas has changed over the decades of diving history from preserves to parks to sanctuaries. The basic goal stays the same: to protect the natural order - the wildness of choice underwater sites.

Such protection is done in the name of conservation, the interests of science, and the good of the public. There are many good reasons for shutting off an area or portion of it from human trespass.

Actually, the names aren't interchangeable, but the general diving public hasn't seemed to distinguish or care about the differences. Divers called them by any of the three names.

A sanctuary is used in a broad sense, in some cases only setting boundaries on an ocean or water area. The idea is to identify such areas, because of their representative abundance of sea life and fragility, for possible restrictions on their use in the future. Next in line would be an underwater park that tries to allow use by humans, but with cautious and caring entry. Boating and scuba diving are often allowed plus the taking of game - but commercial fishing and oil exploration are discouraged.

Preserves usually mean that an area is completely restricted, what is referred to as "no take zones." Almost all trespass is disallowed in order for species to regenerate themselves. The preserve concept can be a permanent designation, or a temporary one to be removed with the regeneration. Temporary designation has been successful. Occasionally, only one specie has a moratorium placed on it, such as abalone. It nearly disappeared in California waters until government, in particular the Fish and Game Department, stepped in to offer protection. A preserve needs scientific management, and diving plays an important role in doing that.

Human presence on ecologically sensitive dryland areas has often had negative effects. In several instances government intervention has taken away or severely restricted public access. For instance, the caves in France with painted walls by prehistoric man have been closed to public access because the breaths of thousands of visitors erased the paint off the walls. Giant redwood trees in California, whose lives extend back several thousand years, topple when tourists compact the soil to get near them. The famous Devil's Hole in Death Valley, a giant cistern of fresh water containing living fossil fish, was fenced-off after divers died exploring it, and teenagers partied there by frying those rare fish for a barbecue. The petrified forest in Arizona, as a National Park, had to be designated a preserve because enough souvenir pieces of petrified wood had been picked to almost denude the grounds of the very thing people came to see. The Underwater World less visible, came later to the environmentalists' attention and, mainly, through the observations of divers both scientific and sport.

The environmental concern movements of the 1970's became a vast public concern as the Sierra Club, Greenpeace, Cousteau Society, and other impassioned groups talked about impact, pollution, ecology, and endangered species. People began to realize that nothing stays the same and although our high-tech society has to progress, it must not at the expense of the natural process of this planet.

Are our feet to touch only asphalt in the future, never to contact the soil? Will the oceans become barren wastelands, Siberias of the sea, if we don't curb the invasion of swelling masses of people? The world population is _expected to double_ by the year 2100.

The abundance once seen in the oceans began to diminish over the years. Sportsmen blamed the commercial fisheries. The commercial people pointed a finger at the abusive growing hordes of recreational fishermen, and fishermen blamed the dumping of waste into the oceans turning it into a potential cesspool.

National Geographic Society Magazine with its beautifully photographed wonders of the world, of the exotic places, of the glorious underwater planet was a recording meter over the years. By the 1990's, it became a doomsday warning voice in part, a sort of media canary to tell us much of the geography was being poisoned and whole species killed off.

Divers in boats were crunching reefs of long lived coral gardens by dropping anchors helter-skelter. Here and there a phenomenon of giant fish schools showed up, such as the 1993 herd of giant marlins off the Atlantic Island of Madeiras. Records were broken and decks piled high with the great billed fish - but three years later, they were all gone and were never seen again in such numbers.

All these things created a growing awareness that resources and creatures were limited, and complete annihilation was possible unless everybody worked together to arrest the destruction.

One approach over the decades of diving history has been to set aside areas and restrict how they are used. America's Great National Parks on land were created with just such goals. Most early days of diving saw limited efforts arise around small underwater areas.

An early and fairly large effort to stem the tide was the creation of John Pennekamp Coral Reef State Park. (Pennekamp was a politician who pushed it through.) This park, off Key Largo, Florida, was an extremely popular and extensively visited coral reef region from the very beginning of diving in the United Sates. Although a large area, seventy-five square miles, bordered by the nutrient-rich Gulf Stream, boats and divers chiseled it up taking game and coral, scrounging for shipwrecks, a dropping anchors without looking or caring. It wasn't so much a pollution thing then, as just a constant impact of people using it carelessly - perhaps, "loving it to death."

Pennekamp became the largest underwater park in the world, a sort of underwater Yellowstone. The park was designated in 1960; and, as Lew Maxwell (his Florida Frogman Shops sent many divers to Pennekamp) told us, "Divers used to have good access to diving sites in Biscayne Bay right off Miami but population impact and pollution drove them to the Keys and in particular, the huge long reef that became Pennekamp Park." Maxwell credits dive shop and boat operators like Steve Klem, a veteran of diving's entire history on Pennekamp Reef, with recognizing the rapid attrition of the reef. The seventy-two acres of campgrounds lured the masses of tourist divers and their boats. Klem realized making friends with the marine life, fish he recognized as individuals, petted and hand fed them, increasingly disappeared, probably victims

National Geogrphic featured Pennekamp Coral Reef State Park in 1962. The cover and issue were dedicated to the first marine park.

of a spear in the hands of a Chicago derived diving-tourist. Coral, favorite stands of it, went back to Ohio, New Jersey and New York as souvenirs. It dawned on Klem and others that the great wonderland of the reef was not inexhaustible and the brakes had to be put on. There wouldn't be any reef for upcoming generations if it was destroyed, and there wouldn't be any diving business. Klem supported the park idea. Other divers, too, realized they might have to forego spearfishing to support the idea.

There was some controversy about how structured an underwater park should be. Trails with markers have been put down in some. Al Tillman wrote for a California magazine in 1970, "I first went to Pennekamp Reef back in 1962. It was great looking around and knowing the wreck sites, coral and fish could be as they were yesterday and the days before - protected. Although some restrictions on taking things were applied, enforcement was haphazard. But I also felt a loss - as an explorer and adventurer. I felt cheated of my chance to

Jerry Greenberg did the story and photography for National Geographic's Pennekamp issue.

discover anything. It's worse when you come on submerged markers that guide you along an underwater trail, telling you what you're looking at. Very educational but the feeling of real exploration, feeling you're the first one on the scene, which Skin and scuba diving is all about, gets robbed away. It all seemed a setup for the see-it-once-and-move-on volume tourist trade."

But in the wilder days, Tillman recalls the attitude of diving instructors who took a break after a Miami NAUI Course in the early 1960's. The group loaded the trunks of several cars with canon balls they'd chopped out of the reef coral. It was Ray Maneri in all innocence who said, "Don't worry, it's just coral, it'll all grow back."

At the time of Florida passing legislation committing the Pennekamp Reef to park status, it seemed like a happy compromise. True wilderness was just disappearing specks everywhere. The traveling hordes could be kept in check by moving in to control the use of natural areas. They would add artificial regulating devices and enforcement schemes, hopefully, stopping somewhere this side of packaged, predictable, plastic, Disneyized fantasy amusement center.

As much as we may praise Cousteau's invention of the Aqua Lung and he saying, "Eureka, it works!", the bringing of volume traffic underwater and the scars it had left brought Cousteau into the 1990's saying as one of his last quotes, "The ocean is dying." Maybe he felt some guilt about putting too many people underwater.

There are many sources to blame if the ocean of divers ends in trouble after fifty years. Certainly, there were divers who were hunters that plucked whole species from the seas while other divers tore up the bottom to bring back wreck artifacts for some dusty museum shelf. When we asked Mel Fisher in the 1980's about this criticism, he responded, "We moved as little of the bottom as possible. The magnetometer helped us pinpoint spots to dig and we made as few holes as possible - if we didn't uncover the artifacts and bring them back, almost everybody would have been deprived of ever seeing them."

The biggest spoilers were probably the dumpers and exploiters of resources - the real monsters. To the first, the ocean was a big bottomless garbage can that could easily absorb nerve gas and raw sewage. To the latter, it was just a holding vault for minerals that couldn't be raped from dryland anymore. As they say, nobody had figured a way to flush the ocean.

"Of all of the things least expected to destroy with fury and thoroughness was the reef's creator, Nature," Captain Don Stewart told the authors. "For six hours on July 23rd, 1975, I watched six foot waves pound the beach near my favorite Karpata Reef (Bonaire, Netherlands Antilles). None but the strongest corals withstood the onslaught of the seas. Sands stirred into suspension, carried offshore, and rained upon even the deepest of corals, whose polyps were suffocated. Entire Brain Corals were dislodged. The eight thousand divers we had directed to Karpata that year, could never have wrought the damage I saw after that storm. I'm glad to have sent divers earlier to pristine Karpata Reef. I know these enthusiasts, in their memories and on film, will remember that precious reef as I knew it from the beginning, and I hope as it will be again for my grandchildren. "

Sticking unnatural things in the ocean drew a lot of controversy. Gustav Dalla Valle, perhaps diving's greatest personality, put an eight-foot statue of Christ with arms outstretched on the reef in Pennekamp Park. It duplicated one underwater in Italy. The Virgin Islands established an underwater park in those early days, putting down engraved plates to explain the sights. In the 1980's, moorings were placed over reefs everywhere to protect them and to allay anchor damage.

Captain Don Stewart, an American with his DIVEPOWER, an organization with the combination of dedication and understanding of the sea, worked with the Council of Underwater Resort Operations (CURO) headquartered in Miami, Florida, and with the Bonaire Government, to create policies that enforced the strict compliance to safeguard Bonaire's marine life and corals. "Enough diving locations were charted so that no site was subjected to overuse. All boats are moored and not anchored. We replant coral life, when deemed necessary," said Captain Don Stewart.

"Bonaire's diving industry began in 1962," explained Captain Don, "when I was shipwrecked off her shores." By 1972, he founded the Aquaventure Dive Complex at Hotel Bonaire. By 1975, the dive-site-moorings were planted. Since then, similar programs of reef management have been initiated with enthusiasm throughout American shores and beyond.

Many divers were soon bobbling on the surface saying, "save our ocean," and effort was underway to create little Edens underwater, sacred places, protected and preserved. The idea of establishing these Paradises was not to mothball them away so no one could use them as the old time conservationists would have us do, but cared for as we did for natural area parks on shore. The caring led to "don't pick the coral" signs but it took away the wildness. Luis Marden, *National Geographic's* legendary underwater photographer, was livid when Florida Frogman Shops owner, Lew Maxwell, put a Florida Frogman ad sign on Pennekamp Reef.

Al Tillman recalls how, with mixed emotions, he put UNEXSO to work in 1966 while trying to protect a small area of Bahamas' reefs. The campaign was to keep pristine a one acre islet called Petersen Cay six miles downshore in a remote area from the Club's location at Freeport. The Cay was gorgeous; white sand surrounded by a splendid array of stag horn coral reefs, the site of many film projects and a paradise for underwater photographers. UNEXSO admittedly had much to be gained, for the Cay was the destination of UNEXSO's most profitable dive trips. Without protection some native Bahamians would have followed their traditional practice of dynamiting the reefs to get fish. UNEXSO got the Bahamas Government to pass an agricultural and Fisheries Act (1967) that disallowed "taking or killing any marine product within a quarter of a mile of the shoreline of Petersen Cay. Product means fish, crawfish, turtle, Conch, crab, sponge, coral, sea fan, sea plume, or marine shell." The UNEXSO staff were appointed wardens to oversee the enforcement of the Act. With such protection (not easily enforced) violations still occurred, but it was the start of a partial solution. But Petersen Cay would never be the wild place it had been when UNEXSO started.

Al Tillman was involved with another underwater park movement in the Philippines in 1970. With Richard Bartlett, Senior and Junior, Tillman worked to develop a China Seas' UNEXSO Club on three islands off the northern tip of the Luzon Peninsula. Then they went with the owner of the islands, Al Lim's blessing, to get President Ferdinand Marcos to designate the island of Fuga and the surrounding quarter mile of ocean as a preserve. It was done and Al Lim took enforcement seriously. When a Taiwan pirate fishing fleet cruised into the restricted area, A Bell Fighter Helicopter was sent to blast part of the fleet out of the water.

Unfortunately, pending insurrection in the Philippines forced Marcos to declare martial law and take over Fuga as one of his retreats - and so the Philippines version of the Bahamas UNEXSO was halted and the first underwater park off shore Fuga was abandoned. By 2000, a Japanese consortium was laying plans to develop Fuga as a destination dive resort.

In California, early 1950's efforts saw the setting aside of ocean preserves. One at Pacific Grove was established by the municipality. Point Lobos Park Reserve and Torrey Pines Park near San Diego were established by the state. Although these were efforts to withstand commercial over exploitation, the SCUBA hunter/diver was on the "enemy list," too. The California Advisory Board on Underwater Parks and Reserves was established in 1968.

The Underwater Parks and Reserves Advisory Board's program operated under the California State Park System. Besides protecting selected underwater areas, it aimed to provide a variety of underwater recreational opportunities focused on diving. Sixteen territories were in place by the year 2000 with many more on the drawing boards. Underwater photography and spearfishing were to be catered to. Interpretive centers told divers what to expect underwater at each location. Once again, many divers feel the sense of going into the unknown has been compromised. The State puts out a list of the parks today with a sample description as follows: "Leo Cabrillo State Park...located on the Los Angeles/Ventura County Line, where there is a fully developed campground, sand and rock beach, reefs offshore and caves in the underwater rock formations."

Some felt that Darwin's law of survival of the fittest should run its course in the ocean, that a preserve was creating a zoolike containment of creatures, a laboratory for marine scientists that would take away from divers the instinctual urge to explore where "no one has been before" and recover what they found. Always, as the population increases, there is compromise.

All these early efforts were indicative of a growing desire to be part of the booming environmental movement that swelled in the 1970's and 1980's. Spearfishing contests of the early days gave way to ocean cleanup dives. By the 1990's, manufacturers of diving equipment had lofted their banners in support of Save the Ocean movements and foundations designed to educate the diving public about the loss of the underwater environment.

Among the many efforts to rescue and protect the underwater world is Ocean Futures, a nonprofit society, first established in 1991 and directed by Dick Bonin under the auspices of SCUBAPRO, a Division of Under Sea Industries, Inc. Later, Jean Michel Cousteau inherited the Ocean Futures movement. The PADI Foundation of which John Cronin is Chairman Emeritus is devoted to preserve and revitalize the marine world. The Cousteau Society, a nonprofit, impactful organization, founded in 1973 gathered moneys to guard and save the seas by supporting the ships, Calypso and Alcyone and their projects. Catalina Conservancy Divers is a strong, powerful group that restores and conserves Santa Catalina Island. Established in 1968, CEDAM International became an early sentry. It is dedicated to Conservation, Education, Diving, Archaeology and Museums. Periodicals, pamphlets, decals, affiliation cards and/or lapel pins show a personal connection to saving the seas.

On September 18, 1999, an international coastal cleanup event was sponsored by See's Candy Company. Dr. Sylvia Earle was the figurehead leader representing the partner sponsor, the Center for Marine Conservation.

Sometimes the big governments don't have to get involved. A prime model of this is Edmonds' (Washington) Dive Park that began in 1971. This site is next to an active ferry landing and contains a 300-foot dry dock sunk in 1935. Divers have been using the area through the 1950's, 1960's and into the 1970's. In December of 1976, there were two diving fatalities and the town mayor decided to close the water area but fanatic divers were not about to be deterred. They lobbied to get access back.

The city backed off but would invest no money nor assume any responsibility. No rules control the park and there are no requirements that divers be certified. Twenty-thousand annual users invade the 27 acres that have rest-floats and two miles of a roped trail system which was installed in 1983. Small boats have been sunk in the park with the last being a donated seventy-foot tug boat put down in 1999. There were also 10,000 tires placed on the bottom. Volunteer divers maintain the park under the dedicated unofficial supervision of Bruce Higgins who works out of a local dive shop.

Some divers like the placement of ropes and concrete blocks to form trails. It is a controlled way to introduce neophytes to the underwater. Classes use it for open water checkouts. Others feel the laying on of structural hands has altered the nature of the area, creating a "virtual reality," where protected marine life alters its natural behavior. They ask, "Is it just another confined aquarium?"

While Edmonds has much marine life, it is mostly of the same kind. Bruce tries to draw more variety putting down milk crates as habitat for shrimp.

All these foregoing efforts have led to the United States government establishing the U.S. National Marine Sanctuaries in the 1990's. They surround the coastal United States including Hawaii and Samoa. Sanctuary, a protected place, was the politically correct word used instead of preserve or park. (A park or preserve can exist within a sanctuary.) The dozen or more sanctuaries existing by the year 2000 were designed to be laboratories for restoration of marine ecosystems. Some have sections set-off as "no take areas," often called preserves, where divers can look and photograph but not touch or take anything.

The Sanctuary System is managed by the National Oceanic and Atmospheric Administration (NOAA). In the forefront has been the "first lady of the deep," former Chief Scientist for NOAA, Dr. Sylvia Earle. Earle has been the key researcher of the sanctuaries under a National Geographic Grant entitled, *Sustainable Seas* (Sustainable implies the limited and intelligent utilization of resources from natural areas.). A whole century has elapsed since the oldest National Park, Yellowstone, was established in 1872 and the Marine Protection, Research and Sanctuaries Act was put in place in 1972. Under it, the first Sanctuary was set up in one square mile surrounding the sunken Civil War metal vessel, The Merrimac, in 230 feet of water off North Carolina. An advanced dive for divers, it's available as a "no take" site for the deep adventurers to see.

The Florida Keys Sanctuary, that includes the old State Park, Pennekamp, covers 3696 square miles of the world's third largest barrier reef.

The Monterey Bay Sanctuary runs for 350 miles along the California Coast and 53 miles seaward. So far it has no "no take" restrictions.

The total Sanctuary System is huge, covering 18,000 square miles. Yet it barely represents one half of one percent of the United States' jurisdiction over the ocean. (Most coastal nations have a territorial sea zone out 12 miles under authority of the shoreline state or territory; another twelve miles contiguous zone to control immigration and sanitation; an economic zone out 200 miles; and a continental shelf zone that covers the seabed but not the overlying water and can extend another 150 nautical miles.

NOAA says that, although marine protection is the key goal, these sanctuaries are not underwater parks. NOAA, being a branch of the Department of Commerce, refers to them as multiple use areas. They were first established to fend off oil exploration. While disallowing drilling, dumping, mining, dredging or removal of artifacts, the Sanctuaries allow some commercial fishing, diving for edibles, setting lobster traps, sport fishing, spearfishing, boating and other types of recreation. Sure sounds like a park! But beware, some are saying, the specter of "no take" preserves always looms in the future. As species diminish there will be pressure for preserve sections in the Sanctuaries.

These natural areas belong to the people not governments or scientists say suspicious divers. People have always been concerned about how many human activities to allow before protection is diluted so there isn't any sanctuary for natural things. Scientists are supposed to come up with answers about sustainability for the century ahead. The 20th Century ended with no idea of what's out there in the water that hasn't been seen, nor whether this last American frontier is still salvageable. (Some divers asked the question, why do tax supported scientists get to do the exploration and get all the surprises?)

The States and the National Fisheries decide the amount of marine life that can be taken from a Coastal Sanctuary, but how this effects indigenous species has to come from scientific studies. A tangled bureaucracy is at work here. Much of the help comes from volunteers, many of whom are divers who help very small Sanctuary staffs.

Out on the Flower Gardens Banks Sanctuary volunteer divers help place coral larvae on scraped sections of the 350 acres of reef to help get information on how to restore reefs. Ten percent of all coral reefs have been destroyed by human impact. At the existing rate destruction could reach 70% over the next few decades.

The Flower Gardens, the northern most coral reefs, 100 miles out off Texas, was the test dive site for the first National Association of Underwater Instructors (NAUI) Course held in Houston in 1960. From the sea floor, hundreds of feet deep, two salt domes thrust up to within fifty feet of the surface. Big and small ships used to throw out coral-damaging anchors on to the domes. Scuba divers saw the scars and lobbied for protective legislation. An underwater video of an oil boat's anchor ripping through coral heads moved Congress to create a fifty-five square mile Sanctuary around the domes in 1992. In 1996 Congress added the Stetson Bank near the coast.

We should look more at the history of Pennekamp, the grand-daddy of all this park/sanctuary thinking. When it was established in 1960, spearfishing, collecting tropical specimens for aquariums, and using wire fish traps were banned. At that time, state territory extended only two miles from shore. The great reef formations were beyond this limit. Damage by treasure hunters forced the State of Florida to go to the Federal government for help.

In 1975 one hundred and thirty-five square miles next to Pennekamp became the Key Largo Sanctuary. In 1981 eight square miles of Loo Key Sanctuary were established. But the State and Federal Governments working together couldn't seem to arrest the pollution pouring into the areas nor the damage from propellers and anchors.

Then in 1989, three big vessels crashed into the reef in 18 days. The United States again, especially with the help of divers, created a new 220 mile-long sanctuary extending from Biscayne National Park to Dry Tortugas National Park in the south Florida State waters. The sanctuary enclosed many waterfront communities. Big and basically invisible, the public didn't know it existed or didn't know the rules for entry.

The 1990's saw a lot of anti-sanctuary attitude as lobster trappers, salvage divers, and others who made a living off the areas resources began chanting "No to NOAA" because they felt the government was trying to kill off the traditional economy and instead create a national tourist park. Indeed, two and a half million tourists affect the area each year; 900,000 people dove on the reef. Tourism brought in a billion plus dollars. Despite the sanctuary intervention, the conditions changed negatively. Algae-blooms were killing off coral; the reefs were suffocating, and visibility in the water had shrunk in half. This was not good for an economy depending largely on tourist divers. Eleven thousand illegal cesspools in the Keys caused much of the degradation. Lobsters were seen to travel up on land to get out of the fecal water. Conchs were once a big harvest for the Keys' divers. By the 1990's they were imported from the Caribbean to supply the famous conch chowder and souvenir-shells.

The government is attempting to bring them back to the sanctuary. Hatchery-grown baby conches are being released - similar to maligned "fake fish" grown in confined tanks and released to the wild. Would any of these domestic raised creatures ever show wild behavior or be as interesting to divers?

A thick three-volume management plan went into effect for the Keys Sanctuary in 1997 that tightened all regulations, including sealed zones from which nothing can be taken. This was a movement back through the park concept to the "no take" preserve idea. Was diving to become just looking through less clear water, and nothing else? Perhaps divers should have spent more time kneeling and praying before Dalla Valle's bronze statue, Christ of the Deep, at Pennekamp.

A dozen other sanctuaries were established under the system in the 1990's, with more to come. By 2000, the office of the President of the United States was rediscovering the sanctuary program. The program had been buried away for decades in NOAA under the Department of Commerce. The Sanctuary was an unclear concept for 25 years. What was protected and what wasn't was never defined. No one in the bureaucracy knew how to manage the oceans. All any one knew in the beginning was that areas had to be defined to stop leasing oil reserves off California, Washington and Massachusetts. This created fights between fishermen and environmentalists. Would fishing, spearfishing, too, be banned? The bureaucracy was promising no bans. However, no permanent sanctuary managers were named until 1990. And they in turn, clashed with community advisory groups. Divers were bewildered by all of this.

Divers have led the way in advocating that future sanctuaries be put around the newly implanted artificial reefs and that the traditional natural dive reefs be left alone. They have wanted government to forget raising The Merrimac and leave it as an open sanctuary, traditionally visited by a half dozen dive charter companies. Divers use the seventeen artificial reefs the State of Georgia has placed.

The Samoa Sanctuary is periled by poaching by locals scuba diving and spearing fish at night. Some divers have just ignored the "no take" preserves and created a bad image of diving's role in conservation. More to be pitied than censured, they resent the loss of a free-range ocean.

A somewhat different situation has developed at the Stellwagon Bank Sanctuary, an 842 square mile area of it just three miles north of Cape Cod. Sanctuary headquarters is at Plymouth, Massachusetts, where the pilgrims landed in 1620. Then lobsters were so abundant, the settlers used them for fertilizer. The area had been overfished for years by seine and trawl nets. The Cod were almost gone forever from Cape Cod. Only a small part of the Sanctuary has been closed to fishing while elsewhere in the world full protection is provided and fish multiply.

The Olympic Coast Sanctuary in the State of Washington is so remote only Indian tribes have fished it, and that sanctuary staffers say they got to in time. Down south, the Channel Islands National Marine Sanctuary covers five islands 25 miles off the California coast near Santa Barbara. This is a scuba divers' Mecca covering 1658 square miles of ocean. It's kelp forests grow at two feet-a-day and are the underwater rain forests of the sea. Seventy commercial fishing boats are allowed in the sanctuary to catch squid, the core of the food chain around the islands. The fastest growing industry using this sanctuary is, you guessed it, tourism: diving, whale watching, and kayaking.

More "blue refuges", as *National Geographic* refers to the sanctuaries, exist in the Farallon Islands off of San Francisco and the Grays Reef off Georgia.

Monterey Bay is the largest sanctuary of them all, spanning 350 miles of California Coastline out to 53 miles offshore. This sanctuary has a large ocean canyon and a multitude of marine life. Scientists are down daily in small submersibles, cruising past tourist-divers, to study all of it. Closed circuit television cameras on the reefs watch marine life and the divers (who someday could suddenly hear on an underwater public address system, "Will the boy in the red wet suit not touch the starfish?") Big brother may be watching what was once a private experience of solitude. Some divers wonder if growing coral polyps on suspended tiles to transplant and restore reefs will be like an artificial golf course. Will there be so many people going down divers will have to get a starting time as they do at a golf course? This may be a fantasized dark view of diving under the many restrictions of a sanctuary. On the other hand without sanctuaries, will we only have pictures of our underwater world to show the grandchildren?

Dr. Sylvia Earle, who is the project director for the Sustainable Seas Expedition of *National Geographic Magazine*, has been at the helm of guiding the sanctuary program over the past several decades. A world famous marine biologist, Sylvia talks about her mother who didn't get to dive until she was 81 years old and berated Sylvia for not getting her to dive earlier. An outstanding diver, Sylvia believes everybody ought to scuba dive to appreciate what we could lose without sanctuaries. She doesn't want to have to answer grandchildren who ask in the future: "Why didn't you do something when the whales and coral reefs were everywhere and now they are gone?"

Pioneer divers interviewed for this history reminisce about when they looked down from the surface and saw kelp jungles so thick one couldn't wiggle through them, and about walls of great fish moving through the water, and abalone and lobster, seeming as though stacked on top of each other in layers. They doubt that will ever be again.

If sanctuaries have a slim possibility of bringing back some of that golden landscape that they first saw, then divers might go ahead and accept the restrictions and hope that Sylvia Earle and her colleagues are right. We can use the ocean and still keep it if we touch with our eyes only.

NOTES

The twelve national marine sanctuaries representing a wide variety of ocean environments are:

Channel Islands: Anacapa, Santa Cruz, Santa Rosa, San Miguel and Santa Barbara Islands, off the coast of California - 1972

Cordell Bank: Northwest of the Golden Gate Bridge - 1989

Gulf of the Farallons: North and west of San Francisco Bay - 1981

Monterey Bay: Central California Coast - 1992

Olympic Coast: Washington State's Olympic Peninsula

Gerry E. Studds Stellwagen Bank: Mouth of Massachusetts

Gray's Reef: Sapelo Island, Georgia

Florida Keys: Northeast to southwest arc between the southern tip of Key Biscayne, south of Miami - 1990

Flower Garden Banks: The coast of Texas and Louisiana

Hawaiian Islands Humpback Whale: Hawaiian Islands - 1992

33

DIVING WITH MONSTERS

DEFINING EVENT: THE CAPTURE OF NAMU IN 1963

The Killer Whale moves in wolf packs killing for food and sport. They slaughter herds of seals, porpoise and other giant whales to appease a voracious appetite. They should be regarded as man eaters. Although no human attacks are recorded, any evidence could have been gobbled down. Divers should leave water immediately if one is sighted.

That information was in one form or another

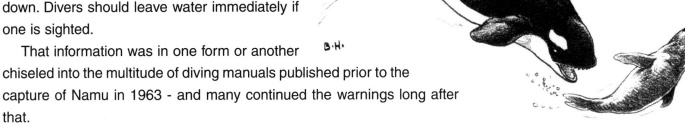

chiseled into the multitude of diving manuals published prior to the capture of Namu in 1963 - and many continued the warnings long after that.

Ted Griffin dispelled the monster label from Killer Whales and got them called Orca by the public. Ted Griffin, who opened an aquarium on the Seattle water front to coincide with the 1962 World's Fair was the first diver, or man, to jump in the water with a 28 foot long monster with two rows of two-inch teeth capable of crushing a Great White Shark. He made a friend of Namu, loved him, hugged him and rode him, a dream he had since childhood. He found that Namu, and the 30 Killer Whales he eventually captured for aquariums around the world were gentle, intelligent and friendly to humans.

In the early years of sport diving, the fear of the unknown and creatures that had formidable weapons, quickness, sharp teeth, were apparently dangerous and to be avoided. There had not been enough reported encounters to verify any vicious propensities. Those that did get revealed were often exaggerated and resulted from divers being in hazardous areas, dirty water, killing fish, putting their hands in holes and touching what shouldn't be touched.

Gary Keffler, a pioneer veteran diver of the Northwest, had been a consultant to Ted Griffin before Ted undertook his in-water-contact with killer whale/monster, Namu. "They appear to be indifferent to divers when we've encountered them...our Mud Shark Diving Club ignores them." Ted Griffin didn't ignore killer whales but showed that our fear out of ignorance kept us enemies. Eventually, the Mud Shark Divers came by to ride and play on Namu.

Namu lived on for three years in captivity, the poster boy for "rehabilitated" monsters. He died from an infection probably contracted from polluted Seattle waterfront water. Namu is a major event in developing sport diving because it swept away the fear of the potentially dangerous creature in the ocean and being afraid of killer whales; the elimination of that monster worry gave divers more confidence and freedom in what was a wild and alien world.

Facing the monster creatures of the deep was a threatening obstacle to going diving throughout human history. Stacked on top of the overall trepidation of drowning and the unseen physiological maladies of diving, there was a mystic quality that frightened most divers but on the other hand drew them irresistibly into the water. No one had any idea what kind of things were down, perhaps a teaming mass of swimming dinosaurs. Would they stay deep or come up to attack divers in the playground of the continental shelf shallows.

What other kinds of monsters were divers in the 1940's and 1950's dreading and the diving books and manuals promoted under dangerous marine life. There's the "terrifying" devilfish that flew out of the water and crushed boats...so the stories go. Divers even spread tales of these giant "horned beasts" settling down on top of divers and pancaking them. Hans Hass's book *Manta* and his films took us around the corner and we began calling the devilfish manta rays and we touched them and swam with them. On the bottom looking up at a manta's silhouette divers felt in the landing path of a stealth bomber.

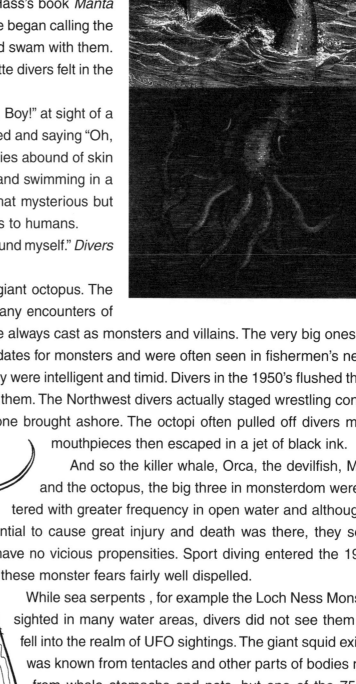

Underwater photographers are saying "Oh, Boy!" at sight of a Manta Ray. In the old days they were wide-eyed and saying "Oh, Oh!" Almost 50-years after Hass's *Manta*, stories abound of skin divers being welcomed by groups of Mantas and swimming in a playful-ballet with them. They remain somewhat mysterious but frequently photographed and filmed as friends to humans.

In the young and basic Hass/Cousteau, "I found myself." *Divers derived courage from those two.*

Another legendary terror of divers is the giant octopus. The movies and adventure magazines showed many encounters of octopi enveloping hard hat divers. Octopi were always cast as monsters and villains. The very big ones up to 28-feet tentacle-to-tentacle were imposing candidates for monsters and were often seen in fishermen's nets. It took scuba divers to finally show that they were intelligent and timid. Divers in the 1950's flushed them out of their rock lairs and grappled with them. The Northwest divers actually staged wrestling contests and awarded trophies for biggest one brought ashore. The octopi often pulled off divers masks and mouthpieces then escaped in a jet of black ink.

And so the killer whale, Orca, the devilfish, Manta Ray and the octopus, the big three in monsterdom were encountered with greater frequency in open water and although the potential to cause great injury and death was there, they seemed to have no vicious propensities. Sport diving entered the 1960's with these monster fears fairly well dispelled.

While sea serpents , for example the Loch Ness Monster, were sighted in many water areas, divers did not see them and they fell into the realm of UFO sightings. The giant squid existed, that was known from tentacles and other parts of bodies recovered from whale stomachs and nets, but one of the 75-foot-long "killing machines with cutting suction cups" had not been seen alive and swimming in the seas.

One other monster that remained a threat to the early divers deserves special consideration and the shark is handled elsewhere as are the smaller dangerous marine creatures.

The controversy rages as to whether all creatures should

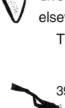

remain in the wild or be put on public display as trained pets. There has always been winning arguments for both sides. Can we ever understand other creatures if we can not make long and prolonged contact, find a friendly rapport; but are we only seeing a diluted caricature of animals in captivity and out of the wild?

Ted Griffin who captured more Killer Whales than any other individual justified taking them out of their native environment with this quote from his book, *Namu*:

"Clearly, public attitudes were changing. For the most part killer whales were no longer ignored, nor feared, nor shot for sport. During Namu's autopsy a 303 Enfield rifle bullet was found lodged harmlessly in his blubber, indicative of the random pot-shots taken at Orca in the past. Personalization of Namu and the public display of killer whales focused the attention of millions on these friendly intelligent mammals. New organizations were formed to capitalize on the changing attitudes. These groups raised money to attract public attention and exert political pressure for the purpose of saving the whales and other wild animals."

Divers owe Ted Griffin some gratitude for removing one of their great monster fears in the beginning.

Unterstüt

34
SHIPWRECKS

DEFINING EVENT: THE ANDREA DORIA

Nothing more blood racing than being on a sinking ship. Being rescued could equal it. <u>Finding</u> the shipwreck is wildly exciting. Walking the sunken decks, as a diver, can be more thrilling.

Shipwreck! Another word in the diver's lexicon that is a clear call to slip on an exposure suit and get wet. Forget the fish, forget the coral scenery, here was...was something to find, a crushed package of enormous human drama, a capsule of history, and maybe, even treasure - but treasure wrecks are in another chapter. The Golden Years of Diving were electric opportunities to stay down with scuba and come across the bones of a fascinating disaster.

Many of our pioneer divers had their imaginations and enthusiasm to get into diving inspired by pictures of intact pirate galleons sitting on the bottom. But the cruel sea in most sinkings absorbs, ingests shipwrecks with erosive encrustations, currents, and storms until they turn to debris, rust dust, bumps in the coral, or sink forever into bottom silt and sand. The reality of sunken ships is that they are best viewed right after they've gone down because after the water environment has had its way, the only trace may be a straight line on the bottom or rust trace or a leather shoe.

In a modern era of robotics going deep without risk to humans, the previous era of an untethered diver getting to be the first visitor looms in the history of sport diving as a marvelous time. Our best adventure stories from diving will always be about self-contained divers crawling through a shipwreck.

Remember if you will, that the shipwrecks we are discussing here are not faux shipwrecks, those big obsolete sea-ships or flying-ships placed on the bottom as "artificial reefs". These ships went down as part of a grand emotional, fearful experience and many of them are filled with mystery and intrigue. It is not knowing what's to be found that awes the diver-it is not an amusement park attraction, completely predictable and over trafficked.

In the 1950's and 1960's when divers were still pondering their equipment and the very idea of breathing underwater, they had no idea of what they'd run into down there. They were diving in places where no one had ever been before and virgin wrecks lay scattered on the bottom everywhere.

It is hard to find a pioneer diver, who at least once, had not descended into the colorless gloom, antennae bristling,

Photo of the sinking Andrea Doria. Peter Gimbel is shown in 1956 (left) and 1975.
Wide World Photos/Blue Gander, Inc.

Ramsey Parks article that ran in Skin Diver Magazine.

Exploration of the Sunken Liner
ANDREA DORIA
By RAMSEY PARKS

expecting a monster, eyes straining when suddenly a ghostly apparition looms large, at the edge of his vision-the clumped remains of a shipwreck. Remember, also, that the world had just finished up the most extensive war, World War II, in all of history and many ships of all kinds had been sunk - and airplanes, too. Shipwrecks sprung from the bottom like mushrooms after a fall rain.

If any shipwreck is to represent the classic best for luring and providing a stage for scuba diving, it was the Andrea Doria. This opulent Italian cruise liner collided with the Swedish liner Stockholm on July 25, 1956 off Nantucket Island, Massachusetts. Fifty-two people were killed, 1,652 rescued. The wreck lies in a divable 225 feet of water. The site is marked with a yellow buoy.

Peter Gimbel launched an expedition to explore the Andrea Doria, to make a documentary film, and to recover whatever valued artifacts could be found. There was talk of treasure but it never came to pass. He used some of diving's top divers and cinematographers of the time. They were: Ramsey Parks, Stan Waterman, Bob Hollis, and Jack McKenney. Part of his film for television was a first in showing scuba divers on a fresh wreck and climaxed with the opening of a recovered safe which yielded...nothing of value. It became a popular, if hazardous, dive site for advanced divers. Dr. Robert Ballard, of the Titanic discovery, made a submersible dive on it over three decades later, but found the current and weather conditions hazardous, too many sharks, and the decaying wreck shrouded in fishnets. An experienced scuba diver, Ballard said, "I don't think it's a safe dive for sport divers...it requires decompression."

And yet over almost fifty years, the Andrea Doria has been a prized wreck diving must-do and a schedule of charter dives have been continuously available.

COUSTEAU'S EARLY SHIPWRECK INVOLVEMENT

Scuba diving on the most ancient ship discovered to that point, was the opportunity of Aqua Lung inventor Jacques Cousteau, who recovered many amphoras, made a film and wrote books about it in 1952. Jacque Yves Cousteau's ship the Calypso sat over the Greek Wine Freighter that sunk around 230 B.C. in 112 to 170 feet of water ten miles from Marseille, France. It was on a shelf extending from a barren Mediterranean Island called Grand Congloue.

Cousteau and crew used a suction pump to dredge up artifacts. They used it mainly to carve amphorae (wine jars) from the wreck. Cousteau knew where the wreck was from a fisherman, who told of "old pots" at the site. With

National Geographic Society support, Cousteau spent five years there recovering 3000 amphorae and initialing the first underwater excavation using free divers and an air lift promising a new era in underwater archeology. Many parts of the ship were lifted, including 200 tons of lead sheathing. Nothing precious was found, like coins. One diver lost his life.

The downside of this famous wreck dive was the use of the Aqua Lung in devastating the divable shipwrecks of the Mediterranean before a public consciousness could be developed about them. Cousteau, actually, salvaged the upper layer of the wreck but did not record the layout intact of the actual site. What may have been lost in revealing information, clues to the times, the history is now gone forever.

Some wrecks had a number of expeditions invade them. The Mahdia Wreck off Tunisia is a prime example of a wreck worked and reworked over the decades.

Sponge divers told French archeologist, Alfred Merlin, a story of what at first he thought were human bodies coming up out of the sand, but it was a graveyard of bronze statues. It was a Roman plunder ship from 90 B.C. returning to Rome with the spoils of war, Greece's best antiquities. Merlin it is said, stumbled across a small encrusted bronze statue in a Tunisian flea market, and knew it was an original. Between 1907 and 1913 after an arduous search for the wreck (sponge fishermen are always very vague with directions), Merlin employed hardhat divers to bring up bronze statues, enough to fill five rooms at the Museum in Tunisia.

The wreck at 93 meters was a decompression dive and rough weather limited time to dive it. By 1948, along came, you guessed it again, Jacques Cousteau. Cousteau with Dumas, Talliez and some French Navy officers went to sea on a ship to supposedly train a staff in diving with the Aqua Lung. Some say Cousteau had a secret agenda - to make a color film of the Mahdia Wreck and use it to publicize the Aqua Lung as a tool for science.

Clint Denn uses a 55 gallon drum and air to bring up ballast stones in Bonaire.

Merlin did not cooperate with Cousteau for he still dreamed of excavating much more of the wreck's cargo that he felt still lay buried. Cousteau had trouble finding the wreck and ended up with only five days to dive it. Aqua Lung divers searched the wreck by hand and brought up amphora and a few other artifacts but no statues. Cousteau sailed away feeling there was much more buried at the wreck site. However, his dives on the Mahdia ship marked the first wreck excavations using scuba. But it was not archaeology, that was yet to be born; underwater archeology is covered in a special chapter.

Unfortunately, Cousteau's work on this wreck got divers everywhere excited about shipwreck discovery. Lots of divers, few archaeologists in the 1950's. Divers found lots of wrecks and picked them apart before scientific study could be applied.

There were 1990's expeditions which established the use of the Global Positioning System for finding the

Sometimes the only personal effects found at a wreck site are shoes.

Mahdia and she would never be lost again. Mensun Bound, an Englishman, covered the Mahdia story in his book, *Lost Ships*, Simon and Shuster, 1998. He was inspired at ten years old by Cousteau's *Silent World*. He describes his first dive on the Mahdia wreck:

"Spread eagled and face down, we let ourselves fall through water. My eyes strained for their first glimpse of the Roman plunder ship...one of the divers turned on his camera lights, and all at once, the columns were illuminated in a crescendo of color that surprised even the fish."

Even the most articulate may wax poetic about first encounters with shipwrecks but even they can not really transpose the great emotional impact into simple words.

Let us run down the most famous and popular true (not deliberately sunk to create artificial reefs.) shipwrecks for sport divers. The emphasis will be on the ones discovered in the pioneer days of diving.

THE RMS RHONE

Go to the Virgin Islands, in particular the British Virgin Islands, forty of them altogether. If you'd gone there just after the Royal Mail Ship Rhone had been sunk by a terrific hurricane in 1857 two years after launching, it would have been then the most important sunken ship as it is today.

And, if you'd gotten there right after it went down, you'd have found the three Murphy brothers in hard hat recovering 60,000 (English pounds) of specie and gold bullion plus cotton bales and very good champagne. It was a treasure wreck and then just a shipwreck.

The 310 foot *Rhone* is broken in several sections. George and Luana Mailer started diving on it back in 1971. Their photographs of it helped persuade the government to recognize it as a national treasure and designate it a National Underwater Park, where coral, souvenirs, game taking are forbidden. It lies at 60 to 80 feet and after 150 years has become a "brilliant display piece of marine life", as George said in 1978.

TRUK LAGOON

Truk Lagoon has the Japanese Imperial Navy, some 50 ships of World War II, in its 70 mile width at depths of 6 to 190 feet. The February, 1944 attack by United States Naval airplanes left a mass graveyard recognized and protected by the Micronesian government. No where in the world, ever before or since, have there been so many wrecks clustered together in shallow, clear water. Not really exploited, as a diving site, until the 1970's, it has become, over the years a diver's mecca, "a dive you must make once before you die". Clark Graham was the key expert on the sunken ships of Truk Lagoon and was there in the 1960's with the Peace Corps before starting up Micronesia Aquatics, as a full service PADI facility. It is a favorite diving place of many of the pioneer divers. Al Giddings who recorded its majesty on film and in *National Geographic Magazine* declared it an out-of-this-world experience.

CAPE GELADOMYA WRECK - TURKEY

In 1958 an United States photojournalist, Peter Throckmorton, went with Turkish sponge divers to locate 30 shipwrecks. The sponge diver leader wanted to blow up a pile of bronze and sell it for scrap. Throckmorton talked him out of it and got the University of Pennsylvania Museum to excavate the site using land standard methods.

This was the first scientific underwater excavation ever planned. It was the real birth of underwater archeology.

A graduate student, George Bass, was appointed Director of the 1961 excavation and went to the local YMCA to learn to scuba dive. National Geographic Society made a grant.

The site was in 100 feet of water and the Bronze Age wreck was completely photographed before bringing up fused clumps of the cargo to study. There were 3515 dives made in examining this time capsule.

George Bass carried on from the 1961 dives on the Cape Giladomya wreck with excavating many wrecks found by sponge divers in divable waters of up to 170 feet. Dr. Bass considered the Father of Underwater Archeology introduced the sonar side scanner which is a towed "eye" that sends out sound waves and record echoes from features on the bottom, called "anomalies". The scanner allowed deeper penetration of the ocean to find wrecks as the shallow ones became more and more scarce. In 1982, a Bass scuba diver found copper ingots of the wreck from 1375 B.C. in depths from 141 to 167 feet. It was the oldest ship ever excavated underwater.

SWEDISH WAR GALLEON

The Swedish War Galleon was only a mile from its launching dock in 1628, when a breeze pushed the top heavy Vasa over and it sank in divable water. The time of 333 years went by before it was discovered in zero visibility and a huge silt mound. It was lifted and preserved intact to become one of the outstanding preservationist efforts ever. For scuba divers in the 1950's, it was an exciting event promising great discovery possibilities for the new breed of divers.

MARY ROSE

The Mary Rose was an "intact recovery" much like the Vasa. A warship of King Henry VIII sank in a gust of wind exposing gun ports to the ocean, as she moved to engage the French enemy in 1545. There she lay in 40 feet divable water near Portmouth, England in 1971 when Brits diver-journalist, Alexander McKee and archeologist, Margaret Rule, located her, after a six-year-search. Over four years, 30,000 dives, and 17,000 artifacts recovered, it was raised and half the hull survives on exhibit today.

SUNKEN CITIES

As scuba divers looked for shipwrecks in places where they gathered lobster and chased fish, earthquakes had sunk seaside cities to provide more hidden mysteries to be solved by the new divers. A former pirate town, Port Royal of Jamaica, a city of 2000 buildings on June 7, 1692 slipped into water up to 40 feet deep. Looter divers were on the ruins within hours. It was not until 1956 that American inventor and diver Ed Link checked it out and found only a mud bottom. Edwin A. Link came back with proper diving gear for salvage and mapped out the walls and streets under the mud. Hundreds of artifacts of normal living were recovered.

Robert Marx with a scuba diving team carried on Link's work in the 1960's bringing up thousands of items to create a special museum for the government. By 1981 marine archeologist Don Hamilton was on the site using hookah divers.

Bradford 'Brad' Luther (Fairhaven, Massachusetts) was into wrecks as a pioneer scuba diver. He was a walking museum of shipwreck information and had dived most of them. Evelyn "Evie" Dudas (West Chester, Pennsylvania) wasn't far behind and the woman who has been down on the Andrea Doria the most times. Here are the East Coast wrecks they feel were the most popular in the pioneer quarter century.

Brad's list: (TKR=Tanker)

TKR CHELSEA, Gloucester

SS ROMANCE, Broad Sound

SS SALISBURY, Graus Ledge

SLOOP J.B.KING, Hardings Ledge

TKR PINTHIS, Marshfield

SCHOONER BARGE POLLSTOWN, Sandwich

TUG WATHEN, Sandwich

TKR PENDELTON, Chatham

SS DIXIE SWORD, Bearses Shoal

SS PORT HUNTER, Hedge Fence Shoal

SCHOONER LUNET, Tarpaulin Cove

SS JOHN DWIGHT, Vineyard Sound

USN YDS, Nomandsland

SS TROJAN, Vineyard Sound

USCGC VINEYARD LIGHTSHIP, Vineyard Sound

TUG TRIANA, Cuttyhunk Island

USN YANKEE, Buzzards Bay

BARGE ANGELLA, Hen & Chickens Reef

HMCS ST. CLAIR, Westport

TKR LELLEWEN HOWLAND, Brenten Reef

SS BLACK POINT, Pt. Judith

GERMAN SUB. U-853, Rhode Island Sound

TKR LIGHTBURN, Block Island

SCHOONER MONTANNA, Block Island

SS ONENDAGA, Watch Hill

YACHT CARMAC, Sugar Reef

Tucker and Mendel Peterson sorting artifacts for shipment to the Smithsonian.

Evie's List:

GERMAN SUB. U-853, Rhode Island Sound

USS SUB. BASS, Block Island, Rhode Island

LINER OREGON, Fire Island, New York

ARMORED CRUISER M.S. SAN DIEGO, Fire Island, New York

REVENUE CUTTER MOHAWK, Sandy Hook, New Jersey

FREIGHTER YANKEE, Sandy Hook, New Jersey

LUMBER FREIGHTER PINTA, Asbury Park, New Jersey

FREIGHTER ARUNDO, Asbury Park, New Jersey

FREIGHTER/PASSENGER DELAWARE, Seaside Heights, New Jersey

PASSENGER MOHAWK, Seaside Heights, New Jersey

FREIGHTER TOLTEN, Seaside Heights, New Jersey

TKR STERN STOLTDAGALI, Seaside Heights, New Jersey -Very popular.

SPANISH MAILSHIP VISCAYA, Barnegat Light, New Jersey

TKR STERN GULF TRADE, Barnegat Light, New Jersey

FLOUR FREIGHTER ALMIRANTE, Atlantic City New Jersey

TKR VARANGER, Atlantic City, New Jersey

PASSENGER CITY OF ATHENS, Cape May, New Jersey/Indian River, Delaware

U.S. DESTROYER JACOB JONES, Cap May, New Jersey/Indian River, Delaware

U.S. PATROL BOAT MOONSTONE, Cap May, New Jersey, Indian River, Delaware

FREIGHTER WASHINGTONIAN, Indian River, Delaware

USN TUG/GUNBOAT CHEROKEE, Indian River, Delaware

GERMAN SUB U-352, North Carolina Coast -Most popular here.

TREASURE THE JAMES BOND WRECK

Dick Anderson was selected Divemaster for the filming of the party reel that would be a celebration projected especially for all who worked on the movie, *Jaws*. The party reel was titled, *Jaws The Revenge*. His position was with the Special Effects Crew in Nassau.

"We were located on a navigable inlet about a half-hour drive from Nassau. Besides just the normal, normal, normal preparation work, a few interesting things did happen. After we started getting things into the water, the Special Effects Coordinator did notice that some of his fifteen "Certified" divers didn't know anything about diving. He decided to charter a dive boat and give everyone a check-out dive.

The dive boat took us to a sunken tug referred to as, The James Bond Wreck. We were anchored next to an impressive drop-off. A guy named Mike, who resented me greatly because he had wanted to be Divemaster, was one of the first to jump in. His weight belt made a speedy descent to 125 feet while he bobbed on the surface like a cork!

Everyone got dressed in and headed for the wreck. I was the last one to go in. The dive boat captain watched as I stuck a pair of 14 inch channel locks in my pocket. "What are you gonna do with those?", he asked. And I said, "Whenever I dive on a wreck I always like to bring up some brass goodie."

And he said, "Anderson, there's been ten thousand divers on this wreck and the last nine thousand, nine hundred and ninety didn't find any brass."

I jumped in. Thirty feet below me I could see the entire sixty foot tug in sparkling clarity. There were a dozen divers hovering over it as though wondering what would happen if they actually touched it!

I dropped down into the stern hatch. The engine room was mainly stripped but there was an array of 2 1/2 inch brass pipe. I didn't want brass pipe. I swam forward through the hull and up into the pilot house. I noticed that the pilot house had a raised false floor. Maybe to make James Bond look taller. The pilot house was bare. I ripped up a few planks from the false floor. Underneath was the tug's original pilot house door with a beautiful brass 12 inch deadlight. (That's a port that doesn't open.)

A couple of the original deckboards were loose and I yanked them up. Lo and behold! There were three 12 inch brass ports (Portholes to landlubbers) screwed to the inside of the hull for some forgotten movie scene. I pulled out my channel locks and freed the three ports. I stirred up so much mud, the inside of the pilot house was black. I picked up the three ports and set them out on the foredeck through the missing front window. A "diver" named Wayne swims by and sees the ports. He can't believe his eyes. With all these divers swimming around he's the only one who spotted these portholes! He picks them up and hefts them. Then he sets them back down and bends his head back to clear his mask. I reach out from the gloom of the pilot house and retrieve the three ports. Wayne looks down. The ports are gone! He clears his mask again. The ports are still gone!

I take the three ports down through the tug and exit through the stern hatch. The dive boat's dive step is thirty feet above me. I bound off the tug and kick like hell for the swim-step. I'm swimming with about thirty or forty pounds of brass and glass. About two feet from the swim step I start to run out of steam. At that very second I feel a hand grab my ankle and boost me upward. It was the hand of a really good diver who worked with the camera crew, Fred Gebler. I thanked him and crawled aboard.

The dive boat captain said, "Wow Anderson, we're never going to take you to any of our good wrecks!" And I said, "You ain't seen nothing yet. Wait 'til this diver Wayne comes up."

Well, Wayne came up. He told everybody that he found three perfect brass portholes but they disappeared when he cleared his mask. Nobody believed him but me.

ATOCHA

Have all the shipwrecks been found with all the scuba divers splashing about on every inch of the divable areas of the continental shelf in discovery 1950's and 1960's, even into the 1980's? It seemed that the divable wrecks, the ones above 200 feet, were finally all discovered with Mel Fisher's long search and ultimate find of the Atocha.

At the same time, the Titanic and the SS Central America discoveries were the start of a new deep era of robotics with no place for scuba divers, the sport divers with simple basic equipment. The Mary Rose was washed up out of the muck in shallow water after all those years by a storm. A number of wrecks over all the years of wreck diving, suddenly appeared on the bottom and where did they come from? Out of the bottom crust of sand, silt, coral, upthrust by the violence of nature. There may be thousands and thousands more that will be coughed up and in the sport diver's range.

Without humans aggressively invading that bottom, the signs of wrecks will appear in the form of ballast stones or timbers or canons. Divers are probably swimming over such sites this very moment.

Even with the advanced technology of sonar picking up bumps or anomalies on the surface of the bottom, there must be a multitude of wrecks not protruding enough to show on the screens. It will be up to nature to reveal those lost ships.

CHINESE JUNKS

The Chinese junks that may have crossed the Pacific Ocean coming to America, giant ships with 3,000-man-crews, are only conceptions of archaeologists. Scuba divers have found pieces of Ming Dynasty pottery in the shallows off the Northwest Islands but no ships. Did the junks arrive there centuries ago? The Meistrel brothers found giant half-ton round boulders with a central groove to hold a rope anchor line lying in shallow water off a popularly dived Palos Verdes, California site. An Archeologist identified them as the type used by Asian junks. There is so much bottom that Skin and scuba divers have rested their hands on. What may well have been a veneer over layers and layers of wreck materials, perhaps a salvage ship on top of a salvage ship on top of a treasure galleon...or just an old fishing boat that was a grand slice of history, a relic to reveal that life was in a sudden moment in time.

STILL THEY'RE WAITING TO BE FOUND

The technology may seem to have pushed the free swimming adventure of the scuba diver out of the ocean and the masses have overrun and over explored the shallows but the ocean is one big mother. She may at anytime regurgitate more antiquities.

HISTORY VS TREASURE

The great issue over who owns all those shipwrecks exceeds that of legal ownership. The wreck hunters over the centuries have enjoyed somewhat heroic status...right into the scuba diving early years. But, there has always been an opposition philosophy that shipwrecks are time capsules of history and what they record belongs to everybody. Somewhere in between the taking of things from these wrecks by whatever means possible, distorting the sites and the archeology purists, who want information with which to construct history, lie the free swimming divers, who were thrilled to discover dramatic things that had sunk from the surface. Forget the history, the possible value of artifacts, divers didn't care...just having the shipwreck remnants was enough. This was part of the divers world and didn't need to be excavated for monetary gain or historic records. The shipwreck was part of the mysterious ocean that divers felt belonged to them. Diving a wreck was a special and different adventure. Most divers felt wrecks ought to be left alone, part of the scenic terrain, that "they owned by rights of going there".

Unquestionably, there have been important identifiable shipwrecks. Most of these are specifically sought and located by research. They are not the ones the divers serendipitously stumbled across.

THE MONITOR

No event in the United States' past is as important to the nation's history as the Civil War. The existence of a Union Navy and a Confederate Navy is best realized by the innovative ironclad ships, in particular the famed Union Monitor. Sunk in 1892, it was not discovered until 1973 in 220 feet of water. Divers worked out of the Edwin Link submersible using helium/oxygen. The Monitor was too fragile to lift to the surface. So in 1975, it was designated as the first marine sanctuary in the United States.

Sam Raymond and HArold Edgerton spent a great deal of time studying relics from the U.S.S. Monitor wreck.

There are some shipwrecks that haven't had national attention but are well-known landmarks to local divers in the different regions. Remember, we are not dealing here with deliberately sunk ships, airplanes, street cars to create artificial reefs.

CALIFORNIA - Pacific storms ravage sunken ships and what's left is covered by the sandy bottom.

YACHT VALIENT, *St. Catherine's Cove, Santa Catalina Island*

PALOS VERDES BARGE, *North of Rocky Point-Palos Verdes*

GAMBLING SHIP STAR OF SCOTLAND, *One mile out end of pier, Santa Monica*

GENERAL WINFIELD SCOTT, *Inside shore Anacapa Island*

CANADIAN GRAIN HAULER DOMINATOR, *Rocky Point-Palos Verdes- Very popular*

Gene Parker with copper fittings made by Paul Revere off the U.S.S. New Hampshire in 1960.

NORTHWEST - By 1975, over 400 wrecks dotted the Puget Sound. Shifting sands reveal new ones every year but the sands will just as quickly reclaim a shipwreck.

THE EDMONDS, *Puget Sound*

POINT FOSDECK, *Puget Sound*

FAMOUS GALLOPING GERTIE BRIDGE, *Tacoma Narrows Bridge*

Bridge collapsed in 1940 and it's a "wreck" still there underwater.

THREE OLD WOODEN GRAVEL BARGES, *Tolmie State Park*

EAST COAST - See the Bradford Luther and Evelyn Dudas lists in this chapter.

*BOSTON SEA ROVERS/*PAUL REVERE SPIKES WRECK

GERMAN SUBMARINE-WORLD WAR II

GREAT LAKES
TOBERMORRY WRECKS

THE KEYS
NUESTRA SENORA DE ATOCHA, *Florida*
SANTA MARGARITA, *Florida*
1715 SPANISH PLATE FLEET REMAINS, *Florida*

BAHAMAS
PAPA DOC WRECK

UNEXSO in 1966 had done its share of galleon graveyard diving and incorporated trips to a ballast bed with old copper nails, as part of their regular trip menu. As is almost always the case, the tourist divers have story-book images of an intact ship in its full glory just sitting upright there waiting for them on the bottom.

Ships just don't last long underwater, worms do their work, salt water erodes, and storms do the rest to make them disappear. So despite lacking the romance of antiquity, fresh wrecks are fully visible and the sinking usually has an exacting story to go with it.

UNEXSO got its Papa Doc Wreck in 30 feet of water and over three months

Al Tillman explores the Papa Doc wreck.

before it was ravished by bad weather and over diving it. Haitian revolutionaries bound to overthrow the vicious regime of Dictator Papa Doc Duvalier were secretly training at the eastern end of Grand Bahama Island. Unbeknownst to the staff, UNEXSO had trained one of its Haitian maintenance workers to scuba dive, who in turn was teaching fellow rebels to be frogmen warriors.

The invasion force had loaded a 30 foot pleasure craft with rifles, dozens of pairs of size 14 army shoes, boxes of bottles of catsup and revolutionary badges and paper propaganda. Unfortunately, a storm struck in the middle of the night and down went the strange "troop ship". It was great fun picking up souvenirs from the shipwreck and visiting divers to UNEXSO still have artifacts in their homes. It was great finding a rifle but the Bahamian government searched for and confiscated the rifles.

It was a safe wreck at an ideal diving depth. It made a fine photographic setting, too. That's the way of shipwrecks coming out of nowhere and disappearing just as fast. But, divers packed up great experiences for their memory banks, then lived in anticipation of one just around the corner of the next storm.

Postscript: Was it a treasure wreck? Rumors persisted but no one was ever sure how much money was on it. Two local divers did buy a rather expensive boat a few weeks after the <u>Papa Doc</u> *sinking!*

THE GOODWILL

Every wreck has its own life's stories. Some of the stories are so enchanting that one would wish the ship would still be alive and well. The grand Goodwill was the largest yacht in the nation's largest marina of Newport Harbor, California, before 1959. Progress of new property development pushed this immense old steel schooner of 161 feet out of that harbor where there no longer was room for her. Pioneer Skin and scuba divers would see the Goodwill temporarily anchored in Bays off shore from Catalina Island to Baja California. What made the sight of this huge sailboat awe-inspiring were thoughts in the mind's eye of dreams of personal fortune, luxury and living a munificent style. She was magnificent to behold! Goodwill was a millionaire's yacht built in the good-times of the roaring 1920's by Bethlehem Steelyard in Wilmington, Delaware, for the Spaulding Sporting Goods Family.

During World War II, the Spauldings turned Goodwill over to the U.S. Navy free of charge to be used as an offshore patrol ship. After the war, the Spauldings didn't want it anymore. The Navy sold her for $20,000 (a paltry price when it cost $1.6 million to build in the 1920's) to a syndicate who planned to convert it into a gambling ship off Acapulco, Mexico. Goodwill had varied assignments in her life, back into service during the Korean War, scientific expeditions and exotic dream trips.

The Goodwill's last trip to Ensenada from La Paz began May 21, 1969. She wasn't exactly in ship-shape. Worst of all, she left La Paz with a fathometer that ceased functioning.

Sad news came Memorial Day Weekend days later, when a rescue helicopter flew over to nearby Geronimo Island not far from the reef that shows up at low tide. There was the Goodwill. No survivors. That reef is 12 miles offshore and 4 miles long, and named the Sacramento after the sidewheeler, Sacramento, that hit a reef in 1872.

Great shipwrecks have been found and photographed and in some cases excavated every year. But they are deep. The free swimming scuba diver has had to be replaced by unmanned robots in a gradual evolution over the years. Unquestionably the ultimate shipwreck in all of history was the dramatic 1912 sinking of perhaps the greatest, largest, most luxurious liner of all time, the Titanic.

Civilization placed a lot of technology, exquisite interior design, sumptuousness of everything into this beauty; it hit an iceberg and sank. Death to a ship does have a domino affect connecting a chunk of humanity. The Titanic changed lives!

Many divers had dreams of discovering the Titanic but only high technology, Robert Ballard and his team were able to suceed.

It was the ultimate fantasy dive for many pioneer scuba divers for many years until Dr. Robert Ballard, operating out of Woods Hole Oceanographic Institute and with plenty of United States Navy help, found the ship broken in two in icy North Atlantic waters at two and a half miles of depth. It was then recorded every which way, was feted in *National Geographic Magazine*, in television specials, and an Oscar-movie-spectacular. Titanic fever raged for several years from 1988 right on through the end of the 1990's. Bob Ballard became an industry with securing private funding to go after more famous wrecks beyond scuba diving range: The German biggest battleship of them all, the Bismark; Centuries old trading ships in the Mediterranean and the Lusitania. He published many books on all of them and even arranged for on-site television broadcasting into classrooms.

Regarding the Lusitania, the flustering currents and depth were the nemesis of Colonel John D. Craig with his team incorporating the knowledge of Gene Nohl, Jack Browne and Dr. Edgar End on their "Lusitania Photographic Project" in 1935. Others, decades later, would finally make dives on the controversial shipwreck. Its sinking by the

Germans got the U.S.A. into World War I.

Unfortunately, Ballard could not get the sophisticated support vessels from public agencies and the United States Navy he had in the search for the Titanic. So recovery of artifacts was not possible for him. The French exploration company that had participated with Ballard in finding the Titanic went ahead with an excavation of loose artifacts from the wreck. Much of it ended up in a traveling exhibit. They have even sold small pieces of souvenir coal from the zillion tons of it laying on the bottom near the Titanic.

Ballard could not be part of the recovery and instead moved to a viewpoint that the Titanic should be designated as some kind of a sanctuary graveyard in respect to the people lost there. To be picked apart, as salvage according to the philosophy, would be a desecration.

Bob Ballard was himself a Boston Sea Rover scuba diver, before he became the Czar of deep water shipwreck exploring. Many scuba divers felt the pangs of loss of a prodigious future diving experience, as robotics took over and the Titanic was now found and too deep. The new Holy Grail of diving shifted to the yet undiscovered sunken continent of Atlantis.

The other celebrated shipwreck discovery and greatest treasure ship ever was the S.S. Central America. Tommy Thompson found and excavated its billion dollar treasure with a well engineered high tech system of robotics. In 1986 this expedition put another nail in the coffin of shipwreck exploration by scuba divers. In rough water at a depth of 2 miles, another dream shipwreck was automatically removed from the search plans of scuba divers.

Despite the disappointment of so many legendary wrecks showing up as deep challenges requiring complex and expensive equipment, scuba divers were still motivated by shipwrecks. There could be more in divable depths uncovered suddenly by the forces of nature.

35

TREASURE WRECKS
BONES OF AN ELECTRIC DIVING MOMENT

DEFINING EVENT: VERO BEACH 1715 FLEET

There it is! Lumps and straight lines. The barely visible remains of a shipwreck, fifty, one-hundred, 300, 3,000 years old. A diver may come upon it serendipitously and while treasure and salvage flashes first through his mind, the dramatic event of the sinking ultimately ignites curiosity. How many died in the sinking? What would it have been like as the ship slipped out from beneath you and the water rose around you? Would you be hoping a rescue was on the way? Or would you give up hope, wonder if you'd drown, freeze to death or be eaten by sharks first? There it is in that encrusted rubble, the lost aspirations and agonies of people in probably the most dramatic moments of their lives.

You are there. The first to be at the ship's and perhaps its passengers', final resting place. This has been the heart thumping "find" moment that diving has made possible. The pioneer days of diving were filled with such experiences and there may yet be more for the free swimming diver. Although the odds have shrunk on striking it rich on an ancient ship, there will be more modern ships that will sink and provide the thrill of exploring a shipwreck. It is an experience that all divers should have.

Spanish galleons represented the bulk of treasure ships in the oceans and the ocean of the West Indies was the wrecking yard.

Spain needed gold and silver to fight wars in the Old World over three centuries - the 1600's through the 1800's. There were emeralds, platinum, copper and jewelry on board these ships that traveled in fleets of a dozen or more to scare off pirates.

They embarked from Central America ports, stopped in Haiti, then moved into the hurricane belt with uncharted reefs and shoals. The galleons had a bad record; only a third ever got back to Spain. Entire fleets went down and there were salvage efforts during ensuing years by the Spanish and English using free divers.

Often the salvage ships sank on top of the treasure wreck leaving confusing layers of ballast rocks and canons. Free divers got shredded on razor sharp corals, pushed by difficult currents, bothered by sharks and endangered by rotting, collapsing parts of wrecks.

Poor records , inaccurate charts, too much romance, too little science over the years made these wrecks undiscoverable. Even if located after boring months of searching, the depth would exceed the limits for a safe workable dive. The ships were buried in sand, encrusted in coral, with no way to pinpoint the treasure itself. Blowing it loose would possibly blow up the booty as well, beyond recovery.

The childhood reading of *Treasure Island* by Robert Louis Stevenson ignited many dreams. Pirates, treasure and sunken ships were the words that exploded the imaginations of youth over the centuries.

Not until the migration of scuba divers into the underseas was the potential for finding treasure there fully realized. Beyond the taking of game and the photography, there was always the lure of finding treasure. For some scuba divers it was the only reason for getting into diving.

The paragon underwater treasure for Peter Throckmorton, marine archaeologist and author of *Diving for Treasure*, is not necessarily the cargo but to him the sunken ship is the treasure. He tells us finding the wreck can be a problem, sometimes to be solved with sonar, sometimes by listening to fishermen's tales. Once found, for example, the wreck at Yassi Ada, where they retrieved 7th century gold coins, the archaeologists were able to re-create a Byzantine trading voyage from these finds.

Patience, perseverance, optimism, arduous research, sacrificing multitudes of dives, and dumb luck were the lot of these divers. Some went about it in their spare time but the successful ones went about it obsessively, compulsively full time.

As scuba divers proliferated, their coverage of the continental shelf at depths safe to dive was extensive. What information couldn't be found in historical records and archives was passed onto them in the stories of old fisher-men.

The treasure diver's situation besides not being one of instant success was one of suffering, disrespect and criticism. Greedy rapists of ship graveyards was a common epithet. Environmentalists and archaeologists turned their critical guns on them and alerted governments to the finds so territorial claims and taxes could be adminis-tered.

There was a swashbuckling air about the treasure divers. They expressed the beliefs of the frontier explorers and pioneers that any treasures belonged to whoever got there first and worked to get it. A lot of these treasure divers would probably have been pirates in times past. Many of them will never be known for it is suspected that much treasure was found and covertly removed without any announcements. It is the great finds by scuba divers over four decades 1950 - 1990, publicized and thus inflamed the interest of all divers, that played such an impor-tant role in keeping sport divers diving.

Here are some of the historical treasure experiences, big and little, that sparked the glitter in divers' eyes:

The major "find" that linked celebrated treasure divers together and nurtured new equipment was the Vero Beach Treasure Fleet of 1715. It is the event that produced the foundation of systematic treasure hunting and recovery.

It is helpful to know something about the two main entrepreneurs of this dramatic event: Kip Wagner and Mel Fisher. Kip was from Ohio and Mel from Indiana. Both had read *Treasure Island* in childhood where "pieces of eight" lodged as a sort of mantra in their subconscious. Kip was doing construction work in the Vero Beach area of Florida and hearing a multitude of treasure stories, the best of which was about an old beachcomber, who found pieces of black scrap metal he used as 'skipping stones'. They were of course "pieces of eight coins" and Kip realized he had been walking past such skipping stones every day as he walked the beach. Eventually, he would move into the water to look and find shipwrecks. It was the King's Treasure Fleet of fourteen galleons that had gone down in shallow water. Fifty-four, white-haired, stocky Kip gathered a team of friends and began to crudely work the wrecks. Some treasure was uncovered but better equipment and know-how was needed.

Enter the other tall, squinty eyed, talented diver, Mel Fisher, who already had a treasure hunter reputation on both coasts. Kip and Mel found kindred souls in each other and merged their two companies Real Eight and Treasure Salvors to do big time treasure hunting, a 50-50 deal. Kip had State permits for working the sites and Mel had a crew of pro-divers, a magnetometer and the mailbox, the L-shaped metal tunnel that used prop wash to blow clear water down to an excavation site as well as dig monster holes in the sand bottom.

Kip Wagner and his team had dredged up a respectable assortment of coins and bars that all together added up to a good find over a couple of years from 1960-1962. Besides joining up with Mel Fisher in 1962, Kip Wagner was still researching and was in touch with a pioneer of diving, Mendel Peterson, historian at the Smithsonian Institute. Peterson nailed Wagner's wreck area as about approximately the site of the 1715 Fleet carrying 14 million pesos of treasure. Backed by stacks of informational material, from many sources, a bonanza from the Spanish archives, he had done the extensive research vital to all treasure hunters.

Fisher had to sell off his dive business, Mel's Aqua Shop, and move family of wife and four children, and his California crew to Florida. Fisher's ace in the hole was Fay Field, an electronics genius and rare shell collector, who developed the magnetometer that located iron shipwrecks (a desirable habitat for a rare spiny oyster Field was seeking).

A year of picking holes in the sand all over the place yielded very little. Just about ready to give it up, Wagner and Fisher merged with yet another group that had found gold coins near a possible wreck site. But this search went on for months until Fisher went out with his mailbox excavation invention. Designed to put clear water on dive site, it astonished Mel to find that it also dug holes in the bottom.

Finally, after an accumulation of much junk over about three months, and with mutiny on his hands, Fisher hit the "glory hole" on May 24th, 1963 which was a "carpet of gold" in a deep trench dug by the mailbox. Despite the revolutionary tech equipment Fisher conceived, the divers brought up 1,033 pieces of gold by stuffing it in gloves and scuba diving up and down. It was chaotic but fear of a storm suddenly appearing to disrupt the bottom at 15 feet drove them to up to six (6) tanks of air over a five hour period in the recovery.

Eventually 2,500 golden doubloons were uncovered at the one site, probably the contents of one chest, its wooden sides eaten away by worms. They dug holes all over the bottom area but could not effectively mark where they had dug so a great redundancy ensued.

The costs of hunting for treasure had to then be paid - by the treasure. Taking the coins brought up to the market place. By this time, it was estimated that despite short working seasons because of storms, approximately $3 million dollars of treasure had been recovered with $14 million or more still lost and recoverable.

Wagner and colleagues sold off the Real Eight Company holdings and went out of business. Fisher did the same and moved Treasure Salvors to Key West to begin his pursuit of another legendary treasure galleon. The Vero Beach Treasure Fleet of 1715 would continue to draw divers to its sunken graveyards for the decades to follow even to the present. And finds are still being made. It may have been out done by finds of greater value in the years to follow but nothing surpasses it as an event for luring divers and keeping divers going under.

THE ATOCHA

Mel Fisher's Nuestra Senora de Atocha is probably the last great treasure wreck find of diving's half century. It is historically impactful because it represents the human effort and long labor of the prospector divers. While some basic low tech equipment played a key role, it was more the hands on, "in the hole," physical presence of scuba divers that pulled it all together.

Mel continued his punching holes in the bottom over a vast suspected area down south of Key West-much to the chagrin of environmentalists and archaeologists. If there was or is some historical correctness to Fisher's system, it is a nebulous thing, and difficult to decide what is most beneficial to humanity.

Mel's wife, Dolores (Deo), is probably the best observer of the stress and sacrifices necessary to treasure hunt. She said, "it has always been this way over all the years going back to Mel's recovery of a galleon canon off the California Coast that turned out to be a sewer pipe. Mel suffered ridicule, disrespect, bankruptcy, criticism and even the sacrifice of the lives of son, daughter-in-law and friends in the long unflinching pursuit of the one great treasure wreck find from way back in the pioneer 1950's until on July 20, 1985, the Atocha became a reality."

Fisher's "Today's the Day" became a famous spirit-lifting battle cry in diving circles, as John Paul Jone's "We have just begun to fight" exists in nautical warfare history. It is an awesome display of determination, never-quitting confidence and searing passion in going after fulfillment of a dream.

In 1985, after a sixteen (16) year search for the grave of a galleon (the Atocha sunk in 1622, with $400,000,000 worth of treasure over 360 years ago) it was no longer lost. All that long search time yielded bits and pieces, a coin here a coin there, an anchor, silver, gold, chains, clues, but in a vast maze of dead ends. It was the mother lode Mel sought and found.

Desperation brought a psychic on board during the search and new high tech equipment was brought in finally to "see the galleon through the bottom with sound waves." Fisher obsessively tried everything.

During all this time, Fisher suffered a barbed shower of criticism and litigation. He was blasting holes in the "sacred bottom of the conservationists" and displacing wreck materials "belonging to" the archaeologists. He was operating in questionable ownership waters off Key West and State and Federal agencies were watching and harassing him. Investors from each new recruitment of funds were questioning, "What a share was in what?" It seemed like over subscription. "This guy (Fisher) sold a whole lot of sizzle but no steak ever gets served", was the cliché grumble of one investor. Later on in the 1990's after the Atocha excavation, complaints kept cropping up about salting the wreck sites to keep back up money flowing and that coins were being counterfeited and sold out of Fisher's treasure store.

Mel Fisher with his gold chain and Atocha treasure relics.

But in the days of chasing the dream, Zale Parry and Al Tillman saw the Fishers off and on; Mel with a gold chain draped around his neck talking confidently in a plush hotel room in Redondo Beach. And another time Christmas Eve in 1976, Al Tillman had stopped by to interview Mel only to find his replica Spanish Galleon Museum sinking into the bay mud and Mel scrambling around trying to make the holiday payroll for his crew. The hunt was always expensive and as talented as Fisher was at selling his dreams to others, it seemed he was always in need.

In 1965 on Flagler Boulevard in Miami, in the rear parking lot of a movie theater showing *Thunderball*, Al Tillman bought some wet, encrusted pieces of eight from Mel. The purchase helped in a minor way keep the perpetual expedition moving onward. "The trunk of the old beat up Cadillac was wired closed and the smell of "under the pier" rose from a bed of back coin clumps. It seemed dark and mysterious and kind of exciting, the perfect setting for a Mel Fisher lure," Tillman recalled.

In the hunt for the Atocha, a major clue found ever so often, real or created, seemed to fuel Fisher's unfaltering quest. A large bronze canon was found by Fay Field, his electronics guru, on a tow over a new area...and it initiated a junk trail in the mud that was followed into deeper water. Fisher's underwater archaeologist, R. Duncan Mathewson III, kept saying, "find the ballast stone!" But small pockets of gold, emeralds and silver were found causing false jubilation about "the Atocha found."

Every Fisher enterprise had always been a family activity. There were times when Mel and Deo had their relatives help them cut and glue wet suits to fill their dive shop business orders. Their four children, daughter Taffi, and sons Dirk, Kim and Kane were personally involved as a team of trained scuba divers, especially on this challenging treasure hunt.

Seven days after Dirk Fisher, oldest son had found five of the Atocha bronze cannon while free diving in deep water and there was an aura of joy that the Mother Lode was at their finger tips, a horrible tragedy struck. It was the dark morning hours of July 20, 1975 when the Northwind, a 74-foot converted ocean-going tug boat used on the hunt, sank. Eight persons were on board: photographers from *National Geographic*, Mel and Deo Fisher's children and crew. Donovan (Don) Kincaid and Kane Fisher were thrown into the sea. Dirk Fisher with his bride Angel and diver Rick Gage were asleep, trapped belowdecks and drowned. Virgalona picked up the survivors.

Deo explained to Zale: "Only much later, we believed what happened to cause the disaster...a faulty valve in the boat's fuel system. Fuel gradually transferred from one side to the other. At the end of the fuel transfer, the boat listed and went over quickly. As on all vessels, we had an occasional nightwatch. All seemed safe. Suddenly, Don Kincaid heard a voice out of the night. He heard, 'Look out up there.' It wasn't long after the message, he was in the water with Kane and the others who survived. In all the grieving that followed, Mel refused to be discouraged. He knew Dirk would want them to continue the work."

But finally Fisher's daily intonation, "Today's the day!", came true on July 20, 1985. (Ten years to the date of the tragic loss of Dirk, Angel and Rick.) At fifty-four (54) feet depth near the edge of a punched crater, divers Andy Matrocci and Greg Wareham saw a two (2) foot high mound of gray "loaves of bread"-silver bars! It was indeed the Atocha and Mel Fisher's life of treasure hunting had reached its climax. Champaign corks popped and Fisher people danced wildly.

Actually, Fisher himself was the last to hear of the find. He was in a local dive shop buying a mask and snorkel so he could dive and keep looking. The mother lode turned out to be seventy-five (75) feet long, thirty (30) feet wide, and four feet deep. It was probably buried under lots of sand and a storm had uncovered it for a short moment in time, plus there was better visibility that day in the underwater murk and so on top of great effort the element of luck was present.

The Atocha salvage was preceded by the find of the galleon, the Margarita. Fisher under the gun from the U.S. Government Agencies about ownership and archaeologists about destruction of history, made the excellent move to have archaeology ensue while the treasure excavation took place. So while 500 feet of gold chain and one emerald worth $1,000,000 highlighted the largest treasure trove ever taken from the sea by divers, a great deal of history-revealing artifacts were scientifically recovered and analyzed. It was determined the Atocha went down in a hurricane because a devious ship builder had used mahogany where tough oak should have been used in the beam-work and worse, he had skimped on nails.

The Atocha stands as a grand beacon luring divers to go treasure hunting over all the decades of free and scuba diving history. Mel Fisher let many scuba divers directly participate in this monumental experience and Mel as a youth reading *Treasure Island* by Robert Lewis Stevenson certainly represents why every child should read.

While there was scientific and pro-salvage involvement, it remains that the core motivations of exploration and discovery, the heart of recreational diving were grandly fulfilled.

MARAVILLA

Robert Marx, who was born in 1935, was Mel Fisher's counterpart in underwater treasure hunting during diving's pioneer years. Another reader, he found his inspiration in the exciting stories of Harry Rieseberg. Living in a sooty harsh Pittsburg built up an urge to run away to the sea.

Marx had some helmet (hardhat) experience in salvage diving as a teenager and got to California to get a taste of skin and scuba diving in the early 1950's. It all seemed to be leading to treasure hunting, especially the lure of the sunken City of Port Royal. It was forcefully printed on his wish list of diving experiences.

He got ample opportunity to dive during three years in the U. S. Marine Corp at various locations. He searched for the Monitor and from its erroneous discovery learned, he had to do research. He did that in the voluminous archives in Spain. It was a treasure house of information.

But even with this great research, it wasn't until he finally found the Maravilla wreck on the Little Bahamas Banks that he evolved into a pro-treasure wreck hunter. Borrowing the salvage vessel of Kip Wagner's Real Eight Company, he worked the Bahamas area with very little luck. Knowing that the Maravilla carried bronze cannons and had lost its anchors, Marx realized the magnetometer geared for ferrous metals would just have to be replaced by digging holes with the blaster, then scuba divers digging with their hands. It was Marx himself, who dug in up to his elbows and brought up artifacts and then a coin. Using a lemon, he found the date -1655. It was the Maravilla.

Marx described the find as being like a "kid in a candy factory". He dug holes and found cannons. They worked ten hours straight but even in the shallow depth of thirty (30) feet, one young diver got bent. Some of the ballast rock was pure silver ore.

Although many salvage attempts had been made over the years, the wreck site was never easily found but some divers later did follow up on Marx and salvage more treasure. Marx went hard at it when he realized word had spread.

Even working in haste, Marx tried to be archaeologically correct by tagging and to photo record things. Divers tended to put emeralds and coins in their mouths.

The Bahamas Government was unhappy and had heard Marx had taken treasure back to the United States instead of Nassau, where they'd get 25% by contract. Marx knew he had to hurry to find the main body of the wreck. He finally did, diving on his own. But with Bahamas police on the way to apprehend him, he decided to cover up the new major site which was two miles from where they'd been excavating. He dragged an anchor and other metal anomalies off the reef and over the side into deeper water.

Marx became a persona non grata and even after he returned the bulk of the treasure to the Bahamas, only his partners were allowed back to pursue more treasure. This was 1974. The found treasure was divided up but Marx would never get back to the wreck. His site of the main portion of the Maravilla with a gold statue of the Madonna and Child listed on the cargo's inventory was never rediscovered. Salvage ships still work the leavings since those first days. Like many wrecks, the full treasure and story is never completely written. Only Sir Robert can really tell the story. It is Marx's Maravilla and stories about it have raced the blood of all divers over the years.

THE SAN PEDRO - THE 16TH CENTURY GALLEON

The San Pedro went down off Bermuda. Edward (Teddy) Tucker changed his 30-year routine of Skin and scuba diving activity of salvage and game taking to recover lots of treasure from this and other wrecks. Mendel Peterson, the diving curator of Naval History for the Smithsonian was there in 1955 for the San Pedro excavation and describes a moment on the wreck - "green fire dazzled...emeralds set in a softly glowing gold cross".

The small island sitting mid-Atlantic attracted many ships running the seas between the old world and the new world. Especially Spanish galleons. A lot of them sunk on the reefs off shore.

Right place, right time, doing the right thing, that was Teddy Tucker. He first found an iron canon in 1951 but didn't get around to finding the big treasure (which was highlighted by The Emerald Cross by itself valued at hundreds' of thousands of dollars) for four more years. He was busy salvaging anchors and propellers. Even after the big find and taking treasure off of other wrecks in the years to follow, he was still a salvor at heart. Some of the treasure wasn't gold nor silver but things like grindstones off the British ship, Caesar. He sold several hundred to a Bermuda resort hotel for elegant terraces.

It was the most valuable wreck found in the pioneer days. Great publicity about it in international media focused many of the new breed of scuba divers on treasure diving.

THE MANTANCEROS WRECK

This wreck is probably the most noteworthy of any found off the Coast of Mexico's Yucatan. It's recovered treasures are somewhat shrouded in mystery and political intrigue.

The famous and infamous Sir Robert Marx surfaces here in his piratical early treasure diving days of the 1950's. The itinerant adventurer had determined to take his lust for adventure and diving prowess to the great Valhalla region of sunken treasure ships, the galleon routes through the Gulf of Mexico.

A good writer, Marx, got Clay Blair, Jr., Editor with *Saturday Evening Post* magazine interested in diving with him in the Mexican waters. Marx had been solo dive-exploring in Cozumel and Yucatan for several years already and located possible wrecks with the Mantanceros Wreck, the best prospect.

Rumors of treasures being fished up and taken to the United States spread to Mexico City where Pablo Bush Romero reigned as unofficial Czar of all diving in Mexico. He was the first to bring scuba into Mexico in 1950 and he formed CEDAM (Conservation - Education - Exploration - Diving) International to promote scientific facets of sport diving.

Bob Marx and Alfonso Arnold direct the recovery of a cannon off the Mantancero wreck in 1959.   *Pablo Bush*

Rights to dive Mexico's heritage ship-wrecks were sought by Marx and Blair but Bush had other ideas and there was a diplomatic flurry between embassies. Pablo recognizing Marx as a cutting edge underwater archaeologist and superdiver arranged joint expeditions to rescue treasure from the Mantanceros with historical artifacts going to the National Museum of Mexico.

How much valuable treasure the Mantanceros yielded remains speculation. A great amount of trade items, 200,000 small artifacts of historical significance is still on display in many places. There were candle snuffers, buckles, and crucifixes. The Skin Diver Magazine Museum had a bronze cross back in 1960 donated by Bob Marx. Al Tillman brought back one for the UNEXSO Museum in 1966 after a diving trip with Pablo Bush. Today in the Scuba America Historical Center on Orcas Island, Washington, a Mantanceros cross is part of the exhibit of a great treasure expedition event in sport diving history.

The Mantanceros wreck is covered in great detail in Clay Blair Jr.'s book *Diving For Pleasure And Treasure*, World Publishing Company, 1960. Marx, Blair and CEDAM headquartered at Acumal which became Pablo Bush's intriguing diving resort in the 1970's. But then it was a wild and undeveloped coastline and virgin diving. The expedition used a boat of Algimiro Arguelles, who had many times over many years seen cannons and anchors with other artifacts along the reef. Captain Arguelles was the one who sold some nineteen miles of shoreline cocoanut plantation to Pablo Bush. In 1996, nearly blind, he skippered Al Tillman and Pablo on another expedition across the Yucatan Channel from Cozumel to Acumal to look for lost artifacts.

An impressive list-of-techniques was learned in the Mantanceros Marx-CEDAM Expedition that became standard practices in later treasure diving:

Hookah was preferred to scuba for stability, how to hack through the hardness of coral, ways to lift artifacts, cleaning and preserving artifacts, and cer-

George Clark, Clay Blair, Jr., Bob Marx and Pablo Bush on Akumal Beach cleaning items recovered off the Matancero wreck in 1959.   *Pablo Bush*

tainly ways of dealing with foreign governments. Marx and Blair followed up the diving with extensive research to identify the ship and its story. As with many treasure seekers, greed turns to curiosity and underwater archaeologists are born. Blair went to the Spanish archives and finally identified the ship. Mantanceros was the Spanish merchant ship's popular name; its registered name was Nuestra Senora de los Milagros. They were able to survey the manifest which listed much in valuable crystal, knives, wine, buckles, spoons but no gold or silver. But who knows...contraband was usually the case with all cargo carrying ships.

Blair and Marx learned and spread the gospel of treasure diving-Do your research and then go diving. The Mantanceros is a landmark treasure dive in diving history and no one will ever know if and how much treasure may have been salvaged off of it since its sinking in 1741 or yet remains encrusted in coral.

THE WYDAH

Clifford had got his turn-on as a boy listening to a fisherman uncle tell of sighting glittering loot in the sands off Cap Cod. Pirate stories included that of the Wydah which was loaded with the booty of thirty (30) captured ships. Barry Clifford did his research and discovered that probably over 3,000 ships had gone down off Cape Cod since the 1700's.

Bits and pieces had washed up on shore over the years. The possibility that all had been salvaged already, as was true of many wrecks, didn't deter Barry's "hunch". Years of diving, expense, and consultation from Mel Fisher's experts on the use of the technology of the time was enough to discourage ordinary divers. What broke the ice was learning that shorelines change, recede. The Wydah was probably 700 feet farther out in deeper water.

There he found it, a huge museum of artifacts with treasure, which was, still remains, the most elaborate window ever found into how pirates lived in their short time in history. Barry Clifford with great intentions made sure all excavations were archaeologically correct. Even so, as usual with treasure finds revealed, the years to follow would see time spent in courts. He hoped to eventually open a pirate museum...and of course, reversing roles, tell his uncle treasure and pirate stories.

LA CONCEPCION

The La Concepcion went down seventy (70) years before the 1715 Spanish Treasure Fleet got spilled over the Florida reefs. Overloaded with treasure and with rotting seams, a hurricane over a number of days drove it off course into the notorious Silver Shoals, a ship wrecking maze of reefs near the Dominican Republic.

Silver Shoals is the most treacherous run for treasure ships anywhere. It is a fabled graveyard for treasure divers. Salvage ships generally ended up sunk on top of treasure ships they were attempting to excavate. The Spanish didn't pursue salvage right away because they were fighting huge battles with pirates. The exact location of the wreck was a muddled mystery. Ships from everywhere searched but no trace was found until an American William Phips came along twenty-four years after the sinking. Phips got backed by an English king and other wealthy Englishmen to take several expeditions to locate the Concepcion.

Outfitted with the latest salvage equipment, a diving bell to supply air to divers, and the directions of a local fisherman, who had sighted the wreck. It was a cannon sticking up from the totally coral encrusted wreck site that put them on the treasure spot. Divers brought up an enormous treasure trove. It was only a part of what was there. Bad weather and pirates forced him to leave the wreck site. Another larger salvage fleet was dispatched for a return expedition. Word had gotten out. Dismayed Phips found dozens of ships working the site upon his return. The easy cache had been found and recovered. The main bulk of the riches were deeply cemented into the reef.

Centuries went by while the location was forgotten. In modern times, Cousteau came to the Silver Shoals looking for the Concepcion but did not find it. Every treasure diver felt he must make a pilgrimage to Silver Shoals. Colonel John Craig wrote of finding black silver stains on reefs in Silver Shoals but believed extensive blasting would be required. Ed Link worked the area too, in the 1950's.

Two-hundred and ninety-one years after the sinking of the Concepcion, in 1978, a professional treasure hunter, Burt Webber, found a silver coin at the lost site. Webber had read the traditional treasure books as a kid and found his first "treasure chest", a slot machine, while he was diving in a stone quarry in Pennsylvania. He also had spent time with Art McKee on expeditions.

The site had been located with aerial photos and Webber designed a small handheld magnetometer. This tool was ten times more sensitive than a towed magnetometer. It, with an enormous amount of research by Webber's partner, Jack Haskins, did the trick.

Much blasting and cutting into the thirty-five to forty-five feet deep reef by divers revealed sand pockets which contained beds of silver coins. Eleven months of work produced 68,000 pieces of eight.

Real treasure divers persevere over years and years. As far as we know, many never make the big find.

EL CAPITANA - ART MCKEE'S WRECK

Someone has to be acclaimed the first treasure hunter of diving. Maybe it was Art McKee, who found mostly adventure in it, but not much treasure. Of course no one is sure about that. A helmet treasure hunter, Art was diving the wrecks of Florida and its Keys back in the 1930's and 1940's. He had the first permit covering all the wrecks from the State but since most of the wrecks were outside the legal three-mile-limit, it proved to be invalid.

When Al Tillman interviewed Art McKee at his Sunken Treasure Museum (A museum built of cinder block like a Spanish Fortress with a sixty-five foot tower from which Art could watch his wreck with a telescope). At Plantation Key in 1975, there was a feeling of being aboard a tattered ghost ship with an old sea captain spinning his exaggerated tales. "It wasn't the treasure. It was the fun of looking! I wish I could do it all over again with SCUBA. I think I had as much excitement as Lieutenant Harry Rieseberg wrote about in I Dive For Treasure. That's the book that got me going even though I found out later, it wasn't too accurate. We all do it, treasure hunters, talk about the exciting things, embellish a bit, because there's plenty of boring times, disappointments, and penance in looking for treasure. The land stuff was terrible but I always enjoyed the underwater part."

McKee worked wrecks others had tried to salvage. He was on the Maravilla, at Port Royal, the sunken city, with Link before Marx. His most famous wreck was the El Capitana, the sunken flagship of a Spanish treasure fleet of 1733. A fisherman friend put him on the wreck, a hill of 250 tons of cantaloupe-sized ballast rock fifteen feet high, forty feet wide and 100 feet long. He picked at it for years even after he found a document that said the Spanish had salvaged all the treasure just following the sinking. Art moved the ballast rock. He accumulated a storehouse of some treasure. Much of it was historical artifacts. A mountain of iron cannons was gathered. He was the first to use an airlift on a treasure wreck. But scuba diving came along in the 1950's and allowed divers who didn't care about any permits to invade all of the wrecks including the Capitana.

Art decided there was treasure to be derived from other people seeing this wreck. He put in Art McKee's Treasures Ashore and eventually took people diving on it for $10.00 a head. "In 1979 I went back out with an impressive amount of the artifacts, especially the cannons and ballast stones. Then I redressed the site so that it really looked like a wreck. We did a good amount of movies, commercials, and still photos. All made on the wreck. I shot some myself with a Bolex. John Craig came down to shoot footage for a television film series called Of Lands and Seas. Mickey Spillane was here too. Divers helped me reorganize the wreck site. We got amazing publicity and the money helped me do all my treasure hunting later on. And of course, get investors."

Art, just as Fisher and Marx to follow, could get divers excited enough to put up money and give up jobs to go with him. He warned them that it was like playing the horses. Once in a great while with Lady Luck you find something. He warned them not to buy a new Cadillac before they went. Art went back, as many as fifty times to one site. His driving interest took him into the use of Link's magnetometer. He worked the entire Caribbean. One ship wreck, The Genovesa, a galleon with fifty-four cannons and three million pesos in gold, sank in the 1700's on Banner Reef near Jamaica, eluded Art McKee. The Genovesa was found by him nine months before his death from a heart attack in 1978, but yielded only a small amount of treasure or artifacts.

Art McKee and the Capitana lit the flame that drew armies of the newly emerging scuba divers into the sea in search of treasure.

CASTRO'S TREASURE HUNTER

A Canadian diver, Glenn Costello, new on the treasure hunting scene, has an exclusive deal with Cuba to recover gold and silver from three centuries of sunken galleons off it's shore. A 70-30 deal. By 1997 using archival research he'd discovered twenty-three ships. Archaeologists have been critical, seeing Costello as another treasure hunter destroying the pristineness of a wreck, before it can be recorded, to just get the gold.

KYRENIA SHIP

Michael Katzev reported on the Kyrenia Ship in *National Geographic Magazine*. A Greek merchant ship of the Fourth Century B.C...."was the oldest sea going ship ever recovered intact." Katzev, a graduate student, with his wife had been working with Dr. George F. Bass, who sent him to dive for Cypress Department of Antiquities for ancient wrecks. At ninety feet they found and excavated the site with scuba. Once again it was a wreck originally discovered by sponge divers. Over 400 amphorae recovered were discovered beneath sand with a metal detector and proton magnetometer. Bates Littlehales was there, as well as, Dr. David I. Owen.

Safety was a big issue (as it would and should be with wreck diving) that in this case would call for work at depth of ninety feet for forty minute periods, twice-a-day for three months. It would set some of the safe practices for all future scuba scientific wreck dives.

One other interesting experience was the solving of a mystery. Pieces of archaeology equipment and artifacts would show up missing from day-to-day. The perpetrator was a resident octopus who stored things in different amphora.

In 1967, George Bass now an Associate Professor of Marine Archaeology returned to the area near his 1957 excavation of the Byzantine wreck to tackle an older Roman ship in about 140 feet of water. *National Geographic* was a sponsor but the U.S. Navy was a major contributor. He took methods and knowledge from the 1950's and new type of equipment. There was a huge airlift, a pinpointing new metal detector and submersible decompression chamber. There was also a plexiglass underwater telephone booth to put by the wreck so divers could duck into it for fresh air and to talk to the surface boat. On the 1950's dives, divers hung on a rope beneath the barge and read pocket books that held up pretty well underwater. The books were in a bucket hanging at ten feet. The 1967 diving would allow four divers to sit in the diving submersible chamber and play chess in relative comfort.

Bass moved on to other wrecks. In particular one called the Negro Boy Wreck at 285 foot depths. It was a very big wreck but for the first time Bass brought in Dr. Harold Edgerton's side sonar scanner and a 600 foot deep submersible. It was the swan song for scuba diving for wrecks; the start of unmanned robotics to do the exploring and excavating.

YORKTOWN WRECKS OF 1781

Some say the American revolution was won in 1781, in the York River of Virginia. That state's first appointed archaeologist John Broadwater led a discovery/excavation to uncover the scuttled ships that represented that historic moment. In the 1970's in twenty feet down with terrible visibility, Broadwater had sponsor National Geographic Society's Bates Littlehales at his side to photograph these shipwrecks partially buried in silt. A wet cofferdam, the first, was built around one of the sunken ships to get thirty feet visibility. Five years of surveying led up to the excavation phase. Most of the nine ships discovered were intact to the waterlines. Broadwater had worked on World War II wrecks in the Marshall Islands, the Civil War Monitor and with Dr. George Bass off Turkey.

The upshot of uncovered artifacts revealed the quarters on board the ship were quite ornate. Thirty shoes were found, a common strangely preserved artifact found on many shipwrecks. But the notched logs uncovered were a real mystery until research showed these types of ships were actually workshops, where parts of fortifications were built for the forces on land. It was also found that these types of ships were not built to precision plans, but helter-skelter or "by rack of eye". Everything was removed from the site except the hull which was buried in sand.

In the bottom of the hull was the usually coal and ballast stones covered with sand. Wooden casks loaded with musket balls were found and gave new information on how casks were made. Sometimes there was valuable trading material from coins to beads - treasure.

Once again scuba divers have laid hands on a possible treasure wreck probably already salvaged just after sinking but still finding artifacts to give us our first real picture of what life was like aboard ships that were at the core of human existence centuries ago.

Many sport divers learned appreciation and caution from the Yorktown wrecks...another step in holding their interest and staying their slash and carry inclinations.

THE SAN DIEGO OFF FORTUNE ISLAND - NEAR MANILA IN THE PHILIPPINES

It was the earliest Asian ship ever found. A French group with National Geographic Society found and investigated it in the 1970's in the Philippines. Blue white Ming Dynasty porcelain valued in the millions by collectors was recovered and went into the Philippine Museum. The rudder was raised from 170 feet and was studied to find it had jammed as the ship headed for shore after being rammed. Outside of the cargo everything else was put back and a discovered wreck still lies there at a divable depth for sport divers.

S.S. CENTRAL AMERICA - THE WILDCAT FREE DIVERS DEMISE

In 1857 the S.S. Central America coming from the California gold rush sunk in a hurricane 200 miles off the Carolinas in 8,000 feet of water. Four-hundred lives were lost, as well as, twenty-one tons of gold.

In 1980 an Ohio engineer, Tommy Thompson, found her after 130 years. Thompson, as a kid, used a flashlight under the covers to fool with tinker toys and constructed his own scuba from a gas furnace regulator. In 1976 before his find, Tommy had gone to work for the "near-sighted Indiana chicken farmer", Mel Fisher. There he learned the chaos of treasure searching...no long term plan, worker turn over, unhappy investor, lawsuits, no search record kept, and how storms scatter remains over many miles. Tommy invented stuff, repaired equipment for Fisher, and decided to put together the "Swiss Army knife" of all the technology, the magnetometer, plus metal detectors, the ROV's with surgical claws.

He passed on the Titanic, Andrea Doria, La Concepcion and decided on the S. S. Central America, as the biggest treasure target in water not subject to government claims. The Church of Scientology was one of his backers. He put together the most planned use of up-to-date technology and made his biggest treasure find of all time. He was careful in his archaeological recording of the wreck site. He composed a large montage picture of thousands of shots of the Central America on the bottom and when he put his "eye loupe to it—" "It was just...it was just...covered with gold! I couldn't believe it! ...naaah, can't be....gotta be a lot of brass."

Gold it was. With the finding and excavation of the S. S. Central America, the boom era of the free diving wildcat treasure diver was over.

FIELD OF PIPES

Barry Clifford found the pirate ship, Wydah, (sunk in 1777) off Cape Cod in 1984. Then in 1998 the diving treasure hunter came up with a mass graveyard of French and pirate warships part of a thirty-five-ship fleet moving to capture Curacao from the Dutch. Clifford got the tip from a fisherman who had seen a "field of pipes" (cannons) off a divable shallow Venezuelan Island reef some thirty-two years before. Clifford was accompanied on the discovery dive by a son of Robert F. Kennedy and a son of Norman Mailer. Treasure hunting has a magnetic allure for celebrities, who were always needed as investors.

BILKED AGAIN AND AGAIN

The Los Angeles Times, October 1998, reported on a common dysfunction of treasure hunting that showed up frequently in the 1990's. A man named Dennis Standefer, who claimed a role in the S. S. Central America treasure salvage of 1988 and gave presentations here and about, was raising money to find and excavate treasure from a Japanese World War II ship sunk off the Northern Philippines. Investor money poured in and Standefer produced nothing over the years but some photos purported to be of sea explorations.

By 1990's conservationists and archaeologists were lobbying for restrictive legislation and treasure hunters were getting together and organizing. A Professional Shipwreck Explorers Association was formed in 1998 with several hundred members, pros and weekend amateurs. One great bilk reported was a treasure hunter's claim to have found the lost treasure of pirate, Jose Caspar, who turned out to be a fictitious character made up by a Tampa real estate promoter in 1922.

Grand daddy of treasure diving, Mel Fisher, who found big treasure in the Atocha wreck in 1987, by 1998 was being accused of salting his sites with "finds" to lure investors.

Back to Standefer, who worked a "worthless" sunken wreck and even had investors come to Philippines to see the excavation work—a short distant away divers were working another 1899 wreck that was yielding silver, making headlines in the Philippines. Standefer had the government permits for the area and moved down to work the other wreck. He brought in a partner and more investment money.

Americans are suckers for treasure stories. Treasure hunters for all the legitimacy of their desire and effort often slide into fantasy to get the financial support needed to activate their dreams. Few sport divers can resist them.

"Until 1980's and 1990's, the study of shipwrecks has been restricted to sites no deeper than two-hundred feet, the limit for scuba divers. That means 97% of world's oceans have never been examined and those depths may hold more history than all the museums of the world combined," mused E.R. Cross, who sought rare shells over treasure wrecks.

TREASURE BEYOND SHIPWRECKS

There is no argument that 5,000 years of maritime trade saturated the bottom of the ocean with shipwrecks and treasure. Hurricanes and war took a huge toll. World War II provided over 900 sunken submarines—a few carried gold and historic art pieces.

But treasure gets dumped into the water for other reasons. High lakes in Mexico are reputed to hold the crown jewels of refugee Aristocracy from Spain while under the bridge of the river going through Reno, the "divorce capital," SCUBA divers recovered a ton of discarded wedding rings. Preserved hard wood logs worth a fortune have been pulled out of the cold depths of the Great Lakes. Cenotes and blueholes everywhere have yielded to divers the sacrificed jewels and relics of ancient civilizations. And, if you've bought a golf ball recently, you can designate as treasure the thousands of golf balls imaginative divers have dredged up from water hazards of thousands of golf courses.

Some divers have made a good living out of recovering bundles of fishing lures or bringing up outboard motors or even whole boats. It doesn't have to be gold to be treasure.

The paragon underwater-treasure for Peter Throckmorton, marine archaeologist and author of *Diving for Treasure*, is not necessarily the cargo but the sunken ship itself. He tells us finding the wreck can be a problem, sometimes to be solved with sonar, sometimes by listening to fishermen's tales. Once found for example, the wreck at Yassi Ada, where they retrieved 7th century gold coins, the archaeologists were able to re-create a Byzantine trading voyage from these finds. That's the treasure!

TREASURE WRECKS AND SHIPWRECK FILMS FROM 1957 - 1971
INTERNATIONAL UNDERWATER FILM FESTIVALS

In many ways the 1957-1971 International Underwater Film Festivals ushered in the focus on underwater photography for the pioneer sport of diving. The subject matter of the films also provided a fairly accurate spectrum of the things underwater that held diver's interests.

Shipwrecks and treasure were only about 10% of the topics covered but next to monsters, sharks and manta rays and such, they were next in line as most exciting and probably were number one on things that lured divers underwater.

Here is a list of the Festival wreck and treasure films:

- (1965) *Tobermory Wrecks* - Jack McKenney
- (1960) *Quest for Treasure* - E. R. Cross
- (1957) *Wrecks of Andros Reefs* - Leon Paddock
- (1959) *The Bottom of the Atlantic* - Peter Gimbel
- (1961) *2000 Years Deep* - London Underwater Research Group
- (1971) *Philippine Treasure Bonanza* - Tim Sevilla
- (1971) *Treasure of Glovers Reef* - Chet Tussey
- (1962) *Diving Into History* - Sidney Wagnall
- (1962) *Sunken Fleet of Marshal Rommel* - Demitri Rebikoff
- (1965) *Point of Antiquity* - Ramon Bravo
- (1970) *Gold From The Winfield Scott* - Dick Anderson
- (1970) *Five Fathoms To A Ships Grave* - Bob Dingman
- (1970) *Treasure From Five Fathoms* - Robert Marx

The past half century of sport diving witnessed the grand fulfillment of many children's dreams as they became adults and ran off to hunt treasure wrecks.

36

DEATH WATCH:
ROLE MODEL DIVERS DIE

DEFINING EVENT: LIMBAUGH'S LAST DIVE

Divers have occasionally died in the act. Some were just poorly trained or panicked or had an ailment that triggered during a dive. Several deaths in close sequence have brought on threatening legislation. The media on a slow news day has often led exploitative movements to restrict diving because it was inherently more hazardous than other sports.

Diving deaths (usually called accidents in the report statistics of diving's own research agencies) shake the confidence of many divers but they have tended to create greater emotional trauma in the families and loved ones who know the diving victim but don't know diving. The victims, the ordinary diving ones, usually appear to have made a stupid decision, short-cutted a procedure or exceeded their capacities.

Connie Limbaugh while serving in the US Army from 1943 to 1944.

The diving deaths we address in this Chapter are about superior divers who have been admired and respected in the diving community. When these role model divers pass on, especially when in the act of diving, all divers tend to realize their own mortality - and that no matter how good they are it could happen to them.

The most shocking death while diving was the last dive of the pioneer-diver-icon, Conrad (Connie) Limbaugh. It happened March 20, 1960, a benchmark year when diving was soaring into a popular attention role in leisure and recreation America. *Sea Hunt*, Cousteau's books and films, and emergence of national diving training converged to make it a banner year. Limbaugh could well have been the third most recognized diver after Cousteau and Lloyd Bridges's Mike Nelson. Certainly divers had elevated Connie Limbaugh to a deified status during the 1950's. Limbaugh was in process at Scripps Institution of Oceanography on the way to becoming a significant marine scientist. He had discovered a number of marine biology phenomena, pioneered films of these things and was the consultant everybody turned to in setting up training programs in the use of scuba.

In 1960 Limbaugh had been sent to Europe under U.S. Navy sponsorship to attend the World Underwater Confederation to which he was elected a director. Cousteau, himself, took him underwing and introduced him to the legendary French Divers Dumas, Falco, LaBan, Portaille, Ruig, Clouzot, Poudevigne, Girault and many others. Limbaugh was America's most esteemed diver and considered an equal among these French veterans.

It was Francis Clouzot and Michel Poudevigne who invited Limbaugh to come dive one of their special underwater caves with an unusual feature - a 70 foot chimney or deep well that ran from ground level to an air pocket in

Conrad Limbaugh and other Bottom Scratchers enjoy a break during a meeting.
Lamar Boren

the filled cave under which was located a cone shaped pile of rocks - the special feature they wanted to show Connie Limbaugh.

Limbaugh was an experienced and expert diver but a relative amateur at cave diving. But a diver is a diver is a diver goes the saying among the super divers; the ones you can throw into vortex of unknown forces and they'll emerge unflustered and with samples of whatever was down there. But cave diving, the idea of a ceiling over one's head, is a daunting twist on clear-shot-to-the-surface diving; there are special rules and special equipment. The National Cave Diving Association of America during the 1960's and 1970's formalized the way to dive caves safely.

We can only assume that these French divers knew the proper procedures and safety equipment. Why didn't they prepare the dive meticulously and carefully? There was no safety line on a reel leading back out of the cave, a partner line attaching the two divers, a compass, backup lights, a redundancy breathing system. Limbaugh was using borrowed equipment except for his camera and red-stripped swim trunks. Although Clouzot, who would stay in the boat over the underwater entrance to the cave, spoke some English and explained the dive plan to Connie; the veteran guide, Connie's partner, Michel Poudevigne spoke only French and Limbaugh only English.

Some knowledgeable divers who had experienced diving in foreign places where they didn't know the languages, have often had to bluff understanding. Al Tillman recalls diving with El Gitano, the legendary diving guide in Cozumel, who kept saying "Tiburones Mis Amigos" and smiling broadly, as they prepared to dive deep off Palancar Reef. "Yeah, yeah," says Al, "sharks, so what!" At 100 feet El Gitano whips out some conch meat and waves it, and here comes a fleet of sharks from everywhere, taking the conch from El Gitano's hand and then a piece he dangled from his flashing teeth. That was "Tiburones my friends," and Al felt some panic, not to show of course, because foreign divers always tend to challenge the traveling acclaimed American divers by showing them the more frightening experiences. Ego and pride forces the stranger in town to go along and show control and calm.

It would seem Limbaugh had every right and motivation to think he could dive with the best divers anywhere, with limited equipment and in strange and perhaps ferocious places. But things do go wrong and the best of divers shouldn't take shortcuts. Perhaps, that's Connie Limbaugh's best legacy - that the best of divers can't cheat on the rules.

Dr. Wheeler North was sent over to France to evaluate what had happened and report back to Limbaugh's sponsors and the University of California State Diving Board. He was taken into the cave with a U.S. Navy representative, Dr. Henry Menard, by the French divers. Bad weather was pounding into the cave and the black, spooky cavern caused disorientation - Menard by 90° at the well and North by 45° in the opposite direction. Looking at the ominous ceiling and jagged walls, Limbaugh was almost forgotten as the question of "What if my scuba fails?" gnawed at North. God, he was glad to see the light from the entrance as they ended this dive. It helped him understand how even a great diver could lose his way in the dark labyrinth.

Actually, only Limbaugh, as it always will be when a diver dies alone, could tell us what happened. Of course,

Connie enjoyed life and loved diving.

we are always interested in the surviving diving-partner-perception of the event. Let us look at Michel Poudevigne's account as relayed to us by Wheeler North:

Poudevigne and Limbaugh were together about 100 feet into the cave at the rock cone which rose 20 feet through the water to the opening of the 70 foot deep well. Connie had been briefed by Francis Clouzot and cautioned if lost to follow the fresh water stream that flowed over the salt water to the entrance. (Were the Clouzot English directions clear? - John Steelquist of Scripps Institution of Oceanography wondered if Connie would have died, if he'd spoken French).

Once again, there was no guideline used or connecting line between the two divers. The French had perhaps over-estimated Connie's ability and failed to use all the safety devices possible... they wanted to treat him as a fellow-pro. Actually, it seemed a simple cave dive, into the well and out, many amateurs had done it.

At the top of the cone, Limbaugh was trying to manage a light and film the well. Poudevigne put his light on the cone and came up to

Connie working in his "office" at Scripps.

Lamar Boren

hold Limbaugh's light. Then handing the light back to Limbaugh, Poudevigne signaled with his hands to "wait" and Connie gave the "OK" signal. The Frenchman dived down to get his own light, then resurfaced to find Limbaugh gone.

He went to the bottom, where water was clearest, expecting to find Limbaugh there. No. His air breathed hard and he went on reserve, making his way out to Clouzot in the waiting skiff - the last remaining hope was gone, Connie was still in the cave. Poudevigne returned to the cave all the way to the well, searching crevices of a different passage as he went, but the air ran completely out.

Clouzot by then was dressed to dive and went into the cave searching with the only remaining tank. He searched the well opening and the cone area. He did not go beyond into the labyrinth of passages and chambers and so he gave up with aching heart.

A flurry of searching attempts were made by firemen and gendarmes and commercial divers. World media picked up the story and everyone was shocked that one of the world's greatest divers could get lost and drown. Surely he had found an air pocket and was waiting there. Cousteau's diving group and the French Navy moved in a mass of equipment. For four days rescue divers ran the cavern's maze with really terrible storm conditions and rotten visibility. Finally, divers were lowered with hookah equipment down through the chimney of the well. They found fin-prints 280 feet back from the cone into the cave. Exactly one week after Connie disappeared, three yellow scuba tanks were sighted, then the hunched form on his side and with all equipment, especially the mouthpiece, still in place.

The who's who of the French diving world was gathered at the top of the well (but not Cousteau?) when tugs on the rope going down signaled they had found Limbaugh's body at 450 feet from the cone.

Wheeler felt it was all a bad dream as he stood nearby and that Limbaugh was infallible. This couldn't have happened to the man who had trained so many of the great pioneer divers, who had battled against the old timer oceanographers to make scuba a fabulous new tool in the study of the oceans.

Limbaugh had just failed a preliminary step to his Ph.D. and was feeling a bit dejected. And the possible thought crossed the minds of some of Connie's colleagues at Scripps that he may have just given up, taken his own life in a place that represented his lifelong passion. Others, knowing his insatiable curiosity, felt Connie got engrossed in the flora and fauna of the cave walls and wandered off in the wrong direction. Wheeler remembered how Connie could pluck marine life from canyon walls others could not see. Once on Santa Barbara Island looking for Indian arrowheads on the beach, seven people found none, while the keen observer, Limbaugh, found four in one of the other's footprint.

Limbaugh was buried in a small fishing village over-looking his beloved ocean with an impressive ceremony, a tribute from the French Nation.

Talking to the many top divers, who knew Limbaugh, it all remains a mystery but there are some note worthy inputs. Jim Stewart, who followed Connie as Chief Diving Officer at Scripps and his good friend, knew Connie, as a confident leader on a dive, and if he made a decision that turned out wrong, he would see it through...which is why he was 450 feet back in the wrong direction. Wheeler North never dove with Limbaugh when he didn't have a huge catch-bag and brought back specimens no one else even saw...so in the cave, he got absorbed in his passion of observing. Wheeler had been on the verge of flying out of Guatemala when a great uneasiness enveloped him at the same time Limbaugh was suffocating from lack of air. Bev Morgan, who found a mentor in Connie in the beginning days of diving, (with a strong friendship that led to Morgan's first born, a girl, to be named Connie Lyn,) on March 20th, 1960, felt a sense of distress and heard Connie calling him. He went outside to ask "Where's Connie?"

Al Tillman recalls, when he and Bev Morgan were taking a final ocean test with Limbaugh in 1953, that they had to swim through the pilings of the Scripps pier without a mask. Al can still remember crashing head-on into piling barnacles and cursing Limbaugh. He was on the pier watching, and when asked, "What did that show?" -

Limbaugh said, "When the equipment isn't there for you, you'd better think, go inside, and find your way. Be able to count on yourself."

Limbaugh died with equipment in place, no panic, thinking, until there was no air. Here's what, we imagine crawling into Connie's mind, thoughts we discern from all the input from those who knew him.

Connie's thoughts and actions went like this:

"I've got some film of this well which was what Michel wanted to show me. Now I want to look at some of the things growing on the cave walls. I noticed some interesting growths on the way in. Michel will pick me up, he's good and I'll be heading out and scrape off some specimens on the way. Mmmh, I should be near the entrance by now...Michel's probably gone on out the other passage. Oh, Oh, I've gone a long ways, a couple of hundred feet it seems and the entrance should be about here. It isn't. The air is coming harder and I'd better go on reserve. That's a nice calciferous growth in that crevice, almost luminescent, better scrape some to take back, no, I'll come back for it. I don't have enough air. I think I've gone the wrong way. I should have picked up that fresh water stream in the top of the cave. There's the water moving in the opposite direction from where I was heading. I've gone a long ways and I don't think I can make the well on the air I have left. Slow down and think. The air is coming too hard. I'm breathing too hard. Best to relax and let the fresh water stream carry me out. I've got my camera still but I set the light down when it went out. I'm not going to drown here in this cave. It would be an embarrassing thing to have happen. I want to get back to my family and there's so much ocean yet to see. We should have taken a safety line in. And what kind of an example am I leaving for everybody who believed in me...but I will not drown, swallow water. I will suck out every molecule of air with dignity. I feel light-headed and my chest is hurting from trying to suck more air out which is now down to nothing. I'm just going to...(darkness)."

Were these the thoughts in Connie Limbaugh's last moments? Maybe. There's an old writers' saying, "We know it's so because we made it up ourselves." With great respect, we felt we'd take a crack at it here.

No one stopped diving, none of the early pioneers, because their superstar of diving had been taken. They all certainly sat with their heads between their knees and with heavy heart to live in their minds-eye the last dive of Connie Limbaugh and how they might have behaved. Most felt they would have done the same things in the given circumstances, same as Connie, but perhaps not as interested in the growth on the cave walls. What it did was make the diving world realize that the very best can fail when all the necessary equipment isn't available and a careful dive plan isn't meticulously rehearsed. Divers all became much more cautious, they felt a new vulnerability.

Diving folklore is full of close calls, near death moments but you'll find those stories elsewhere. It is said that death is a most important moment in living a life. Many want death to come in the midst of doing something they dearly love to do. Let it happen on the playing field or in the ocean or a passionate intimacy.

• Bill DeCourt went out testing new diving concepts, mixed gases and a new scuba in the clearwaters off Cozumel in the 1970's. He was a Chicago inland kid awed by *Sea Hunt's* Mike Nelson. He ended up in San Diego, an award winning underwater photographer and a test diver. Somebody has to take the chances to advance the technology.

• There was Chris Whittaker on the Keller Dive in 1962, a partner with Dick Anderson on the safety and rescue team. Young but with highly regarded experience under certification by the British Sub-Aqua Club which maintained high and rigid standards. He was at a pre-dive gathering at Gustav Dalla Valle's house when he volunteered to team up with Anderson. Al Tillman, whom Keller had asked to recruit the volunteer team, was impressed with the extensive dive-log Chris had kept since starting as a teenager. Chris disappeared while assisting Anderson in a dramatic rescue of Hannes Keller and Peter Small, who had passed out after diving at 1,000 feet. Chris was on his way up from a second dive to 200 feet to signal that the pressure in the bell was secured and it could be pulled up. Fatigue, narcosis, whatever, allowed him to be swept away by a swift current and he was never seen again. Some said he shouldn't have made that second dive to 200 feet, and he was told not to, to get out of the water, but heroes react impulsively in the heat of emergency events and with no fear he went back down with the veteran Anderson, (probably one of the best divers in the world). It was a death that closely followed the loss of Limbaugh. It tended to reinforce a growing feeling that diving demanded a great deal more caution and planning on each dive...and not to let pride interfere with one's thinking while diving.

Al Tillman in interviewing Vince Van Detta in the 1970's about their joint efforts in forging the Los Angeles County Underwater Instructors Program, remembered how Los Angeles County was able to brag that it had never lost a diver. Suddenly in the same summer of 1959, two instructors died while diving. Why? One, Hal Gavenman was herding in his new students on their open water dive off a boat at Catalina Island when he floated into the actuated prop of the diving boat. Not exactly a diving death, but it blew the County's perfect record. Another instructor, Joe McCabe, was working with a crew of other instructors to recover a huge anchor off Catalina. It was deep and he went down alone to secure a life line, and down and down past the anchor and drowned. No one knows why, but narcosis was suspected. The County still hadn't lost a certified diver but two role-model-instructors lost put a dent in the County's shining armor and bragging rights.

• Death can come knocking at your door in the middle of the night. Al Tillman's good friend, Dick Bartlett, whom he had taught to dive and certified as a Los Angeles County instructor, was on his door step back in 1958, sobbing and saying, "I killed my best friend." Dick had been diving with Al at Jade Cove the day before and Al had taken the bus back to his Redondo Beach home while Dick went on to Carmel, California, with all the equipment to visit his best friend. Dick wanted to share this grand new experience with the friend who was a good swimmer and a likely candidate to be a scuba diver. Dick put Al's equipment on him, gave him a few pointers and off they went to the sea. They got separated and Dick came ashore after failing to reconnect. There was Bill's wife and kids anxiously pointing out to a kelp bed where they'd seen someone waving his arm. Dick found Bill entangled in kelp, held down by it until he drowned. He didn't know about surfacing with arms up to spread kelp or that the strands were easily snapped. Al assured Dick, it was not his fault. That just a few years ago, before formal training, the early divers learned scuba by doing it. It was a sobering night, reminding the head of the Los Angeles County Program how fragile life is when one tries what seems to be simple and runs into a crisis that demands prior knowledge. Dick recovered and so did Al but a heightened respect for instruction resulted. It was the case of a role model instructor who truly believed he could by-pass the burden of instruction and escort a friend safely through the scuba experience.

•Not to sound morbid, grim true-tales do teach lessons. Perhaps the learning occurs at a later time. In 1955, Santa Monica Boulevard Camera Shop, Santa Monica, California, had the only photo developing service that Parry Bivens and Zale Parry trusted to develop their 'precious' underwater 16mm footage and 2 1/4" size photo negative film. The movie film was sent to Kodak while Zale's Rolleimarin black and white rolls were developed by Curt Bernard. Curt was the camera shop's dedicated-to-perfection employee, excellent swimmer and borrower of scuba gear to take his own underwater pictures.

Curt had an assignment for a print ad that needed an underwater picture. He had planned to do it on his next day off from work and would arrange to use a friend's scuba gear. Surprised, Zale received the telephone call for the use of scuba gear. By now, she and Bivens had procured two or more of everything. Even though they had never lent any of their gear, (scuba gear is personal, private, like a toothbrush-possession not to lend.) they met with Curt in the Bivens' garage. Curt was handed Zale's personal Northill Regulator, since it breathed so easily, with instructions to lift the right-air-intake hose, if some water should get into the mouthpiece, and 'blow hard' to clear that water, a full tank of air and her weight belt with extra weights. That's all he needed. He left with thanks and a smile. The next evening's news on the radio announced that Curt Bernard, a skin diver, is missing off the coast near Malibu. Zale was devastated. Later they learned that he planned his dive somewhere near Paradise Cove, California. A place where the surge and current are unpredictable. In thinking of how Curt, smart and tough as he was, lost his life that day, the conversation wavered between - the surge rushed his body against the rocks, he was diving alone, he lost the mask and/or mouthpiece of the Northill regulator and/or consciousness and didn't recover. His body was found miles up the coast many days after the horrible radio proclamation. A shivering reflection calls to mind the Shakespearean adage: Never borrow, never lend and you will always have a friend.

• Al Schepperdorf was a champions' champion spearfisherman. During the late 1960's and early 1970's, he won diving competitions galore. He'd won the national championship. He was a world class diver, free diver or scuba. In Mexican waters, 1973, late in the day, shark time, he was off by himself, 200 yards from the boat when a Great White hit on him, a bite so terrible that he quickly bled to death. He may well have been the greatest spearfisherman of them all but took a big risk by himself at a bad time to be spearing fish. Spearfishermen and divers in general have gradually grown to ignore sharks over the years to the point divers are paying for trips to see sharks. But watch out what you wish for, they could show up and behave in a manner that took Al Schepperdorf's life.

• A lot of pioneer divers have passed away...at home over the years. If you gathered the old timers together today, they'd be shouting at each other because diving had damaged their hearing, and they'd be wondering how come with all the diving they did, not knowing much, they didn't die along the way.

Actually, its amazing with the millions of dives that have been made over the years there are so few deaths... and especially, of role model divers who often feel confident enough they can take chances, dive in perilous conditions, and go without complete safety equipment.

Every time we lose an important diver in a diving accident, we'd all best consider it a wake-up call to all divers that they're forever vulnerable.

37
THE DOLPHIN ENCOUNTER

DEFINING EVENT: FLIPPER THE TV SERIES

One of the great human needs is companionship. The search for a real and caring friend, a playmate, can cause a wandering search all of one's life. Mating is such a quest, too, as is finding the near perfect diving partner.

Over the years, we have transferred on occasion our interactive social relationships to animals, such as dogs, cats, and horses. It was natural for divers to expect to find another creature which could serve the purpose - underwater.

Greek and Roman mythology recognized the dolphin (Greek origin) and porpoise (Roman origin) as reincarnation of people of the lost continent of Atlantis, or messengers from God, or alien angels sent via UFO's to teach humans how to live in peace and love. Humans riding dolphins was a favorite theme from Greek mythology.

Right away we'd better get it clarified that the name "dolphin" and "porpoise" have been used interchangeably by researchers and writers. Researchers like "porpoise" because there is a fish called "dolphin". But there is a difference — dolphins have beaked noses, conical teeth and a scythe-like dorsal fin while porpoises have a blunt nose, spade-like teeth and a triangular dorsal fin. Dolphins average seven feet/110 pounds while porpoises are bigger averaging twelve feet/1,000 pounds.

Pioneer dolphin researcher Dr. John Lilly, author Zale Parry and Dr. Oscar Janiger, president of the Dolphin Society in 1998.
Albert Stevens

They are cetaceans, small whales of thirty species that include killer whales, belugas and narwhals. Dolphins have about 200 teeth and porpoise have about 80 teeth. Life spans of both average around 15 - 20 years. The dolphin, the common bottlenose one, that has gained fame for surfing the bow waves of boats, has been around in an aquatic form for 50 million years. Descended from a pig-like land creature, it streamlined itself through evolution into a fish-like form and is now found mostly in a pelagic or open sea environment. But the most important point is that it is the only other creature on the planet that has a brain equal in size to a human's. It is smart, solves complex problems, learns by observation, and seems to have a sophisticated language. It has a nerve system capable of high level thought processes. Although many scientists think the intelligence may be on the level of a dog, others think we can communicate eventually.

Dr. John C. Lilly, a psychiatrist specializing in neurology, caused a great stir back in the 1950's and 1960's pioneering dolphin research and worked hard to establish a "telephone link" because he felt "they had something to tell us." Lilly never gave up on his feelings that dolphins could have an intelligence superior to humans and kept searching for a language link throughout diving's history. Lilly took up scuba diving in the Virgin Islands, had a strong wish-list for human-dolphin interaction, and was one of the pioneers who laid the groundwork for all of our thinking about dolphins not being just another fish in the ocean.

Zale Parry spent time with John Lilly over the years and certainly had her "dolphin rides" experiences. By the end of the 1990's, Zale and John Lilly had gotten together and Zale relates this about Lilly:

"If Hollywood's Central Casting was selecting for the category of a mad scientist, on first appearance John Lilly comes to mind. He is as fascinating and interesting as the dolphins. Speaking with infectious enthusiasm and a twinkle in his eyes, he tells about his studies and relationship with the dolphins with sincere scientific jargon. He is a jovial, happy guy. Anxious to share his tremendous knowledge with anyone with an ear to listen. Most of our visits were in the company of Dr. Oscar Janiger, (one of the first divers to purchase his Aqua Lung from Rene's Sports in Westwood, California,) and Kathy Janiger, Laura Huxley, Albert Stevens and the environmental-intellectual presence of John Allen, plus Abigail Ailing, who were the key figures in the major Biosphere II Experiment in Arizona in the 1980's. (Biosphere I being earth.) Lilly was a guest in my home before a Blue Whale expedition in August 1998. On all of these occasions, John Lilly was up front - center stage with his projects. On the whale trip, he sat in the wheelhouse not far from the Captain. He named the various pods of dolphins, as did our marine biologists, David and Alisa Shulman-Janiger who directed the trip. Only two teenage Blue Whales were sighted, but dolphins were everywhere.

Jordan Klein and Flipper.   *Mako*

"What was John Lilly's most important point or factor concluded out of his years of dolphin research? He discovered the dolphins' ability to produce sounds similar to our speech sounds. In the experiments vocal transactions were started by a human shouting some words over the water of the tank in which the animal was residing. It didn't matter if it was a single word or many words. Eventually, the dolphin in the tank would raise his blowhole out of water, make some sort of a humanoid emission, or whistle or click in a dolphinese style, he explained. He called them "humanoid emissions." The dolphins became very accomplished in repeating a human vocal sound. Lilly explained that on physical examination, the vocal transactions showed them to be quite as complex as the human beings' vocal transactions. It's like Doctor Doolittle talking with the animals. A very, merry Dr. John Lilly."

Of course, it took many years for the general public, and divers, to understand that the dolphin was not a fish. It was a mammal that breathed air, gave birth to a live baby (one at a time after a year long gestation period,) and suckled its young. Evolution pushed the nostrils back on the head of its ancestor until it became a blowhole on top of the head.

The grand discovery finally made, probably through observations of many scuba and skin divers, is that dolphins like to play, play all of the time when not feeding. It's what they do. And they seem to like to play with humans when they feel like it and where they set the rules. Humans were so poorly equipped to swim with them that a bored dolphin could "pick up its marbles" and go home with a swish of its tail, gone deep in seconds, while a diver's awkward movement through the water didn't allow a quick human exit. Certainly, humans have hopelessly tried to keep up by inventing fins and adapting a "dolphin kick". It's dolphins' turf!

Going back to this search for a companion, Ivan Tors, after producing *Sea Hunt*, an underwater Western similar to *Have Gun Will Travel* in the late 1950's, followed it with a kind of wet "Lassie" TV series called *Flipper*, a dolphin (or dolphins) who starred in the action dramas. It was Ricou Browning, *Sea Hunt's* number one stunt man and the *Creature from the Black Lagoon*, who generated the idea, co-authored the book with his brother-in-law, Jack Cowden, and produced the series for Ivan Tors.

Zale Parry, who worked on movie and television shows with Ricou recalls: "Ricou sent his original storybook, *Flipper*, to Ivan Tors, who at the time was producing and wrapping up the series, *Sea Hunt*, in 1961. Ivan gave the book to his wife, Constance, to read and make a book report to him. It was through her excitement and insistence that Ivan created *Flipper*, the movie and the dolphin-story-series for television.

Decision made. Ivan in his Hungarian accent said, 'Okay, Ricou, I vant you to find a brilliantly-trained dolphin. We can start shooting de pilot picture soon."

Ricou had gone to every aquarium, including Marineland of the Pacific. He found that there weren't many aquariums at that time. There weren't any dolphins worthy enough to perform and be filmed on an everyday-basis for a lengthy series either. Ricou explained that on a drive through the Florida Keys, he found Milton Santini, who captured dolphins for aquariums. "Santini always kept one dolphin that would comfort and greet a newly captured one. He couldn't help us either. We finally captured our own. Five of them."

He said that it took six months' training to teach the dolphins to give somebody a ride. "It was difficult. The script called for the dolphin to give boy a ride. Ricou warned: "Flipper was not giving a ride for the boy's pleasure. It was give ride for a fish. Flipper nudged the boy for fish. A nudge, if not attended, could easily be a hard, painful hit. If the dolphin was mistreated accidentally or abused with anger for not following the director/trainer, it would take out its own resentment on the trainers or actors. I've seen it happen. Remember we're working or playing with a mammal that is also a wild animal!"

People think they're doing the right thing by swimming or scuba diving with dolphins. Not true. Somebody will get hurt just as those injured and killed by the so called 'friendly' whales. During the filming of *Flipper* dolphins became popular. Everyone wanted one in the backyard swimming pool. Everyone wanted to protect them. America with its fishing industry tried passing laws to stop killing dolphins. At the time, it was Russia who passed that first law to protect them. I don't believe there will be a serious breakthrough with dolphins in the future. There will be faithful, sidekick dolphins - conditioned ones - that will show up at the beach or resort setting. They'll be friendly but will they become our lifeguards? "I don't think so!" concluded Ricou, the man responsible for Flipper's astonishing accomplishments.

Flipper may have gone too far in taking humans beyond seeing dolphins as the playful-creature that rode the bow of the boat on the way to a diving site. We always seem to want to anthropomorphize, give human interpretation to behaviors of animals. The television show gave Flipper a very human slant. Remember the usual finish where Flipper comes up with a "smile on his face" and that chattering "laugh" - we've been told that Mel Blanc, voice of Bugs Bunny and other Looney Tunes characters, manufactured that distinctive laughing sound for Tors.

So what has been the good of all this for divers? The historic publicity for dolphins has always been very good in giving these big creatures a saintly quality. The mythology had always accented friendships with children and stories of people afloat at sea in rafts. Especially, stories by Second World War sailors aboard ships, about dolphins pushing people and rafts to safety and land. In recent history, the rescued little Cuban boy, Elian Gonzalez, the only survivor of a sinking boat. Elian told of the dolphins that kept vigil near his inner tube-raft when he was floating alone in the big ocean. Some of the stories have dolphins moving in as a pod to fence off a human from attacking sharks and even cases of dolphins ramming a shark in the gills to kill it. No one is sure of the dolphins' exact motivations as to possible human protection, but they do vigorously protect themselves and their young. Ricou Browning may think otherwise but some speculators think that dolphins could become the lifeguards of the future - for divers.

Margaret Bivens, age 3 in 1963, at Marineland of the Pacific.

AMUSEMENT PARK DOLPHINS

Ways to encounter dolphins has taken several forms over the years. Dolphins became the major attractions in oceanariums and aquariums during the 1950's and 1960's. These smart animals learned quickly to perform, leaping high out of the water and giving humans rides - and got rewards of fish and stroking. They perhaps were the actual trainers, doing what they felt like and doing it when they felt like doing it. They easily recognized sounds and hand gestures that would lead to fish rewards if they did what they did anyway to play.

This is the least of possible experiences with dolphins, for they are captive, some of their wild spirit is broken and the encounter is for humans out of the water.

For three decades, 1950's, 1960's 1970's, America was mushrooming amusement parks and water zoos everywhere - people were satisfied to find joy in artificial slides and just watching. Divers were infrequently encountering wild dolphins while diving, and they disappeared when divers tried to jump in their midst when they rode the bow of a moving boat.

Special centers were set up to train dolphins in confined areas and allow tourists to snorkel with them. The encounter was in the water, at least, but once again the captive creature was not the same as a wild one. The most renowned place has been Dolphin Plus in Key Largo, which is a small family operation on a canal with holding pens. They charge $75 for a half hour in the water with the dolphins. Ivan Tors, a great animal enthusiast, spent the early 1980's looking for a large dolphin facility where the animals could be cared for and be used in movies. He almost went to Grand Bahama Island and joined up with UNEXSO to create the facility there, which had a dolphin pool in its original plans. (Eventually, John Englander brought a dolphin experience to UNEXSO in the 1980's whereby captive dolphins would be turned loose to accompany the dive boats out to the reefs, allowing interaction, and the dolphins would return to their pens at the Club where they were fed.) Anthony's Key, the well-known Honduras dive resort, eventually had a similar dolphin experience.

Dr. Oscar Janiger, one of the research directors, with Albert Stevens, of Santa Barbara California's Delphys Foundation and underwater film maker, produced several movies with 1984 Olympic champions. They are Synchronized Swimming Gold Medalist, Tracy Ruiz, and Free Style Gold Medalist, Matt Bionti. Albert told the authors this story. As he was filming Tracy doing water ballet tricks in the open sea near Grand Bahama Island, where a community of dolphins reside, dolphins approached as expected. One of the male dolphins made a sexually motivated move toward her. She accepted the invitation to play and swim with it. When she encouraged an embrace, the dolphin in the same vertical position embraced her by holding her tightly with his pectoral fins. Stevens said, "Everything is an experiment. To walk across the street in Los Angeles is an experiment. Lucky Tracy had the right stuff to be a Gold Medalist. Breath-holding was important this time. Tracy deals with water like no one else on earth. No one on the boat nor anyone could have managed the dolphin like she did. If it was anyone else, they would have drowned. Like a Mozart, there will be none ever like her.

"For the film we floated a small barrel to see if the dolphins would jump over it. Matt Bionti is a big person and super- powerful with the new long swimfins. Matt swam hard and fast and leaped like a dolphin over the small barrel. It didn't take long when a couple of dolphins followed Matt's maneuvers."

Stevens continued his tales with dolphins. When filming for IMAX at Roatan Scuba Diving Resort, he said, "To be in the water with the dolphins at the resort, the trainer/keeper of the dolphins directs the group with full instructions on what to do and what not to do when in the water with the dolphins. The dolphins are familiar with the interactions presented. I had my camera on a float." Stevens continued his story, "the group went in the water, had the fun and in time got out. Then I went into the water alone to take an underwater light reading and approached the float for my camera. One dolphin came too fast, too close to me. He knew the trainer but not me. It changed position, mouth open, jaw clapping, aggressive. Then I got hit in the back like the force of a small truck. I knew it was intentional. Not a mistake. Why did it do that? The routine with the people changed. When people left the water, it meant 'feed me.' I changed the

Zale Parry was one of the first scuba divers to work with dolphins.

act by entering the water immediately after the group got out. Captive dolphins. They could kill you with their interaction. They're in charge."

The Grand Dame of Dolphins, Karen Pryor, in her 1975 book, *Lads Before the Wind*, a Diary of a Dolphin Trainer, writes about her encounters from 1963 to 1971 as a dolphin trainer on Oahu Island, Hawaii. She was put to the test many times by "bullies" and impressed by the dolphins' "almost superhuman mental faculties to be cleverer than man." Karen Pryor, with Tap Pryor's dream and design; with Dr. Kenneth S. Norris, the famous authority on whale, porpoise and dolphin behavior; and with a French-Hawaiian fisherman/naturalist, Georges Gilbert, put Sea Life Park in Hawaii on the map. It is a most successful dolphin meeting- place despite many difficulties when the plan was first initiated.

WILD DOLPHINS

The ultimate encounter, of course, is one underwater with wild dolphins. Most of the contacts so far had been with the bottle nose dolphin, although Karen Pryor trained many Spinner Dolphins during her time. For over thirty years, divers have been in contact with a pod of striped bottle nose dolphins off the Bahamas Banks. Howard Hall, with some divers who came every year to meet these dolphins, said that they sense these divers from miles away and came out of curiosity in the first years. Then familiarity bred friendship - the dolphin had gotten to know them. They brought their babies forth to show them off, as Howard Hall interpreted it. Then the dolphins and humans played keep-away with a red scarf, the dolphins setting the rules it seemed, no snatching the scarf away, it had to be dropped, and Hall suspected it was the dolphins teaching the humans the game. This was a rare interaction in the wild. Until more like-incidents are observed or experienced by divers, no one is sure what any encounter will yield.

Off of Bimini in the 1990's, a young woman trained to be a scuba diver in her physical education class held at UNEXSO in the Bahamas, took divers out north of the island for wild dolphin encounters. It was her diver's dream as a teenager, and now she's living it. Nothing like these great creatures zooming at you out of nowhere in deep blue sea.

Cousteau's team spent many nights on the Calypso after dives, wondering what the dolphins were thinking about man - pity and superiority perhaps. Jacques Cousteau felt that we could never bridge the gap that separates us.

DOLPHIN RAGE

Even beyond that, there is more and more evidence that there is violence behind the fixed smile. Dolphin rage? The warning humans get before a programmed Dolphin Encounter is "don't touch, don't look directly at them, keep arms at side while swimming, don't approach directly, don't get behind the dorsal fin" and more. Besides getting bored, dolphins can get peeved if humans don't play correctly or stop playing before the dolphin is ready to stop. They show anger by a clapping noise made by their jaws. They could butt a diver who does not follow correct nonthreatening procedures. They could even bite. They are wild animals. Forget the discovered equal, if not superior, intelligence. The tail is its fiercest weapon and could easily crush ribs and lungs. Humans can expect too much in interacting with dolphins, assuming too much about the apparent friendliness, and should remember the increasing number of dolphin attacks on people being recorded in 1990's decade. The most repugnant story from Brazil is of people, children, playing with a local dolphin, touching it until it got irritated with the physical contact. Two drunk men tried to put popsicle sticks down its blowhole resulting in one man killed and the other seriously injured. Another aspect of a darker nature is indicated by studies in Florida's Sarasota Bay since 1970. Male dolphins team up to attack other dolphin groups, operating like roving gangs of human hoodlums.

There is still a wonderful mystery about this legendary creature who could be well ahead of people in the power of its intelligence. Will divers crowd dolphins in their favorite places until they turn on humans? Density of a crowded space has proven to incite violence in lab animals. Perhaps, the dolphin may instead very well turn out to be just what Flipper seemed to be. Beyond that, there is a young computer scientist, David Cole, who had been pushing the concept by the year 2000, that dolphins provide therapy for sick and handicapped, especially autistic and retarded children. Dolphins seem to play doctor. With their echo location ability they can touch a human's immune system, give it a boost. Dolphins are certainly not just clowns making us happy, thinks Cole, who is a disciple of John Lilly. He believes echolocation energy resonates in your bones. It passes through you and travels up your spine. This all may be as much of a stretch as New Agers assigning extraterrestrial status to dolphins.

What we can be sure of is dolphins have given divers a chance to swim with a very large animal in the water. One that, if it has an attitude, could have vicious propensities but seems more likely to be a friend to dive with in the wilds under the waves.

NOTES

• Al Tillman figures he spent half of his early life underwater all over the world. The Bahamas especially was four years of daily diving during his overseeing the UNEXSO development. "Dolphins, only saw one or two from a distance while in the water. So they were a rare, very rare encounter in the pioneer days. I think I'm glad after listening to year 2000 stories of the vicious potential they may have."

• Gustav Dalle Valle was asked about dolphins by *Scuba America*, if he'd ever tried to ride one in open ocean. He said, "Do I look like a fool - those are big animals with teeth. I think I was safer in those Italian one-man torpedo submarines during the war."

• Bill Barada recalled how he tried to hold on to one in Florida in 1960's in a tank because he was trying to write scripts for the *Flipper* television series. He shook his head and said, "It kept 'bucking me off' although other people were doing it just before me. It was like a clash of personalities or something."

• John Steele, the renown artist who did so many great *Skin Diver Magazine* covers recalled for Al Tillman in an interview in the 1990's, "It was a strange out of this world experience swimming amidst them. They zoomed and undulated like ballet dancers in space and I never could catch that feeling in a painting no matter how hard I tried. That one experience justified going diving."

• Zale Parry tells of the incident with dolphins when filming a CBS Easter Sunday Special in 1963 with the stars of the *Beverly Hillbillies* television series at the Marineland of the Pacific Oceanarium. The sequence was on the stage of the dolphin arena. Granny expressed to Ellie May that if she dived into the water with the dolphins, she would end up as a shrunken grown-up. Ellie May dressed in a wet suit with a mask and fins, leaped into the tank with the dolphins never to be seen until Zale's three-year old daughter, Margaret Bivens, swam across the tank with a dolphin on each side of her. (Proof Granny was right!) Zale was in the water off camera as a safety for the child. When a third dolphin pushed Zale with great force to a far corner of the tank; Margaret dressed in a wet suit with a mask and fins was helped out of the water by the film crew. It was a successful film take but very scary business. The dolphins protected the baby.

• Like the chameleon's complexion, the changing beliefs in the nature of myths, the scientific interests, and personal encounters with dolphins presents the new era of dolphinology. Divers will play a key role.

38
HUMOR
LAUGHING THROUGH OUR SNORKELS

DEFINING EVENT: DICK ANDERSON

Diving wasn't all physics and physiology. It was a lot of fun even when it was scary and serious.

What made divers laugh over the years? When someone did a dumb thing on a dive? When pompous attitudes got punctured? Great minds have tried to define humor over the centuries and are still on square one. Sometimes what is funny to one person is a dud or distasteful to another. Then again there are stories or incidents that seem to levitate a universal belly laugh.

Way back in the dinosaur days of diving, the 1950's, America was watching and laughing at the slip-on-a-banana peel, slap-stick comedy of Lucille Ball, Jackie Gleason and Milton Berle. *MAD Magazine* tickled people's funny bone with its irreverence toward everything, making fun of icon, John Wayne and diving's own Mike Nelson.

Skin Diver Magazine in those days was not a bundle of laughs, and of course, never intended to be humorous - never was through year 2000. But there were bits and pieces. A Carl Kohler wrote funny things in the Driftwood letter column but his distinctive styled cartoons were the most engaging. One other contributor to *SDM* had an ability to tell a story, any story (written or oral), with a dry wit that might be likened to a hippy Will Rogers. Dick Anderson was a diver who couldn't just tell the facts - he was genetically coded to say everything for, if not a laugh, an appreciative smile.

Carl Kohler did a lot of talking in his column with male and female divers in almost equal numbers with a controversial, wobbling defense for and against what he called the weaker sex of diving. One of the thousands of letters sent to Kohler was from a little boy age 11.

1955 New Yorker cartoon.

Skin diver Magazine

"My mom and dad both like skin diving. There's never any trouble about who gets to go with who at our house because my dad knows who's boss - and besides, my mom helps him with his diving since she's better at it than him. I'm not kidding, either," he wrote.

Kohler's remark: "Tell me kid - how much did your ma pay you to write that letter, anyway?"

Dick Anderson's funniest writings appearing in *Skin Diver Magazine* were true treasures. Here is his malaprop in live-performance that was a comical mistake:

In the early fifties when Dick Anderson worked for Healthways, he did a scuba diving demonstration in a glass tank at the old Pan Pacific Auditorium. After each dive he'd stand on the tank platform and answered questions from the audience.

"Mr. Anderson, what can you tell us about this mysterious 'Red Tide' in Santa Monica Bay that's killing all the fish?"

"I really don't know. I'm not a marine biologist. All I know is that it's a bunch of minute orgasms in the water," replied Anderson. Dick didn't know why his response got such a big laugh until a few minutes later when his friend kicked him in the ankle and said, "Anderson, it's not orgasms - it's organisms!"

Dick said, "Well, I was close!"

It was Dick Anderson's films shown in Film Festivals and shows across America that filled auditoriums with laughter. Some would say the Anderson films didn't show the proper respect for sport diving. They were irreverent but not insulting.

Ripped Off!

By Dick Anderson

Some sonofabitch stole my wetsuit! I hate stealing. The only thing good about it is when you're the one who's doing the stealing. When someone else does it — it's despicable.

Well, I was doing a job near Redondo Pier and I kept my wet suit in a pier storeroom because my landlady seemed to get upset when I dragged the drippy thing home and slopped sand all over her cashmere carpets.

This was no ordinary suit. You've got to be specially suited for making daily 315 foot dives. The three hundred feet was how far I had to swim from the beach to get where I was going, and the fifteen feet was the depth. I had this White Stag Master Diver Suit, complete with leg pockets, that was so flashy and efficient looking that folks on the pier would stop me and ask if I knew Jacques Cousteau.

This suit was medium size, double nylon, black out and orange inside. They make them that way so you can hide a Garibaldi perch inside your suit without the Fish and Game Department wardens finding out. They are also handy for smuggling oranges across the Arizona border.

This suit was customized too, so you can recognize it when you see it. The Master Diver has a fly for those discriminating few who don't like to whiz in their suit. It's handy on the surface *and* underwater, although I wouldn't recommend it when diving in the Amazon; the biting cold is bad enough, but those piranhas are something else. Anyway, some guys don't care about such refinements as a fly. In fact, one magazine editor named Jack once told me, "Hell Anderson, that's the

only time I'm ever warm."

But back to the suit. When you get old and gray and senile, you like things a little easier, so I took the farmer John pants into Dive N'Surf for some custom work. I talked Billy Meistrell into putting a full-length double-slide zipper in the pants front — or maybe it was Bobby Meistrell I talked to. I did learn to tell those twins apart, but they keep changing their names on me.

Well, the pants zipper worked like a whizz. It would zip all the way to the crotch for easy entry, and the bottom slide would allow access to the apparatus for which the access was provided. Folks, there ain't another one like it as far as I know.

Besides the main suit, the culprit also bagged my brand new Sea Glove shorty undersuit that Bobby (or Billy) suggested I buy to replace the soggy one I had been using. *It* even had some custom work. You guessed it — an access hole strategically located to be in concert with the access zip of the suit pants.

The bandit also got my ear-cup hood and my 1/8 inch vest, so I had to get a new one from Bobby — or was it Billy. I didn't mind losing my boots because they were both torn at the seam, but the crook also copped a new can of glue to fix them with. The dirty thief even took six of my favorite wooden hangers, and it took me years to steal them from various fancy hotels around the country.

So, if you ever run across a medium-sized thief wearing the above described suit, you can do any of the following: 1) Punch him in the nose; 2) Send me his name, and if he's skinny and run-down, I'll punch him myself; 3) If you should run across him on a dive boat, wait till the return trip, put his weight belt in his gear bag, and throw the whole thing overboard along with his tank. I suggest you do this while he isn't looking. Then play dumb. That would suit me just fine. ᕙ

It was the way Dick told things that in mouth of others would probably elicit, "I don't get it." But lanky, broad shouldered Dick Anderson, with an inscrutable emotionless face, would put a tilt on almost anything with a sort of cowboy drawl. He was a phenomenal diver but it was his humor that people seem to remember. Wherever it came from, Dick Anderson was the crown prince of comedy in diving's history.

He had a young film audience howling at one of diving's "hazards", getting stopped by the police on the way to a dive and searching his car for a stash of marijuana that he had hid in his snorkel. At the dive there was a dog that dived and making an entry off the side of a boat that ended up with the divers battered and in disarray in a skiff tied along side. Buster Keaton, Laurel and Hardy may have provided some ideas for Dick. They sure were every kid's heroes growing up in the 1930's and 1940's and you could go to comedy school watching their sight gags. Funny is often bad things happening to other people.

There's no doubt that the way to a woman's heart is through her laugh track. Anderson's three wives could all attest to that. Brigitte, his lovely wife through the year 2000 recalls, "Here was one of the first dates with this strange guy who had my family's eyes rolling and it ended up camping beside a river on his claim land. For a week, Dick puttered in the water 'diving' for gold.

He wasn't getting any color that whole time and I was pretty bored although he did keep me entertained when he wasn't trying to find gold. I've got my stuff ready to leave when he calls me down to watch him slosh his gold pan. Pow! There are these small gold nuggets! Suddenly I had gold fever and didn't want to leave. Dick had one of those sly grins on his face so I never knew if he had planted the nuggets. I suspect so since there was a gold engagement ring there, too."

Anderson's humor was never mean or really prankish causing someone else's discomfort. There are wild stories that would make a deacon snort about jokes diving equipment salesmen played on each other. Salesmen were star players for the equipment companies and the best got away with whatever they wanted to do. Booths at the important National Sporting Goods Association Show were where most of the orders for the year were written, but salesmen John Cronin and John McMurphy were down at a corner pub "lifting a few" and regaling each other with funny stories...and plotting pranks. A typical prank reported by Gordon McClymons had Cronin and McMurphy getting a pig's head from the slaughter house and placing it in rival salesman's hotel bed.

The lifeguard crowd that was into diving early were young guys trying to top each other in the prank category. Putting Babe Ruth candy bars into the pool during diving classes emptied the water (..."is that what I think it is!?) Bev Morgan had friends who would stop at nothing. During the frightening Hitchcock film *The Birds*, the playful boys threw a chicken into the crowd from the balcony causing many near heart attacks. The next step was to wait for *Jaws* to appear on the silver screen in the 1970's and the pranksters to get a harmless hornshark or leopard shark and throw it into the pool yelling "shark! shark!".

Some of our best laughs in diving come from pompous self-assured dive leaders getting their

The well read diver.   *Bill Barada*

"knickers in a twist" as our Irish friends say. Nothing would get more guffaws than when a self-important dive instructor would assemble this strange breathing machine with a magician's flourish - only to realize he had put the regulator on upside down. In a publicity shot for the movie, *Underwater*, Jane Mansfield was posed with an Aqua Lung (furnished by René Bussoz) and her enormous chest. When one got past noticing Jane's boobs, even novice divers noticed with great superiority and hilarity that the regulator was upside down.

Al Tillman in his book, *I Thought I Saw Atlantis* told more stories about being a bumbler than being a hero. His pomposity got tweaked a lot he reminisced. He tells of a lecture before a very serious Finish folk group and he wasn't getting much merth from this inherent stoic audience, telling funny things as he showed equipment - suddenly they were roaring with laughter. Tillman quickly searched his mind and memory for what he had said that triggered it when he turned to see his five year old daughter holding up his jock strap she had taken from his gear bag. He also remembers rolling backwards out of a small dive boat only to hang head down looking at the tourist

LIKE THIS—Al Tillman shows his under-water technique in Sportsmen's Show display. Exhibit, sponsored by Los Angeles Examiner, is on three times daily.

The "Little Wet Schoolhouse" was a humorous way to attract people to learn more about diving.

divers on the anchor line waiting for their "divemaster" who had buckled his crotch strap around the boat's railing. That was when he realized you'd better be able to laugh through your snorkel - at yourself.

Many jokes we've had in diving have been conversion jokes, that is they've been adapted to fit diving. An example of that would be a bunch of longtime divers sitting on a boat deck after diving and telling funny underwater stories. Most of these divers had been together for years and the stories had been repeated over and over until they finally just numbered the jokes and shouted out #13 or #27 and the old timers would split their sides laughing. A novice diver along on trip decided to get involved so he shouted out #48 but nobody even smiled. He grabbed one of the veteran divers by the arm and said, "What happened?" "Well," said grizzled old diver, "some guys can tell a story and some can't."

But is there a pure diving joke, not transferred from dry land, that could be called diving's funniest joke or anecdote (which is a long true story joke)? Most old divers would probably come up with the following, (origin unknown) which Owen Lee would charmingly tell and relate in his 1950's book, *The Divers Bible*. It seems there was a diver who had "bought the store", all of the diving equipment on display, the bells and whistles and hanging hardware and had laid out thousands of dollars to be equipped to the ultimate for his first diving experience. At 75 feet he was almost deciding the view was worth all the money when a guy comes floating by without any gear, not even a mask, and the outfitted diver grabs him and writes on his slate, "I bought all this gear and you're here without any"; the ungeared diver grabs the slate, writes on it, "You damn fool, I'm drowning."

Predicaments underwater can be absolutely tragic where someone takes off a tank to slide through a crack in a cave and then can't get back or something like that. Jim Cahill who setup the biggest jobber company of them all, New England Divers, comes pretty close to being Dick Anderson's equal in story telling. He talks "Bawston" with a lilt of his Irish ancestry when he tells about his movie stunt of taking a car off a cliff into the water, which he is supposed to roll out of before it goes over only the door wouldn't open and... well you just have to hear Cahill tell it. Cahill could make you cry and laugh at the same time. His story of lobster diving with good friend and great

diver, Frank Sanger, is priceless. Sanger is minus an arm and a leg but dives like a champion. Cahill notices Sanger is up to his shoulder into a hole. He also notices that a lot of time is going by and Sanger isn't moving. Time ticks by and Cahill goes up to Sanger and looks into his mask to see if he's still awake, or conscious or alive. He sees a tear on Frank's cheek in the mask, then he looks in the hole and Sanger's left hand, his only hand, is locked in the vice-like giant claw of a monster lobster. Once again, it takes Cahill to make this anecdote sing.

The Squid Diddler Dive Club always had a sense of humor. Above is their club house after a particulary spirited meeting.

There was a period, probably the 1970's, when streaking, running through public areas nude, (remember the Academy Awards when a naked man ran across the stage by startled David Niven at the mike who reacted by saying, "...he actually has some short comings?") and mooning, dropping your trousers to show one's bum, was vulgar/funny. Dr. Joe MacInnis, Canada's most publicized diving scientist, was the grand marshall of such shenanigans. It was counterpoint to the serious things he did in diving. With Bev Morgan on a deep test dive in a chamber, he greeted the outside observers at the apex of the dive with his buttocks in the window port and talked Bev Morgan into doing the same. You could expect a MacInnis's dive boat returning to dock and an awaiting crowd of friends to be flashing a lineup of bottoms. MacInnis got Jack McKenney to get up on a limousine roof and moon people leaving one of the big film events in Chicago. MacInnis the Moon King had a dream of having everybody on a landing jet moon the terminal crowd through the windows or do the same through a cruise ship port holes. Many people laughed even while they were saying, "disgusting".

Jim Auxier reminded us of the Film Festival where Jack McKenney's films got their first recognition. It was in the glamorous Santa Monica Auditorium with a LSD hippy, masturbating in the balcony and moaning, who had to be removed. McKenny's films usually had a touch of funny in them, usually by ascribing anthropomorphism to creatures, seeing human behavior in their actions. An example of that would be sound tracking Chubby Checker's "Doin' the Twist" over a mother fish in a quarry twisting and fanning its nest full of eggs or a crab trying to negotiate a slanting deck slipping and sliding like a drunk, and Jack made the most of the analogy. But what Jim recalled, as a keen-eyed printer, was the blunder by our printer of the Festival program in putting a Voit Lung in a U.S. Divers' ad. Just before we opened the doors, Bill Barada, U.S. Divers' promotions manager at the time, came raging in with an advance copy. "You can't use these programs, we'll sue," says he. Auxier said that Al Tillman was going to hand out those programs no matter what, so he went out and got some plain stick-on labels and covered the pictured lung - and didn't plan to charge U.S. Divers for the rest of ad. You can guess what happened. Everybody peeled off the label and laughed. And pompous U.S. Divers got more attention and looked more human than anytime in its history.

There were divers who were just funny being themselves. Gustav Dalla Valle was probably diving's prize character. He was a brawny Italian Frogman during World War II, a champion spearfisherman, and spoke with an accent he never lost and which was hard to understand. He saw humor in lots of things, could laugh at himself, probably giggle would be more accurate - imagine giggles coming from a square-jawed giant. Gustav's stories abound, but Jim Christiansen, who tended to growl out such stories had the same magic way of telling stories as Anderson or Cahill. His Gustav-favorite-story has these two powerful hulks on a flawed boat trip out into the Gulf of Mexico where all power on the vessel shut down and no food supplies had been loaded by boat owner, George

Skin Diver Magazine

Youmans. Hungry and waiting for serendipitous rescue by the Coast Guard or someone, attitudes got a bit grumpy except Gustav seemed in high spirits and didn't complain about hunger. At some point Jim Christiansen noticed crumbs in Gustav's big brush mustache. The next time Gustav went below, Jim followed him and caught him stuffing his mouth. "Oh, Jeem," Gustav startled at being caught but composed, greeted Christiansen, "have a praline." Gustav had been dipping into a huge box of pecan pralines he'd bought in New Orleans to take back to his lady love of the time.

John Gaffney would chortle and fall down laughing at Dick Anderson. John's best laughs were when a rival, competitor "their enemy" had fallen on misfortune, went bankrupt, or distributed a defective product or was being sued. Some felt "the Gaff" had a great sense of humor, was fun to be around, but had little sensitivity for the common folk. The Meistrel twins and their wives were going to a meeting with Gaffney in his oversized convertible and John kept tossing cigarettes and trash out into the street. The Meistrels were the kind of guys whom you make town marshals in the old West, they glowed with integrity. They cared about the environment and didn't like "Gaff's" littering. The next day these serious men, who no one would ever mistake for standup comedians, got several barrels of trash and finding Gaffney's convertible with top down, illegally parked in the alley behind NASDS (National Association of Skin Diving Stores) headquarters, filled the car with litter. Sometimes "getting even" can not harm anyone but just be funny. Bill Hardy at San Diego Divers Supply, when he broke away from Gaffney's autocratic rule of NASDS, took all the NASDS decals and put them in degrading places - if you used the shop toilet, you'd be looking at one of the decals in the bottom of the bowl.

Instruction provided some of the best laughs. At the very first public dive course in 1954 at the Arcadia, California swimming pool, Bev Morgan and Ramsey Parks were instructing - had Mel Fisher in as a guest speaker and to show films on Manatees. The students were breathing from the Aqua-Lungs for the first time and were coming up saying how good they felt and the air sure was a surprise. Bev took one of the units and breathed from it. "Hey, Mel," he called, "see what you think about this." Mel who provided the rentals and air for this class, got that you-know-what eating grin on his face. "Well, Bev, it could be good ole' Black Label Jack Daniels air, sometimes we had more whiskey than water on trips and, well, that's how we rinsed the regulator."

A lot of instructors remember in the old days of "doff and don" or "ditch and recovery" testing of new scuba students, with all the straps of the original scuba units, that young ladies in bikinis would get tangled and end up ditching everything - "we mean everything." Also in the early days of "boot camp training", instructors or their assistants would harass students, pulling off masks and shutting off air. The funny part was that some students were outraged and adept enough to go after their tormenter and turn the tables.

The following are a few jokes and anecdotes from the past of diving that have varying levels of humor and reflect on the culture in American Society at a particular time.

• Diving had its groupies who hung around major diving events and attempted to associate with some of the famous pioneer divers. E. R. Cross told of the pretty young diver who breathlessly asked over her significant bosom, "What was diving like, Mr. Cross, when you were alive?"

• Diving historian, Dr. Sam Miller, decided to ridicule long ordeal stories of divers in his April lst newspaper column. He had himself out diving alone when night fell, a storm hit and equipment was lost - for hours - and then a huge wave swept him up and "deposited him...smack in the middle of Pacific Coast Highway...directly in the path of an oncoming truck, "which immediately ran over me and broke my leg - April Fool!"

• There was a diver who got sued for divorce because husband wanted his wife to get tattooed so he could open a circus. That same diver may be the one whose wife complained about the storing of his gear and catch in the bedroom.

• A funny made-up story they used to tell around the *Sea Hunt* set - stunt man Ricou Browning's daughters had some troubles dating after he starred in a movie. Girls would bring their dates home to meet their father - "This is my Dad, he is the Creature from the Black Lagoon" (Ricou played the Creature in the film), "Creature, my boy-friend - boyfriend, creature."

• Liability and lawyers have been a plague for diving. So divers chastise them by asking "You're diving and find 100 lawyers buried up to their necks in bottom sand, what do you have?"

Two answers: "Good start" or "Not enough sand."

• Dive shops turn a lawyer joke around by asking if you had heard the post office recalled their latest stamps. Why?

Answer: They had pictures of manufacturers on them...people couldn't figure out which side to spit on.

• Why doesn't a whale scuba?

Answer: Cause he got golf balls for Christmas.

• Kid peeing in ocean and mother tells him to stop, Jacques Cousteau wouldn't do that. Kid says, "Dad does it off the boat." Mother says, "That's why we don't eat the lobsters he catches."

• A John Gaffney politically incorrect favorite:

The Nazis taught the Jews scuba diving. First they issue only a 50 pound weight belt and taught a feet-first entry. Not meant to be cruel or anti-Semitic but, of course, it was. Some people would prefer, "The manufacturers taught John Gaffney to dive.......

One cheer-up E-mail that came to *Scuba America*: It went in paraphrase, "As you know my work - is on bottom of sea and I wear a suit to the 'office' - a wet suit. It's cool so to keep warm, a garden hose is shoved down back

Some divers even used humor for marketing their shops.

of the neck and a water heater sucks water out of the sea, heats it, delivers it to me. It's like a jacuzzi. It was going well until a terrible itching struck in my bum and I started scratching. The heater had sucked up a big jellyfish and pumped it into my suit. Up I went missing three decompression stops, scratching and shedding all the way until I surfaced naked to a bunch of laughing faces. Couldn't sit on you know what for days. So when you're having a bad day at the office remember me."

Frank Scalli might have been the shortest icon-diver to be in the sport. His personality was always up and he found humor in everything. When John Cronin hired him to be U.S. Divers National Sales Manager, John met Scalli's 4'11" mother and hugged her, off balance they toppled and rolled down a slight incline with Cronin still hugging her. Scalli shouts in mock horror something like, "Get your hands off my mother, you pervert." Scalli was one of the frequent visitors to the Andrea Doria wreck and he kept going back hoping to "liberate" one of the portholes from six rows of them, but he found they were all dogged down from the inside. He took tools and hit the hinge pins out and grabbed the port hole but it fell inward and wouldn't come through the hole. Scalli held on and struggled with it, wouldn't let go until somebody grabbed him to indicate they were exceeding bottom time. Frank wouldn't let go but as he was pulled away by his buddy, he finally dropped it and Scalli had one of his few down moments - the inside of his mask was wet with tears. He told the story laughingly in later years.

Dewey Bergman is fairly well accepted as the diver who opened up the dive travel business with his Sea and See Company. Dewey went to all these places ahead of the tours he set up. He often had to talk to the native population from a platform the chief would set up for him. So he always told this classic funny story that he said was close to what he'd experienced.

The visiting diver was telling the natives (half who were divers from birth, went to 150 feet with only goggles, and bumped sharks on the nose to scare them off) all about his diving experiences. They shouted "Unka Unka" continuously and the diver thought, "Wow, these dudes really admire me." As he was walking away with the chief through the village cow corral, he asked the chief, "Chief, your people certainly gave me a great reception but what does Unka Unka mean?" Chief says, "Sir, you are sanding in some, it means bull shit, bull shit!"

Given to him by a salesman of the product, Bill Barada tried the "new goggles" in his hotel room. These were one of the first contact lenses for diving to wear without a mask. The lenses looked like clear, halved ping-pong balls that were to be worn by inserting one in each eye socket. Barada was in great pain and try as he might, could not remove them. Fortunately, his buddy came to the door, laughed to see bug-eyed Barada in such a predicament, and assisted in removing the new merchandise from his face. Tragedy turns into comedy.

A sense of humor didn't make a good diver. Boyles Law and such didn't keep anyone in stitches. But like all of life, things to laugh at need to be found to make the great adventure called diving not just exciting but fun. Laughing, - it was what got you through the bad times and helped hold divers into diving over the long run.

NOTES

Dick Anderson's favorite funny diving story is condensed and excerpted here but his raconteur flare is still evident. Without question, this story is a fun read, but out of the mouth of diving's premiere storyteller, it takes wings and pummels the funny bone.

Abalone Divers Get My Goat

When Juan Cabrillo sailed up the California coast in 1542, according to local folklore, he left a few domestic goats on some of the Channel Islands. There have been a lot of goats on Catalina, but they're not over-running the streets of Avalon.

One of the first diving-adventure tales that ever inspired me was about a couple of footloose guys who cruised around Catalina, dived all the time, and ate a lot of abalone and lobster. But that isn't all. When these guys craved red meat they'd spot a tender, young kid on a steep cliff over the water. With one well aimed shot, the kid would fall right into the ocean and the pair would simply cruise over and pull it aboard. That night the kid would serve the purpose his ancestors escaped. He was roasted over a driftwood fire and devoured by ravenous seafarers.

In the late fifties, I palled around occasionally with a couple of actors who like to dive and cruise around Catalina. One was named Dick Norris. Among other things, he is immortalized in that epic, *Beast from 20,000 Fathoms*. It's the classic. The other actor was Britt Lomond. You will remember him as the unlikable Spanish Commandant in the *Zorro* series.

One long weekend we three cruised over to Avalon. Always short of money, we were going to live off the fat of the land. After a lot of lobster and abalone, we decided it was time for some red meat procured in the classic cliff-shot manner. But, by the time we actually got around to doing it, Norris and Lomond had developed other interests. The worldly demeanor of those two glib actors was just too much for the Avalon beach girls to resist, and the guys couldn't bear to pull themselves away. "You go get the goat, Anderson, and we'll interview for some cooks," they said.

I rowed out to my boat and cruised down to the East End. Here steep cliffs rise above the water and narrow rocky beach. I spotted three goats on the face of the cliff.

Dick Anderson photo of daughter Julie that ran in Life Magazine in 1961.

Now, I had always heard that kids were tender and delicious, and that young nannies were okay, and that old rams were tough as U.S. Royals. But hunger had a way of diminishing the negative aspects of the hunt. I figured if I bagged the ram we could pound the steaks like abalone and eat for a month. I sighted in on the ram and fired. Whap! The ram froze for an instant and then peeled off into space. He didn't splash into the water as the old scenario related; he crashed down onto the rocky beach. I couldn't just drive the boat over and hoist him aboard. I'd have to anchor and go get him.

Another problem was getting the big ram out to the boat. I wasn't sure he would float, so I got out an inflatable scuba vest to put on him. Then I stripped to my shorts and swam to shore.

That goat was a lot bigger than I thought. I mean, he weighed something like two hundred pounds. It was a real effort just to drag the carcass down the sloping beach. I put the scuba vest on the goat, fastened it securely and blew it full of air. Then I dragged the ram out as far as I could and started swimming. It wasn't easy. That goat was big and heavy, and had a lot of resistance to the water. I couldn't get a good kick either, because his legs were hanging down in the way. Thoughts of hungry white sharks were trying to overpower my waning macho.

Then, quite suddenly, the afternoon surface chop came up, along with a brisk breeze. I began gasping in a lot of water with each labored inhalation. Next, I was startled almost into coronary arrest by a sudden bump on the leg and dark shapes zipping through the chalky water around me. SHARKS! I thought, and released the goat. It wasn't sharks. It was a group of curious sea lions. At that point I was nearing the low ebb of my goat meat enthusiasm. I grabbed a massive horn and resumed swimming. Somehow I wasn't having much fun. Instead of getting closer, the boat seemed to be getting farther away.

By the time I got the goat to the boat I had sucked in so much sea water, and was so overexerted, I was reeling and almost sick. I climbed aboard and really strained to get the goat up and over the gunnel. It was hopeless. I just let go of the goat and collapsed on the deck for five or ten minutes. After I regained my composure and pulled anchor, the goat, along with my scuba vest, was lost in a sea of whitecaps.

Back in Avalon it took a while to locate Norris and Lomond and their fan club. "Where's the goat, Anderson?," they asked in unison. I told them the story. We went into the Marlin Club. As usual it was noisy, but this evening the noise was mainly concentrated on two slightly inebriated abalone divers who were trying their best to convince a houseful of unbelieving patrons that they had just found a two hundred pound goat, five miles at sea, wearing a scuba vest.

- Diving's funniest story tellers:
    Dick Anderson
    Jim Cahill
    Jim Christiansen
    Frank Scalli

Snicker, laugh, chortle, giggle, grin, smile, chuckle, and guffaw ought to be required skills for all divers along with how to avoid a shark attack or make an unassisted free assent.

39
DARING YOUNG MEN
ON THE WATER TRAPEZE

DEFINING EVENT: THE KELLER DIVE IN 1962

He lifted the round metal hatch in the floor and looked into inky, cold water. It was 1,000 feet deep.

No human being had been there before, uncapsuled, a free swimming diver. As he climbed through the hole and down the ladder extending from the bottom of the bell, the current swirled the United States and Swiss flags he had personally sewn together the day before - he became entangled.

"Damn," he thought, he would not be able to symbolically stick them in the bottom as great explorers have done ceremoniously throughout history. He stripped them loose and let them twist away in the current toward the bottom.

Precious seconds were like molecules of life slipping away. He had to swiftly get back inside the huge cylinder called Atlantis that had lowered him like an elevator to create a breakthrough in modern diving. The year was 1962 and the diver was Hannes Keller.

Al Tillman wrote the eye witness account for *Skin Diver Magazine* immediately following the dive and edited a film of the 1,000 foot dive for the International Underwater Film Festival in 1962. Keller wrote his report, the Coroners Office in Los Angeles had their say, and almost 40 years later, Al Tillman's son, Thomas, took an objective look and presented a comprehensive version over the internet. A composite of those reports and more will be the core of this Chapter.

THE KELLER DIVE

by Thomas Tillman

Two human occupants sat inside the steel cylinder called Atlantis as it was lowered into the waters off Catalina Island, California at precisely 12:06 p.m. on December 3, 1962. This cylinder was destined to make history on that day. The deck of the operations ship, Eureka, was filled with anticipation as Swiss scientist Hannes Keller and British journalist Peter Small descended to be the first human beings to ever set foot on the Continental Shelf, approximately 1,000 feet below the surface. This historic event epitomized scientific triumph under the sea, but would also end in the tragic loss of two men's lives.

The story begins in Switzerland in the late 1950's when Hannes Keller was teaching engineering in his native town of Winterthur. Keller was looking for a hobby to keep him occupied and early attempts at flying proved too costly for the young teacher. He was finally turned on to skin diving by a friend and he focused his efforts and spare time on learning all he could about the sport. He discovered through his research that very little was known about diving science and that the scuba equipment available limited free divers to less than 300 feet. Keller's scientific curiosity led him to come up with the theory that a diver could breathe a different combination of gases than those that make up the air we usually breathe and thereby extend the depth limitations imposed by human physiology. Keller discovered that several scientists, and even the U.S. Navy, had been experimenting for years with mixed gases and an engineer, Arnie Zetterstrom from Sweden, made a successful dive to 528 feet, but died because of mistakes by the support team on the surface. Based on this experiment, Keller went to the University of Zürich to meet with Dr. Albert Bühlmann, who specialized in the respiratory and circulation systems. Bühlmann told Keller that he believed that narcosis was caused by carbon dioxide, and nitrogen, as previously thought. These two scientists agreed to work together and Bühlmann recommended what gases Keller could use to make a safe deep dive. Keller attempted to use these gases by diving to 400 feet in Lake Zürich in a converted oil drum. The dive proved successful without any medical problems. Keller was ready to test the limits of the Bühlmann gas mixture.

Using early computer technology, Keller fed a quarter million computations into an early computer to find ascent times, depths, and decompression procedures. Armed with the secret Bühlmann gas mixture and these new calculations, Keller began to experiment with ever increasing depths. In 1960, he made a 500 foot dive and a two person dive to 728 feet in Lake Maggiore, Italy, breaking the previous record of 600 feet (made by a British Navy helmet diver).

After this record-breaking attempt, Keller was contacted by the U.S. Navy and they gave him a grant to continue his research for potential use in rescuing men off submarines. Keller proceeded to plan the historic 1,000 foot dive to take place off Santa Catalina Island, California. He built the 7'x4.5' Atlantis with a hatch in the bottom so divers could exit and enter at depth.

It should be noted here that Keller was operating on a shoestring budget and making this public event out of the 1,000 foot open water dive in hopes of sponsors coming forward with more financial support. The Atlantis, actually a decompression chamber in itself, should have had a double-lock configuration so medical help could enter quickly after the dive, and in hindsight, this became the major criticism of Keller's experiment in depth.

IBM (International Business Machines) had contacted *Skin Diver Magazine* in the year preceding the dive about helping stage the dive in the Channel between San Pedro and Catalina Island, California. The publishers felt their magazine aimed at sport divers could have a stake in what would happen, the possible use of normal mixed gases to shorten the decompression process. Almost 40 years later, sport divers use of mixed gases would loom the possible successor to atmospheric air diving. Oil exploration was red hot, and many sport divers were being recruited to this new underwater industry. The rough North Seas, in particular, were a great hazard to the working divers trying to follow normal decompression tables after supersaturation.

Skin Diver Magazine assigned their Director of Public Affairs, Al Tillman, to oversee *Skin Diver Magazine's* first involvement in an actual event that could change the nature of diving. Tillman met with Keller at Musso and Franks Restaurant in Hollywood, California. There was Keller, Tillman said, "looking like a freshman sci-

Al Tillman and Hannes Keller while scouting dive sites in the Catalina Channel.

ence student, glasses, spiky-hair, very thin and dressed in casual nondescript clothes". Tillman was caught up in Keller's enthusiasm and confidence but he had a lot of trouble keeping up with the technical explanation of the dive... Al recalls that at the time he felt he was still trying to put the regulator right-side-up on his tank.

"We set up several scouting trips out to the dive site, put together the media coverage and arranged for a safety diving team."

The diving team in the experiment would be Keller (don't ask someone to do what you wouldn't do yourself) and a British Sub-Aqua Club diving journalist, Peter Small, (*Triton Magazine* publisher). The safety team of divers (not expected to have much of a role unless there was some unusual emergency - which, of course, there was) consisted of a young, highly experienced diver, Dick Anderson, who volunteered and Chris Whittaker. Whittaker asked to join the team when a group of significant diving personages was meeting at Gustav Dalla Valle's home. The acceptance of Chris Whittaker was the second major criticism of the dive later on. Whittaker was at that meeting because Peter Small knew Chris' ability and wanted him on the safety team. "Too young," the critics were saying without noting that he had a top British Sub-Aqua Club ranking, an excellent dive log of many experiences and was old enough to fly a fighter jet into combat.

Keller in the outfit he wore on both his 425 foot and 1,000 foot record dives.

Tom Tillman goes on to tell how...

On the morning of December 3, 1962 the Eureka departed from Avalon on Catalina Island bound for an area where the bottom registered a little over 1,000 feet. Small and Keller had made several preliminary dives, one of which was to 300 feet, where Keller and Small swam outside the Atlantis for one hour. Small came down with a mild case of the Bends after one of the preliminary dives but was treated and given the go ahead for the final dive. At around 10:30 a.m., the Eureka was located over the dive site and Small and Keller began preparing for the dive.

A little after 12:00 noon the Atlantis began its decent. Keller and Small switched over to the special gas mixture strapped on their backs at 250 feet. At 12:29 p.m. the Atlantis reached 1,020 feet. Several minutes later the Navy observers and both the American and Swiss crews watched on television screens as the dark figure of Hannes Keller exited the hatch of the Atlantis and made history comparable to Neal Armstrong's first step on the moon or Charles Lindbergh's Paris landing. But that moment also marks the beginning of a series of mishaps that would end in the deaths of Peter Small and Chris Whittaker.

Peter small, Hannes Keller and support crew prepare for the 1,000 foot dive.

Al Tillman's eye witness account went like this in 'his' final report:

I knew Peter Small was mentally composing the lead line on an exclusive *London Telegraph* story as I watched him on the TV monitor. He was sitting in a strange- appearing pressure bell at a depth of 1,000 feet. He and the Swiss scientist, Hannes Keller, were about to set foot where no man had ever been before. It was, perhaps, the greatest diving experiment ever attempted.

I suppose we all held our breath - myself, Peter's lovely blonde wife, Mary, the Swiss crew, the American crew, and the U.S. Navy observers. An army of photographers were on board the Eureka to document the event with still pictures and movies: Lawrence Schiller for *Saturday Evening Post Magazine*; Peter Stackpole for *Life Magazine*; Paul Tzimoulis; Jim Auxier, Harry Wham, Sam Lecocq and Homer Lockwood. Zale Parry with dignitaries from the government and the diving community were on another boat anchored close-by. This was a historical moment...a breakthrough of a depth and time barrier that would allow man to eventually walk unencumbered and perhaps live on the bottom of the sea. At approximately 12:35 p.m., on the TV screen, a fin, a man's legs, his hips and chest, emerged through the bottom of the bell. It was Hannes Keller.

The dark profile hung suspended on the descending ladder while 445 pounds per square inch of seawater exerted its crushing and mysterious powers. Keller dropped the flags that he had planned to ritually plant in this virgin territory. But he went no further, for a series of tragic events had begun at this moment.

Keller said later that he realized from his manometer that there was not enough of his special gas mixture. He was forced to return to the chamber of the bell. Peter Small's story would never contain his sensations of open exposure at 1,000 feet. In fact, it would never be written.

I immediately knew that things had gone wrong. Keller's dreams and place in history hung with him on that ladder. He was not a man to turn back from ultimate

Al Tillman photographing the Atlantis on its descent.

achievement. I had seen Hannes and Peter Small execute the amazing feat of diving to 300 feet and stay there for one hour just two days previous.

The deck of the operations ship, Eureka, suddenly was filled with movement. The murmur of, "Something's gone wrong," stirred the silence. It seemed that the bell had been at its 1,000-foot depth for the intended five minutes. The command was given to bring up the bell. Wet cable spun through the pulleys and the bell filled the TV screens with bubbles as it ascended. I heard later that inside the chamber both men had slumped forward. Communications ceased, and the TV camera inside the bell no longer indicated that life existed there.

I saw the concern on Mary Small's white face. I saw the surface director of operations and Keller's best friend, Fleury Niggli, stride across to the two safety divers. The hatch on the bottom of the bell was not sealed. It was losing pressure, and therefore the bell was being maintained around the 200-foot mark. The divers, Chris Whittacker (19) of England, and Dick Anderson (30) of the United States, had mentally rehearsed their actions in event of this crisis.

I watched the divers leave the Eureka and made sure their return ladder was in place. Their bubbles erupted around the vessel, getting larger as they neared the 200-foot level.

They appeared on the TV screen. I knew how they felt, suspended in open sea, with no orientation to any stable object but the bell. Rapture of the depths can complicate even simple tasks at that depth. They turned off the exhaust valves on the bell and checked the hatch. It appeared closed. The job was done, and they were back on the surface in a total time of less than ten minutes.

But the chamber of the bell was still losing pressure. The hatch was not sealed. The pressure had to be controlled so Keller and Small would properly decompress. Someone would have to go down again.

I was leaning over the side of the ship, ready to assist the divers up the ladder, when someone asked them if they could go back down. I was talking directly to Dick Anderson and told him not to make a second dive. U.S. Navy Commander, N. E. Nickerson, was also urging the divers out of the water. Dick replied that he was well within decompression safety. He was concerned only for those two men whose lives hung at the end of the cable. In times of crisis, courage and the needs of others direct the actions of brave men.

Dick had moved to the cable and was ready to start down. Chris Whittaker had some blood in his mask, and I asked him about it. "A slight sinus squeeze," he said, "but I'm all right. How's Peter?"

He was too concerned with the safety of Peter Small to pay any more attention to warnings. Chris had found a hero in Peter Small many years ago, and I am sure no one could have prevented his heroic second attempt to rescue a man he admired.

Both divers submerged again with the protests still echoing in the air.

The divers appeared on the TV monitor, and then Dick Anderson filled the screen as he worked on the hatch. Dick related to me later the discovery of the tip of a fin which prevented the hatch from sealing. He wedged it back into the bell with Chris' knife. Dick then braced himself, held the hatch tight, and signalled to Chris to surface and tell them to raise the bell. Chris acknowledged the signal and started up. Chris Whittaker was never seen again.

Dick Anderson was finally forced to surface to find out what had happened. "The hatch is closed," he said. "Where's Chris?"

Several other divers were dispatched from a near-by research vessel but only succeeded in cutting off a stabilizing weight below the bell. They were caught in the upward surge of the bell as it rushed to the surface. One diver reported having his watch sucked from his wrist.

There was feverish excitement on deck. It seemed that Keller regained consciousness first and proceeded to take over direction from within the chamber. Hannes

The Atlantis is finally raised out of the water after its 1,000 foot descent. The crew looks on worried over the status of Keller and Small.

Homer Lockwood

administered emergency care to Peter Small under the communicated directions of Dr. Albert Bühlmann on the outside. I watched the amazing Keller on the monitor. He seemed very well indeed, as he efficiently manipulated valves in the close quarters.

It appeared that Peter Small was sitting on the hatch cover and Hannes a little higher on a ledge. When the time came to release the men from their prison of pressure, Keller could not move Small.

Tom Tillman's research account picks up at this point.

At around 1:00 p.m. the Atlantis was lowered onto the Eureka with Keller and Small unconscious inside. Keller awoke at around 1:05 p.m., but Small remained unconscious until 230 p.m. Dr. Bühlmann interviewed both men by phone from the outside. The Eureka was headed for shore by this time. When the Eureka finally arrived and the Atlantis was being lowered onto the Long Beach Pier with Keller and Small still in decompression, Small once again lost consciousness. When the

Atlantis was finally opened around 7:00 p.m., Small had no pulse and was immediately rushed to the Navy Hospital Ship USS Haven where he was pronounced dead. Keller came out with no negative physical effects, but was faced with both the legal questions and the emotional problems that were to result from the loss of two friends during his record dive.

The events of December 3, 1962, despite its tragic aspects, were a historic step toward significantly advancing undersea research. Keller and Bühlmann's work was cornerstone research for much of the mixed gas technology that followed. Keller had proven his theory and brushed aside the long decompression ordeals that preceded his experiment. The oil companies benefited by this new technology because it provided the industry with less cumbersome means of working on the sea floor. The Navy also benefited from their initial investment of funds and personnel with new calculations that advanced their knowledge of submarine rescue procedures.

Al Tillman summed up his feelings as follows:

I saw darkness on December 3, 1962, off the coast of California, even though the sun shined brightly and the water glistened. I saw two brave and heroic men sacrifice themselves for different reasons. Peter Small to help write history; Christopher Whittaker to try and rescue two men whom he respected and admired.

I saw courage and was proud of diver, Dick Anderson, who exceeded what is expected of ordinary men.

I saw Hannes Keller do something that no one has ever done before. He made a giant stride forward in man's conquest of the sea.

Here is Hannes Keller's short personal account of the 1,000 foot dive on December 3, 1962:

We tried to realize a 1,000 foot dive with 5 minutes bottom time as the final attempt of a series of dives. We were two divers, Peter Small and myself, both equipped with the same kind of apparatus and breathing the same gas mixtures. For better safety we were using a submersible decompression chamber.

We were reaching the depth of 1,000 feet and I realized that our gas supply was leaking. I thought the reserve would be sufficient for a couple of minutes, opened the hatch and left the chamber. While getting out of the bell, the U.S. flag which I wanted to plant on the ocean floor entangled with my air hoses. I needed a certain time to get rid of it. Then I went back into the chamber but the tank on my back was empty. I was feeling that things had gone wrong but could manipulate the main valve of air inlet and open the window of my suit after closing the door. It seems that then I lost consciousness from breathing the normal compressed air in the chamber. It was poisoning me with oxygen. Probably Peter Small lost consciousness after me.

The crew at surface pulled us back to 200 feet. I woke up and saw Peter Small was unconscious, and cut his rubber helmet and his suit away. His heart and his respiration seemed normal. I realized that the bell had been lifted on board the "Eureka". During the decompression handled by the crew outside of the chamber, Peter Small recovered after about two hours. He was completely exhausted but answered and reacted clearly. I gave him something to drink and sometimes some oxygen. He seemed to be all right but terribly exhausted. He was very nervous and changed his position every minute. When the ship was at the pier at Long Beach, I asked the crew to lay the chamber on the dock so that it would be easier to get us out of it. When Peter Small was awake he never complained about anything hurting him nor did anything hurt me. When the chamber was lifted on the deck, Peter was unconscious. I didn't try to wake him because I thought that it would be good for him to rest a little bit.

I was sure that we didn't have any decompression sickness or air embolism. At once I was uncertain whether Peter was still breathing or not. I began immediately artificial respiration with the mouth-to-mouth method. I gave the emergency signal and as soon as it was possible ordered them to open the bell and take us out. An ambulance transported Peter Small to a Navy hospital, and Dr. Bühlmann and I accompanied him. Waiting in the hospital, I got the bad information that Peter Small had passed away. We think that he had suffered a heart arrest. I had no symptoms so that we had the opinion that Peter Small was not hurt by a decompression accident. Decompression had been extremely long and careful.

The dive itself didn't hurt Peter Small nor is anything wrong with the gas mixtures. We had done 1,000 foot dives in the laboratory twice and a lot of dives up to 700 feet. Naturally such a dive in a chamber is a very tough thing because we were in heavy suits with two thick underwear-combinations. During compression and decompression, temperature in the chamber moves between 100°F and 20°F within minutes. This alone exhausts the diver. Naturally because these exploits are far ahead of everything that has been done in diving up to now, we can't base our actions on anything available.

Two days before December 3, we successfully performed a dive with one hour bottom time at 300 feet, which never had been done before. After this dive, Peter Small had some light pain in muscles of the legs. We wouldn't have treated him under normal conditions because it was not dangerous at all, and it is quite common after extended dives. But thinking of the 1,000 foot dive on the following Monday we wanted him to be treated in our chamber so that he would be absolutely all right. It is very important to say that his treatment doesn't have anything to do with the fatal accident on Monday.

The medical doctors who examined the body of Peter Small stated the presence of a lot of bubbles in the tissues. It would be wrong to say immediately that this caused the death. It could be that Peter was dead before we opened the chamber, or that at least blood circulation was already minimal. At that moment decompression effect would be reduced to zero and bubbles would appear anyway. Any dead body that has been under pressure develops bubbles.

It is possible that a lot of minor things acted together but we don't know anything for sure, nor did the autopsy give any conclusive evidence.

Keller was taken to the downtown Los Angeles County Sheriffs Headquarters. There he claims he was treated like a prisoner, that the sergeant in charge of questioning told him, "So far we have been kind," but they could easily change the atmosphere if Keller did not agree to talk to the press. Keller, tired and upset after the tragic accidents, agreed to talk to the press.

The newspapers, and especially the *Los Angeles Examiner* on their usual "death watch," dubbed it The Mystery of the Deep, highlighting that the Sheriff's detectives had taken a keen interest in the death of the British Diver, Peter Small. The Coroners Office in Los Angeles had been notorious for taking a high-profile-role in investigations of deaths over the years and newly arrived Dr. Thomas Noguchi became a celebrity star from the Coroners Office. Later he would get worldwide attention for his handling of the Marilyn Monroe death.

Noguchi had no diving background and his autopsy showed nitrogen bubbles in Small's tissues. He decided to blame Small's death on decompression illness. He said, "Peter Small obviously died of gas-embolism." Keller and his physiologist consultant, Dr. Albert Bühlmann, examined all aspects and while it can never be said for sure that some bubbles may have occurred due to decompression, what they finally realized was that Peter Small had probably died of anoxia. Keller in his final report refuted Noguchi's conclusion by pointing out that Small had not removed his mask and was probably without oxygen for 30 minutes. Dr. Bühlmann's revelation to Keller was that it was possible that a person who suffered from anoxia for half an hour could recover for a time (as Small did) and die later...and a dead person will develop bubbles in a decompression procedure, primarily because there is no blood circulation.

Much is speculation on both sides, and no one will ever know the complete story. The complete reports from all sides are in the *Scuba America* archives and will be there for future researchers.

Keller made a great effort not to let critics wash away the three years of effort he'd put in leading up to the 1,000 foot open water dive. He wrote rebuttals to much of the negative opinions, many given to the media before official reports were released. Colonel John D. Craig, who had been part of diving experiments with Dr. Edgar End in the 1930's, was appointed to Chair a Blue Ribbon Fact Finding Committee. Keller took issue with the report as follows in part:

"You speak of obvious violations of diving-safety, gave this information to the world-press, but neither the world-press nor I knew what you were speaking about. You spoke of a safety line for the safety divers without understanding the danger of entanglement with cables and lines to the chamber."

Al Tillman, Larry Schiller, Peter Stackpole and Navy Personnel wait for news from the medical team and discuss the tragic events once back on shore.

Keller questioned the expertise of the Blue Ribbon Committee, citing, in particular, the claim by John Craig to have made a helium/oxygen dive (79%) of one hour at 100 feet pressure with a decompression of two minutes. The U.S. Navy Diving Manual requires 57 minute-decompression for such dives, and Keller believed Craig in his 1938 book, *Danger is My Business*, claimed an experiment that couldn't have taken place and that his writing shows Craig is not familiar with the problems of deep diving.

The Committee, made up of members who were deeply involved in the Los Angeles County Underwater Program, were not invited to be part of the Keller Dive. NAUI Master Divers were used to document the 1,000 foot dive with cameras and were aboard: Jim Auxier, Harry Wham, Paul Tzimoulis, et al. Tension between these Los

Angeles County people and the rival NAUI, as a National Organization moving into Los Angeles, was suspected by some to have triggered the vigorous attack on Keller and on the man Keller listed as his "Chief of Standby Divers and Photography," Al Tillman, who was the President of NAUI at the time.

Dr. Albert Behnke, considered the Father of the U.S.Navy Diving Tables for Decompression, in a 1975 interview reflected on the 1962 Keller dive: "There should have been a double-lock chamber used for the descent, but I admire Keller for challenging the unknown as we did...and we had our share of mishaps in the Navy on the way to getting the tables figured out."

Harry Wham, NAUI instructor and Las Vegas, Nevada, shop owner, was on board the Eureka for the dive, filming it and he said, "I've never seen better organization than what Keller had setup, not even in the big casinos in Vegas."

Keller did have some kind of contract with the U.S. Navy Office of Naval Research and Experimental Diving Unit. Jacques Piccard did the same with the Bathyscaphe, Trieste, when he ran out of money. He and his father had been going deeper and deeper with different untethered submersibles until the Trieste. They were daring men on the deep water trapeze, for no one knew if their vessel would be crushed; nuclear submarines crushed at 1,000 feet as they found out in the Thresher disaster. Finally, in 1960 the Navy reluctantly, (because their rockets were exploding and failing) let Piccard and Lt. Don Walsh take the Trieste down to the deepest part of the ocean, the Mariana Trench off Guam. A side note is that the Navy reneged at the last minute and sent a cancellation message where a disgusted and tired CPO crumpled it up and shoved it in his pocket without showing anyone. Two brave men then plunged into the unknown to a place where no one had ever been before, where at 35,797 feet the 200,000 tons of pressure equaled five battleships pressing down. They were awed at the bottom at what they had accomplished, but the real excitement was seeing a living flat fish with eyes when they lighted the total and absolute darkness. To this point, scientists had mostly agreed there couldn't be a living thing under all that pressure.

So Keller, as Cousteau and Piccard before him, got some help from the U.S. Navy. But the Navy kept a ten-foot-pole distance from actually participating in the 1,000 foot dive; they sent as "observers," Commander N. E. Nickerson, who headed up The U.S. Navy Experimental Diving Unit (EDU) and Dr. Robert Workman, its Chief Medical Officer. Keller's plan, except for the secret formula for mixing the gases, was an open book, fully covered in the media. There was ample opportunity for the hovering experts to step in and correct any flaws.

The aftermath of the Keller dive had some dramatic moments as the impact of the event, like all modern happenings and mishaps, dissolved into the constant barrage of new challenges and discoveries.

• Keller went back to Switzerland where he had been a university professor of mathematics, married a beautiful Japanese woman, served his mandatory military time and supported quietly and less publicly, developed his procedures for reduced decompression in a special laboratory provided for him by sponsors.

• Mary Small, Peter's bride of a few months, grief stricken, committed suicide in the year following the dive.

• Chris Whittaker was a celebrated hero in his home village in England when the entire population turned out for his memorial service. Chris' sister authored a book about him and the dive, entitled *Last Clear Call*, stating the pride they had in Whittaker's bravery and sacrificing himself for his great friend, Peter Small.

• Dick Anderson continued on to be one of diving's most respected professional divers, the best and funniest lecturer on the diving lecture circuit, and much sought-after stuntman and prop designer in the motion picture industry. In 1999 for the motion picture, *Stuart Little*, Dick was credited for engineering the underwater series of guide ropes that followed the ten cables to pull the boats for the action of the sailboat race sequence. The knotted ropes directed the divers in the utter darkness underwater.

• Jim Auxier and Chuck Blakeslee, publishers of *Skin Diver Magazine*, took some criticism from elements in the diving industry because of the deaths. But in their usual style, they stood strong and issued this position statement:

Newspapers and magazines have played sponsoring or supporting roles in many of the great explorations and discoveries of history. When men come forward with daring and brilliant proposals for extending knowledge and understanding our environment, there can be no greater contribution by public media than enabling their fulfillment.

The periodicals of several countries saw merit in the new mixed gas applications for deep and prolonged diving by the young Swiss scientist, Hannes Keller. *Skin Diver Magazine* provided a communications center for the affairs surrounding the now-famous 1,000 foot experimental dive on December 3, 1962. Members of the magazine's staff observed the intricate preparations in the months leading up to this scientific breakthrough. They were there on that legendary day.

• Al Tillman narrated the *Experiment In Depth* film at the 1962 International Underwater Film Festival and exposed it to a hushed and disturbed audience.

Do we stop exploring and discovering this massive unknown world right here on our planet when some things go wrong, people die in the process? Should we have stopped Madam Curie or Lindbergh or our space program? Brave men and women will always risk their lives, and deserve support. They take us past the false images that ships would fall off the edge of the earth or that the bottom of the ocean was solid ice and nothing lived there. Tillman went on from the Keller Dive and NAUI to develop UNEXSO and eventually, write the history of sport diving.

• There is a prehistory to *Scuba America* and its half-century era 1950- 2000, and in some ways several endeavors may exceed the contribution of the 1962 Keller Dive and some of the other achievements that would follow. Our knowledge of the effects of pressures and gases on humans was sparse and in its infancy. The chances taken by divers

Zale Parry and Dick Anderson during a 6 1/2 hour crossing of the Catalina Channel in Healthways Sub. They were the daredevil experimenters of the early devices and theories.

testing the unknown are certainly magnified by lack of information. The risks were enormous.

The exploits of pioneer diver, Max Gene Nohl, are of great importance in how sport diving developed. Nohl, as a MIT student, designed a self-contained diving suit. His passion came of his teenage years of experimenting with bicycle pumps and tin can helmets. Nohl tried everything he invented but his "first S.C.U.B.A." was facing the huge problems of nitrogen narcosis, decompression and being able to carry enough air without relying on a supply hose to the surface.

Nohl was from Milwaukee, Wisconsin, which sits on the edge of Lake Michigan. A Marquette University physiology professor, Dr. Edgar End (M.D.), was also from there. Dr. End provided a breathable mixture of helium-oxygen to solve the aforementioned problems. He did experiments on animals and man (following the pattern, it is rumored of the British diving authorities experimenting with goats and then Irishmen) - those men being himself, Nohl, and John Craig. (Yes, the same Colonel John D. Craig, who Chaired the Keller investigation.)

Some felt End's mixture of gases and Nohl's self-contained equipment, as Fred Roberts states in his book, *Basic Scuba*, was the greatest breakthrough since the design of the standard diving suit in 1837. Dr. End recalled the funny and distressing unforeseen incidents that plagued the diving tests and brought on close calls, near disasters. On one occasion, Nohl was brought up in the suit upside down by the seasick tender team and left that way until the boat could take on storm waves that had come up suddenly and get to the dock.

On the famous record dive to 420 feet by Nohl with End, with Craig and Jack Browne of DESCO fame standing by, the plan was to dive to 350 feet using a safety margin for decompression of 375 feet. Nohl had three high pressure cylinders outside the suit into which he was sealed. One with 80% - 20% mixture of helium-oxygen, and two with pure oxygen. The helium was reused in rebreather style after the carbon dioxide removal. Nohl could carry out a 350 foot for five hours' dive with the system. There was a connection for a surface hose in case of emergency.

Nohl could arrest his descent at any time by a special brake attached to his descending line and reduce partial pressure of oxygen by a valve control. On December 1, 1937 at 12:50 p.m., the 26 year old Nohl started down, stopping at 200 feet to adjust his ear pressure. The telephone cable dropped a loop over Nohl and tangled him with the decent line. He fought it for 26 minutes but had to be raised to surface. Untangled there, he went back in and down to 420 feet, the bottom, in nine minutes. The surface advisors told him to limit the second dive to 220 feet but he shot past to the bottom. Dr. End was forced to adjust the decompression tables. He walked free, unclipped from the descending line for nine minutes, breaking the 22-year-old record by 114 feet. Diving had entered a new era. Later that year, the U.S. Navy would use the helium-oxygen mixture to go to 500 feet; in 1945 Arnie Zetterstrom would go to 528 feet on hydrogen-oxygen; Jack Browne went to a simulated 550 feet with DESCO helium-oxygen suit; then George Wookey to 600 feet in 1956. Only Nohl's dive was made with self-contained equipment.

Actually, Nohl was interested in treasure and salvage and it was why he teamed up with John Craig, who was making underwater movies (both Nohl and Craig would pioneer the diving lecture circuit). They were going after the Lusitania but it never came off. Nohl and Craig used the suit many times but never to such depths as the record, and it proved too unwieldy for their shallower dives around the world. Nohl had formed the American Diving Equipment Company in Milwaukee, selling a unit called the Hydro-Lung which fed air continuously to the diver (these were similar to old DESCO "E" Lung). Nohl switched over to salvage, his first love, until at 49 he died in a 1960 auto accident.

Moving to the early 1940's, we find the Cousteau group putting their lives on the line to find the limits of the Aqua Lung which is the true first scuba because of its demand, open circuit capacity. Cousteau was working with the limited knowledge of gas physiology at that time and came close on several occasions to losing some of his best friends in the tests. Later Cousteau would put his team in deep diving saucers and living in habitats on the bottom, none without a multitude of risks and mishaps.

And women can't be forgotten here. Zale Parry was the test diver for the early experiments of Dr. Parry Bivens, her husband, as he experimented with various gases and developed the portable single-lock and double-lock decompression chambers back in the 1950's. Zale set the world deep diving record for women at 307 feet on air in May 5, 1955. She said that for the dive she didn't sit in a steel capsule to just breathe. There was a list of concise tests to complete. A tablet, pencils, portable typewriter for over-the-phone dictation, small bolts, washers and nuts to put together and reading material were used to test mental proficiency and physical dexterity. It was an all-day-ordeal, with the rise and fall of temperatures the most indelible memory.

Then there's Sylvia Earle, who by herself in the self-contained untethered JIM Suit, walked on the bottom at 1,250 feet in 1979. In 1994, Dr. Earle lamented, "It's ironic that there are more footprints on the moon than there are on the bottom of the sea, and we're only seven miles away."

Others of this ilk, divers who had the blood we all have, a salty solution like ocean water, had some special ingredient that made them dare - and advance our knowledge. Bill DeCourt, who came into diving as a child fan of *Sea Hunt*, became an award winning underwater photographer and professional test diver, died in an experimental dive with a mixed gas unit, the Electrolung, off Cozumel in 1970's. DeCourt had told *Scuba America* in interview:

"When I went from Chicago to San Diego, I was all afire with being Mike Nelson, do what he was doing. When I really got into diving, I started feeling that we were supposed to be there, underwater, maybe become like fish, Cousteau's fishmen, but I knew we had a long way to go and we needed to keep trying things, find out how we wouldn't have to come back up."

Following Keller's dive, Skin Diver Magazine received a lot of letters similar to this one:

January 1, 1963

Dear Mr. Keller,

Being an amateur scuba diver has led me to become interested in spending prolonged periods at deep depths with shorter decompression. When I learned of your experiments I became interested, thus I read the articles containing information about your dives. Here I found little information about the experiments, in fact, some told a different story than others.

Even though I'm only fourteen years old, I think I may be able to develop the simpler pieces of equipment. I think you might be able to use some of my ideas. I know this sounds presumptive but I've thought of practically nothing else for a long time. If I could be of any help to you at all it would make me very happy and no effort on my part would be too great.

Sincerely,

Richard Mooney

Stockbridge, Massachusetts

And so what we have come to find over the decades is that daring and brave people, young men and women come forth to try things that no one has before, stepped into the unknown, put themselves deliberately in harm's way to find new information that has allowed diving to grow progressively better as a safe and exciting experience. Even when some of the events fail, they have been tried and we have learned.

The daring of these people has fueled the minds of more young people each generation and they have continuously come forward to be counted. They in turn have contributed new theories and put themselves in danger to test them. Let it be remembered that the ocean is just as dangerous as the ancient mariners imagined it to be.

Sport diving eventually benefits from all experiments. Knowledge is expanded by them continuously and divers will be safer and their horizons expanded because of it.

40

UNDERWATER SOCIETY OF AMERICA

DEFINING EVENT: *1964 CONVENTION IN MEXICO*

No sport ever produced the opportunity to go off from society and feel really free as skin diving has. Over the decades a lot of that freedom was lost.

It wasn't expected that divers would in part close that freedom themselves by getting together in clubs, regional councils, and nationally, as well as, internationally. Many in year 2000 long for the good old days when a diver just went out into the untouched liquid frontier and saw what no one had ever seen before and didn't have to follow any laws, or rules, or restrictions of society.

Some did it alone and some did it with a small group of friends.

Somehow the groups got bigger, became clubs with political parameters, by-laws, and elected leaders. Of course, with the best of intentions, the politically-minded divers felt that joining together would produce the num-

Council membership drive at the Aportsman's Show. Inset: Patch and logo for the Council.   Homer Lockwood

bers to pressure against government-imposed restrictions. The public and the politicians were in the process during the 1950's and 1960's and beyond of taking the ocean back, curbing the unlimited taking of game and artifacts. The great abundance underwater had an ending point.

A few clubs were trying to ward-off restrictive fish and game laws that would effect divers. Limits and closed seasons were being imposed on fish, abalone, shellfish, and lobster catches. There was always a hue and cry to disallow the use of scuba in taking some game. In Southern California, the Los Angeles Neptunes joined conservation associations and basically stood alone before other clubs through a Council of Clubs joined in. Individuals like Bill Barada, Homer Lockwood, Bill Walker and Woody Dimel were outspoken defenders of diving's access to game.

There were a number of not so famous individuals coming out of the clubs who put a great effort into unifying clubs into a larger body, a Council of Clubs. Some of these Councils were high-profile, well-publicized and from different parts of the country. The Greater Los Angeles Council, Northeast Council, Illinois Council, Florida Skin Divers Association, and Washington State Council were the larger organizations that led the way.

Some clubs resisted the Councils, refused to give up power to such a creation. The Boston Sea Rovers with its powerful Clinic was able to take on the Northeast Council at one point. They pushed into existence another Council for Massachusetts Clubs and caused a turmoil in the formation of USOA as to which Council was to be accepted as representing the clubs and divers of the region. Ultimately, they both were accepted.

In California, a San Diego Council, A Greater Los Angeles Council and a Central California Council tried to unify into a California Council of Councils. But no one wants to give up their power and local control to be part of a larger, cooperative whole. Similar situations plagued the formation of the Society from the onset.

America was rounding off from a stable economy of the 1950's and was amazed and curious about this new recreation of sport diving. It does seem at such a time there's always someone who steps up with an idea and goes ahead and does it. In this case, it was Dick Meyer, President of the Worcester (Massachusetts) Diving Club which was a member of the Northeast Council (Maine, New Hampshire, Connecticut, Rhode Island, and Massachusetts). He pushed and organized into being a National Convention of skin divers and their Councils of Clubs. It was held at the Hotel Bradford (rooms $8 a night) in Boston, Massachusetts on February 21 and 22 of 1959.

A month earlier on January 9th, the World Federation of Underwater Activities (CMAS) was formed in Monaco. It was an appropriate time for such things to happen.

The 1959 "Convention" gave birth to the Underwater Society of America designed to govern over all sport diving activities in America (being on the continent, Mexico and Canada were included) and participate as a member of the World Federation.

The following were at that 1959 Convention: Jacques Cousteau, Jim Dugan, Herb Shriner (diving's first entertainment celebrity into diving), Art McKee, David Owen, Arthur C. Clarke, Dr. Harold Edgerton, Nixon Griffis, and Gustav Dalla Valle.

The following Councils sent representatives:

Northeast Council - Jack Whelan - 50 clubs

Florida Skin Divers Association - Watt Taylor - 30 clubs

Connecticut Council - William Jacobs - 30 clubs

Illinois Council - Carl Hauber - 43 clubs

Ontario Underwater Council - J. Johns - 17 clubs

California (Greater Los Angeles) Council - Bill Barada/Doc Nelson Mathison - 42 clubs

Central California Council - Don Ferrin

Southwest Council - Hal Lattimore/Ray Meisen

Georgia Skin Divers Association - Gene Vezzani

South Council - George Krasle

New Jersey Council - John Brown

Empire State Council - Don Marchese - 52 clubs

Middle Atlantic Council - David Stith

Rhode Island Council - John McAniff

Washington (State) Council - Louis Whittaker

There were official representatives from sixty clubs and 500 "delegates" were registered. Underwater Society of America was formed under a governing board of all Council Presidents or alternates. There were great doubts among many as to whether the councils could cooperate face-to-face and produce a satisfactory union. Committees were formed at the convention to address issues facing diving and ten reports were made. The USOA was very concerned with legislation, instruction, and spearfishing competitions. Dues would be $3.00 a club plus 50¢ for each member; unattached divers came in as associates with no vote for $1.00.

Manufacturers were there to display equipment and help pay for the Boston gathering. It is significant to note that an inter-council unity committee had previously met on January 31, 1959, under the chairmanship of Jim Dugan (Cousteau's representative in America) to pave the way for the convention. Walter Feinberg told us that Dugan tried to alert this enthusiastic group about perils that lay ahead. The bulk of divers were going to come from Massachusetts and so how would they vote? One delegate, one vote and where then would faraway California fit in with its greatest number of divers in the country?

Dugan said, "...anyone could buy this voting procedure by just going down to the local pub and having guys to raise their hands." Dugan had a way with him and may well have been diving's greatest writer. He and Feinberg hammered out a constitution and Dugan coined the name *Underwater Society of America*.

Skin Diver Magazine at this same time was changing format to eliminate individual club reports and cover all clubs material under a section designated for each council. The move strengthened the role of the council and there by USOA in controlling American diving. But the Society wasn't satisfied and tried to put out its own tabloid and lost *Skin Diver Magazine* support.

No one seemed really sure of how USOA would relate to the World Federation. After all, America had the bulk of the divers in the world estimated by some diving analysts at 80%. The World Federation was presided over by the President Jacques Cousteau (of course) with an Executive Board of Serge Bern (USA) as Deputy President; and others from Switzerland, Italy, England, Portugal, and France. One of the key organizers of the 1959 World Federation Congress was Gustav Dalla Valle (USA).

USOA, as a bright and shining idea, would face the horrors of operating by correspondence, a far cry from the electronic world of year 2000. It was slow and ambiguous communication between the 35 members Board of Governors. Carl Hauber of the Illinois Council had become the President and his main job in the year following the 1959 Convention seemed to be trying to convince the diving public that the USOA was the best thing to ever happen to sport diving and would have a tremendous effect but what effect he seemed vague about. Feinberg, in a 1975 interview, said that Hauber just sat on the title until he got a diving job out of it.

Hauber did recognize that divers as individualistic and independent a breed of people as existed anywhere was the reason clubs and councils were hard to form. Despite this Hauber cheer-led the "bright future" of diving through a Society. There would be some rough roads ahead for USOA. Feinberg said diving had to be a strong activity to survive the failings of the Society.

Most of the hopes for USOA to get off the ground hung on the 1960 Convention which was bid for and won by the Southwest Council. It had to vacate the image of being a Northeast affair. George Youmans, President of the Houston underwater Club and the Southwest Council spearheaded the development of the actual first convention under the official USOA direction. Youmans would place the Convention in the new Shamrock Hotel in Houston during the humid, hot, and low rates-August of 1960.

Billed as the first Convention of the USOA (USA was dropped because it would be construed as United States of America and it took away the international potential) because the 1959 "convention" was really the formative meeting to set up USOA.

A Board of Governors met on September 27, 1959 to ratify the Underwater Society of America and over 400 clubs were united officially and legally. "It was the largest organization of its kind ever conceived," said Society Publicity Director, John McAniff. A motion to change the name to American Un-

Joe Dorsey entertains a group of attendees at the "First" Underwater Society of America Convention in Houston, TX in 1960.

derwater Society was narrowly defeated after long tedious discussions of other issues. Don Marchene, Ben Davis, Hal Lattimore and Gene Vezzani were the major advocates of the change proposal. The officers were actually elected at this meeting as follows:

President, Carl Hauber - Illinois Council

Vice President of Competitive Skin Diving, Del Wren - (California)

Vice President, Will Jacobs - Connecticut Council

Secretary, George Krasle - Southern Council

Treasurer, Lee Morton - Washington Council

Law Officer, Hal Lattimore - Southwest Council

Appointments by the President were:

Publicity Director, John McAniff - Rhode Island

Membership Director, C. K. Sherrill - Atlantic Council

Society Historian, Donald Kenley - Middle Atlantic Council

Director of Safety, C. B. Davis - Ontario Council

Nineteen Councils were represented and the major issue besides official ratification and drafting of the Constitution was competitive Skin Diving, which had been under the jurisdiction of the AAU, should be transferred to the Society. It was.

Two Councils were battling for recognition to be on the Board of Governors, the Northeast Council with 50 clubs and the newly formed Massachusetts Council out of twelve clubs. The Boston Sea Rovers were pushing the Massachusetts organization and Jim Cahill, who was then on a State Committee studying diving was a strong supporter. The committee was worried about depletion of lobster fishery by scuba divers, the danger of home-made equipment including the Momsen Lung and the legality of most air stations - issues that a national society should be facing.

A major breakdown for a national organization like the Society is the short term involvement of good leaders. Feinberg analyzed that club and council presidents only last about two years. New ones come in and have to catch-up with issues. By the time they got oriented, they were gone.

The 1960 Houston Convention proved to be the lynch-pin that solidified the idea that clubs through their councils could cooperate on a National level. A major event at the Convention was the first NAUI Instructors Course (National Association of Underwater Instructors) that bonded many of the pioneer instructors together. USOA was still assuming that NAUI would be the training arm of the Society. That didn't quite happen and while USOA, sort of , waffled about with political conflict at the Board of Governors level, NAUI solidified its position as an effective national training program. By 1961 at the next convention in New Orleans, there were demands for more control over NAUI and several individuals and councils had on-going training programs they didn't want pushed aside. Garry Howland and Al Tillman, President of NAUI, were there and they agreed that NAUI would go dead in the water waiting for USOA's large group of political leaders to ever agree and approve anything. They walked away and NAUI went it own way never looking back. Fred Calhoun was asked by the second President, David Stith, of Pennsylvania Council to help develop a program and thereby disassociate with NAUI. Calhoun had developed an excellent training program for USOA that certainly would have been equal to NAUI at the time but he couldn't get the popular vote. He would become a valued leader with NAUI.

The USOA Governors were pretty caught-up in creating a good National Convention and they did for a number of years. Unfortunately, the other areas of concern varied with the different issues geographically. Efforts were made to make diving into a competitive sports field that USOA would coordinate. Spearfishing was losing its popularity with the environmental movement beginning to emerge in America. Killing and taking things from the sea became a questioned outlet for skin and scuba diving. The very core of participation had been diving for family food and then competing for who will get the biggest and most. It represented the great American spirit of conquering the environment and it was slowly slipping into disrepute.

Clubs and Councils began to replace spearfishing meets with Skin and scuba skill's contents, "treasure hunts" with planted things, underwater hockey and of course, the new challenge of taking pictures of the creatures.

Carl Hauber was the first president of the USOA.

But USOA was getting its start just before this transition took place. They sponsored the National Spearfishing Team and officially selected the coach. Certainly divers were interested in how well our spearfishermen would stack-up against the rest of the world.

Feinberg, Bill Barada and Fred Calhoun, who were on the scene of the formation of USOA, felt that the Society made big mistakes. One was letting instruction get away from it. Two was setting the Society up like the United Nations with all those representative votes. Three was not following the British Sub Aqua Club-lead, whereby you could join their club/society before you became a diver. Then the British Sub Aqua Club taught them with a government subsidy. USOA wanted people to train to be divers and then become a member. British Sub Aqua Club eventually had all the divers with its system, but the USA Society never got more than 5% of the divers who

Coles Phinizy, Jordan Klein, Stan Waterman, Dimitri Rebikoff and Al Tillman made presentations at the New Orleans USOA Convention.
Joe Dorsey

were out there.

Fred Calhoun and other presidents who had great reservations about the Society ever becoming the major unifying force in diving said in retrospect why the Society idea failed. "Its conventions were the sole bringing together of the divers, primarily through their clubs, and the exotic locations were exciting venues for divers who had never left their own backyard diving areas. "The presentations at these conventions were weak and poorly organized," said Feinberg and Calhoun, who put on New England Clinics whose content was much more powerful.

Again it is well to remember the size and diversity of America and the difficulty any organization has in unifying interest. The YMCA instruction program was based on a mass of different local YMCAs which just did what they wanted. When anyone looked for leadership in USOA or YMCA, there seemed to be no one dynamic-person in charge. Divers were brought together by the instruction programs and then the shops. The interest in clubs diminished greatly in the 1960's as these other better contacts with divers took over and let divers be individuals.

The 1961 Convention went to New Orleans. The 1962 one was in Philadelphia. Not a lot of divers could afford to travel to these different places and stay the days required. The conventions would be the place where the Board of Governors would kill two birds and have their executive meetings. The 1964 Convention of the Society was probably when the Society was at its zenith and the grand locale was to be Mexico City. It was a pretty exotic happening and many of the dive leaders got to meet each other for the first time, more than at all the preceding conventions. It was also the first awarding of the NOGIs (New Orleans Grand Island) the Society's Hall of Fame System, that to that point had incestuously recognized people within the ranks of founders. The NOGI Awards went to Bill High, George Bond, Coles Phinizy and Al Tillman, achievers from outside the Society's domain.

The Mexico Convention was managed by Mexico's Pablo Bush Romero, founder of CEDAM (Conservation Exploration Diving Archeology Museums) and developer of the dive resort, Akumal. It was Pablo who took key diving-people after the Convention and introduced them to Cozumel which started the resort on its way to being, for a time, the most popular diving venue in the history of diving.

The 1965 Convention went exotic again, setting up in Freeport, Grand Bahama, where Al Tillman was building the UNEXSO facility which didn't quite get open in time to service the Convention. By this time, the old guard was still serving as the Board of Directors and trying to follow the vague mission that had lost its key reasons for the Society's existence along the way.

There was good strong leadership on that Board:

But it never got a chance to really take charge. An incident that the Society tried to forget was staging a Board Meeting underwater on a 25 foot deep reef with a conference table and chairs setup for the board members. Flip Schulke was doing the photos for *Life Magazine*. Many of the divers, when interviewed, felt that the idea lacked some dignity, especially when two Board Members were left out on the reef as the boat returned everybody to the Lucaya docks and the evening parties began - until some asked where the two Board Members were and a search party went out to rescue them.

Al Tillman who did the Film Festivals for both the Mexico and Bahamas Conventions recalls that it seemed conventions were being done for conventions-sake and not serving to ameliorate issues of the field. Tillman felt that the parties had become the major driving force to attract delegates.

Clubs, Councils, the Conventions started downhill at this point. Diving in general was coming off a slack period. America was engaged in international and domestic chaos stemming from a growing Vietnam War, Civil Rights efforts, and the counterculture movement.

USOA never recovered from this descent although good men and women tried to keep it afloat - and they did, barely, for it was in very shallow water. Other forces had moved into positions of power, the training agencies and the dive shops. The manufacturers ran to follow the transition with their support.

The Society hung around and a small following joined or continued to join because it sounded good to say, "Oh, yes, I belong to the Underwater Society of America". The power to govern Spearfishing Competition diminished, instruction was never Society business and no serious legislation needed to be nationally disavowed. Even when the 1972 Los Angeles County Ordinance "raised its ugly head" as Feinberg and Barada told us, the Society was a very small voice in protest.

USOA still existed by year 2000, putting out publicity on its own website.

In its display materials, the year 2000 Society claims to still sponsor the NOGI Awards, conduct a kids poster contest about danger to ocean, oversee competitive fin-swimming (accepted by Olympic Committee for possible inclusion in Athens Olympics 2004), produces beach photo contests, underwater hockey and rugby competition, sponsors the accident research of University of Rhode Island, testifies in legislation threats, has insurance for divers, and puts out a quarterly newsletter, brochures on how to form a club and rules for underwater sports.

And so it survives but is little recognized by the other organizations in sport diving, almost unheard of by individual divers and invisible to the general public. Other attempts were made to just pull individual divers together into a representative organization such as NAUI's National Dive Association which was a place for NAUI certified divers to be further involved with NAUI back in early 1970's but it didn't work and put NAUI into financial difficulties. PADI (Professional Association of Diving Instructors) is still holding onto their certified students with dues; PADI divers get a magazine called *Sport Diving* which followed up another PADI magazine *AQUA* which failed. It has been a major problem of preventing dropout in diving. Every agency has tried to hold divers together after they have been taught. But the idea of a national society of divers has never succeeded.

Clubs had their day, Councils, too, in creating an impact in the early days of sport diving history. The national concept helped pull divers from widely separated localities and get them talking about common problems and issues. But as Bill Barada remembers, "...there was a lot of arguing and positioning for political power and they never seemed to get to the issues."

The USOA did provide a platform for diving leader-types to try themselves out in a larger arena and that experience alone seems to have sent many stronger leaders back to their hometown regions better experienced for the battles of diving. The USOA story had told us what couldn't be done with divers, individualistic, non-joiners that they are.

41

AWARDS

DEFINING EVENT: NOGI

Someone wins and a lot of others lose. That's awards for you. Popularity contests, politically manipulated, all of that.

An award ought to recognize unselfish achievement beyond the call of any duties. It could also recognize amazing bursts of talent that add to the life of society. All of that, too.

Has sport diving awarded its finest and best over the decades of its history? There are some divers who have thumbed their noses at the whole idea, whose attitudes have been in line with the response of the bandit "policeman" in *Treasure of Sierra Madre* - "I don't got to wear no stinking badges." There are other divers who, John Gaffney used to say, "...have good publicists - and manage to get in the pictures at diving affairs." Big Jim Christiansen, who got his share of awards, was uncomfortable with them and would grumble that, "The worst whores in diving campaign for awards, call you up wanting a nomination or your support." Gustav Dalla Valle, who liked a good time as well as anyone, was often approached about receiving some award or another (the requirement was usually that you show up in person to get it.) Gustav would charmingly disdain it by asking, "Wot gud is it? Can you eat it? Can you drink it? So wot gud is it?"

Perhaps we need to differentiate between awards. There are those that are measurable where pounds of fish caught, size, number of dives in a career, are concrete criteria. A contest of diving skills can be measured objectively. That would be called a diving talent award.

The other award is for a diver who produces, organizes, guides an organization, event, new diving concept, invents equipment, and sometimes does many small things that benefit diving over a lifetime of achievements.

Many divers have had to stand and applaud some award recipient about whom they felt, "Why him or her, what about me?" Sometimes these awards are given too soon, a kind of bonus to keep someone working harder, and sometimes too late, after they die. The posthumous award is very popular - dead people can't compete for power.

Name recognition has plenty to do with getting a diving award. Unfortunately, there are many fine achievers "behind the scenes," overlooked because someone else has worked at being recognized. Cousteau's team voted to let Jacques be their public image and spokesman. It could have been Frederic Dumàs, whom we could have accepted as the icon, who created sport diving. We hope this book can go beyond the awards and give attention to many unfamiliar names, the unknowns, who were there on the scene, too, and contributed so much. The unknown soldier who represents the unidentified many who won the war, forget the generals, and so it is in diving.

NOGI STARTS IT ALL

But for this part of the book, we are going to analyze and acknowledge the various award programs.

Diving set up its unofficial "hall of fame" with an Oscar-like statuette called the NOGI. NOGI stands for New Orleans Grand Isle and was spun out of some late 1950's spearfishing contests held off New Orleans in its Grand Isles by two avid divers with big ideas. (They were trying to build oceanariums off the Gulf of Mexico before the idea was popular everywhere). They were Joseph D. "Jay" Albeanese and Louis R. Cuccia.

The two partners went to the Underwater Society of America (the national body representing all divers, but operating through the various regional Councils of Diving Clubs) with an idea that the Society could derive some status attention for recruitment purposes. A big selling point was that they already had an attractive award statuette, hand-carved, that they had used for their regional contests - but they wanted to see national meets through USOA use of the award. The Society wanted a broader concept, recognizing more than spearfishing champions. So Jay and Louis headed up a USOA committee and came up with four categories - Administrative (which later became Distinguished Service,) Sports, Arts, and Science. Jay Albeanese retained rights to the NOGI Program, but Harry Shanks, on behalf of USOA, got the rights from Albeanese's heirs.

The hand-carved statuette lost its sculptor in the 1970's but not before he gave Albeanese a mold. The statuette has since been cast out of polywood.

The NOGI Awards had their inauguration in 1960 at the Houston USOA Convention. NASDS stepped in for awhile to fund the statuettes. *Skin Diver Magazine* provided the statuettes from 1970 on.

The NOGI honors were determined by the USOA Committee in the first years of operation. Jay and Louis were two of the early years' recipients. Well . . . mmh . . . it was their idea and they saw it through.

Since then, nominations are requested in November for the previous year and expected by January 1st. They can be made by any member of USOA but are directly solicited from the past recipients. They must be accompanied by a resume of the nominated party. Past recipients serve as a Board of Trustees to vote on the final list of nominees. The NOGI Awards were fortunate to have a talented lady diver over all of its existence, Mary Edith "Mel" Lillis. Mel managed the awards procedure as USOA's awards Executive Secretary since 1965.

The Director of Awards for the Society was Harry Shanks who since 1967 passionately created NOGI as almost a separate institution from USOA. Harry Shanks had been a key developer of the Chicago Our World Underwater Program and used it as a stage for presentation of the awards. In the 1990's, the DEMA Conference proved to be a greater industry event, and the awards were made at a formal banquet, costing attendees from $35 in 1994 to $75 in 2000. Harry has had to put NOGI's figurative hand out to try and collect donation/membership fees from past recipients of the NOGI in an effort to sustain the awards and give them greater acknowledgment through the media.

ACADEMY OF UNDERWATER ARTS AND SCIENCE

In her acceptance speech for her DEMA Hall of Fame/Reaching Out Award, Zale Parry extended her gratitude to the Academy of the Awards and her diving peers for the prestigious honor at the DEMA Trade Show Breakfast in New Orleans, January 1994. Later that eventful day, while Harry Shanks and Zale were walking the convention floor, Harry said that he would like to place the name "academy" in the title of the NOGI Awards. "The Academy of Underwater Arts and Sciences sounds good, " he expressed to Zale. She responded, "Yes, Harry, but check with Hollywood's Academy of Motion Picture Arts and Sciences for any legal ties." Soon after, Harry Shanks transferred the main sponsor of the awards from the Underwater Society of America to The Academy of Underwater Arts and Sciences. It is not-for-profit and tax exempt. An alliance with Leslie Leaney's Historical Diving Society by 2000 merged the prestige of each into a greater image with better prospects of surviving.

DEMA GIVES AWARDS

NOGI held its own against encroachment by more specialized awards of various defined fields of diving equipment, diving doctor groups, disabled divers associations and by 2000, still could claim the title of diving's "Hall of Fame." But DEMA, (the Diving Equipment Marketing Association) decided in the early 1990's to gain more visibility for itself, as well as extracting support from people they would honor. Insiders say the DEMA Reaching Out Award was very political in the beginning. As Dick Bonin, DEMA's prime mover in its revival in the late 1980's and impresario of SCUBAPRO Company, remarked to us, "It was difficult to get anyone on the recipient list who didn't seem like a full-blooded commercial power in the industry. Some of the DEMA Board of Directors felt there were people who did things to make diving grow who weren't just selling equipment."

The Reaching Out Award was commissioned to Robert L. Straight (1989), who sculpted a pound of sterling

Vero Puccio working on a NOGI.

Andy Rechnitzer has won three NOGI's for his many achievements.

Al Tillman recieves his NOGI in Mexico City.

The inductees in 1968 were Stan Waterman for Arts, Andy Rechnitzer for Science, Terry Lentz for Sports and David Stith for Administration.

Robert Straight designed the sterling Reaching Out Award.

silver into a diver reaching out to a hovering manta ray. The award had more extrinsic value because of the silver, but recipients of both the NOGI and DEMA Awards, a small majority, felt the NOGI statuette impressed their family and friends more. Both, though, are unique and original and quite striking. So far by the year 2000, the report of anyone selling off a NOGI has not come up.

CLUB AWARDS

Dive Clubs, Club Councils, and various regional organizations have a record from the early years of diving of recognizing big contributors and leaders from their own ranks. Most of these people are volunteers. Trying to financially remunerate them usually isn't fiscally feasible, is almost insulting, and can cause dissension. So awards are the way of doing it. It used to be a gold-plated diving figure on a wood pedestal did the trick, and during the 1970's, 1980's and 1990's, clever new ways of designing plaques took over. In the 1990's, the standing etched glass plaque became the prestigious piece of recognition "hardware."

NAUI HALL OF HONOR

NAUI has had a number of annual awards to fete outstanding instructor course graduates, high achieving instructors in the field and other leadership roles. In 2000, the 40th anniversary of NAUI's founding, a Hall of Honor had been established, and a dozen or so long-term veterans of serving NAUI, and being true to it over the decades, were inducted. Al Tillman, NAUI founder, received the agency's only lifetime achievement award by year 2000.

NAUI intended to clear the decks with the first wave into the Hall of Honor, and a very select smaller acceptance would take place each year. No quota and if no deserving candidates exist in any year, then no one goes in the Hall of Honor. The NAUI Board of Directors control it.

As a regional training agency, the venerable Los Angeles County Department of Parks and Recreation Underwater Program, in association with the separately incorporated Los Angeles Underwater Instructors Association, has always given out a plethora of awards, starting with the outstanding graduate of each underwater instructor certification course getting an award and becoming a member of the Board of Directors. The Los Angeles County Program also recognizes its volunteer officers and leaders/staff of UICC's with trophy plaques. They have a Conrad Limbaugh (The Scripps' Chief Diving Officer from 1950's) Award for significant contribution to the birth and growth of diving, a memorial award in the name of one of diving's first heroes.

There have been a number of awards named after

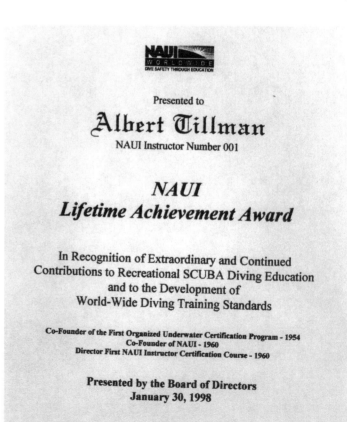

Presented to

Albert Tillman

NAUI Instructor Number 001

NAUI
Lifetime Achievement Award

In Recognition of Extraordinary and Continued Contributions to Recreational SCUBA Diving Education and to the Development of World-Wide Diving Training Standards

Co-Founder of the First Organized Underwater Certification Program - 1954
Co-Founder of NAUI - 1960
Director First NAUI Instructor Certification Course - 1960

Presented by the Board of Directors
January 30, 1998

donors. Anyone could approach an organization with money and an idea and have an award set up with his name on it.

SSI FREQUENT DIVER AWARDS

Scuba Schools International (SSI) came up with a broad stroke award to celebrate frequent divers. Nice idea in that its highest category identified long-term divers who had made 5,000 dives or more, had ten years in the dive industry, plus had made a significant contribution to the industry. It was called the Platinum Pro Award ever since it was started in 1992. It has been showing up on prestigious divers' resumes. To get those 5,000 dives it would roughly take two dives-a-day every day for six years. A log book isn't absolute proof but it helps verify. SSI ended up by year 2000 with 1189 Platinum Pro honorees. They provided polished black with silver engraved cards, elegant lapel pins and gifts. They treated the program with loads of respect.

UNEXSO AWARDS

At UNEXSO in the Bahamas, in the 1960's, visiting divers were trying to rack up feet-in-depth on dives to get on the wall plaque in the UNEXSO Museum. It was the Seven Mile Club and took many dives to make it... Two hundred and fifty foot dives on compressed air which was the UNEXSO specialty in those days. And got you there faster, but it remained a short list with Cousteau's name placed honorarily at the top. Dave Woodward, Chuck Petersen, Jack McKenney and Al Tillman, the staff at UNEXSO, made the list by making up to five dives per day. It was a marketing device to keep people diving, employing the ancient premise of buy a bunch of dives and you get one free. Of course the dives didn't have to be at the UNEXSO Club, and divers took the program seriously and were sending in their pumped-up diving schedules from around the world. Probably only about five other divers/members of UNEXSO ever achieved the seven-mile-goal in the program's short existence. There was a medal issued. Medals are kind of an old-time award, but they still are a respected approach to awards. The spearfishing championships used them, and they have been good enough for the Olympic Games.

PADI HAS AWARDS, TOO

Now we come to the awards that recognize diving performance skills. Spearfishing contests over the years have honored biggest catch - largest fish achievers with "bowling league type" trophies. Mundane and "assembly line" they might have been, but they worked - they seemed to be what the spearfishing divers wanted. The fish may have been eaten or given away, but the trophies were on the mantel. That told family and friends that what a spearfisherman went off and did, the invisible sport, had some substance.

Underwater photography, spearfishing's counterpart, the underwater paradox of hunter-versus-artist, lent itself well to a new avenue of recognition in diving. There was the picture or film representing diving skill and artistic skill, a concrete result to be judged and presented for public-view over and over. Getting a picture published was a kind of an award and opportunities abounded for the amateur in the early days of diving. But it was the contests covering prints, slides and films put on locally and regionally, starting in 1957 with the Los Angeles Original Underwater Photographic Society Chapter and the film festivals, initiated with the International Underwater Film Festival in "Hollywood," produced by Zale Parry and Al Tillman that were important. Plaques and medals were the awards with extra-large, elaborate ones given in film festivals. The Film Festival in Los Angeles/Hollywood during its fourteen-year life introduced to the public the world's best underwater photographers. It served as a virtual Hall of Fame, selecting the Underwater Photography of the Year in the world. The physical award was far exceeded by the honor which remains the highlight of many famous divers' biographies.

The Boston Sea Rovers, one of the earliest clubs, had some good organizers in its membership, and under people like Walter Feinberg and Frank Scalli produced an annual "clinic" that featured the big names in diving. It rivaled the International Underwater Film Festival as a major social event for the diving public. Dive leaders kept in touch by attending the clinics. As for awards, the Boston Sea Rovers had recovered some metal spikes made by Paul Revere (the "British are coming, the British are coming" guy) from a wreck site back in the 1950's, and important divers recognized for significant achievements received one of these spikes mounted on an engraved wood base. Eventually, the club ran out of authentic spikes and had to go to replicas. They were the first "big event" to host and honor Jacques Yves Cousteau. Silver bowls eventually replaced the spikes.

Jacques Cousteau was the most popular recipient over diving's historic 50 years, the collector of the most awards and deservedly so. The attendance of Jacques Cousteau at any event gave it an important prestige aura that would market the event in the coming years. Cousteau's physical hardware- awards ended up in 2000 with his widow, Francine, and various diving museums regard them with lust.

Many foundations and nonprofit organizations emerged with the environmental movement and gained full momentum in the 1980's and 1990's. While Cousteau evolved into the very vocal advocate for protection of the seas in his later years, Dr. Sylvia Earle appeared to have been assigned the role of Cousteau's ecology successor. By the late 1990's, there were more awards for environmental efforts than any other category for divers. The various foundations knew that giving an award was good for a short run of publicity.

OCEAN FUTURES AWARDS

Ocean Futures, a nonprofit "ocean advocacy network," was DEMA's (Diving Equipment and Marketing Association) designated environmental organization initiated in the 1980's. By the late 1990's Jean-Michel Cousteau Institute and the Free Willy Keiko Foundation inherited Ocean Futures and made a thunderous call to the global community to "Protect the Ocean and You Protect Yourself" with a list of choices from clean water for all to preservation and protection of our ocean future. In 1996, its Chairman, John Englander, was at the White House shaking hands with President Bill Clinton for a grand coming out exposure. By 1997, the organization was giving its lifetime leadership award on behalf of the ocean environment to . . . you're right again. . . Jacques-Yves Cousteau. Englander, who played a key role in reviving NAUI at one of its low periods and ran UNEXSO in the 1970's and 1980's, got this award started, called The Oceanus Award. It's an intricately designed, colorful mixed-media trophy. The first one went to actor, Ted Danson, in 1996. High-profile celebrities getting awards is a surefire way to get instant recognition for a sponsoring agency.

Awards certainly have an impact on some divers, the ones who receive them, although E. R. Cross, who gathered quite a few later in life, had something to say about them. Cross told us, "I seemed to have gotten my awards later in life than others. I could have used them earlier to help support interest in some of my projects, but I never did anything with any award as an incentive. The best things in diving, I always felt, got done when the doers didn't even think who was going to get the credit." Its good to know that by the end of the 1990's, the Historical Diving Society, had a E. R. Cross Award as their top recognition for diving contributions.

Has there been a major impact of awards on the growth and development of diving? Does the general diving public pay much attention to them? We'd like to say the research this book has done says "Yes" to both of those questions. The real impact, and there is one, is that awards are a fuel to activate the engines of diving's prime movers and shakers. The physical award, a symbol of honor from peers and colleagues, sits on desks and mantels across the land, reminding those honored leaders that someone cares about what they did, mostly unselfish and always passionately, to make things better in diving. They seem to say, "Thanks a million, but are you through yet?"

Perhaps all of us worry too much about who's getting credit for what happened in diving. It's a fact of life that we all, overtly or secretly, deep down, like to get credit. If it comes in the form of a nicely designed piece of hardware with a standing ovation, most of us won't say, "No, I'm not deserving, give it to someone else."

NOGI AWARD RECIPIENTS

Jay Albeanese	Richard Anderson	Oscar Asturias
Jim Auxier	Art Bachrach	Robert Ballard
Bill Barada	George Bass	Albert Behnke
George Benjamin	Peter Bennett	Dewey Bergman
Chuck Blakeslee	George Bond	Dick Bonin
Lamar Boren	Alfred Dove	Lloyd Bridges
Ernest Brooks II	Jim Brown	Recou Browning
Pablo Bush	Scott Carpenter	Jim Christiansen
Cathy Church	Jim Church	Ron Church
Eugenie Clark	Robert Clark	Roger Cook
Richard Cooper	Jacques Cousteau	Jean-Michel Cousteau
Phillipe Cousteau	John Craig	John Cronin
E. R. Cross	Louis Cuccia	Gustav Dalla Valle
Ben Davis	Helen Turcotte Davis	Jefferson Davis
Ralph Davis	Robert Dill	David Doubilet
Harold Drake	James Dugan	Sylvia Earle
Harold Edgerton	Glen Egstrom	Bernard Empelton
John Ernst	Jack Faver	Louis Fead
Walter Feinberg	Frank Fennell	John Fine
Elliot Finkle	Mel Fisher	Rick Freshee
John Gaffney	Andre Galerne	John Geiszler
Al Giddings	Peter Gimbel	Dennis Graver
Nixon Griffis	Melville Grosvenor	Howard Hall
Bill Hamilton	John Hardy	Carl Hauber
Walt Hendrick, Sr.	Bill High	Genaro Hurtado
Nick Icorn	Bert Kilbride	Jordan Klein
Ian Koblick	Emory Kristof	Christin Lambertsen
E. H. Lanphier	Terry Lentz	Mel Lillis
Connie Limbaugh	Ed Link	Bates Littlehales
Dick Long	John McAniff	Jack McKenney
Joe MacInnis	Luis Marden	Robert Marx
James Miller	Bev Morgan	Zale Parry
Chris Nicholson	Chuck Nicklin	Flip Nicklin
Wheeler North	Phil Nuytten	Dan Orr
Ralph Osterhout	David Owen	Duke Pawlowicz
John Perry	Mendel Peterson	Coles Phinizy
Jacques Piccard	John Rawlings	Dimitri Rebikoff
Andy Rechnitzer	George Ruggieri	Rick Sammon
Frank Scalli	Nancy Sefton	Harry Shanks
Charles Shilling	Gene Shiinn	Richard Slater
Lee Somers	James Stewart	David Stith
Kathryn Sullivan	Phillipe Tailliez	Bob Talbot
Ron Taylor	Valerie Taylor	Lee Tepley
Albert Tillman	Ivan Tors	Teddy Tucker
Paul Tzimoulis	Art Ullrich	Otto Van Der Aaue
Eugene Vezzani	Don Walsh	Stan Waterman
Lowell Weicker	Morgan Wells	Ralph White
Robert Wicklund	Robert Workman	George Youmans

DEMA'S REACHING OUT AWARD RECIPIENTS

1989	1990	1991
Jacques-Yves Cousteau	E. R. Cross	John Cronin
Dr. Glen Egstrom	Bill and Bob Meistrell	Sam Davison, Jr.
Jack McKenney	T.A. "Mike" Kelly	Dr. Sylvia Earle
Stan Waterman	Albert Tillman	

1992	1993	1994
Dick Bonin	Scott Carpenter	Jim Auxier
Ralph Erickson	Dr. Eugene Clark	Chuck Blakeslee
Michael Kevorkian	Zale Parry	Lloyd Bridges
Arnold Post		Jean-Michel Cousteau
James Stewart		

1995	1996	1997
Robert Gray	John McAniff	Joe Dorsey
	Bev Morgan	Dr. Hans Hass
	Fred Weiss	Paul Tzimoulis
		Frank Scalli

1998	1999	2000
John Gaffney	Clive Cussler	Cathy Church
Bob Clark	Al Giddings	Bob Hollis
Captain Don Stewart	Howard Hall	Gordon Shearer
	Ron Merker	

BOSTON SEA ROVERS DIVER OF THE YEAR AWARD

1956 Edward Pansewitz	1957 Peter Gimbel	1958 James Cahill
1959 James Dugan	1960 George Bond	1961 Harold Edgerton
1962 Hannes Keller	1963 Pablo Bush Romero	1964 Alan Krasberg
1965 Kip Wagner	1966 Scott Carpenter	1967 Stan Waterman
1968 Joseph MacInnis	1969 Al Giddings	1970 Melville Bell Grosvenor
1971 George Benjamin	1972 Paul Tzimoulis	1973 Smokey Roberts
1974 Jack McKenney	1975 David Doubilet	1976 Luis Marden
1977 Rick Frehsee	1978 Eugenie Clark	1979 Sylvia Earle
1980 Robert Ballard	1981 Larry Emmerson	1982 Elga Anderson
1983 Frank Scalli	1984 Don Stewart	1985 Walt Hendrick, Sr.
1986 Rusty Murray	1987 Argo/Jason Jr.	1988 Emory Kristof
1989 Stan Waterman	1990 John Stoneman	1991 Walt "Butch" Hendrick, Jr.
1992 Ruth Dixon Turner	1993 Dee Scarr	1994 Nick Caloyianis
1995 Bill Curtsinger	1996 Wes Pratt	1997 Bill Hamilton
1998 Frank Fennell	1999 Jordan Klein	2000 John Cronin

Top award getters in diving history

Dr. Eugenie Clark

Jacques Yves-Cousteau

Sylvia Earle

Dr. Hans Hass

Dr. Andreas Rechnitzer

Stanton Waterman

SCUBA AMERICA HISTORICAL CENTER AWARD In Diving Literature

Nominees for Year 2000

James Dugan	Jacques Yves-Cousteau	Dr. Hans Hass
Sir Robert Marx	Dennis Graver	Dick Anderson
Albert Tillman	Clive Cussler	

INTERNATIONAL SCUBA DIVING HALL OF FAME

2000 is the inaugral year under sponsorship of the Cayman Islands. Honorees from around the world, who have made a major contribution to the development of recreational scuba diving.

Lloyd Bridges/US	Jacques-Yves Cousteau/France	Ben Cropp/Australia
E. R. Cross/US	Dr. Jefferson C. Davis, Jr./US	Gustav Dalla Valle/Italy
Sylvia Earle, Ph.D./US	Bernie Eaton/UK	Emile Gagnon/France
Al Giddings/US	Hans and Lotte Hass/Austria	Jack Lavanchy/Switzerland
Jack McKenney/Canada	Bob Soto/Cayman Islands	Ron and Valerie Taylor/Australia
Al Tillman/US	Stan Waterman/US	

WOMEN DIVERS HALL OF FAME

2000

Susan Bangasser, Ph.D.
Tamara Brown
Cathy Church
Cathy Cush
Evelyn Bartram Dudas
Dr. Caroline Fife
Regina Franklin
Anne G. Giesecke
Mehgan Heaney-Grier
Norma Hanson
Jill Heinerth
Lise Kinahan
Dr. Ann Kristovich
Capt. D. Karin Lynn, CEC, USN
Devonna Sue Morra, Ph.D.
Patti Schaeffer Mount
Betty Orr
Ellen J. Prager, Ph.D.
Norine Rouse
Dee Scarr
Marguerite St Leger-Dowse
Valerie Taylor
Hillary Viders, Ph.D.
Kathy Weydig
Andrea Zaferes

Capt. Janet Bieser
Bonnie Cardone
Eugenie Clark. Ph.D.
Helen Davis
Sylvia Earle, Ph.D.
Dolores Fisher
Dottie Frasier (May)
Linda Gray
Michele Hall
Lotti Hass
Edith Hoffman
Jennifer King
Barb Lander
Connie Lyn Morgan
Denise J. Morrissette
Jan Neal
Zale Parry
Vreni Roduner
Betsy Royal
Commander Bobbie Scholley
Tanya Streeter
Dr. Ruth Turner
Kay Walten
Frankie Wingert

Jana Bradley
Jennifer Carter
Cindi Courter
Sue Drafhal
Mary Ellen Eckhoff
Mary Jo Ferris-Fischer
Lynn Funkhouser
Brigit Grimm
Erika Leigh Haley
Hillary Hauser
Maria Hults
Capt. Marie E. Knafelc, Ph.D.,M.D.
Mel Lillis
Ella-Jean Morgan
Patty Newell-Mortara
Erin O'Neill
Alese O. Pechter
Carol Taylor Rose
Lorraine Bemis Sadler
Jeanne Bear Sleeper
Dr. Maida Beth Taylor
Dr. Karen Van Hoesen
Renee Westerfield
Jill Yager, Ph.D.

42

Sea Hunt
Diving's Ultimate Recruiting Poster

Defining Event: Balsa Wood Diving Tanks

The *Sea Hunt* television series came along at a point in time when television itself was just emerging as the great mass entertainment media of all time and the viewing public was extremely receptive to the portrayal of lone wolf type of heroes.

Westerns were extremely popular. *Sea Hunt* in many ways was an underwater Western movie. It also was at a time when scuba diving was just starting to pick up significant numbers of people. The personal ownership of your own regulator and tank had started to become a part of the American life-style. Everything was ripe and primed for a Mike Nelson to come on the scene and become the inspiring hero. *Sea Hunt* came along and personalized the experience of going underwater. It gave everybody someone to emulate. It gave them a hero that they could identify with and pretend to be and fantasize about and try to behave like when they went underwater.

Because it was not filmed in color, it did not convey the emotional impact that the color films and movies have done, but *Sea Hunt* conveyed the adventure aspect, the unknown aspect, and the challenge. *Sea Hunt* continued to play on television through the 1970's around the world.

Watched by the same kind of kids that loved sports, *Sea Hunt* made scuba diving into a sport. It reached not just divers. It created divers. More of the people on our 'founding fathers and mothers list' were promoted into diving by *Sea Hunt* than by any other single motivation.

"I wanted to be Mike Nelson," sighed that generation of divers who watched the popular television show *Sea Hunt* as children.

We interviewed the early divers and when *Sea Hunt* came up, they winced. Those on the 'founding roster' took diving seriously in the 1950's. They thought the show took a number of liberties and the main character came off as a sort of comic hero. The second generation, who watched it wide-eyed as children, became the pioneer divers of the 1960's and 1970's and praised the show as leading them into diving.

PEOPLE BEHIND THE SCENES

Zale Parry and Al Tillman were both intimately part of the production of *Sea Hunt*. Ivan Tors, the originator of *Sea Hunt*, *Flipper* and dozens of other films and animal projects was a good friend. The model for Mike Nelson was Commander Francis "Doug," "Red Dog" Fane and he, too, was a close friend. Lloyd Bridges, Ricou Browning, Courtney Brown, Lamar Boren, Paul Stader and the rest of the production staff were friends beyond the television series and into other aspects of sport diving. Together Zale and Al feel they have a deep and broad view of the *Sea Hunt* story.

THE MIKE NELSON ROLE MODEL

The *Sea Hunt* history should start with Doug Fane, who was the public image of the military frogman and is often credited with creating the UDT (Underwater Demolition Team) from which many of our best sport divers graduated into civilian life. The book, *The Naked Warriors*, and movie, *Underwater Warrior*, starring Dan Dailey were actually Fane's life story.

Ivan Tors was introduced to Doug Fane by Parry Bivens and wife, Zale Parry, during their business of selling

Director Leon Benson (seated) and Ivan Tors in 1963.

Lamar Boren

the Navy and civilians portable recompression/decompression chambers in 1955. Doug Fane was getting ready to retire from the U. S. Navy, when Tors recognized the potential for an action series that takes place underwater. "Vot vill you do as a civilian, Doug?", asked Ivan in an excited voice still laced with a Hungarian accent after forty years in the United States. "I'll probably get a boat and hire myself out on diving jobs; do some police work if contacted," was Fane's growling devil-may-care reply.

The pilot for the *Sea Hunt* series, began with the film, *Underwater Warrior*. Zale Parry recalls that MGM and the producers of Ivan Tors Production Company flew in a DC-7 propeller-engine airliner to the Hawaiian Islands. Record flying time 8 hours in September 1957. The first location was the Hawaiian Village Hotel, the tallest building along Waikiki. Commander Fane appropriated a Pacific Fleet Minesweeper before getting Zale Parry, who played Fane's wife in the film, thoroughly interviewed and checked out in the Barber's Point Tower. "No woman was going to sink the U.S. Navy's Pacific Fleet" were the undertones. Three weeks of underwater and topside filming was completed using almost every Hawaiian Island. The minesweeper carried all the UDT equipment, rubber rafts, scuba gear, crew and cast. The first officer assigned to that ship was given leave to allow accommodations for 'the girl' on board.

"During that time, underwater island hopping in search for good water was necessary for certain scenes required in the script. They ran into murky water, sometimes too much current for the action required, or nature's underwater stage was just not to the liking of the director, Andrew Marton, of King Solomon's Mines fame. A scheduled U.S. Navy submarine joined us for a full day's shooting. We were in 60 feet of water off the Island of Molokai for that one. The submarine submerged very slowly while Lamar Boren captured every angle. The star, Dan Dailey, performed well in the submarine escape hatch sequence. When we finished the day's work, we were allowed to stand on the deck of the sub while it surfaced very, very slowly. An eerie experience. When we were ankle-deep in water, Dailey performed a Broadway stage soft-shoe-shuffle while still wearing UDT garb with fins and those of us next to him joined the dance. This was serious fun!," recalls Zale Parry.

SHARK FOOTAGE

Doug Fane arranged for his finest, and strongest UDT swimmers to be part of the cast. The frogmen were: Leonard E. "Big Mac" McLarty, George Gionnatti, Walter Otte and Jon Lindbergh. After the three weeks were up, Fane and the UDT men with the cameraman, Lamar Boren, flew to the Marshall Islands where the filming of the shark sequence for Underwater Warrior took place. "They sniffed us like dogs," Fane explained in a short film, *Sharks*, made out of some of the reels of footage. What was shown was the actual footage. Nothing faked. Fane bouncing around by himself with swarming sharks, hand feeding them, probably the first diver to ever jump in and do it - and from it derived another name for Fane, "Fearless Francis". As the hardened frogmen under him said in awe, "the guy's one tough dude." Fane became a key consultant for the *Sea Hunt* show in its beginning. The shark footage from the Marshall Islands showed up in the *Sea Hunt* series and gave the series its most authentic "bite".

Dan Dailey, and the other cast of characters, Ivan Tors and the entire MGM crew returned to the Mainland while Zale, John Florea, associate producer/photographer, Courtney Brown, Jack Harris and Navy men remained in Hawaii for additional footage.

Making pictures underwater is physically consuming. Anyone, who has done work of any kind for a full day can testify how much physical effort goes into it - all the time wearing full gear, while boarding and dropping off boats dozens of times a day. Finally, when the production was moved to Silver Springs, full air tanks were delivered underwater. Changing tanks was easy. Remember how the actors dressed - weight belt first? Criticism of the procedure rang loudly from the diving public who knew "Safety first - weights last". Film production could not wait for proper procedure to remove weights to secure tank straps under the weight belt.

Courtney Brown

THE AFFORDABLE ACTOR

Now Ivan needed an affordable, veteran actor, who was athletic to be the main character, Mike Nelson. There was Lloyd Bridges, a journeyman actor, who more often played villain parts and leading man roles had eluded him. Lloyd was blonde, well-built, looked great in a wet bathing suit in the sun. But he didn't dive at the time. So while he would be the perfect image of Mike Nelson on the surface and underwater closeups, a veteran diver stand-in, Courtney Brown, would do the actual diving footage.

Although females were brought in for guest roles, Tors recruited an actress to be Bridges co-star and assume all the underwater stunt work. Zale's recollections were as follows: George Wilhelm had telephoned Zale to call Producer Ivan Tors immediately. George was the Associate Producer for Jack Douglas Productions and Jack had just finished his series, Kingdom of the Sea, with Zale and Col. John D. Craig. Thus, George, who was very familiar with Zale's work and being in contact with Hollywood's producers made the connection with Tors.

Without demonstrating her acting or aquatic ability, Zale was hired by Tors over the telephone. Their first meeting was for a family dinner and evening chat in Tor's home in Beverly Hills. Husband, Parry Bivens, University of California Berkeley-graduate engineer, underwater photographer and medical student at the time, was signed on, too. Tors was very excited to have found both of them. They were saturated in the scientific phases of diving and well- soaked with underwater experiences. Furthermore, they had a fast Jeffries speed boat that Tors used to search for filming locations along the Los

Zale Parry and Lloyd Bridges in Sea Hunt.

Bridges Collection

Angeles County coastline and the close-by Channel Islands.

Zale tells of many assignments before the actual first episode. She was Tor's 'girl Friday'. Zale followed through on permits to be acquired for filming on city or county property, searched for best possible "deal" for dive equipment to be used, checked the first few scripts for technicalities, and performed topside as well as underwater when the film was being shot in Hollywood or Marineland of the Pacific Oceanarium. The pace became frantic once it was known that the schedule called for one episode to be 'in the can' every few days. It didn't take long before two units were at work. The topside unit and the underwater unit. Not always in the same location or state. The female character changed topside while Zale became the underwater double more frequently. There were a few other underwater doubles, after Zale's seventh month of pregnancy and the Meistrell brothers had the job of placing V's-of-rubber on each side of Zale's black wet suit to disguise that reality. Courtney Brown's wife, Wendy Wagner, Ginger Stanley, Frances Dwight and Patsy Boyette pitched-in for Zale for a few episodes.

WANTED: A GREAT UNDERWATER PHOTOGRAPHER

Ivan knew that he needed the best underwater photographer he could get and there was that original Bottom Scratcher already acclaimed in Hollywood for his underwater photography for *Underwater*, with Jane Russell - Lamar Boren. A barrel-chested bull of a man, Lamar, came on duty in charge of underwater photography and general diving patriarch to everybody who had to dive connected with the TV show.

This was not an eight to five o'clock job. Film was shot from a time-slot after sunrise until sunset. When it rained, they'd watch the rain drops dimple the surface. Filming continued. No submersible pressure gauges were used but each one could tell when the breathing became labored. It's a miracle none of the divers developed the bends. Lamar went on to fame winning the Motion Picture and Television Academy Award for underwater photography in *Thunderball*.

Lamar Boren with underwater camera housing.

Ricou Browning was a graceful, strong swimmer, platform and underwater diver out of Florida waters. He really knew the territory and knew the owners of Silver Springs, where much of the underwater filming took place. Tors hired him to be their location diving expert. (Ricou would eventually be the star in the *Creature from the Black Lagoon*.)

Ricou's sense of humor kept everyone in good spirits long after everyone was tired and still had film to burn for the day's shoot. It was Ricou, who surfaced to check on meal time. He would skin dive with the message "LUNCH" written on paper, tucked in his face plate and deliver the message on one breath-hold dive to each person underwater.

DON'T DO THIS AT HOME

Sea Hunt was on television screens, the original series from 1957 to 1960 and then showed up in syndicated reruns. Throughout America, experienced divers found fault with some of the diving behavior of Mike Nelson. - Hey! Why is he diving alone? How about "always dive with a buddy?" With Lamar, Ricou, Zale and Courtney on the set, really foolish things like putting a regulator on upside down or going in without a weight belt were avoided. But boys, and even some girls, let their imaginations soar and identified with the super hero Nelson. This character was a grand counterpart to the comic book hero, Submariner, and while hardhat diving was intriguing, the diver looked like a robot. Mike Nelson was a real human being, his body visible and, despite the mask, showed emotional facial expressions to them all the time. Kids didn't want to know that Lloyd Bridges registering concern with furrowed brow amidst a swarm of sharks and sawfish, was being shot close-up through a window at Marineland of the Pacific or the unusually small glass tank on a stage in the Hollywood studio. Kids said, wow, when Mike Nelson slung his air tanks over his shoulder like they were balsa wood - which as studio props - they were! However, Bridges learned this technique with the real tanks by watching Courtney Brown perform this maneuver, when dressing for a dive. Sometimes, the hero would leap in the water with one tank and then be seen swimming with two at which the adult veteran divers would hoot (Of course, none would admit to watching the show.) but the kids loved it, flaws and all.

Lloyd Bridges in an episode of Sea Hunt with son Jeff.

Bridges Collection

A lot of bad or incorrect diving procedures needed to be caught before any expensive filming. Back in the idea stage and then in reviewing the script. The first couple of shows resulted in some complaints from adults, mostly parents, that the show needed warning footage about "not trying anything we're doing here at home" or that diving requires special training and supervision. To avoid possible lawsuits that might result from people treating *Sea Hunt* like a training film, Ivan Tors felt a point of authority was needed that would screen the scripts for technical flaws. Al Tillman in 1957 was heading up the Los Angeles Underwater Program and had written the manual, *Underwater Recreation*. Ivan had also seen Al's *Little Wet Schoolhouse* tank show at the Los Angeles Sportsmen Show. Zale Parry, who actually did technical advising on the first two shows and worked with Al on the International Underwater Film Festivals, influenced Tors into retaining Tillman, as technical advisor on all the forthcoming scripts.

SCRIPT DETECTIVES

Tillman recalls playing detective on the red covered scripts that came every week for four years: "big obvious things like Mike staying down all day on a couple of tanks of air or giving the correct hand signal to say he was out of air underwater. It was more difficult to determine how authentic a fist fight would be underwater just from reading the script."

Al had a favorite script and Zale a favorite episode. Al picked Script No. 53B by Art Arthur with title "Ransom". Mike is retained by the police to uncover some kidnapped electronic tapes in the maze of canals of Venice, California. The kidnappers chase Nelson up and down the canals trying to speargun him from a boat. "It wasn't Dostoevsky" sighed Al, "but it was always interesting to see how they'd take the usual story and make it fit scuba diving." This was a story where questions were asked before the script. - Could Mike with a bum regulator breathe directly from the tank? -Yes. Al had to go test that one. The other idea was could Mike lose his mask and still see some way underwater? -Yes, he could cup his hands over his eyes, breathe a big bubble into them and voila, he would see.

This is how the synopsis was written by Art Arthur for Ivan Tors: "Mike Nelson is hurriedly summoned — via pistol shots — from his underwater work by Police Chief Al Clark, head of the Police Department in a small California town. Tanks and all, Mike is thrust out of sight into the back of an unmarked Police car. He learns that a ransom is about to be paid in some manner involving water — and he may be needed. The ransom, $100,000 is being paid by Howard Stoneham, head of Stoneham Electronics. It is not being paid for a human being, however — but to ransom six stolen 'Memory Tapes' without which Stoneham's electronic computers are paralyzed. To replace them would cost at least one million dollars. The Police Chief's hunch turns out to be right. Stoneham tosses the money, in a waterproofed box, from a bridge into a lagoon in a very unique part of Southern California called "Little Venice" — full of crisscrossing lagoons and small-boat canals. But by the time the Chief's car reaches the bridge, it is too late for Mike to overtake whoever retrieved the box when it plunged underwater. However, Mike does find a tiny but baffling fragment of something he cannot identify — rubbed on a bridge piling. Later Mike establishes that the fragment is part of the insignia of a local skindiving club called the Neptunes — but in doing so he alarms Don and Cassie Gilliam — who clearly intend him no good. Mike follows a lead that the money box is still hidden underwater — and locates it in a dangerous area. Without realizing it, he has started a radio signal which tips off Don and Cassie Gilliam On reaching the scene, they just miss running Mike down in their speed-boat. Then, using an "electronic ear", the speedboat follows Mike as he tries to get away along the bottom of the canal. Mike is lucky to escape twice when spears are fired down at him from a spear gun. But his air is just about gone. In a daring maneuver he disables the speedboat, evades revolver shots when he reaches the surface and,

Lamar Boren filming an underwater Sea Hunt fight scene in Silver Springs, Florida. *Mozert/Boren*

in a final knife fight, helps to bring Don and Cassie into custody."

Zale's choice of episodes was one she'll never forget. It is one of her favorites because a part of it became true to life itself. The underwater gymnastics with divers and equipment were no play acting. It was done in the second year of the series. The synopsis for this program reads as follows:

"Beautiful but reckless Gracie Bond enrolls in Mike's class for skindiver instructors. She promptly flunks out when her underwater antics nearly cost her life. Vengeance-bent, she finds an opportunity to invite Mike to accompany her on a dive to an underwater cave. Gracie lets half the air out of Mike's tank, then waits for the chance to save his life and thus assert her diving superiority — but the maneuver perilously backfires.

How Mike Nelson, with two lives in the balance, pits his resourcefulness against great odds, creates a fever-pitch climax.

This story was death defying in truth. Two lives were in jeopardy. If you ever happen to watch a rerun of this story, hold your own breath to get the feeling of water, water all around with no gills to breathe.

The location is the large underwater cave at Silver Springs, Florida. The crew and cast are ten feet into the cave from the arched entrance.

The June 27, 1959 issue of TV Guide featured Sea Hunt.

As Mike Nelson (Courtney Brown) and Gracie (Zale) are swimming through the cave, Gracie waits for a chance to save Mike's life. The maneuver perilously backfired. What you witness, really happened! Zale's (Gracie's) regulator is rigged with a loose intake hose clamp on her regulator. As she follows Courtney (Mike) through a debris of broken tree branches, the loop of her breathing hose on the right side (the good-air side), hooks unto a branch. The deliberately loosened clamp releases the hose from the connection to the first stage of the regulator. Gracie is now breathing water and reaches ahead to grab one of Mike's fins for immediate attention. Courtney play acting attached Zale's hose. While both of them were buddy breathing and siphoning water and air in their mouths, Zale coughed from water that went down the wrong pipe. She motioned to ascend. She knew she could do it. She had ascended without air on other occasions. But Lamar Boren, the cameraman, saw the trouble through the lens. He handed the camera over to the person next to him, grabbed Zale's swim suit strap, held her down to prevent her from doing a free ascent from ten feet out of the cave and sixty feet to the surface. Lamar shared his air with Zale until Zale recovered by coughing into the water and gasping for air on a bite of shared air. Upon surfacing the underwater director, Paul Stader, said to Zale, "You scared the daylights out of all of us. We thought we lost you forever. Now go do it again!"

Courtney Brown in a 1975 interview reminisced about all the films he was in but said *Sea Hunt* was his best experience. As Lloyd Bridges stand-in and doing all of the underwater stunt work, he was always amused when he saw the edited film. The film editors through crosscutting in close-up of Bridges making faces shot through a studio tank's glass window and footage of Courtney underwater tweaking tiger shark's tails certainly looked like the same guy all the way through. There's lots of waiting around on a movie and when it's waiting around underwater, as it was with *Sea Hunt*, the cast and crew would pull boredom-pranks. Courtney said sneaking up and shutting off someone's air was continuously done. It got the best reaction when someone was using line to tie a tiger shark's tail to a coral head in order to tire them. That's when shutting off air was really fun. There was mooning, too. Like the postman on his day off, Courtney went wall diving!

Kent "Rocky" Rockwell, author of a soon to be published book, *Sea Hunt*, was asked about his favorite episode. He replied, "All the episodes that Zale appears in." He mentioned that Lloyd Bridges had no favorite...they were all the same to him.

Tillman's job back-stepped to the idea stage before a script was finished. Art Arthur, a key producer/writer for *Sea Hunt*, would call Al in the middle of the night to check out technical questions that would make a script idea work or not work. "Al, sorry, ...but if I put a baby in a sealed box would there be enough good air to get it down the Amazon River a few miles?" Al even thought up some weird ideas to submit on his own. There was one about Mike Nelson going to a European Castle to verify a giant TV Quiz show's jackpot winner's contested answer. Mike had to find out how the army inside the castle snuck out and whipped the attacking enemy troops. Wearing armor to weigh them down, they took large oaken buckets and breathed the air therein, as they walked the bottom under the castles moat. The writers said it was a good thing Al had a regular day job to fall back on. Ivan Tors didn't go along with Al's diving Gorilla story either, where a promoter wants to stage a fight between the gorilla and a Great White Shark. High production costs, but for decades Art Arthur would tell people that if anyone could teach a gorilla to dive it was Tillman. Coles Phinizy picked up the quote for a *Sports Illustrated* article in 1967.

SCUBA WAS THE REAL STAR

We think everybody had a lot of fun watching a scuba diver put into harm's way, following the common plot lines of cops and robber or Westerns. But it was scuba itself that kept the fans glued to the set. This brand new machine that let man become a fish - almost. Bridges made the character come to life and he became a surrogate career counselor for the second and third generation of divers. The old crustacean crowd of skin divers out of the 1940's grumbled about "this dipstick doing dumb things on this new TV thing." But those new kids on the block wanted to do just what Mike Nelson was doing when they grew up - and many of those rabid fans did just that.

Bill DeCourt was one who packed up everything and transplanted himself from Chicago to San Diego so he could emulate Mike Nelson. DeCourt was a gold medal winning underwater photographer and a test diver for experimental diving gear. He died in Cozumel testing a new breathing device using exotic gases. It was the way Mike would have liked to go.

Kent "Rocky" Rockwell was a devoted *Sea Hunt* fan as a kid, too. He told us that he would hurry home after school to do his homework first, so that he would not miss any part of the television series. We met him at a diving pioneers photo shoot for the premiere issue of *AQUA* Magazine in 1997. He could well have stood with Cross, Morgan, Anderson, Parry, Tillman, Stewart and the Meistrells except he was only about nine or ten years old when *Sea Hunt* was riding its crest.

Rocky has chased across the country tracking all the principals involved with *Sea Hunt*. For every story we had on *Sea Hunt*, Rocky had a dozen more and it'll all be in Rocky's *Sea Hunt* book. Rockwell may well turn out to be sport diving's best historian. So he too became Mike Nelson and did some fascinating diving. Running a shop in Las Vegas for example and getting the call to recover a kid who'd disappeared down a flooded mine shaft while riding a motorcycle. He brought up the kid, the motorcycle, and two other bodies probably left behind by the Mafia.

Old timers might scoff at the overly melodramatic *Sea Hunt*, but it produced some important divers like DeCourt, Rockwell and a long list more.

COULD BRIDGES REALLY DIVE?

The inevitable question always arises because the Mike Nelson character was so inspirational to so many divers in the early days of diving history: Could Lloyd Bridges really scuba dive? The answer is no. He came into the show not as a diver but as a fine actor and ended a respected career as a virtuoso comic actor. His Izzy, personal trainer character, on *Seinfield* in the 1990's was uproarious. While he started in *Sea Hunt* as a non-diver, he got exposed to all the best divers for a number of years, even had training by the Meistrells of DiveN'Surf/Body Glove fame. So did he then become a master diver? No. In 1967 at the height of his continuing fame as Mike Nelson, Lloyd brought his really All American Family of wife, Dorothy, sons Beau and Jeff, box office actors, and daughter, Cindy, to the Underwater Explorers Club in the Bahamas to go diving. The boys and Lloyd did scuba dive and were - well OK at it. Bridges took Al Tillman, who ran UNEXSO, aside and said, "You know it's embarrassing to have everybody expecting me to be a super diver every place I go, but

Lloyd, Judy, Beau, Wendy and Jeff Bridges with Dave Woodward and Al Tillman at UNEXSO.

frankly I'm not that comfortable with it, meaning I guess I'm not a bad actor."

Dick Anderson hung around with actors because he did a lot of movie work. He got to know Lloyd Bridges and went to Catalina Island with him after he'd taken some training. Dick recalled that Bridges was very nervous and as they anchored finally said, "Dick, you know I'm not really a diver... I'm not really Mike Nelson." Dick patted Bridges on the back and said something like "don't worry, I am."

Lloyd Bridges remained, throughout the 50 year history of diving, an inspiring hero in the public's minds and received many diving awards for creating a luring, exciting, ultimate- recruiting vehicle for the sport. To some he and *Sea Hunt's* Mike Nelson were a greater influence than Cousteau.

MORE ATTEMPTS AT UNDERWATER FILMS

Ivan Tors continued after *Sea Hunt* with his ZIV Productions to feature scuba as a theme element with the successful *Flipper* series. Ricou Browning gets the credit here for creating *Flipper*. Ricou told us that the idea popped into his head when he saw his kids watching *Lassie* and thought, "Why can't we have a boy and a dolphin?" Ricou with his brother-in-law, Jack Cowden, wrote a *Flipper* story over the duration of a weekend. He intended it for a children's book but no publisher was interested. Then Ricou presented the concept to Ivan Tors, with whom he had worked with during the duration of the *Sea Hunt* production. Two *Flipper* films were made, which launched the delightful long-running series.

There are many noted divers whose paths crossed into the creation of the *Sea Hunt* series. Some of the villain divers were played by Parry Bivens (Zale's husband), Connie Limbaugh, "Big John" McLaughlin, Norm Bishop and Jon Lindbergh. Great credit goes to cameraman, Lamar Boren; the role model for Mike Nelson, Francis Fane; Ricou Browning and Courtney Brown safety divers and stand-ins for Lloyd Bridges. Jordan Klein played a significant role in providing a vast array of underwater props that gave the television series its authentic and dramatic look.

The Aquanauts was another series where scuba, as a theme element, was used. Jeremy Slate was one of the original "Aquanauts". In 1976 he had written in reply to our questionnaire that "I'm constantly surprised, after all these years especially, to find that our show did indeed entice a great number of people to that quiet, beautiful

In the late 1980's MGM tried to bring Sea Hunt back. Cinematographer Paul Mockler reviews the day's shotting schedule with Gary Ruhl (the stunt double for Ron Ely who played Mike Nelson) and UNEXSO President John Englander.   *UNEXSO*

world below the surface. As recently as a month ago, I was approached on the beach (Hawaii, where he lived) by a man in his early thirties, who told me that he had spent the last 15 years as an avid scuba diver as a direct result of having watched *The Aquanauts* as a young teenager. He was pleased to see "Larry Lahr" still walking the waters edge and alive and kicking."

"When I was offered the role in *The Aquanauts* by Ivan Tors, I was naturally thrilled, but until then had never used scuba gear, although I was a skin diver in the Navy in 1946 and later a lifeguard and swimming teacher in Rye, New York. Needless to say, I didn't mention that I never used scuba. And..I'll never forget that occasion - momentous to me, but hidden from everyone else - when I dropped off the fantail of the camera barge wearing eighty-five pounds of strange equipment and trying to behave as if I'd been doing it for years. Happily, I kept my mouthpiece in my mouth and in the split second it took me to plunge into the Pacific and suck in my first breath of bottled air, I knew I was in love with scuba."

"That love lasted passionately for over a year, and then the series was cancelled. I recall two pertinent features of *The Aquanauts* which you might find informative. *Sea Hunt* was running concurrent with our show, but ours was the first to use the single hose regulator. Also, contrary to *Sea Hunt*, we made it a point, except in dire exigencies, never to dive alone, which endeared us to many concerned scuba instructors."

Al Tillman remembers training Ron Ely and Keith Larsen, who were being groomed to be diving leads. Neither Ron nor Keith really had their hearts in it while they were being trained in backyard pools. Not being able to afford a second scuba unit, Tillman took them ocean diving by tying a rope around their waist, like a leash, and pulling them around underwater while they used the one scuba unit and he snorkeled. Both were good athletes and eventually were good divers. Ron Ely even got a shot at being Mike Nelson in an attempt to revive the *Sea Hunt* series decades later but the producers failed to get network support.

Actually, scuba as a strange new invention was the real star of *Sea Hunt* and a great actor made everybody believe that they could go scuba diving also. *Sea Hunt* was in black and white in the 1950's and the great color panorama of the underwater world wouldn't arrive until the documentaries shifted the public's fascination. Scuba had become less a startling invention and just a tool for viewing the strange sights underwater.

Nothing in television in the area of underwater drama ever again approached *Sea Hunt's* influence in the sport of sport diving.

ABOUT VOLUMES II, III AND IV

The agony and ecstasy of compiling lists of "the best" is the ultimate challenge to all historians. At some point in time they have to stop publishing telephone books of every diver who has passed this way, stop cutting bait and get the line in the water.

There are many events and people deserving recognition in this huge generational family of diving. The authors of this book tried to put sentiment aside, personal antagonism, politics, but despite objective research over all the 50 years of diving history, there is a tendency to be influenced by personal contacts. Good friends, relatives, diving partners can be vouched for from first hand experience and in most cases supported by extensive poling of celebrated divers by *Scuba America* over the years.

The major roster of the Blue Ribbon Founders of sport diving is a best effort at being fair and rewarding the deserving. Even the authors' "antagonists" were treated without prejudice.

And so beyond these first events we have acknowledged in Volume I will be a Volume II of the 50 Blue Ribbon, most impactful people as follows:

Jacque Yves-Cousteau	E. R. Cross	Al Giddings
James R. Stewart	Richard E. Anderson	Bob & Bill Meistrel
Bev Morgan	Zale Parry & Dr. Parry Bivens	Albert Tillman
Jim Auxier & Chuck Blakeslee	Bill High	Paul Tzimoulis
Dr. Eugenie Clark	Dr. Sylvia A. Earle	Sir Robert F. Marx
John Gaffney	Jim Christiansen	Dick Bonin
Gustav Dalla Valle	Ralph Ericksen	John Cronin
Bernie Empleton	Frank Scalli	Jordan Klein
Stan Waterman	Dr. George F. Bond	Jon Hardy
Dennis Graver	Dr. Hans Hass & Lottie Hass	Ben Davis
Mel Fisher	Luis Marden	Ricou Browning
Jim Cahill	Connie Limbaugh	Dr. Andreas Rechnitzer
Pablo Romero Bush	Tom Mount & Patti Mount	Jack McKenney
Jack Ackerman	Dr. Joseph B. MacInnes	Nick Icorn
Fred Calhoun	Dr. Glen H. Egstrom	Ron Church
Cmdr. Francis Douglas Fane	Bill Barada	Bob Soto
James Dugan	Bob Clark	Ivan Tors
Lloyd Bridges	Courtney Brown	Garry Howland

Volume III will recognize a second 50 influencing founders to include such pioneers as Dr. Hugh Bradner, Dr. Edgar End, Col. John D. Craig, Gene Nohl, Dr. Wheeler North, Dr. Lee Somers, Sam and Don Davidson, and more.

Volume IV will finish up the 100 Blue Ribbon Events with Celebrity Divers, Women in Diving, Dry and Wet Suits, Scripps Institution of Oceanography, Diving Equipment Marketing Association (DEMA), and Diving in Television and movies, and more.

To be placed on the mailing list for future volumes send a note to Whalestooth Publishing, 131 Bond Mill Road, Olga, WA 98279.

Zale Parry - Albert Tillman

ORDER FORM

QTY	Title	Total
	Scuba America Vol. One $49.95	
	I Thought I Saw Atlantis (softcover) $14.95	
	I Thought I Saw Atlantis (hardcover) $39.95	
	Subtotal	
	Shipping $6.00 for the first book, $1.50 each additional book	
	Sales Tax (WA residents add 7.7%)	
	Total Enclosed	

WE ACCEPT CHECK, MONEY ORDER OR VISA/MASTERCARD

___ Check Enclosed

___ Credit Card Number_____ exp_____/_____

Name_____

Address_____

City_____ State_____ Zip_____

Whalestooth Publishing
131 Bond Mill Road
Olga, WA 98279
(360) 376-6621 fax
www.whalestooth.com

Quantity discount available!